Age discrimination ha

G000125517

Age Discrimination Handbook website

www.ageconcern.org.uk/agediscriminationlaw

This book is accompanied by a comprehensive website hosted by Age Concern. The site covers:

- Amendments to the regulations made after 1 October 2006 (eg amended pension provisions expected in December 2006).
- Updates on domestic and European case-law.
- Useful statistics and sources of evidence to support applications.
- Worked examples covering a range of employment scenarios of the steps that need to be taken to identify evidence of discrimination, prepare an application, and rebut defences from employers.
- Details on ordering further copies.
- Links to resources on age discrimination.

Declan O'Dempsey is a barrister at Cloisters, London. He specialises in public and employment law, trade union cases, discrimination, and human rights. Amongst his publications are *Employment Law and the Human Rights Act 1998* (Jordans, 2001) and *Disability Discrimination: the Law and Practice* (Sweet & Maxwell, 1996). He regularly lectures and teaches on all the Framework Directive strands both in the UK and abroad. Declan is vice-chair of the Bar Disability Committee and a member of the Bar Law Reform Committee. He was the first Employment Law Caseworker at the Free Representation Unit (FRU).

Schona Jolly is a barrister at Cloisters, London, specialising in employment and discrimination law and has particular expertise in domestic and international human rights and equality issues. Schona writes and lectures on all aspects of her practice, at home and abroad. She is author of *Addressing Age Barriers*, a consultation paper for Age Concern England.

Andrew Harrop is Head of Policy at Age Concern England (ACE) where he leads the charity's work on employment, education and equality issues. He is co-author of *Your Rights: working after 50* (ACE, 2006) and *An Age Equality Duty* (ACE, 2004). He led Age Concern's work on the implementation of the directive, as a member of the Department of Trade and Industry's age advisory group, and was responsible for key changes to the detail of the regulations. He has successfully influenced Government policy on a range of other issues, including proposals for further age equality legislation, upper age limits on student loans and the duties of the Commission for Equality and Human Rights.

The Legal Action Group is a national, independent charity which campaigns for equal access to justice for all members of society. Legal Action Group:
- provides support to the practice of lawyers and advisers
- inspires developments in that practice
- campaigns for improvements in the law and the administration of justice
- stimulates debate on how services should be delivered.

Age discrimination handbook

by Declan O'Dempsey, Schona Jolly and
Andrew Harrop

 Legal Action Group
2006

This edition published in Great Britain 2006
by LAG Education and Service Trust Limited
242 Pentonville Road, London N1 9UN
www.lag.org.uk

British Library Cataloguing in Publication Data
a CIP catalogue record for this book is available from the British Library.

ISBN 10: 1 903307 48 1
ISBN 13: 978 1 903307 48 1

Printed and typeset by Hobbs the Printers, Totton, Hampshire SO40 3WX

Foreword

I have been very fortunate to work with each of the authors on the issues which this book addresses. I have worked with Andrew Harrop and Age Concern to discuss how they should respond to the developing policy on age discrimination regulation. I have worked with Schona Jolly specifically on issues of comparative age discrimination protection and I am working with Andrew and Declan O'Dempsey on the first case to review the compatibility of the regulations with the European Framework Employment Equality Directive. Both Schona and Declan are valued colleagues in my Chambers. So I am very aware of the rigour and insight of the contribution that all three make to this work, which could not be more timely.

The European Commission's Green Paper 'Confronting Demographic change: a new solidarity between generations'[1] pointed out that in 2009 the youngest cohort of workers 16 – 25 would fall below the last major cohort 55 – 65 for the first time. It added that while the overall population of Europe will grow to 2025 before starting to drop, the growth will be patchy and the downward trend will become noticeable in specific areas much sooner. It predicted that between 2005 and 2030 the total working age population (18 – 64) will drop by 20.8 million. That is not far short of the total working population of Great Britain.

These stark economic facts demonstrate in a few words how concepts of ageing, and of what it means to have a working life, must change or will be changed for us.

Some lawyers and social policy activists have already started to think hard about the consequences of these changes. Their actions have been spurred on by the introduction of laws to outlaw discrimination in relation to age in the employment field.

All three of the authors have been prominent in the first rank of those who have been undertaking this work. They have collective experience in relation to comparative approaches to the problems which are confronting us. They understand and have been closely

---

involved in the policy debates which underlie the current laws and so are closely aware of the faults and their good points. As a team they are uniquely qualified to undertake the task of explaining the interrelationship of policy and law in this developing field.

The task they have undertaken is not an easy one. The new regulations have already been criticised for their complexity and the Government has already promised a review by 2011 of the controversial provisions limiting their effect at and beyond 65. The debate in relation to that limitation is itself a reflection of the fight between the desire to hold on to hard won rights to a happy and long retirement and the economic necessities of a state threatened with a diminishing and ageing workforce.

The debate as to how to resolve these issues will take time and it is essential that it is well informed. This book will make a very important contribution to that debate as well as to the understanding of the law.

It is thus with great pleasure that I welcome its publication.

Robin Allen QC
Cloisters
October 2006

Preface

Age discrimination can be seen as one of the last frontiers in unfair treatment at work. It is the most widely practiced and most socially acceptable form of workplace discrimination, even though its victims face devastating consequences, sometimes never working again. Now, for the first time, legislation had been introduced to outlaw and regulate age discrimination. Not before time; it is more than thirty years since sex and race discrimination became unlawful, and a decade since age discrimination legislation was first promised by the Labour Party in opposition.

The new law however is highly complex and in some respects flawed. Partly this is because age discrimination poses some unique issues. However most of the loopholes and complications are a result of the numerous exemptions introduced at the urging of employer organisations. This means that that even experienced employment advisers will need a helping hand to support their work with clients.

In this book we have attempted two main goals. We have tried to give advisers a practical tool which will enable them to represent their clients in this new, and unintuitive form of anti-discrimination law. We have also tried to give an understanding of the process leading to the formulation of the current laws. In attempting the first, we have tried to cross-refer between age and other strands of discrimination law as much as possible, and use relevant examples of the law in practice. In respect of the second, we have taken advisers through the European law underlying the Employment Equality (Age) Regulations 2006 and have tried to show where we think there are tensions between what was intended by the Framework Directive and what was implemented in UK legislation. We hope that those reading this book will find materials to inspire arguments for the workplace and the tribunals, enabling those who suffer from this iniquitous form of discrimination to find a voice and use it.

We have tried to state the law as at 1 October 2006, taking into account later developments where we could or referring readers to the accompanying website (www.ageconcern.org.uk/agediscriminationlaw) where we could not.

As with all books, the help and advice of colleagues and friends is invaluable and the authors would like to thank various members of Cloisters for their help: Robin Allen QC, Rachel Crasnow, Anna Beale, Joel Donovan, Jacques Algazy, William Latimer Sayer as well as Jagdip Jagpal. We would also like to thank current and former colleagues at Age Concern England particularly Nony Ardill, Richard Baker, Helena Herklots, Gordon Lishman, Susie Munro, Sujata Ray, Ella Saltmarshe and Ellen Sharp, as well as Professor Dominic Abrams at the University of Kent. Age Concern England also held a series of seminars which were invaluable in formulating our approach to the new laws. We would like to thank Isabelle Chopin and the Migration Policy Group together with Equinet for the opportunity to speak at and attend many international seminars on the Framework Directive. In particular we are grateful to Colm O'Cinnneide for his insights on age. Needless to say those being thanked are not responsible for any mistakes there may be in the book, but have encouraged and helped the authors with their understanding of the new law.

Finally the authors would like to thank their families and friends for their support, encouragement and tolerance during the writing of this book in particular Clare Cozens, Katie Ghose and the Jolly family at large.

Declan O'Dempsey
Schona Jolly
Andrew Harrop

October 2006

Contents

Table of cases

Table of Statutes

Table of statutory instruments

Table of European legislation

Abbreviations

ACAS	Advisory Conciliation and Arbitration Service
Age Regs 2006	Employment Equality (Age) Regulations 2006
ANH	artificial nutrition and hydration
CAB	Citizens Advice Bureaux
CBI	Confederation of British Industry
CEHR	Commission for Equality and Human Rights
CMD	Case Management Discussions
COREPER	Committee of Permanent Representatives
CRE	Commission for Racial Equality
DDA 1995	Disability Discrimination Act 1995
DDP	
DfEE	Department For Education and Employment
Disability Discrimination Regs 2004	
Dispute Regs 2004	Employment Act 2002 (Dispute Resolution) Regulations 2004 SI No 752
DLR	Discrimination Law Review
DRA	default retirement age
DRC	Disability Rights Commission
DTI	Department of Trade and Industry
DWP	Department of Work and Pensions
EA 2002	Employment Act 2002
EAT	Employment Appeals Tribunal
ECHR	European Convention on Human Rights
ECJ	European Court of Justice
EDT	effective date of termination
EE (RB) Regs 2003	Employment Equality (Religion or Belief) Regulations 2003 No 1660
EE (SO) Regs 2003	Employment Equality (Sexual Orientation) Regulations 2003 No 1661
Employment Tribunals (C&R) Regs 2004	Employment Tribunals (Constitution and Rules of Procedure) Regulations 2004 No 1861
EOC	Equal Opportunities Commission
EPPS	Employers' Pension Provision Survey
ERA 1996	Employment Rights Act 1996

ET Procedure Regs 2004	Employment Tribunals (Constitution and Rules of Procedure) Regulations 2004 SI No 1861
ET Rules 2004	Employment Tribunals Rules of Procedure 2004
FALMPOW	Factors Affecting the Labour Market Participation of Older Workers
GOR	genuine occupational requirement
ILO	International Labour Organisation
ITEPA 2003	Income Tax (Earnings and Pensions) Act 2003
LFS	Labour Force Survey
LSC	Legal Services Commission
MRS	mandatory retirement age
NSF	National Service Framework
NGO	non-governmental organisation
ONS	Office of National Statistics
OPS	occupational pension scheme
PCP	provision, criterion or practice
PHA 1997	Protection from Harassment Act 1997
PHR	Pre-Hearing Review
PI	personal injury
PIU	Performance and Innovation Unit
PQE	post qualification experience
Religious Belief Regs 2003	Employment Equality (Religion or Belief) Regulations 2003 SI No 1660
RRA 1976	Race Relations Act 1976
SAYE	Save As You Earn
SDA 1975	Sex Discrimination Act 1975
Sexual Orientation Regs 2003	Employment Equality (Sexual Orientation) Regulations 2003 SI No 1661
SOCA	Serious Organised Crime Agency
TULR(C)A 1992	Trade Union and Labour Relations (Consolidation) Act 1992

CHAPTER 1

Context and history

Key points

- Age discrimination in employment is widely reported by both individuals and employers, in all aspects of the employment relationship.
- Ageist thoughts and feelings are ingrained, even among victims of age discrimination.
- The United States has had age discrimination law since the 1960s and there have been calls for UK legislation since the 1980s.
- In the late 1990s the Labour Government adopted a voluntary code of practice on age diversity, despite promising legislation while in opposition.
- Age discrimination was included in the Treaty of Amsterdam and the Framework Directive despite limited support from Member States.
- The UK Government took more than five years to prepare the implementing regulations, with major delays caused by controversy over mandatory retirement ages.

Age discrimination in employment

1.1 Age discrimination is sometimes described as the last frontier in the struggle for workplace equality. For more than thirty years Britain has had legislation outlawing sex and race discrimination. In that time the place in society of women and people from minority ethnic backgrounds has changed immeasurably. Equality law drove discriminatory practices underground and made stamping down on workplace sexism and racism a business necessity. But over time the legislation did more than that; it helped change hearts and minds. By sending out a signal about what was socially acceptable, and by establishing norms of workplace behaviour, the 1970s discrimination legislation contributed to shifts in beliefs and attitudes across society. The long road to sex and race equality may not be over, but looking back, the glass is certainly 'half full'.

1.2 More recently, legislation on disability, trans-gender identity, and in 2003, sexual orientation and religion or belief, reached the statute book. These laws have reflected and reinforced society's changing views about groups who had been left on the margins. In the last decade there has been a transformation in attitudes towards disabled people, lesbians, gay men and bisexuals. Sadly developments with respect to minority religious groups have been significantly less positive.

1.3   Now it is the turn of age. As with other areas of equality, new legislation, in part, results from significant shifts in attitudes and practices over recent years; but the law will also entrench and drive forward further change. The aim should be for age-based decision-making to be just as exceptional and unacceptable as treating people differently because of sex or race today. We will know that age discrimination legislation has worked when we can look back on early 21st century Britain and view forcing people to retire as a curious historical anachronism; akin to our view of forcing women to stop working at marriage.

What is age discrimination in employment?

1.4   Age discrimination in employment can be overt and deliberate, or it can be subtle and unintentional. It can affect people of any age, depending on the context; all that matters is being the 'wrong' age for the circumstances. It can take the form of individual decisions made by employers or colleagues, or it can be embedded into the policies and systems of an organisation. It can be based directly on age, or be the result of the indirect effects of provisions that appear to treat everyone alike. Put simply, age discrimination is any workplace practice that disadvantages people of a particular age.

1.5   When Age Concern asked people in 2004 whether they had recent experience of age discrimination, 28% of adults said they had. The highest incidence was from people aged under 25 and between 55 and 65, the points where most people enter and leave the labour market.[1] Another survey from 2001 found that one in four people aged between 50 and 69 report having experienced age discrimination in work or when applying for a job.[2]

Recruitment and selection

1.6   People talk about age discrimination in recruitment more than in any other sphere of employment. Youthful and mature workers consistently report being disadvantaged by their age in applying for jobs. For example, in 2006 when Age Concern launched Heyday, a membership organisation for people in their 50s and 60s, it asked around

---

1   *How ageist is Britain?* Age Concern England, 2005.
2   *Evaluation of the Code of Practice on Age Diversity in Employment,* Department for Work and Pensions, 2001.

60,000 potential members whether they thought their age would count against them in applying for a job. An astonishing 70% said that it would and a further 25% said it might, with only 5% saying their age would have no effect.

1.7   Individuals' perceptions are backed up by reports of employer practices. Even after 15 years of government campaigning against age discrimination 10% of employers openly admit to using age as a criterion for making recruitment decisions. With many employers unaware that they are discriminating, or unwilling to own up to it, this figure is likely to be the tip of the iceberg. The position is even worse for people in their 60s since almost three in ten recruiting employers openly apply upper age limits in recruitment.[3]

1.8   There are wide ranging effects from discrimination in recruitment. First, it leads to people being out of work against their wishes. Discrimination is certainly one explanation for why there are around a million over-50s wanting work (although there are other reasons, such as health and skills problems). In total if all these people were able to move into work it would add around £30 billion to economic output.[4] Second, it makes it harder for people to move jobs. This means that mature workers can stay on with an employer longer than either side may want. It also leads to people getting stuck in jobs beneath their abilities, unable to find work that matches their skills. This is one cause of the 13% 'age pay gap' – the difference in the hourly wage of full-timers aged over 50, compared to those in their 40s.

Promotion

1.9   Compared to recruitment, there has been less research and debate on discrimination in promotion. Nevertheless, age discrimination in promotion is widespread, and also tends to affect young and old alike. Of employers with recent experience of promoting staff, 5% admit to using age as a criterion for promotion, while younger employees are also affected by employers imposing length of service requirements. With half of employers not having any criteria for promotion at all there is also wide potential for ageist decision making on a case-by-case basis.[5]

3   H Metcalf and P Meadows, *Survey of employers policies, practices and preferences relating to age*, Department of Trade and Industry and Department for Work and Pensions, 2006.

4   *Age Concern's Response to A New Deal for Welfare*, Age Concern England, 2006.

5   H Metcalf and P Meadows, *Survey of employers policies, practices and preferences relating to age*, Department of Trade and Industry and Department for Work and Pensions, 2006.

1.10   Discrimination in promotion is often linked to a wider culture of ageism within organisations. If an employer has lower expectations of older workers, he or she may assume that an employee will not want development and promotion; they will offer them fewer opportunities and, unsurprisingly, the employee is less likely to develop; moreover the expectations of the employer are likely to rub-off on the employee whose horizons may narrow as a result. This process is particularly associated with the use of fixed retirement and pension ages, which can create a 'countdown culture' in the years beforehand.

1.11   One of the early cases under Ireland's Employment Equality Act 1998 saw a civil servant win an age discrimination claim after being overlooked for promotion.[6]

Training and education

1.12   Older employees are significantly under-represented in training at work. Of workers aged 50–59, 23% report recent participation in training, compared to 30% of 25–49-year-olds. This lower participation rate is in part caused by employer policies.[7] Around 1% of employers admit using age as a criteria for selection for training, and 8% take account of the time an employee has before retirement.[8] However, more often ageism in training results from the shared expectations of employer and employees; managers do not encourage older workers to train, and employees do not request training.

1.13   There are similar problems in adult learning provided by colleges and universities, which are also covered by the Employment Equality (Age) Regulations 2006. There is a significant problem with take-up in work-related learning among people over 50 (although participation in adult vocational training begins to tail-off from the 30s onwards). There is also an ageist culture within much of the adult learning world, with older learners being seen as less deserving than younger adults. In recent years Age Concern has heard of marketing campaigns being explicitly targeted at younger age groups, and the timing of classes being shifted to reduce the number of older learners. On top of this, there are examples of direct age discrimination in the government's

6   *Gillen v Department for Health and Children*, ET CDEE/2000 1027, labour Court ADE/03/15 determination 0412.

7   P Meadows and Volterra Consulting, *The economic contributions of older people*, Age Concern England, 2004.

8   H Metcalf and P Meadows, *Survey of employers policies, practices and preferences relating to age*, Department of Trade and Industry and Department for Work and Pensions, 2006.

rules for the funding of adult learning. For example, many apprenticeships are only available to people up to the age of 25. In 2003 the government committed to removing this barrier over time, but then in 2006 it proposed yet more discrimination in the shape of a new entitlement to free A Level equivalent qualifications for under-25s.[9] A financial incentive for taking A Level equivalent qualifications is only available up to the age of 30.

Pay and benefits

1.14 Age discrimination in pay is at present an issue of both direct and indirect discrimination. 14% of employers admit taking age directly into account when setting pay (of whom 11% use youth rates). But on top of this, one-third of employers use incremental pay scales, which are likely to indirectly discriminate against younger people with fewer years of service. A further third have performance-related pay, where decisions are susceptible to the age-related prejudices of managers.[10]

1.15 The most important non-pay benefit is an occupational benefit. For pensions, talking about discrimination is problematic because treating people of different ages differently is an essential part of their design. Put crudely, if the same amount of money is put in for people of different ages, they will get different pensions out. If the same amount of pension is promised for people of different ages, different amounts of money need to be put in. However on top of this basic design, there are examples of unfair age-based practices. For example, one-third of schemes apply a maximum age for joining.[11]

1.16 Other forms of benefits, such as leave entitlements and fringe benefits such like insurance, may also have age limits. This was the source of much discussion by employers in the lead-up to the new legislation, however it is rare in practice. Only 2% of employers have age-based leave entitlement and 1% have upper age-limits on benefits. Even where there has been official approval for discrimination in benefits it has been rare. Only 8% of employers offering sick pay above the statutory level apply an upper age limit, even though the statutory sick

---

9 *Twenty-first century skills: realising our potential,* Department for Education and Skills, 2003; *Further Education: Raising Skills, Improving Life Chances,* Department for Education and Skills, 2006.

10 See H Metcalf and P Meadows, note 8 above.

11 H Metcalf and P Meadows, *Survey of employers policies, practices and preferences relating to age,* Department of Trade and Industry and Department for Work and Pensions, 2006.

pay scheme included a limit of 65 until the Employment Equality (Age) Regulations 2006 came into force.[12]

Redundancy

1.17   Age discrimination in redundancy works in two ways. It can disadvantage the person being selected for redundancy, particularly where they are selected for compulsory retirement against their wishes, or it can appear to benefit the person being made redundant, for example where someone receives a redundancy package that is not available to people of other ages. Even the second category often leads to long-term financial hardship since people made redundant in their 50s often struggle to find work again. This sort of voluntary redundancy has often been regarded as a 'kind' way to ease out older workers. It may benefit individual workers, but it entrenches ageist attitudes and practices within the organisation.

1.18   Age discrimination is widespread in selection for compulsory redundancy. Age itself is a factor in redundancy decisions in 14% of cases where employers have selection criteria. Other factors that are likely to disadvantage older workers are also used including length of service and salary (51% and 5% of cases, respectively). On the other hand, younger workers can also be disadvantaged by the use of a 'last in, first out' criterion (which features in 28% of selection criteria). Age is less often included as a criterion for voluntary redundancy arrangements (appearing in 8% of selection criteria) although length of service is used more often (15%).[13]

1.19   Age and length of service are common features of criteria for redundancy payments, including the statutory scheme (which remains largely unchanged by the new regulations). Around a quarter of employers with policies or recent experience of redundancy report taking age into account in setting compensation, while close to half report using length of service.[14]

Retirement

1.20   Retirement can mean two very different things. First, it is voluntary exit from work, often accompanied by entitlement to a pension and

12   H Metcalf and P Meadows, *Survey of employers policies, practices and preferences relating to age,* Department of Trade and Industry and Department for Work and Pensions, 2006.

13   See note 9.

14   See note 9.

welcomed by the employee. Second, it can also mean compulsory dismissal by an employer, solely on grounds of age, against the wishes of an employee. In between these two positions, some people report that their retirement was 'part wanted, part chosen', with the policies and culture of an employer (alongside personal circumstances) dictating a decision that might have been different other things being equal. More than half of retirements before the state pension age are against people's wishes (often on health grounds) as are around one third of retirements at state pension age.[15]

1.21   Forced retirement remains surprisingly widespread. 37% of employers use mandatory retirement ages, and they are particularly common in larger organisations and in the public sector: 71% of employers with less than 50 staff do not use mandatory retirement ages, compared with 44% of employers with over 250 staff; 64% of private sector employers do not use mandatory retirement ages compared with 34% of public employers. In most cases mandatory retirement ages appear to be relics of history. Looking at those employers with fixed retirement ages 70% could not give a reason for this and a further 14% said the reason was historic or when asked said 'we just do'.[16]

1.22   It is difficult to calculate the number of people who are actually forced out of their jobs each year by a mandatory retirement age. Around 150,000 workers reach their 65th birthday each year and Age Concern estimates that between 5,000 and 25,000 are forced to retire. It is easier to detect the impact on forced retirement on overall employment patterns (measures of this sort take into account the wider implications of scrapping retirement ages, including shifts in expectations, voluntary decisions and recruitment patterns). A 2003 survey showed that where employers do not have a mandatory retirement age(MRA) 18% of people retire after state pension age, compared to 7% where MRAs are in use.[17] This result reflects similar research in the United States which suggests that scrapping mandatory retirement ages there led to an increase in the number of workers aged over 65 of between 10 and 20%.[18]

---

15 A Humphrey et al, *Factors affecting the labour market participation of older workers*, Department for Work and Pensions, 2003.

16 H Metcalf and P Meadows, *Survey of employers policies, practices and preferences relating to age*, Department of Trade and Industry and Department for Work and Pensions, 2006.

17 A Humphrey et al, *Factors affecting the labour market participation of older workers*, Department for Work and Pensions, 2003.

18 T von Wachter, 'The end of mandatory retirement in the US: effect on retirement and implicit contracts', Center for Labour Economic, Working Paper no 49, University of California, Berkeley, 2002.

The ageing workforce

1.23 So the evidence shows that age discrimination is extremely wide-spread. The irony is that by discriminating on grounds of age, employers are shooting themselves in the foot. Today discrimination reduces the pool of talent open to employers to recruit from – we have already seen that there are around one million people over 50 wanting work. But in the future, excluding older people will not simply be unwise; it will have serious consequences for businesses and the wider economy.

1.24   Most people are now familiar with the idea that the British population is ageing. Our life expectancies are growing longer and fertility rates have fallen from the peaks seen between the 1940s and the 1960s. The implications of population ageing for the supply of labour should be obvious, but many employers have not woken up to the changes ahead. Over the next decade, as the population grows by 2.7 million people, there will be a modest *decline* in the number of adults aged under 50. Meanwhile the number of people aged 50 to 69 will rise by 2 million. They will offer a growing pool of workers, available to those employers who do not let ageist prejudice get in the way.[19]

1.25   On the other hand, if the status quo continues and employers do not make more use of older peoples' skills the damage that could be caused to the economy can hardly be over-stated. If there is no rise in the share of older people in work over the next ten years, then the ratio of workers to non-workers in the population will fall alongside the decline in the proportion of people aged 16 to 49. This would depress the annual rate of economic growth. On the other hand if, over the next 10 or 15 years, employers reach out to older workers, there is the potential to employ an extra million people over 50. If this happened then the ratio of workers to non-workers would remain static and economic output would be unaffected by demographic change.[20]

Ageism

1.26 Ageism is everywhere. Sometimes it is completely in the open. People use offensive language about older people – how about 'coffin dodger'?

19 2004-based principal population projections, Government Actuary Department, 2005.

20 *Age Concern's response to a new deal for welfare*, Age Concern England, 2006.

– when equivalent descriptions of minority ethnic groups or disabled people are socially unacceptable throughout most of society. Similarly, many people express derogatory views about older people which either have no factual basis or are gross generalisations. This can be illustrated by two examples from the workplace. First, it is often said that older workers are less likely to be able to acquire new skills.[21] Second, employers frequently assume that older workers' mental or physical capabilities are lower than those of younger adults.[22] Both these assumptions are wrong. Young people suffer from similar generalisations, for example with regard to inexperience and lack of responsibility.

1.27   Ageism can also be hidden – either where people disguise their ageism or where it is subconscious and they are not aware of it themselves. In *Freakonomics*, Stephen Levitt's surprise hit of 2005, the study of hidden (or 'implicit') ageism was brought out of the psychologist's laboratory and into the TV studio. Levitt described how, in the US version of the *Weakest Link*, contestants' voting decisions were, on average, biased against older panellists. At the stage of the game where it is in participants' interests to vote for poor performers, older people were likely to be chosen even when younger adults had performed worse. But when contestants would benefit by choosing top performing rivals (to eliminate the competition) they tended to choose lower-performing older contestants. Subconsciously the panellists simply did not want to be around older people.[23]

---

21   This is untrue, older people who participate in training courses are just as likely to qualify (P Meadows and Volterra Consulting, *The economic contributions of older people*, Age Concern England, 2004).

22   Here an entire age group is stereotyped on the basis of the small minority of older employees who struggle, almost always due to identifiable health problems. The reality is that, as we age, some aspects of our capabilities decline gradually (eg physical agility and high-speed mental processing) while others improve (eg abilities linked to relationship-building and experience). But overall the differences in abilities within age groups massively outweigh average differences between people of different ages; changes in individuals' capabilities scarcely show up in terms of job performance. (P Meadows and Volterra Consulting, *The economic contributions of older people*, Age Concern England, 2004; S Ray, E Sharp, D Abrams, *Age discrimination: a benchmark of public attitudes*, Age Concern England, 2006).

23   S Levitt and S Dubner, *Freakonomics*, Penguin, 2005 pp77–79. The *Weakest Link* is a popular British general knowledge quiz show. At the end of each round contestants vote for one of their fellow participants to be ejected from the contest, supposedly on the basis of their performance.

Defining ageism

1.28   The term 'ageism' was coined in 1969 by Robert Butler, the Director of the US National Institute on Aging. He defined it as a combination of three connected elements. These were:

- prejudicial attitudes towards older persons, old age and the ageing process;
- discriminatory practices against older people;
- institutional practices and policies that perpetuate stereotypes about older people.[24]

1.29   He was thinking of ageism in terms of the attitudes held by people, the way they behave as a result of these attitudes, and the institutional norms that foster both discriminatory attitudes and practice.

1.30   Since 2004, Age Concern has been carrying out a programme of research on ageism, and has tried to break down Butler's concept into different categories. The charity defines 'ageism' itself as the stereotypes and prejudices people hold about older people (whether open or hidden). The practices that result from these attitudes, at both personal and institutional level, are described as 'age discrimination'. So, ageism refers to beliefs and attitudes; age discrimination is about actions.

1.31   Campaigners for older people also refer to 'age equality', which Age Concern describes as the equal participation in society of people of every age, based on respect for the dignity and value of each individual. Barriers to age equality include ageist attitudes, and the discriminatory practices that result from them, but age-related inequality can also stem from other sources of disadvantage (such as differences in health or education between generations). It can be helpful to think of 'institutional ageism' when the outcomes an organisation or system achieves for people of different ages are unjustifiably different, even where this is not the intention of the people providing the services. The concept of institutional ageism is useful because unequal outcomes are often linked to unacknowledged attitudes or the ageist culture of an organisation. For example, when institutions treat different people identically when their needs or preferences are different, this is frequently related to ageism.[25]

---

24   J Wilkinson and K Ferraro, 'Thirty Years of Ageism Research' in T Nelson (ed) *Ageism: stereotyping and prejudice against older persons*, Massachusetts Institute of Technology, 2002.

25   Where people of *different ages* are treated alike despite their differences this is often because older people have been ignored in the design of services. Where a group of *older people* are treated alike despite being very different this is often linked to stereotyping, which lumps older people together.

Ageist stereotyping and prejudice

1.32   What do we mean by ageist stereotyping and prejudice? *Stereotyping* is
a tool of cognition which involves categorising into groups and attributing characteristics to these groups. Stereotypes are necessary for processing huge volumes of information, which would otherwise overload
us, and they are often based on a 'grain of truth' (for example, the
association between ageing and ill-health). However, they cause harm
when the content of the stereotype is incorrect with respect to most of
the group; or where a stereotype is so strongly held that it overrides evidence which shows that an individual does not conform to it. Stereotypes are used to interpret the world around us. For example, age-based
stereotypes prime us to draw very different conclusions when we see
an older and a younger adult with, say, back pain or a limp. We might
well assume that the younger person's condition was temporary and
treatable, following an accident; while the older person's condition
was chronic and less susceptible to intervention. On average this might
be true, but plenty of older people have accidents and recover quickly.
This assumption may have no consequence if we make it in the blink
of an eye as we are passing someone in the street; but if it is held by
health professionals offering treatment, or managers thinking about
occupational health, it could inappropriately influence their actions
and lead to age-related discrimination.

1.33   *Prejudice* is a type of emotion which is often linked to the cognitive process of stereotyping. It can involve the expression of derogatory
attitudes, which may then lead to the use of discriminatory behaviour.
The example of the Weakest Link helps to explain the difference
between stereotyping and prejudice. Where older contestants were
rejected in the belief that they were poor performers this could well be
the result of stereotyping. But older people were also voted for at the
stage in the game where it made sense to target the best performers.
This can only be explained by a subconscious emotional reaction to
older people; in this case the prejudice took the form of distaste and a
desire to exclude oneself from the company of older people.

1.34   This subconscious desire to separate ourselves from older people,
which may be linked to fears about our own ageing, is one driver for
the whole process of stereotyping; the desire for distance leads to older
people being seen as 'other'. Evidence of this distancing of older people
comes from a survey on ageism carried out by Age Concern in 2004.
It showed that people are more likely to attribute stereotypes to older
people than younger people, indicating that older people are more
often seen as a homogenous, separate group. Moreover two-thirds of
respondents said that under-30s and over-70s have little or nothing in

common. 45 to 54 year-olds – aged half-way between 30 and 70 – were more likely to have close friends under the age of 30 than over the age of 70, and even among 55–64-year-olds, one-third reported having no friends over 70.[26]

1.35   Stereotyping and prejudice against different groups in society does not take the same form. Age-based prejudice and stereotyping usually involves older people being pitied, marginalised or patronised. This is described as 'benevolent prejudice' because the tendency to pity is linked to seeing older people as 'friendly' but 'incompetent'. This is similar to the prejudice most often directed against women and disabled people. Age Concern's survey revealed strong evidence of 'benevolent prejudice'. 48% said that over-70s are viewed as friendly (compared to 27% who said the same about under-30s). Meanwhile only 26% believe over-70s are viewed as capable (with 41% saying the same about under-30s).

1.36   'Hostile prejudice' based on hatred, fear or threat (which often characterises attitudes linked to race, religion and sexual orientation) is less common with respect to age issues. But there are examples, including excessive rhetoric regarding inter-generational competition, and violence against vulnerable older people, which can be motivated by sub-conscious hostility or fear. Equality campaigners are often wary of drawing comparisons between different forms of inequality. But it is unquestionably true that abuse and neglect experienced by vulnerable older people (which is closely linked to hostile prejudice) kills more people each year than the shocking but relatively isolated cases of public violence motivated by race, religion or sexual orientation.

1.37   The impact of 'benevolent' and 'hostile' prejudice can be equally severe but tends to be different. The warmth felt towards older people means there is often public acceptance that they are deserving of preferential treatment – for example, concessionary travel. But the perception of incompetence means older people can be seen as 'not up to the job' or 'a menace on the roads', when there is no evidence to support this. Benevolent prejudice also leads to assumptions that it is 'natural' for older people to have lower expectations, reduced choice and control, and less account taken of their views. To take one example, people over the age of 65 are not entitled to the mobility element of Disability Living Allowance because it is assumed they do not have the same need as younger people to be mobile.

26   S Ray, E Sharp, D Abrams, *Age discrimination: a benchmark of public attitudes*, Age Concern England, 2006. Note that some of this distancing results not from personal choices but institutional and social factors (which may in themselves arise from ageism).

Internalised ageism

1.38   Although stereotypes and prejudices are usually held in relation to groups we see as 'other', they can also be held by people about themselves. The main victims of ageism – older people – often hold ageist attitudes. This is because stereotypes and prejudices are acquired when people are young, when older people are 'others'. These stereotypes become internalised so that as people age they can remain prejudiced against older people, without being aware of it. One effect of this is that older people do not identify with their chronological age or with categories and concepts linked to age. This reduces an older person's ability to recognise or challenge ageism and may be one reason why people aged over 65 tend not to believe that age discrimination is a serious issue.[27]

1.39   Research also shows that the impacts of internalised ageism can reduce people's functioning, health and wellbeing. For example when older people are told that they are being compared to younger people (this 'primes' thoughts and feelings about age) their cognitive and physical performance is measurably reduced. Interestingly this effect does not occur when people have close friendships with younger adults, and so are less likely to hold age-related stereotypes.[28] There is also good evidence that holding positive attitudes to ageing is important for health and wellbeing in later life. A fascinating US study has even shown a link between positive attitudes to ageing and improved life expectancy.[29]

Action against age discrimination before 2000

Before the 1990s

1.40   In the United States, age discrimination law (for people over 40 only) was part of the 1960s civil rights settlement alongside legislation on race and gender. President Johnson issued an Executive Order covering

---

27   S Ray, E Sharp, D Abrams, *Age discrimination: a benchmark of public attitudes*, Age Concern England, 2006.

28   *Age discrimination beyond the workplace, Age Concern seminar series*, Age Concern England, 2006; T Nelson (ed) *Ageism: stereotyping and prejudice against older persons*. Massachusetts Institute of Technology, 2002.

29   BR Levy, MD Slade et al, 'Longevity Increased by Positive Self-Perceptions of Aging' *Journal of Personality and Social Psychology* (2002) 83, (2): 261–270. *Promoting mental health and wellbeing in later life, a first report from the UK Inquiry into Mental Health and Wellbeing in Later Life*, Age Concern England, 2006.

age discrimination in employment in 1964 and this was followed in 1967 by the Age Discrimination in Employment Act.[30] In the UK, however, there was little pressure to include age discrimination legislation in the mid-1970s alongside the Sex Discrimination Act 1975 and the Race Relations Act 1976. This was at a time when the employment rates for men in their 50s were as high as for younger men and the concept of 'ageism' was unfamiliar.[31] From its inception, however, the Sex Discrimination Act was sometimes used to challenge age discrimination; as early as 1977 an upper age limit of 28 for entry into the civil service was found to be indirect sex discrimination.[32]

1.41　　　In the 1980s there were some calls for age discrimination legislation, for example from the Unemployment Alliance.[33] However, from the early 1980s onwards the Conservative government responded that legislation would not be 'beneficial or practicable'.[34] In the late 1980s there was increased discussion about age discrimination in employment. The Institute of Personnel Management included age in its Code of Practice from 1987.[35] In 1988 the Campaign Against Age Discrimination in Employment was established by a group of people who felt they had been victims of age discrimination.[36] Age discrimination was also discussed by the House of Commons Employment Select Committee in its 1988 inquiry 'Employment Patterns of the Over 50s'. The committee's recommendations fell well short of a call for age discrimination legislation, but included proposals that employers who impose age restrictions on recruitment should always be challenged by the Employment Service; that the Confederation of British Industry (CBI) and the government should mount a campaign emphasising the value of older workers and challenging discrimination; and that the government should review its own practices on retirement ages and early pension entitlements to give more choice about the age of retirement.[37]

30　Special Committee on Aging, United States Senate, *Developments in aging: 1999 and 2000*, Vol I, United States Congress, 2001.

31　B Byetheway, *Ageism*, Open University Press, 1995, p299.

32　*Ms Price v Civil Service Commission*, 1997.

33　E McEwen (ed) *Age – the unrecognised discrimination, views to provoke a debate*, Age Concern England, 1990, p93.

34　E McEwen (ed) *Age – the unrecognised discrimination, views to provoke a debate*, Age Concern England, 1990, p86; the quote is from Peter Morrison, Minister of State for Employment in 1984.

35　Ibid pp94–95.

36　See www.caade.net.

37　*Employment patterns of the over-50s: second report*, House of Commons Employment Committee, Session 1998/1999.

1.42   Conservative ministers repeatedly spoke out against age discrimination in employment. The 1988 white paper *Employment in the 1990s*
criticised the wastefulness of employers who ruled out applicants on
grounds of age. Ministers also warned against age discrimination in
communications to employers and in speeches.[38] The government also
took some limited action on age discrimination, in response to the 1988
select committee report. Employment Service guidance already
instructed jobcentre staff to try to persuade employers not to use age
restrictions, but in January 1989 the guidance was tightened 'to ensure
that where an employer insists on an age restriction, the Employment
Service seeks to persuade him to treat it as a preference rather than an
absolute requirement. The service will also contact an employer if a
recruit becomes available who is suitable in all respects other than age'.[38]
At the same time, age limits on civil service recruitment were removed.[40]
The most significant reform of 1989 came, however, in the budget. The
Chancellor of the Exchequer, Nigel Lawson, announced that rules
restricting State Pension eligibility to people who had retired or had
low earnings would be removed.[41] In retrospect, this reform came to
be seen as the lifting of a directly discriminatory barrier to employment.

The 1990s

1.43   From 1992 onwards the government began to step up action on age
discrimination in employment. Perhaps surprisingly, older workers
found an enthusiastic champion in Ann Widdecombe MP, a Department
of Employment minister between 1993 and 1995. An Advisory Group on
Older Workers was established in December 1992 and the following
year the 'Getting On' initiative was launched with a five-point plan for
employers to avoid ageism. This was followed up with a booklet for
employers, drawing on the experience of companies with mixed age
workforces, as well as regional workshops. Further action was taken in
1995 with the publication of *Too Old ... Who Says?*, a guidance booklet for
individuals, and the promotion of good practice to recruitment agencies.[42]

---

38   Hansard, col 437, 16 May 1990; col 40, 7 May 1991; E McEwen (ed), *Age – the
unrecognised discrimination, views to provoke a debate*, Age Concern, 1990 p84.

39   Hansard, col 64, 6 June 1989.

40   Hansard, col 565, 23 May 1995.

41   Hansard, col 307, 14 March 1989; Social Security Act 1989, Fiscal Studies, Vol
11, No 3, August 1990; R Disney and S Tanner, *The abolition of the earnings rule
for UK pensioners*, IFS working paper, April 2000.

42   Hansard, col 418, 4 Dec 1992; col 435, 4 Nov 1993; col 143, 2 May 1995; col
565, 23 May 1995; col 817, 23 May 1995; col 131, 17 Oct 1995.

1.44   During this time, the government remained firmly opposed to age discrimination legislation. In June 1994 the Department of Employment published *An international overview of employment policies and practices towards older workers* which included research into the policies and practices towards older workers in 22 countries, including Canada and New Zealand. Ministers concluded that 'the research found no evidence that anti-discrimination legislation has been successful in improving either the economic activity rates of older workers or their employment prospects'.[43]

1.45   The government's caution in proceeding to legislation reflected a wider reticence current at the time. The influential Carnegie Inquiry into the Third Age recommended in 1993 that voluntary initiatives should be adopted, and legislation only considered if employers failed to act. Even Age Concern expressed caution about age discrimination legislation, calling in 1990 'for a start to be made in this country through making upper age limits in recruitment advertising illegal'.[44]

1.46   Age discrimination in recruitment advertising was widely seen as the top priority for action on age discrimination. In 1987 the Equal Opportunities Commission had carried out a survey on age discrimination in recruitment advertising, which showed that a quarter of adverts had upper age limits, usually of 45 or lower.[45] Similar findings were reported throughout the early-1990s and the Carnegie Inquiry made a series of recommendations on advertising and initiated a campaign to reduce the use of age limits.[46] This voluntary approach was largely successful, with overt age limits in recruitment advertising becoming much less common over the course of the 1990s.

1.47   Age restrictions in recruitment advertising were the target of several private members bills, for example the Employment (Upper Age Limits in Advertisements) Bill of 1996, sponsored by Labour backbencher David Winnick and, once Labour was in power, the 1998 Employment (Age Discrimination in Advertisements) Bill, introduced by Linda Perham MP. These bills sought to outlaw age discrimination in job advertisements only, partly as this was seen as a top priority and partly

---

43   Hansard, col 565, 23 May 1995; Joanne Moore, Barbara Tilson, Gill Whitting, *An international overview of employment policies and practices towards older workers*, ECOTEC Research and Consulting Ltd, Employment Department Research Series no 24.

44   E McEwen (ed), *Age – the unrecognised discrimination, views to provoke a debate*, Age Concern England, 1990 p86.

45   Equal Opportunities Review, 25, 1989.

46   *The third age: the continuing challenge, a report to mark the end of the second stage of Carnegie's work on the third Age*, 1996.

because anything more radical would stand no chance of gaining government support.

1.48 These bills were two of a series of attempts to introduce legislation on age discrimination from the backbench and opposition benches of both houses of parliament. In 1998 Linda Perham described her 1998 bill as 'Parliament's ninth opportunity in 15 years to put on the statute book legislation that begins to address age discrimination'.[47] These bills were mainly designed simply to raise awareness of the issue. For example, in March 1997 the Conservative MP Quentin Davis – normally a staunch de-regulator – introduced an age discrimination 'ten minute rule' bill (ie a procedural device to raise debate, with no real chance of becoming law).[48] In 1989 the Labour frontbench proposed that a new clause be added to the Employment Bill to outlaw discrimination on grounds of age.[49] A decade later it was a Labour government that would resist similar moves to amend mainstream employment legislation when the Liberal Democrats put down amendments to the 1999 Employment Relations Bill.[50]

The Labour Party in opposition

1.49 The Labour Party in opposition was positive about age discrimination legislation, and at times led calls for change. In its 1992 manifesto it said 'anti-discrimination law will be strengthened and we will consider as part of that law outlawing discrimination in employment on the grounds of age'.[51] During the 1992 to 1997 Parliament, Labour hardened its position. The 1994 Labour Party *Charter for employees* committed 'to expand existing anti-discrimination legislation and provide new opportunities for removing discrimination on the grounds of race, sex, disability and age in recruitment, promotion, redundancy and retirement for men and women up to the age of 65'.[52] In 1996, during the debate on David Winnick's private member's bill, the Labour frontbench spokesperson Ian McCartney confirmed this, saying:

> The Labour Party's position is quite clear. This Conservative Government may not accept my hon. Friend's Bill, but an incoming Labour Government

47 Hansard, col 1396, 6 Feb 1998.
48 Hansard, col 885, 19 Mar 1997.
49 Hansard, col 57, 6 June 1999.
50 Hansard, col 930, 30 March 1999.
51 *It's time to get Britain working again*, Labour Party Manifesto, 1992.
52 Quoted in Richard Worsley, *Age and employment, why employers should think again about older workers*, Age Concern England, 1996.

will introduce comprehensive legislation to make age discrimination in employment illegal. We shall consult on the legislation.[53]

1.50   This statement proved to be a millstone for Labour ministers once in office, when the new government decided to pursue non-legislative options. While in opposition, Labour's support for legislation led organisations such as Age Concern to call much more vociferously for a change to the law, and they were joined by mainstream commentators such as the Law Society's Employment Committee.[54] The Labour Party's 1997 manifesto was however more circumspect than previous statements, stopping short of a definitive commitment to legislation:

> We value the positive contribution that older people make to our society, through their families, voluntary activities and work ... In work, they should not be discriminated against because of their age ... We will seek to end unjustifiable discrimination wherever it exists.[55]

The Labour Party in government

1.51   Once in office Labour moved quickly. On 22 May 1997 Andrew Smith MP, the Minister for Employment, announced that the government would consult on age discrimination:

> The Government are strongly opposed to age discrimination at work. We shall be consulting widely to obtain a consensus on how we can best proceed to achieve that ... The role of legislation must be examined ... Before we proceed to legislate, we shall need to consult interested parties, groups that would be affected, including those representing elderly people, employers and those with expertise. We strongly believe that age discrimination is wrong, and we shall implement proposals to stop it.[56]

1.52   Over the following 15 months the government's ambivalence on legislation shifted to outright opposition. In August 1998 Smith published *Action on age,* a report setting out the conclusions of his consultation and announcing that legislation was being ruled out. The government said 'on balance, there was no consensus of opinion on legislation and a strong case for legislation was not made during the consultation'. The report listed arguments in favour of legislation including

---

53   Hansard, col 618, 9 Feb 1996.
54   *Age, discrimination and employment law, a report of the Law Society's Employment Law Committee,* March 1996.
55   *Because Britain deserves better,* Labour Party Manifesto, 1997.
56   Hansard, col 826, 22 May 1997.

the role it would play in changing attitudes; the broad support of managers and employees for new law; the success of age discrimination law in other countries; and the case for establishing parity with sex, race and disability equality. The report also presented robust evidence of age discrimination, reporting that 5% of older workers reported being discriminated against in making a job application. The arguments against that won the day were that it would add to regulation and employment costs; that unscrupulous employers would find ways around the law or take discrimination underground; and that there would need to be so many exemptions that the law would end up as a half measure. The government also argued that the overseas evidence on age discrimination law was inconclusive.[57]

1.53   This announcement came as little surprise. Earlier in 1998 the government had refused to support Labour backbencher Linda Perham's private member's bill on age limits in recruitment advertising. It had also announced that it would consult on the introduction of a non-statutory Code of Practice on age diversity. A working group to advise on the code was established and the code was issued in draft in October 1998.[58] There were two crumbs of consolation for advocates of legislation. The Employment Service announced an outright ban on upper age limits in jobcentre recruitment advertising; and the government pledged to raise the upper age limit for entitlement to a higher education student loan from 50 to 55. The *Action on age* report also promised that the government would monitor the code and carry out a full evaluation in early 2001.

1.54   There was a further development in December 1998 when the Prime Minister was caught off guard at Prime Minister's Questions. Without a brief to hand he said that the government stood by the commitment to introduce legislation made in opposition.[59] This led to a written statement from the Prime Minister a fortnight later, which re-opened the door to eventual legislation:

> Given this Government's busy legislative programme, the Code of Practice is an effective measure that will challenge employment practices that unfairly discriminate against employees on the grounds of age. The impact of the Code will be evaluated and this will inform future plans for legislation in this area.[60]

---

57 *Action on age – report on the consultation on age discrimination in employment,* Department for Education and Employment, 1998.

58 *Consultation on A Code of Practice for Age Diversity in Employment,* DfEE, 1998.

59 Hansard, col 879, 2 Dec 1998.

60 Hansard, Commons Written Answers, 15 December 1998.

1.55   Following consultation the Code was launched by the Prime Minister in June 1999. The government reported that the initial launch of the code was a success; 34,000 copies were issued over the summer and a poll in September reported that 70% of employers were aware of the code.[61] For campaigners for age discrimination law it seemed that there would be no chance of further progress until at least 2001. To their surprise, by the end of 2000 age discrimination law was not just being discussed, but had actually been approved. And against all the expectations in 1997, the new law came from Europe rather than domestic legislation.

The Treaty of Amsterdam and the article 13 Directives

The Treaty of Amsterdam

1.56   Since the 1950s the remit of the European Community has encompassed sex discrimination in employment. Article 119 of the EC Treaty stated that member states should 'maintain the application of the principle that men and women should receive equal pay for equal work' (the original rationale for the provision had far more to do with cross-border competition than feminism). In the mid-1970s there were two further developments; the European Court of Justice ruled that article 119 should have direct effect and the council approved the 1976 Equal Treatment Directive.

1.57   By contrast, until the late-1990s the EC had no competence with respect to discrimination on other grounds (with the exception of equality between citizens of member states). The 1992 Maastricht Treaty required the union to respect human rights as general principles of community law, but this did not extend its competence into new areas of employment discrimination. This limited scope for action became a growing concern as fears about racism grew across the union in the 1990s. In advance of the 1996 Intergovernmental Conference which would revise the treaties, the official advisory committees of the union, the Economic and Social Committee and the Committee of the Regions both recommended a new treaty provision outlawing discrimination on a wider number of grounds. Age was very much at the periphery of these discussions.

61   DfEE Press Releases, 14 June 1999, 6 September 1999.

1.58   While the Conservatives were in office the United Kingdom remained opposed to a new treaty article on discrimination. Most other member states supported extending protection to race and religion, but there was initial opposition to the article covering disability, let alone sexual orientation and age. However, during the Irish presidency in the second half of 1996 there was significant movement, with member states proposing a new equality provision covering a longer list of issues. Older people's organisations led by Eurolink Age, an EU-wide network, lobbied member states and the European Parliament to see age included in the list. Their case was helped by the poor record of the European institutions on age discrimination, which had only recently removed an upper age limits of 35 for recruitment into senior grades. No government was a real advocate for including age in the article, but few member states had strong objections either. So when Labour came to power in May 1997, and the UK gave its backing to article 13, the draft that was finally approved referred to six strands, including age:[62]

> Without prejudice to the other provisions of this Treaty and within the limits of the powers conferred by it upon the Community, the Council, acting unanimously on a proposal from the Commission and after consulting the European Parliament, may take appropriate action to combat discrimination based on sex, racial or ethnic origin, religion or belief, disability, age or sexual orientation.[63]

Proposals for legislation and the government's reaction

1.59   Article 13 came into force in May 1999 and by November the European Commission had consulted and was ready with proposals for action. The package included two draft directives, one covering race equality across all areas of community competence, and the other covering equal treatment in employment across five strands.[64] There was also a proposal for a Community Action Programme to promote equality.

---

62 *EU proposals to combat discrimination*, House of Lords European Union Select Committee, 9th report, session 1999/2000; K Ghose, *Beyond the courtroom, a lawyer's guide to campaigning*, (Legal Action Group, 2005).

63 EC Treaty, art 13.

64 The Commission decided not to absorb the existing gender directives into the proposals. The overlap between the race and employment directives was subsequently removed.

Extract from Explanatory Memorandum to the Commission Draft Directive (November 1999)

The aim of this proposal is the establishment of a general framework for the respect of the principle of equal treatment between persons irrespective of race or ethnic origin, religion or belief, disability, age, or sexual orientation within the European Union. The areas covered by the proposal are access to employment and occupation, promotion, vocational training, employment and working conditions and membership of certain bodies.

In spite of the fact that demographic trends make it essential to ensure that as high a percentage as possible of people of working age are in jobs, a recent survey of 11 European countries identified five sets of discriminatory measures in the employment field which particularly affect older people: loss of employment, discrimination in recruitment, exclusion from special unemployment measures, exclusion from training and discrimination at retirement.

Concrete examples of the above include, in particular, the establishment of maximum recruitment ages (other than those mentioned in Article 5(d)), the limitation of older workers' training rights concerning new technologies, the right to promotion, or dismissals of older workers within the context of restructuring.

The Commission believes that the proposal for a Community framework directive on employment equality fully complies with the principle of proportionality. First, the Commission has decided to follow a step-by-step approach, based on the successful precedent of Community legislation on sex equality ... All grounds of discrimination are apparent in employment and occupation matters. Employment and occupation also constitute people's main guarantee for social inclusion, for full participation in economic, cultural and social life and for the enjoyment of basic human rights and freedoms. For this reason, a horizontal proposal covering the area of employment and occupation is considered appropriate.

Second, the scope of the present proposal covers all discriminatory grounds referred to in Article 13 except sex and does not rank them in any way. This absence of a qualitative hierarchy among the discriminatory grounds is of particular importance in cases of multiple discrimination. Therefore, it is consistent with the structure and apparent purpose of Article 13.

1.60   The British government reacted warmly to the proposals. David Blunkett, the then Secretary of State for Education and Employment, commented: 'we must ensure that any new legislation gives maximum protection from discrimination, but that it is also practically workable and easy to use for employers. Our support for these important measures shows that we continue to be at the forefront of European action to fight discrimination effectively'.[65] Despite the caveat regarding employers, this was quite a u-turn from the government's commitment to exclusively non-legislative action on age discrimination.

1.61   The government's position was indeed contradictory, with ministers supporting both the new code of practice and inclusion of age within the Directive. The government commented cryptically that its negotiating strategy would 'take account of an evolving domestic policy'.[66] The then minister for employment, Tessa Jowell MP said in her initial written comments on the Directive: 'The Government is open to making necessary and proportionate changes in this area [regulation on employers] to promote equal opportunities if the case is made. However, the need to avoid unnecessary and burdensome regulation will remain a priority in the Government's considerations. It will also be guided by assessments of the progress which can be achieved through non-legislative means such as codes of practice.'[67] In July she added: 'we have made it clear that [the Code's] impact will be evaluated before a decision about legislation is taken. The evaluation is due to be completed towards the middle of next year'.[68]

1.62   To add to this confused picture, in April 2000, the Cabinet Office published *Winning the generation game,* an important report on the contributions of people aged between 50 and state pension age. The report came from the Performance and Innovation Unit (PIU), an in-house government think-tank, and the recommendations were 'to' government rather than official policy commitments. However, they clearly showed the government thinking on age discrimination legislation was shifting from 'if' towards 'when'.

---

65   DfEE Press Release, 25 November 1999.

66   *EU proposals to combat discrimination,* House of Lords European Union Select Committee, 9th report, session 1999/2000.

67   House of Commons European Scrutiny Committee, Seventh Report, Session 1999/2000, 2 February 2000.

68   Hansard, European Standing Committee C, 24 July 2000.

Extract from *Winning the generation game*
There is some activity in the European Union on various forms
of discrimination including age. Article 13 of the Treaty of Amsterdam extended EU competence in the field of equal opportunities, previously limited to gender, so that the Council of Ministers
may 'take appropriate action to combat discrimination based
on sex, racial or ethnic origin, religion or belief, age or sexual
orientation'. The European Commission published three proposals under this article in November 1999, including one dealing with direct and indirect discrimination in employment on all
of the grounds covered by article 13 (except sex).

It will be important to monitor developing EU proposals and
to consider the extent to which they meet the potential need
identified for legislation in this area. At present the proposals
are, in a number of respects, inconsistent with the UK Code of
Practice. It will also be important to bear in mind that agreement of the EU proposals will be subject to unanimity and
negotiations are likely to take some time.

The conclusion that this study has reached is that age discrimination legislation would have a positive effect on British
culture and would build – as other discrimination Acts have – on
a growing sense of public interest and concern about the issue.
The scale of the impact on employers' behaviour is hard to measure and would depend on the model of legislation adopted. But
the absence of legislation on age, when it exists for gender, race,
and disability, sends a powerful message that age discrimination
is taken less seriously.

**Conclusion 5: The Government should make clear that it will
introduce age discrimination legislation if evaluation of the Code
of Practice on Age Diversity shows that it has not been effective.** That is, Government should decide to legislate unless a
clear shift in attitudes and behaviour has occurred.

1.63   The government's ambivalence was in part possible because ministers
and officials assumed there would be a lengthy negotiation period before
the Directive was approved. Early reports suggested that the directives
were unlikely to be agreed quickly. The PIU report and ministerial statements suggested that the UK would be quite happy to let discussions drift
into 2001 to give time for the code of practice to be evaluated.[69]

69   *EU proposals to combat discrimination,* House of Lords European Union Select
Committee, 9th report, session 1999/2000.

Negotiation and scrutiny

1.64 The government was caught by surprise when rapid progress was made on the directives. This was prompted by events in Austria, when Jörg Haider's far-right Freedom Party came second in the October 1999 elections. After protracted negotiations, the Freedom Party joined a coalition government in February 2000, to the consternation of other EU member states. The union was determined to show its commitment to tackling racism and under the Portuguese presidency the race Directive was agreed in the first half of 2000. There was a knock-on impact on the Framework Directive, with Tessa Jowell commenting in July 2000 that 'negotiations ... have been taken forward much more quickly than we anticipated. That acceleration of pace was due to decisions made by the Portuguese and the French presidencies. The French presidency made it clear that it intends to reach agreement on the proposal by 17 October or 3 November [2000]'.

1.65 With this political context the Labour government was hardly going to be singled out by rejecting progress on equality legislation. At the 17 October Employment and Social Affairs Council Tessa Jowell joined ministers from other member states in approving the Directive, setting to one side her comments in the summer that legislation would wait until the code of practice had been evaluated.

1.66 The process that led to the agreement of the Directive was severely criticised by the House of Lords European Union Committee.[70] The draft directive was the subject of negotiations for almost a year, but these took place almost entirely behind closed doors, with a Council of Ministers working group in the lead. The European Commission did not issue updated versions of the Directive as negotiations progressed, so independent scrutiny by national parliamentarians and commentators was impossible. In addition, the Lords argued that UK ministers had failed to set out all their major negotiating positions when questioned by parliament.[71]

1.67 Under article 13 the European Parliament had the power to suggest amendments to the directives. However, MEPs were only permitted access to the original draft, which was hopelessly out of date by the time the Parliament approved their amendments on 5 October 2000.

---

70 The following account is drawn form the House of Lords European Union Committee, Fourth Report, Session 2000/2001, 19 December 2000.

71 Committees of both houses did at least have a chance to debate the original draft of the framework directive before it was approved. Not even this was possible for the race directive.

The day before the ministerial meeting, in a Byzantine twist, the Commission published the Parliament's amendments to the November 1999 version of the Directive (complete with the Commission's recommendations on which should be accepted) as a new official version of the draft directive. This was in full knowledge that the draft which would be discussed the next day bore no resemblance to the one MEPs had debated. Not surprisingly, Tessa Jowell described the Parliament's amendments as 'largely irrelevant' and the official Commission text was ignored in the subsequent negotiations.

1.68   The text put before ministers was the outcome of three meetings of the Committee of Permanent Representatives (COREPER, the committee of member states' ambassadors to the EU) in the fortnight leading up to the Council. Ministers then debated the final wording into the night on 17 October until 'political agreement' on the Directive was established. Press reports suggested that negotiations lasted six hours, during which time it remained unclear whether a deal would be reached. In the end the Council was said to have bowed to the pressure of member states holding out the prospect of a veto.

1.69   Tessa Jowell suggested to the Lords committee that the rapid pace of negotiations, and the eagerness of the French Presidency to reach agreement at the 17 October Council, had helped the government to secure 'our negotiating objectives ultimately on all grounds'. On the other hand, UK parliamentarians worried about the implications of such last minute negotiations: 'the net result may well be poorly drafted and inadequate legislation that leads to severe problems in interpretation and implementation'.

1.70   And what were those 'bottom lines' the government was so eager to secure? Some had little relevance to age equality, for example an exemption for public security, order or health, and support for the Irish government in strengthening safeguards for ethos-based discrimination by religious organisations. However, amendments with relevance to age discrimination included an exemption for the armed forces with respect to age and disability, and a new provision offering protection to occupational pension schemes from regulation on age discrimination. But, the most significant deal that night – and one fiercely opposed by the Commission – was the negotiation of an extended implementation period for the new age discrimination provisions.

1.71   So the UK's price for the fast-track approval period was an extremely long implementation period. Tessa Jowell had said back in July: 'we have also been exploring the scope for extending the implementation period, which is currently two years. We attach considerable importance to having a longer transposition period, which would allow time for culture change and change of practice in preparation for the legislation.' She was very successful on this point and came away with a three-year implementation period for the outlawing of discrimination on grounds of religion or belief and sexual orientation, but an additional three year extension for age and disability.[72] The result would be that the UK would not be required to implement age discrimination law until December 2006 – 12 years after the Labour Party's 1994 commitment to introduce legislation.

1.72   What is surprising is that this long implementation period was not the result of unanimous business lobbying. The CBI was firmly opposed to any form of legislation, but other employer organisations had much more mixed views. The Institute of Directors, the Employers Forum on Age and the Federation of Small Business all reported that their members were fairly evenly divided on the case for legislation. Members of the Chartered Institute of Management and the Chartered Institute of Personnel and Development were broadly supportive of a new law.

1.73   When the negotiations were over, ministers were challenged on whether they had been bounced into age discrimination legislation:

Question: Minister, turning to the issue of the EU Directive on Equal Treatment and the Government's plans for [age] legislation, which came first? The EU Directive or the Government's desire to legislate? In other words, did you jump or were you pushed?

Ms Hodge: I think the answer is they came together. We committed ourselves in our manifesto to tackling age discrimination. We tried first working through the code and, although we think it has been effective, I have said before I think speed is of the essence in this, given the demographic changes and the extent of disadvantage, so there was a happy togetherness.

We have always said that if the code was not sufficiently effective, then we would go further. That is what we are now doing. The European directive has come together quite neatly for that and we very successfully negotiated this long transposition period of six years which will give us time to develop from that best practice.[73]

---

72 A minister accidentally reported this 'success' to the Director General of Age Concern, in the belief that she was telephoning the CBI.

73 *Age Discrimination in Employment*, House of Commons Education and Employment Select Committee, 7th report, session 2000–2001.

Age discrimination in the draft Framework Directive

1.74   The inclusion of age discrimination legislation in the November 1999 proposals had in fact been by no means a foregone conclusion. As in 1997, when article 13 was being negotiated, there were few enthusiastic advocates for age equality. The impetus for covering all the article 13 grounds in the draft directive came mainly from the European Commission itself, as the House of Lords report describes:

> It may indeed be that in certain Member States there is little desire to combat discrimination on some of these grounds – for instance, age or sexual orientation. However, as Mme Quintin [the Commission spokesperson] pointed out, 'the heads of state and governments have ... put sexual orientation in the context of article 13'. In other words, an initial commitment to combating discrimination on all the grounds included in article 13 has already been made by all the Member States, and is embodied in the EC Treaty. Mme Quintin asked, 'would it have been wise ... for the Commission to decide not to cover one ground which had been agreed by the heads of state and governments to put in article 13?' The Commission clearly believes this is the most opportune moment to capitalise on the Council's commitment by adopting an instrument granting some form of protection, however limited, to all the groups. In Mme Quintin's words, 'we needed to cover all the grounds of discrimination in article 13 and to go as far as politically possible in each'.

1.75   By contrast, Eurolink Age, the network of older people's non-governmental organisations (NGOs), was initially opposed to the inclusion of age in the draft legislation. It believed that any age legislation would be too weak to be effective:

> Eurolink Age expressed doubt ... about the likelihood of obtaining unanimity in Council on any form of binding measures on age discrimination. We stressed that the best way forward would be for the action programme to prepare the political ground with appropriate actions to justify subsequent legislative proposals in this field.[74]

1.76   Confirming the network's fears, the Commission's draft directive did indeed propose that protection from discrimination on grounds of age should be significantly more limited than other grounds. Article 5 (what would become article 6 of the final directive) outlined the scope of exemption:

---

74   *EU proposals to combat discrimination*, House of Lords European Union Select Committee, 9th report, session 1999/2000.

Article 5: Justification of differences of treatment on grounds of age

Notwithstanding point (a) of article 2(2), the following differences of treatment, in particular, shall not constitute direct discrimination on grounds of age, if they are objectively and reasonably justified by a legitimate aim and are appropriate and necessary to the achievement of that aim:

(a) the prohibition on access to employment or the provision of special working conditions to ensure the protection of young people and older workers;

(b) the fixing of a minimum age as a condition of eligibility for retirement or invalidity benefits;

(c) the fixing of different ages for employees or groups or categories of employees for entitlement to retirement or invalidity benefits on grounds of physical or mental occupational requirements;

(d) the fixing of a maximum age for recruitment which is based on the training requirements of the post in question or the need for a reasonable period of employment before retirement;

(e) the establishment of requirements concerning the length of professional experience;

(f) the establishment of age limits which are appropriate and necessary for the pursuit of legitimate labour market objectives.

1.77   The Commission's explanation of the proposal said:

> ... the existing law of the Community and Member States tends to suggest that it is only in very exceptional circumstances that ... a difference of treatment could be justified. This article provides a non-exhaustive list of differences of treatment on grounds of age which shall not constitute direct discrimination, provided that they are objectively justified. It is intended, both to limit the possibilities of claiming justification in cases of direct discrimination to exceptional situations concerning the ground of age, and to ensure that this limited range of exceptions respects the principles of necessity, proportionality and legitimacy as laid down by the European Court of Justice as regards the notion of indirect discrimination. Therefore, Member States may allow differences of treatment on grounds of age other than those listed in article 5, in accordance with their legal traditions and political priorities, provided that they are appropriate and necessary to attain a legitimate aim. With respect to age,

article 5 does not exclude the application of the genuine occupational qualification justification.[75]

1.78   The Commission's stated intention was therefore that direct age discrimination should be permitted in a 'limited range of exceptions' that would have to comply with the European Court of Justice's established test for indirect sex discrimination. The Commission's representative explained to the House of Lords European Union Committee that article 5 was 'designed to fix clear limits, to insist on the principles of objective justification, necessity and proportionality, and to give some indicative examples in order to clarify the type of exception which is envisaged, and provide certainty concerning the most widespread and clearly justified examples'.[76]

1.79   But the sweeping nature of the six (non-exhaustive) examples suggested that in practice the Directive would permit age discrimination across a very wide range of areas. Eurolink Age reacted with fury to article 5 arguing that it provided 'employers with the opportunity of pursuing a policy of discrimination against workers based on their age, defeating the very purpose of the package of measures in the fight against discrimination'.[77]

1.80   They pointed in particular to examples (e) and (f) of article 5 which had only been included at a late stage at the behest of Germany. Eurolink Age argued that the proposal would 'not produce any clear benefits for older workers in Europe who currently suffer from age discriminatory practices' and that examples (d) and (f) in particular might 'have the effect of legalising age discrimination in Europe'. But despite the network's opposition to article 5, and their earlier concerns about introducing legislation at all, they recommended that age should be included in the Directive subject to 'proper adaptation'.[78]

1.81   Concerns with article 5 were widely shared in the UK. The House of Commons Scrutiny Committee commented: 'given the Commission's assurance that there is no prioritisation of the grounds for discrimination ... we are struck by the number of exemptions for age discrimination in [the draft directive] ... We seek the Minister's views

75   *Proposal for a Council Directive establishing a general framework for equal treatment in employment and occupation,* Commission of the European Communities, 25 November 1999, COM(1999) 565 final.

76   *EU proposals to combat discrimination,* House of Lords European Union Select Committee, 9th report, session 1999/2000.

77   *Agence Europe* No 7625: 3 and 4 January 2000.

78   *EU proposals to combat discrimination,* House of Lords European Union Select Committee, 9th report, session 1999/2000.

about whether there is, in fact, an implicit hierarchy in the proposals.'[79] Tessa Jowell accepted that the draft article 5 could have the effect of legalising age discrimination and said that for this reason the government was negotiating for it to be amended to deliver genuine protection from discrimination.[80]

1.82   The House of Lords report on the proposals was even more critical. Its recommendation on age discrimination stated:

> Article 5 of the framework Directive entirely fails to achieve the Commission's goals of providing clear limits and certainty in the field of age discrimination. As drafted, there is a strong possibility that it would do more harm than good, effectively legalising age discrimination throughout the Community. There appears to be no coherent pattern in the list of justifications ... the Government should seek to ensure that any exceptions to the principle of equal treatment irrespective of age are clearly defined and justified.

1.83   In its response, the government agreed with the concerns about the range of justifications proposed: 'we believe that provisions relating to age require considerable modification and improvement, and agree that as drafted they could legitimise age discrimination'. So although ministers were unsure about whether they wanted age legislation, if they were going to have it, they wanted it to work.

Shaping article 6

1.84   In the negotiations leading up to approval of the Directive there were considerable changes to the drafting of what was to become article 6. There was agreement on most of the article at official level in advance of the ministerial meeting, and the article was not one of the key areas of dispute on 17 October 2000. The exception is that Britain was able to insert an additional clause creating a wide-ranging exemption with respect to occupational pensions.

1.85   The list of examples changed considerably in wording, but rather less in terms of scope. Paragraphs (a) and (d) of the draft article 5 became paragraph (a) and (c) of article 6 (although the reference in paragraph (a) to 'prohibition from access to employment' was replaced with the more ambiguous phrase 'the setting of special conditions on access to employment'). Paragraphs (b), (c) and (e) were replaced with a single general example 'the fixing of minimum conditions of age, pro-

79 *House of Commons European Scrutiny Committee*, Seventh Report, Session 1999/2000, 2 February 2000.

80 Hansard, European Standing Committee C, 24 July 2000.

fessional experience or seniority in service for access to employment or to certain advantages linked to employment'. This catch-all paragraph did not represent a significant tightening of the scope for discrimination. Finally paragraph (f) was omitted and its content absorbed into the body of the article.

1.86   The main text of the article was re-worked in several important ways. First, someone had noticed that difference of treatment relating to length of service would constitute indirect rather than direct discrimination, so the specific reference to direct discrimination in the draft disappeared. Second, the final wording made it clear that any form of unequal treatment (not just those listed in the examples) could be potentially lawful. The important new caveat was however the phrase 'within the context of national law'. This made it clear that it was for member states to prescribe the boundaries of acceptable direct discrimination within their own national legislation.

The 'test' for justifying direct discrimination – the draft and final directive compared

Draft article 5
Notwithstanding point (a) of article 2(2), the following differences of treatment, in particular, shall not constitute direct discrimination on grounds of age, if they are objectively and reasonably justified by a legitimate aim and are appropriate and necessary to the achievement of that aim ...

Article 6(1)
Notwithstanding article 2(2), Member States may provide that differences of treatment on grounds of age shall not constitute discrimination, if, within the context of national law, they are objectively and reasonably justified by a legitimate aim, including legitimate employment policy, labour market and vocational training objectives, and if the means of achieving that aim are appropriate and necessary. Such differences of treatment may include, among others ...

1.87   Age campaigners accepted that the drafting had improved, but felt that article 6 did little to close the loopholes in the draft directive. Peers were similarly critical. They said:

> Age discrimination is a particularly complex area, and it would not have been appropriate for a framework Directive to have addressed it in great detail. However, we are concerned that the justification of difference of

treatment on grounds of age is so broad that it may lead to damaging unpredictability and inconsistency between Member States. On the other hand, the fact that legislation against age discrimination is now in place is itself a major breakthrough, and it may be that article 6, as a derogation from the principle of equal treatment, will be interpreted narrowly. We welcome the Government's assurance that there will be very full consultation before the Directive is implemented.[81]

Article 6: Justification of differences of treatment on grounds of age

1. Notwithstanding article 2(2), Member States may provide that differences of treatment on grounds of age shall not constitute discrimination, if, within the context of national law, they are objectively and reasonably justified by a legitimate aim, including legitimate employment policy, labour market and vocational training objectives, and if the means of achieving that aim are appropriate and necessary.

Such differences of treatment may include, among others:

(a) the setting of special conditions on access to employment and vocational training, employment and occupation, including dismissal and remuneration conditions, for young people, older workers and persons with caring responsibilities in order to promote their vocational integration or ensure their protection;

(b) the fixing of minimum conditions of age, professional experience or seniority in service for access to employment or to certain advantages linked to employment;

(c) the fixing of a maximum age for recruitment which is based on the training requirements of the post in question or the need for a reasonable period of employment before retirement.

---

81 House of Lords European Union Committee, Fourth Report, Session 2000/2001, 19 December 2000.

UK implementation

Cross-strand consultation

1.88   The long process of implementation began soon after approval. In January 2001 the Department for Education and Employment set out its initial views on implementation in a memorandum to a House of Commons select committee inquiry on age discrimination.[82] The note explained that the government intended 'to take full advantage of the long implementation period' and currently anticipated that 'legislation implementing the Directive would not come into force until December 2006'. The six-year period would give time 'to consult closely and extensively with employers, individuals and expert groups [and] to prepare clear, workable and beneficial age legislation'. The government also mentioned the need to prepare clear guidance and give employers time to prepare (in the event, barely six months of the six years was set aside for this). No timetable for the process was set out.

1.89   The note also commented on the key issue of derogations:

> We have not yet decided how the derogations provided for in the Directive will be transposed into national law. We intend to carry out an extensive consultation exercise before making firm decisions in this respect, or before starting to prepare draft legislation. But it should be borne in mind that the derogations are permissive only, and are likely to be construed narrowly by the European Court of Justice. It will therefore not be open to the Member States to provide for sweeping, open-ended exceptions that would undermine the whole purpose of the Directive. This Government would not want to do so in any event; indeed we are committed to developing workable legislation which will produce a fair balance between the legitimate needs of employers on the one hand, and the need to eliminate age-related prejudice on the other.

1.90   On the key issue of mandatory retirement ages, the government explained there was no derogation and they would be 'unlawful unless employers can show that they are objectively justified – in accordance with criteria specified in legislation transposing the Directive'. This interpretation of the directive's implications for retirement was in marked contrast to the eventual position adopted in the regulations.

1.91   The following month, the department announced it was setting up the Age Advisory Group, a stakeholder forum that would advise

---

82   House of Commons Education and Employment Select Committee, Seventh Report, Session 2000/2001, 21 March 2001.

the government on the shaping of the law.[83] This was followed in December by the government's first consultation on the article 13 directive *Towards equality and diversity*.[84] This sought views on proposals for legislation on all five grounds covered by the directives. With respect to age, the paper only aimed to identify the key issues and promised further consultation in late 2002 (later postponed to summer 2003). The paper set out the terms of article 6 and explained that 'A key goal of this consultation is to identify which types of treatment are acceptable and which are not'. It asked what age-based practices might be acceptable in the areas of recruitment, selection, promotion, training, occupational requirements, pay and non-pay benefits, redundancy and retirement. The questions did not refer to the detail of the article 6 test, or ask stakeholders whether age-related practices could be objectively justified.

1.92   The consultation also explained that the directives would be implemented through secondary legislation:

> The process of implementing the Directives is made even more complex by their differences in scope, timing and impact. With this in mind, we intend to prepare separate items of legislation for each of the strands and to use regulations under section 2(2) of the European Communities Act 1972 to implement the Directives, where practicable. This will help us to manage the process of implementation in a way which allows sufficient time for consultation and preparation, but without missing important deadlines.

1.93   This was perhaps an inevitable decision, given the greater flexibility regulations would afford the government. Many equality campaigners and parliamentarians had, however, hoped for an act, both to give the opportunity for detailed scrutiny and to open the possibility of introducing legislation beyond the scope of employment.

The Commission for Equality and Human Rights

In May 2002 the Government announced it was considering options for the future of equality institutions in light of the article 13 Directives. This led to vigorous debate on the pros and cons of establishing a single equality body that would cover all six grounds of discrimination, absorbing the three existing equality commissions (the Equal Opportunities Commission, the

---

83   DfEE press release, 14 February 2001.
84   *Towards equality and diversity, implementing the Employment and Race Directives,* Office of the Deputy Prime Minister, 2001.

Commission for Racial Equality, and the newly established Disability Rights Commission). In October the Women and Equality Unit published a consultation *Equality and Diversity: Making it Happen* which set out three options: a single equality body working across all strands; a shared gateway bringing the existing commissions together; and an overarching commission, sitting above strand-specific institutions. The tone of the paper made it clear that the Government's preference was for a single body. In October 2003 the Government confirmed that a single Commission for Equality and Human Rights would be established and a White Paper followed in May 2004. Legislation was introduced in 2005 which eventually became the Equality Act 2006. Broadly speaking the commission will have the same responsibilities with respect to the age regulations as the existing commissions do for discrimination law in other areas. In particular, the act enables the Commission to issue a statutory code of practice on the regulations for the first time. The Commission is due to begin work in Autumn 2007.[85]

1.94   In October 2002 the government (by now responsibility had transferred to the Department of Trade and Industry) published *Equality and diversity: the way ahead.*[86] This outlined the policy decisions the government had made in response to the 2001 consultation. It did not cover the age-specific elements of implementation but set out the general framework that would apply to all grounds of discrimination. The key concepts of direct and indirect discrimination, and victimisation, would be the same across equality legislation. There would also be provisions on harassment, genuine occupational requirements and positive action for all grounds of discrimination. The paper shaped the regulations on sexual orientation and religion or belief, which came into force in December 2003. In many areas these would be identical to the age regulations when they were eventually approved.

---

85 *Equality and diversity: making it happen,* Department of Trade and Industry, 2002; *Fairness for all, a new Commission for Equality and Human Rights,* Department of Trade and Industry, 2004; Equality Act 2006.

86 *Equality and diversity: the way ahead,* Department of Trade and Industry, 2001.

The *Age Matters* consultation

1.95 The next stage in the development of the age regulations came in July 2003 with the publication of *Equality and diversity: age matters*. This was the first consultation specifically on age discrimination legislation. In two important respects the proposals differed from the eventual regulations.

1.96 First, the paper proposed that direct discrimination should only be permitted in circumstances prescribed by the regulations. The approach the government outlined was to include a 'closed list' of acceptable aims which an employer could attempt to rely on when offering an objective justification:

> Therefore we propose that, whilst outlawing age discrimination generally, the legislation should:
>
> • provide that certain discriminatory practices will be capable of justification by reference to specific aims set out in legislation; if
> • employers and others with obligations under the Directive can show that the practices are appropriate and necessary.[87]

1.97 The paper consulted on five possible aims:

(a) health, welfare, and safety – for example, the protection of younger workers;

(b) facilitation of employment planning – for example, where a business has a number of people approaching retirement age at the same time;

(c) the particular training requirements of the post in question – for example, air traffic controllers, who have to undergo 18 months theoretical and practical training at the College of Air Traffic Control, followed by further on the job training;

(d) encouraging and rewarding loyalty;

(e) the need for a reasonable period of employment before retirement – for example, an employer who has exceptionally justified a retirement age of 65 might decline to employ someone only a few months short of 65 if the need for, and the cost and length of, training meant that the applicant would not be sufficiently productive in that time.

1.98 This approach was criticised by representatives of employees and older people who argued that the broad scope of the aims would open up huge loopholes in the legislation. On the other hand, some employer organisations suggested that the aims were too prescriptive, with the CBI arguing that the legislation should permit reference to aims not

---

87 *Equality and diversity: age matters*, Department of Trade and Industry, 2003 para 3.16.

cited in the list.[88] In later consultations the government sided with employers and created an open-ended test for direct discrimination, identical to the provision for indirect discrimination.

1.99   The second major area where change occurred was the government's approach to mandatory retirement ages. *Age Matters* proposed that mandatory retirement ages should be unlawful unless exceptionally justified. However it also asked whether a 'default' retirement age of 70 should be introduced, at which point employers would not need to justify retirement dismissals.

1.100   Responses to the consultation showed strong opposition to the idea of the default retirement age of 70. Representatives of older people argued that no default should be permitted, as forced retirement constituted a fundamental breach of the principle of equal treatment. They were joined by trades unions in arguing that adopting the age of 70 would set a dangerous precedent for future increases in occupational and state pension ages. Broadly speaking employer organisations welcomed the proposed default age, but argued that it should be set at 65 rather than 70. They were joined in this position by some trades unions, who were more concerned about securing occupational pension schemes than the rights of the minority of their members who wished to work after 65.

Consultation on mandatory retirement ages

1.101   Following *Age matters* there was an extended delay to consider the retirement issue, accompanied by intense pressure from lobbyists on all sides. Ministers finally decided to support the employer position. The policy chosen was essentially to maintain (and not improve) the law on retirement for people over 65. Mandatory retirement up to the age of 65 would have to be objectively justified, but retirements at or after 65 would be lawful. The only caveat was that the department would introduce a 'right to request' procedure which would require employers to ask workers if they would like to stay on.

1.102   At the outset of the implementation period there had been little indication that retirement ages would be a uniquely problematic element in outlawing age discrimination. Article 6(1) of the Directive did not cite retirement ages in the examples of practices that might be objectively justified. The only reference to retirement ages was in

---

88   *Age Concern's response to Equality and diversity: age matters,* Age Concern England, 2003; *CBI response to Equality and diversity: age matters,* Confederation of British Industry, 2003.

recital 14 ('this Directive shall be without prejudice to national provisions laying down retirement ages'). However, throughout the consultation process the government stated that the UK did 'not have a national mandatory retirement age' and it did not suggest it would rely on this recital.[89]

1.103   Initially there was no suggestion that retirement would be subject to a special exemption. Retirement ages were seen as one of a number of existing business practices where behaviour would need to change once the Directive came into force. The Government had pushed for a six-year implementation period precisely because they recognised that employers would need to make adjustments to these sorts of practices. At the time the Directive was adopted a Department For Education and Employment (DfEE) memorandum to a House of Commons select committee said that mandatory retirement ages 'will be unlawful unless employers can show that they are objectively justified – in accordance with criteria specified in legislation transposing the Directive'. In oral evidence Margaret Hodge, the Parliamentary Under-Secretary for Employment, confirmed this (quoting from the brief her officials had prepared) saying that the new law would mean 'compulsory retirement based on age would only be possible where it is objectively justified by a legitimate aim'.[90] This remained the government's position in December 2002 when the pensions green paper said: 'Under the Directive compulsory retirement ages are likely to be unlawful unless employers can show that they are objectively justified'.[91]

1.104   In the 2001 consultation the government had sought preliminary views on retirement with the aim of identifying circumstances in which employers might need to rely on retirement ages. The paper asked four questions on retirement:

(a) Do you think employers should be able to require people to retire at a certain age?

(b) If so, do you think there should be any legal limits placed on their right to do so?

89   *Equality and diversity: age matters*, Department of Trade and Industry, 2003 para 4.9. In 2001 Margaret Hodge MP, Parliamentary Under-secretary for Employment, said 'there is no such thing as a national retirement age' (House of Commons Education and Employment Select Committee, Seventh Report, Session 2000/2001, 21 March 2001).

90   House of Commons Education and Employment Select Committee, Seventh Report, Session 2000/2001, 21 March 2001.

91   *Simplicity, security and choice*, Department for Work and Pensions, 2002.

(c) What concerns, if any, do you have about current retirement practices?

(d) In your opinion, what would be the advantages and disadvantages if there were no fixed retirement age?[92]

1.105   At this stage the government did not indicate what mechanism might be used to permit mandatory retirement ages, and there was no indication that an exemption for retirement might be introduced. The government was setting out to establish the practical pros and cons of policy options, and did not state the parameters of what might be lawful, or ask for views on this question. This approach was understandable, given the importance of opening up debate to non-legal audiences and enabling the government to gather a wide range of views and experience.

1.106   However, this set the tone for many of the discussions that were to follow. The debate about retirement ages did not take place in the context of the legal framework of the Directive. Many of the concerns expressed by employers' representatives were based on the premise that any move away from current practice would have a negative impact on business operations and should be resisted. Organisations representing older people had to remind other stakeholders that the aim of the Directive was to achieve equal treatment and that this would inevitably require some changes in practice. They emphasised that the implementation process had to identify policies that were objectively justified under the legal test set out in the Directive. It was not enough to select a discriminatory policy in response to the expressed preferences or beliefs of one party or another.

1.107   It was only with the publication of *Age matters* in 2003 that the government raised the possibility of a blanket exemption for retirement ages, alongside a permissive approach where employers could objectively justify practices on a case-by-case basis. The proposed age of 70 would however have had lower discriminatory impact than the eventual decision to select 65; only a third as many people are in work aged over 70, compared to 65.[93]

1.108   The government did not set out a detailed objective justification for this proposed exemption. It said:

Some businesses have said that allowing the default option of a retirement age of 70 might allow them to manage their workforces effectively and

92   *Towards equality and diversity*, Office of the Deputy Prime Minister, 2001 para 15.19.

93   Labour force survey, Spring Quarter, 2003.

operate productively – providing them with more certainty when it comes to workforce planning.

Some businesses have argued that staff appraisal systems may not be sufficiently sensitive or objective to be able to tackle effectively the declining performance and productivity of some older workers. There may be implications for business and the resources they would have to deploy to manage an ageing workforce, and it might also raise health, welfare, and safety issues – for employees, and the general public if they are put at risk. But others have argued that age is not a reliable indicator of ability or of risk, and that inclusion of a default age could help to perpetuate age discriminatory beliefs.[94]

1.109   It is interesting to note that the reasons advanced in support of the policy in 2003 were different from those the government relied on for its objective justification of the eventual exemption. Neither the inadequacy of appraisal systems for addressing the performance of older employees nor health, welfare and safety reasons were mentioned when the legislation was placed before Parliament in 2006.[95] This was presumably because the government concluded that these arguments were based on generalised, stereotyped assumptions about older workers. In any event a DTI-commissioned literature review published alongside *Age matters* had shown clear evidence that capability does not decline for most people in their 60s.

1.110   Following the 2003 consultation no public statements were made on retirement ages for over 18 months. In *Age matters* the government had said it intended to introduce the regulations around two years in advance of their implementation (ie, at the end of 2004).[96] However following the close of the *Age matters* consultation it soon became clear that progress had stalled. In April 2004 the *Financial Times* reported disagreement between the DWP and the DTI on whether to adopt a default retirement age.[97] Then in July the *Financial Times* – again reporting on the dispute between the DTI and DWP – revealed for the first time the package that would in due course become government policy.[98]

1.111   With the two departments unable to reach a way forward, it was agreed that the issue would be referred to a taskforce of senior figures from both sides of industry, chaired by Rita Donaghy of ACAS. With

94 *Age Matters* (2003), paras 4.26 and 4.27.
95 Employment Equality (Age) Regulations 2006, Notes on Regulations, Department of Trade and Industry, 2006.
96 *Age Matters* (2003), para 1.21.
97 *Financial Times*, 24 April 2004.
98 *Financial Times*, 8 July 2004.

the taskforce meeting, Alan Johnson, the new Secretary of State for Work and Pensions, tried to nudge proceedings forward by commenting on the record, in a Sunday Times interview:

> The national retirement age should be abolished so people have the right to work as late in life as they like, the new pensions secretary has said. Alan Johnson, who was promoted to the cabinet in a reshuffle earlier this month, said Britain should follow the example of America and take the step in order to tackle ageism at work. His argument, which came in his first newspaper interview since being appointed, could lead to a clash with cabinet colleagues and employers. Patricia Hewitt, the trade and industry secretary, is said to want companies to remain able to impose a cut-off for workers between the ages of 65 and 70. The Confederation of British Industry wants a 'default' retirement age of 65, so that companies can still pension people off. However, Johnson said: 'My instinctive feeling has always been that, compared with America, we are a pretty ageist society. In America they don't have an ageist approach. I've always felt it would be much healthier if we had that system here.' The US outlawed age discrimination in 1967 and abolished compulsory retirement for most workers in 1986.[99]

1.112   By mid November it was becoming clear that the taskforce would not be able to reach agreement.[100] The outcome of the taskforce's debate was leaked on 13 November:

> A taskforce set up to resolve the thorny issue of whether companies can set fixed retirement ages threw the decision back to ministers after it failed to reach a consensus yesterday. The Department of Trade and Industry said the taskforce had 'completed its work' and that Rita Donaghy, its chairman, would report to ministers shortly, outlining its irreconcilable differences. The taskforce, made up of industry, the unions and age lobby groups, was set up last year [sic] after ministers failed to agree on how to implement European laws banning age discrimination, which come into force in 2006 ... With no agreement reached it now falls to Patricia Hewitt, trade and industry secretary, to settle the issue. DTI officials are strongly sympathetic to the argument that fixed retirement ages should be abolished, as argued by business ... However, ministers in the Department for Work and Pensions appear determined to stick to a 'no-default retirement age' position and are adamant that simply setting a higher one – such as 70 – is not an answer. But Downing Street may be reluctant to force such an unpopular move on business ahead of a general election. Members of the taskforce speculated yesterday that the government's final position may be to end fixed retirement ages but with five years' notice. This would give industry the time to adjust to the new rules while giving individuals 'the right to request' to work in the meantime.

99   *Sunday Times*, 26 September 2004.
100   *Financial Times*, 12 and 13 November 2004.

1.113 The DWP and DTI now finally had to agree on a joint recommendation to put to the rest of government. On 28 November the Sunday Times revealed the contents of a leaked letter apparently setting out the agreed position of the two departments.[101] Under this agreement compulsory retirement ages were to be abolished. However, the departments agreed to defer this change for five years until 2011.

1.114 This, however, was not the end of the matter. The joint recommendation of the two secretaries of state was rejected by colleagues elsewhere in government. According to the rumour mill, it was the Prime Minister himself who decided that the CBI should be given what they wanted. He was no doubt conscious of the need to appear even-handed in advance of the General Election and wished to avoid accusations of imposing excessive regulation; earlier in the year Tony Blair had made high profile concessions to trades unions at the Labour Party National Policy Forum meeting in Warwick. On 14 December 2004 the news was confirmed in a Ministerial Statement to parliament:

> We have carefully balanced the arguments on all sides, and have decided that the legislation, which will come into force in autumn 2006, will provide for a national default retirement age of 65 and a right for employees to request working beyond the set retirement age. The decision to have a national default retirement age will be reviewed after five years.
>
> In setting the default age, we have taken careful note of a number of representations we received in the course of consultations which made it clear that significant numbers of employers use a set retirement age as a necessary part of their workforce planning. While an increasing number of employers are able to organise their business around the best practice of having no set retirement age for all or particular groups of their workforce, some nevertheless still rely on it heavily.
>
> Furthermore, our consultations have demonstrated that if all employers only had the option of individually justified retirement ages at the time the legislation was introduced, this could risk adverse consequences for occupational pension schemes and other work-related benefits. Some employers would instead simply reduce or remove benefits they offer to employees to offset the increase in costs.[102]

1.115 So after a protracted period of policy development and consultation the government had arrived at the position originally advocated by employer representatives. Neither the 2000–2002 position – that retirement ages were likely to be unlawful unless justified – nor the 2003 consultation option – of permitting mandatory retirement at 70 – had found favour. Even the compromise reached between the DTI and

---

101 *Sunday Times*, 28 November 2004.
102 House of Lords, Hansard, col WS78, 14 December 2004.

DWP – that mandatory retirement ages at 65 should be permitted, but only as a transitional measure until 2011 – had been rejected.

1.116   During all this manoeuvring, government representatives hardly discussed the thorny issue of whether the default retirement age option was lawful. After the decision had been made the DTI declined to release its legal advice, following a Freedom of Information request by the Third Age Employment Network. It will be for the courts to decide whether the exemption for retirement ages is objectively justifiable under the Directive (a legal challenge is already underway). What is certain however is that the government's legal interpretation of the Directive changed substantially during the process of policy development, in light of the pressure it was under. The process of objective justification was made to fit the demands of changing policy, rather than policy development being constrained within parameters set by the legal test.

The draft regulations

1.117   Once the hiatus caused by the retirement age controversy was over the DTI moved rapidly to finalise the draft regulations. They appeared in July 2005, alongside another consultation paper *Equality and diversity: coming of age*.[103] In the intervening months the department had fleshed out its proposals for the retirement age exemption and the 'right to request'. In response to lobbying from Age Concern the government announced one important concession – the retirement provisions would include a six months notice period to prevent retirement dismissals taking place 'out of the blue'. The draft legislation filled out the detail in a number of areas where the government had until then said little. These provisions included:

- a complicated set of exemptions from indirect discrimination on grounds of length of service;
- exemptions permitting the use of length of service in calculating redundancy pay, so long as employers' arrangements were similar to the provisions of the statutory redundancy scheme;
- an exemption for recruitment over the age of 65 (a corollary of the exemption for retirement);
- the introduction of detailed exemptions for occupational pensions, including some provisions that went beyond the scope of article 6(2);

103   *Equality and diversity: coming of age*, Department of Trade and Industry, 2005.

- an exemption for invalidity benefits aimed at implementing the provisions of article 6(2);
- an exemption for young adults paid below the adult rate of the National Minimum Wage;

1.118   Finally the draft regulations confirmed that the upper age limit on protection from unfair dismissal and for entitlement to redundancy pay would be removed. In the case of redundancy pay this was a change of policy from *Age matters* which had envisaged that entitlement to redundancy pay would end at the default retirement age. These reforms were a belated vindication for John Rutherford and Samuel Bentley, two older workers who since 1998 had been challenging the legality of the existing upper age limits contained in the Employment Rights Act 1996, by arguing that they constituted indirect sex discrimination. In 2006 the House of Lords eventually rejected their challenge, but not before the test case had highlighted the injustice of imposing upper age limits on employment rights.

Statutory redundancy pay

1.119   In the *Coming of age* consultation the government had reserved its position on one outstanding area of controversy. This was the question of how the existing statutory redundancy pay scheme should be revised to ensure it was age equal. In *Age matters* the government's view had been that the scheme's length of service criteria could be objectively justified but that the directly discriminatory element of the rules, which linked compensation to an employee's age, would have to be removed. They had proposed that workers of all ages should receive one week's pay per year of service. This was an improvement for some young adults, but it represented a cut for older workers who were entitled to one-and-a-half week's pay for each year of service over the age of 41. In 2003 organisations representing older people and trade unions had opposed this levelling-down, arguing that older workers should not lose out, given the difficulties they faced in finding work after being made redundant. Ministers were sympathetic to this argument, but were also mindful that 'levelling up' compensation to one-and-a-half weeks' pay for people of all ages would be costly for employers.

1.120   The issue was shelved until Autumn 2005. At this stage DTI officials proposed a cost-neutral option of 1.2 weeks' pay per year of service for workers of all ages. Employee representatives continued to hold out for 1.5 weeks' pay, while employer organisations dug-in on the issue of regulatory burden. The CBI broke the impasse by producing a controversial legal opinion which argued that the existing scheme could be objectively justified, on the basis of the greater labour market disadvantage experienced by older workers. The government let pragmatism prevail over age equality and decided to accept the CBI's position. Litigation on this issue seems inevitable.

The regulations

1.121   The Employment Equality (Age) Regulations 2006 were finally published in March 2006. They received cursory scrutiny in committees of both the Lords and Commons and were then approved by positive resolutions of both houses. They were signed into law by the Parliamentary Under-Secretary of State, Gerry Sutcliffe MP, on 3 April 2006.

1.122   There were few major changes in policy between the *Coming of age* proposals and the final regulations. However there were significant shifts in drafting, particularly in the schedules which set out the detail of the retirement procedure and the exemptions for occupational pensions.

1.123   The key changes between the 2005 draft regulations and the 2006 legislation were as follows.

Direct discrimination

1.124   Three examples of potentially justifiable direct discrimination (inspired by the article 6.1 examples) were removed, following complaints that they were unclear. This left the new legislation with identical provisions for the justification of direct and indirect discrimination.

Mandatory retirement

1.125   The government significantly amended the provisions on retirement and the right to request procedure. The most important change was to extended protection to people with normal retirement ages over 65. Age Concern had highlighted the unfairness of employers being able to dismiss people between 65 and a normal retirement age above this age. The charity also argued that permitting retirement dismissals before a normal retirement age would be a regression from the protection available under Employment Rights Act 1996 s109, and therefore incompatible with article 8 of the Directive.

1.126   There were other more technical changes. The draft regulations had introduced the concept of 'planned retirement' (retirements at 65, a normal retirement age, or with six months' notice); where a dismissal did not take place on a planned retirement date the burden would have been on the employer to show that it was on grounds of retirement. The final regulations did away with the idea of 'planned retirement' with all employers instead being expected to give six months' notice, whether or not the retirement was at 65 or a normal retirement age. But the final legislation also gave employers greater leeway to show that retirement was the reason for dismissal if six months' notice had not been given.

1.127　The draft regulations enabled employees to prove that retirement was not the reason for dismissal ('the employer would not have dismissed the employee ... but for some other reason than retirement').[104] This would have offered protection to people who could show that they would have been dismissed for redundancy or capability grounds. Following criticism from employment tribunal chairs, this provision was removed leaving individuals with no way of arguing that a dismissal was not a retirement as long as the correct process had been followed.

1.128　The duty to consider procedure was amended, again to make it a purely procedural exercise. In the draft regulations employers had been required to consider requests for continued employment 'in good faith'.[105] This requirement was removed, meaning that employers could comply even if they gave no real consideration to a request. The duty by now bore little resemblance to the 'flexible working' provisions, which require employers to give substantive reasons for their decisions based on a prescribed list (and are reinforced by protection for indirect sex discrimination). The minimum time before a dismissal for making a request was increased from six weeks to three months, but employees did gain the right to be accompanied to the meeting where the request would be discussed.

Other changes

1.129　The detail of the provisions on length of service and for redundancy payments changed considerably following criticism from employers (although in the case of redundancy pay the new provisions did little to stop the complaints). The loosely defined exemption for invalidity benefits was replaced with an exemption specifically relating to life assurance. Most significantly, there was a major redraft of the exemptions on occupational pensions, partly to close discriminatory loopholes which had been identified in the course of the consultation.

104　Proposed Employment Rights Act 1996 s98ZA(9).
105　Proposed Sch 6 para 6(1).

European Union law

> **Key points**
> - The principle of equality.
> - The treaty and directive.
> - Principles of interpretation.
> - Concepts of discrimination in the directive.
> - Derogations from the principle of equal treatment.
> - Justification of differences in treatment based on age.
> - Remedies and enforcement under the directives.
> - Procedure for applications for preliminary rulings.

Legislative basis for age discrimination

2.1   The principle of equality has long been considered a fundamental pivot in European law. Originally, it was found to be a necessary component of the creation of a common market ensuring free movement of goods and services, labour and capital. What is now article 141 of the EC Treaty established the principle of equal pay for men and women for equal work. Its aim was said to be the avoidance of a situation in which undertakings established in states which had implemented the principle of equal pay might suffer a disadvantage in competition with undertakings that did not have to observe the principle due to non-implementation by their home state.

2.2   The article was said to form part of the social objectives of the community (to ensure social progress and the constant improvement of living and working conditions) and was therefore a part of the foundation of the community.[1] The principle of equality then was described as a fundamental personal human right, respect for which was one of the general principles of community law.[2]

2.3   The Treaty of Amsterdam (the Treaty establishing the European Community) introduced a new provision, article 13. Article 13 clarified that the Community has competence in anti-discrimination issues. It provides:

> Without prejudice to the other provisions of this Treaty and within the limits of the powers conferred by it upon the Community, the Council, acting unanimously on a proposal from the Commission and after consulting the European Parliament, may take appropriate action to combat discrimination based on sex, racial or ethnic origin, religion or belief, disability, age or sexual orientation.

1   Case 43/75 *Defrenne v SABENA (No 2)* [1976] ECR 455.
2   Case 149/77 *Defrenne v SABENA (No 3)* [1978] ECR 1365.

2.4 Article 13 forms the basis for the law prohibiting age discrimination in the workplace.[3] The Framework Directive is a key part of the action that has been taken pursuant to article 13.

Using EU law

2.5 Section 2 of the European Communities Act 1972[4] makes European Community law part of domestic law. European Community law takes precedence over domestic law where the two are in conflict.[5] It is important to distinguish between provisions of Community legislation which may be relied upon in all circumstances; those that can only be relied upon against an emanation of the state and those which can only be relied upon for their interpretive effect.

The treaty provisions

2.6 Article 13 confers competence on the Community to introduce Community legislation in respect of the discrimination themes mentioned in it. It also paves the way for broader based anti-discrimination measures to be introduced. Treaty provisions create private rights and obligations for individuals, which are enforceable by those individuals before their national courts regardless of whether the member state has acted to implement the particular Community standard into its national law. Treaty provisions, such as articles 141 and 39, are directly effective. If it has this 'direct effect' individuals may assert EC law before national courts in order to invoke their Community rights. The European Court of Justice (ECJ) developed this concept in *Van Gend & Loos*.[6] Treaty articles can be invoked against a member state in national courts.

3 Much of what follows is based on the EC Commission's proposal for the Framework Directive COM (1999) 565 final (1999/0225 (CNS)), 25.11.99 Brussels.

4 As amended by the European Communities (Amendment) Act 1993.

5 *Van Duyn v Home Office (No 2)* [1975] 3 All ER 190.

6 Case 26/62, *Van Gend & Loos v Nederlandse Administratie der Belastingen,* 1963 ECR 1, [1963] 2 CMLR 105 (1963). The *Van Gend & Loos* company had imported chemicals from Germany into the Netherlands and was charged with an import duty. It argued the duty had been increased since the time of coming into force of the EEC Treaty, contrary to article 12 of the EEC Treaty. The ECJ asserted that 'independently of the legislation of Member States, Community law ... not only imposes obligations on individuals but is also intended to confer upon them rights which become part of their legal heritage'.

Provisions such as the principle of non-discrimination on the basis of nationality, are directly effective within the scope of the matters dealt with in the treaty.[7] The Community treaties have the status of primary legislation in all member states.[8] In addition to the treaty provisions there are other forms of legislation which can be relied upon.

Secondary legislation

2.7   *Regulations* are issued by the Council or Commission. They are directly applicable, so an individual can rely upon them in domestic courts. They are binding in their entirety on member states and take precedence over all domestic law.

2.8   *Directives*, by contrast, are expressed in terms of policy aims and leave the member state with a discretion as to how the objective is to be implemented into domestic law. They are also issued by the Council or Commission, have a similar level of binding force to regulations. An individual can rely directly on a provision of a directive against the state or an emanation of the state if it satisfies the following conditions:

a)   it is sufficiently clear and precise;
b)   it is unconditional;[9]
c)   the time limit for the implementation of the directive by the member state has expired;[10]
d)   the state has failed to implement the directive correctly or at all.[11]

2.9   The ECJ expanded the doctrine of direct effect from the treaty provisions by confirming that EC regulations are directly applicable and also by establishing the direct effect of decisions and directives.[12] The result of that development is that individuals can assert treaty provisions and these three forms of EC law in national courts directly against the

---

7   Case 36/74 *Walrave and Koch v Association Union Cycliste Internationale* [1974] ECR 1405.
8   They are the highest form of law for member states (see *Costa v ENEL* [1963] ECR 1).
9   See Case 41/74 *Van Duyn v Home Office* above.
10   Case 148/78 *Criminal proceedings against Tullio Ratti*, para 47. However, in *Mangold* [2006] IRLR 143 the ECJ ruled that it was not necessary to wait for the expiry of the implementation period in certain cases.
11   Case 8/81 *Ursula Becker v Finanzamt Münster-Innenstadt* [1982] ECR 53.
12   Case 39/72 *Commission v Italy*, 1973 ECR 101, [1973] 3 CMLR 439 (regulations); Case 9/70, *Franz Grad v Finanzamt Traunstein*, 1970 ECR 825, [1971] CMLR 1 (decisions); *Van Gend & Loos*, 1963 ECR 1 (directives). See Cases C-6/90 & C-9/90, *Francovich v Italy*, 1991 ECR I-5357, 1–5408, 2 CMLR 66 (1991).

state[13] and decisions, treaty articles and regulations can be invoked directly by an individual in a national court against other individuals (horizontally). Although directives can give individuals rights that they can enforce against their respective governments, they do not have this 'horizontal' direct effect. The court has stated that directives are only binding on the member state to whom they are addressed and therefore they cannot be used against individuals or non-state entities.[14] The directive provisions can be relied upon against any emanation of the state. This will cover any public sector organisation (such as a local authority or an NHS trust).[15] Obviously the government, local authorities, the police and other emergency organisations will be covered. In *Foster v British Gas*[16] the ECJ stated that:

> It follows from the foregoing that a body, whatever its legal form, which has been made responsible, pursuant to a measure adopted by the state, for providing a public service under the control of the state and has for that purpose special powers beyond those which result from the normal rules applicable in relations between individuals is included among the bodies against which the provisions of a Directive capable of having direct effect may be relied upon.[17]

2.10   The underlying principle in *Foster* and other cases is that the state may not benefit from its default in respect of anything that lies within the sphere of responsibility which by its own free choice it has taken upon itself, irrespective of the person through whom that responsibility is exercised.

13   A concept known as *vertical direct* effect.

14   See Case 152/84, *Marshall v Southampton & South-West Hampshire Area Health Authority*, [1986] ECR 723, 749, 1 CMLR 688. Marshall, an employee of the Health Authority, was dismissed in 1980 on the ground that she had passed the normal age of retirement applicable to women. The Authority's policy was that female employees were to retire at age 60 and males at 65. UK legislation did not impose any obligation on women to retire at 60, because payment of the state or occupational pension would be deferred until actual retirement. She complained that her dismissal violated the Equal Treatment Directive 1976 before the employment tribunal. The court held that the binding nature of a directive exists only as against the state or states to which it is addressed. It could therefore be used by Ms Marshall as against the Health Authority as it was an emanation of the state.

15   *Foster and others v British Gas plc* (1990) IRLR 353 defined it as: 'a body, whatever its legal form, which has been made responsible, pursuant to a measure adopted by the state, for providing a public service under the control of the state and has for that purpose special powers beyond that which result from the normal rules applicable in relations between individuals'.

16   [1991] ICR 84.

17   Para 20 of the judgment.

Duty to interpret national law

2.11   The duty to interpret national law in conformity to Community law stems from the following considerations:[18]

i) the member states' obligation arising from a directive to achieve the result envisaged by the directive and their duty under the EC Treaty to take all appropriate measures, whether general or particular, to ensure the fulfilment of that obligation is binding on all the authorities of Member States including, for matters within their jurisdiction, the courts;[19]

ii) in applying national law, in particular legislative provisions which were specially introduced in order to implement the Directive,[20] the national court is required to interpret its national law, so far as possible, in the light of the wording and the purpose of the directive in order to achieve the result pursued by the treaty.[21]

2.12   It is not yet clear whether the provisions of the Directive will be considered to be of direct effect as they relate to age.[22] However, even if a provision of the directive ultimately proves not to be of direct effect the courts and tribunals remain under a duty to construe the anti discrimination regulations in accordance with it.[23]

---

18   Starting with Case 14/83 *Von Colson and Kamann v Land Nordrhein-Westfalen* [1984] ECR 1891, para 26.

19   This obligation derives from article 249(3) and article 10 EC Treaty (see Case 105/03 *Criminal Proceedings against Pupino* [2005] 3 WLR 1102).

20   As was the case with the Age Regulations 2006.

21   *Marleasing SA v La Comercial Internacional de Alimentacion SA* (Case C-106/89) [1990] ECR I-4135, 4159, para 8; *Wagner Miret v Fondo de garantia salaria* (Case C-334/92) [1993] ECR I-6911, 6932, para 20; *Faccini Dori v Recreb Srl* (Case C-91/92) [1994] ECR I-3325, 3357, para 26, and *Connect Austria Gesellschaft fur Telekommunikation GmbH v Telekom-Control-Kommission* (Case C-462/99) [2003] ECR I-5197, 5236, para 38.

22   In particular the effect of article 6.1 may be to render article 2 not of direct effect in respect of age because it renders direct discrimination capable of justification by reference to aims which potentially will vary from state to state. However, this question will need clarification from the ECJ.

23   See Case 14/83 *Von Colson and Kamann v Land Nordrhein-Westfalen* [1984] ECR 1891, [1986] 2 CMLR 430, ECJ, where a directive had no direct effect on the parties to the case, however the ECJ stated that in dealing with national legislation designed to give effect to a directive: 'It is for the national court to interpret and apply the legislation adopted for the implementation of the directive in conformity with the requirements of Community law, in so far as it is given discretion to do so under national law'.

2.13 If the UK has failed to transpose the directive properly as regards age, time limits do not apply to a claim relying directly on the directive.[24] National courts cannot wait until national implementing legislation is passed. They must ensure the full protection which persons derive from the direct effect of Community law.[25]

2.14 In relation to primary legislation, in *Pickstones v Freeman*[26] Lord Oliver stated:

> It must, I think, be recognised that so to construe a provision which, on its face, is unambiguous involves a departure from a number of well-established rules of construction. The intention of Parliament has, it is said, to be ascertained from the words which it has used and those words are to be construed according to their plain and ordinary meaning. The fact that a statute is passed to give effect to an international treaty does not, of itself, enable the treaty to be referred to in order to construe the words used other than in their plain and unambiguous sense. Moreover, even in the case of ambiguity, what is said in Parliament in the course of the passage of the Bill, cannot ordinarily be referred to to assist in construction. I think, however, that it has also to be recognised that a statute which is passed in order to give effect to the United Kingdom's obligations under the E.E.C. Treaty falls into a special category and it does so because, unlike other treaty obligations, those obligations have, in effect, been incorporated into English law by the European Communities Act 1972.

2.15 He went on to indicate that if the relevant legislation can be interpreted to give effect to the obligations under the treaty, it should be. More recently the Court of Appeal has held in relation to the Employment Equality (Sexual Orientation) Regulations 2003[27] that they had to be construed purposively so as to conform as far as possible with the directive and any challenge to them had to be resolved in light of what the court considered to be the true construction of the relevant provisions.[28]

2.16 In discharging its duty to give a purposive construction to directives (and to regulations issued in order to comply with the obligations imposed by directives) so as to achieve the intended outcome, a national court has the flexibility to supply into the national provision, by

---

24 Case C-208/90 *Emmott v Minister for Social Welfare and A-G* [1991] ECR I-4269, [1991] 3 CMLR 894, ECJ.

25 Case C-184/89 *Nimz v Freie und Hansestadt Hamburg* [1991] ECR 297, [1992] 3 CMLR 699, ECJ.

26 [1988] 3 WLR 265 at 283.

27 SI No 1661.

28 *R (on the application of Amicus) v Secretary of State for Trade and Industry* [2004] IRLR 430.

necessary implication, words appropriate to comply with those obligations.[29]

2.17 In *Litster* the House of Lords was prepared to insert words into domestic regulations. The House of Lords held that the courts of the United Kingdom were under a duty to give a purposive construction to the Transfer of Undertakings Regulations 1981[30] in a manner which would accord with the decisions of the ECJ on the directive and where necessary implying words which would achieve that effect. Advisers should bear in mind the possibility that words could be added to the Employment Equality (Age) Regulations 2006 in order to achieve the result required by the directive.

Claim against the state

2.18 Where an individual cannot rely on the provisions of the directive directly (for example, against a private employer), and where the domestic provision cannot be interpreted to give effect to the directive the individual may have a claim against the state. The individual may obtain compensation from the state for the loss and damage they have suffered by the failure to implement.[31] A claim may be brought in the High Court for breach of statutory duty under the European Communities Act 1972 for failure to implement the directive. In order to succeed, the claimant would have to show that:

i) the relevant rule of law was intended to confer individual rights;
ii) breach of that rule was serious; and
iii) there was a direct causal link between the breach and the loss suffered by the individual.[32]

2.19 Further, as a result of the case of Haim[33] public authorities may be liable for damages for breach of EC law in addition to or in substitution for member states themselves on the basis set out above. Whether UK law would permit a qualification body or other emanation of the state (such as a health authority) to be substituted as defendant in a *Francovich* claim using these principles remains to be seen.

29 *Litster and others v Forth Dry Dock & Engineering Co Ltd & another* [1989] IRLR 161, HL.
30 SI No 1794.
31 Cases C-6/90 and C-9/90 *Francovich and Bonifaci v Italy* [1991] ECR I-5357, [1992] IRLR 84, ECJ.
32 *Brasserie du Pecheur SA v Germany* (C46/93) [1996] QB 404.
33 *Haim v Kassenzahnärztliche Vereinigung Nordrhein* (C424/97) [2002] 1 CMLR 11.

Interpreting the regulations by reference to the directive

2.20   It will be necessary to rely on principles derived from the directive to show the way in which the Employment Equality (Age) Regulations 2006 should be interpreted, to challenge the regulations or supplement them (as against emanations of the state) where they fail to implement the Framework Directive properly. Whether a relevant provision of national law was made before or after a directive, the national court must interpret the domestic provision so as to comply with the directive.[34] As seen above, the interpretative duty is a very strong one indeed[35] and tribunals should be directed to the preamble of the directive where necessary. The preamble sets out the purposes of the directive which are to be achieved. In respect of age the preamble refers to international instruments, policy objectives and treaty provisions for its purposes.

Provisions of Community law relating to age discrimination

2.21   The first point to be noted is that the source of anti-discrimination law in the European Union regarding age is not the directive. The ECJ stated in *Mangold*:[36]

> 74 In the second place, and above all, Directive 2000/78 does not itself lay down the principle of equal treatment in the field of employment and occupation. Indeed, in accordance with article 1 thereof, the sole purpose of the directive is 'to lay down a general framework for combating discrimination on the grounds of religion or belief, disability, age or sexual orientation', the source of the actual principle underlying the prohibition of those forms of discrimination being found, as is clear from the third and fourth recitals in the preamble to the directive, in various international instruments and in the constitutional traditions common to the Member States.
>
> 75 The principle of non-discrimination on grounds of age must thus be regarded as a general principle of Community law. Where national rules fall within the scope of Community law ... and reference is made to the Court

---

34   Case C-106/89 *Marleasing SA v La Comercial Internacional de Alimentacion SA* [1990] ECR I-4135, [1992] 1 CMLR 305, ECJ and *Finnegan v Clowney Youth Training Programme Ltd* [1990] 2 AC 407.

35   See para 2.11 above.

36   [2006] IRLR 143.

for a preliminary ruling, the Court must provide all the criteria of inter-pretation needed by the national court to determine whether those rules are compatible with such a principle.[37]

2.22   The aim of the Framework Directive is the establishment of a gen-eral framework for the respect of the principle of equal treatment between persons irrespective of religion or belief, disability, age, or sexual orientation within the European Union. The areas covered by the directive are access to employment and occupation, promotion, voca-tional training, employment and working conditions and membership of certain bodies.

2.23   The article 13 foundation also refers to the prohibition of discrim-ination on the grounds of sex. However, Community legislation on equal opportunities and equal treatment of men and women in mat-ters of occupation and employment already had a basis in article 141 of the treaty. There was also the directive[38] on the implementation of the principle of equal treatment for men and women as regards access to employment, vocational training and promotion and working conditions.[39] No further Community legislation was thought necessary therefore in respect of sex discrimination.

2.24   Where a case involves an apparent conflict between the require-ments of equality in respect of age and the requirements of equality in respect of sex, it is worth remembering that articles 2 and 3 of the treaty place equality between women and men among the explicit objectives of the Community, and obliges the Community in all its tasks to aim to eliminate inequalities and promote equality between women and men. There is however no hierarchy (yet established) in terms of the anti-discrimination rights (see para 14.88).

2.25   The Commission[40] identified five sets of discriminatory measures in the employment field which particularly affect older people:

1) loss of employment;
2) discrimination in recruitment;

---

37   Case C-442/00 *Rodriguez Caballero* [2002] ECR I-11915, paras 30–32.
38   Directive 76/207/EEC of 9 February 1976.
39   There is also the often overlooked 86/613/EEC of 11 December 1986 on the application of the principle of equal treatment between men and women engaged in an activity, including agriculture, in a self-employed capacity, and on the protection of self-employed women during pregnancy and motherhood.
40   In its original proposal for the directive: Commission's proposal for the Framework directive COM (1999) 565 final (1999/0225 (CNS)), 25.11.99 Brussels (see para 1.59).

3) exclusion from special unemployment measures;
4) exclusion from training; and
5) discrimination at retirement.

2.26 The Commission pointed to examples of such practices as the establishment of maximum recruitment ages, the limitation of older workers' training rights concerning new technologies, the right to promotion, or dismissals of older workers within the context of restructuring. There was therefore a need for a directive. Disability affects older people and lower socio-economic groups disproportionately. It is always worth considering therefore whether an issue of disability discrimination arises in an appropriate case.

2.27 It is worth considering why it was appropriate for the Community to issue legislation in this area. Particularly in relation to justification for age discrimination, the justification for EU intervention has significant consequences. The existence of explicit powers conferred by article 13 of the treaty did not mean that Community legislation could be justified. Article 5 of the treaty, permits the Community to act only if and in so far as the objectives of the proposed action *cannot be sufficiently achieved by the member states* and can, therefore, by reason of the scale or effects of the proposed action, be better achieved by the Community. The question of whether prohibitions on discrimination should be left to the member states raises the question of whether a member state should be permitted divergent scope, content and enforceability in those laws. The Commission stated: 'The essential question here is to what extent such a divergence puts at risk, within the scope of Community competence, the effectiveness of the fundamental principle of equality in employment.'[41] The aim behind the adoption of Community law in this field is to give an 'unequivocal statement of public policy leaving no doubts as to the stance which European society has adopted towards discriminatory practices'.[42] The Commission therefore stated (and the EU Parliament accepted) that action in this area was not to be left to the member states individually under the principles of subsidiarity and proportionality as the objectives of a Community framework on employment equality can be better achieved by the Community.

2.28 Taking into account that anti-discrimination measures exist to some extent in all member states the Commission concluded that it was vital that the level nature and focus of Community action 'should take account of the different national situations in so far as this is

41 COM (1999) 565 final above, p5.
42 COM (1999) 565 final above, p5.

compatible with the aims and objectives of that Community action'. The Commission adopted a 'step-by-step' approach. The wording of the directive is 'sufficiently broad to accommodate the different circumstances of member states, in particular their different policy preferences and priorities'. However, it is clear that divergence in content of the rights involved was not the intention of the Directive. The Commission stated that the Framework Directive establishes a limited number of requirements, which allow member states considerable flexibility to both maintain existing and well established national arrangements and encourage, where possible, their implementation by collective agreements.

The provisions of the Framework Directive relevant to age discrimination

1) The preamble

2.29   The preamble to a directive provides an essential reference point, namely the social purpose of the Directive. The Directive is always to be interpreted so as to give effect to that social purpose. The starting point for the Directive is that:

> (4) The right of all persons to equality before the law and protection against discrimination constitutes a universal right recognised by the Universal Declaration of Human Rights, the United Nations Convention on the Elimination of All Forms of Discrimination against Women, United Nations Covenants on Civil and Political Rights and on Economic, Social and Cultural Rights and by the European Convention for the Protection of Human Rights and Fundamental Freedoms, to which all Member States are signatories. Convention No 111 of the International Labour Organisation (ILO) prohibits discrimination in the field of employment and occupation.

2.30   The concept of equality set out in these instruments is aimed at providing equality in practice and to that end some measures of positive discrimination based (among other grounds) on age may be deemed not to be discrimination.[43] This is the approach that is adopted in article 7 of the directive. Significantly, paragraph 6 of the preamble provides:

> (6) The Community Charter of the Fundamental Social Rights of Workers recognises the importance of combating every form of discrimination,

---

43   See ILO Convention 111 article 5.

including the need to take appropriate action for the social and economic integration of elderly and disabled people.

2.31 The Charter of Fundamental Rights of the European Union contains the prohibition of discrimination on grounds of age[44] and the recognition of the rights of the elderly.[45] Those rights are to lead a life of dignity and independence and to participate in social and cultural life. In addition article 35 requires in general terms that the minimum age of admission to employment may not be lower than the minimum school-leaving age. The preamble indicates that more favourable working conditions can be afforded to young people admitted to the workforce. It provides that:

> ... young people admitted to work must have working conditions appropriate to their age and be protected against economic exploitation and any work likely to harm their safety, health or physical, mental, moral or social development or to interfere with their education.

2.32 The preamble provides in paragraph 11 that discrimination based on age may:

> ... undermine the achievement of the objectives of the EC Treaty, in particular the attainment of a high level of employment and social protection, raising the standard of living and the quality of life, economic and social cohesion and solidarity, and the free movement of persons.

2.33 The over-arching purpose of the equality principles to be applied therefore are to maximise employment and social protection. Although these are high level statements, they demonstrate that a measure which restricts access to employment will require to be justified against the damage it does to those aims. Thus if a law means that no protection is given against dismissal on the grounds of age to an age defined proportion of the workforce, it will be necessary for the state to justify that law against the fact that it makes independent, economically active citizens less economically active and more dependent.

2.34 In paragraph 25 the preamble provides that:

> the prohibition of age discrimination is an essential part of meeting the aims set out in the Employment Guidelines[46] and encouraging diversity in the workforce. However, differences in treatment in connection with age may be justified under certain circumstances and therefore require specific provisions which may vary in accordance with the situation in Member

---

44 Article 21.

45 Article 25.

46 These are the aims of employability, entrepreneurship, adaptability and equal opportunities.

States. It is therefore essential to distinguish between differences in treatment which are justified, in particular by legitimate employment policy, labour market and vocational training objectives, and discrimination which must be prohibited.

2.35   This paragraph of the preamble sets an important limit on the way in which differences in treatment in connection with age can be justified. The directive requires specific provisions to be made by member states. Those provisions are permitted to vary between member states. However, they must distinguish between differences in treatment which are justified and discrimination which must be prohibited. Justification may be by reference to legitimate employment policy, labour market and vocational training objectives. However the preamble suggests that the state's laws must indicate particular justified differences in treatment. Against that approach the use of a generic provision justifying any difference in treatment based on age by reference to a legitimate aim would be unlawful.[47] Paragraph 13 provides that the Directive does not apply to social security protection schemes. In addition, by paragraph 14, the Directive is without prejudice to national provisions laying down retirement ages. There are no such national provisions in the UK.

2.36   Paragraph 37 provides a clear statement of the way in which the directive is to operate. The objective of the directive is to create within the Community a level playing field as regards equality in employment and occupation. Paragraph 37 records the policy agreement between the member states that this objective cannot sufficiently be achieved by member states. The implication of this reference to the principle of subsidiarity[48] is that although member states can provide justifications for direct discrimination which are relative to the situation in their particular state, the differences in justification must not be such as to undermine the attainment of a level playing field as regards equality between the various member states. Thus if one state adopts a very loose or non-specific law permitting justification of direct discrimination for the purposes of achieving an economic or labour market advantage over other states, that will undermine the objective of the directive. Such a law will be capable of attack by reference to the directive. By reason of the scale and impact of the action, the objective of realising the level playing field as regards employment and occupation equality needed to be achieved at Community level.

47   See paragraphs 5.5 onwards.
48   See EC Treaty article 5.

2) The articles

2.37 Article 1 of the Directive sets out its purpose. It provides a general framework for combating discrimination on the grounds of various matters including age as regards employment and occupation. This is done with a view to putting into effect in the member states the principle of equal treatment. 'Equal treatment' means that there must be no direct or indirect discrimination whatsoever on the grounds of age.[49] The definition of the principle of equal treatment contained in article 2.1 is consistent with the definition provided by article 2.1 of directive 76/207/EEC of 9 February 1976 and is intended to be interpreted in the same way. The requirement that there should be no discrimination whatsoever[50] indicates that even the smallest amount of influence by a discriminatory factor is to be taken into account. Query whether this means that minor or trivial discrimination is permitted.

Direct discrimination

2.38 Direct discrimination under the directive occurs where 'one person is treated less favourably than another is, has been or would be treated in a comparable situation, on any of the grounds ...' protected by the directive. The directive links the treatment with the protected ground rather than any personal status of the claimant.[51] It is concerned to establish whether age has played any role whatsoever in the less favourable treatment. Article 2.1(a) requires that a comparison can be made between the situation of the claimant and that of either an actual or hypothetical person in a comparable situation. The ground for the treatment must be age. In the context of age the question of whether the situation of one person is comparable to that of another may be difficult.

2.39 For example, where a small difference in age can be shown it may be that this will be significant in one context but not another. If there is a specific age at which a benefit ceases to be available or becomes

---

49 Framework Directive article 2.1.

50 This is interpreted in the UK as meaning that there should be no discrimination of a more than minor or trivial nature, see *Igen Ltd v Wong* [2005] ICR 931. Guideline 10 in *Barton v Investec Securities Ltd* [2003] ICR 1205 makes it clear that in order to discharge the burden of proof the Respondent will have to prove on the balance of probabilities, that the treatment was in no sense whatsoever on one of the protected grounds. The Court of Appeal held (*Igen* para 37) that this was the same as saying that discrimination must not have been a significant influence on the treatment (the test proposed in *Nagarajan v London Regional Transport* [1999] ICR 877).

51 Thus the Directive prohibits discrimination on the grounds of age, whether that is the age of the complainant or another person. See paras 4.12–4.18.

available, a very small age difference may result in a difference of treatment and may constitute age discrimination. On the other hand there will be situations in which such a small chronological age difference may not indicate that the treatment was on the grounds of age. This will arise where the basis for the age related treatment is not based on a specific age, but is based on the more amorphous concept of an age group defined by characteristics other than chronological age. If the employer discriminates against 'young' people, there will be a group of people who are neither young nor old. The boundaries of these groups will be difficult to establish and will depend on the perception of the employer about the individuals who are on the periphery of the age group. A difference of a few days in age is unlikely to make a difference to the treatment in such circumstances. A difference in the characteristic which leads the employer to classify a person as 'young', on the other hand, will. The directive captures both differences in treatment based on strict chronological age and those based on perceived age characteristics (for example, being middle-aged).

2.40   In respect of age, article 2.1(a) must be read as subject to article 6 which provides for justification of differences in treatment on the grounds of age.[52]

Indirect discrimination

2.41   Indirect discrimination is deemed to occur where an apparently neutral provision, criterion or practice would put persons having a particular age at a particular disadvantage compared with other persons unless:

> (i) that provision, criterion or practice is objectively justified by a legitimate aim and the means of achieving that aim are appropriate and necessary.

2.42   The definition of indirect discrimination in paragraph 2(b) is inspired by the case-law of the ECJ in cases involving the free movement of workers.[53] According to this definition, an apparently neutral provision, criterion or practice will be regarded as indirectly discriminatory if it is *intrinsically liable* to adversely affect a person or persons on the grounds referred in article 1. That it is intrinsically liable may be proven on the basis of statistical evidence or by any other means that demonstrate that a provision would be intrinsically disadvantageous for the person or persons concerned.

---

52 See below para 2.59 onwards.
53 See *O'Flynn v Adjudication Officer*, Case C-237/94, judgment of 23 May 1996 [1996] ECR 2417 and para 4.22 onwards.

2.43   The emphasis on an objective justification in cases of indirect discrimination is put on two elements. Firstly, the aim of the provision, criterion or practice which establishes a difference of treatment must
deserve protection and must be sufficiently substantial to justify it
taking precedence over the principle of equal treatment. Secondly, the
means employed to achieve that aim must be appropriate and necessary. The definition of indirect discrimination should be construed in
conjunction with the general rules on the burden of proof set out in article 10. It is for the claimant to prove the disadvantage, and intrinsic likelihood of such disadvantage, it is for the respondent to prove all the
elements of justification.

Harassment

2.44   Harassment is deemed to be a form of discrimination.[54] It occurs when
unwanted conduct related to any of the protected grounds takes place
with the purpose or effect of violating the dignity of a person and of creating an intimidating, hostile, degrading, humiliating or offensive
environment. Such conduct can take different forms, ranging from
spoken words and gestures to the production, display or circulation of
written words, pictures or other material. This behaviour must be of a
serious nature and create an overall disturbing or hostile working
environment. There is no need for the unwanted conduct to emanate
from the employer or from a person for whom the employer has
responsibility. It is arguable that the social purpose of the directive
can only be fully achieved if harassment by a third party in a situation
over which the employer has control is actionable against the employer
when it fails to exercise that control.

> EXAMPLE: Two waitresses in their 50s are working at a reception
> at which a comedian, well known for his mother-in-law jokes and
> jokes about age, is performing. As the evening wears on, they are
> subjected to a foreseeable barrage of personal comments about
> their age while they move among the tables. The employer could
> foresee that this would be the result of placing them in this situ-
> ation but did nothing to prevent the harassment to which they
> are subjected by the comedian and members of the audience.[55]

54 Article 2.3.
55 Cf the facts of *Burton v De Vere Hotels Ltd* [1997] ICR 1 which approached the
    same problem using principles of vicarious liability and direct discrimination.
    This approach was overruled in *Pearce v Mayfield School* [2003] UKHL 34;
    [2004] 1 All ER 339; [2003] ICR 937; [2003] IRLR 512. It may now be available
    under the various implementing regulations.

2.45　The wording of the article suggests that harassment is a third type of prohibited discrimination. It stipulates that harassment is deemed to be a form of discrimination within article 2.1. Some may wish to argue that therefore it must either be direct discrimination or indirect discrimination. The article makes clear however that it is deemed to be a form of discrimination, rather than that such treatment must be analysed according to the factors relevant to one or other form of discrimination. The article does not simply serve to treat it as prima facie discrimination of one type or the other, but as a form of discrimination. In the UK the laws implementing the directive do not allow harassment to be justified. An employer might wish to argue that such laws failed to implement the directive. The employee would riposte that the directive is to provide minimum standards of protection and it is open to the member states to define harassment.[56]

2.46　The matters that need to be established for harassment indicate that a comparator is not required.

Instructions to discriminate

2.47　An instruction to discriminate against persons on grounds of age is deemed to be discrimination.[57] The directive raises the question of what constitutes an instruction to discriminate. Clearly an instruction to something which is justified age discrimination is not an instruction to discriminate under the directive. The concept of an instruction to discriminate would clearly include an instruction to apply an unjustified age neutral provision, criterion or practice (PCP) which placed people of a particular age at a particular disadvantage but not an instruction to apply a justified PCP. The circumstances in which article 2.4 may be relied upon may need clarification.

Public order, etc derogations

2.48　The directive is without prejudice to measures laid down by national law which, in a democratic society, are necessary for public security, for the maintenance of public order and the prevention of criminal offences, for the protection of health and for the protection of the rights and freedoms of others.[58] This principle, being a derogation

---

56　Article 2.3 provides: 'In this context, the concept of harassment may be defined in accordance with the national laws and practice of the Member States.'

57　Framework Directive article 2.4.

58　Framework Directive article 2.5.

from an individual right (equal treatment) laid down in the directive, must be interpreted strictly. Further, any derogation from equal treatment must observe the principle of proportionality. Any such derogation must remain within the limits of what is appropriate and necessary for achieving the aim in view (here the listed aims) and requires the principle of equal treatment to be reconciled as far as possible with the requirements of public security, for the maintenance of public order and the prevention of criminal offences, for the protection of health and for the protection of the rights and freedoms of others.[59]

2.49   The directive does not cover differences of treatment based on nationality. It is without prejudice to provisions and conditions relating to the entry into and residence of third-country nationals and stateless persons in the territory of member states. Thus it cannot affect the immigration status of a third country national. It is without prejudice to any treatment which arises from the legal status of the third-country nationals and stateless persons concerned.[60] This last point gives rise to the question whether an illegal contract (as a result of immigration restrictions on the employee) can nullify the right of the employee to seek redress for age discrimination. In *Vakante v Addey and Stanhope School Governing Body*[61] an asylum seeker whose immigration status did not permit him to work complained of race discrimination consisting of dismissal and a failure by the employer to permit him training opportunities and other benefits, facilities and services. The employment tribunal rejected the claim because the contract was illegal and the complaints were so closely bound up with the contract. The Court of Appeal upheld that view. It would appear that if the same issue arose in relation to a non-EU national who complained of age discrimination, but whose immigration status rendered the contract illegal he would not be able to bring a claim of age discrimination. The refusal of the tribunal would arise from his status as a third country national.[62]

2.50   By article 3.3 the Directive does not apply to payments of any kind made by state schemes or similar, including state social security or social protection schemes. Article 3.4 provides that member states may provide that the directive, in so far as it relates to discrimination

---

59 *Johnston v Chief Constable of the Royal Ulster Constabulary* [1987] QB 129; [1987] ICR 83 at paras 36–38.

60 Framework Directive article 3.2.

61 [2005] ICR 231; [2004] EWCA Civ 1065.

62 *Vakante* sought to rely on the Race Directive, Directive 2000/43, but it was not in effect at the time of the events (nor of the tribunal's decision).

on the grounds of disability and age, shall not apply to the armed forces. The UK has taken advantage of this provision to remove the armed forces from the scope of the regulations.

Scope of the Directive

2.51   The Directive applies to all persons, as regards both the public and private sectors, including public bodies.[63] The list of areas to which the Directive applies is extensive and bears some comparison with the scope of the Employment Equality (Age) Regulations 2006:

a) conditions[64] for access[65] to:
   i) employment;
   ii) self-employment;
   iii) occupation;
b) access to all types and to all levels of vocational guidance, vocational training, advanced vocational training and retraining, including practical work experience;
c) employment and working conditions, including dismissals and pay;
d) membership of, and involvement in, an organisation of workers or employers, or any organisation whose members carry on a particular profession, including the benefits provided for by such organisations.

2.52   There will be a certain amount of debate as to what constitutes vocational training. In the context of legal work, for example, working as a volunteer is often seen as a way of entering the profession or gaining skills.[66] It may be that such volunteer work will be regarded as vocational training or practical work experience in certain situations where it is closely associated with entry to a profession or job.

---

63 Within the limits of the areas of competence conferred on the Community (Framework Directive article 3.1).
64 Whatever the branch of activity and at all levels of the professional hierarchy (Framework Directive article 3.1).
65 Including selection criteria and recruitment conditions and including promotion (Framework Directive article 3.1).
66 In the UK there have been divergent views on the status of volunteers (see *Murray v Newham Citizens Advice Bureau* [2001] ICR 708 and *South East Sheffield Citizens Advice Bureau v Grayson* [2004] ICR 1138) and see para 14.30 onwards.

Genuine occupational requirement

2.53 The preamble to the directive states that in very limited circumstances, a difference of treatment may be justified where a characteristic related to age constitutes a genuine and determining occupational requirement (GOR), when the objective is legitimate and the requirement is proportionate. Such circumstances should be included in the information provided by the member states to the Commission.[67] Note that the preamble views GORs as a justification of discrimination. Clearly there is an overlap with justification under article 6.

2.54 A difference of treatment which is based on a characteristic related to age will not constitute discrimination where, by reason of:

a) the nature of the particular occupational activities concerned; or
b) the context in which they are carried out,

such a characteristic constitutes a genuine and determining occupational requirement. However the objective must be legitimate and the requirement must be proportionate.[68]

2.55 Age will be a GOR only if it is necessary to be of a particular age to perform a particular job, or if there is some characteristic which is objectively related to age which is necessary to perform the particular job. It is difficult to see a circumstance in which being of a particular age will be necessary to perform the particular role. This is because performance of any role depends generally on the person's abilities rather than any extraneous characterisation of them. The only exception to that principle is where there is a qualification that it is necessary to have to be permitted to perform a job. However it will seldom be the case that the possession of a qualification can be said to be related to age in the way that is required for the age characteristic to be a GOR. Article 4 is a general provision in which the onus lies on the defendant to justify why an exception from the normal provisions relating to discrimination is appropriate in the particular circumstances. It permits the judge to determine each case on individual merit. However the circumstances in which the justification is to be used are to be notified by the member states to the Commission. Thus there will necessarily be a limited set of circumstances in which the justification can apply in any particular member state. Proof of matters

---

67 Preamble, para 23.
68 Directive, article 4.1.

along the lines of a Canadian bona fide occupational requirement is needed in our view:[69]

a) The treatment must be based on an article 1 related characteristic.

b) Such treatment will not be discrimination if either by reason of the particular occupational activities concerned or of the context in which they are carried out, the following conditions are fulfilled:

   i)   the defendant has an honest and good faith belief that the GOR is necessary for the fulfilment of the legitimate aim of the employer (the characteristic must be a genuine occupational requirement);

   ii) the characteristic is a determining occupational requirement. Possession of the characteristic or failure to possess it cannot be accommodated in another way, so that the person cannot engage in the occupation without (or with) that characteristic;

   iii) the insistence of the defendant that the characteristic is a requirement of engaging in the occupation must be in pursuit of a legitimate aim; and

   iv) requiring the characteristic for engaging in the occupation is proportionate to the aim pursued.

2.56   The UK has chosen to introduce the concept of a GOR, but has not specified acceptable GORs. It appears therefore that the GOR defence is available across the scope of the 2006 regulations. As the requirements for justification of direct discrimination are similar, and if anything less stringent than those using GORs, it is thought that resort

---

69   *Terry Grismer v The British Columbia Council of Human Rights & The British Columbia Superintendent of Motor Vehicles and the Attorney General of British Columbia* [1999] 3 SCR 868 and see *British Columbia (Public Service Employee Relations Commission) v BCGSEU* ('the *Meiorin* case') [1999] 3 SCR 3, where the Supreme Court of Canada adopted the following approach:

54. Having considered the various alternatives, I propose the following three step test for determining whether a prima facie discriminatory standard is a BFOR. An employer may justify the impugned standard by establishing on a balance of probabilities:

(1) that the employer adopted the standard for a purpose rationally connected to the performance of the job;

(2) that the employer adopted the particular standard in an honest and good faith belief that it was necessary to the fulfilment of that legitimate work-related purpose; and

(3) that the standard is reasonably necessary to the accomplishment of that legitimate work-related purpose. To show that the standard is reasonably necessary, it must be demonstrated that it is impossible to accommodate individual employees sharing the characteristics of the claimant without imposing undue hardship upon the employer.

to GORs will be rare, and a successful application of a GOR will be very rare.

2.57 There is a further GOR available in article 4.2 whereby member states can keep existing certain national legislation or provide for future legislation incorporating national practices existing at the date of adoption of the directive. The laws or practices must relate to occupational activities within churches and other public or private organisations the ethos of which is based on religion or belief. The laws or practices must provide that a difference of treatment based on a person's religion or belief will not constitute discrimination where, by reason of the nature of these activities or of the context in which they are carried out, a person's religion or belief constitute a genuine, legitimate and justified occupational requirement, having regard to the organisation's ethos. The difference of treatment on the basis of religion or ethos must be implemented taking account of member states' constitutional provisions and principles, as well as the general principles of Community law, and should not justify discrimination on another ground. Therefore it is not possible to use a religion and belief GOR to justify age discrimination.

2.58 In *R. (on the application of Amicus) v Secretary of State for Trade and Industry*[70] certain trade unions applied for the annulment of the provisions of the Employment Equality (Sexual Orientation) Regulations 2003.[71] These regulations implement the sexual orientation aspects of the directive. The unions challenged the provisions for exceptions to the general prohibition of discrimination on the grounds of sexual orientation on the basis of GOR, including occupation for the purposes of an organised religion and benefits dependent on marital status. The implementation survived this challenge.[72]

Justification of differences of treatment on grounds of age

2.59 Article 6.1 provides in part:

> 1. Notwithstanding Article 2(2), Member States may provide that differences of treatment on grounds of age shall not constitute discrimination, if, within the context of national law, they are objectively and reasonably justified by a legitimate aim, including legitimate employment policy, labour

70 [2004] EWHC 860; [2004] IRLR 430. The GOR provisions in the Sexual Orientation Regulations were required to be construed very narrowly. The same principles will apply to regulation 8 of the Age Regulations 2006. See *Amicus* judgment at para 115 onwards.

71 SI No 1661.

72 See para 3 for discussion of the implementation of GORs in the Age Regulations 2006.

market and vocational training objectives, and if the means of achieving that aim are appropriate and necessary.

2.60   The Commission in proposing the directive took the view that because equal treatment is a fundamental principle, any difference in treatment which is based explicitly on one of the grounds specified in article 1(1) should normally be regarded as discriminatory. It is in this context that article 6.1 should be considered. The Commission reflected that the existing law of the Community and member states tends to suggest that it is only in very exceptional circumstances that such a difference of treatment could be justified. It is suggested that this indicates that the use of justifications for direct age discrimination should therefore be exceptional and not mundane.

2.61   Article 6.1 provides a list of certain matters which may constitute justified age discrimination. They are simply examples:

> Such differences of treatment may include, among others:
>
> (a) the setting of special conditions on access to employment and vocational training, employment and occupation, including dismissal and remuneration conditions, for young people, older workers and persons with caring responsibilities in order to promote their vocational integration or ensure their protection;
> (b) the fixing of minimum conditions of age, professional experience or seniority in service for access to employment or to certain advantages linked to employment;
> (c) the fixing of a maximum age for recruitment which is based on the training requirements of the post in question or the need for a reasonable period of employment before retirement.

2.62   The original draft of the article was intended to provide:

> ... a non-exhaustive list of differences of treatment on grounds of age which shall not constitute direct discrimination, provided that they are objectively justified. It is intended, both to limit the possibilities of claiming justification in cases of direct discrimination to exceptional situations concerning the ground of age, and to ensure that this limited range of exceptions respects the principles of necessity, proportionality and legitimacy as laid down by the European Court of Justice as regards the notion of indirect discrimination. Therefore, Member States may allow differences of treatment on grounds of age other than those listed in article [6], in accordance with their legal traditions and political priorities, provided that they are appropriate and necessary to attain a legitimate aim.[73]

2.63   The Commission intended therefore that the laws introduced by the member states should allow 'differences of treatment on grounds of age'

---

73   See paras 1.74–1.87 above.

in a 'limited range of exceptions'. It is doubtful that a general test of whether treatment is appropriate and necessary to attain a legitimate aim fulfils this requirement. Rather the legislation should specify the treatment that is permitted or limit the range of exceptions to the principle of equal treatment.[74] In the Opinion of the Committee on Citizens' Freedoms And Rights, Justice And Home Affairs,[75] the Rapporteur Thomas Mann (draftsman Joke Swiebel) stated:[76]

Article [6] – Justification of differences of treatment on grounds of age

The formulation of this article in the proposal for a directive shows the drafters to have been in two minds: on the one hand, it is proposed that possible exceptions to the prohibition on discrimination on grounds of age should be subject to a justification test, while on the other hand a non-exhaustive list of exceptions is given. This could give the impression that these variants of age differentiation have already passed the justification test, but that is not the case. Thinking about the social importance of the age factor is rapidly changing, which is just one of the reasons why it is not expedient to adopt a fixed list of exceptions. Your rapporteur proposes deleting the list of possible exceptions from Article [6] so as to create an open assessment system. The Member States must, however, be required to review periodically whether the age criteria in use still comply with the justification test in the directive and inform the Commission of this.[77]

2.64 This model of abolition of the possible list of exceptions was not pursued in the final directive.[78] At the least this indicates that the member states should specify the treatment that is justified, rather than applying a general test for justification.

2.65 The extended reflection on the scope of justification of age discrimination suggests two matters:

a) that the UK's attempt at implementation of justification of direct age discrimination is flawed in that it fundamentally undermines the intention of the directive by permitting a general non-specific test of justification of age discrimination;

b) that even if the UK's implementation survives challenge on that basis, the test for justification of direct age discrimination will be

74 See regulation 3 in the Age Regulations 2006; para 5.33.

75 A5-0264/2000.

76 Page 82 – the proposed amendment (38) was not adopted.

77 See 14 September 2000 Opinion of the Committee on Citizens' Freedoms And Rights, Justice And Home Affairs for the Committee on Employment and Social Affairs on the proposal for a Council directive establishing a general framework for equal treatment in employment and occupation (COM(1999) 565 – C5-0068/2000 1999/0225 (CNS)).

78 See paras 2.34–2.36 above.

very much more stringent than that for indirect discrimination because it is seen as limited to a narrow set of circumstances and it should be viewed as an exception to the principle of equal treatment.

2.66   The question of whether there has been proper implementation of the directive by regulation 3 is currently the subject of litigation before the administrative court.[79]

Positive action on age

2.67   The directive[80] provides for positive action in very much stronger terms than is permitted in the UK. Article 7 permits, but does not require, member states to maintain or adopt specific measures to prevent or compensate for disadvantages linked to age. Where this is to be done with a view to ensuring full equality in practice, it does not breach the principle of equal treatment. These measures would include those that promote the integration of young people, and the transition from work to retirement, for example. The purpose of any such measures must be to achieve substantive equality, in the sense that the principle of equal treatment does not simply require that everyone is treated identically. Rather the principle permits the removal by positive action of inequalities that have been identified. However as always, strong measures of positive discrimination will have to be justified as proportionate and necessary. The UK's version of positive action is restricted to training and encouragement.[81]

Minimum standards

2.68   A technical, but highly important, article of the directive is article 8 which provides that member states may introduce or maintain provisions which are more favourable to the protection of the principle of equal treatment than those laid down in the directive. It also stipulates that the implementation of the directive shall under no circumstances constitute grounds for a reduction in the level of protection against discrimination already afforded by member states in the fields covered by this directive.[82] Existing law which has the effect of

---

79   *R on the application of The Incorporated Trustees of the National Council on Aging v The Secretary of State for Trade and Industry* (Admin Ct CO/5485/2006).

80   Article 7.

81   See para 6.19 onwards for a discussion of the UK law.

82   Article 8.2.

protecting against certain species of less favourable treatment, such as unfair dismissal law, must therefore be preserved in scope.

Remedies and enforcement

2.69   There are two main conditions for effective legislation implementing equal treatment provisions. A victim of discrimination must have an effective personal remedy against the person or body who has perpetrated the discrimination. There must also be adequate mechanisms in each member state to ensure adequate levels of enforcement. Thus persons who consider themselves wronged must have the possibility of pursuing their claims through an administrative and/or judicial procedure to enforce their right to equal treatment, even after the employment relationship has ended.[83] Article 9 of the directive provides

Article 9 – Defence of rights

1. Member States shall ensure that judicial and/or administrative procedures, including where they deem it appropriate conciliation procedures, for the enforcement of obligations under this Directive are available to all persons who consider themselves wronged by failure to apply the principle of equal treatment to them, even after the relationship in which the discrimination is alleged to have occurred has ended.

2.70   Article 9.2 provides that member states must ensure that associations, organisations or other legal entities which have, in accordance with the criteria laid down by their national law, a legitimate interest in ensuring that the provisions of the directive are complied with, can engage, either on behalf or in support of the complainant, with his or her approval, in any judicial and/or administrative procedure provided for the enforcement of obligations under the directive. In the UK it is intended that the Commission for Equality and Human Rights (CEHR) will deal with the age strand of discrimination. Age focussed groups are able to support claims made by individuals in the UK, but cannot bring claims on behalf of claimants. The law does not permit such groups to join in litigation in support of the complainant at first instance. The Commissions (CRE, DRC, EOC) have been recognised as legitimate interveners by the Court of Appeal.[84] It is arguable that the UK has failed to implement the directive properly in this respect as the duty on the UK is to permit the organisations to engage in any judicial procedure in support of a claimant who approves their involvement.

---

83   See para 3.78 for a discussion of the implementation in the UK of this principle.

84   See *Igen* above, para 2.37.

2.71   Article 9.3 preserves national rules relating to time limits for bringing actions as regards the principle of equality of treatment. There is a
three-month time limit set under the 2006 Regulations for the bringing
of claims. That is consistent with the other equality strands and the
directive does not require more generous time limits to be operated in
respect of age.

Burden of proof

2.72   The Commission noted, in introducing the directive, that normally,
the burden of proving a case rests on the plaintiff. However, obtaining
evidence in discrimination and employment law cases, where the relevant information is often in the hands of the defendant, can be very
problematic. There is therefore an article dealing with the burden of
proof. It sets out how the burden of proof shifts to the defendant in
accordance with the case-law of the ECJ.[85] The original Commission proposal was that 'the burden of proof reverts to the defendant once the
plaintiff has established factual evidence of less favourable treatment
caused by apparent discrimination'. Article 10 provides:

   1.   Member States shall take such measures as are necessary, in accordance
        with their national judicial systems, to ensure that, when persons who
        consider themselves wronged because the principle of equal treatment
        has not been applied to them establish, before a court or other compe-
        tent authority, facts from which it may be presumed that there has been
        direct or indirect discrimination, it shall be for the respondent to prove
        that there has been no breach of the principle of equal treatment.

   2.   Paragraph 1 shall not prevent Member States from introducing rules
        of evidence which are more favourable to plaintiffs.

   3.   Paragraph 1 shall not apply to criminal procedures.

   4.   Paragraphs 1, 2 and 3 shall also apply to any legal proceedings
        commenced in accordance with article 9(2).

   5.   Member States need not apply paragraph 1 to proceedings in which it
        is for the court or competent body to investigate the facts of the case.

2.73   The provisions for reversal of the burden of proof are much more
familiar to common lawyers than to those from a civil code country.
Detailed guidance has been given on the application of the burden of

---

85 Danfoss, Case C-109/88, judgment of 17 October 1989 [1989] ECR 3199, para
    16; *Enderby v Frenchay Health Authority*, Case C-127/92, judgment of 27
    October 1993; [1993] ECR 5535, APRs 13 and 14 and *Royal Copenhagen*, Case
    C-400/93, judgment of 31 May 1995 [1995] ECR 1275, para 24.

proof provisions as they will apply in the UK.[86] Note that recital 31 in the preamble makes clear that it is not for the respondent to prove that the plaintiff is of a particular age.

Victimisation

2.74 Victimisation, under the directive, is seen, not as a species of discrimination, but as a necessary adjunct to enforcing the principle of equal treatment. Member states are required[87] to introduce such measures as are necessary to protect employees against dismissal or other adverse treatment by the employer as a reaction to a complaint within the undertaking or to any legal proceedings aimed at enforcing compliance with the principle of equal treatment. The article appears to require the implementing law to do the following:

a) protect against dismissal as a reaction to an internal complaint or legal proceedings; and

b) protect against adverse treatment as a reaction to those matters.

2.75 There is no requirement that the law should provide that the adverse treatment be *worse* than the treatment of another in similar circumstances who had not made (or assisted) an internal complaint, or brought (or assisted in the bringing of) a legal complaint.[88] The UK model of discrimination victimisation fails to protect as it does not capture adverse treatment unless that treatment is worse than the treatment given to another real or hypothetical person. The implementing law should only require that a causal link be shown between adverse treatment and the complaint or proceedings. There is no need for a comparator.[89]

Information, bargaining and NGOs

2.76 The directive requires governments to engage in ensuring the dissemination of information concerning rights, down to an appropriate level, for example the level of the workplace.[90] Governments are also enjoined to encourage social dialogue between the social partners.[91]

---

86 See para 11.90 onwards.
87 By article 11.
88 Compare the approach in *Aziz v Trinity Taxis* [1989] QB 463 and *Chief Constable of the West Yorkshire Police v Khan* [2001] IRLR 830.
89 See the discussion of victimisation under the Age Regulations 2006, para 4.43.
90 Article 12.
91 Article 13.

They must engage in dialogue with non-governmental organisations (NGOs) concerning anti-discrimination measures.[92]

3) Final measures

2.77   The final measures of a directive are often overlooked because they appear to contain fairly high level obligations on states. This is not the case. Member states have to carry out a review of their existing legislation and if existing legislation offends against the principle of equal treatment it must be made to conform.

Penalties

2.78   Article 17 deals with the nature of the laws that must be introduced. It provides:

> Member States shall lay down the rules on sanctions applicable to infringements of the national provisions adopted pursuant to this Directive and shall take all measures necessary to ensure that they are applied. The sanctions, which may comprise the payment of compensation to the victim, must be effective, proportionate and dissuasive.

2.79   In order to comply with the directive, national law must provide 'effective, proportionate and dissuasive' sanctions for violation of national anti-discrimination norms. Sanctions 'may comprise the payment of compensation to the victim'. The requirement that sanctions must be effective, proportionate and dissuasive means that all forms of damages (including punitive damages) must be available to the person whose claim is well founded. The ECJ stated:

> ... it has been consistently held since *Marshall v Southampton and SW Hampshire Area Health Authority* ... that a Directive cannot of itself impose obligations on an individual, in this case a private-sector employer, and thus cannot be relied upon as such against such a person. However, it has also been consistently held since [Case 14/83 *Von Colson and Kamann* [1984] ECR 1891] that the Member States' obligation arising from a Directive to achieve the result envisaged by the Directive and their duty under Article 5 of the Treaty of Rome [now Article 10 EC] to take all appropriate measures, whether general or particular, to ensure the fulfilment of that obligation are binding on all the authorities of Member States including, for matters within their jurisdiction, the courts. As follows from *Marleasing SA v La Comercial Internacional de Alimentación* 1990 ECR I-4135, paragraph 8, and *Wagner Miret v Fondo de Garantía Salarial* 1993 ECR I-6911, paragraphs 20 and 21, in

92   Article 14.

applying national law, in particular legislative provisions which, as in the present case, were specially introduced in order to implement the Directive, the national court is required to interpret its national law, so far as possible, in the light of the wording and the purpose of the Directive in order to achieve the result pursued by the third paragraph of Article 189 of the Treaty.[93]

2.80   Further, the court stated in *Von Colson*:[94]

It follows from [article 6] that Member States are required to adopt measures which are sufficiently effective to achieve the objective of the directive to ensure that those measures may in fact be relied upon before the national courts by the persons concerned.

2.81   Advisers should note that it is the objective of the directive which is the standard by which the effectiveness of the measure is to be judged. Second, any measure introduced must in practice be capable of being relied upon by the individual. This standard has implications for the clarity and accessibility of the law implementing the Directive.[95] The ECJ stated:

Although ... full implementation of the directive does not require any specific form of sanction for unlawful discrimination, it does entail that the sanction be such as to guarantee real and effective judicial protection. Moreover it must also have a real deterrent effect on the employer.[96]

2.82   The sanction must, in the ordinary case, have a real deterrent effect on the employer. A study of the various cases gives no constant idea of what the ECJ considers the requirement that the remedies under the directive be 'effective, proportionate and dissuasive' means.[97] What seems to be a common concept may be used in a different way in different fields of application.[98]. However it is clear from cases such as *Marshall II*, a proposed sanction or remedy can be tested for effectiveness by reference to the aim proposed under a directive. In the case of directives aimed at equality, *Marshall II* provides useful guidance:

Article 6 [of EC Directive 76/207] does not prescribe a specific measure to be taken in the event of a breach of the prohibition of discrimination, but

---

93   *Coote v Granada Hospitality Ltd* (C185/97) [1998] ECR I-5199.

94   At p1907, para 18.

95   See discussion of retirement provisions, chapter 9.

96   Further at p1908, para 23.

97   See Christa Tobler *Thematic Report Remedies and Sanctions in EC Non-Discrimination Law* June 2005 para 2.3 www.migpolgroup.com or www.publications.eu.int.

98   See *Aknlagemynidgheden v Hansen & Soen I/S* [1990] ECR I-2911, Italy v Commission C 297/02 of 23 September 2003.

leaves Member States free to choose between the different solutions suitable for achieving the objective of the Directive, depending on the different situations which may arise.

24 However, the objective is to arrive at real equality of opportunity and cannot therefore be attained in the absence of measures appropriate to restore such equality when it has not been observed. As the Court stated in paragraph 23 of the judgment in *Von Colson and Kamann,* cited above, those measures must be such as to guarantee real and effective judicial protection and have a real deterrent effect on the employer.

25 Such requirements necessarily entail that the particular circumstances of each breach of the principle of equal treatment should be taken into account. In the event of discriminatory dismissal contrary to Article 5(1) of the Directive, a situation of equality could not be restored without either reinstating the victim of discrimination or, in the alternative, granting financial compensation for the loss and damage sustained.

26 Where financial compensation is the measure adopted in order to achieve the objective indicated above, it must be adequate, in that it must enable the loss and damage actually sustained as a result of the discriminatory dismissal to be made good in full in accordance with the applicable national rules.[99]

2.83   The second requirement that the remedy must be **proportionate** must be seen in the context of the third requirement which is that the remedy must be **dissuasive of discrimination**. The Basic Principles and Guidelines on the Right to a Remedy and Reparation for Victims of Gross Violations of International Human Rights Law and Serious Violations of International Humanitarian Law,[100] articles 15–20 deal with the types of compensation and remedy that should be available for gross violations of international human rights law. It is clear from article 20 that compensation should include any economically assessable damage, such as:

a) physical or mental harm;
b) lost opportunities, including employment, education and social benefits;

---

99   C 271/91 *Marshall v Southampton and South West Hampshire Area Health Authority ('Marshall II')* [1990] 3 CMLR 425.
100   CHR res 2005/35, UN Doc E/CN.4/2005/ L.10/Add.11 (19 April 2005), adopted 16 December 2005 by General Assembly resolution 60/147 of 16 December 2005. Article 23 of the UN Universal Declaration of Human Rights created an international human right to work, and to free choice of employment. That freedom is to be enjoyed without discrimination on other status (article 7) which would include discrimination based on age.

    c) material damages and loss of earnings, including loss of earning potential;

    d) moral damage;

    e) costs required for legal or expert assistance, medicine and medical services, and psychological and social services.

2.84   Where a person has suffered financial loss from discrimination, a system of compensation for breach of an anti discrimination measure cannot be capped. Where **compensation** is awarded to penalise breaches of the prohibition of discrimination, such compensation has to be more than nominal so as to guarantee effective protection and to provide a deterrent to employers.[101] The UK system of compensation for breach of the consultation on retirement provisions is capped at eight weeks' pay.[102] It is arguable that this is a breach of the requirements of the directive as it does not permit a tribunal to consider that had consultation taken place properly a different outcome would have been achieved and to compensate fully for that different outcome.[103] If the steps in the UK retirement procedure are subject to the requirement of non-discrimination this may not matter because the employee can claim compensation for the lost chance of further employment in those proceedings.

References to the European Court of Justice

2.85   Where there is a question concerning the proper interpretation of a provision of Community law the ECJ can give a preliminary ruling.[104] The power of the employment tribunal to make references to the ECJ derives directly from the treaty. Any court may make a reference if it considers that a decision on the interpretation is necessary to enable it to give judgment. A distinction is drawn between courts of last instance, which *must* make a reference to the ECJ unless the EC law issues are

---

101 *Von Colson v Land Nordrhein-Westfalen* (14/83) [1984] ECR 1891.

102 See para 9.89.

103 Ie, a lost chance of further employment.

104 By article 234 EC Treaty. Where a question of interpretation is raised before any court or tribunal of a member state, that court or tribunal may, if it considers that a decision on the question is necessary to enable it to give judgment, request the ECJ to give a ruling thereon. Where any such question is raised in a case pending before a court or tribunal of a member state, against whose decisions there is no judicial remedy under national law, that court or tribunal shall bring the matter before the ECJ.

acte clair.[105] National courts have the widest discretion in referring matters to the ECJ if they consider that a case pending before them raises questions involving interpretation, or consideration of the validity, of provisions of Community law, necessitating a decision on their part.[106]

2.86   The ECJ has stated that 'a reference for a preliminary ruling may prove particularly useful, at an appropriate stage of the proceedings, when there is a new question of interpretation of general interest for the uniform application of Community law throughout the Union, or where the existing case-law does not appear to be applicable to a new set of facts'.[107] In the UK this discretion has been the subject of guidance from the Court of Appeal:

2.87   Is the reference 'necessary'?

i) The point of European law must be conclusive, in the sense that it is necessary for the tribunal to give judgment in the case before it in the sense that if the provision of European law bears one interpretation judgment will be given one way, and if it bears another, the judgment will go the other way.

ii) Is there a previous ruling of the ECJ on the same point? If so, a reference is not necessary, unless the court or tribunal considers that the previous ECJ ruling may have been wrong or if there are new factors that ought to be brought to the ECJ's notice.

iii) If the point is 'acte claire' there is no need for a reference. This means that the point is reasonably clear and free from doubt, so that the court or tribunal simply needs to apply the European law provision.

iv) The facts of the case should be decided first. As a rule, the tribunal will not be able to tell whether it is necessary to decide a point until all the facts are ascertained. The rule is a general rule[108] and there will be some situations in which a reference will be appropriate before facts are found (as for example where it is not possible to

---

105 'Acte clair' means that the correct application of EC law is so obvious as to leave no scope for any reasonable doubt as to the manner in which the question raised is to be resolved.

106 Case 166/73 *Rheinmühlen-Düsseldorf v Einfuhr- und Vorratsstelle für Getreide und Futtermittel* [1974] ECR 33, the ECJ held (at para 4).

107 It is for the national court to explain why the interpretation sought is necessary to enable it to give judgment. See OJ C143/1, 11.6.2005, (2005/C143/01) *Information note on references from national courts for a preliminary ruling.*

108 Particularly in discrimination cases there may be situations in which a reference can be seen to be necessary at an earlier stage (namely the stage at which the primary facts are established or agreed).

determine what the relevant facts are without the interpretation of the European law provision).

2.88 Should the discretion to make a reference be exercised? The following factors should be taken into account:

i) The length of time it will take to get a ruling. Very considerable delays are occurring in the ECJ. The time taken to obtain a judgment in a preliminary ruling case has been rising[109] and is likely to increase as a result of the accession of ten new member states in May 2004.

ii) Avoid overloading the court. The right to make a reference should be exercised sparingly.[110]

iii) The question should be formulated clearly and relate solely to the interpretation of the European law provision. The facts should be found and stated clearly before the question is referred.

iv) Unless the point is really difficult and important the tribunal or court should determine it. There is a sliding scale: Where the national court is not a court of last resort:

1) a reference will be most appropriate where:
    a) the question is one of general importance; and
    b) where the ruling is likely to promote the uniform application of the law throughout the European Union;

2) reference will be least appropriate where:
    a) there is an established body of case law which could readily be transposed to the facts of the specific instance case; or
    b) where the question turns on a narrow point considered in the light of a very specific set of facts and the ruling is unlikely to have any application beyond the instant case.[111]

v) The expense to the parties should be taken into account. This will particularly be a factor in a jurisdiction in which costs will not automatically follow the outcome of the case.

---

109 *Viking Line Abp v International Transport Workers Federation & The Finnish Seamen's Union* [2005] EWHC 1222 (Comm).

110 Advocate General Jacobs in Case C-338/95 *Wiener SI GmbH v Hauptzollamt Emmerich* [1997] ECR-I 6495 warned against overloading the ECJ with references.

111 In *Trinity Mirror* [2001] EWCA Civ 65, Chadwick LJ applied the *Else* test (at para 51 of his judgment), but said that it was necessary to have regard also to the observations in *Wiener*. See also *R v Commissioners of Inland Revenue ex p Professional Contractors' Group & Others* [2002] EuLR 3296 and *R (on the application of Federation of Technological Industries and others) v Customs and Excise Commissioners & Another* [2004] EWCA Civ 1020.

vi) If both parties want the point to be referred the court or tribunal should have regard to their wishes, but should not give them undue weight. There should be some hesitation if one of the parties does not want a reference to be made.[112]

2.89 In *R v International Stock Exchange ex p Else*,[113] Lord Bingham MR gave further guidance on the reference of questions to the ECJ which he regarded as giving the essence of the above guidelines:

> I understand the correct approach in principle of a national court (other than a final court of appeal) to be quite clear: if the facts have been found and the Community law issue is critical to the court's final decision, *the appropriate course is ordinarily to refer the issue to the Court of Justice unless the national court can with complete confidence resolve the issue itself.* In considering whether it can with complete confidence resolve the issue itself the national court must be fully mindful of the differences between national and Community legislation, of the pitfalls which face a national court venturing into what may be an unfamiliar field, for the need for uniform interpretation throughout the Community and of the great advantage enjoyed by the Court of Justice in construing the Community instruments. If the national court has any real doubt it should ordinarily refer.

2.90 Where a court or tribunal decides to make a reference it may invite the parties to agree the terms of the questions to be referred. The court or tribunal can decide the final wording of the question. The order of reference will contain a judgment setting out the facts and identifying the issues of law. The order should explain why the reference is appropriate. The questions are attached to the order.

2.91 The decision by which a national court or tribunal refers a question to the ECJ for a preliminary ruling takes the form of an order of the tribunal. The secretary to the employment tribunal then sends a copy of the order to the registrar of that court.[114] This order serves as the basis of the proceedings before the court and must contain such information as will enable the ECJ to give a reply which is of assistance to the national court. Moreover, it is only the actual reference for a preliminary ruling which is notified to the parties entitled to submit observations to the court, in particular the member states and the institutions, and which is translated.

---

112 *Bulmer v Bollinger* [1974] Ch 401 per Lord Denning MR at 419–425.
113 [1993] QB 534.
114 See rule 58 of the Employment Tribunals (Constitution and Rules of Procedure) Regulations 2004.

2.92   Due to the need to translate the reference, it should be drafted simply, clearly and precisely, avoiding superfluous detail. A maximum of about ten pages is often sufficient to set out in a proper manner the context of a reference for a preliminary ruling. The order for reference must be succinct but sufficiently complete and must contain all the relevant information to give the court and the parties entitled to submit observations a clear understanding of the factual and legal context of the main proceedings. In particular, the order for reference must:

- include a brief account of the subject-matter of the dispute and the relevant findings of fact, or, at least, set out the factual situation on which the question referred is based;
- set out the tenor of any applicable national provisions and identify, where necessary, the relevant national case-law, giving in each case precise references (eg page of an official journal or specific law report, with any internet reference);
- identify the Community provisions relevant to the case as accurately as possible;
- explain the reasons which prompted the national court to raise the question of the interpretation or validity of the Community provisions, and the relationship between those provisions and the national provisions applicable to the main proceedings;
- include, where appropriate, a summary of the main arguments of the parties.

2.93   In order to make it easier to read and refer to the document, it is helpful if the different points or paragraphs of the order for reference are numbered. The referring court may, if it considers itself to be in a position to do so, briefly state its view on the answer to be given to the questions referred for a preliminary ruling. The question or questions themselves should appear in a separate and clearly identified section of the order for reference, generally at the beginning or the end. It must be possible to understand them without referring to the statement of the grounds for the reference, which however provides the necessary background for a proper assessment.

2.94   The parties, the Commission and member state governments, may give their written submissions to the court. This must be done within two months of the date on which the ECJ notifies them of the registration of the case. There may be an oral hearing, after which the Advocate-General gives an opinion and suggests to the court the answer that should be given. The opinion is very influential in terms of providing more reasoning than will appear in the judgment subsequently (if the Advocate-General's opinion is followed). It should be noted, however, that the Advocate-General's opinion does not bind the court and is sometimes rejected.

2.95   If a reference is made by the employment tribunal, it is possible to get exceptional funding from the Lord Chancellor. If the Employment Appeals Tribunal (EAT), or any other court makes the reference, legal aid may be available. There is minimal legal aid available from the ECJ which an applicant may be able to obtain by writing to the court setting out financial circumstances.

CHAPTER 3

Scope of the Age Regulations 2006

The Employment Equality (Age) Regulations (Northern Ireland) 2006 (SI No 261) implement the Framework Directive for Northern Ireland. In principal respects they mirror those for England, Wales and Scotland. Certain differences are noted at www.ageconcern.org.uk/agediscriminationlaw.

Key points

- The Age Regulations 2006 cover employees, self-employed people, office holders, members of trade organisations and employment agencies.
- They cover all courses at further education or higher education colleges or universities. However, the regulations govern post-16 education only, so schools are excluded.
- Vocational training, and anyone offering it, will be covered (except schools).
- The regulations apply to job applicants, as well as people who apply for placements on vocational training courses and application to become a member of a trade organisation.
- Key exclusions from scope include those serving in the military, naval or air forces of the Crown.
- Unpaid volunteers are not covered by the regulations.

Introduction

3.1   This chapter sets out the scope of the Employment Equality (Age) Regulations 2006, dealing with the range of areas which are affected by the age discrimination legislation. The scope of the regulations goes beyond merely employment relations, affecting both post-16 education as well as the provision of vocational training. The law governing age discrimination does not, as yet, extend to the provision of goods and services or schools. However, a proposal for a directive relating to discrimination in the provision of goods and services has recently been issued and it is dealt with in more detail in chapter 14.[1]

Employment to which the regulations apply

3.2   The most obvious impact of the new legislation will be felt on employment relations. Discrimination can operate before someone is employed, in the application stage, during employment and, in some situations, even post-employment. 'Employment' is defined as meaning 'employment under a contract of service or of apprenticeship or a contract personally to do any work'.[2] Related expressions, such as

---

1   www.ace.org.uk/AgeConcern/Documents/Age_Directive_on_Goods_facilities_and_services_final1.pdf.
2   Reg 2(2).

employee or employer, are construed according to the general definition of employment set out. An employer can include a person who has no employees at the time that he or she is seeking to employ an individual, and accordingly, the regulations will apply in respect of prospective employment applications[3] even where the employer is currently without staff.

3.3   However, there is an obligation for a claimant to be able to show that he or she is personally obliged to provide some personal service. There remains a test of 'minimum obligation'. In *Mingeley v Pennock & Ivory*,[4] the Court of Appeal held that an independent taxi driver, whose only connection with the respondents was in respect of buying radio services, could not complain of race discrimination since there was an absence of any obligation on his part.[5]

3.4   The correct test is:

- Is there at least a 'minimum obligation' to perform work?
- What is the 'dominant purpose' of the contract?

3.5   When considering the minimum obligations it is important to identify what exactly the obligation on the claimant was. What was the work the person was obliged to perform?[6] When considering dominant purpose, tribunals will consider, as a matter of fact, whether the exchange of monies for services is predominantly for the provision of services rather than the performance of work or labour.

3.6   In *Kelly v Northern Ireland Housing Executive*,[7] the House of Lords held that 'employment', as defined in 'contract personally to execute work' could cover work done by an independent contractor.

Police

3.7   Holding the office of constable is treated as employment by the chief officer of police, or in respect of any act done by him or her in relation to a constable or that office.[8] Anything done by that constable in the performance, or purported performance of the constable's functions shall be treated as done in the course of his or her employment by the chief

---

3   Reg 2(3).
4   [2004] IRLR 373, CA.
5   See the discussion in chapter 8.
6   See para 6.35. See also *Cotswold Developments Construction Ltd v Williams* [2006] IRLR 181, EAT; *Express and Echo Publications Ltd v Tanton* [1997] IRLR 367, CA and *MacFarlane v Glasgow City Council* [2001] IRLR 7, EAT.
7   [1999] 1 AC 428.
8   Reg 13(1)(a).

officer of police.[9] The police authority will be treated as the constable's employer in respect of any act done by it in relation to that constable or office.[10]

3.8   Extended definitions of 'chief officer', 'police authority' and 'police cadets' are found in regulation 13.[11]

3.9   Any constable or other person who has been seconded to the Serious Organised Crime Agency (SOCA) is treated as employed by SOCA and any acts done in the performance or purported performance of the duties under that secondment, will be treated as having been done in the course of employment by SOCA.[12]

Application to Crown employment

3.10   The regulations apply to Crown employment as they apply to employment by private individuals. All references to a contract of employment and/or dismissal in the regulations can also be taken to include references to terms of service and/or termination of Crown employment accordingly.[13] 'Crown employment' means service for the purposes of a Minister of the Crown or government department, other than the service of a person holding a statutory office, and it includes service on behalf of the Crown for the purposes of holding a statutory office or purposes of a statutory body.

3.11   The regulations apply, in the same way as they would to an act done by a private person:

a) to an act done by or for purposes of a minister of the Crown or government department; or

b) to an act done on behalf of the Crown by a statutory body, or a person holding a statutory office.[14]

3.12   Parts 2 to 4 of the Crown Proceedings Act 1947 apply[15] to proceedings against the Crown under the regulations as they apply to proceedings

---

9 Reg 13(2). Note that these provisions are now consistent with amendments made to the Race Relations Act 1976 and Sex Discrimination Act 1975 s17 as a result of Sex Discrimination Act 1975 (Amendment) Regulations 2003 SI No 1657 reg 2. This section reversed the decision and analysis of the Court of Appeal in *Chief Constable of Bedfordshire Police v Liversidge* [2002] IRLR 651.

10 Reg 13(1)(b).

11 Reg 13(6) and (7).

12 Reg 14.

13 Reg 44(2).

14 Reg 44(1).

15 Reg 44(6).

in England and Wales which are treated as civil proceedings against the Crown.[16]

Application to House of Commons/House of Lords staff

3.13 The regulations cover employment as a relevant member of House of Commons and House of Lords staff, as they do to employment generally set out in the regulations.[17]

Self-employed individuals

Barristers

3.14 Barristers and their clerks, within England and Wales, are covered by regulation 15. It is unlawful for a barrister or his or her clerk, in relation to any offer of pupillage or tenancy, to discriminate against a person:

a) in the arrangements which are made for the purpose of determining to whom the pupillage or tenancy should be offered;
b) in respect of any terms on which it is offered; or
c) by refusing, or deliberately not offering, it to him.[18]

3.15 It is also unlawful for a barrister or his or her clerk, in relation to a pupil or tenant in the set of chambers in question, to discriminate against him or her:

a) in respect of any terms applicable to him or her as a pupil or tenant;
b) in the opportunities for training, or gaining experience, which are afforded or denied to him or her;
c) in the benefits which are afforded or denied to him or her; or
d) by terminating his or her pupillage, or by subjecting him or her to any pressure to leave the chambers or other detriment.[19]

3.16 It is also unlawful for a barrister or his or her clerk, in relation to a pupillage or tenancy in the set of the chambers in question, to subject a pupil or tenant (or someone who has applied to be either) to harassment.[20]

---

16 By virtue of section 23 of the Crown Proceedings Act 1947, except that section 20 of that Act would not apply (removal and transfer of proceedings). The provisions of Part 5 of that Act applies to proceedings against the Crown in Scotland by virtue of regulation 44(7).
17 Regs 45 and 46.
18 Reg 15(1).
19 Reg 15(2).
20 Reg 15(3).

3.17   It is unlawful for 'any person, in relation to the giving, withholding or acceptance of instructions to a barrister, to discriminate against any person by subjecting him to a detriment' or harassment.[21] Potentially, barristers' clients or instructing solicitors, where they are responsible for giving or withholding instructions, or where they directly instruct a member of the Bar pursuant to the Direct Access scheme, could be pursued for discrimination under this regulation. There are equivalent provisions under the sex race, and disability legislation.[22]

Advocates

3.18   Similar provisions are made in regulation 16 for advocates in Scotland as for barristers in England and Wales, except they cover only those aspects which relate to the advocate's pupil, as well as an identical anti-discrimination provision in respect of giving, withholding or accepting instructions to the advocate.[23]

Partnerships

3.19   Despite considerable concern during the consultation period as to how these regulations would apply, within the commercial context, to partnerships, they are included within the scope of the legislation.[24]

3.20   Concerns were raised at the consultation stage that the regulations appeared to be treating 'partnerships' too much in the same way as employment relationships, when there were fundamental differences between them. In particular, there was concern that regulation 17, unlike regulation 7 dealing with applicants and employees, contained no provisions relating to 'partners' operating outside Great Britain. Respondents sought clarification that a partner working overseas in a firm which had its head office or principal place of business in the UK would be protected by the regulations. Failure to do this, it was said would lead to overseas firms having an advantage over UK-based ones.[25] This has not been amended or clarified in the final draft of the regulations.

3.21   The regulation applies both to firms, as defined in section 4 of the Partnership Act 1890, as well as to limited liability partnerships.

---

21 Reg 15(4).
22 Sex Discrimination Act 1975 s35A(3) and s35B(3); Race Relations Act 1976 ss26A(3) and 26B(3); Disability Discrimination Act 1995 s7A.
23 Reg 16(4).
24 Reg 17.
25 See *Equality and Diversity Coming of Age: Report on the Consultation on the draft Employment Equality (Age) Regulations 2006*, para 3.22.

References to partners are construed as references to general partners, within the context of limited partnerships, as defined in section 3 of the Limited Partnerships Act 1907.[26] References to a partner in a firm are also treated as references to a member of the limited liability partnership.[27]

3.22   It is unlawful for a firm, in relation to a position as partner in the firm, to discriminate against a person:[28]

a) in the arrangements they make for the purpose of determining to whom they should offer that position;

b) in the terms on which they offer him or her that position;

c) by refusing to offer, or deliberately not offering, him or her that position; or

3.23   It is also unlawful for a firm, in relation to a position as partner in the firm, to subject to harassment a person who holds, or has applied for, partnership.[29] These provisions would apply equally where persons were proposing to form themselves into a partnership.[30]

3.24   Where a person already holds the position of partner, it is unlawful for a firm to discriminate:[31]

i) in the way they afford the person access to any benefits or by refusing to afford, or deliberately not affording, the person access to them; or

ii) by expelling the person from that position, or subjecting the person to any other detriment.

3.25   It is also unlawful for a firm to expel a partner from that position, or subject him or her to any other detriment.[32] Expulsion means terminating that person's partnership by the expiry of any period, which would include a period expiring by reference to an event of circumstances, where the partnership was not renewed immediately afterwards on the same terms.[33] Expulsion also is defined as meaning the termination of a partnership by any act of his or hers (including giving

---

26 Reg 17(5).
27 Reg 17(6).
28 Reg 17(1).
29 Reg 17(2).
30 Reg 17(3).
31 Reg 17(1)(d).
32 Reg 17(1)(d)(ii).
33 Reg 17(8)(a).

notice) in circumstances where he or she is entitled to end that partnership without notice by reason of the conduct of other parties.[34]

3.26   The discrimination provisions set out in regulation 17(1) are said not to apply where, if the partner's position was that of employment, an exception pursuant to the genuine occupational requirement could be made.

3.27   The regulations require that the termination of the partnership of a partner by reason of the partner reaching a retirement age be justified by reference to the fact that it is a proportionate means of pursuing a legitimate aim. It must be justified under regulation 3(1) as an instance of direct discrimination on the grounds of age. The exception relating to dismissal from employment by reason of retirement at the normal retirement age (or 65 where there is none) does not affect partners in partnerships.[35]

Contract workers

3.28   It is unlawful for a principal, in relation to contract work at an establishment in Great Britain, to discriminate against a contract worker:[36]

a) in the terms on which the principal allows the worker to do that work;
b) by not allowing the worker to do it or continue to do it;
c) in the way the principal affords the worker access to any benefits or by refusing or deliberately not affording him or her access to them; or
d) by subjecting the worker to any other detriment.[37]

3.29   It is also unlawful[38] for a principal to subject a contract worker to harassment.[39]

3.30   A 'principal' is defined as meaning:

> ... a person ('A') who makes work available for doing by individuals who are employed by another person who supplies them under a contract made with A. Contract work means work so made available and contract

---

34   Reg 17(8)(b).
35   Reg 30(1).
36   Reg 9.
37   For detailed discussion of these concepts in the context of employment see chapters 7 and 8.
38   Reg 9(2).
39   Defined in chapter 4.

worker means any individual who is supplied to the principal under such a contract.[40]

Office holders

3.31   Traditionally the holder of an office was not regarded as an employee or any kind of worker.[41] The extension of protection to office holders reflects the scope of the Council Directive 2000/78/EC of 27 November 2000 *establishing a general framework for equal treatment in employment* ('the directive'), and recognises the various forms that occupation takes.[42] The provisions in respect of office holders are set out at length in regulation 12. It extends protection to those who do not qualify as employees, but are 'officer holders'.[43] The regulation applies to any office or any post to which persons are appointed to discharge functions personally under the direction of another person, and in respect of which they are entitled to be remunerated.[44] A holder of an office or post will be regarded as discharging his or her functions under the direction of another person if that other person is entitled to direct him or her as to when and where he or she discharges those functions.[45] For the purposes of this regulation, 'appointment' to an office or post does not include election to that office or post.[46] This means that councillors or those seeking to become councillors will not be covered.[47] 'Entitled to remuneration' does not include entitlement to payment of expenses incurred in the carrying out of the post, or by way of compensation for the loss of income or benefits he or she may have received from any

---

40   Reg 9(5). See *Harrods Ltd v Remick* [1998] 1 All ER 52; [1998] ICR 156; [1997] IRLR 583 – will apply to cover workers for a concessionaire in a department store if they are subject to the store's approval.

41   See cases such as *Arthur v Attorney-General* [1999] ICR 631 and *Knight v Attorney-General* [1979] ICR 194 (lay magistrate).

42   See article 3 of the directive.

43   Amendments made to the sex and race legislation in 2005 employ the same phrasing, and see *Perceval-Price v Department of Economic Development* [2000] IRLR 380; [2000] NI 141.

44   Reg 12(8)(a). As to 'remuneration' the starting point appears to be that it is monetary consideration. However see below, para 3.32. Query whether remuneration is to be construed so as to include any valuable consideration.

45   Reg 12(9)(a).

46   Reg 12(10)(a).

47   See *Triesman v Ali* [2002] ICR 1026; [2002] IRLR 489 where, in addition, a political party was said not to be a qualification body.

person had he or she not been carrying out the functions of the office or post'.[48]

3.32 This does not mean, however, that every worker who is not an employee will be covered. The crucial word in the definition is 'remuneration'. Consider the following cases: In *Melhuish v Redbridge CAB*,[49] in relation to the definition of 'employee' under section 230 of the Employment Rights Act (ERA) 1996, the Employment Appeals Tribunal (EAT) held that a volunteer worker, who had no contract of employment, no holiday entitlement or sick pay or notice requirements, and to whom the disciplinary and grievance procedures did not apply, had no contract of employment and was not an employee. The fact that he attended training courses did not begin to provide any kind of similar consideration to remuneration, as was said to be necessary in the decision of MacKenna J in *Ready Mixed Concrete v Minister of Pensions and National Insurance*,[50] A similar decision was reached in *South East Sheffield Citizens Advice Bureau v Grayson*,[51] where the Employment Appeals Tribunal (EAT) held that volunteer advisers working for the Citizens Advice Bureau (CAB) were not 'employees' employed under a contract of service within the meaning of section 68(1) of the Disability Discrimination Act 1995. In order for a volunteer to be an 'employee', it is necessary to be able to identify an arrangement under which, for valuable consideration, the volunteer is contractually obliged to render services or work personally for the employer. In this case, where there was a volunteer agreement undertaking for a usual minimum weekly commitment of six hours, the crucial question was whether this undertaking imposed an obligation on the CAB to provide work for the volunteer to do, whether the volunteer was personally obliged to do that work and whether there were any notice requirements.

3.33 Regulation 12 also applies to any office or post to which appointments are made by (or on the recommendation of or subject to the approval of) a minister of the Crown, a government department, the National Assembly for Wales or any part of the Scottish administration. Recommendations can be either positive or negative.[52]

48 Reg 12(9)(b).
49 [2005] IRLR 419, EAT.
50 [1968] 2 QB 497, HC.
51 [2004] IRLR 353.
52 Reg 12(10)(d).

3.34   However, this regulation will not apply to a political office.[53] Nor will the regulation apply in respect of cases which deal with applicants and employees,[54] or contract workers,[55] or barristers and advocates,[56] or partnerships[57] either under these regulations, or where those relevant regulations would apply but for the operation of other provisions within the regulations.

3.35   Regulation 12 establishes unlawful acts which correlate to those imposed on employers in respect of employees.[58]

Overseas employment

3.36   Employment must be at an establishment in Great Britain.[59] Overseas employees may be excluded from the scope of the regulations in all the anti-discrimination legislation. Both employment and contract work will be regarded, for the purposes of the regulations (and the other discrimination legislation) as being at an establishment in Great Britain if the employee works wholly or partly within Great Britain.[60]

3.37   Employment is regarded also as being within Great Britain, even if the employee works wholly outside Great Britain so long as the employee's employer has a place of business at an establishment in Great Britain, the work is conducted for the purposes of the business carried out at that establishment and the employee is ordinarily resident in Great Britain either at the time of the employee's application for the job, or at any time during the course of his or her employment.[61]

3.38   The regulations also have effect in relation to any ship, aircraft or hovercraft belonging to or possessed by Her Majesty in right of the United Kingdom government as it would to any ship, aircraft or hovercraft, as set out in regulation 10(3) generally.[62]

---

53   Defined at length in reg 12(10)(b).
54   Under reg 7.
55   Under reg 9.
56   Under regs 15 and 16 respectively.
57   Under reg 17.
58   See para 3.71 below and chapter 8 generally.
59   Regs 7 and 9, Great Britain includes such of the territorial waters of the United Kingdom as are adjacent to Great Britain, reg 2.
60   Reg 10(1)(a).
61   Reg 10(2).
62   Reg 44(5).

3.39   In *Saggar v MOD*,[63] the Court of Appeal held that in determining whether or not an applicant worked 'wholly or mainly outside Great Britain', the relevant period is the whole of the period of employment. 'Employment' is considered to be the entire relationship between the employer and employee. Although the right to present a complaint to an employment tribunal has to be considered by reference to the employment situation at the time, there is no express or implicit requirement that, in deciding whether a claimant works mainly or wholly outside the UK, account should be taken only of where the claimant did his or her work during the period of time to which the discrimination complaint relates.

3.40   In *Ministry of Defence v Gandiya*,[64] the EAT held that the de minimis principle applied so that a brief visit to Great Britain by an individual who worked mostly abroad was insufficient for jurisdiction purposes. However, an individual who works mostly in Great Britain, but who complains about an act of discrimination occurring on a brief visit outside Great Britain should be permitted to bring a discrimination claim here.

3.41   In relation to a claim brought under ERA 1996 s94(1) not to be unfairly dismissed, the House of Lords have held, in *Lawson v Serco*[65] that this right generally applies to an employee who is working in Great Britain at the time of his or her dismissal. In respect of peripatetic workers, such as airline pilots, international consultants and salesmen, the solution adopted under the former 'ordinarily works outside Great Britain' of treating the base of a peripatetic employee as his or her place of employment for the purposes of the statute remain valid. It was stressed that the terms of the contract were not always helpful in deciding this matter and what has to be considered is the conduct of the parties, and the actual operation of the contract in practice.

3.42   It is arguable that the limitation on employment being at an establishment in Great Britain may contradict article 39[66] of the EC Treaty, concerning the right to freedom of movement of workers.[67]

---

63 [2005] IRLR 618, CA.
64 [2004] ICR 1708, EAT.
65 [2006] IRLR 289, HL.
66 Formerly article 48.
67 See correlative argument under race discrimination in *Bossa v Nordstress Ltd* [1998] ICR 694; [1998] IRLR 284.

Miscellaneous

3.43 Relevant 'employment' also includes employment on board a ship, if that ship is registered at a port of registry in Great Britain,[68] as well as employment on an aircraft or hovercraft if they are registered in the United Kingdom and operated by a person who has his or her principal place of business, or is ordinarily resident in the United Kingdom.[69] There are specific provisions dealing with employment which involves working on the Frigg Gas Field.[70]

Potential respondents

Employers

3.44 Public and private employers, including charities and not-for-profit organisations to mention just a few, as well as the police are covered. Essentially a person will be an employer if they are in a contractual relationship with another by which the other undertakes personally to perform work and the employer undertakes to give a valuable consideration for that work.[71]

Trade organisations

3.45 Trade unions and employer organisations fall within the scope of these regulations.[72] Trade organisations are defined as 'an organisation of workers, an organisation of employers, or any other organisation whose members carry on a particular profession' (which includes any vocation or occupation) or trade for the purposes of which the organisation exists.[73] These can include employer organisations, professional or vocational organisations as well as trade unions. A professional organisation can exist either for the purpose of carrying on the profession or for the purposes of the profession. The words in regulation

---

68 Reg 10(3)(a) see *Haughton v Olau Line* (UK) [1986] ICR 357; [1986] IRLR 465.
69 Reg 10(3)(b).
70 Reg 10(4), (5), (6).
71 See discussion in chapter 8 and paras 3.2–3.6 above.
72 Reg 18.
73 Reg 18(4).

18 are wide enough to cover either interpretation.[74] It is unlawful for a trade organisation to discriminate against a person:[75]

a) in the terms on which it is prepared to admit the person to membership[76] of the organisation; or

b) by refusing to accept, or deliberately not accepting, the person's application for membership.

3.46 It is also unlawful for a trade organisation, in relation to a member of the organisation, to discriminate against a person:[77]

a) in the way it affords the person access to any benefits or by refusing or deliberately omitting to afford him or her access to them;

b) by depriving the person of membership, or varying the terms on which he or she is a member; or

c) by subjecting the person to any other detriment.

3.47 Again, discrimination by way of harassment, in relation to a person's membership or application for membership of the organisation, is unlawful.[78]

---

74 In *1 Pump Court Chambers v Horton*, UKEAT/0775/03/MH, 2 December 2003, before Burton J, the EAT considered barristers chambers to be trade organisations within the same wording in the Disability Discrimination Act 1995 (prior to the 2004 amendments) s13. The EAT considered that the organisation of barristers in chambers was the way in which the practice as a barrister was facilitated, so that joining chambers was plainly for the purposes of the profession. Similarly, barristers joined chambers in order to carry on their profession. Chambers were therefore trade organisations (affirmed in this respect [2004] 3 All ER 852; [2005] ICR 292, CA).

75 Reg 18(1).

76 In order to determine what a member is, it is necessary to look at the rights and duties of a member of the organisation, for example the organisation's constitution. In *1 Pump Court*, above, the Court of Appeal noted that no pupil had the right to attend a chambers' meeting nor could he be a member of a sub-committee or an officer. The responsibilities and liabilities of members did not apply to pupils. In addition any professional code should be taken into account if appropriate. The Court of Appeal stated that its interpretation accorded with the Code of Conduct of the Bar which prohibited a pupil from holding himself out as or becoming a member of chambers ([2004] 3 All ER 852; [2005] ICR 292 (Laddie J dissenting)).

77 Reg 18(2).

78 Reg 18(3).

Qualifications bodies

3.48 Qualification bodies are brought within the scope of the regulations.[79] They are described as 'any authority or body which can confer a professional or trade qualification',[80] but it does not include governing bodies of institutions of further and higher education[81] and importantly, it does not provide for schools (by their proprietors) to be included.[82] Profession can include any vocation or occupation as in the context of trade organisations.[83]

3.49 It is unlawful for such bodies to subject to harassment a person who holds or applies for a professional or trade qualification.[84] It is also unlawful for qualification bodies to discriminate against a person:[85]

a) in the terms on which it is prepared to confer a professional or trade qualification[86] on him or her;

b) by refusing or deliberately not granting any application by him or her for such a qualification; or

c) by withdrawing such a qualification from him or her or varying the terms on which he or she holds it.

Vocational training providers

3.50 Vocational training, and the providers of such training, fall within the scope of the regulations, within regulation 20.

3.51 The definition of vocational training follows the same approach adopted for the religion or belief and sexual orientation regulations,

---

79 By virtue of reg 19.

80 Defined further in reg 19(3) as 'any authorisation, qualification, recognition, registration, enrolment, approval or certification which is needed for, or facilities engagement in, a particular profession or trade'.

81 See further reg 23.

82 Reg 19(3).

83 In *Triesman v Ali* [2002] EWCA Civ 93; [2002] ICR 1026; [2002] IRLR 489 the Court of Appeal held that in selecting or allowing a person to be nominated as a party candidate, the Labour Party was not a 'qualifying body' within the meaning of the Race Relations Act 1976 s12. The Court of Appeal also expressed the view that it was doubtful whether being a local councillor amounted to being engaged in an 'occupation' and held that it certainly did not amount to being engaged in a 'profession'.

84 Reg 19(2).

85 Reg 19(1).

86 'Qualification' does not cover the appointment of a duly qualified professional to carry out remunerated work on behalf of a client such as when a solicitor is appointed to represent a client (see *Kelly v Northern Ireland Housing Executive* [1999] 1 AC 428; [1998] ICR 828; [1998] IRLR 593).

which prohibit discrimination by training providers. A 'training provider' is defined loosely as 'any person who provides, or makes arrangements for the provision of training'.[87] However, it does not include training provided by employers for persons he or she employs,[88] the governing bodies of institutions of further and higher education[89] or a proprietor of schools in relation to any registered pupil.[90] Education of pupils in schools is excluded since this is not vocational training within the meaning of the directive.[91]

3.52   'Training' means:[92]

a) all types and all levels of training which would help fit a person for any employment;
b) vocational guidance;
c) facilities for training;
d) practical work experience provided by an employer to a person whom he or she does not employ; and
e) any assessment related to the award of any professional or trade qualification.

3.53   'Vocational training' has been held by the European Court of Justice (ECJ) in the context of free movement rights to cover a course in the art of strip cartoons run by an institution providing advanced artistic education, if the course prepares students for a qualification for a specific profession, vocation or job or if it provides them with the special skill for the exercise of such a profession vocation or job.[93]

3.54   It is unlawful for a training provider to discriminate against any person seeking or undergoing training:[94]

a) in the arrangements the training provider makes for the purpose of determining to whom he or she should offer training;
b) in the terms on which the training provider affords a person access to any training;

---

87 Reg 20(4)(e).
88 Reg 20(4). This is covered by reg 7(2).
89 Reg 20(4), and see further the cross-reference to reg 23.
90 Reg 20(4).
91 Explanatory Memorandum, para 4.1.
92 Reg 20(4).
93 *Gravier v Liège* (C 293/83) [1985] 3 CMLR 1. University education in veterinary medicine came within the definition of 'vocational training' *Blaizot v University of Liege* (C24/86). See also, in relation to vocational training *R v Secretary of State for Education ex p Connon* [1996] COD 454 and *R v Inner London Education Authority ex p Hinde* (1985) 83 LGR 695. The essence is that the training course should be designed or intended to equip the trainee for a career or a job.

c) by refusing or deliberately not affording a person such access;

d) by terminating a person's training; or

e) by subjecting a person to any other detriment during his or her training.

3.55   There is an exception made if the training would only fit a person for employment which, by virtue of the provisions made for genuine occupational requirement, the employer could lawfully refuse to offer the person seeking training. It is difficult to imagine where such a situation may arise. For example, where a mature actor is said to be required to play an elderly person, is not the key factor that the aspiring younger actor could appear to be much older, by way of make-up and technology? However, it may be that there are valid concerns in respect of some particular professions, such as fire-fighters and pilots and in any event, where statute requires age limits to be set, those limits will take precedence.[95]

3.56   Harassment by the training provider in relation to a person seeking or undergoing training is also unlawful.[96]

Institutions of further and higher education

3.57   Regulation 23 applies to the following type of educational establishment in England and Wales:[97]

a) institutions within the further education sector;[98]

b) universities;

c) institutions within the higher education sector which are not universities.[99]

3.58   Within Scotland, the following types of educational establishment are included within the provisions of the legislation:

a) colleges of further education, under the management of a board of education;[100]

b) colleges of further education maintained by an education authority;[101]

---

94   Reg 20(1).

95   For genuine occupational requirements, see further at para 6.2.

96   Reg 20(2).

97   Reg 23(4).

98   Within the meaning of Further and Higher Education Act 1992 s91(3).

99   Within the meaning of Further and Higher Education Act 1992 s91(5).

100 Within the meaning of Further and Higher Education (Scotland) Act 1992 s36(1), boards of management being defined in Part 1 of that Act.

101 In the exercise of its further education functions in providing courses of further education pursuant to Education Scotland Act 1980 s1(5)(b)(ii).

c) any other educational establishment (not being a school) which provides further education;[102]
d) institutions within the higher education sector;[103]
e) central institutions.[104]

3.59 It is unlawful for the governing bodies of relevant educational establishments to discriminate against a person:[105]

a) in the terms on which it offers to admit the person to the establishment as a student;[106]
b) by refusing or deliberately not accepting an application for the person's admission to the establishment as a student; or
c) where the person is a student of the establishment:
   i) in the way it affords him or her access to any benefits;
   ii) by refusing or deliberately not affording him or her access to them; or
   iii) by excluding him or her from the establishment or subjecting him or her to any other detriment.

3.60 There is an exception made if the training would only fit a person for employment which, by virtue of the provisions made for genuine occupational requirement, the employer could lawfully refuse to offer the person seeking training.[107] It is difficult to imagine where such a situation may arise.

3.61 It is unlawful for the governing body of the establishment to harass a student at the establishment, or to harass someone who has applied for admission to the establishment.[108]

---

102 Within the meaning of Further and Higher Education (Scotland) Act 1992 s1.
103 Within the meaning of Further and Higher Education (Scotland) Act 1992 Part 2.
104 Within the meaning of Education Scotland Act 1980 s135.
105 Reg 23(1).
106 See the race relations case of *Orphanos v Queen Mary College* [1985] AC 761; [1985] IRLR 349 (allegation of indirect race discrimination based on the charging of higher fees for admission to university). As to how an argument relating to direct age discrimination might be approached, see the Human Rights Act 1998 case of *R (on the application of Mitchell) v Coventry University* [2001] EWHC Admin 167 [2001] ELR 594 in which the challenge to overseas nationals paying university fees was made on the basis of nationality discrimination in access to education. It was held to be reasonably and objectively justified.
107 Reg 23(3).
108 Reg 23(2).

Employment agencies

3.62   'Employment agencies' are defined as a person who, for profit or not, provides services for the purpose of finding employment for workers, or supplying employers with workers.[109] They do not include schools, or institutes of further or higher education.[110]

3.63   It is unlawful for an employment agency to discriminate against a person:[111]

a) in the terms on which the agency offers to provide any of its services;
b) by refusing or deliberately not providing any of its services; or
c) in the way it provides any of its services.

3.64   As with training providers, there is an exception made to exclude discrimination where it relates to employment which the employer could lawfully refuse to offer the person in question, pursuant to the genuine occupational requirement provisions, set out in regulation 8.[112] However, there is a defence in respect of liability for employment agencies, where they can prove that they:[113]

a) acted on reliance on a statement made to it by the employer to the effect that, it could lawfully refuse to offer the person in question employment, by reason of the operation of the genuine occupational requirement provisions; and
b) it was reasonable for the employment agency to rely on that statement.

3.65   Any person who 'knowingly or recklessly' makes such a statement which is in a material respect false or misleading commits a criminal offence and will be liable on summary conviction to a fine not exceeding level 5 on the standard scale.[114]

3.66   It is unlawful for the employment agency to harass a person to whom it provides its services, or who has requested it to provide its services.[115]

---

109   Reg 21(6)(a).
110   Reg 21(6)(a)(i) and (ii).
111   Reg 21(1). See also para 4.58 onwards.
112   Reg 21(3).
113   Reg 21(4).
114   Reg 21(5).
115   Reg 21(2).

Secretary of state

3.67 It is unlawful for the secretary of state to discriminate against any person by subjecting a person to a detriment, or to subject a person to harassment, in respect of the provision of facilities or services under section 2 of the Employment and Training Act 1973 (assisting persons to obtain employment).[116]

Scottish Enterprise/Highlands and Islands Enterprise

3.68 It is unlawful for Scottish Enterprise or Highlands and Islands Enterprise to discriminate against any person by subjecting the person to a detriment, or to subject a person to harassment, in respect of the provision of facilities or services under the provisions of section (3) of the Enterprise and New Towns (Scotland) Act 1990, which are also provisions in respect of assisting people to obtain employment.[117]

Applicants

3.69 The following applicants are covered in varying degrees by the regulations:

- job applicants;
- applicants for an office or post;
- applicants for a vocational training course;
- applicant members of trade unions;
- applicants to post-16 educational establishments, such as colleges of further education or universities.

Job applicants

3.70 This topic is dealt with in chapter 7 on recruitment, and in chapter 8 on employment.

---

116 Reg 22(1).
117 Reg 22(2).

Applicants for an office or post

3.71   It is unlawful for a relevant person, in relation to an appointment to an office or post to which regulation 12 applies,[118] to discriminate against a person:

a) in the arrangements which he or she makes for the purposes of determining to whom the appointment should be offered;

b) in the terms on which he or she offers the person the appointment; or

c) by refusing to offer the person the appointment.[119]

3.72   Refusal includes deliberate omission.[120] Although an exception is made for genuine occupational requirements etc, in circumstances where the office or post constitutes employment, pursuant to regulation 8,[121] it is difficult to imagine where such a requirement may be justifiable in these circumstances.

3.73   A 'relevant person' is defined as being any person with the power to make or terminate appointments to the office or post, or to determine the terms of the appointment.[122] It may also be any person with power to determine the working conditions of a person appointed to the office or post in relation to opportunities for promotion, transfer, training or for receiving any other benefit.[123]

3.74   Where appointments are made to an office or post by a Minister of the Crown, a government department, the National Assembly for Wales or any part of the Scottish administration, or upon whose recommendation or approval such appointment relies (and such recommendation could be negative[124]), any person or body who makes those decisions will be covered by the scope of regulation 12.[125] In respect of these appointments, it is also unlawful to discriminate in the arrangements made by the relevant person for the purposes of determining who should be recommended or approved in relation to the appointment, or in the making or refusing of recommendation or approval in relation to the appointment.[126]

---

118   See above, para 3.31.
119   Reg 12(1).
120   Reg 12(10)(e).
121   Reg 12(5).
122   Reg 12 (10)(c)(i).
123   Reg 12(10)(c)(ii).
124   Reg 12(10)(d).
125   Reg 12 (10)(c).
126   Reg 12(2).

3.75   It is also unlawful for a relevant person to subject an individual to harassment who is seeking or being considered for appointment to an office or post,[127] or who is seeking or being considered for a recommendation or approval to an office or post where such appointment, recommendation or approval is made by a minister of the Crown, a government department, the National Assembly for Wales or any part of the Scottish administration.[128]

Applicants for a vocational training course

3.76   By regulation 20(1), it is unlawful to discriminate against any person seeking training in respect of the arrangements made for determining to whom training should be offered or the terms on which access to training is provided or by refusing or deliberately not affording the person access to training on grounds of the applicant's age.

Applicant members of trade unions

3.77   This is set out in regulation 18(1) and makes it unlawful for a trade organisation to discriminate against a person in the terms on which it is prepared to admit the person to membership of that organisation, or by refusing to accept or deliberately not accepting his or her application for membership on grounds of age. It is also unlawful for a trade organisation to subject an applicant to harassment on grounds of age, which could be on grounds of someone else's age.

Relationships which have come to an end

3.78   Protection against discrimination would not be complete if it stopped with the ending of the relevant relationship. A career can be destroyed by a bad reference from a prejudiced previous employer, for example. The directive makes clear that:

> Member States shall ensure that judicial and/or administrative procedures, including where they deem it appropriate conciliation procedures, for the enforcement of obligations under this Directive are available to all persons who consider themselves wronged by failure to apply the

127   Reg 12(4)(b).
128   Reg 12(4)(c).

principle of equal treatment to them, even after the relationship in which the discrimination is alleged to have occurred has ended.[129]

3.79 The regulations prevent any further acts of discrimination (by subjection to a detriment) or harassment, following the end of a relevant relationship, such as the employment relationship, where the discrimination or harassment arises out of and is closely connected to that relationship.[130] The obvious examples, other than post-employment harassment, may include providing a poor reference on grounds of age. A 'relevant relationship' is a relationship during the course of which an act of discrimination against, or harassment of, one party to the relationship by the other party to is unlawful by virtue of any provision of Part 2 (namely all acts set out within the context of the relationships set out in this chapter).[131]

3.80 The protection against post-termination discrimination and harassment includes any protection against discrimination and harassment over a relationship which has come to an end before the coming into force of the regulations. The relationship must have been a relationship during the course of which an act of discrimination against, or harassment of, one party by the other would be unlawful after the coming into force of the regulations.[132] In other words, if it was the type of relationship that now gives rise to protection against post termination discrimination and harassment, it will give rise to protection against post termination acts which occur after 1 October 2006. If the act of post relationship discrimination occurred before that date, no cause of action will have existed. The regulations are not retrospective.

3.81 Chapter 8, dealing with discrimination in employment, deals with post-employment discrimination in more detail. Those provisions, and interpretations, can be applied across the discreet areas of discrimination following the end of a relationship.

Exclusions from personal scope

3.82 The following groups of people are excluded personally from the scope of the regulations: service in any of the naval, military or air forces of the Crown (including regulars, full-time and also part-time reservists,

---

129 This principle was developed in *Coote v Granada Hospitality Ltd* (C185/97) [1998] All ER (EC) 865 [1999] ICR 100; [1998] IRLR 656.

130 Reg 24.

131 Reg 24(1).

132 Reg 24(3).

when acting in their military capacity).[133] These exclusions are lawful under the directive.[134]

Statutory authority

3.83   Where legislation provides for acts to be done, based on a criteria of age, they will not be unlawful by operation of regulation 27 which states that the regulations will not render unlawful any act done in order to comply with any statutory provision.[135] For example, it will not be unlawful to refuse a 15-year-old a place on a driving course, due to other laws governing driving age.[136]

3.84   Since age criteria are used widely in legislation, such as for purchasing alcohol or driving vehicles, those age limits would be given the absolute protection of statutory authority. For example, an employer in the business of car sales would not be discriminating against a 16-year-old employee if he prevented that employee from driving prospective clients around in the showroom cars, since the employer would be protected by legislation which prevents a 16-year-old from driving.

National security

3.85   Nothing in the regulations would render unlawful an act done if it was done for the purposes of safeguarding national security, if the doing of the act was 'justified by that purpose'.[138] No guidance is given on justification. However it is suggested that justification must require proof that the requirement for the act for the purposes of safeguarding national security must be a necessary and appropriate, proportionate means of achieving that aim as in other derogations.[139]

---

133   Reg 44(4).
134   2000/78 EC article 3.4.
135   Reg 27.
136   See paras 6.5–6.12 for a full discussion of this exception.
137   See paras 90–92 of the notes to the Regulations.
138   Reg 28.
139   See chapter 5 generally for a discussion about justification, and para 6.13 for this topic.

Positive action

3.86 See chapter 6 for a full discussion of the operation of the positive action provisions.

Validity of unlawful contractual terms

3.87 A term in a contract which purports to exclude or limit any provision of the regulations is unenforceable by any person in whose favour the term would operate ordinarily.[140]

3.88 By virtue of regulation 43 of and Schedule 5 to the regulations, a term of a contract is void where:

a) its inclusion renders the making of the contract unlawful by virtue of the Age Discrimination Regulations;
b) it is included in furtherance of an act which is unlawful by virtue of the regulations;
c) it provides for the doing of an act which would be rendered unlawful by the regulations.[141]

3.89 Examples would include a term in a contract which provides for a discriminatory advertising regime would be void.

3.90 A term which constitutes, or is in furtherance of, or provides for, unlawful discrimination or harassment against a party will not be void, but will be unenforceable.[142] For example, a term in a contract with a 55-year-old man which stated that he would not be able to use his employer's gym facilities between 7pm and 9pm would not be enforceable in a court of law.

3.91 These provisions apply irrespective of whether the regulations were in force at the date the contract was entered into. However, where the contract was made before 1 October 2006, these provisions of Schedule 5 Part 1(1)–(3) do not apply in relation to any period before that date.[143]

---

140 Reg 43 and Sch 5 Part 1(1)(3).
141 See parallel provisions in reg 35 and Sch 4 Part 1(1)(1) of the Sexual Orientation Regs 2003 SI No 1661 and Religious Belief Regs 2003 SI No 1660.
142 Reg 43 and Sch 5 Part 1(1)(2).
143 Reg 43 and Sch 5 Part 1(1)(4).

3.92   In addition, any rule of an undertaking which furthers discrimination will be void.[144]

Liability for the acts of others

Vicarious liability of employers and principals

3.93   Vicarious liability of employers is dealt with at paras 8.84–8.87 in chapter 8.[145]

Liability for agents

3.94   Anything done by a person as agent for another person with express or implied authority of the principal is treated as having been done by both the agent and the principal.[146]

3.95   The principal will not mount a successful defence by arguing that he or she did not give the agent authority (whether express or implied) to discriminate. It is sufficient if the agent is given authority to do an act which may be carried out, irrespective of whether it is done in a lawful or discriminatory fashion.[147]

---

144   See Part II Sch 5 to the regulations. Similarly, collective agreement terms which have this effect are voided (see chapter 12 for a discussion of this and its uses).

145   And see reg 25(1).

146   Reg 25(2).

147   *Lana v Positive Action Training in Housing (London) Ltd* [2001] IRLR 501, EAT.

CHAPTER 4

Types of discrimination

> **Key points**
> - Discrimination can be direct or indirect.
> - Both kinds of discrimination can be justified, which differs from direct discrimination in other strands of equality legislation.
> - Discrimination can also take place by way of victimisation or harassment.
> - There is provision dealing with instructions to discriminate and aiding unlawful acts.
> - Direct and indirect discrimination must take place on grounds of the complainant's age, or apparent age, for it to be an unlawful act.
> - Harassment, by contrast, can take place on grounds of anyone's age in order to be an unlawful act.
> - Comparators, actual or hypothetical, feature strongly in any discrimination claim.

Introduction

4.1   There are five types of discrimination created by the Employment Equality (Age) Regulations 2006:

1) direct discrimination;
2) indirect discrimination;
3) victimisation;
4) harassment;
5) detriment arising from instructions to discriminate.

This chapter also considers aiding unlawful acts.

4.2   The provisions relating to each of these types of discrimination are in certain respects similar, and in some cases identical, to those appearing in other equal opportunities legislation, and case-law is largely inter-changeable. The key difference from all other discrimination provisions normally encountered is that justification of both direct and indirect discrimination is permitted.

4.3   Before embarking on the discussion of the various forms of age discrimination it is useful to try to get a clear idea of what we mean by 'age'. Age must, it is suggested, mean chronological age, rather than any other concept. Other age concepts can be defined by reference to chronological ages, although there may be overlaps between various age concepts. Thus youth can be correlated to a number of different age brackets, but depends on a subjective perception. It also depends on context. A young shop assistant is in a completely different chronological age grouping to a young judge (in the UK). Similarly, there will be a correlation between a range of chronological ages and the concept of being old, but again there will be a subjective perception at work. Age discrimination legislation must deal with the impact of such subjective perceptions and with the application of transparent chronological age requirements.

4.4   *Direct discrimination* is treatment which is based on a person's age or perceived age, thus reflecting the two concepts of age applied in society. *Indirect discrimination* is based on the idea that a person belongs to an age group. Indirect discrimination then is the idea that the employer applies a provision, criteria or practice (PCP) to persons not of the same age group as the complainant. However, sometimes the two will overlap. Thus if I make a rule that anyone aged between 20 and 30 will not receive a certain benefit, the complainant, who is aged 23, does not get the benefit because his age falls within that bracket. That would be an example of direct age discrimination as the treatment is based on the complainant's age. If I make a rule that anyone with less than 15 years' experience in a profession should not be appointed to an employed post, that is a criterion which I am happy to apply to anyone, but is likely to place those in the age bracket 20–30 at a particular disadvantage. That would be an example of indirect discrimination. If I next make a rule that anyone between 20 and 25 will not get the benefit and that anyone between 25 and 35 will not get the benefit, all I have done is to create two different age categories. If you happen to fall into either of them due to your current age you will not get the benefit simply by virtue of your age. It remains direct discrimination despite the fact that I am prepared to apply the less favourable treatment to more than one age bracket.

Direct discrimination

4.5   Direct discrimination takes place where, on grounds of B's age, A treats B less favourably than he treats or would treat other persons,[1] and A cannot show the treatment to be a proportionate means of achieving a legitimate aim.

---

1 Reg 3(1)(a).

> EXAMPLE: Employer A will only allow individuals between the ages of 20 and 30 to go on paid training courses relating to their employment. B is aged 31. B and all individuals outside the age bracket are treated less favourably on the grounds of their age (if they want to go on a training course) since they do not have access to the same training opportunities as their colleagues.

4.6   Direct discrimination involves, to some degree, a two-step test,[2] although the Employment Appeals Tribunal (EAT) has recently re-affirmed that it is not always necessary for tribunals to adopt a two-stage approach when considering discrimination claims.[3] The claimant must show that he or she has been less favourably treated than the appropriate comparator (or hypothetical comparator[4] *and* that such treatment was *on the grounds of his or her age*. This is not a simple causation or 'but for' test. The tribunal must ask itself why the claimant was treated in a particular way rather than whether 'but for the claimant's age', the claimant would have been treated differently.[5] Although in some cases it may be helpful to ask tribunals to adopt a specific two-stage approach, in many cases it is simpler for the tribunal to ask just one question: Did the claimant, on grounds of his or her age, receive less favourable treatment than others? Often, it is very difficult to separate the two stages out, and a common sense application of the test will prevail.[6]

4.7   Discrimination need not be conscious and it may be the result of inbuilt or unrecognised prejudices.[7] The existence of unrecognised

---

2   See *Shamoon v Royal Ulster Constabulary* [2003] IRLR 285, HL.

3   *Brown v London Borough of Croydon*, UKEAT/0672/05, 20 February 2006.

4   See paras 4.25–4.30.

5   See *Shamoon v Royal Ulster Constabulary* ibid; *Chief Constable of West Yorkshire Police v Khan* [2001] IRLR 830, HL; *Nagarajan v London Regional Transport* [1999] IRLR 572.

6   See further *Dresdner Kleinwort Wasserstein Ltd v Adebayo* [2005] IRLR 514. However it is worth reminding a tribunal that particularly in a new area of discrimination law, one's instincts and 'common sense' are a poor substitute for an analytic approach. There is a danger in asking the generic 'why' question that the role that the prohibited ground plays in the treatment. In that context it is useful to remember what the EAT in *Peake* said 'In truth, no guidance can be got from instinctive feelings; rather the reverse. Such feelings are likely to be the result of ingrained social attitudes, assumed to be permanent, but rendered obsolete by changing values and current legislation' (*Peake v Automotive Products Ltd* [1977] ICR 480).

7   *Bahl v Law Society* [2003] IRLR 640, approved by the Court of Appeal, [2004] IRLR 799. See further *Dresdner Kleinwort Wasserstein Ltd v Adebayo* ibid.

prejudice (in the sense of assumptive thinking) will be key in age discrimination cases. The stereotypes surrounding old age tend to be a mixture of positive regard concerning honesty or morality, but negative in relation to capability. In relation to youth stereotypes surrounding dependability, lack of leadership skills and the like are also prevalent.[8]

> EXAMPLE: An employer has two members of staff doing the same work for the same period of time and whose appraisals are in fact very similar. The employer is considering which of them to promote. One is 35 and the other is 55. The employer considers that his staff will take orders more easily from the older applicant. The employer concludes that the younger member of staff lacks the gravitas needed to do the job.

4.8   The discriminatory conduct need not be the sole or even the principal reason for the discrimination.[9] It is sufficient that discrimination is a contributing cause in the sense of a significant influence.

4.9   When considering whether discrimination has occurred, the tribunal must consider the totality of the evidence.[10]

4.10   Advisers should adopt some care in relying on case law dealing with proving direct discrimination[11] before *Barton v Investec Henderson Crosswaithe Securities Ltd,*[12] as approved (and amended in part) by the Court of Appeal in *Igen v Wong.*[13] Earlier case-law referred to the (different) burden of proof provisions before they were changed in respect of most aspects of UK discrimination law and whilst some of the general principles still exist, when advising and running a claim for discrimination pursuant to the Age Discrimination Regulations, advisers should refer to the guidelines set out in *Barton,* as amended in *Igen.* Burden of proof is dealt with in detail in chapter 12.

---

8   For guidance on unconscious discrimination (from race relations) see *Anya v University of Oxford* [2001] EWCA Civ 405, [2001] ICR 847 and *King v Great Britain China Centre* [1992] ICR 516 and see paras 1.26–1.39.

9   *Bahl v Law Society* ibid. See further *Dresdner Kleinwort Wasserstein Ltd v Adebayo* ibid.

10   *Bahl v Law Society* ibid. See further *Dresdner Kleinwort Wasserstein Ltd v Adebayo* ibid.

11   See *Dresdner Kleinwort Wasserstein Ltd v Adebayo* ibid.

12   [2003] IRLR 332.

13   *Igen ltd v Wong, Chamberlin Solicitors v Emokpae; Brunel University v Webster, EOC CRE and DRC intervening* [2005] IRLR 258, CA.

4.11   However, ultimately proving that there has been discrimination means that a causative test has to be satisfied. The complainant has to show that he or she has suffered the less favourable treatment *on grounds of his or her age*. Properly expressed, the test is 'what was the reason for the treatment, whether conscious or unconscious?'.[14]

On grounds of B's age

4.12   Direct discrimination occurs under the regulations when on grounds of B's age, A treats B less favourably than he treats or would treat other persons. The regulations permit the causative link in respect of *direct discrimination* to be on grounds of B's own age, or B's apparent age.[15] The Consultation Paper, *Coming of Age*, points out that direct age discrimination can include discrimination based on the perception of someone's age, irrespective of whether that perception is right or wrong.

> EXAMPLE: The employer is a firm of solicitors. D, the boss, refuses to allow a junior lawyer access to significant clients on the grounds that he thinks she is 'barely 25'. In fact, she is 35. She may be able to claim direct discrimination on grounds that he considered her to 'look' too young to perform corporate deals. In that example, what justifications might the employer try to use?

4.13   Regulation 3 purports to implement the principle of equal treatment in the Directive. However, regulation 3 fails to implement article 2 because it requires proof that the treatment occurred on the grounds of B's age, rather than on the grounds of age, which may be the age of a person other than B.

> EXAMPLE: Thus A denies B promotion because B is married to C who is younger than her and belongs to an age group about whom A has prejudiced views (for example that they are shallow and self seeking). This is on the grounds of age, but not on the grounds of B's age.

14 *Constable of West Yorkshire Police v Khan* ibid.
15 Reg 3(3)(b).

4.14 By contrast to the restrictive wording for direct discrimination, in respect of harassment,[16] the test permits the causative link to be extended to someone else's age. The intention of the difference in wording may be to exclude discrimination by association from the definition of direct discrimination, but to include it in harassment. This contrasts sharply with the position in race discrimination and in relation to sexual orientation or religious belief.[17]

4.15 Associative discrimination *is* covered under the provisions for direct discrimination under the Race Relations Act (RRA) 1976 since the definition of 'racial grounds' has been held to cover any reason or action based on race and is not limited to the race of the person alleging less favourable treatment.[18] Accordingly, if A suffers less favourable treatment on the grounds that she cares for an elderly person (ie someone else's age), there will be no act of unlawful discrimination pursuant to these regulations.

4.16 The Directive requires that protection be given against less favourable treatment on grounds of age. Less favourable treatment on the ground of a third person's age is covered by this formula.[19] So, for example, if a project leader happens to have older workers forming the majority in his teams and is not promoted because of this, the regulations will not permit him to bring a claim of direct discrimination since the less favourable treatment has not been on the basis of *his* age. The Framework Directive has not been implemented properly in this respect. If, however, the project leader was harassed because of the older employees in his team, he would be able to bring a claim for unlawful harassment since there is no need for the age to be that of the person being harassed.

4.17 A person who has been treated less favourably as a result of the age of a third person (for example, because of having teenage

---

16 Reg 6.
17 There is no express provision covering associative discrimination in either the Employment Equality (Religion or Belief) Regulations 2003 SI No 1660 or the Employment Equality (Sexual Orientation) Regulations 2003 SI No 1661. However, the DTI explanatory notes state that 'on the grounds of' includes associative discrimination.
18 *Show Boat Entertainment Centre Limited v Owens* [1984] IRLR 7, and *Weathersfield Ltd v Sargent* [1999] IRLR 94.
19 The words 'on the grounds of' have been transposed directly into the definition of discrimination provided in the Employment Equality (Religion or Belief) Regulations 2003 and Employment Equality (Sexual Orientation) Regulations 2003. Both these regulations purport to implement the provisions of the directive.

children about whose behaviour the employer makes negative assumptions), cannot rely directly on the provisions of the Directive against a private employer. However, taking the project leader above, if employed by a local authority or other emanation of the state, the person could seek to argue that the provisions of article 2 of the Directive are sufficiently clear and precise to permit him or her to rely directly upon them against the employer, the state.[20]

4.18   A similar situation arose in the context of disability discrimination. Direct discrimination is only actionable under section 3A(5) of the Disability Discrimination Act (DDA) 1995, where less favourable treatment occurs *on the ground of* the disabled person's disability. The case of *Coleman v Attridge Law*[21] has been referred, direct from the employment tribunal, to the European Court of Justice (ECJ) for a preliminary ruling on the question of whether discrimination by way of association with a disabled person, or associative discrimination, is prohibited by the Equal Treatment Directive. Subject to appeal, a preliminary ruling should be expected by the end of 2007. Clearly the same argument arises in relation to age discrimination and an early reference for a preliminary ruling on this point should be sought.

Indirect discrimination

4.19   Indirect discrimination takes place where A applies to B a provision, criterion or practice which A applies or would apply equally to persons not of the same age group as B,[22] but

i) which puts or would put persons of the same age group as B at a
    particular disadvantage when compared with other persons; and
ii) which puts B at that disadvantage,

and A cannot show the provision or practice to be a proportionate means of achieving a legitimate aim.[23]

4.20   Indirect discrimination can be a more subtle form of discrimination, whereby a particular practice or rule, either by intent or default, prevents a group of individuals, on the basis of a common factor such as age or sex or race, from having access to opportunities (such as to employment

---

20 See *Marshall v Southampton & South West Hampshire AHA*, 152/84 [1986] IRLR
    140, ECJ.
21 Decision of London South Employment Tribunal dated 17 February 2006,
    before Chair Ms Stacey sitting alone.
22 The PCP, as they are known, must be apparently neutral as regards age (see
    Directive article 2.1(b)).
23 Reg 3(1)(b).

itself, or promotions and benefits etc) that others would be able to access without the same barriers. A common example, for the purposes of the Age Regulations 2006, would be by reference to length of service, or by reference to a requirement of a certain number of years' experience.

4.21   A complainant of indirect discrimination has to show three things:[24]

1) the existence of a provision, criterion or practice; and
2) that such provision, criterion or practice has a disproportionate impact on those of the complainant's age; and
3) that the complainant has been put at a disadvantage.

> EXAMPLE: An employer advertises a vacancy where only individuals with GCSEs (no equivalent qualifications) may apply. This would exclude all prospective applicants who had O Levels or equivalent, rather than GCSEs since the GCSE system only came into operation relatively recently. Accordingly, individuals over the age of about 35 would be particularly disadvantaged.

4.22   The Directive's concept of indirect discrimination was introduced by the Commission in the following way:

> The definition of indirect discrimination in paragraph 2(b) is inspired by the case-law of the European Court of Justice in cases involving the free movement of workers.[25]

4.23   And:

> According to this definition, an apparently neutral provision, criterion or practice will be regarded as indirectly discriminatory if it is intrinsically liable to adversely affect a person or persons on the grounds referred in article 1. The 'liability test' may be proven on the basis of statistical evidence or by any other means that demonstrate that a provision would be intrinsically disadvantageous for the person or persons concerned.[26]

4.24   The concept of indirect discrimination at work was set out in *O'Flynn* (a case on free movement of workers) as follows:

> 18. Accordingly, conditions imposed by national law must be regarded as indirectly discriminatory where, although applicable irrespective of nationality,

---

24 See further *Allonby v Accrington and Rossendale College and others* [2001] ICR 1189, in particular the judgment of Sedley LJ, CA; see further *Spicer v Spain* [2004] EWCA Civ 1046.

25 Page 8 of *Proposal for a Council Directive Establishing A General Framework for Equal Treatment in Employment and Occupation* (Brussels 25.11.1999) COM (1999) 565 Final. *O'Flynn v Adjudication Officer*, Case C-237/94, judgment of 23 May 1996 [1996] ECR 2417.

26 *Proposal* ibid p8.

they affect essentially migrant workers (see Case 41/84 *Pinna v Caisse d' Allocations Familiales de la Savoie* [1986] ECR 1, paragraph 24; Case 33/88 *Allué and Another v Università degli Studi di Venezia* [1989] ECR 1591, paragraph 12; and Le Manoir, paragraph 11) or the great majority of those affected are migrant workers (see Case C-279/89 *Commission v United Kingdom* [1992] ECR I-5785, paragraph 42, and Case C-272/92 *Spotti v Freistaat Bayern* [1993] ECR I-5185, paragraph 18), where they are indistinctly applicable but can more easily be satisfied by national workers than by migrant workers (see *Commission v Luxembourg*, paragraph 10, and Case C-349/87 *Paraschi v Landesversicherungsanstalt Wuerttemberg* [1991] ECR I-4501, paragraph 23) or where there is a risk that they may operate to the particular detriment of migrant workers (see Case C-175/88 *Biehl v Administration des Contributions* [1990] ECR I-1779, paragraph 14, and Case C-204/90 *Bachmann v Belgium* [1992] ECR I-249, paragraph 9).

…

20. It follows from all the foregoing case-law that, unless objectively justified and proportionate to its aim, a provision of national law must be regarded as indirectly discriminatory if it is intrinsically liable to affect migrant workers more than national workers and if there is a consequent risk that it will place the former at a particular disadvantage.

21. It is not necessary in this respect to find that the provision in question does in practice affect a substantially higher proportion of migrant workers. It is sufficient that it is liable to have such an effect.[27]

4.25   Therefore where an apparently age-neutral provision criterion or practice is intrinsically liable to disadvantage a particular age group, there is no need for statistical evidence. An advert for a solicitor with three years' post qualification experience, for example, would intrinsically disadvantage those aged between 21 and 26/27. This would not require statistical evidence.

4.26   However, if statistics are available, the claimant can support his or her claim by statistical and factual evidence which illustrates a disproportionate impact.[28] The new definition does not require proof of proportions of groups being unable to comply with requirements. Other types of helpful evidence may include expert reports, general research papers etc. This may assist in showing that a PCP intrinsically disadvantages an age group. Statistical evidence could be obtained via the questionnaire[29] and/or disclosure procedures. Where it is not clear

27   *Proposal for a Council Directive Establishing A General Framework for Equal Treatment in Employment and Occupation* (Brussels 25.11.1999) COM (1999) 565 Final.

28   *Barry v Midland Bank plc* [1999] IRLR 581, HL.

29   See chapter 10 generally.

that the PCP intrinsically disadvantages an age group, statistics should be obtained on the appropriate pool. See para ?? below for detail on selection of the appropriate pool for comparison. Although there will usually be only one logical pool for comparison in each case, there may be situations where more than one pool is possible, necessary or desirable.[30]

4.27   It is for the respondent/defendant to show that the provision, criterion or practice can be objectively justified. Since the test is objective, it is not a defence for an individual merely to claim that they believed the provision criterion or practice was necessary.[31]

4.28   'Age group' is defined as meaning a group of persons defined by reference to age, whether by reference to a particular age or a range of ages.[32] It is only in the context of direct discrimination that perceived age can be used. In the context of indirect discrimination, the age group will generally be constructed by reference to a chronological age or ages. Other features might pick out a chronological age group. 'Those who remember ABBA first time around' clearly picks out an age group because it is a not-so-coded reference to a period in history and having first-hand memories of that period in history as a result of being alive at the time. Such definitions may be important, for example, in the context of redundancy selection. Suppose I want to retain 'those who know how to do manual record entry [or other skill]' because the computer system I work with can sometimes break down and when it does the company has to resort to manual record entry and file keeping. That is a knowledge which younger people may never have acquired. The reference to that skill criteria therefore picks out a band of ages who will be advantaged (and hence another band which will be disadvantaged). Such disadvantage will be intrinsic in the cases of ages for whom the skill has never been needed, and less so for those ages where there will be some memory of exercising the skill on a sporadic or more regular basis (in relation to whom it might be advisable to have statistics to prove the disadvantage).

4.29   Advisers should be aware that any case-law (relating to other indirect discrimination legislative provisions) which refers to the former legal definition of indirect discrimination, where there was a need to show that, for example under the Sex Discrimination Act (SDA) 1975, a woman could not comply with a particular standard, nor that the

---

30 *Allonby v Accrington and Rossendale College* [2001] IRLR 364, CA.

31 See chapter 5 for discussions of the approach to justification.

32 Reg 3(3)(a).

standard was a form of 'requirement or condition',[33] may not be of direct application, although general principles may still be helpful. The newer test, found across the discrimination legislation generally, mirrors the wording of the Equal Treatment Directive and reduces the need to rely on statistical evidence so heavily. Case-law prior to 2001, as to what will and will not constitute indirect discrimination should be used with some caution.

4.30   'Provision, criteria or practice' (PCP) is not defined. This should allow advisers a wider discretion in arguing that a particular approach falls foul of the discrimination provisions. For example a practice can be any work place practice. It may be something that has never been written down or formalised. In a particular work place those with greatest length of service may get first choice whether to do overtime. This is simply the product of a series of personal decisions by a succession of the immediate managers over a number of years. The practice of offering first choice on overtime to those with greatest length of service is likely to disadvantage those with shorter length of service. These are likely to be the younger members of staff.

Comparators

4.31   Regulation 3(3) provides that:

> A comparison of B's case with that of another person under paragraph (1) must be such that the relevant circumstances in the one case are the same, or not materially different, in the other.

4.32   Direct discrimination is a 'like for like' comparison. This means that when comparing how someone has been treated with another person, there is a need to compare situations that are the same, or not materially different.

4.33   The 'relevant circumstances' include those which the alleged discriminator takes into account when deciding to treat the complainant as he or she does, or would treat him or her.[34] For example, if an employer dismisses a 58-year-old woman who persistently takes

---

33 Sex Discrimination (Indirect Discrimination and Burden of Proof) Regulations 2001 amended the SDA 1975. The Employment Equality (Sex Discrimination) Regulations 2005 SI No 2467 amend the definition of indirect sex discrimination again and now is worded almost identically to the provisions set out in the Age Regulations 2006. Both definitions now reflect the EC Equal Treatment Directive 2002/73/EC.

34 *Shamoon v Royal Ulster Constabulary*, ibid.

Monday mornings off for GP visits. The correct comparison would be with a younger employee who also persistently takes a similar amount of time off for GP visits. The questionnaire should therefore seek to establish information concerning the relevant circumstances. For example, was the younger woman dismissed or merely warned? Were the GP visits in respect of an intermittent illness or was the younger woman visiting the GP because of a disability etc?

4.34   One difficult issue will be the extent to which an age difference itself may constitute a relevant circumstance. Much will turn on context. For example, in the above example if the age difference is one month, can it be said that there is a relevant difference in age? Is the younger woman the correct comparator if the perception of the employer is that both women are of the same age? On the other hand, in another example, a difference of a day may be a relevant difference in age. If there was a justified trigger age for receipt of a benefit on dismissal and the two women are dismissed at the same time, the fact of the age difference will be a relevant circumstance because one will obtain the benefit and the other will not. The other woman's age will be a relevant circumstance in this case because the rule being imposed contains the particular clear trigger age whereas in the disciplinary example no such trigger age is employed and the concept of age being considered will be a vaguer concept.

4.35   Comparators can be actual or hypothetical. An actual comparator will be a named person who was actually treated better. However, in most cases, it is likely that the claimant will need to ask the tribunal to consider how a person of a different age would have been treated in similar circumstances. The tribunal will need to construct a 'hypothetical comparator'. Advisers should be aware that where a claimant relies on an actual comparator only, he or she may not succeed if the circumstances of the actual comparator are shown to be materially different.[35] This could substantially weaken a claim. The choice of comparator should be thought through fully before pleading any discrimination claim. It is advisable to argue in the claim form for both actual comparators and for a hypothetical in the alternative.

4.36   It is for the claimant to show that the hypothetical comparator would have been treated more favourably. The claimant must establish the primary evidence from which the tribunal can draw conclusions or inferences. In comparing the claimant's situation to that of a hypothetical comparator, however, evidence about how other individuals

---

35 *Shamoon v Chief Constable of the Royal Ulster Constabulary* [2003] UKHL 11, [2003] ICR 337.

were actually treated could be crucial in establishing how a hypothetical comparator would be likely to be treated.

4.37   Sometimes, it can be helpful to produce statistical evidence in direct discrimination cases, where a complainant wants to show that he or she has suffered direct discrimination because of general treatment of a particular group.[36]

> EXAMPLE: Susanne, 46, claims that she has been excluded from opportunity for promotion in her company because of her age. She can demonstrate that everyone under the age of 35 is treated better than she is, and moreover she can demonstrate that there has been a consistent pattern of treating employees over 35 less favourably. She may want to produce statistical evidence that could support her claim, and ask the tribunal to draw inferences, from all the surrounding facts, that she has been treated less favourably on grounds of her age.

4.38   Although the test for discrimination is expressed as a two stage test,[37] it may be simpler in certain cases for the tribunal to consider all the evidence in the round. In *Shamoon*, Lord Nicholls suggested that employment tribunals may sometimes be able to avoid arid and confusing disputes about the identification of the correct comparator by concentrating primarily on the reason why the claimant was treated as he or she was, and postponing the less favourable treatment issue until after they have decided why the treatment was afforded.

4.39   The requirement for comparators also exists in respect of indirect discrimination.[38] B can argue that A would apply the (or did apply the) PCP to persons not of the same age group as B, so the issue of hypothetical comparators arises again. Like has to be compared with like.

4.40   If the complainant identifies the PCP, the complainant may argue that the PCP is intrinsically likely to disadvantage persons of the same age group as the complainant when compared with others whose circumstances are the same or not materially different but who belong to a different age group. The complainant will have to be able to show either an actual person who belongs to a different age group or a hypothetical comparator.[39] Thus if an employer decides that only employees

---

36   *West Midlands Passenger Transport Executive v Singh* [1988] IRLR 186, CA.

37   See para 4.5.

38   See further *Spicer v Government of Spain* [2004] EWCA Civ 1046, concerning indirect race discrimination.

39   The group can be defined by reference to a single age (for example 'being 29'). Similarly an age group can be constructed by a negative ('not being 29') or by reference to a relationship to a particular age ('being younger than 30').

with savings over a particularly high level can have access to a preferential investment rate, it can be argued that this is intrinsically liable to favour older workers who are liable to have more by way of savings than younger employees. The identification of the relevant circumstances for comparison may be difficult in relation to such an example. If the comparison is made between an age group, 50+, and another age group 20–30, the argument appears more plausible. If, however, the comparison is made between 50+ and everyone else, it appears less so, as it does not follow from being 50+ that a person will have any savings which those under 50 will not have. This is a key difference between age and other strands where membership of groups tends to be clear cut.

4.41   Once the complainant has identified the relevant provision, criterion or practice, he or she can identify the correct pool of individuals upon whom the effect of the provision, criterion or practice is going to be assessed. The choice of pool is said to be a question of logic, rather than discretion or fact-finding.[40]

4.42   If unable to demonstrate that discrimination is intrinsically likely, the next step becomes to focus on the pool. In order to decide who should form the pool, it will generally be necessary to consider what qualifications are required to do the work. It will therefore be necessary to consider who the relevant total number of individuals are that would be affected (positively or negatively) by the provision, criterion or practice, and then ascertain who would be disadvantaged by it. The relevant total is the number of people to whom the person (such as the employer) applies or would apply the provision, criterion or practice.[41] Determining the correct pool for comparison is a matter of fact for the tribunal. Claimants should consider all the possible pools which the tribunal may consider of its own motion at the hearing to avoid being taken by surprise, without the correct evidence at the hearing. It may be necessary to have a pre-hearing review on the question of the correct pool.[42]

EXAMPLE 1: An employer advertises a post for a 'person with 3–5 years' post-qualification experience'. She chooses these qualifications because the position is made vacant by a person leaving who has five years' post qualification experience and the employer takes the view that the replacement should be able to take up where the leaver left off at about the same level of skill. This criteria is intrinsically likely to disadvantage those between 18 and 26

---

40 See *Allonby v Accrington and Rossendale College*, ibid, at para 17 of the judgment.
41 See *Jones v University of Manchester* [1993] IRLR 218.
42 See chapter 12.

because of the likelihood of a person of that age group being newly qualified in this way. However, it will not be intrinsically likely to disadvantage those in older age groups (for example).[43] Suppose the complainant is 27. The complainant is likely to need to produce statistics on how the PCP impacts on people from his age group. The relevant people will be those with the relevant qualifications. The tribunal will then look to see how many of them have 3–5 years' post-qualification experience. They are the appropriate pool for comparison.

EXAMPLE 2: Employer A demands that all applicants for promotion must have a qualification in media studies. He will not accept any other qualifications. This intrinsically puts all applicants for promotion over the age of 50 at a disadvantage since media studies did not exist at the time they were becoming qualified. However, for younger employees proving that the PCP places their age group at a disadvantage will require reference to the impact of the PCP on that age group. If employee, B, who is 46 and has no qualification in media studies, wishes to bring a claim to the employment tribunal for indirect discrimination, B can argue that the numbers of those in the age group 45+ who are disadvantaged by the PCP is higher than the numbers of those in the age group below 45. However only those who are otherwise in the running for promotion will be relevant to this pool. The pool for comparison will comprise all those who have all the other qualifications for promotion and who are below 45.

Victimisation

4.43   Discrimination by victimisation is a way of challenging an individual who subjects another individual to a disadvantage because they have brought a claim (or suspect they will, or know that they intend to bring a claim) for age discrimination to the courts or tribunals, or because they threaten to support another person in such an action, or because they have done anything under or by reference to the age discrimination regulations, or because they allege that the individual or employer

---

43 It is arguable however that at the other end of the age spectrum the PCP in question again can be taken intrinsically to disadvantage people in that age group as they are much less likely to have the band of PQE being sought, unless the advert makes it clear that this is a minimum service requirement.

has done something, or someone else has done something contrary to the regulations. This is known as a 'protected act'.

4.44 The legal sense of victimisation differs from the layman's interpretation. However, for the purpose of the regulations, it has the same definition and meaning as given to victimisation across the other discrimination legislation.

4.45 The concept of victimisation implements article 11 of the Directive. This provides that the states must introduce 'such measures as are necessary to protect employees against dismissal or adverse treatment by the employer as a reaction to a complaint within the undertaking or to any legal proceedings aimed at enforcing compliance with the principle of equal treatment'. This requires proof of adverse treatment as a reaction to a complaint.

4.46 The regulations provide that A discriminates against B, if A treats B less favourably than A treats or would treat other persons in the same circumstances, and does so by reason that B has:[44]

a) brought proceedings against A or any other person under or by virtue of the regulations;
b) given evidence or information in connection with proceedings brought by any person against A or any other person under or by virtue of the regulations;
c) otherwise done anything under or by reference to the regulations in relation to A or any other person; or
d) alleged that A or any other person has committed an act which (whether or not the allegation so states) would amount to a contravention of the regulations,

or by reason that A knows that B intends to do any of those things, or suspects that B has done or intends to do any of them.

> EXAMPLE: B says she will give evidence in a case before the employment tribunal for age discrimination brought against her employer, A, by another employee, C. A refuses to promote B unless she withdraws her support to C. That is an act of unlawful victimisation.

4.47 Under the regulations there needs to be a comparison made for the purposes of successfully bringing a discrimination by victimisation claim. The correct comparison would be between the treatment given to the

44 Reg 4(1).

complainant who had done a protected act and the treatment given to another employee or individual who had not done a protected act. However, the Directive has not been adequately transposed since there is no requirement for a comparator for victimisation within the body of article 11 of the Directive.

4.48   All that the person needs to establish under the Directive test is that the protected act caused detrimental treatment, rather than that it caused the person to be treated less favourably than another actual or hypothetical comparator. It may be that a reference to the ECJ should be sought on this point. Clearly the regulations do not constitute what is necessary to protect against adverse treatment if a comparison is required. In some cases where that comparative treatment cannot be shown by reference to an actual or hypothetical comparator the claim will fail where a claim based simply on the fact that adverse treatment was given as a result of the protected act would not fail.

4.49   There is a defence specifically provided within the regulations which is that regulation 4(1) does not apply to treatment of B by reason of any allegation made by him or evidence or information given by him, if the allegation, evidence or information was false and not made (or as the case may be, given) in good faith.[45]

> EXAMPLE: B says she will give evidence in a case brought by another employee, C, against their employer, A. However, B does not actually believe A has committed an act of discrimination and simply gives evidence in an attempt to force A to give her a pay rise that she has been seeking. A disciplines her for misconduct since he knows that B's evidence is malicious. That is unlikely to be an act of victimisation since B's evidence is false and made in bad faith. Both of these requirements must be fulfilled before the defence is established, so that it is not enough for the employer to show that a true allegation was made for ulterior purposes.

4.50   Regulation 4(1)(d) is likely to be construed fairly narrowly, in line with the other discrimination provisions. The Court of Appeal has held that the wording of s4(1)(d) in the SDA (which is almost identical to that in the Age Regulations 2006) must be applied literally. The allegation relied on does not have to state explicitly that an act of discrimination has occurred, but the asserted facts must be capable of amounting in law to an act of discrimination by the employer. In *Waters v Metropolitan*

---

45   Reg 4(2).

Police Commissioner,[46] the Court of Appeal upheld the tribunal and Employment Appeals Tribunal's (EAT's) decision that the appellant police constable's complaint that she had been victimised by her employer contrary to SDA 1975 s4(1) by being subjected to a detriment because she alleged she had been sexually assaulted by a male colleague must be rejected. As the alleged sexual assault had not been committed in the course of her colleague's employment, the employer could not be deemed to be vicariously liable for it. Accordingly, the allegation of victimisation was not in respect of an act by the employer which 'would amount to a contravention of' the SDA 1975 within the meaning of s4(1)(d).

4.51   In *Chief Constable of West Yorkshire Police v Khan*,[47] a detective sergeant of Indian origin brought a complaint for race discrimination (alleging failures to promote him) to the tribunal. Before the complaint was heard, he applied for a promotion in another police force who asked the West Yorkshire Police for a reference. The Chief Constable replied, 'Sergeant Khan has an outstanding industrial tribunal application against the Chief Constable for failing to support his application for promotion. In light of that, the Chief Constable is unable to comment any further for fear of prejudicing his own case before the tribunal'. Consequently, the sergeant amended his claim to include one for victimisation. The lower courts held that the failure to provide a reference had been unlawful victimisation. The House of Lords disagreed since the reference was not withheld 'by reason that' the sergeant had brought discrimination proceedings, but rather because the employer temporarily wanted to preserve his position. On the facts of that case, the evidence established that once the litigation had concluded, the reference request would have been complied with. The key question is not a 'but for' test but rather a subjective test: Why did the alleged discriminator act as he did? What, consciously or unconsciously, was his reason?[48]

4.52   Although a strict 'but for' test will not be applied, it will be difficult to succeed in a claim of victimisation without being able to establish the respondent/defendant's motive or impetus. However, the employer has no defence simply because the complainant cannot prove that there was conscious motivation because of the protected act: Unconscious motivation will suffice.[49]

---

46 [1997] IRLR 589, CA.
47 [2001] IRLR 830, HL.
48 Per Lord Nicholls.
49 *Nagarajan v London Regional Transport* [1999] IRLR 572, HL.

Instructions to discriminate

4.53 Article 2.4 of the Directive states blandly that 'an instruction to discriminate against persons on [age] grounds ... shall be deemed to be discrimination within the meaning of [article 2.1.]'. By virtue of regulation 5, a person, A, discriminates against another person, B, if A treats B less favourably than he treats or would treat other persons in the same circumstances because:

a) B has not carried out (in whole or in part) an instruction to do an act which is unlawful by virtue of the regulations; or

b) B, having been given an instruction to do such an act, complains to A or any other person about that instruction.

4.54 There is a difference between the provisions governing instructions to discriminate in the new regulations compared with those found in SDA 1975 s39, RRA 1976 s30 or DDA 1995 s16C.[50] The latter makes it unlawful *for a person who has authority over another person*, or in accordance with whose wishes that other person is accustomed to act, to instruct him to do any unlawful discriminatory act, or to procure or attempt to procure the doing by him of such an act. SDA 1975 s40, RRA 1976 s31(1) and DDA 1995 s16C also make it unlawful to induce or attempt to induce a person to do any unlawful discriminatory act. No directly comparable provisions appears in the regulations, or indeed in the Religion or Belief Regulations 2003 or the Sexual Orientation Regulations 2003. However, the provisions governing instructions to discriminate are arguably broader than those in the older statutes.

4.55 The key difference between the wording in regulation 5 and that in the older statutes is that there is no requirement under the regulations for the instructions to come from someone who is in a position of authority. The new regulations effectively cover the situation where any member of the public comes in and instructs a person who would be covered by the scope of the regulations (notably an employee, or a person charged with admissions to vocational training or the education sector, excluding schools) to commit an act that would be unlawful pursuant to these regulations. For example A, who works in a public house instructs a colleague, B, not to employ women 'of a particular age'. A has no particular authority over B since they are at the same level of seniority.

4.56 However, there would only be a cause of action under the regulations if A then treated B less favourably because he had refused to

---

50 No such provision appears either in the Religion or Belief Regulations 2003 or the Sexual Orientation Regulations 2003.

carry out the instruction (in whole or part), or complained to A or anyone else about having been given that instruction. So, if A (who happens to be in charge of the rota) then refused to allow B flexi-working, which everyone else enjoyed, because B had employed a woman 'of a particular age', or because B had complained to other colleagues about the instruction, regulation 5 would apply. However, if B refused to carry out the instruction, and A decided he would not take any further action, there would be no cause of action under the regulations whereas by virtue of SDA 1975 s39, for example, the mere fact of the instruction, or the attempt to procure the unlawful act, would have been enough to constitute an unlawful act.

4.57   The appropriate comparator would be somebody who was prepared to go along with the unlawful instruction.[51]

Aiding unlawful acts

4.58   Regulation 26 provides that a person who knowingly aids another person to do an act made unlawful by the regulations, will be treated as himself committing an unlawful act. This provision also appears in both the SDA 1975, RRA 1976 and DDA 1995.[52] 'Aid' is used in the everyday sense of the word and it has no special or technical meaning in this context (help, assist, co-operate, collaborate etc).[53] A person aids another if the help is both substantial and productive or whether it is not, so long as the help is not so insignificant as to be negligible. However, a person may knowingly aid another to do an unlawful act without inducing the other to do an unlawful act, or procuring an act of discrimination.

4.59   A person who knowingly aids another person to do an act which is made unlawful by the regulations is treated as if he or she himself or herself committed that unlawful act.[54]

4.60   A person does not knowingly aid another to do an unlawful act in the following circumstances:[55]

a) the person acts in reliance on a statement made to him or her by that other person that the act would not be unlawful; and
b) it was reasonable for him or her to rely on that statement.

51 See *Weathersfield Ltd v Sargent* [1999] IRLR 94.
52 Sections 42(1), 33(1) and 57(1).
53 *Anyanwu v South Bank Student's Union* [2001] IRLR 391, HL.
54 Reg 26(1).
55 Reg 26(3).

4.61   If a person knowingly or recklessly makes a false or misleading statement that it would not be unlawful for another individual to do an
act, they may be committing an offence which is punishable by a fine
not exceeding level 5 on the standard scale.[56]

4.62   Knowledge is an additional element in relation to whether there
has been 'aiding' of an unlawful act, in accordance with the decision in
Hallam v Avery.[57] On the facts of this case, a local authority had agreed
to hire out rooms to a gypsy couple for their wedding reception. The
police warned the local authority that they had experienced problems
with gypsy weddings in the past. The local authority sought to impose
further conditions on the hiring of the room which was found, at first
instance, to be an act of discrimination. The Court of Appeal considered
that there was insufficient evidence that the police had been aware
that the local authority would go on to treat the couple less favourably
on grounds of their race, following the police advice. It was held that
recklessness was insufficient since the police had to know they were
aiding an act of discrimination. That position has not changed in
respect of the age regulations, where reckless aid will not suffice. The
House of Lords, in the *Hallam* case, decided it on a different basis.[58] It
was held there that the fact that a respondent had been 'helpful' did not
necessarily permit a court or tribunal to conclude that they had aided
an act of discrimination since aiding an act required a degree of
involvement, possibly in the decision itself.

Harassment

4.63   Harassment is defined as A engaging in unwanted conduct which has
the purpose or effect of:

a) violating B's dignity; or
b) creating an intimidating, hostile, degrading, humiliating or offensive environment for B.

4.64   For the purposes of the regulations, such conduct will be unlawful if
such harassment is *on grounds of age*.[59] There is no requirement that for
harassment to occur, the basis of that conduct is the age of the person
making the complaint. This is a contrast from the provisions governing

---

56 Reg 26(4). See also para 3.62 onwards.
57 [2000] ICR 583, CA, and see further *Sinclair, Roche & Temperley v Heard* [2004]
IRLR 763, EAT.
58 [2001] ICR 408, HL.
59 Reg 6(1).

direct discrimination, where the discrimination must be 'on grounds of B's age'. This could mean that harassment on account of someone else's age could occur, and be treated as unlawful under the regulations. For example, an employee is bullied at work on the grounds that her partner is perceived to be a 'toy-boy' and immature because of his age.

4.65   Conduct will only be regarded as harassment where, having regard to all the circumstances, including in particular the perception of B, that conduct *should reasonably be considered as having the effect* of violating B's dignity, or creating an intimidating, hostile, degrading, humiliating or offensive environment for B.[60] The insertion of a criterion of reasonableness into the test of harassment is controversial.[61] There is no equivalent in the Framework Directive.[62]

4.66   The consultation on harassment gave a rather strange suggestion as to what might not constitute harassment: 'where a person makes light-hearted jokes about his own age, and another person simply repeats that comment to him in the same context'. Whilst this may be evidence that the claimant did not believe that what was said constituted harassment, it does not follow simply from the fact that a person refers to him or herself in a socially acceptable but discriminatory way that it does not constitute harassment for others to refer to him or her in that way. A better approach to what might constitute harassment is given in the ACAS booklet, *Tackling discrimination and promoting equality – good practice guide for employers*. This was written in the context of the other strands of discrimination and harassment but there is no suggestion that the examples of behaviour it provides should not be applicable in an age context. Obviously the ground of the conduct must be age:

- physical contact which is unwanted (eg, patting a younger employee);
- coercion, isolation or 'freezing-out' (eg, deliberately using speech associated with youth culture to isolate an older employee);
- offensive jokes (jokes using age stereotypes, such as jokes about memory and older people);
- unwelcome remarks about a person's dress or appearance (eg, 'mutton dressed as lamb', 'are you having a mid-life crisis?' or by reference to era or seriousness);

60 Reg 6(2).
61 The same wording appears in the Sexual Orientation Regulations 2003 No 1661. It mirrors the newly inserted SDA 1975 para 4A(4) (giving effect to article 2(3) of the EC Directive 2002/73/EC), which reads 'Conduct shall be regarded as having the fact mentioned [above] only if, having regard to the circumstances, including in particular the perception of B, it should reasonably be considered as having that effect'.
62 Article 2(3) of the directive, ibid.

- shouting at staff;
- personal insults (eg, references to 'dinosaurs', 'wet behind the ears' etc on a repeated basis);
- persistent criticism (eg, 'you don't know you've been born');
- setting impossible deadlines.

4.67   Harassment cannot be justified.

4.68   How far is too much? Is one rude comment sufficient to establish a case of harassment? The short answer is that it may be, depending on the circumstances, particularly where the comment or conduct was objectively degrading, demeaning, hostile etc.[63] One person's silly joke may be offensive to another, but would that be enough to be considered harassment? Factors to consider include:

- How often has the remark or conduct taken place? The cumulative effect of a series of incidents will be relevant.
- Was the comment made in the presence of others, and if so, would other individuals have considered the comment or conduct insulting or humiliating to the intended victim?
- Did the remark in some way demean, or humiliate the recipient? How did he or she feel at the time, or later? The subjective perception of the recipient remains important.[64]
- Was the recipient indeed offended or humiliated etc? Did the recipient make his or her objection clear, and if so how?
- Was the comment designed to offend? Motive and intention can be useful in ascertaining discrimination, although it is not necessary to demonstrate a desire to humiliate, affront or offend.
- If the comment was not designed to offend, did it form part of a culture of 'banter'? If so, was the recipient a willing participant in those conversations? That might, but not in all cases, demonstrate that he or she was not offended or is not likely to have been genuinely offended or insulted by the remarks made.
- Did the recipient complain at the time? In some cases, the detriment or disadvantage caused by the discriminatory conduct may be so obvious that the lack of any contemporaneous complaint may be irrelevant in all the circumstances[65].

---

63 *Reed and Bull Information Systems Ltd v Stedman* [1999] IRLR 299, EAT; *Chief Constable of the Lincolnshire Police v Stubbs* [1999] IRLR 81, EAT; *Institu Cleaning Co v Heads* [1995] IRLR 4.

64 See, eg, *Driskel v Peninsula Business Services Ltd* [2000] IRLR 151.

65 Ibid.

4.69 The objective nature of the test lends assistance to claimants. In *Moonsar v Fiveways Express Transport Ltd*,[66] the EAT considered that, in a case where a female employee considered she had been harassed by the downloading of pornographic images by male colleagues in her office, viewed objectively, such behaviour clearly had the potential effect of causing an affront to a female employee working in a close environment, and as such would be regarded as degrading or offensive to an employee, as a woman. It was clearly potentially less favourable treatment and a detriment clearly followed from the nature of the behaviour. Since there was evidence before the tribunal that the claimant found the behaviour unacceptable, the fact that she did not complaint to her employers at the time did not afford the employers a defence since the behaviour was so obvious. The burden then shifted to the employers to show that there was not less favourable treatment, for example that the claimant was a party to the conduct or enjoyed what was happening. Ageism is currently socially acceptable in many contexts (compared to eg, racism) but the purpose of the Regulations is to challenge the attitudes, so 'common sense' will not always be a reliable guide.

4.70 Tribunals should not carve up complaints of harassment into a series of specific incidents to try to measure the harm or detriment in relation to each. The course of conduct must be considered as a whole.[67]

4.71 Tribunals may have to resolve complicated issues of fact. In particular, there may be issues as to whether conduct is welcome or unwelcome. It is not necessary that a complainant make clear in advance that a particular form of remark or conduct is unwelcome. Since the test contains both subjective and objective elements, the tribunal has to determine whether by words or conduct the complainant has made clear that particular conduct is unwelcome. Further, it should consider whether any reasonable person would understand the complainant to be rejecting the conduct, and if so, any continuation of the conduct generally should be regarded as harassment.[68]

4.72 It must be remembered that harassment in the sense described above is only unlawful in employment situations where it takes place in the course of employment. This can prove difficult to determine. Often, harassment takes place in the form of social gatherings, which could be after office hours or outside the workplace. Tribunals will

---

66 [2005] IRLR 9.
67 See *Reed and Bull Information Systems Ltd v Stedman* [1999] IRLR 299, EAT.
68 See *Reed and Bull* ibid.

need to consider whether the circumstances demonstrate that what is taking place is an extension of employment.[69]

4.73   The Directive states that harassment is deemed to be a form of discrimination when unwanted conduct related to age takes place with the purpose or effect of violating the dignity of a person and of creating an intimidating hostile, degrading or humiliating or offensive environment.[70] Under the new definition of harassment it is an open question whether the employer is liable to an employee for harassment by failing to protect employees against harassment by customers. The Directive requires member states to define harassment so as to achieve the objective of protection where unwanted conduct takes place. It does not have to be unwanted conduct by the employer or a person for whom the employer is responsible. One House of Lords decision has been taken to create a difficulty in this area. Under the Regulations employers may not be liable, according to the circumstances, of acts of harassment by third parties, even where the employer could have taken steps to prevent or reduce the effect of the harassment.[71] However, the Directive suggests that the employer may be liable when unwanted conduct related to age takes place with the effect that the working conditions are offensive and which the employer does not prevent.

4.74   An employer may be vicariously liable for an employee who harasses another employee, subject to the provisions of regulation 25. This is further discussed in chapter 8.

4.75   If an employer fails to investigate an act of harassment when it is raised with him or her, and but for the complainant's age would have so investigated it (ie fails to investigate on grounds of the complainant's age), the employer may have committed a further act of discrimination.[72]

4.76   A person who knowingly aids another person to do an act made unlawful by the regulations shall be treated for the purposes of the regulations as doing an unlawful act of the like description.[73] An employee who knowingly fosters and encourages a sustained campaign of bullying and unlawful discrimination will be regarded as having subjected a complainant to a detriment for which both that

---

69 See *Chief Constable of the Lincolnshire Police v Stubbs* [1999] IRLR 81, EAT.
70 Article 2.3 of the directive and article 3.1(c) applying the directive to employment and working conditions.
71 *MacDonald v AG for Scotland* [2003] ICR 937 para 31, disapproving *Burton v De Vere Hotels* [1997] ICR 1.
72 *Home Office v Coyne* [2000] ICR 1443, CA.
73 Reg 26(1).

employee and his or her employee can be held jointly and severally liable. However, in order to 'aid' an act of unlawful discrimination, a person must have done more than merely create an environment in which discrimination can occur. However, where there is evidence that a discriminatory culture has been allowed to flourish, that may be sufficient to demonstrate complicity.[74]

4.77 The Protection from Harassment Act (PHA) 1997 creates both civil liability and criminal offences of harassment. Harassment may also give rise to a tortious action at common law.[75] The purpose of this statute is to protect victims of harassment, whatever form the harassment takes, wherever it occurs and whatever its motivation. The Act seeks to provide protection against bullying at work and away from work. Section 1 prohibits harassment in these terms:

(1) A person must not pursue a course of conduct –
   (a) which amounts to harassment of another, and
   (b) which he knows or ought to know amounts to harassment of the other.
(2) For the purposes of this section, the person whose course of conduct is in question ought to know that it amounts to harassment of another if a reasonable person in possession of the same information would think the course of conduct amounted to harassment of the other.

4.78 Certain courses of conduct are excepted including where, in the circumstances, it was reasonable to pursue the course of conduct.[76] 'Harassment' is not defined in the Act, but it includes causing anxiety or distress. A course of conduct means conduct on at least two occasions.[77] Harassment may be of more than one person.

4.79 The prohibition applies as much between an employer and an employee as it does between any other two persons. Although the victim must be an individual, the perpetrator may be a corporate body.[78]

4.80 Section 3 gives victims of harassment a civil remedy in respect both of actual breaches of section 1 and also threatened breaches.[79]

---

74 *Gilbank v Miles* [2006] IRLR 538, CA.
75 *Wong v Parkside Health NHS Trust* [2003] 3 All ER 932, CA; *Hunter v Canary Wharf Ltd* [1997] AC 655, HL; *Khorasandjian v Bush* [1993] QB 727, CA.
76 Protection from Harassment (PHA) 1997 s1(3).
77 PHA 1997 s7(2), (3).
78 See *Majrowski v Guy's and St Thomas NHS Trust* [2006] UKHL 34 which also establishes the vicarious liability of the employer for harassment under the PHA 1997.
79 In relation to which an injunction may be sought.

This means a single act of harassment may have occurred, which is not in itself a course of conduct, and the victim may fear repetition. Section 3 provides:

> (1) An actual or apprehended breach of section 1 may be the subject of a claim in civil proceedings by the person who is or may be the victim of the course of conduct in question.

> (2) On such a claim damages may be awarded for (among other things) any anxiety caused by the harassment and any financial loss resulting from the harassment.

4.81   An award of damages under this section is not discretionary. The effect of section 3(1) is to render a breach of section 1 a wrong giving rise to the ordinary remedies the law provides for civil wrongs including an entitlement to damages for any loss or damage sustained by a victim by reason of the wrong. Such an award is subject to the principles of causation and mitigation.[80]

---

80 See chapter 12.

CHAPTER 5

Age discrimination justifications

> **Key points**
> - Age discrimination, whether direct or indirect, may be justified.
> - Justification requires proof of a legitimate aim.
> - Justification requires proof that treatment of the claimant is appropriate and necessary to pursue the legitimate aim.
> - There are differences between the approach in the Framework Directive and in the Age Regulations 2006.
> - The role of ACAS guidance.
> - Checklist on justification of direct and indirect discrimination.

Introduction

5.1   In this chapter we will look at the concept of justification used in the Employment Equality (Age) Regulations 2006. The underlying thinking of the consultation paper, *Coming of Age*, was that it should be exceptional to justify direct discrimination, but that there should be circumstances in which justification could take place.

5.2   Regulation 3 of the 2006 regulations creates a test for justification that applies both to direct discrimination and to indirect discrimination:

> ... and A cannot show the treatment or, as the case may be, provision, criterion or practice to be a proportionate means of achieving a legitimate aim.[1]

5.3   The alleged discriminator must show that the treatment etc is a proportionate means of achieving a legitimate aim. In broad terms this sets a high hurdle for justification of direct discrimination because if the legitimate aim can be achieved by non-discriminatory means this should be used in preference. The discriminatory effect of the treatment must be outweighed significantly by the benefits of a legitimate aim.

5.4   The legitimate aim must correspond with a reasonable need on the part of the employer. One of the debates about the 2006 regulations is the extent to which economic factors such as business needs and efficiency will be legitimate aims. However, the employer will not be able to argue the expense of complying with the regulations as a valid reason justifying less favourable treatment.

---

1   Reg 3(1).

The Directive

5.5   In order to understand the nature of the justification permitted by regulation 3, it is important to understand the provisions of the directive on which the concept of justification is said to be based: the Framework Directive. The preamble to the directive states:

> (25) The prohibition of age discrimination is an essential part of meeting the aims set out in the Employment Guidelines and encouraging diversity in the workforce. However, differences in treatment in connection with age may be justified under certain circumstances and therefore require specific provisions which may vary in accordance with the situation in Member States. It is therefore essential to distinguish between differences in treatment which are justified, in particular by legitimate employment policy, labour market and vocational training objectives, and discrimination which must be prohibited.

5.6   The purpose of the directive therefore is to permit the member states to implement *specific* provisions stating the circumstances in which differences of treatment in connection with age may be justified. The requirement on the member states is to distinguish between justified differences in treatment and discrimination which must be prohibited. Regulation 3(1) does not do this in respect of direct discrimination. Instead a general test is used and national law does not draw the distinction by means of specific provisions between discrimination which is unlawful and justified differences in treatment. This is a fundamental problem with the UK's implementation of the legislation.

Justification under the Directive

Justification of indirect discrimination

5.7   Indirect age discrimination occurs where an apparently neutral provision, criterion or practice (PCP) puts or would put persons having a particular age at a particular disadvantage compared with other persons unless the provision, criterion or practice is objectively justified by a legitimate aim and the means of achieving that aim are appropriate and necessary.[2] In the context of indirect discrimination the directive does not make reference to any specific provisions within the context of national law but permits a general test.

---

2 Article 2.2(b).

Justification of direct discrimination

5.8   Direct age discrimination may be justified but the approach of the Directive is much more restrictive. Differences of treatment on the grounds of age may be justified 'if, within the context of national law, [differences of treatment on grounds of age] are objectively and reasonably justified by a legitimate aim, including legitimate employment policy, labour market and vocational training objectives, and if the means of achieving that aim are appropriate and necessary'.[3] There appears to be a distinction drawn in the language of the Directive between the justification of indirect discrimination which can be on the basis of any legitimate aim and the justification of direct discrimination which must be objectively and reasonably justified by reference to a legitimate aim within the context of national law. Read in the context of the preamble, the requirement is that 'differences in treatment in connection with age may be justified under certain circumstances and therefore require specific provisions which may vary in accordance with the situation in Member States'. A general justification of direct age discrimination does not appear to be warranted by the Directive, as it does not constitute a specific provision. An issue for early consideration will be whether regulation 3 of the 2006 regulations transposes article 6.1 properly or at all.[4]

5.9   Assuming that a general test is permissible, the next issue is what standard the Directive sets for the justification of direct discrimination. In *Kutz-Bauer v Freie und Hansestadt Hamburg*,[4a] the European Court of Justice (ECJ) considered justification of laws resulting in indirect sex discrimination under Directive 76/207. Using that as a model of justification, an age based difference of treatment would not constitute discrimination if it was justified by objective factors which are unrelated to any discrimination based on age.[5] In *Kutz-Bauer* the complainant challenged a public service collective agreement which offered part-time work for older employees up to pensionable age. Since pensionable age differed as between men and women, the female complainant could only avail of the scheme up to 60, but could have continued until 65 had she been male. The ECJ provided guidance to the national court concerning the legitimate aim pursued by Germany of

---

3   Framework Directive article 6.1.
4   See *R (on the application of the Incorporated Trustees of the National Council for Ageing) v Secretary of State for Trade and Industry* (Admin Ct CO/5485/2006).
4a C-187/00 ECR 2003, page I-02741 of judgment, 20 March 2003.
5   See *Kutz-Bauer* para 50, and the guidance at paras 55–60.

providing part time work for older employees. The aim was to combat unemployment by offering maximum incentives for workers who were not yet eligible to retire to do so thus making posts available.

5.10   The ECJ stated in relation to objective justification:

> It is necessary in that regard to ascertain, in the light of all the relevant factors and taking into account the possibility of achieving by other means the aims pursued by the provisions in question, whether such aims appear to be unrelated to any discrimination based on sex and whether those provisions as a means to the achievement of certain aims, are capable of advancing those aims (see, in that regard, Case C-167/97 *Seymour-Smith and Perez* [1999] ECR I-623, paragraph 72).[6]

5.11   However:

> Mere generalisations concerning the capacity of a specific measure to encourage recruitment are not enough to show that the aim of the disputed provision is unrelated to any discrimination on grounds of sex or to provide evidence on the basis of which it could reasonably be considered that the means chosen are or could be suitable for achieving that aim (*Kutz-Bauer*, paragraph 57).[7]

5.12   Furthermore:

> Moreover, to concede that budgetary considerations may justify a difference in treatment between men and women which would otherwise constitute indirect discrimination on grounds of sex would mean that the application and scope of a rule of Community law as fundamental as that of equal treatment between men and women might vary in time and place according to the state of the public finances of Member States (*De Weerd and Others*, cited above, paragraph 36, and *Jorgensen*, cited above, paragraph 39).

5.13   In that case, the Court also referred to *Hill and Stapleton v The Revenue Commissioners and the Department of Finance*[8] which held that increased costs cannot justify discrimination. The court stated in *Hill and Stapleton*:

> So far as the justification on economic grounds is concerned, it should be noted that an employer cannot justify discrimination arising from a job-sharing scheme solely on the ground that the avoidance of such discrimination would involve increased costs.

---

6   *Helga Kutz-Bauer v Freie und Hansestadt Hamburg* Case C-187/00 ECR 2003 Page I-02741 para 51.

7   *Erica Steinicke v Bundesanstalt fur Arbeit* Case C-77/02 11 September 2003 para 64.

8   Case C243/95.

5.14   The language of the Directive also mirrors the test for justification used in cases under article 14 of the European Convention on Human Rights (ECHR). In the *Belgian Linguistics* case,[9] the European Court of Human Rights stated that a difference in treatment would not constitute discrimination for article 14 purposes where an objective and reasonable justification could be argued. Drawing analogies from that and other cases, what is meant by objective and reasonable justification is that very weighty reasons would have to be put forward before a difference of treatment could be regarded as compatible with the fundamental principle of EU law prohibiting age discrimination.[10] Matters such as the existence of a sustained practice would not constitute objective and reasonable justification for direct discrimination.

5.15   In general terms, article 14 discrimination could be justified by pursuit of a 'legitimate aim' and if there is a 'reasonable relationship of proportionality between the means employed and the aim sought to be realised'.[11] For example, the European Court of Human Rights has rejected an argument that to levy contributions to child benefit from unmarried childless women would impose an unfair emotional burden on them as it might equally well apply to unmarried childless men or to childless couples. In *Van Raalte v Netherlands*[12] it held that even if the desire to spare the feelings of childless women of a certain age could be regarded as a legitimate aim, the objective could not provide a justification for the gender based difference of treatment. The reason was simply not sufficiently weighty.[13] Objective and reasonable justification was found not to exist in *L v Austria*[14] in which the court considered the unequal age of consent. The Austrian law made an offence of homosexual acts of adult men with consenting adolescents between the ages of 14 and 18. It did not criminalise the

9   (1968), (1979) 1 EHRR 252
10   See *Bughartz v Switzerland* (1994) 18 EHRR 101 at para 27:
     'The Court reiterates that the advancement of the equality of the sexes is today a major goal in the Member States of the Council of Europe; this means that very weighty reasons would have to be put forward before a difference of treatment on the sole ground of sex could be regarded as compatible with the Convention.'
11   *Gaygusuz v Austria* (17371/90) (1997) 23 EHRR 364.
12   (1997) 24 EHRR 503.
13   By contrast, see *Jane Smith v United Kingdom* (25154/94) (2001) 33 EHRR 30 where it was held that the significance of environment preservation aims outweighed the discrimination to a gypsy family's rights in respect of planning matters.
14   13 BHRC 594.

equivalent for women. The court said that the issue was whether there was an objective and reasonable justification why young men in the 14–18 year age bracket needed protection against any sexual relationship with adult men, whereas women in the same age bracket did not need protection against relations either with adult men or women. Without objective and reasonable justification, the maintenance of a higher age of consent for homosexual acts than for heterosexual acts breached article 14.

5.16 The analogy with human rights provision cannot, however, be taken to its extreme conclusion as this may lead away from the objective of the directive. The concept of age equality is still in its infancy and the level of justification that is required under article 14 may not indicate the level required under the Directive. A view may be taken that there is a hierarchy of human rights and a distinction to be drawn between the rights which are seldom if ever acceptable grounds for differences in treatment (eg gender) and which prima facie appear to offend notions of the respect due to the individual and those which merely require some rational justification (for example grounds of ability, education, wealth, occupation).[15] The likelihood is that utilitarian justifications will be permitted more readily in respect of the second category and will usually depend upon considerations of the general public interest. The second consequence of this distinction is a courtly deference. While 'the courts, as guardians of the right of the individual to equal respect, will carefully examine the reasons offered for any discrimination in the first category, decisions about the general public interest which underpin differences in treatment in the second category are very much a matter for the democratically elected branches of government'. Discrimination on the grounds of old age was recently described as a borderline case between the two. 'But there is usually no difficulty about deciding whether one is dealing with a case in which the right to respect for the individuality of a human being is at stake or merely a question of general social policy.'[16] That approach is very much at odds with the underlying principle of the directive which is fundamentally concerned with the dignity of the individual. It is suggested that such individual rights fall firmly into the first of the suggested categories of discrimination (see para 14.83 onwards).

---

15 *Massachusetts Board of Retirement v Murgia* (1976) 438 US 285.

16 *R (on the application of Carson) v Secretary of State for Work and Pensions* [2005] UKHL 37; [2006] 1 AC 173.

Mangold v Helm

5.17   The importance of the right being infringed seems to play an important role in determining the level of justification by way of objective and
reasonable justification that must be offered. In the context of the
Directive, the ECJ has held that the principle of non-discrimination
on the grounds of age is one of the general principles of community
law.[17]

5.18   The case of *Mangold v Helm* was the first case to reach the ECJ
under the Directive and deals with the age ground. It is an important
case in the context of the introduction of age legislation which differ-
entiates between age groups (such as the new retirement dismissal
provisions discussed later).[18]

5.19   Mr Mangold was employed by Rüdiger Helm, a lawyer, under a
fixed-term contract taking effect on 1 July 2003. He was aged 56 at the
time and clause 5 of the contract provided:

> 1. The employment relationship shall start on 1 July 2003 and last until 28
> February 2004.
>
> 2. The duration of the contract shall be based on the statutory provision
> which is intended to make it easier to conclude fixed-term contracts of
> employment with older workers (the provisions of the fourth sentence,
> in conjunction with those of the first sentence, of para. 14(3) of the TzBfG
> ...), since the employee is more than 52 years old.
>
> 3. The parties have agreed that there is no reason for the fixed term of
> this contract other than that set out in para. 2 above. All other grounds
> for limiting the term of employment accepted in principle by the
> legislature are expressly excluded from this agreement.

5.20   A few weeks after commencing employment, Mr Mangold brought
proceedings against Mr Helm claiming that because this clause limited
the term of his contract, was incompatible with the Framework Agreement on fixed-term contracts and with the age discrimination provisions in the Framework Employment Directive 2000/78/EC. German
law (para 14(3) of the TzBfG, the German law on part-time working and
fixed-term contracts) permitted such arrangements. That law was said
to implement the directive (and one relating to fixed term contracts).
The German law permitted these arrangements in order to promote
employment among older workers. The law in general limited the

17   *Mangold v Helm* [2006] IRLR 143.
18   Chapter 9.

maximum term of a fixed-term employment contract to two years and provided that within that limit, the contract could be renewed at most three times. In relation to those aged over 60, these conditions did not apply 'if the employee has reached the age of 60 when the fixed-term employment contract begins'. In 2001 the age of 60 was reduced to 58 by amendment. The law thereafter stated:

> A fixed-term employment contract shall not require objective justification if when starting the fixed-term employment relationship the employee has reached the age of 58. It shall not be permissible to set a fixed term where there is a close connection with a previous employment contract of indefinite duration concluded with the same employer. Such close connection shall be presumed to exist where the interval between two employment contracts is less than six months. Until 31 December 2006 the first sentence shall be read as referring to the age of 52 instead of 58.

5.21   Germany, like the UK, did not implement the Framework Directive by 2 December 2003, the primary implementation period but made use of a permissible three years extension (ending in December 2006). Such extensions were permissible 'in order to take account of particular conditions'.

5.22   The Munich Labour Court referred questions to the ECJ for a preliminary ruling and in particular:

> 2. Is Article 6 of ... Directive 2000/78 ... to be interpreted as precluding a provision of national law which, like the provision at issue in this case, authorises the conclusion of fixed-term employment contracts, without any objective reason, with workers aged 52 and over, contrary to the principle requiring justification on objective grounds?

5.23   Advocate General Tizzano delivered the Opinion on 30 June 2005 and the ECJ subsequently ruled that the successive reductions of the age above which the conclusion of a fixed-term contract is permissible without restrictions were justified by the need to encourage the recruitment of older persons in Germany.

5.24   The Advocate-General[19] took the view that it was open to a claimant to use the general principle of equality contained in EU law to challenge national rules. This principle requires that 'comparable situations must not be treated differently and different situations must not be treated in the same way unless such treatment is objectively justified' by the pursuit of a legitimate aim and provided that it 'is *appropriate and necessary* in order to achieve' that aim. The Advocate-General stated that under article 6.1, in order to determine whether a provision

19   Paras 84–85 of the Advocate-General's opinion.

constitutes age based discrimination there must be analysis of whether there is differential treatment. If so the court should ask whether it is justified by a legitimate aim and is appropriate and necessary in order to pursue that aim. The Advocate-General considered that the German law pursued a legitimate aim, aimed at enhancing the employability of unemployed older workers who, 'according to the official figures cited by the commission, have particular trouble finding new employment'. Where the German law, which allowed persons over 52 to be employed on fixed term contracts (whether or not they were previously unemployed), failed was that it was not an appropriate or necessary means of pursuing that aim. The measure went beyond what was necessary in order to enhance the employability of older workers. The legitimate aim could not be thrown into doubt[20]. However, the ECJ considered that although the member states have a broad margin of appreciation in respect of the means used to achieve the directive's aims, the means used in that case were not appropriate or necessary.

5.25   The court held that Community law, and, in particular, the age discrimination provisions in article 6(1) of the Framework Employment Directive 2000/78, precludes a provision of domestic law which authorises, without restriction, the conclusion of fixed-term contracts of employment once the worker has reached the age of 52 except where there is a close connection with an earlier contract of employment of indefinite duration concluded with the same employer. The court noted that article 6(1) provides that member states may provide that differences of treatment on grounds of age 'shall not constitute discrimination, if, within the context of national law, they are objectively and reasonably justified by a legitimate aim, including legitimate employment policy, labour market and vocational training objectives, and if the means of achieving that aim are appropriate and necessary'. The legislation in Germany introduced a difference of treatment on the grounds directly of age.

5.26   Although the purpose of the legislation was plainly to promote the vocational integration of unemployed older workers, which was a legitimate public interest objective, the means used to achieve that objective could not be regarded as appropriate and necessary.

5.27   The court held that 'observance of the principle of proportionality requires every derogation from an individual right to reconcile, so far

---

20 Judgment paras 59–60.

as is possible, the requirements of the principle of equal treatment with those of the aim pursued'.[21]

5.28   In *Mangold* the legislation resulted in a situation in which all workers who reached the age of 52, without distinction, whether or not they were unemployed before the contract was concluded and whatever the duration of any period of unemployment, could lawfully be offered fixed-term contracts of employment which could be renewed an indefinite number of times. Insofar as the legislation took the age of the worker concerned as the only criterion for the application of a fixed-term contract of employment, when it had not been shown that fixing an age threshold, as such, regardless of any other consideration linked to the structure of the labour market in question or the personal situation of the person concerned, was objectively necessary to the attainment of the objective of the vocational integration of unemployed older workers, it must be considered to go beyond what is appropriate and necessary in order to attain the objective pursued.[22] Such national legislation could not, therefore, be justified under article 6(1) of Directive 2000/78.[23]

5.29   It is against the light of that concept of justification that regulation 3 must be interpreted.

5.30   A very important part of the *Mangold* ruling is the remark that the principle of proportionality requires every derogation from an individual right to reconcile, so far as possible, the requirements of the principle of equal treatment with those of the aim pursued. The *Lommers* case demonstrates what is meant. There the ECJ considered a challenge to Dutch law under which nursery places were only available to the children of female civil servants save in cases of emergency when a male could apply for a nursery place for his child. The ECJ stated (para 39):

> Nevertheless, according to settled case law, in determining the scope of any derogation from an individual right such as the equal treatment of men and women laid down by the Directive, due regard must be had to the principle of proportionality, which requires that derogations must remain within the limits of what is appropriate and necessary in order to achieve the aim in view and that the principle of equal treatment be reconciled as far as possible with the requirements of the aim thus pursued (*Johnston*, paragraph 38; *Sirdar*, paragraph 26, and *Kreil*, paragraph 23).

5.31   In giving guidance to the national court on questions surrounding proportionality, the ECJ noted that the Dutch law, 'whose aim is to

21 Judgment para 65.
22 See, to that effect, case C-476/99 *Lommers* [2002] IRLR 430, para 39.
23 See [2006] IRLR 143 at para 64 ff.

abolish a de facto inequality, might nevertheless also help to perpetuate a traditional division of roles between men and women'. It then
went on to consider the view that 'if the aim of promoting equality of
opportunity between men and women pursued by the introduction of
a measure benefiting working mothers can still be achieved if its
scope is extended to include working fathers, the exclusion of men
from its scope would not be in conformity with the principle of proportionality'. It next took account of the insufficiency of nursery
places, the fact that female civil servants endured waiting lists and
that there was no guarantee of the female civil servants gaining a
place. The court made the point that the law 'does not have the effect
of depriving the male employees concerned, any more than other
female staff who have not been able to obtain a nursery place under
the nursery places scheme subsidised by the Ministry of Agriculture,
of all access to nursery places for their children, since such places
still remain accessible mainly on the relevant services market'. One
other factor considered was the fact that 'the measure at issue does not
totally exclude male officials from its scope but allows the employer to
grant requests from male officials in cases of emergency, to be determined by the employer'. The court went on to consider the situation
of male officials who are bringing up children on their own. The court
stated:

> In this respect, a measure which would exclude male officials who take care
> of their children by themselves from access to a nursery scheme sub-
> sidised by their employer would go beyond the permissible derogation
> provided for in Article 2(4), by interfering excessively with the individual
> right to equal treatment which that provision guarantees. Moreover, in
> relation to those officials, the argument that women are more likely to
> interrupt their career in order to take care of their young children no
> longer has the same relevance.

5.32   In *Lommers* there was an express derogation in article 2(4).[24] The court
in *Mangold*, in referring to the justification of direct discrimination
as a derogation from the principle of equal treatment clearly signifies
that the circumstances in which such justification can take place are
rare. If treated as a derogation from the principle of equal treatment,
the concept of justification for direct discrimination will need to be
construed narrowly.

---

24   The directive shall be without prejudice to measures to promote equal
opportunity for men and women, in particular by removing existing
inequalities which affect women's opportunities.

Justification of direct discrimination under the Age Regulations 2006

5.33 Regulation 3 provides that direct discrimination will be justified where the person accused of discriminating can show the treatment be a proportionate means of achieving a legitimate aim. The language of the Directive points to the intention that the justification of direct discrimination should rarely be available. In EU case-law, 'proportionate' is explained in terms of the measure being appropriate and necessary.[25] Thus an act which is based directly on age should be justified only where it can be shown that:

i) the action/treatment is given in pursuit of a legitimate aim;
ii) the treatment is a proportionate means of pursuit of that aim.

ACAS guidance

5.34 In this area it needs to be remembered that the ACAS guidance (or any other guidance available from the DTI, Employers' Forum on Age or other sources) has only persuasive effect. Strangely there are no provisions for the creation of a statutory code of guidance such as is found in race, sex or disability discrimination. It may be that in due course this role will be taken up by the Commission for Equalities and Human Rights.[26] However, that is still a long way off. In the meantime, ACAS and others have mirrored what was said in the consultation process, but is not reflected in the wording used in the regulations concerning justification of direct discrimination.

5.35 ACAS makes the point[27] that treating people differently because of their age will only be justifiable in exceptional circumstances, which it seeks to list. There are specific exceptions which are dealt with in the next chapter of this book, but it also stated:

> You may treat people differently on the grounds of their age if you have an objective justification. An objective justification allows employers to set requirements that are directly age discriminatory. Remember that different treatment on grounds of age will only be possible exceptionally for good reasons.

25 C-157/96 *R v MAFF, ex p NFU* [1998] ECR I-1211 and C-222/84 *Johnston v RUC* [1986] ECR 1651 Case C-144/04 *Mangold v Helm* (see para 65).
26 Provision in made under sections 14 and 15 of the Equality Act 2006 for a statutory Code.
27 In *Age and the workplace* (2006) p 30.

5.36   The respondent will need to provide real evidence to support any claim of objective justification. Assertion alone will not be sufficient and each case must be considered on its individual merits. Both direct and indirect discrimination will be justified if it is 'a proportionate means of achieving a legitimate aim'.

Legitimate aim

5.37   The ACAS guidance also tries to answer the question 'what is a legitimate aim?' by reference to suggestions made in the consultation process, but not drafted into the 2006 regulations. It suggests:[28]

What is a legitimate aim?

A legitimate aim might include:

- economic factors such as business needs and efficiency
- the health, welfare and safety of the individual (including protection of young people or older workers)
- the particular training requirements of the job.

A legitimate aim **must** correspond with a real need of the employer – economic efficiency may be a real aim but saving money because discrimination is cheaper than non-discrimination is not legitimate.

The legitimate aim cannot be related to age discrimination itself.

The test of objective justification is not an easy one and it will be necessary to provide evidence if challenged; assertions alone will not be enough.

5.38   These suggestions are useful guidance mirroring the way in which legitimate aims have been treated in justification in other areas of anti-discrimination law. Thus the ECJ in *Bilka Kaufhaus* provided a strict test for justification, requiring that measures 'correspond to a real need on the part of the undertaking, are appropriate with a view to achieving the objectives pursued and are necessary to that end'.[29] Economic factors such as business needs and considerations of efficiency may also be legitimate aims. However, discrimination will not be justified merely because it may be more expensive not to discriminate.[30]

---

28 *Age and the workplace* (2006) p31.

29 *Bilka Kaufhaus* [1987] ICR 110 at 36.

30 *Hill and Stapleton v The Revenue Commissioners and the Department of Finance* Case C243/95 [1999] ICR 48.

An aim which is tainted with any kind of discrimination or is otherwise unlawful should nullify the justification.[31]

EXAMPLE: The respondent imposes a rule that no staff may be over 35 because the clients with whom they are to work are younger than that and, the employer argues, there is an atmosphere in the hairdressing salon created by having a young group of staff.

5.39 Has the respondent demonstrated a real need? The aim being pursued is the maintenance of a 'young atmosphere' in the salon. Is that a legitimate aim? It is unlikely to be because it makes reference to an age related concept for the purposes of trying to justify age discrimination. The aim should be neutral as to age. However if the age related aim itself can be justified, such an age reference will be unobjectionable. In the salon example the employer's aim is profit by appealing to certain age related assumptions. That is unlikely to be a legitimate aim.

5.40 The DTI's initial public consultation *Age matters*, suggested such factors as:

- health and safety;
- the facilitation of employment planning;
- encouraging and rewarding loyalty;
- training requirements; and
- the need for a reasonable period of employment before retirement.[32]

5.41 These were said to be legitimate aims which might exceptionally justify directly discriminatory treatment. However these are simply examples and their appearance in the consultation document does not give them particular status. In any event some of them are hopelessly vague (such as workforce planning). Others, such as health and safety raise more problems than they solve.

---

31 The ECJ in the sex discrimination case of *Helga Kutz-Bauer v Freie und Hansestadt Hamburg* Case C-187/00 ECR 2003 Page I-02741 para 51 stated that where a purportedly indirectly discriminatory provision is said to be justified, the aims must be unrelated to any discrimination based on sex. The Consultation Paper gave the example of a retailer of trendy fashion items wanting to employ young shop assistants because it believes that this will contribute to its aim of targeting young buyers. Arguably trying to attract a young target group will not be a legitimate aim, because this has an age-discriminatory aspect built into it. Generally it must be right than a legitimate aim is legitimate in that there is no breach of any law involved in it!

32 UK Department of Trade and Industry, *Equality and Diversity: Age Matters* (London: DTI, 2003), para 3.15.

5.42   In *Hurley v Mustoe*[33] the EAT emphasised the danger of unsupported evidence about the characteristics of a particular class of person (there men with children) being considered by tribunals.[34]

Health and safety

5.43   The danger is that the employer will think that it is promoting health and safety as an aim, but in fact a series of assumptions have been made about the health and safety implications of being a particular age or over a particular age.[35] For example, as Age Positive points out:

> Health is influenced by many factors, particularly lifestyle, activity and nutrition. Although risk of illness or disease may increase with age, this is not always the case. In fact the good news is that the general health of older adults is improving, suggesting that the risk of certain diseases may be decreasing.

5.44   An employer who wishes to rely on health and safety to justify the withdrawal of a particular type of work on the basis of health risks related to age will have to have statistical evidence in support and major consequences resulting from the manifestation of the health risk before more serious forms of discrimination could be justified.[36]

33   [1981] ICR 490.

31   July 2003.

34   The Canadian Supreme Court case of *McKinney v University of Guelph* [1990] 3 SCR 229 illustrates an approach to employment planning and, arguably, some of the risks of assumptive thinking in this area. The court considered that the use of a mandatory retirement age in an academic field had (in the terms of the directive) a legitimate aim of continuing faculty renewal (in the context of a tenured system) and of ensuring that universities remain centres of excellence on the cutting edge of new discoveries and new ideas. The court therefore considered that the retirement age was in pursuit of a legitimate aim. Second, the SCC considered whether the impairment of the right to equality was minimally impaired [ie whether the interference was proportionate and necessary]. Caveat: how many of these 'justifications' are based on assumptions about the nature of young and old thought? Immanuel Kant, for example, produced his greatest (and ground breaking) philosophical tome *The critique of pure reason* very late in his life.

35   Age Positive issued *Age, health and employability – the facts, not the myths* on 28 July 2006 (available on Age Positive's website).

36   See *MacDonald v Regional Administrative School Unit No 1* (1992), 16 CHRR D/409 (PEI Bd Inq). There a Canadian Board of Inquiry upheld mandatory retirement of school bus drivers at age 65. Expert medical evidence indicated that, as a group, those over 65 are more likely to have accidents, and that it is impossible to test individually to determine who is likely to have health problems or create risks for others. This was a justification based on evidence relating to the age group.

5.45   More generally, it is often claimed that there are health risks connected with ageing and that capability and performance declines. One
economist conducting a review of literature for the DTI summarised
what the literature shows in the following way:

- 'The evidence suggests that, except in a very limited range of jobs,
  work performance does not deteriorate with age, at least up to the age
  of 70. Since few people are employed beyond that age, there is virtually
  no evidence about work performance after the age of 70.
- The positive effects on performance of experience, interpersonal skills,
  and motivation generally offset the adverse effects of loss of speed,
  strength and memory.
- Where performance does decline with age, the falling average scores
  for older people seem to be driven by the marked deterioration of a
  small number of individuals rather than by a decline across the whole
  cohort.
- Older workers have the same ability as younger workers to master
  new skills, but they learn more slowly and can be helped by different
  training methods.
- Employers may need to introduce new performance monitoring and
  management systems, which will add to business costs.'[37]

5.46   Arguments based on health and safety matters will therefore have to
be very specific. The claimant's adviser should ensure that the questionnaire seeks specifics of any claimed health and safety purpose
legitimation of discriminatory treatment. Arguments based on
productivity claims which are not properly evidenced will fail.

Facilitation of employment planning

5.47   The government's notes on the draft regulations purport to give some
content to 'workforce planning' in the context of retirement ages.[38] In
the explanatory memorandum the use of the default mandatory
retirement age is justified on the basis that:

> ... it provides a target age against which employers can plan their work –
> including the recruitment, training, and development of employees and the
> planning of wages structures and occupational pensions against a known
> attrition profile – and employees can plan their careers and make
> adequate plans for retirement.[39]

37 Pamela Meadows *Retirement ages in the UK: a review of the literature*, 2003
    Chapter 3.
38 Draft Employment Equality (Age) Regulations 2006, Notes on Regulations,
    para 100.
39 Employment Equality (Age) Regulations 2006, Explanatory Memorandum,
    para 7.10.

5.48   The aim of workforce planning, will arise principally in this context. It is very difficult to see how the mere fact that the employer wants to plan the workforce can justify very much as it is contentless. It could lead to unnecessary argument on whether the act was done for the purpose of employment planning. What appears to be indicated is age related employment planning – no doubt to alleviate the impact of having many people retiring at the same time on a pension fund or on a workforce is a legitimate aim. If the concept of facilitation of employment planning is left vague there is a risk that it will encourage assumptive thinking under its guise. The question is not whether an employer is planning employment, but what is the aim for which the employer is planning the workforce. It will be in relation to that aim that the discriminatory provision must be justified. Thus an employer might want to plan the workforce to retain the ones with the best memories. Underlying that may be an assumption that memory declines whereas:

> evidence demonstrates that any variation in brain functioning in older adults is not decreased function but simply different from younger adults. In fact mental functions can even improve with increased experience.[40]

Where an employer restricts recruitment to persons below a particular age, this may be justified by reference to the need to retain staff in that position for a reasonable period before retirement.

Encouraging and rewarding loyalty

5.49   Another of the suggested examples was 'rewarding loyalty'. Rewarding loyalty would not be a legitimate aim in and of itself however. The employer would have to be able to point to some other business benefit which he perceives to be fostered by loyalty.[41] Avoiding high turn over of staff might be a legitimate aim justifying, for example, the use of seniority. The employer would probably be able to produce objective evidence that a high turn over of staff affects staff morale and lowers productivity even in a low skilled work force.[41a]

---

40   *Age, health and employability – the facts, not the myths,* Age Positive, 2006.

41   See *Nikoloudi* Case C 196/02 [2005] ECR I-1789. There the ECJ remarked that length of service could reward loyalty when used in the context of access to benefits in a collective agreement. However, use of length of service will not be automatically justified by this aim.

41a See the length of service exemptions discussed at para 6.41 onward.

Examples from the Directive

5.50 Finally, the Directive gives an exemplar list of justified direct discrimination. These are:

(a) the setting of special conditions on access to employment and vocational training, employment and occupation, including dismissal and remuneration conditions, for young people, older workers and persons with caring responsibilities in order to promote their vocational integration or ensure their protection;

(b) the fixing of minimum conditions of age, professional experience or seniority in service for access to employment or to certain advantages linked to employment;

(c) the fixing of a maximum age for recruitment which is based on the training requirements of the post in question or the need for a reasonable period of employment before retirement.

5.51 The clear theme running through these directive examples is that steps aimed at aiding vocational integration related to age are to be permitted. Positive action can be justified on this basis as well as the other basis set out in the Directive.[42] A proportionate seniority related rewards structure may be maintained by a business in terms of access to benefits and conditions of access to benefits reflecting seniority may be set. Finally it is a legitimate aim that (whatever the retirement age is), the employer is permitted to refuse to take someone on who will need training the costs and time for which would be disproportionate to the amount of working time the employer could expect to obtain from the worker before retirement.[43]

The treatment is a proportionate means of pursuit of a legitimate aim

5.52 It is for the employer to identify a legitimate aim and to show that the treatment is a proportionate means of pursuing the legitimate aim.

5.53 ACAS explains that in order for treatment to be proportionate 'what you are doing must actually contribute to a legitimate aim, eg if your aim is to encourage loyalty then you ought to have evidence that the provision or criterion you introduce is actually doing so'. By the same token, claimants' advisers should seek such evidence by questionnaire answers and disclosure. The employer will have to possess some record

42 Reg 29 and Framework Directive article 7.
43 See chapter 8 for a discussion of reg 7.

or paper trail demonstrating that the PCP does actually encourage loyalty. The employer should be asked for any staff surveys that have been carried out to find out whether there is any evidence that a particular practice does contribute to the aim pursued.

5.54   The discriminatory effect of the treatment or PCP should be measured. The greater the number of people from the claimant's age group that are adversely affected by it, and the seriousness of its impact on any individual worker, the harder it will be for the employer to justify the provision, criterion of practice.[44] Has the employer taken account of the detriment to the employee and those in the same position as the employee? The employer's decision to treat an age group in a particular way may carry obvious detrimental consequences to all of the group as well as to the individual claimant. Is there any evidence that this impact was considered? Did the employer do anything to mitigate it? For example an employer decides that there should be a new retirement age below 65 (the previous one) and seeks to introduce it. There is no evidence that the employer has considered phasing in retirement for the group who in the immediate future will be required to retire. The requirement to retire may have altered the plans of members of that group who may wish to work longer because of financial constraints. The employer who provides nothing by way of mitigation of the impact is likely to be unable to justify the less favourable treatment that it represents.

5.55   The ACAS guidance states that to be proportionate, the discriminatory effect of the treatment or PCP should be significantly outweighed by the importance and benefits of the legitimate aim. The claimant should therefore in the questionnaire seek details:

a) of what legitimate aim or aims the Respondent claims the treatment or PCP furthered;

b) whether it is admitted that the treatment or PCP had a discriminatory effect either by resulting in less favourable treatment compared to another relevant person or a hypothetical person or placing persons from an age group at a disadvantage compared to persons not in that age group;

c) what were the benefits of the legitimate aim (unless these are obvious);

d) what evidence is there relating to the striking of a balance between the discriminatory effect and the alleged benefits of the aim.

44 See, for example, *London Underground Limited v Edwards* (No1) [1995] ICR 574.

> EXAMPLE: An example which demonstrates the process of bal-
> ancing impact against the employer's needs is *London Under-
> ground v Edwards (No1)*. The appellant was a single parent,
> working for the Underground as a train driver employed on a
> three-shifts-a-day system. She could meet her childcare respon-
> sibilities by shift swapping. Then a new roster system was intro-
> duced with longer shifts and extended over more days. The
> unsocial hours premium was also stopped. She was then given
> a choice of working under the new system or dismissal. She
> accepted voluntary severance because she could not work the
> new system and the Underground refused to guarantee that she
> could carry on shift swapping.
>
> On her complaint of sex discrimination the tribunal held that
> the Underground could not objectively justify the application of
> the new system. They could have made provision to cater for
> single parents without significant financial implications. In fact
> they had previously contemplated introducing a scheme for
> single parents, so it was clearly feasible.

5.56   The ACAS guidance states that the employer should have no reasonable
alternative to the action that is being taken to achieve the legitimate
aim. It states that if the aim can be achieved by less discriminatory
means, or by means that do not discriminate at all, these other means
should take precedence. Thus if the claimant is aware of other means
whereby the aim could be achieved the questionnaire should seek to
obtain the employer's reasoning (and evidence) as to why those other
means are not available or why they cannot be made available and used.

5.57   In the context of direct discrimination the case-law relating to indirect discrimination in other areas may provide some indication of how
the requirement of justification will be interpreted under regulation 3.
It is important to recall that the scope for justification of direct age
discrimination is intended to be narrow in that it is regarded as a derogation from the principle of equal treatment.[45]

5.58   The test is set out in the context of equal pay in *Bilka-Kaufhaus*:[46]

a) Do the grounds put forward by the employer explain the treatment
in question?

---

45 See the ECHR article 14 cases above at para 5.17 and *Mangold* above at para
5.17.
46 [1987] ICR 110 (at para 36).

b) Does the treatment decided upon correspond to a real need on the part of the undertaking?

c) Is the treatment appropriate with a view to achieving the objectives pursued and necessary to that end?

5.59   The UK courts have rejected the idea that this test means that the employer must show that the treatment is the only means of achieving the aim.[47] The tribunal must evaluate the justification offered by the respondent by seeking to establish whether it meets the *Bilka* test. In *Hampson v Department of Education and Science*[48] the House of Lords held that justification requires an objective balance between the discriminatory effect of the practice, provision or criteria and the reasonable needs of the employer.

5.60   Does the information put forward justify the treatment? The simplest example of whether the explanation would not justify the treatment would be where the employer is merely making a generalised assumption about people of a particular age group without any evidence. Often this will be an assumption about capability. If there is no evidence to support the asserted justification, the tribunal should simply reject it as incapable of providing justification.

> EXAMPLE: The respondent bus company introduces a rule that none of its bus drivers may be over 55. The aim of this rule is public safety. The respondent has come across statistics demonstrating that over the age of 55 there is an increased risk of heart attack. Is this a legitimate aim? Clearly. Pursuant to this rule the respondent dismissed the claimant with contractual minimum notice. The claimant loses all his pay and benefits and must look for another job. As against that discriminatory impact, the tribunal must consider whether dismissal was an appropriate and necessary means to achieve the aim of public safety. This will involve consideration of whether there was another way to achieve the aim.

---

47 *Barry v Midland Bank plc* [1999] ICR 319 (at page 336B) and see *Rainey v. Greater Glasgow Health Board* [1987] ICR 129 and *Webb v Emo Air Cargo* (UK) Ltd [1993] ICR 175.

48 (1989) IRLR 629.

5.61 It is suggested that the test requires as a minimum the critical evaluation of the issues.[49] In *Hardys and Hansons plc v Lax*[50] a woman became pregnant and requested to be allowed to work part-time or on a job share on return from maternity leave. This request was rejected. The employment tribunal found that there was no objective justification for refusing to allow the job to be split. The employers argued that they had a margin of discretion because the treatment had to be reasonably necessary. This meant, they argued, that the tribunal should simply consider whether their response fell within the band of reasonable responses. The Court of Appeal rejected this approach. It should be noted that although a band of reasonable responses might be an inappropriate test for the general test of justification, employers will seek to argue that it is an appropriate approach to the question of whether regulation 32 (justification of use of length of service) applies.[51]

5.62 The tribunal must make its own judgment upon a fair and detailed analysis of the working practices or the situation and business considerations involved. In constructing a questionnaire the claimant should seek to put in place the means of that analysis by seeking details of the working practices or any business considerations that have been mentioned during the course of the case. Thus the tribunal will have to make judgements on the alternatives available to the employer if the employer did not maintain the discriminatory practice.

EXAMPLE: In the bus driver example above, the bus company could be pressed to explain why medical checks could not be carried out more accurately so as to monitor for the risk of heart conditions over the age of 55. The tribunal will be interested in the robustness or validity of the employer's practices (for example, the frequency of medical checks).

5.63 The tribunal will be concerned to look at and evaluate the practical problems which may or may not arise from not engaging in the discriminatory treatment in the context of a particular business. The claimant should therefore be seeking to find out what practical

---

49 Ie has the employer demonstrated a real need or objective for the treatment or measure which is legitimate? If there was such a need, the seriousness of the discriminatory impact of the treatment or measure on the claimant, and whether the need for the treatment or measure is sufficient to outweigh the discriminatory impact on the claimant.

50 [2005] IRLR 668.

51 See chapter 6.

problems are being suggested arise out of a non-discriminatory alternative. How seriously would behaving in a non-discriminatory manner hamper the managerial discretion of the employer?

5.64   Employment tribunals must reflect the detail of their consideration in their judgements. An appellate tribunal or court will seek evidence from the judgment that the employment tribunal engaged in the proper evaluation of the justification. It must be clear from the decision that the tribunal has understood what the needs of the business are. Therefore, questionnaires should be used at an early stage in the proceedings to ascertain exactly what business needs are being asserted, what the details of them are and how they are said to justify. These are matters which otherwise spring out of a witness's mouth at a hearing, or after the case has progressed to disclosure (creating problems around seeking further disclosure for the claimant). It is better, it is suggested, that any reliance on business needs be firmly limited by use of the questionnaire procedure.

5.65   As we have seen, the employer cannot merely assert, without evidence, the existence of a legitimate aim or a policy which has been followed. The tribunal is entitled to evaluate that policy. The employer will not be able to plead ignorance of any discriminatory effect. There should be evidence[52] of the importance of the policy, practice or criterion to the employer and why it is necessary for the employer to have it. Again, this is a focus for scrutiny and the employer should be questioned about it in the questionnaire and made to disclose documents concerning it. Likewise the necessity for the policy to be constructed in the way it is or for the practice to be as it is should be investigated. The employer should produce evidence of why it was necessary to apply the treatment, or PCP to the claimant and others in the form or manner it was applied.

---

52   See *Whiffen v Milham Ford Girls' School* [2001] ICR 1023 at 1028: 'The generally accepted test for justification is set out in *Bilka-Kaufhaus GmbH v Weber von Hartz* (Case 170/84) [1987] ICR 110, the ratio of which is set out in *Staffordshire County Council v Black* [1995] IRLR 234, 237: 'the test is that set out in *Bilka-Kaufhaus GmbH*: namely is the difference in treatment based on objectively justifiable grounds: are the measures chosen appropriate to achieve the aims of the undertaking and are they necessary to achieve those aims?' Subsequent authorities have stressed the desirability (if not quite necessity) of there being evidence to establish these matters.'

Time at which justification is to be judged

5.66 Finally, the wording of the 2006 regulations in respect of justification permits after the event justifications[53] to be presented by the employer. Such arguments should receive careful scrutiny. The job of the respondent will have been made considerably more difficult if questions concerning justifications that were considered at the time and any other matters relied upon are asked. A tribunal will be sceptical at the least of an employer's justification in such circumstances.

Practical points concerning justification

1) The grievance should expressly challenge the question of justification.

2) Early and detailed use of the questionnaire procedure will ascertain the scope of the employer's defence and identify areas for subsequent disclosure.

3) Advisers should argue that the standard for justification of direct age (and indirect discrimination) discrimination requires the following elements to be considered and should structure disclosure around these points:

   a) What is the difference of treatment?/ What is the provision criterion or practice?

      i) how was the claimant treated/what is the age group concerned?

      ii) how was this worse treatment than an actual or hypothetical comparator/how is the age group intrinsically (or disproportionately) disadvantaged by the PCP?

   b) Is it based on age?/Is it age neutral?

      i) in the case of indirect discrimination how was the claimant disadvantaged?

   c) What has the respondent offered as the justification for the treatment/PCP?

      i) Is it possible to identify an objective for it?

      ii) Is the objective or aim a lawful one?

      • Is the aim tainted by other discrimination or illegality?

---

53 See from the field of equal pay, *Cadman v Health and Safety Executive* [2004] IRLR 971, CA and *British Airways v Starmer* [2005] IRLR 862, CA.

iii) If so, are the means adopted (PCP/treatment) to achieve that aim appropriate and necessary for the achievement of that aim?

- How does the treatment or PCP contribute to the achievement of the aim?
- What is the discriminatory impact of this PCP or treatment?
- Is there an alternative means available of achieving the aim of the employer which would have lesser a discriminatory impact?
- Is the aim sufficiently serious so as to outweigh the infringement of a fundamental individual right of the claimant to equal treatment?

CHAPTER 6

Exceptions to age discrimination

> **Key points**
> • The exceptions represent derogations from the principle of equal treatment and are therefore to be construed narrowly.
> • Individual exceptions are discussed below.
> • Use of an exception requires the employer to prove all elements of the exception.

Introduction

6.1   In this chapter we will look at the express exceptions contained in the Employment Equality (Age) Regulations 2006. These are derogations from the principle of non-discrimination and are to be construed narrowly. It should be recalled that the regulations provide for the justification of direct and indirect discrimination. These exceptions therefore are to be used by the employer as the first defence. The second will be that even if one of these exemptions does not apply, the treatment etc was a proportionate means of achieving a legitimate aim.

Partial exceptions from Parts 2 and 3

Recruitment over retirement age

6.2   If a person's age is greater than the employer's Normal Retirement Age (or in default 65) the employer may refuse to employ him or make discriminatory selection arrangements. If the person will reach that age within 6 months of the date of the job application, the employer may also treat him in these ways. This issue is developed in more detail in para 7.45 onwards.[1]

Genuine occupational requirements

6.2A   Certain provisions of Part 2 are limited by regulation 8 which provides:

> 8. (1) In relation to discrimination falling within regulation 3 (discrimination on grounds of age)–
>   (a) regulation 7(1)(a) or (c) does not apply to any employment;
>   (b) regulation 7(2)(b) or (c) does not apply to promotion or transfer to, or training for, any employment; and

---

1 Regulation 7(4).

(c) regulation 7(2)(d) does not apply to dismissal from any employment, where paragraph (2) applies.

(2) This paragraph applies where, having regard to the nature of the employment or the context in which it is carried out—

    (a) possessing a characteristic related to age is a genuine and determining occupational requirement;

    (b) it is proportionate to apply that requirement in the particular case; and

    (c) either—

        (i) the person to whom that requirement is applied does not meet it, or

        (ii) the employer is not satisfied, and in all the circumstances it is reasonable for him not to be satisfied, that that person meets it.

6.3   The directive provides by article 4:

Occupational requirements

1. Notwithstanding Article 2(1) and (2), Member States may provide that a difference of treatment which is based on a characteristic related to any of the grounds referred to in Article 1 shall not constitute discrimination where, by reason of the nature of the particular occupational activities concerned or of the context in which they are carried out, such a characteristic constitutes a genuine and determining occupational requirement, provided that the objective is legitimate and the requirement is proportionate.

6.4   It is suggested that this provision will be of limited application in employment, with most employers seeking to justify discrimination under the test set out in regulation 3. However it should be noted that it operates to render only the following lawful. Discrimination in relation to:

- arrangements made for determining to whom employment should be offered;[2] or
- refusing to offer, or deliberately not offering employment;[3] or
- in respect of promotion or transfer to or training for any employment;[4] or
- dismissal from any employment.[5]

2 Reg 7(1)(a).

3 Reg 7(1)(c).

4 Reg 7(2)(b) and (c). Note that it does not permit discrimination in relation to opportunities for receiving any other benefits.

5 Reg 7(2)(d).

It does not permit discrimination by way of 'other detriment' such as suspension. Arguably, any characteristic which is related to age will bring the GOR into play. It is suggested that characteristics which objectively can be shown to relate to age are scarce.

There is nothing in the Directive warranting the inclusion of the words 'the employer is not satisfied and in all the circumstances it is reasonable for him not to be satisfied' in regulation 8(2)(c)(ii). The question is an objective one rather than a 'band of reasonable responses' test.

General exceptions from Parts 2 and 3

Exception for statutory authority

6.5   Age requirements appear in a wide variety of legislation, for example, in relation to licence requirements. Parts 2 and 3 of the regulations do not render unlawful any act done in order to comply with a requirement of any statutory provision.[6] 'Statutory provision' means any provision (whenever enacted) of an Act or an Act of the Scottish Parliament, an instrument made by a minister of the Crown under an Act or an instrument made under an Act or an Act of the Scottish Parliament by the Scottish Ministers or a member of the Scottish Executive.

6.6   Similar provisions exist in other anti-discrimination legislation. However there are differences. Section 41(1)(c) of the Race Relations Act 1976 provides an exemption for any act of racial discrimination done '(c) in order to comply with any condition or requirement imposed by a Minister of the Crown (whether before or after the passing of this Act) by virtue of any enactment'. In *Hampson v Department of Education and Science*[7] the House of Lords considered Balcombe LJ's judgment in the Court of Appeal, Lord Lowry describing as apt the following:

> Similarly if a Minister of the Crown imposes a condition or requirement compliance with which could lead to racial discrimination – see section 41(1)(c) of the Act of 1976 – he can be made answerable in Parliament for his action. If what is done is not necessary to comply with a statutory requirement, then there can be no valid reason why it should not have to be justified before an industrial tribunal.[8]

6   Reg 27.
7   [1991] 1 AC 171; [1990] 3 WLR 42.
8   [1989] ICR 179 at 188.

6.7 The better view is that 'in order to comply with' means that the act complained of in its doing and in the way it was carried out, must have been one which was reasonably necessary in order to comply with any condition or requirement of the statute or order. This would include carrying out the duties or other necessary functions.[9] The House of Lords concluded that the words 'in pursuance of any instrument' in the context of section 41(1)(a) of the Race Relations Act 1976 were limited to those acts which are done 'in necessary performance of an express obligation contained in the instrument and do not also include acts done in exercise of a power or discretion conferred by the instrument'.

6.8 However Lord Lowry in *Hampson* stated that he did not quite accept the 'equiparation of the words "in pursuance of" with the phrase "in order to comply with"'.[10] Unfortunately no reasoning was given for this statement. In *Hampson* the House of Lords considered expressly the words 'in pursuance of', but the same reasoning applies to the words 'in order to comply with a requirement of any statutory provision' in regulation 27 of the Age Regulations 2006. Almost every discretionary decision of a statutory body is taken against a statutory background. However it is only those actions which are reasonably necessary in order to comply with a requirement that fall within the exemption. Note also that it must be a statutory *requirement*. Thus if there is an element of discretion anywhere in the process of compliance, the exemption will not apply.

6.9 Regulation 27 does not exempt acts of age discrimination done in order to further a statutory power. Moreover, the exemption applies where the act is done in order to comply. That means that the act is done with the purpose of complying with the requirement. The mere fact that there is a legislative requirement which could have justified the act does not exempt the act. The act must be carried out with the purpose of compliance. The directive permits member states to specify differences of treatment which are based on age but which are to be treated as justified in pursuit of a legitimate aim. Such statutory authorisations to discrimination on the grounds of age must be measured against that requirement of the directive. Where, therefore it is claimed that an act of age discrimination is committed in order to comply with a legislative requirement, regulation 27 should be construed narrowly.

9 See *GMC v Goba* [1988] ICR 885 at 894.
10 1990] 3 WLR 42 at 53.

6.10   A good example of a requirement of a statute is the requirement on the employer to afford minimum contractual notice. Employment Rights Act (ERA) 1996 s86(1)(b) provides that the notice required to be given by an employer to terminate the contract of employment of a person who has been continuously employed for one month or more is not less than one week's notice for each year of continuous employment if his period of continuous employment is two years or more but less than twelve years up to a ceiling of 12 weeks' notice.[11] The employer is obliged to give someone with seven years' service at least seven weeks' notice. If the contract is more generous than this, but bases length of notice on length of service, this will have to be justified under regulation 3.

6.11   The Save As You Earn (SAYE) legislation requires a participant in a share scheme to be able to exercise his option either:

a) when he retires at the specified age for the purposes of the plan which cannot be lower than 60 or higher than 75; or
b) at any other age at which the participant is 'bound to' retire in accordance with the terms of their employment.[12]

6.12   In order to comply with the SAYE legislation therefore the employer must permit the retiring employee to exercise their options. Other staff who are leaving before that date cannot complain that those retiring are permitted to exercise their options as this is permitted by the employer in order to comply with the legislation.

Exception for national security

6.13   There is an exemption for acts done for the purpose of safeguarding national security, if the doing of the act was justified by that purpose[13]. In the Sex Discrimination Act (SDA) 1975 and the Race Relations Act (RRA) 1976 there used to be provisions permitting the secretary of state to issue a certificate that an act was done for the purposes of

---

11 The 12-week ceiling may have to be justified by the UK, but probably can be.
12 The concept of being bound to retire is given further clarity by the retirement dismissal provisions. An employee is bound to retire in the sense of being obliged at the instance of his or her employer at the normal retirement age. That of course is a different concept from the contractual retirement age. However, if there is a contractual provision which constitutes the normal retirement age (see para 9.30) this will be the date at which the employee is bound to retire in accordance with the terms of their employment. A person whose contract does not set such a date will not be bound to retire in this sense.
13 Reg 28.

safeguarding national security. Such a certificate was said to be conclusive evidence of this fact. However, in *Johnston v Chief Constable of the RUC*[14] the European Court of Justice (ECJ) held that such opacity was incompatible with the principles of the Equal Treatment Directive.[15] The issue now under those Acts is the same as that under regulation 28: Does the aim of protecting national security justify the act in question?

6.14 The directive provides at article 2.5:

> 5. This Directive shall be without prejudice to measures laid down by national law which, in a democratic society, are necessary for public security, for the maintenance of public order and the prevention of criminal offences, for the protection of health and for the protection of the rights and freedoms of others.

6.15 Regulation 28 must therefore be construed in the light of this provision of the Directive. It mirrors the approach under the European Convention on Human Rights (ECHR) to qualified rights. The concept of public security, within the meaning of the treaty articles cited in the preceding paragraph, covers both a member state's internal security[16] and its external security.[17] In situations that relate to the safeguarding of national security, the legislature is to be afforded a wide area of judgment within which to strike a balance between competing considerations.[18] This may extend to the refusal of the state to provide information.[19]

14 Case 222/84 [1986] ECR 1651, IRLR 263.

15 76/207 EC, in particular article 6 requiring the states to introduce measures necessary to enable everyone who considers that they have been the subject of discrimination to bring a claim before the national courts.

16 See *Johnston* above.

17 See *Sirdar v Army Board* [2000] ICR 130 para 17 and Case C-367/89 *Richardt and 'Les Accessoires Scientifiques'* [1991] ECR I-4621, para 22, Case C-83/94 *Leifer and Others* [1995] ECR I-3231, para 26, and *Kreil (Social policy)* [2000] EUECJ C-285/98 [2000] ECR I-69, para 17.

18 *Leander v Sweden* [1987] 9 EHRR 433 at para 59, for example, and *Devenney v UK* [2002] 35 EHRR 24 at para 29. Note however that the right under regulation 28 is not now a procedural right bringing article 6 of the ECHR into play. The focus of the tribunal should be on the relationship of proportionality between the act done and the aim pursued.

19 See the discussion of the relevant principles in the context of a refusal by the Chief Constable to give disclosure of reasons for a vetting decision in *Chief Superintendent & Anor v Barracks* [2005] UKEAT 0394_05_1810, and see the discussion in the *Court of Appeal Barracks v Chief Superintendent & Anor* [2006] EWCA Civ 1041. The Court of Appeal pointed out that it was the Respondent's risk in the litigation if it did not produce its explanation for the discrimination allegation.

6.16   An employer may be faced with a situation in which it is told that it cannot employ a person as a result of national security considerations. Although it is anticipated that such a situation will be very rare in age discrimination cases, it is suggested that the employer will in all cases have to be able to justify the act as proportionate to the aim of safeguarding national security.[21]

6.17   Where there is a need to explore the facts underlying an assertion that an act of age discrimination was carried out in order to safeguard national security, a minister of the Crown may, if he considers it expedient in the interests of national security direct the tribunal to hear matters in private, exclude the claimant/claimant's representative from all or part of the proceedings, or take steps to conceal the identity of a particular witness.[22] However these powers are confined to Crown employment proceedings. Where such a direction has been given (or where the tribunal has taken the point of its own motion) the proceedings are dealt with under Schedule 2 to the employment tribunals rules of procedure. Where a claimant/representative has been excluded provision is made for a 'special advocate' to be appointed.[23]

6.18   More common will be the need to hold proceedings in private where it is alleged by a private employer that matters of national security are raised by evidence that has to be called to give the justification for an act of discrimination. In those circumstances the tribunal has power to hear evidence in private.[24]

Exceptions for positive action

6.19   The directive provides:

> Article 7 – Positive action
>
> 1. With a view to ensuring full equality in practice, the principle of equal treatment shall not prevent any Member State from maintaining

21 The difficulties that this presents for all parties can be seen from the discussion in the context of unfair dismissal in *B v BAA plc* [2005] UKEAT 0557_04_1905 (19 May 2005).
22 Rule 54 to the Employment Tribunal Rules of Procedure under the Employment Tribunals (Constitution and Rules of Procedure) Regulations 2004.
23 Rule 8 of Schedule 2 to the Employment Tribunals (Constitution and Rules of Procedure) Regulations 2004. Such a person is put in the strange position of not being able to communicate a great deal of information to the client or other excluded person without permission from the tribunal.
24 See rule 16(1)(a) of the Employment Tribunal Rules of Procedure under the Employment Tribunals (Constitution and Rules of Procedure) Regulations 2004.

or adopting specific measures to prevent or compensate for disadvantages linked to any of the grounds referred to in Article 1.[25]

6.20   The regulations do not do this. Instead of introducing specific measures to prevent or compensate for disadvantages linked to age discrimination, the regulations introduce a generic measure. However the article is permissive rather than mandatory.

6.21   The directive permits the proportionate use of age distinctions (to compensate for disadvantages) which should be deemed to be objectively justified if such measures are the result of 'specific measures ... introduced or adopted by a member state'.

6.22   Regulation 29(1) provides an exception for a limited form of positive action. Nothing in Part 2 or 3 renders:

> unlawful any act done in or in connection with–
> (a) affording persons of a particular age or age group access to facilities for training which would help fit them for particular work; or
> (b) encouraging persons of a particular age or age group to take advantage of opportunities for doing particular work;
>
> where it reasonably appears to the person doing the act that it prevents or compensates for disadvantages linked to age suffered by persons of that age or age group doing that work or likely to take up that work.

6.23   The regulation does seek to compensate for disadvantages linked to age discrimination. It does not permit positive discrimination. Regulations permitting positive discrimination would have been permissible under article 6 of the Directive.[26]

6.24   Measures such as 'New Deal' programmes, which have been available on different terms to the under-25s and over-50s, with the aim of integrating deprived and socially excluded groups into the workforce can be justified either as positive action measures or under article 6.1. There are upper age limits placed upon apprenticeships, student loans, or access to Jobcentre Plus and New Deal advice and training.[27]

---

25 The Commission's proposal (see chapter 2) required that equal treatment results in real equality. Thus equal treatment will also imply the recognition of special rights for specific groups of people.

26 Article 6(1)(a) makes it clear that the directive recognises that the promotion of vocational integration and the protection of vulnerable groups is a legitimate aim.

27 For a summary of how the positive action provisions operate under the directive see Colm O'Cinneide's *Thematic report: age discrimination and European law*, published by Office for Official Publications of the European Communities ISBN 92-894-9698-3.

6.25   The concept of positive action has been discussed in the context of sex discrimination on several occasions by the ECJ.[28] Some guidance can be obtained from these authorities but it is important to bear in mind that the age discrimination principles under the directive go very much further towards justifying specific measures of positive discrimination. With that warning in mind it is helpful to look at some of the cases.

6.26   In *Kalanke v Freie und Hansetadt Bremen*[29] a man attacked a German law to the effect that when considering an assignment to a position in a higher pay, remuneration and salary bracket, 'women who have the same qualifications as men applying for the same post are to be given priority if they are under represented'. Within each bracket there had to be 50% women, otherwise under-representation existed. The domestic court found that the man was equally well qualified as the successful woman and that she had received preference pursuant to the domestic law. The ECJ held that a national law which gave a specific advantage to women to improve their ability to compete on the labour market so as pursue a career equally was consistent with article 2(4) of 76/207/EC. Absolute and unconditional priority for appointment or promotion however on the facts went beyond the limits of the exception in article 2(4) and since there was no individual hardship rule limiting positive discrimination where 'unbearable hardship' to the male competitor was produced, the law was not consistent with article 2(4).

6.27   The ECJ has also held[30] that a similar selection criteria which had a saving clause[31] did not breach article 2(4). There needed to be an objective assessment of the candidates taking account of all the criteria specific to each. The criteria shifting the decision in favour of the tied man needed to be discrimination neutral.[32]

28 See *Kalanke v Freie Hansestadt Bremen*, Case C-450/93 [1995] ECR I-3051, *Marshall v Land Nordhein-Westfalen*, Case C-409/95, judgment of 11 November 1997 [1997]; ECR I-6363, *Badeck v Hessischer Ministerprasident* Case 158/97 [2000] ECR I 1875 and IRLR 432, *Abrahamsson v Fogelqvist* Case 407/98 [2000] ECR I-5539; [2000] IRLR 732, and *Lommers v Minister van Landbouw, Natuurbeheer en Visserij* C 476/99 [2004] 2 CMLR 49; [2002] IRLR 430 and the EFTA Court of Justice case of *EFTA Surveillance Authority v Norway* (E1/02) [2003] 1 CMLR 23; [2003] IRLR 318.

29 Case 450/93 [1995] ECR I-3051; [1995] IRLR 660.

30 *Marschall v Land Nordrheinwestfalen* Case 409/95 [1997] ECR I-6363; [1988] IRLR 39.

31 'Unless reasons specific to an individual candidate tilt the balance in his favour'.

32 See also *Badeck v Hessischer Ministerprasident* Case 158/97 [2000] ECR I-1875; [2000] IRLR 432.

6.28   In *Abrahamsson v Fogelqvist*[33] a Swedish rule requiring the appointment of a suitably qualified person from the under represented sex before a better qualified person of the other sex, 'unless the difference between the applicants' qualifications was so great that positive discrimination would be contrary to the requirement of objectivity in the recruitment process', failed because the 'scope and effect' of the savings clause could not be precisely determined. The selection of a candidate from among those who are sufficiently qualified was ultimately based on the mere fact of belonging to the underrepresented sex (even if the merits of the candidate are inferior to those of a candidate of the opposite sex). In the context of age such a selection process would have to be justified by reference to the proportionate pursuit of a legitimate aim. For that justification to succeed the basis for the application of the preferential rule would have to be clear. Proportionality is not simply achieved by a recitation that proportionality must be observed. A savings clause such as the one in *Abrahamsson* would provide no basis.[34]

6.29   In terms of the regulations, measures of positive *discrimination* can be justified if they are in pursuit of a legitimate aim and are a proportionate means of achieving that legitimate aim.[35] Whereas a strong argument can be made in most circumstances that the legitimate aim must be free of age discrimination, it is arguable that where the aim of the PCP or treatment is the achievement of substantive equality,[36] this is a legitimate aim.[37] The employer would have to be able to show that the means adopted to achieve this aim were proportionate.

6.30   If an employer is carrying out monitoring of the workforce by age, it may become apparent that there is an under representation of an age grouping within that workforce. Provided that the age grouping categories are rational ones, the employer may reasonably reach the conclusion that there is a need for training or encouragement of those within that age group. In judging whether the respondent reasonably believes 'that it prevents or compensates for disadvantages linked to age suffered by persons of that age or age group doing that work or

33   Case 407/98 [2000] ECR 1-5539; [2000] IRLR 732.

34   For further consideration of positive action under EC law see also *Lommers v Minister van Landbouw, Natuurbeheer en Visserij* [2004] 2 CMLR 49; [2002] IRLR 430, and *Schnorbus v Land Hessen* (C79/99) [2000] ECR I-10997.

35   See reg 3. Of course positive action under regulation 29 does not need such justification.

36   Such as measures aimed at the professional integration of young people.

37   See *Archibald v Fife Council* [2004] UKHL 32, [2004] 4 All ER 303 [2004] ICR 954; [2004] IRLR 651 at paras 60–61 judgment. *Coming of Age* included promotion of the employment of older workers as a legitimate aim.

likely to take up that work' the tribunal should bear in mind that it has to be able to identify the disadvantages linked to age. The respondent should be able to give some evidence that it has applied its mind to the point.

Trade organisations

6.31   Nothing in Part 2 or 3 makes unlawful an act done by a trade organisation[38] in or in connection with–

(a) affording only members of the organisation who are of a particular age or age group access to facilities for training which would help fit them for holding a post of any kind in the organisation; or

(b) encouraging only members of the organisation who are of a particular age or age group to take advantage of opportunities for holding such posts in the organisation,

where it reasonably appears to the organisation that the act prevents or compensates for disadvantages linked to age suffered by those of that age or age group holding such posts or likely to hold such posts.[39]

6.32   Further a trade organisation may do any act in or in connection with encouraging only persons of a particular age or age group to become members of the organisation where it reasonably appears to the organisation that the act prevents or compensates for disadvantages linked to age suffered by persons of that age or age group who are, or are eligible to become, members[40].

Exception for retirement

6.33   The exception for retirement is one of the most controversial aspects of the regulations and has been given a chapter dealing with the rather Byzantine choreography surrounding dismissal for retirement, the scope of the regulations prohibition on age discrimination and requests to carry on working.

6.34   The basic points to note about the provision is that regulation 30 applies in relation to an employee within the meaning of section 230(1) of the 1996 Act, a person in Crown employment, a relevant member of

---

38 See reg 18.

39 Reg 28(2)

40 Reg 28(3). Youth and Student recruitment will be permissible if the trigger criteria are satisfied therefore.

the House of Commons staff, and a relevant member of the House of Lords staff.[41]

6.35 This is an area in which the distinction between employees and workers may be of considerable importance. If a person is not an employee, the 'employer' will have to justify dismissal for retirement. If a person is an employee the employer may not have to justify dismissal for retirement.

6.36 Where there is a contract there will be mutual obligations between the parties. The irreducible minimum of obligation necessary to create a contract of service is some obligation on the employer to provide work and on the employee to do the work when offered.[42] A contract for services may exist simply on the basis of a letter of appointment appointing for a fixed term of three years, terminable on notice. If the letter of appointment indicates an obligation on the worker and provides an open ended opportunity to work during the term of the agreement that may be sufficient. The tribunal must assess whether there are such mutual obligations on the facts of each case.[43]

6.37 In the ordinary case the question is whether the employer is under an obligation to provide work and the worker to do it when offered.[44] However in order to determine whether there are mutual obligations it is necessary to see what obligations the worker undertakes. These may be generic or specific in nature, but both will be obligations forming the contract in response to the consideration offered by the employer. There will not be mutual obligations where the performance of duties under the contract are neither personal nor compulsory.

6.38 If it is established that the person who was dismissed from the contract is an employee, then consideration needs to be given to whether the age discrimination provisions in Parts 2 or 3 apply to render unlawful the dismissal of a person at or over the age of 65 where the reason for the dismissal is retirement. Regulation 30(2)

41 Reg 30(1). It does not apply therefore to a person who engages in a contract for services. The 'retirement' of such persons is governed by regulation 3 and must be justified as the pursuit of a legitimate aim.

42 See *Carmichael v National Power plc* [1999] 1 WLR 2042; 1999] ICR 1226; [2000] IRLR 43 where the House of Lords approved the approach of the Court of Appeal in *Nethermere v Gardiner* [1984] IRLR 240 and *Clark v Oxfordshire Health Authority* [1998] IRLR 125.

43 See *Younis v Trans Global Projects Limited* [2005] UKEAT 0504/05/0212 and see *Byrne Brothers v Baird* [2002] ICR 667, *Stephenson v Delphi Diesel Systems Ltd* [2003] ICR 471 paras 10–14 and *A D Bly Construction Ltd v Cochrane* (UKEAT 0243/05/MAA).

44 See *Mingeley v Pennock & Ivory* [2004] IRLR 373, para 14.

provides that Parts 2 and 3 do not apply where the reason for dismissal is retirement. However the determination of what the reason for the dismissal is in this context is determined by regulation 30(3). This provides that whether or not the reason for a dismissal is retirement shall be determined in accordance with sections 98ZA–98ZF of the 1996 Act. The details of this process are explored in chapter 9.

Exception for the national minimum wage

6.39   There is an exemption for the national minimum wage. A relevant person[45] ('A') may be remunerated in respect of his work at a rate which is lower than the rate at which another relevant person ('B') is remunerated for his or her work where–

a) the hourly rate[46] of the national minimum wage for a person of A's age is lower than that for a person of B's age; and

b) the rate at which A is remunerated is below the single hourly rate for the national minimum wage prescribed by the secretary of state under section 1(3) of the National Minimum Wage Act 1998.[47]

6.40   There is an exemption for discrimination against an apprentice[48] who is not a relevant person in so far as the apprentice may be remunerated in respect of his work at a rate which is lower than the rate at which an apprentice who is a relevant person is remunerated for his work.[49] In

---

45   'Relevant person' means a person who qualifies for the national minimum wage (whether at the single hourly rate for the national minimum wage prescribed by the secretary of state under National Minimum Wage Act 1998 s1(3) or at a different rate).

46   The hourly rate is prescribed in regulation 11 of the National Minimum Wage Regulations 1999 SI 584 and that rate has most recently been amended by regulation 2 of the National Minimum Wage Regulations 1999 (Amendment) Regulations 2005 SI No 2019.

47   Reg 31(1).

48   By regulation 31(3) 'apprentice' means a person who is employed under a contract of apprenticeship or, in accordance with regulation 12(3) of the National Minimum Wage Regulations 1999 SI No 584, is to be treated as employed under such a contract. The NMW Regs 1999 were amended by SI 2000 No 1989 and SI 2004 No 1930. Thus those employed under National Traineeships, Modern Apprenticeships, Foundation Modern Apprenticeships or Advance Modern Apprenticeships are included as apprentices. See *Flett v Matheson* [2006] EWCA Civ 53. More generally on apprentices see *Dunk v George Waller and Son Ltd* [1970] 2 All ER 630, *Wallace v C A Roofing Services Limited* [1996] IRLR 435, *Thorpe v Dul & Ors* (No 1) [2003] ICR 1556, *Whitely v Marton Electrical Ltd* [2003] ICR 495.

49   Regs 31(2).

other words apprentices who are not entitled to the National Minimum Wage may continue to be paid at a lower rate than those that are entitled.

Exception for provision of certain benefits based on length of service

6.41 There are two types of exception to the anti age discrimination scheme relating to benefits based on length of service:[50]

a) *less than five years' service:* the employer ('A') can put any worker ('B') at a disadvantage compared to another worker ('C') in relation to the award of a benefit by A, to the extent that the disadvantage is suffered because B's length of service is less than that of C the comparator.[51]

b) *length of service exceeding five years:* If B's service exceeds five years, A must have a reasonable belief that the way in which he uses the length of service criterion in relation to the award in question fulfils a business need of the undertaking.[52]

6.42 The consequences of this exception are that the employer may discriminate in relation to the opportunities for gaining the benefit on the basis of age between workers. The role of the reasonable belief criteria in relation to persons with more than five years' service presents certain difficulties. First, this exception is a derogation[53] from the principle of equal treatment and as such is to be construed narrowly. Therefore the tribunal in considering whether the belief of the employer was reasonable will have to apply a high standard of scrutiny to whether it reasonably appeared to the employer that the way in which he uses the length of service criterion in relation to the award in question fulfils a business need of the undertaking. However, second, it is clear that this test requires the tribunal to make a judgment on what appeared to A to be the case at the time A decides to use the criterion of length of service in relation to the award of a benefit to workers.[54] It is therefore a time sensitive test. It will not be open to the employer to assert

---

50 In reg 32.

51 Reg 32(1).

52 Reg 32(2).

53 Under article 6.1 of the directive.

54 See reg 32(3). A has to use one of two methods of calculation of length of service at the time A decides to apply the length of service criterion to access/ enjoyment of a benefit.

the exception without having applied some thought at the time of the application of the differential treatment. Third it is a test which relates to the justification of the use of length of service in relation to a particular award to categories of staff. Although it is time sensitive, A will not have to justify the difference in treatment between specific workers which may arise as a result of the application of the criterion.[55]

On 3 October 2006 the ECJ ruled that length of service as a factor in calculating pay could be justified although it discriminated indirectly on grounds of sex against women. It pointed out however that length of service is a surrogate for increasing skill at the job coming with experience. Where the woman could show that there was doubt whether length of service correlated to increased skill etc, the employer would have to justify the use of length of service as a factor resulting in unequal pay. Similarly where the use of length of service over compensates older workers, because they do not in fact get proportionately more skilled with longer service, the younger (shorter served) employees will be able to challenge the use of length of service as unreasonable (and so not falling within this exception) and not objectively justified (so that regulation 3 does not justify their treatment).

6.43   The ACAS code (which is not a statutory code and so only has persuasive value) suggests:

> In order to meet these requirements employers would need evidence from which they can conclude there is a benefit to the organisation. This could include information the employer might have gathered through monitoring, staff attitude surveys or focus groups for example.[56]

6.44   It is suggested that this approach is correct. In order to raise an objective justification for discrimination it is necessary for the employer to produce some evidence that the treatment was a proportionate means of achieving a legitimate aim.[57] The same approach should hold good where the employer seeks to rely on an exception. Without such a level of scrutiny it would be possible for the exception to be abused by employers. The approach is also consistent with the narrow construction of exceptions as derogations from an individual right to equal treatment.

---

55 This approach is consistent with the Advocate-General's in *Cadman v HSE* C17/05, opinion delivered 18 May 2006 at para 49.

56 *Age and the workplace* p32. See appendix E.

57 See chapter 5.

6.45   'Benefit' does not include any benefit awarded to a worker by virtue of his ceasing to work for A. The ACAS guidance points out that the exception does not cover contractual redundancy benefits.[58] Clearly redundancy payments are benefits awarded to a worker by virtue of his or her ceasing to work for A. Less clear is the case of notice payments. On one reading, they are payments paid by virtue of ceasing to work for A, but on another reading they are payment for work done during the notice period. Payments in lieu of notice, on the other hand, are payments clearly made by virtue of ceasing to work for A. The better view is that such lieu payments are made by virtue of the worker ceasing to work for A. The cause of their payment is ceasing to work for A. The length of notice itself will be a benefit falling under this exception.

Methods of calculating length of service

6.46   There are two ways of calculating the worker's length of service in these circumstances open to A. A can either calculate:

a) the length of time the worker has been working for him doing work which A reasonably considers to be at or above a particular level (assessed by reference to the demands made on the worker, for example, in terms of effort, skills and decision making); or
b) the length of time the worker has been working for him in total.

6.47   On each occasion on which he decides to use the criterion of length of service in relation to the award of a benefit to workers, it is for A to decide which of these definitions to use to calculate their lengths of service.[59] There should therefore be a paper trail demonstrating this decision making process. If there is not, a tribunal will be in a position to infer that this exception does not apply and if necessary that the attempt to use it constitutes unjustified indirect discrimination. This means that the claimant should immediately ask about this decision in the

---

58 See *Age and the workplace* (2006) p34. Reproducerd at appendix E.
59 Reg 32(3). This raises very difficult issues akin to those raised by equal value claims of the assessment of the particular level of work by reference to the demands made on the worker for example in terms of effort skills and decision-making. However, the method mentioned is merely indicative, and the employer simply has to be able to show that his view that the worker is at that particular level is a reasonable one. Mercifully the mechanism for assessment of equal value has not been applied in this context, but this provision is likely to give rise to confusion. It is likely therefore that employers will opt to use the second method in many cases.

questionnaire in any case which may involve differentiation on the basis of length of service in relation to benefits. As there is a risk in any case that the employer will have chosen the first more complex method of differentiating between workers, the questionnaire should ask for details (should that be the case) of what work B or C have been doing and the factual basis on which A considers that work to be at or above a particular level. The questionnaire should seek details of any assessment by A by reference to the demands made on the worker. A may have conducted an analysis based on effort, skills and decision making, so the questionnaire should verify the method used and ask in particular for any details of the assessment based on effort, skills or decision making.

6.48   For the purposes of this calculation of the length of time a worker has been working for A:[60]

a) A must calculate the length of time in terms of the number of weeks during the whole or part of which the worker was working for A;

b) A may discount any period during which the worker was absent from work (including any period of absence which at the time it occurred was thought by A or the worker to be permanent) unless in all the circumstances (including the way in which other workers' absences occurring in similar circumstances are treated by A in calculating their lengths of service) it would not be reasonable for him to do so;[61]

c) A may discount any period of time during which the worker was present at work ('the relevant period') where:

   i) the relevant period preceded a period during which the worker was absent from work; and

   ii) in all the circumstances (including the length of the worker's absence, the reason for his absence, the effect his absence has had on his ability to discharge the duties of his work, and the way in which other workers are treated by A in similar

60 Reg 32(4).
61 This will raise issues particularly in cases involving disability questions. The employer may owe a duty to make reasonable adjustments in respect of the absence of a disabled person and will be under a duty to make a reasonable assessment (including making reasonable inquiries of the disabled person) of what adjustments the disabled person needs.

circumstances) it is reasonable for A to discount the relevant period.[62]

6.49   If an employer has a rule which permits it to discount any period of time during which the worker was present at work preceding a period during which the worker was absent from work, this rule may be rendered void by paragraph 4 of Schedule 3A to the Disability Discrimination Act (DDA) 1995. This provides that 'any rule made by an employer for application to all or any of the persons who are employed by him or who apply to be, or are, considered by him for employment' is void where the rule is included in furtherance of an act which is unlawful by virtue of Part II of the DDA 1995 or where the rule provides for the doing of an act which is unlawful by virtue of Part II of the DDA 1995. It is suggested (modestly) that it would not be reasonable for A to have a rule which contravened the DDA 1995 in this way. Similarly if the way in which the 'impact on abilities' consideration operated was discriminatory in some other way, it would not be reasonable for A to discount the time preceding the absence.

6.50   There is a danger that employers will seek to exclude benefit differentials which are based on discounted lengths of service in situations where an element of discrimination has entered into the calculation of the length of service. The questionnaire should in appropriate cases seek to find out how any discounting has occurred. Since this may not be obvious from the outset it is recommended that the questionnaire include such questions where there is any doubt as to how the length of service has been calculated.

Continuity of service between employers

6.51   For the purposes of calculating the total time the worker has worked for A (method b) above), a worker shall be treated as having worked for A during any period during which he worked for another if:

a) that period is treated as a period of employment with A for the purposes of the Employment Rights Act (ERA) 1996 by virtue of the operation of ERA 1996 s218;[63] or

---

62 Reg 32(4). The provision in reg 32(4)(c) raises extremely difficult issues which are explored below.
63 The provisions dealing with the effect of a change of employer on continuity of employment.

b) were the worker to be made redundant[64] by A, that period and the period he has worked for A would amount to 'relevant service' within the meaning of section 155 of that Act.[65]

Workplace benefits

6.52   A great deal of concern has been expressed by some in the run up to the introduction of the Regulations concerning a variety of workplace benefits which are based on length of service. The type of benefits which are regularly affected by length of service will include:

- incremental salary scales;
  - salary based on age for young workers;
  - extra days of holiday;
  - notice periods;
  - amount of contractual sick pay;
  - leave of absence;
  - bonuses for long service;
- certain share scheme provisions.

6.53   Once the claimant ('C') has more than five years' service, C may challenge the use of incremental salary scales, leave of absence, sickness schemes, additional holiday regimes, and the other matters on the basis that they indirectly disadvantage his age group. Taking pay as an example, C can argue that incremental schemes are intrinsically liable to disadvantage his age group. The employer would have to be able to show that it had a reasonable belief that the way in which it uses the length of service criterion in relation to pay fulfils a business need of the undertaking. Perhaps the encouragement of loyalty will be cited. There is a danger, however, that age discriminatory attitudes of the workforce the expectation that pay rises with seniority are what

---

64   Ie dismissed for redundancy within the meaning of ERA 1996.

65   In relation to any person to whom the Redundancy Payments (Continuity of Employment in Local Government, etc) (Modification) Order 1999 SI No 2277 (as amended) applies, section 155 has effect as if continuity was measured as 'employed in relevant service'. In this context 'relevant service' means one of two things. First it can mean continuous employment by an employer specified in the Redundancy Payments (Continuity of Employment in Local Government, Modification Order 1999 (Sch 2). Alternatively it if immediately prior to the relevant event a person has been successively employed by two or more local government employers (specified in Sch 2 Pt II), such aggregate period of service with such employers as would be continuous employment if they were a single employer. It does not matter therefore whether the employee is a local authority worker, the same rules for calculation of continuity apply.

create the danger of disloyalty should the employer not maintain the length of service related pay structure. If all that was available was objective regulation 3 justification there would be a risk that such pay schemes could not be justified without reference to a discriminatory aim. Incremental salary scales will probably fall under this exception, depending on the size of the increments at particular points on the scale. The employer will bear the burden of showing a reasonable opinion that such pay increases reflect a level of experience, encourage loyalty, or maintain motivation (without reference to a discriminatory aim). In the context of incremental pay increases, the advocate-general recently noted that:

> A provision working to the disadvantage of younger or older workers, neutral on its face, could also constitute indirect discrimination based on age. In the present case, although the question has not been raised by the referring court, it is not inconceivable that recourse to the length-of-service criterion in a pay system could, in certain circumstances, lead to indirect discrimination on grounds of age. Inherent in the concept of indirect discrimination is a requirement that there should be a substantive notion of equality.[66]

6.54 The employer's use of the criterion of length of service in relation to any particular pay award will therefore be subject to a test of reasonableness. If all that the increments are doing is giving greater pay to those with greater service, without regard to the relevance of the experience or skills this gives them, there will need to be some evidence that the payment can reasonably be believed by the employer to affect loyalty. The level of evidence that will satisfy this test will not be very high. However, it must be doubted whether it would be a legitimate business

---

66 *Cadman v Health and Safety Executive* C15/05 at para 23. On 3 October 2006 the ECJ departed from the Attorney-General's recommended answer to the specific questions before it concerning equal pay. However it did not deal with this point. The formulation of the exception in the Regulations means that if a worker can show reason to doubt that length of service corresponded to increased skill at the job, the employer will have to show that its use of length of service for the category of employee in question was a reasonable use. If it cannot do that it will have to justify use of the length of service as a criterion in pay as a proportionate pursuit of a legitimate aim. In doing so it will not be able to rely on a general justification of the use of length of service. It will have to show that in relation to the specific job, using length of service justified the particular pay differential arising from it. So if a person does a job where the level of skill and ability at 5 years is the same as that at 15 years, it will be difficult to justify a very great pay difference purely on the 10 year difference in service. Employers will probably seek to justify on the basis of rewarding loyalty.

need to maintain the discriminatory expectations of the workforce. The employer will therefore need to look at why the workforce think that the incremental differentiation of two people doing the same relatively skilless job is important. If there is evidence that the workforce believe that the greater the length of service the greater the skill or knowledge this may be sufficient.

6.55   The second area of concern[67] was that of differential pay for young workers. This practice will almost certainly be captured by the five-year rule, which does not require further justification. In the very few cases where there is a direct age condition built into the terms and conditions of an employee whereby it might be possible for the worker to have more than five years' service and yet have less favourable pay, it is very difficult to see what business needs could justify the practice. Objective justification would probably not be available either. This is because the rationale for a young person's pay differential will be connected to the acquisition of skills. In almost every job the relevant skills would be acquired in the first five years.

The exemption on length of service for pay does not cover all potential areas of indirect discrimination in pay arrangements. Many pay systems have the effect of treating workers of different ages unequally, even if they are not based on age or length of service. For example performance-related pay schemes are often linked to length of service, as workers are usually eligible for a maximum annual increment. This means that only long-serving employees can be eligible for the higher salaries within a pay band. Another potential area of indirect discrimination is the widespread practice of matching a new recruit's previous salary. Since people in their 40s tend to be paid more than people in their 20s this could result in indirect discrimination. In both these examples, employers might well be able to offer objective justifications. However in these cases they would need to meet the full test of proportionality rather than the easier test designed for justifying service-related pay arrangements. If the experience of equal pay on grounds of gender is anything to go by, this could be an area of extensive and complex litigation.

6.56   Slightly different considerations may apply to notice periods. These may fall within the statutory exception (above) if they simply mirror the minimum statutory notice requirement. Most employers are more generous. They may allow increasing periods of notice depending on length of service. If the notice period is treated as a

---

67 Expressed in consultation by the Engineering Employers' Federation.

benefit (for example because payments are made during it or because the employee is allowed time off during it to look for other work), it is likely to be treated as one which is awarded on the worker ceasing to work for A. In those circumstances the exception for benefits based on length of service will not apply and the length of the notice period must be justified under regulation 3. Even if the notice period is not treated as a benefit awarded by virtue of the worker ceasing to work for A, once over five years C can challenge these as indirectly discriminatory to those of C's age group having shorter service than others doing the same job. What is the employer's justification for maintaining the differential? The need for staff retention, ironically, is probably the key, whether it is to be justified under regulation 3 or the exception. If the employer provides the same notice (or conceivably a merits-based system of notice) to people doing the same job, it can be argued that this means that employees have less job security and hence will feel less loyal to the employer. However without any staff opinion being sought on the matter the employer may have to resort to other means of proving the business need (or legitimate aim) on which to base a reasonable opinion that having differential notice periods based on length of service will retain staff (or to demonstrate that a legitimate aim is being pursued proportionately). The difficulty with all of these arguments is of course that the differential may make more junior staff feel under-valued for doing the same work. An employer would have to balance those two considerations. Finally, the payment of pay in lieu of notice would have to be justified under regulation 3 in any event as it is clearly paid by virtue of the worker ceasing to work for A.

6.57　　How should the employer approach the justification of length of service-based benefits? It is suggested that an objective justification should be sought first under regulation 3. If the employer can justify the use of length of service as a proportionate means of achieving a legitimate aim, no question of discrimination will arise. However if that cannot be done, and the length of service criteria involves service over five years in length, the employer will need to conduct an analysis of the relevant terms and conditions identifying:

a) the role that length of service plays in the allocation of the benefit;
b) the business need that this fulfils – identifying whether that need involves any discrimination itself or not;
　　i) if the business need discriminates in any way the exception will not apply;
　　ii) if the business need does not discriminate how exactly does the

use of length of service relate to the business need? The employer will need at this point to gather evidence of the way in which:

- the benefit affects the workforce (for example in terms of loyalty);
- the benefit recognises (and if so how this is relevant) experience and/or skills;
- the differential in benefit impacts on the age groups within the workplace.

c) the way in which the evidence gathered justifies, in the opinion of the employer, the continued use of the differential length of service in allocation of the benefit. The more objective the opinion can be made the more likely it is to withstand scrutiny from a tribunal whose view of its reasonableness will be tempered by the discriminatory impact the use of the criterion has on the disadvantaged age group.

6.58   The fact that the employer has a paper trail dealing with the reasoning process leading to the reasonable belief will suggest that the opinion is a reasonable one and should be recommended as good practice.

6.59   Slightly different considerations may apply in relation to share schemes. These benefits may affect people during or after their employment. A period longer than five years under the statutory Save as You Earn Plan ('SAYE') and a period longer than 18 months under the statutory Share Incentive Plan ('SIP') is not permitted. The use of length of service in relation to such schemes will generally involve justification of use of length of service over five years. In other words the employer would have to demonstrate their value in relation to a business need and that the opinion that they furthered that need was reasonable. The same is true of any of the length of service requirements relating to share benefits which are not covered by the exception for statutory authority[68]

---

68   Further detail on the issue of the treatment of shares is beyond the scope of this book. However, see the extremely useful analysis *Age discrimination and employee share schemes* by Nicholas Stretch, CMS Cameron McKenna and PLC Pensions and Incentives available, on subscription, at http://employment. practicallaw.com/8-203-8766?item=8-203-8766 (homepage:http://employment. practicallaw.com/main.jsp).

Exception for provision of enhanced redundancy payments to employees

6.60 There is an exception for the provision of enhanced redundancy payments to employees. ACAS states that because the statutory redundancy scheme will not substantially change (except in respect of the years worked when an employee was below 18 or over 64), both the statutory authority exemption and regulation 33 make it clear that, even though statutory redundancy payments are calculated using age-related criteria, such payments are lawful.

> The exemption linked to statutory redundancy payments is for an employer who wants to make more generous redundancy payments than under the statutory scheme. It allows the employer to use one of the methods specified, based on the statutory redundancy scheme, to calculate the amount of redundancy payment. An employer can use a different method of their own to calculate the amount of redundancy payment, but if it is based on length of service and if an employee brings a discrimination claim under the regulations, the employer will have to objectively justify it insofar as age discrimination arises.[69]

6.61 The exception applies in the following way. It is lawful under the regulations Parts 2 and 3 for an employer:

a) to give a qualifying employee[70] an enhanced redundancy payment which is less in amount than the enhanced redundancy payment which he gives to another such employee if both amounts are calculated in the same way;

b) to give enhanced redundancy payments only to those who are qualifying employees because either they are volunteers in a redundancy situation who would have been eligible for a redundancy payment had they been dismissed, or to those who have been dismissed.[71]

---

69 *Age and the Workplace* pp33–34.
70 'Qualifying employee' means – (a) an employee who is entitled to a redundancy payment by virtue of section 135 of the 1996 Act (the worker is dismissed by reason of redundancy or laid off or kept on short time so as to give rise to a right to a redundancy payment); (b) an employee who would have been so entitled but for the operation of section 155 of that Act (two years' employment); (c) an employee who agrees to the termination of his employment in circumstances where, had he been dismissed he would have fallen into one of these two categories.
71 Or a lay off/short time situation giving rise to a right to a redundancy payment.

6.62   However, the amount must be calculated in accordance with ERA 1996 s162 which provides that the redundancy payment must be calculated by determining the number of years the employee has been continuously employed by reckoning backwards from the date of the dismissal.[72] The employer must then award 'the appropriate amount'. However, where the employer intends to pay an enhanced redundancy payment, there is no limit on the amount that may be allowed for a week's pay,[73] and he may multiply the appropriate amount allowed for each year of employment by a figure of more than one. Thus the employer could decide to award one months' pay for each completed year of continuous service. The employer would be entitled to differentiate between the age groups in employment by applying the same age differential approach as is found in the statutory redundancy scheme as amended. In other words, the employer must calculate the redundancy payment thus using one month's pay rather than one week's pay:

a) one and a half months' pay for a year of employment in which the employee was not below the age of 41;

b) one month's pay for a year of employment below 41, in which he was not below the age of 22; and

c) half a month's pay for a year of employment in which the employee was below 22.

The employer may then apply a multiplier to the resultant figure.

EXAMPLE: To take a simple example:
The employer decides to pay a week's actual pay of £300 for each continuous year worked. Employee A who is 46 has worked 4 years. The employer must calculate A's enhanced redundancy payment by applying a multiplier of 1.5 to each of those continuous years (ie, 4 x 1.5 x 300). At the end of that process the employer may apply a multiplier of eg 2.

Employee B is 36 and has worked 4 years also on £300 per week. B's enhanced redundancy calculation would be 4 x 1 x 300 x 2.

---

72 The date the termination takes effect is used in relation to a person who has volunteered for redundancy for this purpose (reg 33(5)).

73 The amount of a week's pay is currently capped under the ERA s227 at £290 see SI 2005 No 3352.

> Finally any years in excess of 20 continuous years of employ-
> ment are to be ignored.[74] So C who is 65 has worked 25 years
> for the company and is also on £300 per week. C's redundancy
> payment would be based on 20 x 1.5 x 2.

6.63   The only aspect that is permitted to disadvantage a person by reference to age, is the application of the multiplier mirroring the statutory redundancy scheme. It would not be permissible to differentiate
in terms of the other variables of calculation on the basis of age.

6.64   Some redundancy schemes do not have the differential structure
used by the statutory scheme. In these schemes the employer will pay
a package based purely on length of service and salary. There will be no
multiplier differentiating between age groups. Such packages will
have to be objectively justified under regulation 3. They are less explicitly discriminatory, as they are not based on age banding. They do,
however, contain an element of indirect discrimination requiring justification. A legitimate aim may be available for their use. They probably further loyalty, particularly during economically difficult times
for the employer. At such times a more generous redundancy package
may lessen the risk of those who can leave early for an employer with
better prospects. The question for the tribunal in such cases will be
whether their use was proportionate considering that both the long
served and short served employee are being made redundant. Both
might have important jobs to do in the workplace and there may be a
question as to the rationality of awarding more money irrespective of
the importance of the job being done by the employee. Employers
using such schemes should be able to demonstrate that the aim and the
proportionality of the use of the enhancement has been considered.

Exception for provision of life assurance cover to retired workers

6.65   Sometimes a worker retires early due to ill health. Certain ill health
schemes involve the employer continuing to provide life assurance
cover for that worker. Such workers will not, in fact retire either at any
normal retirement age or the age of 65 as they have already done so.
Under regulation 34 an employer is allowed to stop providing life
cover when the worker reaches the age at which he would have retired
had he not fallen ill (ie the normal retirement age or the age of 65).

74   See ERA 1996 s162(3).

6.66   If A arranges for workers to be provided with life assurance cover after early retirement on grounds of ill health it is lawful:

a) for A to arrange for such cover to cease when the applicable normal retirement age in relation to any such workers at the time they took early retirement, is reached;

b) in relation to any other workers, for A to arrange for such cover to cease when the workers reach the age of 65.[75]

6.67   'Normal retirement age', in relation to a worker who has taken early retirement, means the age at which workers in A's undertaking who held the same kind of position as the worker held at the time of his retirement were normally required to retire.

6.68   Note that the exemption operates to allow the employer to set a general principle. It would not apply where there was no evidence that the employer intended it to apply to all cases. The exception in other words must be pre-planned rather than sought in response to a situation which has arisen.

Practical points

1) The burden of proof that one of these exceptions applies falls entirely on the respondent (save in certain respects concerning dismissal for retirement dealt with subsequently).

2) The claimant should therefore ensure that the factual background to the use of these exceptions is firmly established.

3) Where there is a margin of discretion to be disputed the fact that these are derogations from the principle of equal treatment requires the exception to be construed narrowly.

4) It is only precisely the subject matter of the exception that is taken outside the scope of the regulations. The process surrounding the application of an exception will generally not be outside the scope of the regulations. If therefore the employer seeks to establish that one of the exceptions applies, advisers should give careful consideration to exactly what remains under the scope of the regulations.

5) Where the respondent fails to show that an exception applies it may seek to argue that the treatment arising from the supposed application of the exception was in fact justified. The claimant will therefore need to address issues of general justification in any case where an exception is pleaded.

---

75   Reg 34(1).

CHAPTER 7

The recruitment process

> **Key points**
> - The Age Regulations 2006 apply from advert onwards.
> - There is an exception for recruitment over 65.
> - Good practice indicates areas for examination by claimants using the questionnaire procedure.

Introduction

7.1   In this chapter we will examine:

a) what are the unlawful acts of discrimination in relation to recruitment;

b) the process of recruitment itself and how an employer can try to avoid age discrimination;

c) the points that can be raised on a questionnaire concerning the various stages of the recruitment process;

d) the exception to protection against age discrimination in recruitment for persons over 65.

7.2   There is general recognition that older workers may find it harder to re-enter the labour market because of negative stereotypes, even though they are still productive.[1] Younger workers also may be subject to similar prejudices. It is therefore imperative that employers combat age-related prejudice by ensuring staff are fully trained on equality and age discrimination.

7.3   In what follows reference is made to the ACAS guidance. It should be remembered that the ACAS code does not have any stipulated evidential value in the courts or tribunals in relation to age. There is no equivalent provision of the Employment Equality (Age) Regulations 2006 establishing the special status given to the DRC, CRE or EOC codes. However, the ACAS code could be taken into account as carrying obvious persuasive power and sometimes as a guide for the perplexed.

Age discrimination in recruitment

7.4   Regulation 7(1) provides that it is unlawful for an employer in relation to employment by him at an establishment in Great Britain, to discriminate against a person in any of the following ways:

---

1   For a review of the statistical literature including that relating to productivity see Pamela Meadows *Retirement Ages in the UK, a review of the literature* (2003) and see paras 1.6–1.8.

a) in the arrangements the employer makes for the purpose of determining to whom he or she should offer employment;
b) in the terms on which the employer offers that person employment;
c) by refusing to offer, or deliberately not offering, the person employment.

We will examine these in turn.

Arrangements the employer makes for the purposes of determining to whom he or she should offer employment

7.5 The term 'arrangements' covers everything done for the purpose of determining who should be offered the job. Word-of-mouth recruitment would constitute an arrangement. If the employer has an age homogenous workforce, that profile is likely to be maintained if word-of-mouth recruitment is used. It is difficult to see how word-of-mouth recruitment can be objectively justified.

Advertisements

7.6 Whether an advertisement would be covered by 'arrangements' at first sight might appear moot, as it is covered by other provisions in other discrimination legislation. However the directive[2] requires the regulations to cover conditions for access to employment.[3] The regulations do not have a separate regulation to deal with advertisements. Arrangements therefore will cover advertisements which are a condition of access to employment.[4]

7.7 Adverts that contain overt age requirements will need to be justified as instances of direct discrimination. Referring to 'young graduates' or 'bright young things' would, for example, be difficult to justify.[5] Adverts for recent graduates will run the risk of being indirectly discriminatory and will accordingly need to be justified. Similarly, the advert/recruitment charm-offensive known as the 'milk round' targets young people and will need justification. An advert that seeks a certain level of

2 2000/78 EC.

3 Directive article 3.1(a).

4 See chapter 2 for the interpretive arguments to be used. Even without recourse to Community law, logically the arrangements would include the advert (see the Scottish IT decision *Brindley v Tayside Health Board* [1976] IRLR 364 said to be wrong because the Sex Discrimination Act (SDA) 1975 covers adverts by another section enforceable only by the Equal Opportunities Commission (EOC)).

5 The ACAS guidance states that the term 'graduate' can be code for someone in their early 20s, so advertisements should make it clear that it is qualifications that are relevant, and not age. Limiting recruitment to university 'milk rounds' alone should be avoided and should be enhanced with a broader recruitment strategy.

experience in an area runs the risk of discriminating indirectly against younger applicants. The requirement for experience of a particular length must be justified.

7.8   A discriminatory advert is likely to put a prospective employee off applying for the job in the first place.

> EXAMPLE: An advert, which refers to the need for a young dynamic person to fulfil the role, may cause Barbara who is 63 not to apply for the role in the first place. She has suffered a detriment as a result of the arrangements the employer makes in relation to recruitment. She may have a remedy under the regulations.[6]

7.9   Clearly a person in that situation has lost the chance of obtaining employment with the employer. If the discriminatory element of the advert arises from the application of an employer's rule, which may be applied to the applicant on the next occasion a vacancy arises, in the example above it may be in Barbara's interests to make an application both in respect of the discrimination she has suffered and in respect of the fact that the rule may be applied to her in future. If the employer is large enough and controls local employment opportunities, an application will be worthwhile.

7.10   In Ireland, one of the first cases brought under the Employment Equality Act 1998 under the ground of 'age' was decided in February 2001. The Office of the Director of Equality Investigations found against the airline Ryanair in a case brought by the Equality Authority involving a job advertisement for a Director of Regulatory Affairs, seeking a 'young and dynamic professional ... the ideal candidate will be young and dynamic ...'.[7] Ryanair claimed that 'young' was a state of mind rather than a chronological age. They claimed that despite the fact that the word 'young' had been used twice in the advertisement, there was no mention of age limits, nor any intention to discriminate. They added that the word 'young' had juxtaposed the word 'dynamic' in both places, and the key qualities they were looking for were passion and ambition. The Equality Officer held that the word 'young' may reasonably have been understood to exclude people who were not young, and further that the words 'young', 'middle aged' and 'old' did describe particular ages in the context of the Equality Act.

---

6 That remedy may be under regulation 7, discussed below, and if the advert is the result of an employer's rule, under Schedule 5.

7 *Equality Authority v Ryanair* EE/2000/19.

7.11   An example given by ACAS is where a fashion retailer, focusing on trendy clothes for young people, seeks a young sales assistant, typically so that they can be closer in age to the customers and better understand needs and requirements, as well as portray the young, trendy image of the retailer. The guidance suggests that that would be discriminatory. Concerns have been expressed about this example[8] by some who argue that there may be a legitimate aim such as pursuit of a particular age group of customers, which may render an age restriction appropriate in these circumstances. Although attracting a young clientele may be a legitimate aim (as there is no restriction on discrimination in relation to goods and services) it does not follow that having 'young' staff is a proportionate means of achieving that aim. The youth of the staff represents a short-hand either for acceptability in the client's mind or for skills and knowledge of the client group. If the former, the age restriction will not be a proportionate means of pursuing a legitimate end. It amounts to saying that if the clients do not want an old looking person, the employer does not have to employ them. If the latter, there is no reason why the employer should not simply seek people with the relevant skills whether or not they fall within the target age group.

7.12   Insistence that candidates possess certain qualifications in recruitment which were not available decades ago, such as media studies or even GCSEs, may be indirectly discriminatory.

EXAMPLE: A small hotel in Bournemouth is recruiting for a Tourism Manager. One of the key criteria is that the applicant has a degree in trade and tourism, and no substitute qualification is accepted. An accountancy firm, also in Bournemouth, advertises for a junior financial assistant. It also requires that the applicant has a degree in trade and tourism, without the possibility of any substitute qualification. The requirement for a degree in trade and tourism excludes any applicants who took their university degrees more than 15 years ago, since that degree did not exist at that time. The small hotel may be able to justify its requirement on grounds of the nature of its business and particular circumstances. It is unlikely that the accountancy firm would be able to do the same. However, in both cases, it may be difficult to justify the exclusion of any equivalent degrees or work experience.

---

8 Which also occurs in the Consultation Paper as an example of an impermissible justification of discrimination.

EXAMPLE: In a case involving the Republic of Ireland's Employment Equality Act 1998, the Equality Officer found that an advertisement for a Senior Financial Analyst, requiring 2–3 years of experience, was indirectly discriminatory since the complainant was told that he was too senior for the position, despite the fact that the advertisement claimed that someone of more than 2–3 years' experience would be capable of doing the job. The company alleged that the experience requirement, which had not been stated to be a maximum level of experience, was a genuine requirement and therefore the complainant's 20 years' experience was too great for the post.[9]

7.13   In constructing the questionnaire the claimant's adviser will want to obtain information about the ways in which the respondent did or did not seek to avoid discrimination on the grounds of age or indirect discrimination. The employer should:

i) ensure that all staff responsible for recruitment have received training in the respondent's age equality policy and equal opportunities policy;

ii) ensure that all opportunities for employment/promotion and training are open equally to all candidates and that selection is on merit;

iii) review the rules, requirements, conditions or practices relating to the post to be advertised to see whether they place any age group at a disadvantage, and if so whether they can be justified. The employer should have evidence that this review was carried out. There should be a paper trail;

iv) create a job description prior to the advertisement being put out which has been scrutinised to see whether any issue of direct or indirect age discrimination arises on it, and if so how such an issue can be justified:[10]

- Does the job description overstate any duty or responsibility in a way that may select out one age group or another?
- Was the job description based on what the previous post-holder was actually doing? If it was supposed to, was there any monitoring of what the previous incumbent actually did by the employer?

9 *Noonan v Accountancy Connections,* Office of the Director of Equality Investigations, EE/2003/254, 2004.

10 The ACAS guidance recommends that references to age in job descriptions or candidate specifications, and asking for a particular number of years experience should be avoided.

v) that there is a person specification which describes the skills, knowledge, abilities and qualifications, experience and qualities that are considered necessary/desirable (stating which) for performance of the duties in the job description satisfactorily. The relative importance of each criterion should be made clear. It is sensible to have more than one person drawing up the person specification and job description so as to avoid the terms used becoming more subjective than they need to be:

- Is the length of experience required by the person specification longer than is warranted by reference to the proficiency in the skills indicated? The person specification may promote a criteria that is only desirable to one which is necessary.
- The questionnaire can seek to find out why each necessary specification is required.
- A person specification which indicates objective qualities is likely to be more difficult to challenge than one which (for example) states that the successful candidate will have 'gravitas', 'leadership' or similar.

vi) that the advertisement accurately reflects the job description and requirements of the person specification;

vii) that the advertisement is directed to publications which have an age diverse audience rather than restricting publication to those that are likely to be seen only by particular age groups.

The procedure after response to the advertisement

7.14   The scope of the concept of arrangements means that recruitment policies, procedures and practices must ensure equality of opportunity for all ages, unless there is a justifiable reason for a distinction being drawn between people of different ages. The Claimant should check, using the questionnaire procedure if available about the training and merit matters mentioned above.

Application form

7.15   The application form is clearly an arrangement for the purposes of determining who should be offered. A standard application form should be used. Personal details such as age should be kept on a detachable part of the form.[11] They should not be made known to the

---

11 The ACAS guidance recommends that age or date of birth should be removed from application forms and included in diversity monitoring forms to be retained by the employer's personnel department.

members of the selection panel. Certain age matters may have to appear on the application form if relevant and justified.

7.16   The matters sought from the candidate should relate to the matters in the person specification/job description. The application form can ask for the age of the candidate if that is relevant and justified only. For the majority of jobs it will not be relevant.

7.17   An employer who asks for photographs of applicants runs a substantial risk both in relation to age and race discrimination of being accused of making prejudicial judgements based on these factors. It is sensible not to request photographs unless the looks of the person are strictly relevant to the job. Thus a model's facial looks may be relevant for a facial modelling job. They would not be relevant if the model's face was not to be photographed (for example because the model was required to do an advertisement for hand worn jewellery).

7.18   An employer would be able to indicate that it would not employ someone over the normal retirement age or 64.5 years of age in default. If this is to be done it may be permissible for the employer to indicate what the normal retirement age is and ask the 'yes/no' question whether the applicant confirms that they are younger than six months prior to that date. The employer will have to justify (and very often will be able to justify) requiring dates of jobs and qualifications as these may give rise to assumptions as to age and age related competence being made.

7.19   Shortlisting needs to carried out in a way to avoid biased decisions being reached.[12] The tribunal will be interested in answers to questions such as:

- Was the shortlisting carried out after a marking scheme was devised and agreed?
- Was it applied consistently?
- Did those carrying it out have age equality training relating to recruitment?

7.20   From details of education and the dates on which qualifications were obtained it may be that those conducting the shortlisting will make assumptions about the capabilities of candidates of certain ages. Those conducting the shortlisting will have to ensure that such assumptions play no role in their deliberations. If it is considered that an age related characteristic is relevant there should be some evidence of the justification for its inclusion as a factor in the shortlisting decision. There is of course a danger that those shortlisting, if they are able to ascertain

12 See *Saunders v Richmond upon Thames Borough Council* [1978] ICR 75; [1977] IRLR 362.

age from the application form, will apply stereotypes such as that the older worker is likely to be less capable than the younger worker, or that such a worker is likely to be less flexible than the younger worker. Equally younger applicants for managerial roles may face the stereotype that leadership comes with age.

7.21   If possible more than one person should shortlist. The marking system should be agreed in advance along with the cut off score for selection. The applications should then be assessed with consistent use of these systems. The markers should reach independent conclusions and award a mark before discussing the final mark to be awarded. These are all ways in which the prejudice of one person can be prevented from tainting the judgement of the other. The selection should be based on what is in the form, or formal assessment reports if applicable. Psychological reports, such as psychometric tests, should only be used as one part of the selection process and should be properly validated in order to avoid age biased references in the tests.

7.22   Employers should consider what instructions are given to employment agencies. Where recruitment agencies are instructed by a client employer to discriminate on grounds of age, the agency should obtain the client's justification in writing.

Tests and assessment centres

7.23   Many employers include tests in the recruitment process. The test should only test relevant matters. Certain tests will favour younger workers, such as those involving quick reaction times. As Pamela Meadows summed up the statistical literature:

> There have been a very large number of studies of the effect of ageing on capacity.[13] The evidence from gerontologists, especially in laboratory tests, consistently finds that on average ageing reduces:
>
> • hearing
> • vision
> • lung capacity
> • muscular strength
> • bone structure
> • speed of activity and reaction
> • memory.

---

13 Jablonski et al (cited in Meadows), Levine (ibid), and Warr (ibid) all review a large number of studies of ageing, capacity and productivity. Warr alone reviewed more than 100 different studies. Thus the findings which cite these three sources are based on consistent findings across a large number of studies. See Pamela Meadows *Retirement ages in the UK: a review of the literature* (2003) p17.

7.24   However, performance in comprehension and knowledge tests improve up to the age of at least 70 and verbal meaning tests demonstrate performance improves or remains stable with age. Therefore the employer needs to be able to justify the type of test that is applied. Clearly even if it discriminates indirectly because it emphasizes some skill which is not evenly distributed over age groups, providing the skill is relevant to the job in question, it should be justified as a proportionate means of selecting staff.

The interview

7.25   The interview presents the greatest opportunity for discrimination on the basis of unspoken assumptions based on the interviewee's age. Obviously the conduct of the interviewer will be covered.[14] However, interviews for promotion or for other internal movement will not be covered by the provisions relating to 'arrangements' in recruitment.[15]

7.26   The interview is very often the point at which assumptions about workers play a significant role:

> The evidence based on the perceptions of managers and colleagues as well as some independent studies by researchers measuring performance in the workplace suggests that older workers:
>
> - work harder and more effectively
> - think before acting
> - have better interpersonal skills
> - work better in teams
> - are less likely to leave
> - have lower rates of absenteeism
> - have better motivation
> - have fewer accidents
> - have more experience
> - have better knowledge of the company and its products.[16]

7.27   Some of these views are based in objective experience, and others will not be. Insofar as they are beneficial to older workers they are detrimental to younger workers. The employer should attempt at least to explore whether there is an objective basis for any such beliefs by those engaging in the recruitment process.

14   *Tower Hamlets London Borough Council v Rabin* [1989] ICR 693 (words of discouragement at the interview).

15   By analogy with *Clymo v Wandsworth London Borough Council* [1989] ICR 250; [1989] IRLR 241.

16   See Pamela Meadows *Retirement ages in the UK: a review of the literature* (2003) p20.

7.28   The claimant should try to establish the ages of the panel of people interviewing. There is some evidence suggesting that younger age groups are unlikely to have friendships with older age groups and vice versa.[17] If particular questions indicating an age bias were asked at the interview the claimant should try to establish that the words were spoken and seek any justification for their use. They may reveal stereotypes such as the belief that older workers make better managers than younger. Without anything more such a belief is difficult to justify in objective terms.

7.29   Examples of potentially (and rather blatant!) discriminatory questions at interview include: 'At your age, what do you hope to gain from this job?', or 'You know this job takes a lot of energy, do you think at your age you still might have what it takes?'[18]

7.30   The EAT has held that appointing a person to conduct interviews was part of the arrangements made for the purpose of determining who should be offered the post. In a sex discrimination case, the complainant applied for a job and was interviewed by a shop manager who made it clear that he did not want to employ a woman. However, the decision ultimately did not lie with him but she was told to ring back to find out whether she had got the job. The district manager who was to make the decision decided in the meantime that the post was not to be filled. On ringing, the complainant was told that the job had been taken. The employer was held liable for the discriminatory behaviour of the shop manager.[19]

7.31   Those involved in interviewing should conduct the interview on the basis of the application form, job description, person specification, the results of any tests taken and the agreed weight to be given to each of the job criteria. A careful employer will have ensured that interviewers have received training on identifying when they are making a stereotyped assumption about a person based on age. There should be a trail of disclosable documents generated by the arrangements made for

17   S Ray, E Sharp, D Abrams, *Age Discrimination: A benchmark of public attitudes*, Age Concern England, July 2006. Questions about close, positive social contact with either younger people (under 30) or older people (over 70), revealed that friendships across age groups were limited.

18   It may be safer to have questions written down in advance so that the same or similar questions are asked to all candidates. Questions should be about the job in hand, rather than personal questions, which could inadvertently lead to discrimination.

19   See the sex discrimination case of *Brennan v J H Dewhurst Ltd* [1984] ICR 52; [1983] IRLR 357, EAT see also *Roadburg v Lothian Regional Council* [1976] IRLR 283.

selection. Thus in addition to the job description, person specification, shortlisting notes, there should be notes of the interview. There may also be notes of discussions between the interviewers.

7.32   Questions asked at interview will clearly fall under the term 'arrangements'.[20] Discouraging words have been held to be a detriment[21] and may be less favourable treatment in the arrangements made in order to select. In order to avoid age discrimination, the panel conducting the interview should decide in advance the relevance of any theme that is to be pursued in questioning. Before asking any question the justification for asking it should be borne in mind. If the suggestions made above have been followed the employer is more likely to be able to avoid discrimination because its actions will be capable of an objective justification.

7.33   A difficult issue will be whether the retirement plans of a prospective employee will be relevant.

> EXAMPLE: Lesley is newly 64 on the day of the interview. The employer asks when Lesley intends to retire. Lesley replies at the age of 70. The employer picks another employee aged 63 who intends to retire at age 65 (which is the employer's normal retirement age) because the employer does not want the trouble of an employee who wants to carry on working after 65. The employer cannot rely on regulation 7(4)[22] because the applicant has more than six months before reaching age 65.

7.34   The employer may be able to justify asking about retirement plans but if the normal retirement age is 65 for this employer, it is clear that his proximity to the retirement age was the reason for the employer's choice. The exception relating to recruitment operates on the basis that the applicant must not be within six months of the normal retirement age. However, where the training requirements of the job are such that by the time the employee has completed them, there will not be sufficient time for the employer to gain from employing the employee (for example, because he will not get back the training costs), the employer is likely to be able to justify not offering the employment to the person with the shorter time to retirement.

20 See *Saunders v Richmond-upon-Thames London Borough Council* [1978] ICR 75 as to the fact that asking discriminatory questions could constitute 'arrangements'.
21 *Simon v Brimham Associates* [1987] ICR 596; [1987] IRLR 307, CA.
22 See para 7.45 onwards.

7.35   On the other hand, as the example shows, the applicant's intention was to work until 70. He would intend to request to work after age 65. Whilst the employer is not obliged to consider that request in good faith, if and when it is made, the tribunals have to determine how the employer's intention to refuse any request for continued working should affect its consideration of recruitment discrimination nearing retirement. The better view is that the employer will not be able to justify failing to offer the applicant the job solely on the basis of proximity to the normal retirement age (or 65 where none exists). The tribunal will have to consider whether the applicant for the job would have been retained. The applicant has at least lost a chance of persuading the employer to grant an extension. It is suggested that the maintenance of a normal retirement age of 65 is an aim which is unaffected by considerations of whether the applicant for employment will eventually make a request for an extension of employment. It is enshrined in regulation 30 in a particular way (discussed in Chapter 9). Refusing to employ a person because the employer might have to consider an application not to be retired is not a proportionate means of achieving the aim of retiring people at 65.

7.36   Another difficult issue is the extent to which the employer making its policy clear in the recruitment process that it does not retain people after the normal retirement age in any circumstance can be justified. Clearly this would discourage those nearing retirement from pursuing an application. The same question would arise as to whether the employer can justify an approach which goes beyond the recruitment exception. In certain employments a longer training period might be required, so that the employer would argue that there is not a reasonable period of valuable work prior to retirement despite the fact that the employer would obtain more than six months' work from the employee. It is suggested that merely stating 'we do not retain employees after [the normal retirement age]' cannot be justified on this basis.

7.37   What can be justified is an indication of the precise basis on which a particular length of service prior to the retirement age is required. Thus 'because of the need for, and cost of training, we will not employ persons who cannot offer at least 6 months post training work prior to [the normal retirement age]' might be more justifiable.

7.38   Arrangements will also cover how the person is treated on coming to the interview by reception staff.

> EXAMPLE: Phillip, who looks old – he has lines on his face, white hair and thin-looking skin – goes for a job interview at the local GP surgery. The receptionist assumes that he is a patient because the doctor has many elderly patients. When the receptionist realises his error, he makes discouraging remarks about the practice because he does not want to work with an older person who he does not think would be 'fun' and tells Phillip that he is unlikely to fit in.

7.39   It is important, therefore, that those conducting the physical arrangements for the interview are aware of avoiding age stereotyping.

7.40   Finally, references should be checked for all candidates, and not just for older candidates or those for whom it is considered further checks may be appropriate, without substantial reason.

> EXAMPLE:[23] Whilst being interviewed, a job applicant says that she took her professional qualification 30 years ago. Although she has all the skills and competences required of the job holder, the company decides to take up her references where it would not have done so in the case of a younger person. This is direct discrimination, for which the applicant can bring a claim to the tribunal. If it decided to take up the reference because of the age of the qualifications, this might be indirect discrimination which would warrant justification. If the qualifications are not such as to lose effectiveness with time, there will be no justification for taking them up in her case and not in everyone's case.

7.41   There should be a considerable amount of documentation available for disclosure in an age recruitment case:

> Employers need to make arrangements to keep application forms, and documents relating to each stage of the recruitment process, for 12 months, in case of any complaints about decisions or procedures, or requests for the information under the Data Protection Act 1998, or, where appropriate, the Freedom of Information Act 2000. The documentation should include:
>
> a) records of discussions and decisions by members of the selection panel; for example, on marking standards or interview questions;
> b) notes taken by each member of the panel during the interviews; and

23   Taken from the ACAS Guide for Individuals on the Age Discrimination Regulations, at p2.

c) each panel member's marks at each stage of the process; for example, on the application form, any selection tests and each interview question.[24]

In the terms on which the applicant is offered employment

7.42 Regulation 7(1)(b) refers to the offer of employment rather than the terms on which employment is afforded once employment has started. A complaint relating to terms within a period of employment would be brought under regulation 7(2)(a).[25] The act only becomes unlawful if there is unjustified discrimination involved. Thus where one of the exceptions[26] applies or the employer can show that the term is a proportionate means of achieving a legitimate aim then the terms will be lawful.

7.43 If the terms are unlawful under this provision but the claimant has accepted the employment, pursuant to a collective agreement, the claimant should make an application under paragraph 5 of Schedule 5 to the regulations, to the effect that the claimant believes that a term of a collective agreement is void and will be applied to him in the future (or permits an unlawful act which will be done to him in the future). He must also show that at the time of issuing the proceedings the term would be unlawful if applied to him.

By refusing to offer, or deliberately not offering, the person employment

7.44 Regulation 7(1)(c) may apply to internal applications for posts. Therefore where a person is refused a promotion because of age an action may be brought under this provision.[27] More obviously it will apply where employment is refused on external application. Similar evidence gathering considerations will apply in this case to a case involving discriminatory arrangements.

The exceptions to protection

7.45 The regulations follow a scheme in which the dismissal from, or recruitment to employment of a person of 65 or older is not subject

---

24 This general guidance is modelled on the Commission for Racial Equality (CRE)'s statutory Code on Employment (2006) para 4.30.
25 By analogy with *Clymo* above.
26 See chapter 6.
27 See *Timex Corpn v Hodgson* [1982] ICR 63, [1981] IRLR 530, EAT a case of internal selection for posts in a redundancy process.

to the prohibition against discrimination. These exceptions only apply to employment.[28] The net effect of these provisions is that persons of 65 and older will be more likely to be unemployed or self employed.

7.46   By Regulation 7(4) if a person's age is greater than the employer's normal retirement age (or 65 in the absence of an employer's normal retirement age) it is not unlawful for the employer to discriminate against him in the arrangements he makes for the purposes of determining to whom he should offer employment. Equally he may refuse to offer (or deliberately not offer) that person employment.[29] In these respects the employer may also discriminate against anyone who, within a period of six months *from the date of his application to the employer,* would reach the employer's normal retirement age or, 65 if the employer does not have a normal retirement age.[30]

EXAMPLE: Tarik, who is 64 but will be 65 in four months' time, wishes to apply to Sam's Fishmongers for a job. Sam's Fishmongers has a retirement age of 65 for its employees. However, Sam is worried that the expense of recruiting and training Tarik, who has never worked in a fishmonger's before, will be too great since he would have retired Tarik at age 65 in any event. He rejects Tarik for the position on grounds that had Tarik been an employee, he would have dismissed him for mandatory retirement at 65. That will not be an unlawful act under regulation 7(1)(a) or (c). However, if Tarik had just turned 64, there would be no defence for the employer if the reason for not recruiting him was by reason of his age.

7.47   However, in the example above it should be noted that it does not matter why Sam does not want to employ Tarik, provided it is otherwise legal. Suppose that Sam thinks that everyone over 60 is a burden on the workplace. He can reject Tarik as an applicant. When challenged he can then assert that it is not unlawful to discriminate against Tarik in refusing to appoint him because of Tarik's age. This gives rise to the following situation. Tarik may have gone to an interview at which his age became apparent and during the course of which Sam stated that he would only employ him if he was willing to work for half the pay his

---

28   And employment in the Houses of Parliament etc.
29   Reg 7(4)(a).
30   Reg 7(4)(b).

co-workers would receive. This offer of the terms on which Sam is prepared to employ Tarik is actionable under regulation 7(1)(b). Having decided to make an offer, Sam must make it on the same terms as he would make to a person not of Tarik's age.

At an establishment in Great Britain

7.48   The provisions relating to recruitment apply in relation to employment by the employer at an establishment in Great Britain. Regulation 10 provides

> 10. – (1) For the purposes of this Part ('the relevant purposes'), employment is to be regarded as being at an establishment in Great Britain if the employee–
>   (a) does his work wholly or partly in Great Britain; or
>   (b) does his work wholly outside Great Britain and paragraph (2) applies.
> (2) This paragraph applies if–
>   (a) the employer has a place of business at an establishment in Great Britain;
>   (b) the work is for the purposes of the business carried on at that establishment; and
>   (c) the employee is ordinarily resident in Great Britain–
>   (i) at the time when he applies for or is offered the employment, or
>   (ii) at any time during the course of the employment.
> (3) The reference to 'employment' in paragraph (1) includes–
>   (a) employment on board a ship[31] only if the ship is registered at a port of registry in Great Britain, and
>   (b) employment on an aircraft or hovercraft only if the aircraft or hovercraft is registered in the United Kingdom and operated by a person who has his principal place of business, or is ordinarily resident, in Great Britain.

7.49   Regulation 10(1)(a) contemplates that the relevant period for determining whether the applicant did his work wholly or mainly outside Great Britain is the whole period of employment. 'Employment' is the entire relationship between employer and employee. It extends over a period of time. Normally the employment should therefore be taken into account as a whole and not in segments.[32] The requirement that the

---

31   See *Deria v General Council of British Shipping* [1986] ICR 172.
32   *Saggar v MOD* [2005] EWCA Civ 413 para 27, which discusses *Carver v Saudi Arabian Airlines* [1999] ICR 991, *Haughton v Olau (UK) Ltd* [1986] ICR 357 and *Deria v General Council of British Shipping* [1986] ICR 172.

claimant be employed at an establishment in Great Britain also applies in relation to contract work as it applies in relation to employment.[33]

Exception for genuine occupational requirement etc

7.50　Regulation 8(1) provides that discrimination on grounds of age under regulation 3 shall not be unlawful in certain respects relating to recruitment. The employer can discriminate in relation to the arrangements for appointment and in relation to appointment[34] where, having regard to the nature of the employment or the context in which it is carried out the following requirements are met:

a) possessing a characteristic related to age is a genuine and determining occupational requirement;

b) it is proportionate to apply that requirement in the particular case; and

c) either:

　i) the person to whom that requirement is applied does not meet it; or

　ii) the employer is not satisfied, and in all the circumstances it is reasonable for him not to be satisfied, that that person meets it.[35]

7.51　It is very difficult indeed to think of a characteristic relating to age which is determinative in this way. However where an employer seeks to argue for a normal retirement age which is below 65, it is arguable that in fact the employer is suggesting that that age is a genuine occupational requirement (GOR) for the job. Thus in the light of medical statistics concerning the rate of heart attack after a certain age, and employer might, in an appropriate case be able to argue that the characteristic of having an increased chance of heart attack meant that the employer could not take the risk of having the applicant do particular work where the consequences of the manifestation of that risk would be the deaths of other people. However most employers will simply seek to argue that there is objective justification for the use of the criterion and will not resort to GORs.

33 In relation to contract work, references to 'employee', 'employer' and 'employment' are references to (respectively) 'contract worker', 'principal' and 'contract work' as those terms are respectively used in regulation 9.

34 Ie reg 7(1)(a) or (c).

35 Reg 8(2).

Discrimination in employment

Key points

- The Age Regulations 2006 cover terms and conditions, promotion, benefits, dismissal and any other detriment.
- A dismissal will not be unlawful if the reason for dismissal is retirement at or over the age of 65 years, where the reason for the dismissal is retirement so long as the statutory procedures are complied with.
- Equality training on age is crucial to avoid concerns over discrimination.
- Equality policies should be updated to include the new age provisions.
- Performance appraisals are likely to have a stronger, and more necessary, role.
- There are particular issues relating to redundancy dismissals, in particular unfair selection.
- The statutory disciplinary, dismissal and grievance procedures apply.

Introduction

8.1   Employment relations are at the heart of the new Employment Equality (Age) Regulations 2006 and discrimination on grounds of age is unlawful at each stage in the employment relationship. Older workers may possess skills and experience which are valuable in the workplace, which are often underestimated by employers.[1] A report commissioned by the Age Partnership Group and the Department of Work and Pensions states that 'Older adults are often discriminated against in the workplace on the basis of stereotypes about ageing. Many of these stereotypes may not be accurate or recognise the benefits of employing older workers, although they may influence the recruitment and retention of older individuals'.[2] The Office of National Statistics indicates that nearly a third of the labour force will be over 50 by 2020.[3]

---

1 See www.facoccmed.ac.uk/library/docs/ppageemp.pdf for *Position paper on age and employment* by the Faculty of Occupational Medicine of the Royal College of Physicians, August 2004.

2 Report No HSL/2005/20: www.hse.gov.uk/research/hsl_pdf/2005/hsl0520.pdf.

3 DTI Age Legislation Fact Sheet No 1.

8.2　　The regulations are intended to cover largely the same ground as the other key discrimination provisions in force, save that there are provisions for justification, even for direct discrimination.[4] Rights under the discrimination legislation act independently of the contract of employment. Part 2 of the regulations deal with discrimination in employment. However, the key provisions are found in regulation 7:

> 7(1) It is unlawful for an employer, in relation to employment by him at an establishment in Great Britain, to discriminate against a person–
>> (a) in the arrangements he makes for the purpose of determining to whom he should offer employment;
>> (b) in the terms on which he offers that person employment; or
>> (c) by refusing to offer, or deliberately not offering, him employment.
>
> (2) It is unlawful for an employer, in relation to a person whom he employs at an establishment in Great Britain, to discriminate against that person–
>> (a) in the terms of employment which he affords him;
>> (b) in the opportunities which he affords him for promotion, a transfer, training, or receiving any other benefit;
>> (c) by refusing to afford him or deliberately not affording him, any such opportunity; or
>> (d) by dismissing him or subjecting him to any other detriment.
>
> (3) It is unlawful for an employer, in relation to employment by him at an establishment in Great Britain, to subject to harassment a person whom he employs or who has applied to him for employment.
>
> (4) Subject to paragraph (5), paragraph 1(a) and (c) does not apply in relation to a person–
>> (a) whose age is greater than the employer's normal retirement age, or, if the employer does not have a normal retirement age, the age of 65; or
>> (b) who would, within a period of six months from the date of his application to the employer, reach the employer's normal retirement age, or, if the employer does not have a normal retirement age, the age of 65.
>
> (5) Paragraph (4) only applies to a person to who, if he was recruited by the employer, regulation 30 (exception for retirement) could apply.
>
> (6) Paragraph (2) does not apply to benefits of any description if the employer is concerned with the provision (for payment or not) of benefits of that description to the public, or to a section of the public which includes the employee in question, unless–
>> (a) that provision differs in a material respect from the provision of the benefits by the employer to his employees; or
>> (b) the provision of the benefits to the employee in question is regulated by his contract of employment; or
>> (c) the benefits relate to training.

4 See chapters 3–5.

(7) In paragraph (2)(d) reference to a dismissal of a person from employment includes reference–

(a) to the termination of that person's employment by the expiration of any period (including a period expiring by reference to an event or circumstance), not being a termination immediately after which the employment is renewed on the same terms; and

(b) to the termination of that person's employment by any act of his (including the giving of notice) in circumstances such that he is entitled to terminate it without notice by reason of the conduct of the employer.

(8) In paragraph (4) 'normal retirement age' is an age of 65 or more which meets the requirements of section 98ZH of the 1996 [Employment Rights] Act.

Employment

8.3 'Employment' has a broad definition in discrimination law, and its definition is set out more extensively in chapter 3 on scope. It can cover employees (in the ordinary sense of the word) as well as contract workers, workers or even office-holders in specified positions.[5]

Qualifying period

8.4 There is no requirement that a person has been employed for any specific length of time when bringing a claim for discrimination in employment. Indeed, prospective employees are entitled to bring claims where they consider they have been unlawfully discriminated against in the arrangements made for interviews and other arrangements for the purposes of determining to whom work should be offered, or in the terms on which that employment is offered or by refusing to offer or deliberately not offering employment.

Employment at an establishment in Great Britain

8.5 This is discussed in chapter 3 on scope.[6]

---

5 See paras 3.2–3.13 and 3.31.
6 And see para 7.48.

Prohibition of direct and indirect discrimination

8.6 As in all other areas of discrimination law, the regulations prohibit direct and indirect discrimination on grounds of age in recruitment and selection arrangements, the terms on which employment is offered as well as the terms of employment per se, promotions, transfers, training, general detriment and dismissal.

8.7 However, unlike the other discrimination strands, *both* direct and indirect discrimination can be justified where the employer can show that the treatment is 'a proportionate means of achieving a legitimate aim'.

Proportionality

8.8 This is discussed in detail in chapter 5 on justification. The ACAS guidance sets out a useful summary to what tribunals and courts will consider when justification is attempted by respondents/defendants:

- What you are doing must actually contribute to a legitimate aim, eg if your aim is to encourage loyalty then you ought to have evidence that the provision or criterion you introduce is actually doing so.
- The discriminatory effect should be significantly outweighed by the importance and benefits of the legitimate aim.
- You should have no reasonable alternative to the action you are taking. If the legitimate aim can be achieved by less or non-discriminatory means then these must take precedence.[7]

Legitimate aims

8.9 Examples of legitimate aims might include:

- economic factors such as business needs and efficiency;
- the health, welfare and safety of the individual (including protection of young people or older workers);
- the particular training requirements of the job;[8]
- the vocational integration of individuals of a particular age;
- the need for a reasonable period of employment before retirement.[9]

---

7 *Age and the workplace* (2006) p30.
8 These three examples are taken from the ACAS Guidance (see para 5.43 onwards). Reproduced at appendix E.
9 These two examples are taken from DTI Age Legislation Fact Sheet No 2.

8.10 A legitimate aim must correspond with a real need of the employer. Although cost savings may constitute a real need, and a genuine aim, as ACAS puts it, 'saving money because discrimination is cheaper than non-discrimination is not legitimate. The legitimate aim cannot be related to age discrimination itself'.

8.11 Note that the government has aimed for a 'light touch implementation' of the Framework Directive 'that strikes the right balance between tackling age discrimination effectively by giving important new rights for individuals, whilst allowing businesses to continue to operate productively, but fairly'.[10] It remains to be seen whether the courts will try to effect that 'light touch' in their construction of legitimate aims and justification generally. Further detail on, and examples of, proportionality and legitimate aims is found in chapter 5 on justification.

8.12 An employer has a defence to certain types of direct discrimination under the regulation 8 genuine occupational requirement (GOR) provisions in respect of:

- arrangements made for determining to whom employment should be offered; or
- refusing to offer, or deliberately not offering employment; or
- in respect of promotion or transfer to or training for any employment; or
- dismissal from any employment,

where there is a genuine and determining occupational requirement, which it is proportionate to apply in the particular case and the person to whom that requirement is applied does not meet it, or the employer is satisfied, and in all the circumstances, it is reasonable for him not to be satisfied that the person meets it. This is considered in chapter 6 on exceptions.

Specific areas of discrimination within employment

Recruitment, advertising and engagement

8.13 The recruitment process is dealt with in chapter 7, in relation to the process of recruitment. The discussion of discrimination relating to terms and conditions and other employment terms will also apply to certain aspects of recruitment.[11]

10 EP para 7.2, Explanatory Memorandum.
11 See paras 8.14–8.17 below.

Terms and conditions

8.14 It is unlawful to offer or set discriminatory terms and conditions in respect of prospective or actual employees[12]. These could be express or implied terms, agreed in writing or orally. Express terms could be found in the letter of appointment or in the written contract of employment. They may also be found in other documents, such as employee handbooks, policies or additional memos etc sent to employees throughout the course of their employment, as well as documents which may be in the general domain.

8.15 Key express terms and conditions which could be offered or set out in a discriminatory manner may include:

- rates of pay, and modes of pay (how often, by what means etc);
- holiday and holiday pay;
- sick pay;
- notice pay;
- working hours;
- job duties;
- job descriptions;
- disciplinary rules;
- grievance procedures.

> EXAMPLE: A contract of employment contains a clause that allows the employer to vary the rates of pay at his discretion. There is a sign on the notice board which states that employees over 50 will not be entitled to pay increases until further notice. It is likely that the condition relating to pay would be unlawful.

8.16 The implied term of mutual trust and confidence is most often cited by employees as leading to the breakdown of an employment relationship, causing the employee to resign and claim constructive unfair dismissal. The employer, or indeed the employee, must not, without reasonable and proper cause, conduct him or herself in such a manner likely to destroy or seriously damage the trust and confidence between the parties. Examples of the employer's actions which could cause or contribute to this breakdown would be any discriminatory act, such as harassment, bullying or abuse, as well as inappropriate, detrimental behaviour on grounds of age.

12 Reg 7(1)(b) and (2)(a).

> EXAMPLE: A construction company has employed 100 workers of varying ages to work on a particular site. John, who is 42, has been working on this site for the last 3 years. Without reason or warning, the employer puts up a notice saying that 'for health and safety reasons, no worker over the age of 40 is allowed to work on the site, and must re-locate to office duties only'. This could constitute direct discrimination. Terms and conditions relating to health and safety are dealt with below.

8.17　Any term in an employment contract which purports to limit or exclude the operation of the Age Regulations 2006 will be unenforceable by any person in whose favour that term would operate ordinarily.[13]

Promotion and training

8.18　It is unlawful for an employer to discriminate against his employees, or to refuse or to deliberately not afford them, opportunities which he affords them for promotion, transfers, training or receiving other benefits.[14] Employers must ensure that opportunities for promotion and job-related training or development are advertised to everyone and available for everyone in a fair and equal manner, regardless of age. ACAS advises that the training should be monitored to ensure no age group is left out.

8.19　Training should be provided in such a manner that it is accessible to all employees, regardless of age. This includes considering the format and location of the training to ensure that there are no barriers to any particular age group participating. An example given in the ACAS guidance is that if the training given is computer-based, no assumptions should be made that everyone will be fully competent using a PC. This example itself may be problematic, since it implies that older people may not be computer-literate. Making assumptions based on age is a key contributor to disadvantage, and therefore discrimination, faced by workers.[15] In each scenario, employers will need to be sure they make no such assumptions and enquire sensitively into individual circumstances. Younger workers, for example, may be disadvantaged if they do not have their driving licences and the training requires personal transport. Suitable provisions should be made accordingly.

13　Reg 43 and Sch 5 Part 1 para 1(3).
14　See reg 7(2) and paras 8.25–8.31.
15　See paras 7.23 and 7.26 for some potential assumptions based on research into managers' attitudes.

8.20   Promotion based on seniority or length of service *may* discriminate against younger workers, unless objective justification for such a requirement can be shown (see *Lockstep* at para 8.24 below). Promotion should be awarded fairly and without bias. A merit-based system tends to operate more fairly amongst all employees. However, where vacancies or transfers are made available through internal mechanisms, a careful record of informal and verbal references from managers, supervisors and departmental heads should be kept since those references would be covered by the regulations and should be non-discriminatory.

8.21   There is some question as to whether experience requirements (for promotion or vacancies etc) will discriminate against younger applicants or employees. ACAS considers that such requirements may be discriminatory. However, where proportionate experience requirements can validly be justified, it is difficult to see how employers are not entitled to look for minimum experience requirements. It may be valid to seek, for example, at least two years' experience in a particular setting or type of employment, but discriminatory to seek 15 years' experience. It all comes down to proportionality, and the employer's genuine needs and aims.

8.22   In a case in the Republic of Ireland, *McCormick v Dublin Port Company*,[16] Ms McCormick claimed she had not been offered promotion on grounds of age. She had joined the company in 1959 as a clerk typist, and following competitive interviews, had worked her way up to an executive position. In 1992, she unsuccessfully applied for an internal promotion for a senior executive position, despite having considerable direct experience of the job. The person appointed was 17 years younger than her. Between 1993 and 1996, a further six individuals were promoted, who were all between the ages of 25 and 36. She was unsuccessful again in her attempt to be promoted in 1998, and again, the individual appointed was 34. Ms McCormick herself was now 57 years old. Four further promotions of personnel between 30 and 36 followed. Age discrimination in respect of promotions became unlawful in Ireland in 1998, with the Employment Equality Act 1998. She brought a claim under the Act, which was unsuccessful since the Equality Officer considered she had not established a prima facie case of discrimination. Although Ms McCormick was much older than the candidates appointed, there was no statistical evidence or plausible explanation for a discriminatory policy towards employees of 50 years and over.

8.23   In *Morris v Canadian Armed Forces,* a case brought before the Canadian Human Rights Tribunal, Mr Morris claimed that he had not been promoted to the rank of Master Warrant Officer, because of his age

16   EE/2000/008, 22 October 2002.

(he was 46 at the time). Although the Armed Forces claimed that it was because he had not scored sufficiently highly on the Merit Lists, his Performance Evaluation Report had deemed him highly suitable for the promotion. The tribunal found in Mr Morris' favour, finding that there was no reasonable explanation for the discriminatory acts as proven.

Lockstep

8.24 'Lockstep' is common practice in law firms, and is used as a system of remuneration. Under this system, each partner's remuneration is based on seniority, rather than merit-based performance testing. There was some concern at the consultation stages of the Regulations that this system would fall foul of the new legislation since pay increases would be based on chronological seniority rather than merit or performance criteria. Systems based on chronological seniority will have to be justified as they call for an explanation of the differential treatment of different age groups identified by length of service. It may be that many will be justified. In a lockstep situation, the aim is to distribute profits, thus fulfilling business needs as well as rewarding loyalty, or experience and potentially motivation of partners and employees. Whether any particular lockstep system is justified will depend on its detail.

Benefits

8.25 Employers must not discriminate in the allocating, access or awarding of benefits to employees. Benefits can include facilities and services and should be construed in the ordinary sense of the word. They could include items such as vouchers and tokens, provision of company car, gym membership etc, access to financial advisers etc.

8.26 Many employers offer company benefits as a means of encouraging loyalty and long service. By virtue of Regulation 32, there is no requirement for employers to justify any benefits linked to length of service up to five years. Beyond five years, it must reasonably appear to the employer that the way in which he or she uses the length of service criterion fulfils a business need of the employer's undertaking, for example by encouraging motivation or loyalty or rewarding the experience of some or all of the workers. The five-year limit appears arbitrary and was criticised as such at the consultation stage. It remains to be seen how it will bite in practice.[17]

---

17 Many benefits are affected by this exception. In particular service related pay increments (whether used as sole criterion or with performance increments) will be affected (see para 6.52 and following).

8.27   Length of service can be calculated by the employer in one of two ways:[18]

a) the length of time the worker has been working for the employer doing work which he or she reasonably considers to be at a particular level (assessed by reference to the demands made of the worker, for example in terms of effort, skills and decision making); or
b) the length of time the worker has been working for the employer in total.

8.28   On each occasion the employer decides to use the length of service criterion in relation to the award of a benefit to workers, it is for the employer to decide which is the definition to use to calculate their length of service.

8.29   The provisions about unlawful discrimination in respect of access to benefits in regulation 7(2) do not include benefits of any description if the employer is concerned with the provision (for payment or not) of benefits of that description to the public, or to a section of the public which includes the employee, unless:

a) that provision differs in a material respect from the provision of the benefits by the employer to his employees; or
b) the provision of the benefits to the employee in question is regulated by his contract of employment; or
c) the benefits relate to training.

8.30   Where the claimant is a former employee, as opposed to an existing employee, failure to provide a non-contractual benefit will constitute discrimination only in exceptional circumstances, where the discrimination is alleged to have taken place in the opportunity to receive benefits.[19]

8.31   The Explanatory Memorandum[20] states that benefits that recognise length of service are widely supported, and the government recognises the positive role they play in rewarding loyalty, providing incentive and helping motivation. However, it remains to be seen whether employers will still be forced to justify such length of service requirements in other areas such as for promotions.[21] The idea that promotion should be given to the person with the longest service runs against any merit based selection system. It would be very difficult to justify as the proportionate pursuit of a legitimate aim.

---

18 Reg 32(3).
19 *Relaxion Group plc v Rhys Harper* [2003] ICR 867.
20 Para 7.15.
21 See chapter 6 for a discussion of this exception in detail.

Performance appraisals

8.32   Performance appraisal systems will need to be strengthened and used far more widely with the onset of the new regulations since they are a far more accurate method of workforce planning than age limits, which tend by their nature to be arbitrary. Transparent use of these systems will also need to apply to the whole workforce irrespective of age in order to avoid accusations of age discrimination. Performance appraisal systems must be drawn up and conducted without bias or discrimination as to age. They must also be transparent. Employees should know what is expected of them, and how they are being measured. It is also important that objective criteria are used and implemented to measure performance, and that there is consistency applied to all employees. Similar systems could be used in certain industries as a means to overcoming perceived 'normal' age limits for certain jobs.

> EXAMPLE: A large construction firm hires most of its workers on site for labouring work. The work is physically demanding and often dangerous, requiring a good level of physical fitness and sound motor skills. The firm has set a maximum age for their on-site workers but accepts workers of any age for off-site administrative work and less physically demanding roles. The firm feels that, if challenged, it can objectively justify this approach. However, the HR Director suggests that some older workers are as capable, or more capable, of meeting the physical demands of the job than some younger workers. Consequently, the firm adopts a 'performance appraisal' approach to recruitment, where appropriately skilled workers of any age must show that they are physically fit enough to meet the demands of the job, rather than using an objective justification based upon an arbitrary age.[22]

8.33   The ACAS guidance highlights the problem with people having preconceptions or making assumptions based on age.

> If these preconceptions appear in performance appraisals through use of inappropriate comments – such as 'does well despite their age' or 'shows remarkable maturity for their age' – they will undermine the whole basis of a fair appraisal system. Such comments could also lead to further discrimination when decisions about promotion or work allocation are being made.

22 Example taken from DTI Age Legislation Fact Sheet No 2.

8.34   The guidance gives this example:

- Two candidates have done equally well for the post on offer so the selectors decide to review previous assessments to try and draw a fair distinction between them. On one they read: 'Despite his many years with the company, John remains capable and enthusiastic' and 'John does very well considering his age'. There are no such comments against Mark's assessment.

8.35   Appraisals may demonstrate more subtle types of discrimination. For example, a manager might remark 'I would have expected greater aptitude for the role from someone with so many years' experience in the role'. Length of service is very often used as a proxy for age. Here the employee is being criticised simply on the basis of an expected level of aptitude after a certain time period. However, if the task is one which is basic and only minimum improvements are seen in performance after an initial learning period, the remark could be acting as a cypher for the person's age. If the employee's performance is the same as a younger person's, the fact of longer experience at the job should not be taken into account in determining whether the performance is adequate or not unless it can be objectively justified.

8.36   Conversely, the manager who gives a better appraisal to a younger person because he or she considers that, for one so young or inexperienced, their performance is better than average, is making a comparison with an age component built into it. The use of the age component will have to be justified. Otherwise the employees with longer experience, who will tend to be older, could have a justifiable basis of complaint. Thus it will be legitimate for the claimant, when constructing the questionnaire, and when seeking disclosure from the respondent, to seek comparative marks for persons with different ages/lengths of service doing the same job.

8.37   Similarly, the employer should have established a neutral basis for objective-setting. The younger employee can complain of age discrimination if the older employee's objectives or targets are easier to obtain. The employer may have done this because the older employee is nearing retirement, for example. However, the employee's performance should be judged on the same basis. If the younger employee's performance would result in him or her being subjected to a capability procedure, the same result should occur for the older employee exhibiting exactly the same performance. If the employer fails to treat the older employer in the same way it will have to justify the difference in treatment.

Dismissal

8.38   If dismissal is on grounds of age (outside the permitted exceptions relating to retirement), it will be unlawful unless objectively justified.[23]

8.39   Dismissal is given the same extended meaning that is found in the other discrimination legislation, by virtue of regulation 7(7). It includes the termination of employment by the expiry of any period, immediately after which the employment is not renewed on the same terms. This can include expiration of any period expiring by reference to an event or circumstances. Additionally, dismissal is said to include termination of employment by any act of the employee, including giving notice, in circumstances where he is entitled to terminate the employment without notice by reason of the employer's conduct. In practical terms, this means that there is an express provision related to resignations in response to fundamental breaches of contract, enabling the employee to resign and claim constructive unfair dismissal.

8.40   If the act of dismissal is an act of direct discrimination on the grounds of the claimant's age, this means that it was not carried out in pursuit of a legitimate aim and/or that it was not a proportionate means of pursuing a legitimate aim. It is likely in those circumstances that the dismissal will be unfair for the purposes of the Employment Rights Act (ERA) 1996. In this respect the theoretical possibility that also exists in other parts of the discrimination framework, namely that the dismissal whilst an act of unlawful discrimination, may be fair, is unlikely to have any practical application.[24]

8.41   By virtue of regulation 30, a dismissal will not be unlawful if the reason for dismissal is retirement at or over the age of 65 years, where the reason for the dismissal is retirement. Whether or not the reason for dismissal is, in fact, retirement must be determined in accordance with ERA 1996 ss98ZA–98ZF. Because compulsory retirement is a dismissal, the provisions in the ERA 1996 on unfair dismissal are changed so that a genuine retirement conducted in accordance with the detailed rules set out in Schedules 6 and 7 to the regulations (which include the necessity to follow certain procedures) will be a fair dismissal.[25]

8.42   In July, 2001, the Labour Court in Ireland found in favour of a woman who was dismissed by a firm of solicitors on age grounds.

---

23 Reg 7(2)(d).
24 For these see *Timex Corpn v Hodgson* [1982] ICR 63, EAT; [1981] IRLR 530; *Clarke v Eley (IMI) Kynoch Ltd* [1983] ICR 165; [1982] IRLR 482, EAT.
25 See further para 8.94 below and chapter 9.

The female worker was told that she was being made redundant because it had been decided to 'take on a young girl who could be trained to do her job'.

Redundancy dismissals

8.43   Length of service is a commonly used criterion in redundancy situations. Whilst this always has had the potential to be discriminatory on other grounds, notably sex, it could now create distinct problems for younger workers. The onus, therefore, will lie on employers to develop tighter, more sophisticated selection systems.

8.44   There are generally three main causes of redundancy situations: (i) where the business as a whole has closed down, or (ii) where the particular workplace where the employee was employed has closed down, or (iii) where the redundancy is wholly or mainly attributable to the fact that the requirements of that business for employees to carry out work of a particular kind, or to carry out work of a particular kind in the place where the employee was employed have ceased, diminished or are expected to cease or diminish.[26] In essence, this amounts to a cutting down of the workforce for reasons of cost efficiency and diminished requirements.[27]

8.45   If an employee is dismissed on grounds of redundancy, the employee is entitled to a statutory redundancy payment if he or she:

- is an employee;
- has continuous service; and
- has been dismissed for redundancy.

There is a statutory presumption that a dismissal in these circumstances is for redundancy unless the employer proves the contrary.[28]

8.46   Pursuant to regulation 33, it is not unlawful for an employer to give a qualifying employee an enhanced redundancy payment which is less in amount than the employer gives to another such employee if both amounts are calculated in the same way.[29]

8.47   If the employee unreasonably refuses an offer of suitable alternative employment, he or she will lose the right to receive the statutory redundancy payment.

---

26   ERA 1996 s139(1)(b).
27   *Murray and another v Foyle Meats Ltd* [1999] IRLR 562, HL.
28   ERA 1996 s139(1)(b).
29   See para 6.60.

8.48   The Employment Appeals Tribunal (EAT) has set out guidelines in assessing the fairness or otherwise of a redundancy dismissal in *Williams v Compare Maxam Ltd.*[30] The tribunal should consider:

a) whether the redundancy situation was genuine (although the tribunal is not permitted to consider the economic or commercial reasons justifying or leading to the redundancy);
b) whether the employer failed to consult, properly or sufficiently or at all;
c) whether the employee was unfairly selected; or
d) whether the employer failed to offer suitable alternative employment if such vacancies were available (there must be at least an attempt by the employer to consider alternative employment).

Discriminatory selection for redundancy

8.49   For the purposes of the regulations, the key point of interest lies in the question of unfair, and discriminatory selection for dismissal. It should be noted, however, that direct discrimination could occur at any stage of the *Williams v Compare Maxam* list, for example there could be a discriminatory refusal to offer alternative employment to an employee on grounds of age, or the redundancy explanation could have been contrived to get rid of a particular employee on grounds of age. There are two key areas in respect of unfair selection which employers must consider:

a) selection of the pool from which employees will be selected;
b) selection criteria to apply to those individuals in the pool.

8.50   The pool must be selected fairly, reasonably and without discrimination. It must be objectively justifiable. For example, an employer who decides that the pool will consist of all the 'old folk' is likely to discriminate against older workers, unless that can be validly justified. A pool which is based on a factor that places persons of a particular age group at a disadvantage would have to be justified. Thus redundancies from those with a particular skill which has not been taught for a number of years due to falling demand would have to be justified as a proportionate means of pursuing a legitimate aim.[31]

30 [1982] IRLR 83, and *Mugford v Midland Bank plc* [1997] ICR 399 and others.
31 Pooling in this way might result in an indirect discrimination claim which might not be justifiable. The pool of those with an obsolete qualification would be an irrational pool if those having the qualification had, in many cases gained other skills to replace that obsolete qualification. Basing the pool on the possession of the obsolete skill would then primarily pick out the older workers and would need to be justified.

8.51   The selection criteria also must be objectively justifiable. Multiple selection criteria are more likely to be objective than singling one person out, on the basis of one criterion alone. Subjectivity, especially where there may be a risk of unconscious prejudice or discrimination, needs to be eliminated as far as possible. There are many standard selection choices, such as attendance, and performance.[32] A 'last in, first out' policy could be discriminatory towards certain categories of workers, and particularly younger workers. This system has been used by some employers traditionally and employers now will have to consider the impact it will have on sections of their employees. Where discriminatory impact has been assessed as negative, then it may remain a valid system of selection. The size of the employer, and the resources available to it, remain relevant for the tribunal's assessment of what was reasonable in the circumstances, but notwithstanding size, unjustifiable discrimination will not be lawful. If the criteria employed by the employer do discriminate, it is open to the employer to seek to justify that discrimination as proportionate. In considering whether the treatment or application of the PCP was proportionate, the administrative resources and business needs of the employer will be taken into account in reaching a conclusion.

8.52   Criteria could also be indirectly discriminatory against a particular age category of worker. Experience in a new skill which older workers generally have not had will be a criteria which will indirectly discriminate against those whose training took place after the new skill started to be taught. On the whole such discrimination is likely to be justified. However a question will arise about the extent to which an employer should pursue alternatives to redundancy. If the new skill is very easy to obtain, the discriminatory impact on one age group may render it a disproportionate means of achieving redundancies.

8.53   Where claimants are concerned that a redundancy dismissal has been discriminatory towards them, the questionnaire process should be used to obtain the selection pool and criteria, and to force the employer to state his reason as to why the employee was selected for redundancy. Inconsistency with disclosed documents or later evidence may allow the tribunal to draw a negative inference about the employer's conscious or unconscious reasoning.

8.54   The following is a checklist relating to some general matters for consideration in a questionnaire relating to a redundancy dismissal:

1) Did the employer audit the criteria being used for selection for

32 See below, this can be a highly subjective criterion.

direct or indirect age discrimination? If any was discovered was there a justification for its inclusion?

2) If performance assessments were included, have these been audited for age discrimination?

3) Do the criteria for selection arise out of a collective agreement? If so do any of the relevant rules of the agreement give rise to unlawful discrimination, or facilitate it? If so consider whether the rule is void under Schedule 5 and consider making an application under Schedule 5 for future relief from its application (if reinstated or re-engaged).

4) Were the staff responsible for selection trained in equal opportunities? In particular, were they trained in age discrimination avoidance? Were they trained in the application of the respondent's equal opportunities policy and its application to the redundancy selection process?

5) Were considerations of age balance taken into account in determining the impact of the redundancies? If a decision was reached that a balance of age groupings should not be maintained, what was the reason for that decision?

6) If aptitude tests are being used, how has the employer ensured that age bias will not enter into these tests: are they based on one person's opinion? How has consistency of approach between those testing been achieved?

7) Are objective criteria being applied to determine who should be redeployed?

Subjection to any other detriment

8.55 This is a tidying-up provision, which enables a claimant to complain that there has been other forms of discrimination on grounds of age.

8.56 Although there is no precise definition of 'detriment', it broadly implies that the employee has suffered a disadvantage. It is unlikely that a trivial disadvantage would suffice. The House of Lords, in *Shamoon v Chief Constable of the Royal Ulster Constabulary (Northern Ireland)*[33] stated that it would be sufficient to show that a reasonable employee would or might take the view that they had been disadvantaged in the circumstances in which they had to work. Lord Scott added that this test must be applied from the victim's point of view.

8.57 There is no requirement to show that there has been a financial or physical consequence as a result of the unlawful treatment. However,

33 [2003] IRLR 285, HL in particular Lord Hope's speech at paras 31–37.

the claimant must demonstrate that there has been some disadvantage to them. An unjustified grievance cannot amount to a 'detriment'.

8.58 A detriment remains a detriment even if there is some compensation for suffering it.[34] The employer cannot buy the right to discriminate. The only issue is whether something valued in the sense indicated in *Shamoon* has been refused to the claimant or others have received an advantage or facility. It is not necessary for the claimant to have any right under contract or statute to the advantage.[35]

8.59 Certain types of behaviour will obviously constitute a detriment. Age abuse will more generally be dealt with under the harassment provisions, but may also indicate attitudes of the worker concerned. 'Relic', 'dinosaur' and the like may in time come to have the same status as racial abuse does today. However, it is likely that employers will want to argue that such language is harmless banter and does not indicate anything about the basis for decision making.

8.60 Segregation by age is not separately dealt with under the regulations. However if a person was transferred to another post on the basis of age (for example because younger workers felt uncomfortable working with an older worker) this is likely to constitute direct age discrimination which will have to be justified.[36] Segregation itself will constitute direct discrimination if it is involuntary. However, age segregation can come about as a result of workplace practices. Thus all of the older workers end up working in a particular area because when a person retires from the employment the longest serving member of staff is asked to take that person's place by the other workers. This is likely to result in the older members of staff working together. If there is no good reason for such a practice the employer should consider taking steps to break up that arrangement. Whilst not discriminatory in itself it is likely to lead to discrimination should any adverse decisions have to be made in relation to that workplace.

---

34 In *Jeremiah v Ministry of Defence* [1980] ICR 13 dirty work in the colour blasting shop was compensated by an additional payment, but a detriment still existed as only the men were required to work there if they did overtime. The women were not required to do their overtime there.

35 See *Iske v P&O European Ferries (Dover) Ltd* [1997] IRLR 401.

36 Thus if a member of staff is being harassed on age grounds and the manager's reaction is to move the person subjected to the harassment to a less interesting job this will constituted discrimination on the grounds of age (see *Deson v BL Cars Ltd* EAT 173/80).

Disciplinary and competence matters

Disciplinary matter

8.61 One area which consistently throws up problems in terms of discrimination is the discriminatory application of disciplinary sanctions. This is because, in part, of the way in which conduct is viewed by the employer or fellow employees. Thus what might appear as rational argument over a point when set down on paper becomes insolence when placed in the mouth of a 19-year-old. The same words uttered by the 45-year-old manager offended by them to a colleague would not arouse any offence. It is an area in which stereotypes have a practical impact.

> EXAMPLE 1: There is a stereotype that elderly people are more moral than younger people. A manager faced with a decision as to which of two people has committed an act of misconduct should be careful before assuming that the older person is more likely to be truthful about what happened. If that conclusion is reached, there should at least be some justification given for the belief.
>
> EXAMPLE 2: A young worker claims that she has been sexually harassed at work. The complaint is against a worker in his 60s. The manager's views on the plausibility of such harassment by an older worker may be based on assumptions such as the importance of respect in the generation to which the older worker belongs ('older people are more courteous'), or the manager's perception of the interest of that age group in sexual matters.

8.62 As with other areas of discrimination there is a risk that employers will regard complaints from certain age groups less seriously than those from others.

Competence matter

8.63 In a case in which competence is being considered, there is a danger of stereotypical thinking about older employees. There are a number of stereotypes surrounding age. For example, a manager may have information that the claimant, who is in her 50s, was responsible for a particular task and that task has not been done. The manager believes that as a person gets older their memory starts to fail and so concludes that claimant forgot to do the task. If the claimant had been in her

30s the manager would not have considered this as the immediately plausible explanation and would have assumed that there would be an explanation based on something other than competence.

8.64   Where there is a question of putting a person through a capability procedure age stereotypes can also play a difficult role. Clearly a younger worker will feel rightly aggrieved on seeing an older worker who is every bit as incapable as the younger worker avoiding competence procedures when the younger worker is being put through them. The same standard of competence or capability should be applied to all workers regardless of age, unless there is an objectively justifying reason for the differential treatment on grounds of age.

8.65   Finally the probationary period of employment is a period during employment where the parties to the relationship determine whether the decision to employ the claimant was correct. The newly employed person must frequently spend a considerable period of time being assessed and trained. Although every new employee has to go through this process it can be argued that the system disadvantages the age group that changes employment most frequently. This is likely to be one of the younger age groupings. The practice of having probationary periods will have to be justified in objective terms. Clearly for some jobs a probationary period will be appropriate because it gives enough time for all the training and the assessment of skills to be carried out. However for others a probationary period will have been retained simply because it has been used in other jobs and gives the employer the option of not continuing the employment relationship for any (lawful) reason. It is likely that tribunals will want to retain the probationary period, as justified by such an aim. However it is arguable that, as with many other strands of discrimination, the probationary period permits too much scope for subjective decision making and stereotypical thinking. Using a probationary period to see whether an employee would 'fit in', for example, would probably not be a legitimate aim.

Health and safety

8.66   The Framework Directive states at article 6(1) that differences in treatment may be 'objectively and reasonably justified by a legitimate aim, including legitimate employment policy, labour market and vocational training objectives, and if the means of achieving that aim are appropriate and necessary'. The following example is given:

The setting of special conditions on access to employment and vocational training, employment and occupation, including dismissal and remuneration conditions, for young people, older workers and persons with caring responsibilities in order to promote their vocational integration or to ensure their protection.

8.67 Accordingly, the health, welfare and safety of the individual (including protection of young people or older workers) could be a legitimate aim that could justify direct or indirect discrimination.[37] The importance of the legitimate aim that is being pursued should be weighed up against the discriminatory effects. It is arguable that where the legitimate aim is the protection of people's lives and safety, a bigger discriminatory effect will be permissible than where the legitimate aim is merely rewarding employee's loyalty. Take, for example, health and safety considerations for bus drivers reaching a particular age. Before mandatory retirement can be justified, it would be necessary for the employer to be able to show that there is a real (and random) risk that, after a particular age, the risk of heart attack increases significantly so that the passengers' lives are put at risk.[38]

8.68 The Royal College of Physicians' Occupational Medicine Faculty has recognised that workplace adaptations for the older worker require an objective evidence-based assessment of functional capacity in order to avoid unsubstantiated prejudice in the workplace. Whilst this is true of any age group, there is a requirement for objective and effective systems of health monitoring, rehabilitation after illness, job analysis, skill assessment, job coaching and retraining as well as job matching, which should lead to an effective management system that prevents discrimination and prejudice. It is worth also considering the findings of a report produced by the Health and Safety Laboratory, available from the Health and Safety Executive, *Facts and misconceptions about age, health status and employability*[39] in this regard.

8.69 Pre-employment health screening is not dealt with expressly in the regulations. This is a common feature used in some places of employment. It will form part of the arrangements captured by regulation 7(1)(a). By screening for certain health-related and medical conditions, there is a possibility that some segments of the older workforce could be excluded. This topic was raised during the initial consultation

---

37 See further the ACAS guidance.
38 Note, however, that in such cases there would have to be evidence of a particular risk to health which was also increased by age. Such health statistics will depend crucially on whether a group correlating to a potential working population is chosen or whether it includes much older people who are unlikely to be economically active. If the health risk is predictable in individuals it would be proportionate to have individual health checks rather than a mandatory retirement age.
39 Report No HSL/2005/20: www.hse.gov.uk/research/hsl_pdf/2005/hsl0520.pdf.

process for the Disability Discrimination Act (DDA) 1995. The government then considered that employers should be entitled to use whatever recruitment procedures best fitted their needs.[40] Issues of age and disability may be linked. Indeed, there could be some interesting challenges ahead where both sets of discrimination provisions are used simultaneously. Medical examinations, screenings and questionnaires are likely to constitute "arrangements" for the purposes of deciding to whom employment should be offered. As a general rule, whilst employers remain lawfully able to use pre-employment health screening, they must be able to justify doing so.

References and post-employment discrimination

8.70   Regulation 24 makes acts of post-employment discrimination unlawful where the discrimination or harassment 'arises out of and is closely connected to' the employment relationship.

8.71   Although there is rarely a contractual obligation on employers to provide references, failure to provide references could be discriminatory if such failure (either during or post employment) is on grounds of age. The key discrimination authority is the House of Lords decision in *Rhys-Harper v Relaxion Group plc; D'Souza v London Borough of Lambeth; Jones v 3M Healthcare Ltd,*[41] although it is overtaken by the insertion of amendments to the Sex Discrimination Act (SDA) 1975[42] (and the other equality provisions), which are replicated in regulation 24 of the age regulations. However, despite the new statutory provisions, their Lordships' reasoning in respect of whether the act of discrimination or harassment 'arises out of or is closely connected' to the relationship is helpful.

8.72   Failure to provide a reference on grounds of age both during and post-employment is likely to be discriminatory unless the reason can be objectively justified. In *Coote v Granada Hospitality Ltd,*[43] the European Court of Justice (ECJ) held that a failure to provide references because the employee had brought or threatened to bring legal proceedings alleging discrimination constituted victimisation.

8.73   If an employer does provide a reference to a third party (or internally, for promotions, transfers or access to other benefits), the employer is

---

40   HC Deb Standing Committee E, col 151.

41   [2003] IRLR 484.

42   Sex Discrimination Act 1975 (Amendment) Regulations 2003 SI No 1657.

43   C-185/97, [1998] IRLR 656.

under a duty of care to provide a true, accurate and fair reference.[44] Nor must the employer give an unfair or misleading impression, even where the facts set out are accurate. It is in this area where employers (through their managers, supervisors, human resources etc) must take great care not to make comments that could be discriminatory, or make presumptions relating to age.

> EXAMPLE: Laura writes a reference about Robin, stating 'He is really rather energetic, considering his age'. This contains assumptions that older people will not be energetic, and minimises or even negates her positive comments on Robin. The provision of that reference could be discriminatory.

8.74 Since an employee, or former employee, or a third party could sue the employer if a negligent reference is given, great care must be taken to ensure a reference is factually accurate. It is advisable to make negative statements only where there are supporting grounds to do so, such as through an investigation process, or where the employee has been disciplined, or where that individual has cause to know about his or her employer's concerns. Manifest unfairness or unreasonableness in the giving or refusal to give a reference could lead to a tribunal concluding that there has been discrimination.

8.75 Discrimination in the giving or refusal to give a reference can take place after employment has ended, by virtue of regulation 24.

8.76 In *Chief Constable of West Yorkshire Police v Khan*,[45] the House of Lords held that employers ought to be able to take steps to preserve their position in pending discrimination proceedings without laying themselves open to a charge of victimisation. In that case, the Chief Constable was found not to have victimised the complainant sergeant in the refusal to provide a reference since, on the facts, that refusal was only temporary, allowing the proceedings to terminate before a reference was in fact provided. A key question is whether the employer would have refused the reference request if the litigation had been concluded, whatever the outcome. If the answer is no, the reason for the refusal is likely to be the existence of pending proceedings rather than the fact that the employee complainant commenced them. However, if on the facts, the real reason for the refusal is that the employee had in fact commenced proceedings, there is likely to be a finding of discrimination by victimisation.

44 *Bartholomew v Hackney LBC* [1999] IRLR 246, *Spring v Guardian Assurance plc* [1994] IRLR 460.
45 [2001] IRLR 830, HL.

8.77   It may be possible to seek disclosure of the references through the questionnaire procedure, which would enable a claimant to decide better whether or not to bring a claim for post-employment discrimination. The time limits always must be borne strictly in mind when considering pre-action questionnaires. Since they are automatically extended by three months if a grievance letter is lodged within the normal time limit (three months from provision of reference), it will usually be safer to lodge a grievance early if there is any indication of impending proceedings.

8.78   An act of discrimination or harassment may run over the end of the employment relationship so as to form a continuing act with post relationship harassment[46] provided that entire course of conduct has sufficient proximity to the relationship to warrant protection having regard to the purpose of the legislation.

EXAMPLE: A self-employed model is harassed by an employee of the hiring party on the grounds of age. After the hire is finished the employee continues to send abusive text messages to the effect that the model is too old to continue to be a model (a persistent theme). Such behaviour would have sufficient proximity to the relationship to warrant protection as it arises out of the relationship.

Equality policies

8.79   Best practice dictates that all companies or organisations, regardless of size, have an Equality Policy, which is publicly available to all employees and on which employees are trained and updated periodically. This helps reduce the likelihood of discrimination, victimisation and harassment taking place. From an employer's perspective, it could help to limit liability if a claim is brought to the tribunal, since regulation 25(3) allows an employer a defence to a claim of vicarious liability where the employer can prove that he or she took such steps as were reasonably practicable to prevent the employee from committing a discriminatory act. In respect of this defence, tribunals will always consider whether an Equality Policy exists (which must be updated now to include age), the terms of that policy, how accessible the policy was to the staff and in particular the employee said to have committed the act of discrimination or harassment, and whether training to that individual had been provided in the implantation of that policy. In

---

46 *Bhs Ltd and anor v Walker and anor* EAT, 11.5.05 (0001/05).

practice, where no policy exists, and there has been little or no training on equality issues, it is difficult for employers to succeed in a defence to a claim for vicarious liability.

8.80   The training that will have to be given in respect of the equal opportunities policy of a company will have to reflect the much more flexible concept of discrimination that is employed in age discrimination. Managers will have to get used to showing that although a decision may have some age impact that impact is justified by reference to the aim of the managerial action and that it is proportionate to that aim. This means managers will have to get used to conducting balancing exercises between the interests of the affected age group and the needs of the business. In grievance hearings and during other challenges to decisions they will have to have evidence of the decision making process. Managers in public authorities should already have had some training in dealing with such balancing of rights when considering the human rights of those with whom they have to deal. A similar process is engaged when considering justification of direct discrimination. It underlines the need for objective, evidence based decision making.

8.81   It is vital that those employees who make decisions relating to the employment of others (recruitment, selection, day-to-day activities about work allocation, appraisals, quality and standards etc) understand the organisation's policy on age discrimination. Supervisors and managers should be trained in recognising and dealing with bullying and harassment.

8.82   The policy should contain a clear statement of purpose, and a definition of discrimination, harassment and victimisation. It should give examples of what could constitute discriminatory behaviour, and set out clearly why discrimination and harassment is hurtful and unacceptable. The policy should explain what employees should do if they consider they are the victims of harassment, bullying or discrimination, whether by reference to another specific policy, or in a clear series of steps set out within the Equality Policy.

Instructions to commit unlawful acts

8.83   By virtue of regulation 5, where an employer, A, or a fellow employee, B, requires an employee, D, to carry out an act which would be unlawful conduct pursuant to the age regulations, and then A or B treats D less favourably than he or she would treat other persons in the same circumstances because D refused or did not carry out that instruction, or because D complained about having been given that instruction, A or

B's actions constitute unlawful discrimination. This is dealt with in more detail in chapter 4.

> EXAMPLE: Mr Q owns company X. He is looking to hire new recruits and has decided that he only wants young, attractive people between the ages of 20 and 25. He has no real reason for this other than the fact that he wants to be surrounded by young, beautiful people. He instructs Mr D to refuse to hire anyone outside of those age groups. Mr D refuses to carry out this instruction and hires the best person available for the job, who happens to be in his 30s. Mr Q then refuses to allow Mr D to continue in a recruitment and selection role. Mr Q's behaviour would constitute unlawful discrimination.

Vicarious liability

8.84　By virtue of regulation 25, employers are liable for any unlawful act committed by an employee in the course of his employment, whether or not it was done with the employer's knowledge or approval.[47]

8.85　A problem in practice can be the distinction between whether an act, particularly in respect of harassment, was committed in the course of employment. If harassment is clearly committed outside of the workplace and working hours, arguably it may not have been committed in the course of employment.[48] However, in practice, if there is a pattern of harassment, even if it takes place practically outside of the workplace and working hours, there may be knock-on effects at work which impact upon the relevant employee's, or indeed other employees' employment. In those circumstances, a complainant could argue that the employer is liable for acts of discrimination that take place 'at work' rather than merely when they are committed in the workplace.

8.86　However, an employer has a defence available under regulation 25(3), if the employer can prove that he or she took such steps as were reasonably practicable to prevent the employee, who is alleged to have committed a discriminatory act or harassed the complainant, from doing that act. The tribunal will consider whether appropriate steps have been taken to discipline employees who have been found guilty of unlawful discrimination.[49] The EAT has held that if there existed steps

---

47　Reg 25(1).
48　See *Sidhu v Aerospace Composite Technology Ltd* [2000] IRLR 602, CA, *Jones v Tower Boot Co Ltd* [1997] ICR 254, CA.
49　See *Balgobin v Tower Hamlets London Borough Council* [1987] ICR 829.

which would have been reasonable to take, the respondent must take them if he or she wants to succeed in making out the defence, even if he or she cannot show that those steps would have prevented the discrimination or harassment from taking place.[50]

8.87   In *Hawley v Luminar Leisure Ltd*[51] the appellant was visiting a nightclub when one of the doormen hit him so hard that he fell to the floor and suffered serious personal injury. The doorman was not employed by the nightclub, but by a security company to whom the nightclub had subcontracted its security arrangements. The Court of Appeal held that the nightclub exercised sufficient control, in a practical and effective sense, to make the nightclub the 'temporary deemed employer' for the purposes of a finding of vicarious liability. Factors that the court took into consideration included the fact that the doormen were supervised by the manager of the nightclub and provided detailed guidance to them in respect of admissions into the nightclub, as well as subjecting them to the nightclub's code of conduct.

Liability for the acts of third parties

8.88   The key case is *MacDonald v Advocate General for Scotland*,[52] which disapproved *Burton v De Vere Hotels Ltd*.[53] Where an employee is subjected to acts of discrimination or harassment or bullying by third parties, the employer is not liable simply because he had some or some sufficient control over the circumstances in which the discrimination or harassment took place to have prevented it from happening. In that case, a school was not liable for the taunting of a teacher by a pupil on grounds of her sexual orientation. Where the employer will be liable is in circumstances for which the employer failed to intervene in contravention of the regulations themselves.

EXAMPLE: If a teacher complained to her employer that she was being bullied on grounds of her age by pupils, and the school did not respond to her complaint in the same way as it did to a younger teacher, that in and of itself would be an act of unlawful discrimination. However, the pupil's bullying itself would not be an act of harassment for which the school could be sued under the age regulations.

50 See *Caniffe v East Riding of Yorkshire Council* [2000] IRLR 555, EAT.
51 [2006]EWCA Civ 18, 24 January 2006.
52 [2003] ICR 937, HL.
53 [1997] ICR 1.

8.89   The decision in *Pearce v Governing Body of Mayfield Secondary School*[54] was made under the pre-directive regime. Article 2.3 provides:

> 3. Harassment shall be deemed to be a form of discrimination within the meaning of paragraph 1, when unwanted conduct related to any of the grounds referred to in Article 1 takes place with the purpose or effect of violating the dignity of a person and of creating an intimidating, hostile, degrading, humiliating or offensive environment. In this context, the concept of harassment may be defined in accordance with the national laws and practice of the Member States.

8.90   This does not require that the unwanted conduct is sourced in law or in fact the employer. The aim of the provision is to ensure the dignity of the worker by protecting the worker from such unwanted conduct. It is arguable that the decision in *Pearce* does not affect the ability of the worker to make the employer liable in situations in which the effect of an omission on the part of the employer is to cause unwanted conduct having the effects mentioned in the article. Although the state has power to define harassment, that definition must be such as to achieve the objective aimed at by the directive.[55]

Aiding unlawful acts

8.91   A person who knowingly aids another person to do an act which is made unlawful by the age regulations is treated as if he or she had committed that unlawful act.[56] This expressly includes an employee or agent for whose act the employer or principal is or would be liable (but for the operation of the regulation 25(3) defence), who will be deemed to aid to the doing of the act by the employer or principal.[57] This means that the employee may also be liable in his or her own personal capacity, even if the employer succeeds in establishing a regulation 25(3) defence.[58] See also paras 4.46–4.50 in chapter 4.

---

54 *Pearce v Mayfield Secondary School Governing Body* [2003] UKHL 34; [2004] 1 All ER 339; [2003] ICR 937; [2003] IRLR 512.
55 See chapter 2 for further discussion of this point.
56 Reg 26(1).
57 Reg 26(2).
58 *Crofton v Yeboah* [2002] IRLR 634.

Changes to the Employment Rights Act 1996

8.92 The upper age limit to unfair dismissal claims is removed. The tapering-down provisions which reduce the award in the period leading up to the previous upper age limit are also removed.

The removal of the upper age limit means that a dismissal for capability (for example) over the employer's normal retirement age will be subject to exactly the same consideration by the tribunal as a capability dismissal below that age.

8.93 Retirement for employees aged 65 or over is dealt with in more detail in chapter 9. Because compulsory retirement is a dismissal, the provisions in the ERA 1996 on unfair dismissal are changed so that a genuine retirement conducted in accordance with the detailed rules set out in Schedules 6 and 7 to the regulations (which include the necessity to follow certain procedures) will be a fair dismissal.

8.94 The principal changes affecting redundancy payments set out in Schedule 8 are:

- the lower age limit is removed;
- the upper age limit of 65 is removed;
- both the two-year qualification period and the maximum of 20 countable years will remain;
- the tapering down rule is removed;
- the Redundancy Payments Regulations 1965[59] permitting the offset of certain pension and lump sums are revoked;
- length of service as a criterion is retained.

Statutory dismissal, disciplinary and grievance procedures

8.95 The statutory disciplinary, dismissal and grievance procedures will apply in cases of age discrimination. The procedures and accompanying rules are set out in the Employment Act (EA) 2002 and the Dispute Resolution Regulations 2004.[60]

8.96 Employers are required to follow minimum dismissal or disciplinary procedures when dismissing an employee or taking relevant disciplinary action. Employees are required to lodge a grievance before bringing a claim for age discrimination (in most cases) to the employment tribunal. The procedures are complicated and there remains a great deal

59 SI No 1932.
60 The Employment Act 2002 (Dispute Resolution) Regulations 2004 SI No 752.

of uncertainty about how they apply to particular cases. Advisers are advised to adopt a cautious approach and ensure that grievances are lodged in a timely and complete manner.

8.97   The EA 2002 is amended[61] so that regulation 36 (age discrimination in the employment field) will be added to the list of tribunal jurisdictions to which:

- section 31 applies for adjustment of awards for non-completion of statutory procedures, by insertion at the end of EA 2002 Sch 3;
- section 32 applies for complaints where the employee must first submit a written grievance to the employer in order to bring a claim to the tribunal, by insertion at the end of EA 2002 Sch 4;
- section 38 applies in relation to proceedings where the employer has failed to give a statement of employment particulars, by insertion at the end of EA 2002 Sch 5.

Statutory dismissal and disciplinary procedures

8.98   The standard dismissal and disciplinary procedures apply when the employer first contemplates dismissing or taking relevant disciplinary action against an employee.[62] There is a standard and modified procedure. The latter applies when the employer has dismissed the employee already for gross misconduct and it was reasonable for the employer to have dismissed the employee before speaking to him or her.[63] Relevant disciplinary action includes an actual dismissal, including failure to renew a fixed-term contract. It will not apply to constructive dismissal so long as the employer has not instigated disciplinary action first, in which case the dismissal and disciplinary procedures will apply.

8.99   The employer should follow the checklist set out below:

- The employer should send a Step 1 letter setting out the employee's alleged conduct or characteristics or other circumstances which lead him or her to contemplate dismissing or taking other relevant disciplinary action, and invite the employee to a meeting.
- It is advisable to set out the basis for the grounds in the letter, including relevant redundancy criteria or the basis of the evidence in a misconduct dismissal, such as the investigation report. In any event, this must be done before the meeting.

---

61 Age Regs 2006 Sch 8 para 36.
62 Dispute Resolution Regs 2004 reg 3(1).
63 Dispute Resolution Regs 2004 reg 3(2).

- The employee must have a reasonable opportunity to consider his or her response before the meeting.
- The employee must take all reasonable steps to attend the meeting.
- At Step 2, the meeting must be held in a reasonable location and at a reasonable time. This includes holding the meeting within a reasonable period.
- The meeting must be conducted in a manner which enables both employer and employee to explain their case.
- Following the meeting, the employer must notify the employee of the decision and the right to appeal.
- At Stage 3, if the employee wishes to appeal, he must inform the employer.
- The employer must then invite the employee to an appeal meeting, which must be held at a reasonable time (including within a reasonable period) and at a reasonable location.
- As far is as reasonably practicable, the employer should try to ensure that a more senior manager conducts the appeal than at the original grievance hearing.
- The meeting, again, must be conducted in a manner permitting both sides to explain their concerns.
- Following the appeal hearing, the employer must notify the employee of the final decision.

8.100   Each step, action or decision in the process must take place without unreasonable delay.[64]

8.101   The worker has a right to be accompanied to a grievance hearing by a work colleague or trade union official.[65]

8.102   If the employee, the employer or the employee's representative cannot attend the grievance or the appeal meeting for reasons which were not reasonable foreseeable at the time the meeting was arranged, the employer must set a new date. If a new date is fixed and again, a party (or representative) cannot attend for unforeseeable reasons, each party is deemed to have complied with the procedure and nothing further has to be done.[66]

8.103   Under the modified procedure, the employer must send the employee a letter setting out the employee's alleged gross misconduct which has led to the dismissal and the basis for considering the

---

64   EA 2002 Sch 2 para 12.
65   Note that this right is derived from Employment Relations Act 1999 s10: There are different remedies if the employer fails to allow the colleague or trade union official.
66   Dispute Resolution Regs 2004 reg 13.

employee was guilty of gross misconduct.[67] If the employee wishes to appeal, he or she must inform the employer, and the same steps in respect of the appeals procedure under the standard dismissal and disciplinary procedures are followed.

8.104   A recent decision of the EAT, *Silman v ICTS (UK) Ltd*,[68] should be noted for its rejection of the submission that if new allegations of misconduct come to light during the course of the disciplinary hearing, that is a new matter which should be the subject of a letter by the employer identifying this conduct as a potential grounds for dismissal in order to comply with EA 2002 Sch 2 Part 1. The EAT held[69] that it is not necessary to create unnecessary technical hurdles for either employer or employee. The purpose, it said, of the procedures was to ensure that there is a proper and fair opportunity for the parties to seek to address any disciplinary issue and other matters which may lead to dismissal prior to the matter ending up in litigation before the employment tribunal. It was considered that frequently, evidence might emerge in the course of a disciplinary hearing that identifies potentially disciplinary conduct which, although closely related to the original alleged misconduct, is a variant of that. 'Shifts in the focus of the case will not lead to an obligation for the employer to write fresh missives on each occasion'. However, where a wholly distinct act of misconduct arises at some stage of the disciplinary or investigative process, employers would be required to comply with the procedures afresh.

Statutory grievance procedures

8.105   The statutory procedures relating to grievances will apply to individuals wishing to complain about breaches of their rights under the regulations. The main purpose of the procedure is to give employees an opportunity to bring their grievance or concerns to the attention of their employer before they bring any claims before the tribunal. There are strict time limits about when grievances must be brought, if the employee is not to be barred from bringing a claim about age discrimination to the employment tribunal (see chapter 11). Broadly, employees should bring their grievances as soon as is possible and/or appropriate and they must bring them within three months (four months at the latest if they are to have any chance of the tribunal

---

67   See EA 2002 Sch 2 paras 4–5 and 11–13.
68   UKEAT/0630/05/LA, 6 March 2006.
69   At para 22.

considering their claims) of the date of dismissal, or the act of discrimination, whichever is being complained about (see chapter 11).

8.106 There is both a standard procedure as well as a modified procedure, which is shorter but can only be used in specific, limited circumstances.

8.107 The employee is required to send a written grievance, in accordance with the statutory provisions in order to bring any claim relating to age discrimination before the tribunal. If he or she does not comply fully with the grievance procedure, his or her compensation may be reduced, even if the case is successful.

8.108 If the employee is claiming that only the act of dismissal (or failure to renew a fixed-term contract) was an act of discrimination, there is no requirement to lodge a grievance. However, if the employee has resigned and claims constructive dismissal, the grievance procedure does apply and he or she must bring a grievance, in accordance with the relevant provisions.[70]

8.109 In general, employees should ensure that they bring a grievance relating to any aspect of their employment, or any treatment of them in the course of their employment, which they consider has been discriminatory. It is arguable whether it is necessary to bring a grievance for harassment or actions taken by a fellow colleague, rather than the employer itself, since the wording of the regulations define a grievance as being 'a complaint by *an employee* about action which *his employer* [our italics] has taken or is contemplating taking in relation to him'. However, although there is as yet no authority on the point, the view of these authors is that it is advisable, if not strictly necessary, to bring a grievance in such circumstances so that there could be some attempt at conciliation by the employer without the need to bring the matter to the tribunal.

8.110 The modified grievance procedure applies when the employee has left his or her employment, where the standard grievance procedure was not previously completed and where the parties agree in writing that the modified procedure should apply.[71]

---

70 Age Regs 2006 Sch 8 para 36 provides that the age regulations are one of the tribunal jurisdictions in respect of which the employee must first submit a statement of grievance to the employer. Sch 8 para 64 inserts dismissal where retirement is either the reason or the principal reason into the list of those dismissals under regulation 4 of the Dispute Resolution Regs 2004 (dismissals to which the dismissal and disciplinary procedures do not apply).

71 Dispute Resolution Regs 2004 reg 6(3).

Standard grievance procedure

8.111 The Dispute Resolution Regulations 2004 only state that the employee must 'set out the grievance in writing'. It is not necessary to write the word 'grievance' in the letter, although it is preferable to mark the word 'grievance' clearly, and this should alert the employer better to his or her own obligations. Although there is no statutory guidance on the content and nature of the grievance complaint, the employee must inform the employer of the basis for the grievance before the grievance meeting is held. It is preferable that this is done on the body of the initial grievance letter.

8.112 In *Canary Wharf Management Ltd v Edebi*,[72] the EAT debated what was meant by 'grievance' within the meaning of the Employment Act in respect of whether a grievance had been raised under the DDA 1995. It is a useful case for advisers to consider when dealing with the issues of a grievance, and in particular, the timing, form and content of a grievance. The EAT's conclusions are referred to under the appropriate paragraphs below.

8.113 The Step 1 grievance is a minimal requirement to actually state that there is a grievance, and the essence of that should be what the employee communicates to the employment tribunal later on. There is no requirement for the employee to indicate that he expects or wants the grievance to be dealt with, since there is no requirement that he actively invoke the process. By contrast, the modified procedure requires both the grievance and the basis for the grievance to be set out in writing and sent to the employer. Once those requirements are met, the onus falls on the employer to arrange a meeting to deal with the grievance, although in respect of the standard procedure, at that stage, the employee will then have to notify the employer of the basis of that grievance.[73]

8.114 Ideally, the grievance should contain some or all of the following:
• the key facts;
• the key players, actors and instigators of the discrimination;
• the dates(where possible) or timings of incidents;
• the nature of the conduct;
• if discriminatory remarks have been made, it is preferable that they are set out as fully and clearly as possible;

72 UKEAT/0708/05/DA, before Elias J sitting alone.
73 *Canary Wharf Management v Edebi*, UKEAT/0708/05/DA, at paras 21–22 of the judgment.

- whether this is a continuing act, and if so, the history of the complaint;
- if the discrimination is said to be on grounds of age, and if possible why.

8.115   Complaint about an act can include a failure to act.[74]

8.116   There is flexibility in the form of the grievance. It may be raised in a resignation letter, or after the dismissal has taken place,[75] or raised by a solicitor in a communication to the employer's solicitor. It is immaterial whether other issues are raised at the same time as the complaint.[76] The discrimination questionnaire (see further chapter 11) does not constitute a grievance letter.[77]

8.117   Employees should follow this **checklist:**

- The employee should send a Step 1 letter to their employer, setting out the gist of the complaint.
- The employer must invite the employee to a meeting. Both the timing and the locating of the meeting must be reasonable, and held within a reasonable time from the sending of the grievance.
- If the employee wishes to add more substance to the basis of his or her complaint, this is the most appropriate time to do so, although it generally makes sense for all details to be included in the Step 1 letter at the outset.
- The employer must have a reasonable opportunity to consider his or her response before the meeting.
- At Step 2, the meeting takes place, which should be conducted in a manner permitting both sides to explain their side of the story or concerns.
- After the meeting, the employer must notify the employee of the decision, and inform the employee of the right to appeal.
- At Step 3, the employee must inform the employer if he wishes to appeal the decision.
- The employer must then invite the employee to an appeal meeting. Again, the timing and location of the meeting must be reasonable, and it should be held within a reasonable period.

---

74 *Galaxy Showers Ltd v Wilson* [2006] IRLR 83, EAT.
75 Which is one of the conditions for application of the modified procedure.
76 *Canary Wharf Management Ltd v Edebi,* note 73 above.
77 Dispute Resolution Regs 2004 reg 14.

> - The employee must take all reasonable steps to attend the appeal meeting.
> - So far as is reasonably practicable, the employer should try to ensure that a more senior manager conducts the appeal than at the original grievance hearing.
> - The meeting, again, must be conducted in a manner permitting both sides to explain their concerns.
> - Following the appeal hearing, the employer must notify the employee of the final decision.

8.118   Each step, action or decision in the process must take place without unreasonable delay.[78]

8.119   The worker has a right to be accompanied to a grievance hearing by a work colleague or trade union official.[79]

8.120   If the employee, the employer or the employee's representative cannot attend the grievance or the appeal meeting for reasons which were not reasonably foreseeable at the time the meeting was arranged, the employer must set a new date. If a new date is fixed and again, a party (or representative) cannot attend for unforeseeable reasons, each party is deemed to have complied with the procedure and nothing further has to be done.[80]

Modified grievance procedure

8.121   Under the modified procedure, the employee must set out in writing the grievance, and its basis, and send this to the employer. The employer then must send the employee a written response.[81]

8.122   In individual circumstances, the employee may or may not wish to be interviewed by the employer following the termination of his or her employment. If this applies, the employee should state that at the outset, and invite the employer to make any findings on grounds of facts, documents or his own investigations.

---

78 EA 2002 Sch 2 para 12.
79 Note that this right is derived from Employment Relations Act 1999 s10. There are different remedies if the employer fails to allow the colleague or trade union official.
80 Dispute Resolution Regs 2004 reg 13.
81 EA 2002 Sch 2 paras 9–10.

Consequences of not following the statutory procedures

8.123 Three consequences stem from not following the grievance procedure, but they only arise if the employee wants to bring a claim before the employment tribunal, since the procedures are not implied into the contract of employment:

   i) automatic unfair dismissal;
   ii) adjustment of compensation;
   iii) lack of jurisdiction, barring claims before the employment tribunal.

Automatic unfair dismissal

8.124 If the employer does not follow or complete the statutory dismissal and disciplinary procedures, and the non-completion of the procedure is wholly or mainly attributable to the employer's failure to comply with those requirements, the employee can claim automatic unfair dismissal under ERA 1996 s98A, if he or she has at least one year's service.[82]

Adjustment of compensation

8.125 If the employer or the employee fails to comply with either of the statutory procedures, compensation can be increased or reduced by between 10% and 50%. For example, if the employer has failed to comply with the procedures, then the employee, assuming he or she is successful in winning the tribunal case, could have his or her compensation increased by between 10% and 50%. If it is an automatic unfair dismissal, there is also a minimum of four weeks payable for the basic award.[83] If the employee has failed to comply with procedures (beyond lodging the Step 1 grievance letter of which failure to comply in the relevant time scales will lead to the claim being barred for want of jurisdiction), but nevertheless goes on to win his or her case, his or her compensation could be reduced by between 10% and 50%.

8.126   In what way can the employee fail to comply with the procedures? Once he or she has lodged the Step 1 grievance, which is the basic minimum requirement before bringing a claim to the tribunal, he or she could fail to attend the grievance hearing without reasonable cause, or fail to set out the basis of the complaint, having simply lodged a bare grievance. There is lack of clarity as to whether the employee is required to submit an appeal once the employer has informed him

82 ERA 1996 s108.
83 ERA 1996 s120(1A).

or her of the right to an appeal, since the wording of the procedure is unclear. Although the point has not yet been clarified, it is advisable for employees to follow the procedure all the way through, unless there is very clear and good reason for them not to do so (such as threatening conduct from the employer) in order to avoid unnecessary reduction of their compensation.

8.127   There is no guidance on the sliding scale of increase or reduction by 10–50%. The following factors are likely to be helpful:

- whether non-compliance was deliberate;
- manner of non-compliance. In *Sutton v The Ranch*,[84] the employment tribunal at first instance awarded an uplift of 50% where the employer had deliberately prevented the employee from attending a grievance hearing, refused to allow her a companion and then refused altogether to comply with the procedure;
- conduct of both parties;
- timeliness of compliance.

Employment tribunal claim to be barred for want of jurisdiction

8.128   By section 32(2), the employment tribunal has no jurisdiction where it concerns a matter relating to age discrimination in the employment field (except purely dismissal by the employer as set out above), and *the grievance requirement has not been complied with*. In other words, if the employee wishes to raise a complaint of age discrimination (except for a pure employer-instigated dismissal), and has failed to set out the grievance in writing and sent the statement or a copy of it to the employer,[85] the tribunal has no jurisdiction to hear the complaint.

8.129   Step 1 of the standard grievance procedure is a minimal requirement and is basically that the employee should set out in writing a complaint relating to age discrimination, and that he makes the same complaint to the employer as he does to the employment tribunal. In respect of Step 1 of the standard procedure, there is not even a need for that to be substantiated with evidence since that requirement arises at Step 2 of the procedure.[86] However, as set out above, it is preferable that grievance letters do set out the basis for the complaint. In respect of the

---

84 UKEAT/0072/06, uplift awarded at first instance and unaffected at appeal.

85 This is the requirement identified in paragraph 6, which is the Step 1 of the Standard Procedure, or paragraph 9 which is Step 1 of the modified procedure, which requires the grievance and the basis for it to be set out in writing and a statement or copy of it sent to the employer.

86 See *Canary Wharf Management v Edebi*, note 73 above.

modified procedure, both the grievance *and* the basis for it must be set out in writing and a statement or copy of it sent to the employer.

8.130 The content of the complaint must be broadly that which is raised before the employment tribunal, although technical arguments about precision are unlikely to be greeted happily.[87] It is, however, necessary that the employers, on a fair reading of the grievance statement and having regard to the particular context in which it is made, can be expected to appreciate that the relevant complaint is being raised.[88] It is vital, however, to make it clear that the complaints raise the question of age discrimination, otherwise the employers may argue that they simply could not have been expected to understand that the issues complained about arose in this manner.

8.131 EA 2002 s32 requires the employee to have sent the employer a written statement of grievance, and waited at least 28 days for the employer to respond. If that has not taken place, the employment tribunal will not hear the complaint.

8.132 If the grievance has been raised properly, then in certain circumstances, the time limit for lodging a complaint with the employment tribunal is extended by a further three months. So long as a Step 1 grievance letter has been sent to the employer within the normal employment tribunal time limit (which is three months in most cases), the time limit for presenting a claim to the tribunal is extended by three months. So, for example, if the employee considers he has been harassed on grounds of age, which was the cause of his resignation, and therefore wishes to claim constructive dismissal, he must present a grievance to the employer within the normal time limit for bringing a claim for unfair dismissal, which is three months. If he does that, the time limits for presenting a claim to the employment tribunal are extended by three months automatically, pursuant to regulation 15(1) and (3)(b) of the Dispute Resolution Regulations 2004. It does not matter whether the procedures have been complied with by the employer or remain incomplete at the time the employee presents his or her claim.

8.133 In *Singh t/a Rainbow International v Taylor*,[89] the EAT held that the statutory extension of time under regulation 15(1) of the Dispute Resolution Regulations 2004 means three months, and not three months less one day.

---

87 See *Canary Wharf Management v Edebi*, note 73 above, at para 24 of the judgment.
88 Ibid, at para 25 of the judgment.
89 UKEAT/0183/06/MAA, 24 May 2006, before HHJ Birtles.

8.134   Although there is no maximum time limit prior to lodging the claim with the tribunal, the grievance must be extant. The employer may argue that a grievance is no longer outstanding since it has been dealt with, or the employee has not pursued it in circumstances where it may properly be inferred he no longer wishes to have it determined. In those circumstances, it would be necessary for the employee to raise the complaint in writing again.[90]

8.135   Advisers should ensure the following **checklist** is followed:

- Does the standard or modified grievance procedure apply?
- If the standard procedure applies, did the employee present a grievance?
- If so, when?
- If this has not been done before employment ended, or within three months of the act of discrimination:
  - a grievance should be lodged immediately;
  - 28 days should then be waited before lodging a claim before the employment tribunal.
- If the modified procedure applies, the employee or the adviser should send a statement of grievance, including the basis of the grievance to the employer within the normal time limit, which is generally three months from the date of the act complained of.

---

90 *Canary Wharf Management v Edebi*, note 74 above.

CHAPTER 9

Retirement

Key points
- Dismissal where retirement is the reason is not an unlawful act of discrimination and is not unfair.
- The reason for the dismissal must be found in accordance with the statutory procedure.
- The employer may create a normal retirement age above 65 or below it. It must be justified. If none is set, 65 is the retirement age.
- The employer must write to the employee 6-12 months before the proposed date of retirement informing of the date and of the right to request to continue working;
- The employer must consider a formally made request to continue working.
- The process leading up to the retirement dismissal remains subject to the Age Regulations 2006.
- The exception for retirement does not apply to office holders or other non-employees.

Introduction

9.1   Retirement is a termination of employment due to age. One of the most controversial areas in the new Employment Equality (Age) Regulations 2006 is the provision made for retirement of employees at the age of 65. Regulation 30 provides:

Exception for retirement

30(1) This regulation applies in relation to an employee within the meaning of section 230(1) of the 1996 Act, a person in Crown employment, a relevant member of the House of Commons staff, and a relevant member of the House of Lords staff.

(2) Nothing in Part 2 or 3 shall render unlawful the dismissal of a person to whom this regulation applies at or over the age of 65 where the reason for the dismissal is retirement.

(3) For the purposes of this regulation, whether or not the reason for a dismissal is retirement shall be determined in accordance with sections 98ZA to 98ZF of the 1996 Act.

9.2   It is debatable whether this provision is compatible with the Framework Directive. The matter is likely to be settled by early litigation which has been issued by Heyday, a branch of Age Concern England.[1]

1   *R on the application of the Incorporated Trustees of the National Council for Aging v The Secretary of State for Trade and Industry* (Admin Ct CO/5485/2006).

9.3   What follows assumes that the current formulation of the regulations survives challenge.

9.4   The ACAS guidance summarises the situation:

> The Regulations set a default retirement age of 65 (to be reviewed in 2011). This means you can retire employees or set retirement ages within your company at or above 65. Retirements or retirement ages below the default retirement age will need to satisfy the test of objective justification (see page 30). However, you do not have to have a fixed retirement age. Indeed, there are many business benefits to adopting a flexible approach to the employment and work patterns of older workers. Employees will have the right to request to continue working beyond their retirement date and you have a duty to give consideration to such requests. Think about each request on an individual basis – taking into account opportunities to vary the employee's hours or the duties they perform. You are under no obligation to agree to such requests.

9.5   The provisions concerning retirement represent some of the most complex procedures that have been introduced in respect of an anti-discrimination right, save perhaps for the equal pay provisions.[2] They represent an intra-governmental compromise between the Department of Work and Pensions (DWP) and the Department of Trade and Industry (DTI). The former wished to get rid of retirement ages (because of the implications for drawing of pensions) the latter wished to impose the least possible burden on business.[3] Finally, the Regulatory Impact Assessment of March 2006 stated:

> This approach aims to promote greater choice for older workers without an unnecessary burden on business – many of whom rely on retirement ages as an important means of workforce planning – and to avoid adverse effects on occupational pensions and other employment benefits.

9.6   And in discussing the various options for the treatment of retirement discrimination the Regulatory Impact Assessment stated:

> d. A national DRA [default retirement age] of 65 and allowing employers to set an EJRA, and also giving employees a right to request to work beyond their employers' retirement age (if they have one) or 65 (if the employer chooses to make use of the DRA).

> 18. Failing to implement the Directive (i.e., doing nothing) would leave the UK non-compliant with the European Directive. Option d is the closest to legislation to maintain the status quo.

---

2   They are more complex, for example, than the family friendly provisions on which they are said to be modelled.

3   See the Regulatory Impact Assessment March 2006. See the discussion at paras 1.101–1.116.

9.7   It is not the intention of this book to explore the rather Delphic reference to greater choice for older workers. However, the only choice that appears to be conferred on older workers is the choice to ask the employer if they can carry on working after age 65 (if that is what they want to do). They were already able to do that. The Regulations appear to do little to improve the lot of those reaching age 65 and certainly provide limited protection to a worker whose employer gets the dismissal procedure right. Note that even if the procedure is followed, only the dismissal is removed from protection. Each step prior to dismissal may need to be justified under regulation 3. For example, the decision not to extend a person's contract after retirement may require justification if age/an age stereotype is a factor. There is to be a review of the retirement arrangements in 2011, so that the government's current position could be summed up in the Augustine saying 'Lord make me holy, but not yet'. For the next few years, however, the system described below is the system practitioners will have to use.

Exception for retirement

9.8   In the UK there is no compulsory retirement age. There has also been no national default retirement age (DRA). Employers have been able to dismiss an employee after the date on which the employee reaches the normal retiring age in that employment without breach of the unfair dismissal legislation. What the new provisions state is that if the employer dismisses on the date on which the employee reaches the normal retirement age or in default of one, age 65 and if the employer follows the correct procedure, the reason for dismissal is deemed to be retirement and *the dismissal* is also not capable of being found to be an act of age discrimination. Whether this is lawful in the light of the Framework Directive is highly contentious.[4]

9.9   Regulation 30 states that nothing in Part 2 or 3 of the regulations renders unlawful the dismissal of an employee[5] at or over the age of 65 where the reason for the dismissal is retirement.[6] The regulation applies only in relation to employees, those in Crown employment and various parliamentary staff.[7] Other workers' dismissals for retirement must be objectively justified.

4 See *Mangold v Helm* [2006] IRLR 143.
5 For the purposes of the ERA 1996.
6 Reg 30(2).
7 Reg 30(3). Thus partners, office holders and workers are not affected.

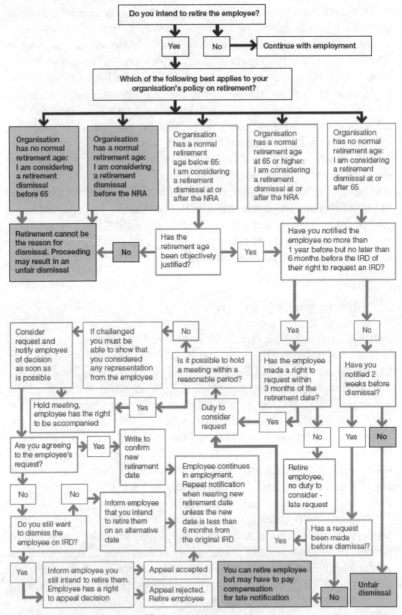

Notes: NRA means normal retirement age   IRD means intended retirement date

8   For intended retirement date see para 9.52 onwards.

Source: Reproduced from *Age and the Workplace*, ACAS, 2006 pp48 and 49.

9.10 Having established that the person is an employee in the sense given to that term in the Employment Rights Act (ERA) 1996, the next step in determining whether the claimant has been dismissed for retirement is to establish the reason using the statutory scheme. The discussion now goes into a consideration of that scheme.

9.11 The ACAS guidance summarises the scheme in the following way:

Fair retirement

A fair retirement is one that:
- takes effect on or after the default retirement age (or on or after the employer's normal retirement age – if there is one) and
- where the employer has given the employee written notice of the date of their intended retirement and told them about their right to request to continue working. ...

If the employer's normal retirement age is below the age of 65, it must be objectively justified.

For the retirement to be classed as 'fair' you need to have informed the employee in writing of their intended retirement date and of their right to make a request to work beyond retirement age at least six months in advance (but no more than 12 months before the intended date).

If they do make such a request, you must have followed the correct procedure for dealing with it.

9.12 Before setting out to describe the scheme in linear prose, a quick visual overview may help (*shown on opposite page*):

Finding the reason for dismissal – amendments to the ERA 1996

9.13 The reason for dismissal is determined in accordance with a process introduced into the ERA 1996 in ss98ZA–98ZF. Where these do not exclusively apply, the reason for dismissal for unfair dismissal purposes will be the set of psychological causes or facts operating on the mind of the employer.

A reason for the dismissal of an employee is a set of facts known to the employer, or it may be beliefs held by him, which cause him to dismiss the employee.[9]

9 Cairns LJ in *Abernethy v Mott Hay and Anderson* [1974] ICR 323 at 330 and *W Devis & Sons Ltd v Atkins* [1977] ICR 662, HL). Cairns LJ also said in the *Abernethy* case:

'If at the time of the dismissal the employer gives a reason for it, that is no doubt evidence, at any rate against him as to the real reason, but it does not necessarily constitute the real reason'.

9.14   The first change that the regulations introduce to the ERA 1996 is that retirement becomes a potentially fair reason for dismissal.[10] The normal method of determining what the reason for dismissal is, in which the burden of proof lies on the employer, is made subject to the statutory provisions which determine whether retirement is the reason for dismissal.[11]

9.15   The legislation envisages several possibilities. The employee might be dismissed before the retirement age is reached. He or she might be dismissed on the retirement age or after it. If retirement is asserted to be a factor in the dismissal, that is to be approached by considering which of the following most aptly describes the situation of the employee and employer.

Determining the reason for dismissal where retirement is a factor

Case 1: No normal retirement age – dismissal before 65th birthday

9.16   The first situation to consider is where there is no normal retirement age.[12] Section 98ZA(1) ERA 1996 specifies that if there is no normal retirement age and the 'operative date of termination'[13] falls before the employee's 65th birthday, the tribunal cannot take retirement to be the reason (or a reason) for the dismissal.[14] In other words, if the dismissal takes effect before the 65th birthday, the reason cannot be retirement. The implication of such a finding is that the exception in regulation 30 does not apply and the age related dismissal is likely to be both unfair and an act of unlawful age discrimination, even if it purported to be a retirement.

---

10   ERA 1996 s98(2)(ba) inserted by Sch 8 Part 1 para 22.

11   ERA 1996 s98(2A).

12   'Normal retirement age', in the context of ERA 1996 s98 in relation to an employee, means the age at which employees in the employer's undertaking who hold, or have held, the same kind of position as the employee are normally required to retire (ERA 1996 s98ZH). See para 9.30 below.

13   'Operative date of termination' means (a) where the employer terminates the employee's contract of employment by notice, the date on which the notice expires, or (b) where the employer terminates the contract of employment without notice, the date on which the termination takes effect.

14   NB, for the purposes of the unfair dismissal provisions only. Of course if the reason was retirement, that will not be an excluded act of direct discrimination and the employer will have to be able to justify it as a species of direct discrimination. For unfair dismissal purpose age by itself is not a potentially fair reason.

> EXAMPLE: Mark works as a panel beater. He is 64. He takes a day sick due to a cold. On return to work his employer states that he is getting too old to do the job and retires him on the spot, bemoaning the fact that Mark would not have taken a day off in previous years. The employer does not have any normal retirement age for panel beaters. In fact Mark is able to do his job properly and could have worked for the employer for another five or six years before he wanted to retire (due to his financial situation). Mark will be able to claim unfair dismissal but also, because the employer is not allowed to assert retirement as a reason for dismissal and it is clear that the dismissal is on the grounds of the employer's stereotypical assumptions concerning age and capability, Mark will be able to assert that his dismissal was an act of unjustified direct age discrimination.

Case 2: No normal retirement age and operative date on or after 65

9.17 Where the employee has no normal retirement age, and the operative date of termination falls on or after the date when the employee reaches the age of 65, section 98ZB applies to the dismissal. The Act envisages several different scenarios depending on whether and the extent to which, the employer has followed the procedure in the Regulations relating to retirement dismissals.

Scenario 1: paragraph 2 notification

9.18 Where the employer has notified the employee in accordance with paragraph 2 of Schedule 6 to the 2006 regulations, and the contract of employment terminates on the intended date of retirement, retirement of the employee is taken to be the only reason for the dismissal by the employer and any other reason shall be disregarded[15]. Paragraph 2 of Schedule 6 to the 2006 regulations provides:

> 2.– (1) An employer who intends to retire an employee has a duty to notify the employee in writing of–
> (a) the employee's right to make a request; and
> (b) the date on which he intends the employee to retire, not more than one year and not less than six months before that date.

---

15   ERA 1996 s98ZB(1) and (2).

> EXAMPLE: Harriet is given notice by her boss, Frank, ten months before her 65th birthday that Pompeii Ltd is going to retire her on her 65th birthday and that she has a right to ask to carry on working after that date. Harriet does not want to do this and makes no request. After the end of her employment she decides that the dismissal was an act of age discrimination and seeks to assert that Frank made the decision to retire her based on his perception of the capabilities of people over 65 (Frank was always talking about how their powers declined). Harriet will not be able to assert capability as a reason for dismissal before the employment tribunal and will not be able to assert that the dismissal was either unfair or an act of age discrimination.

9.19   Provided the correct notification procedure is followed, it does not matter why that procedure was followed. No matter how discriminatory the reason for the decision to implement a retirement dismissal, provided the employer gets the procedure right, the employee has neither unfair dismissal rights nor age discrimination protection, in respect of the dismissal.

Scenario 2: paragraph 2 notification, but premature termination

9.20   Where the employer has notified the employee in accordance with paragraph 2 of Schedule 6 to the 2006 regulations,[16] but the contract of employment terminates before the intended date of retirement, retirement of the employee shall not be taken to be the reason (or a reason) for dismissal.[17] The retirement reason is not even treated as part of the set of reasons for dismissal. The fact that dismissal was because of the claimant's age will, however, be treated as one of the reasons for the dismissal. This will allow the claimant to bring a claim for age discrimination. The employer will have to try to justify the dismissal objectively.

> EXAMPLE: James receives notification from Frank that Pompeii Ltd wants to retire him on his 65th birthday and telling him he can ask to carry on working. He does want to do so. He sends in a written request to Frank saying how humiliating he finds it to have to ask to carry on, but stating that he wants to continue

16   See para 9.18 above.
17   ERA 1996 s98ZB(3).

> working indefinitely. Frank does not consult the personnel department but arranges a meeting at which he ridicules the reasons put forward by James whilst he considers them. He says that there is no way that he will agree to James carrying on working after 65 because everyone knows that after 65 capability decreases and he wouldn't want a dinosaur like James being dead weight around the place. James has pointed out in his letter that his work performance has been appraised as good consistently over the previous five years. Frank is unmoved and says that no, really, it will not do, James must go. James is infuriated by this and resigns, having lodged a grievance and given Frank enough time to respond before issuing proceedings.[18] At his tribunal Pompeii Ltd will not be able to assert that the reason for the dismissal was retirement. James will be able to assert that the reason for the constructive dismissal was unlawful age discrimination.

Scenario 3: no paragraph 2 notification and termination before the intended date

9.21 If the employer has not notified the employee in accordance with paragraph 2 of Schedule 6 to the 2006 regulations, and although there is an intended date of retirement in relation to the dismissal, the contract of employment terminates before it, retirement of the employee shall not be taken to be the reason (or a reason) for dismissal.[19]

9.22 There can be an intended date of retirement where the employer notifies the employee of the intended date of retirement more than

18 Employment Act 2002 Sch 4 is amended so that an employee wishing to complain of age discrimination must first submit a statement of grievance to their employer (Schedule 8 paragraph 36). Any employee who brings a claim relating to their right to work beyond their normal retirement age without going through the statutory grievance procedures will face the risk of a tribunal reducing their compensation by at least 10% and up to 50%. However, by regulation 4(1)(f) (inserted by Schedule 8 paragraph 64 to the regulations) the grievance procedure requirements do not apply if the reason (or if there is more than one, the principal reason) for the dismissal is retirement of the employee. So complaints of dismissal where retirement is the principal reason will not need to go through the grievance procedure. However, claims that dismissal was on the grounds of age or where retirement is deemed not to be a reason will. The constructive dismissal of a person resigning because of being treated poorly during the process will be subject to the grievance regime.

19 ERA 1996 s98ZB(4). For paragraph 2 notification see para 9.18 above.

14 days before the date on which the retirement is due to take effect.[20] There can also be an intended date of retirement where the employee notifies the employer of the date due to a reasonable belief that it is the date of retirement.[21]

9.23   Where the employer in fact terminates the contract prior to that date, retirement cannot be taken to be any reason for the dismissal. However, age can be taken to be a reason for the dismissal and Part 2 of the regulations will apply to the dismissal.

> EXAMPLE: After Jack was given notice of dismissal for retirement (and the intended date of retirement) three weeks before his 65th birthday, he goes into Frank's office and, in front of Barbara the personnel officer, threatens to go to the local press with the goings-on at the previous year's Christmas party, unless he is kept on. An argument ensues and Jack hits Frank. He is summarily dismissed for gross misconduct. Clearly retirement is not a reason for the dismissal. Jack will be able to assert (with whatever prospect of success) that the true reason for dismissal was his age, and the desire of Pompeii Ltd to get rid of older employees.

Scenario 4: no paragraph 2 notification – all other cases

9.24   The three earlier scenarios cover (a) the situation in which proper notification is given and the contract terminates on the retirement date, (b) where proper notification is given but the contract terminates earlier than the retirement date and (c) the situation in which proper notice is not given and the contract terminates before the intended date. In all other cases, where the employer has not notified the employee in accordance with paragraph 2 of Schedule 6 to the 2006 regulations, particular regard shall be had to the matters in section 98ZF when determining the reason (or principal reason) for dismissal.[22] This scenario will cover situations in which less than 6 months notice has been given of the intention to retire and the contract terminates on the intended retirement date.

9.25   The matters are:

a) whether or not the employer has notified the employee more than 14 days before the operative date of termination;[23]

20 Sch 6 para 4.
21 Sch 6 para 1(2)(c)(ii). For 'intended date of retirement' see para 9.52 below.
22 ERA 1996 s98ZB(5).
23 In accordance with Sch 6 para 4. For operative date of termination see note 13 above. For 'intended date of retirement, see para 9.52.

b) if the employer has notified the employee more than 14 days before the operative date, how long before the retirement date the notification was given;

c) whether or not the employer has followed, or sought to follow, the procedures[24] relating to the holding of a meeting with the employee to discuss a request to carry on working within a reasonable period of the request.[25] These include notifying the employee of the decision on the request as soon as reasonably practicable after the meeting or consideration.[26]

9.26 This provision is supposed to be aimed at technical failings. Regulation 30 excludes the operation of Parts 2 and 3 of the regulations where retirement is *the reason* for the dismissal. It does not apply where retirement is the principal reason but not the reason for the dismissal. Therefore, it is possible for the tribunal to conclude that the reason for dismissal remains retirement where there has been a failure to notify the employee of the date on which the employer intends the employee to retire. In such a case, regulation 30 will preclude any argument that the dismissal was an act of age discrimination.

EXAMPLE: William is given notification of the intention to retire him five months before his 65th birthday because Barbara, Pompeii Ltd's personnel officer, has been on holiday and dealt with it immediately after she came back. The tribunal accepts that although paragraph 2 notification has not been given, Pompeii tried to ensure that William was notified of his right to request, discussed that request with him at a meeting and, two days later, refused the request. The tribunal would be entitled to conclude that retirement was the reason for dismissal. Regulation 30 would therefore preclude an argument concerning age discrimination.

---

24 In Sch 6 para 7. See para 9.81 onwards.
25 If a meeting is not practicable the employer must consider the written representations of the employee.
26 'As soon as reasonably practicable' is a very stringent test (used also in the Employment Act 2002 (Dispute Resolution) Regulations 2004 SI No 752 regs 7(4)(c), 8, and 13 (failure to attend a meeting)). It is anticipated that the same level of procedural stringency will be required in respect of both procedures. See *Palmer v Southend-on-Sea Borough Council* [1984] 1 All ER 945, [1984] ICR 372, CA.

9.27   By contrast:

> EXAMPLE: June is given one month's notification and when she requests to carry on working she is given a meeting only two weeks before the date of retirement. She then waits until the day before the retirement is due to take effect when a letter arrives telling her that her request has been refused. She argues that the real reason for her dismissal was capability and age discrimination because the employer had made remarks about these aspects during the meeting. It would be open to a tribunal to find that retirement was not a reason for dismissal, but that the employer had tried to employ a retirement dismissal procedure to get rid of an employee whose capability was mistrusted on the grounds of her age. In those circumstances retirement would not be a reason; regulation 30 would not apply and a finding of unjustified direct age discrimination would be possible.[27]

9.28   The last example illustrates one other point arising out of the way which section 98ZB is drafted. The section requires that particular regard should be had to the matters set out in section 98ZF. This means that the tribunal is entitled to have regard to all other matters, but it must have particular regard to those matters. Thus if the employer holds discussions with the employee, but does not hold them in good faith, that could be a matter to which the tribunal could have regard in determining whether retirement (as opposed to age) was the reason for the dismissal. However that possibility only arises because the employer has initially failed to notify the employee in accordance with paragraph 2 of Schedule 9.

Case 3: normal retirement age – dismissal before that age

9.29   If there is a normal retirement age and the operative date[28] of termination falls before the date on which the employee reaches it, retirement shall not be taken to be a reason for the dismissal. It is disregarded for unfair dismissal purposes.[29] In these circumstances regulation 30 will

---

27   The question of whether the dismissal was unfair would be dealt with under ERA 1996 s98ZG (see ERA 1996 s98(3A)). See para 9.50.

28   The date on which the employer's notice expires or on which summary dismissal takes effect (Sch 6 para 1(1)). See note 13. For 'normal retirement age' see para 9.30.

29   ERA 1996 s98ZC.

not apply. Therefore the dismissal of the employee before the normal retirement age will have to be justified if it is alleged that the dismissal was an act of age discrimination.

> EXAMPLE: Sidhu Ltd has a normal retirement age of 60 for its clinical staff. Alison is 59 and 8 months. The managing director decides to serve notice on her in line with her contract. She is entitled to three months' notice. Due to the wording of the letter, notice expires a day before her 60th birthday. Sidhu Ltd cannot assert retirement as the reason for dismissal.

Normal retirement age

9.30 A 'normal retirement age' is, in relation to an employee, the age at which employees in the employer's undertaking who hold, or have held, the same kind of position as the employee are normally required to retire.[30] The concept of a normal retirement age replaces the concept of a normal retiring age which was previously used in the ERA 1996. It is not clear whether this change in wording is designed to create a change in approach to how to ascertain that age. It is suggested that the case-law that was used to determine the normal retiring age will continue to determine the normal retirement age.

9.31 The residual age of 65 only applies if there is no normal retirement age.[31] Where there is a contractual retiring age, that is likely to be presumed to be the normal retirement age unless that presumption is rebutted by evidence of significant departure from it in practice. If evidence shows a higher age at which relevant employees regularly are retired and which they have reasonably come to regard as their normal retirement age, that age replaces the contractual age.[32] Similarly, if the evidence shows that the contractual age has in practice been abandoned but that relevant employees retire at a variety of ages, then there is no 'normal retirement age' and so the residual rule applies.[33] It has sometimes been accepted that a contractual retirement age has been 'abandoned' by evidence of significant departure from the contractual age rather than a wholesale departure.[34]

---

30 ERA 1996 s98ZH.
31 *Barnet London Borough v Nothman* [1979] ICR 111.
32 See *Jayawardane v Customs and Excise Commissioners* [2003] EWCA 1194. The test is not the individual's expectation.
33 *Waite v Government Communication Headquarters* [1983] ICR 653.
34 *Secretary of State for Scotland v Meikle* [1986] IRLR 208.

9.32   Whether there is a normal retirement age is judged by reference to employees in the employer's undertaking who hold, or have held, the same kind of position as the employee. It is necessary to determine this group and not to sub-divide it. It then becomes necessary to determine what was the reasonable expectation of the group as a whole in respect of its retirement age.[35]

9.33   It is possible for an employer to change retirement age policy and create a new normal retirement age by changing the date at which employees normally expect to be retired. This will have to be justified if it shortens the working life of the group of employees.[36] Moreover, the employer cannot simply change a contractual retirement age as a matter of policy. It must not breach the employee's contract. If there is no lawful variation of the existing contractual age, the employer's change will be ineffective to vary the normal retirement age, save to the extent that it raises the age. It may not lower it below that contractual age.[37]

9.34   Where a policy change produces a band of lower ages at which employees are expected to retire which is not definite enough to produce a new, lower retirement age, the residual age of 65 applies.[38]

9.35   There can be a normal retiring age where a general policy is subject to individual exceptions, particularly where they are limited in time and of essentially a transitional nature.[39] There can be a 'normal retirement age' (other than 65) in the case of one particular individual. It is not necessary for there to be a group of employees in an appropriate case.[40]

35   *Brooks v British Telecommunications plc* [1992] IRLR 66.
36   See *Department of Health and Social Security v Hughes* [1985] ICR 419. Now the change will have to be justified by reference to a legitimate aim and be shown to be a proportionate means of achieving that aim.
37   *Bratko v Beloit Walmsley Ltd* [1995] IRLR 629.
38   *Swaine v Health and Safety Executive* [1986] ICR 498.
39   *Barclays Bank plc v O'Brien* [1994] ICR 865.
40   In *Wall v British Compressed Air Society* [2004] IRLR 147 the claimant was until his dismissal at the age of 67, the director general of the respondent. He complained of unfair dismissal, contending that he had a contractual retirement age of 70. The company argued that, on the assumption that he had a contractual retirement age of 70 and that his office of director general was a unique position, his contractual retirement age was not his 'normal retiring age' for the purposes of section 109(1)(a) of the Act. The Court of Appeal held that the word 'normal' in this context did not necessarily require the existence of one or more comparators. If it did then a unique employee could never rely upon his contractual retiring age in order to establish a 'normal retiring age'. Where an employee had a contractual retirement age, there was no need for comparisons to be made with other employees holding the same position before a normal retiring age could be established.

9.36   Because the normal retiring age is generated in this way, it does not necessarily transfer on a TUPE transfer to the new employment. An employee's contractual rights under his pre-transfer contract of employment cannot define or 'freeze' his pre-transfer normal retiring age so as to transfer it along with his pre-transfer contractual rights. It is the normal retiring age of employees in the position of the employee at the time of his dismissal that is relevant.[41] This may have altered after the transfer. That may be so in particular because, although the contractual age transfers, the expectation of the new group of workers to which the claimant belongs after the transfer rebuts the presumption that the contractual age is the normal retirement age.

Case 4: normal retirement age of 65 or more and dismissal at or over 65

9.37   If the employee has a normal retirement age which is 65 or more and the operative date of termination falls on or after the normal retirement age, a number of possibilities arise.[42] These involve the notification of the rights to request and of the intended date of retirement.

Scenario 1: proper notification of intended date of retirement and right to request

9.38   If the employer notified the employee in accordance with paragraph 2 of Schedule 6 to the 2006 regulations and the employment terminates on the intended date of retirement, *retirement is the only reason* and any other reason must be disregarded.[43] However, in those same circumstances if the employment terminates before the intended date of retirement, *retirement is not a reason* for dismissal.[44] If the employee is constructively dismissed before the intended date he may argue the dismissal was unlawful age discrimination and unfair. The employer cannot assert retirement as a reason for the termination.

---

41   *Cross v British Airways plc* [2006] EWCA Civ 549 at para 37 ff.
42   ERA 1996 s98ZD. For operative date of termination see note 13.
43   ERA 1996 s98ZD(2). For 'intended date of retirement' see para 9.52.
44   ERA 1996 s98ZD(3).

EXAMPLE: Ray's employer Learnfast Education Ltd has a normal retirement age for its teachers of 68. Ray is a teacher; he is 67 and 5 months. Learnfast serves notice of retirement on him, saying that there is not much call for Latin teaching these days. Ray agrees, but after the dismissal takes effect he brings a claim for unfair dismissal on the basis of being unfairly selected for redundancy. Ray cannot assert redundancy as a reason for dismissal in these circumstances.

9.39   However:

EXAMPLE: When Ray hears that the true reason for termination of his employment is that he is no longer required for teaching purposes, he is extremely upset and resigns. He argues that his is an age-related dismissal because the employer decided to use the retirement process as a way of avoiding paying a redundancy payment to him or allowing him to redeploy to other teaching opportunities with Learnfast. It could only seek to use the process because of his age and therefore he argues that the dismissal was age-related.

Scenario 2: failure to notify properly

9.40   If the employer has not notified the employee in accordance with paragraph 2 of Schedule 6 to the 2006 regulations,[45] then:

1) if there is an intended date of retirement in relation to the dismissal, but the contract terminates before the intended date of retirement, *retirement is not a reason for dismissal;*[46]
2) in any other case of failure to notify, regard is had to the severity of the breach to determine the reason or principal reason. The tribunal must in particular have regard to:[47]
   a) whether or not the employer has notified the employee more than 14 days before the operative date of retirement;[48]

---

45   Ie because he has given either no notice, less than 6 months' notice, or too much notice (more than 12 months').
46   ERA 1996 s98ZD(4). The consequence is that the dismissal is subject to the anti-discrimination provisions of regulation 7. For 'intended date of retirement' see para 9.52.
47   ERA 1996 s98ZF.
48   In accordance with Sch 6 para 4. For operative date of retirement see note 13.

b) if the employer has notified the employee more than 14 days before the operative date, how long before the retirement date, notified by that notice, the notification was given;

c) whether or not the employer has followed, or sought to follow, the procedures[49] relating to the holding of a meeting with the employee to discuss a request to carry on working within a reasonable period of the request.[50] These include notifying the employee of the decision on the request as soon as reasonably practicable after the meeting or consideration.[51]

9.41 As stated above,[52] the tribunal may have regard to other matters and, indeed, must have regard to all matters that are relevant to the dismissal.

Case 5: normal retirement ages below 65

9.42 Section 98ZE applies where there is a normal retirement age for the employee, set below 65, and where the operative date of termination falls on or after the employee reaches the normal retirement age. If the retirement age cannot be justified dismissal will constitute an unlawful requirement and retirement will not be a reason for the dismissal for the purposes of unfair dismissal. However, if the employer can justify having that normal retirement age and the retirement age does not constitute unlawful age discrimination, the four situations below must be considered. The employer will have to demonstrate that the normal retirement age was adopted in pursuit of a legitimate aim and was a proportionate means of achieving that aim. The policy may be challenged under regulation 7 and/or under paragraph 4 of Schedule 5 of the Regulations.

---

49 In Sch 6 para 7. See para 9.84.

50 If a meeting is not practicable the employer must consider the written representations of the employee.

51 'As soon as reasonably practicable' is a very stringent test (used also in the Employment Act 2002 (Dispute Resolution) Regulations 2004 SI No 752 regs 7(4)(c), 8, and 13 (failure to attend a meeting)). It is anticipated that the same level of procedural stringency will be required in respect of both procedures. See *Palmer v Southend-on-Sea Borough Council* [1984] 1 All ER 945, [1984] ICR 372, CA.

52 See para 9.28.

Scenario 1: justified retirement age and proper notification

9.43   Where there has been notification in accordance with paragraph 2 of Schedule 6 to the 2006 regulations and the contract terminates on the intended date of retirement, retirement *is the only reason for the dismissal* and other reasons are disregarded.[53]

Scenario 2: justified retirement age, termination before date of retirement

However, where there was proper notification but the contract was terminated before the intended date of retirement, retirement is *not a reason* for the dismissal.[54]

Scenario 3: justified retirement age, but no proper notification and termination before intended date

9.44   Where the employer does not notify in accordance with paragraph 2 and there is an intended date, but the contract terminates before it, retirement is *not a reason* for the dismissal.[55]

Scenario 4: justified retirement age – all other cases

9.45   In all other paragraph 2 non-compliance situations, regard is to be had to the severity of the non-compliance when determining the reason or the principal reason for dismissal.[56] The tribunal in particular must have regard to:

a) whether or not the employer has notified the employee more than 14 days before the operative date of retirement;[57]

b) if the employer has notified the employee more than 14 days before the operative date, how long before the retirement date, notified by that notice, the notification was given;

c) whether or not the employer has followed, or sought to follow, the procedures[58] relating to the holding of a meeting with the employee to discuss a request to carry on working within a reasonable period

---

53   ERA 1996 s98ZE(4).
54   ERA 1996 s98ZE(5).
55   ERA 1996 s98ZE(6).
56   ERA 1996 s98ZE(7).
57   In accordance with Sch 6 para 4. For operative date of retirement see note 13.
58   In Sch 6 para 7.

of the request.[59] These include notifying the employee of the decision on the request as soon as reasonably practicable after the meeting or consideration.[60]

9.46 Note that if the reason for dismissal is in part something other than retirement on this analysis, regulation 30 will not apply and a claim for unlawful discrimination using regulation 7 (and unfair dismissal[61]) is possible.

What is excluded in the dismissal process by regulation 30?

9.47 For the purposes of considering whether a dismissal for retirement amounts to an unlawful act of age discrimination it is important to remember that:

a) if the retirement procedure is followed, the reason for dismissal will be retirement;

b) if the reason for dismissal is deemed to be retirement, regulation 30 takes the dismissal outside the scope of the regulations.

9.48 It does not follow that any other activity of the employer during the process of discussion or leading up to dismissal is outside the scope of the regulations.

> EXAMPLE: Edward is given proper notification of retirement by his boss, Frank of Pompeii Ltd. He is given seven months' notice of the intention to retire him on his 60th birthday, in line with the company's normal retirement age. However, Frank indicates that if he was prepared to take a 30% pay cut, the company would retain him after that time because there is nothing wrong with his work but of course older workers are less productive and so the company can only continue to employ him if he is

---

59 If a meeting is not practicable, the employer must consider the written representations of the employee.

60 'As soon as reasonably practicable' is a very stringent test (used also in the Employment Act 2002 (Dispute Resolution) Regulations 2004 SI No 752 regs 7(4)(c), 8, and 13 (failure to attend a meeting)). It is anticipated that the same level of procedural stringency will be required in respect of both procedures. See *Palmer v Southend-on-Sea Borough Council* [1984] 1 All ER 945, [1984] ICR 372, CA.

61 However, if retirement is a reason for dismissal the fairness of the dismissal is to be determined in accordance with section 98ZG, for which see para 9.50.

cheaper than his co-workers. Edward agrees to the terms but is very unhappy. He sees his local law centre, who advise him of his rights. The day after his new contract is entered into, Edward starts proceedings for age discrimination based on the new rate of pay compared with his co-workers. Pompeii Ltd would have to justify the difference in pay by reference to a legitimate aim and show that it was a proportionate means of achieving that legitimate aim.

9.49   In the earlier example of Frank and James (see para 9.20) when Frank abuses James during the meeting to discuss James's request to carry on working, that may amount to harassment if it created the requisite atmosphere. Even if the paragraph 2 notification procedure is correctly followed, the employer can still be liable for acts of discrimination relating to any request to extend the contract. If found liable for discrimination in the process the employer will be obliged to compensate the employee for the lost chance of working beyond retirement.

Fairness of a retirement dismissal

9.50   So far we have considered principally the impact which the determination of the reason for dismissal has in terms of whether Parts 2 and 3 of the regulations apply to the dismissal. The dismissal itself may be an unfair dismissal. If the employer shows that the reason *or principal reason* for the dismissal is retirement, the question of whether the dismissal is fair or unfair is determined in the following way.[62] The retired employee is deemed to be unfairly dismissed *if and only if* the employer has failed to comply with one of the following procedural requirements:

a)   The requirements concerning notification by the employer to the employee of retirement. There is a continuing duty to notify the employee in writing until the fourteenth day prior to the operative date of termination.[63]

b)   If the employer receives a request from the employee, the employer is obliged to consider the request in accordance with a set procedure contained in paragraphs 7–9 of Schedule 6 to the 2006 regulations.[64] If the employer fails to comply with that obligation, the

---

62   ERA 1996 s98(3A) – the method is set out in section 98ZG.
63   Sch 6 para 4 contains the continuing duty. Para 2 is the primary duty.
64   See para 9.84.

dismissal will be unfair. Similarly, by paragraph 7 the employer is obliged to hold a meeting to discuss the request within a reasonable period after receiving the request. The duty may be breached by the employer not taking all reasonable steps to attend the meeting in circumstances in which it was practicable to do so. However, if it is not practicable to do so, the employer may consider the request without the meeting provided that he considers any representations made by the employee. The notice of the decision of the employer must state any period of further employment or whether the employment will continue indefinitely. If the decision is that the request is refused, the decision must confirm that the employer wishes to retire the employee and the date on which the dismissal is to take effect. If the employee has specified a period for which he wants to remain employed and the employer will not grant that period, the notice of decision must state the shorter period and must notify the employee of the right to appeal. A refusal decision must also notify the employee of the right to appeal. All these notices must be written and must be dated.

> EXAMPLE: Grace receives a decision letter stating that her employment will continue 'until next year'. This neither gives a date certain nor states that the employment continues indefinitely. The following year she is given a week's notice. The dismissal is unfair.

c) Under paragraph 8 of Schedule 6 to the 2006 regulations, the employer must allow the employee to appeal either a refusal of the request or of the length of the future employment. The employer must hold a meeting with the employee to discuss an appeal within a reasonable period after the date of the notice of appeal. Both must take all reasonable steps to attend it. If it is not practicable to hold the meeting within that reasonable period and the employer considers any representations made by the employee, the employer does not have to hold the meeting. He or she must give the employee notice of the decision as soon as is reasonably practicable after the date of the meeting/consideration as the case may be. The notification must state whether the appeal is accepted (and if so, how long the employment will continue). If the decision is to refuse the appeal the notice must state that the employer wishes to retire the employee and the date on which the dismissal is to take effect. The notices must all be written and must all be dated.

9.51   By virtue of section 98ZG, the tribunal must find that there has been an unfair dismissal if *any* of the above obligations have not been complied with. Clearly, there are many procedural ways in which a dismissal which is otherwise clearly for retirement purposes may become technically unfair throughout this process. Note however that this does not mean that the dismissal is also an act of age discrimination. This is because the paragraph 2 notification requirement may have been met in such a way that the reason for dismissal is in fact retirement. Regulation 30 therefore excludes a claim for unlawful discrimination. However, the process after paragraph 2 may have been defective in one of the ways described above. The notification claimant will have lost the chance of persuading the employer that he or she should be retained. Compensation will be assessed on the basis of what the reasonable employer would have done in that situation.[65] The employer cannot simply rely on the existence of the statutory procedure to limit the loss. The tribunal will consider whether a reasonable employer would have been persuaded to permit the claimant to carry on working. The compensatory award will be capped at the current limit.[66]

Intended date of retirement

9.52   We have mentioned the concept of the intended date of retirement on several occasions during the above discussion. It is an important concept for the purposes of both the right to request and the determination of the reason for a dismissal. 'Intended date of retirement' is dealt with in the following ways:

a)   It is the date notified to the employee in the notice issued by the employer between 6 and 12 months before the intended date which specifies the intended date of retirement and which tells the employee of the employee's right to make a request to continue working.[67]

---

65   See, for example, *Sawyer v London Borough of Southwark & ors* [1999] UKEAT 238_98_2302: 'Any application of the *Polkey* case would involve a consideration of a hypothetical situation based upon the question, "What would have happened if the Respondents had behaved reasonably?".'

66   See chapter 12. Compensation for failure to notify properly is discussed at para 9.88 onwards.

67   Sch 6 para 1(2)(a).

EXAMPLE: Stan's employer, Frank, writes to him seven months before Stan's 65th birthday stating that Pompeii Ltd intends to retire Stan on his 65th birthday. However, Frank fails to let Stan know that he has a right to make a request to continue working. No intended date of retirement is set.

b) If the employer has failed to comply with the requirement, he or she has a continuing duty to notify the employee of these matters in writing until the 14th day before the operative date of termination. Where the employer notifies a date prior to the 14th day before the operative date of termination and either no request is made or a request is made after the notification, the intended date of retirement is the date notified by the employer.[68]

EXAMPLE: Pompeii Ltd's personnel officer Barbara notices the error in the original letter from Frank to Stan. Three weeks before Stan's 65th birthday she writes to Stan stating that the date of termination really will be his 65th birthday and notifying him that he has a right to ask to be allowed to continue working for Pompeii Ltd.

c) If the employer has not notified a date within the 6–12-month window before the intended date of retirement (or if the notice is defective in that it does not tell the employee of the right to request to continue working), the intended date of retirement will be the date contained in any request to continue working after the date which the employee notifies the employer that he or she has reasonable grounds to believe the employer intends to retire him or her.[69] Of course if the employer has notified the employee already (and there are more than 14 days before the intended date), the intended date is the one named by the employer.

EXAMPLE: Ken, Stan's co-worker, is also coming up to 65. He received one of Frank's letters telling him that he would be retired at 65 but not naming the date or telling him of the right to request. He writes to Barbara stating that he thinks he is going to be retired on his 65th birthday. He gives the date. He asks to be allowed to continue working. The date is the one named by Ken.

---

68 Sch 6 para 1(2)(b).
69 Sch 6 para 1(2)(c).

d) If a date has been identified by one or other of these means but either a later date is agreed as a result of the various meetings that the procedure requires or an earlier date is mutually agreed then the date identified by that agreement is the intended date. Similarly, if the employer gives notice to the employee that the employee's employment will continue for a further period and specifies the length of the period or the date on which it will end, the date named by the employer is the intended date. This may happen as a result of the meeting to discuss the request or as a result of the appeal against the decision of the employer concerning that request.[70]

9.53   In these circumstances the employer is not required to give the employee a further notice in respect of a dismissal taking effect on the agreed date if that date is less than 6 months after the original date.

> EXAMPLE: Stan is in his last week before his 65th birthday. Frank calls him in and tells him that they are having the meeting in response to the written request he made to carry on working after his retirement date. Frank says that Stan can carry on work-ing until five months after Stan's 65th birthday. Stan is some-what disgruntled and cannot understand what is happening, but he agrees to the new date. Pompeii Ltd will not have to serve a fresh notice on Stan.

9.54   Another situation in which the employer is not required to give the employee a further notice in respect of a dismissal taking effect on an agreed date is where that date is earlier than the original date.

> EXAMPLE: Ken is fed up at having to write to his employer in the way he has had to, and wants to leave. Barbara and he agree that he can do so with a week's notice (so that a farewell party can be arranged). Obviously Pompeii Ltd will not have to serve a notice on Ken.

Dismissal before notification of decision on request

9.55   Where an employer has had a request to continue working from the employee but the employer dismisses the employee for retirement in accordance with the original notification on or before the date on

70   Sch 6 para 3.

which the employer notifies the employee of his decision on the request, the contract continues in effect for all purposes.[71] The contract continues until the day following that on which the decision notice[72] is given.[73]

9.56   If the employer fails to give the decision notice at all, therefore, the contract will continue for the purposes of the payment of wages. The employer's dismissal will be ineffective for the purposes of ascertaining the date on which the dismissal took effect for the purposes of ascertaining whether it is a dismissal for retirement. If the dismissal did not take effect on the 65th birthday, the provisions of section 68ZB will not apply, so that (without more) the act of serving the notice and bringing the contract to an end would be an act of unlawful age discrimination (unless it could be justified objectively). Paragraph 10 avoids this consequence in two ways:

i)   by stipulating that the day following the day on which the decision notice is given supersedes what would otherwise have been the operative date of termination according to the original notice of intention to retire the employee. It also becomes the intended date of retirement;[74]

ii) by stating that the continuation of the contract of employment is disregarded when determining the operative date of termination for the purposes of ERA 1996 ss98ZA–98ZH.[75]

EXAMPLE: Frances receives a retirement notice stating that she will be retired in seven months' time on 10 July 2007 (her 65th birthday). She writes to the employer making a request that she should be allowed to continue working. She has a meeting with her employer, but then hears nothing. There is no decision. 10 July 2007 comes and goes, and she writes to the employer on several occasions both before and after asking what is happening. She is ignored. She issues proceedings on 30 September 2007 in the tribunals for the following:

a) unlawful deductions from wages;

---

71 Sch 6 para 10(1). This includes the purpose of calculating continuous employment (para10(2)).
72 Under Sch 6 para 7(6).
73 Sch 6 para 10(2).
74 Sch 6 para 10(3). Paragraph 1(2)(e) states that this date becomes the intended date of retirement.
75 Sch 6 para 10(4).

> b) age discrimination;
> c) unfair dismissal.
>
> On receipt of the papers, the employer writes back rejecting her request. This arrives with Frances, via the tribunal, on 14 October 2007. 15 October 2007 becomes the intended date of retirement. However, for the purposes of determining whether the reason for dismissal was retirement for unfair dismissal purposes and for the purpose of determining whether the dismissal is actionable as age discrimination, the operative date of dismissal remains 10 July. Nevertheless, Frances will be able to claim for unlawful deductions from wages from 11 July to 15 October. Her unfair dismissal claim may also survive.

9.57　The contract remains in force for all purposes, so that if there is a pay rise during that time, the benefit of it will come to the claimant. Similarly, if the workforce is TUPE transferred to a new employer, the claimant's contract will be transferred.

Right to request and duty to consider

9.58　In the discussion so far there has been mention of the concept of a right to request to continue working and to a duty to consider that request. These are rather grand titles for rather skeletal rights. Where there is an intended dismissal for retirement, Schedule 6, which sets out the procedure to be followed if an employee is to be retired, applies. Employers will have new time bound responsibilities to inform employees of their 'right to request' and they will have a 'duty to consider' all such applications. Where an extension of work is agreed, the 'right of request' and 'duty to consider' will remain in place when retirement is next considered.

The procedure

9.59　If the employer intends to retire the employee he must[76] notify the employee in writing of the latter's right to make a request[77] and the date on which he or she intends to retire the employee. This must be

---

76　By Sch 6 para 2.
77　'Request' means one under paragraph 5: it is a request not to retire on the intended date of retirement.

done not less than 6 and not more than 12 months before the date on which he intends to retire the employee. The paragraph is clear that this notice requirement is an absolute one. It does not matter what other information is available about retirement, from a contractual term to information about retirement from other sources or about the right to make a request.[78]

EXAMPLE: Sims Allcock, solicitors, provides information to its clients on the retirement process, which is stored on its intranet. Human resources also ensured that information leaflets were sent to each member of staff about the retirement process. Frances Cole, a legal secretary, types letters concerning retirement on a daily basis and has often expressed an interest in the retirement process. She was employed after the regulations were in force and human resources included a term in her contract notifying her that Sims Allcock's normal retirement age is 65. The term is worded so as to stipulate that Sims Allcock gives and Frances accepts six months' notice prior to her 65th birthday that the contract will terminate for retirement on that day. Sims Allcock therefore does not serve a letter notifying her in accordance with paragraph 2 of Schedule 9. The effect of this is that when she is dismissed on the day after her 65th birthday on arrival at the office, there is no intended date of retirement. The tribunal will have particular regard[79] in determining the reason for dismissal to the facts that (a) no notification of dismissal took place of any kind; and (b) there had been no attempt to follow the procedure relating to retirement. The tribunal may have regard to other matters. However, if it reaches the conclusion that there were other reasons for dismissal as well as retirement, regulation

---

78 Sch 6 para 2(2).
79 ERA 1996 s98ZF. The requirement that the tribunal has particular regard to the matters set out in that section will need to be tested. Does it mean that matters such as an innocent mistake combined with the intention to follow the procedure can or cannot outweigh the failure to follow procedure? The phrase 'particular regard to' occurs in section 12(4) of the Human Rights Act 1998 emphasising the importance of article 10 of the European Convention on Human Rights (ECHR) in consideration of interim relief applications. It is suggested that similarly under ERA 1996 s98ZF the procedural matters are to be given particular importance, so that an employer should not be able to say that the reason for dismissal is retirement where there has been a major breach of these procedural requirements.

> 30 will not apply and a claim for unlawful age discrimination
> (and unfair dismissal) may proceed. The term of the contract
> may also be void insofar as it is an attempt to contract out of
> the provisions of the regulations,[80] or is in furtherance of an act
> which is unlawful by virtue of the regulations.[81]

Notification given of intention to retire or anticipatory request made by employee

9.60   There is a continuing duty to notify the employee of the intention to retire him or her up until 14 days before the date on which the dismissal is to take effect.[82] After that time it is too late to notify the employee properly.

Scenario 1: parties agree before discussion meeting or appeal meeting

9.61   Assuming, however, that the employee was either notified between 6 and 12 months before the operative date of retirement or between 6 months and 14 days before the operative date of retirement, it is possible that the parties will agree a new date for dismissal. That agreement may arise:

a) as a result of the request to carry on working (before any meeting);
b) as a result of an appeal against a decision concerning continued working (before the appeal meeting).

9.62   In those circumstances, if the agreement gives rise to a date less than six months after the original date, no further notification of intention to retire need be given by the employer.[83]

---

80 See Sch 5 para 1(1), (2) and (3).
81 The inclusion of the contract term may only be known to be unlawful if the purported justification for its inclusion (seeking to ascertain the retirement date) fails to justify.
82 Sch 6 para 4.
83 Sch 6 para 3(2)(a).

Scenario 2: decisions arising from decision or appeal meeting

9.63 Aside from agreements, an extension o f employment may occur as a result of the meeting or appeal. The employer is entitled to consider the case put forward by the employee and may decide to give the employee either an indefinite extension of the contract or a time limited extension. The employer must notify the employee of the decision in writing. Where a time limited extension is for less than six months, no further notification of the intention to retire the employee need be given by the employer.[84] There is no requirement to give reasons. However if the refusal to grant an extension is challenged as an act of discrimination, the employer will struggle to show an innocent explanation for the refusal without them. Prudent employers will give reasons for the refusal. Such reasons will need to be objectively justified.

EXAMPLE: Stuart and Gloria are both given notification of intention to retire them. Stuart makes a request to continue working after retirement age, pointing out that employees with his particular skills cannot now be found. Immediately after his employers read his request, they accept that this is the case and immediately agree his request that his contract will continue indefinitely. Gloria does not include that kind of detail in her request but requests to work until she is 70 (she is now 65). However, the employer holds a meeting to discuss her request at which she makes the point that removing her will deprive the company of some substantial customer goodwill. The employer accepts her point but notifies her that her request to continue working until she is 70 is refused. It notifies her of its decision to retire her on her 66th birthday, using the intervening year to train up a replacement.

9.64 In both of these examples a new notification of retirement would subsequently have to be served on the employee. However:

EXAMPLE: Dr Watt is a scientist working with Bung Ltd on their deep frying food technology. He is notified of the intended retirement properly and makes a request to carry on working after that retirement date. There is a meeting at which he states that

---

84 Sch 6 para 3(1)(b).

certain processes are known to him alone and he will take them with him if he cannot do so indefinitely. Bung Ltd does not accept his case for indefinite continued work but notifies him that he will be retired at age 65 and 4 months (the intervening 4 months being used as a hand-over for the knowledge he possesses). They do not need to serve a new notification on him. Dr Watt may challenge the amount of the extension and Bung Ltd will have to justify its decision.

Scenario 3: employee raises the issue within six months of operative date but before employer notifies

9.65   The procedure also allows an employee to raise the issue of retirement him or herself if no notification has been given to the employee by six months before the operative date. Here too there may be an agreement as a result of the request by the employee to carry on working that the date for dismissal should be different to the one the employee reasonably believes is the one on which the employer wishes to dismiss. This may occur either before any discussion meeting (or appeal meeting) or as a result of a decision arising out of such meetings.[85] If the amount of the extension agreed or notified is less than six months, then no further notification of intention to retire the employee need be given.

Scenario 4: parties agree an earlier date

9.66   Finally, the procedure envisages that the parties may agree an earlier date.[86] For example the employee may have found another job after being notified of the intention to retire. The employee may ask the employer to leave before the intended retirement date.[87] If the employer agrees, it is not required to serve a fresh notice on the employee.

EXAMPLE: John Fettle works for Language Plus Ltd, managing EFL teachers. He was given 12 months' notice of intention to retire him on his 65th birthday. He immediately starts looking for other work and is interviewed by a local school requiring teachers for

85   Sch 6 para 3(1) and (2).
86   Sch 6 para 3(1)(c).
87   See para 9.52.

> the next academic year. They require him to start three months before his 65th birthday. Although this means that there are eight months before the new termination date, Language Plus is not required to give him a further notification of intention to retire.

9.67   Dates reached by agreement become the intended date of retirement.[88]

Consequences of an extension

9.68   Suppose that the employer fails to comply with the primary notification duty, which is to notify at least six months before the operative date. Notification does not take place until three weeks before the operative date. The same day the employee makes a request in writing. The employer realises that it is in breach of the notification procedure and decides to grant an extension for 5 months 1 week from the original date on the same day. This gives an extension which is less than 6 months from the original date. The employee wishes to argue that the subsequent dismissal is unfair and that the reason for it is age so that the principal reason is not retirement.[89]

9.69   The new date set by the extension notice becomes the intended date of retirement. When looking at section 98ZF, the tribunal will be obliged to have particular regard to the fact that the employer notified the employee in accordance with the continuing duty to notify. It must also consider how long before the intended retirement date notification was given. If the originally notified date was the intended retirement date, that would be three weeks, in our example. If the extension date becomes the intended date, in our example, the employer is considered to have given only just under six months' notification of intention to retire the employee. However, the tribunal will also have to consider whether the employer followed the procedure for the discussion and appeals meeting. It will also be able to consider the reasons why the employer acted in the way it did.

> EXAMPLE: Alf has not been notified of his dismissal by retirement until three weeks before the operative date. He seeks an indefinite extension and the employer realises that it is in breach of the regulations. It seeks to agree with him an extension of five months before holding the discussion meeting. Alf refuses to agree,

---

88   Sch 6 para 3(3).
89   Under ERA 1996 s98ZF.

pressing for his indefinite extension. The employer holds the meeting, discusses the retirement and decides that Alf should be given a four-month extension, notifying him of the new date for dismissal. It rejects Alf's appeal against this decision. It does not need to give him a fresh notification of intention to retire. It is still in breach of the requirements of paragraph 2, but may argue that in substance Alf has had extra employment. The tribunal may have regard to this, but may also have regard to the fact that it appears that the discussion was not a genuine discussion but was motivated by the employer's desire to dismiss him taking advantage of the retirement procedure and without incurring any real risk that the reason for dismissal might be found to be for reasons other than simply retirement. The discussions may be evaluated by the tribunal.

Continuing duty to notify

9.70   Suppose that the employer has not given notice of the intention to retire the employee at least six months before the intended date of retirement. Paragraph 4 stipulates that there is a continuing duty to notify the employee in writing which continues up to the 14th day before the date on which the dismissal is to take effect. The requirements of that notice are the same as in the six-month notice. It must state the date and state the right to request to carry on working.

9.71   This stipulation is significant when considering the degree of breach which has occurred. It demonstrates that failure to give notice is not simply a one-off failure but is a breach which grows in seriousness the closer to the operative date of dismissal the parties get. This should reflect in the level of damages payable when notification has not occurred.[90]

9.72   The consequences of failing to comply with paragraph 2 (6+ months' notification of intended retirement date) can be that the reasons for the decision fall to be considered under section 98ZF.[91] It will be a matter of degree whether the reason for retirement is held to be the only reason or whether there are other reasons (even if the retirement is the principal reason). Thus if the employee argues that stereotypes surrounding age were part of the reason for attempting to employ the

90   See paras 9.88–9.92 below.
91   See paras 9.24 and 9.40 above.

retirement process and the tribunal accepts that these formed part of the reasoning, regulation 30 will not apply and the tribunal will have to consider whether the improperly notified dismissal was in fact unlawful age discrimination.

9.73   Where a tribunal is determining whether retirement was the reason for dismissal under section 98ZF it must apply the burden of proof provisions.[92] The consequence of finding that age stereotypes formed part of the reason for dismissal is that the tribunal could conclude that unlawful discrimination has taken place in respect of that dismissal.[93] Therefore, if the employee shows a difference in age and the fact that a real or hypothetical comparator was not dismissed using the retirement procedure (albeit defectively) the tribunal may infer age discrimination from the failed attempt to use the retirement procedure. Regulation 37 requires the tribunal to draw that conclusion unless the employer can show that it did not commit an unlawful act of discrimination. In other words the employer will have to justify the dismissal by reference to it being a proportionate means of achieving a legitimate aim. The employer will have to try to argue that it was trying to implement the retirement process, which is a legitimate aim and that the means employed (dismissing the employee with short notification and on the basis of the 'stereotype') are proportionate to that end. Against this the employee may argue that the regulatory scheme gives one route by which the employer may dismiss for retirement without having to justify that dismissal or the factors that lead to it. The tribunal will have to consider the discriminatory impact on the employee of the dismissal and balance that against the desire of the employer to follow the retirement procedure (together with the degree of default).

Formal request to carry on working after retirement

9.74   The employee can make a request to the employer not to be retired on the intended date of retirement.[94] This is a formal request which must comply with certain requirements. The employee must propose that his or her employment should continue after the intended date of retirement either indefinitely, for a stated period or until a stated date.

---

92 Reg 37 and see para 9.24 above.
93 If it reaches this conclusion retirement is not the only reason for dismissal and regulation 30 does not apply.
94 By Sch 6 para 5.

> EXAMPLE: Ros Sims writes to her employer on receipt of the notification of intention to retire stating that she wants to carry on working to a date that can be mutually agreed between her employer and herself. Unfortunately she has thereby failed to make any request as she has neither proposed indefinite working, a date or stated a period of time.

9.75   Curiously, if the employer has not yet complied with the duty to notify of the intention to retire the employee, but the employee believes that there is a date[95] on which the employer intends to retire him or her, the regulations require that the request identifies that date.

> EXAMPLE: Grace is suspicious in the final six months before her 65th birthday that her employer intends to dismiss her on that date. In her request to carry on working she must say that she thinks the employer intends to dismiss her on her 65th birthday.

9.76   The request must be in writing and, contentiously, it must state that it is made under paragraph 5 of Schedule 6 to the regulations 2006. This raises the question of when something states that it is done pursuant to a provision. On the face of it, the wording seems very specific[96] so that it would not be possible to accept anything less. However, the consequences of such an interpretation would be to render all but the most formalistic requests invalid as requests under paragraph 5.[97] Union representatives, and advice centres should consider providing standard forms for requesting an extension of employment which expressly mention paragraph 5 of Schedule 6 to the regulations. Similarly an employer's age equality policy should include a request letter which may be used by the employee for this purpose. A tribunal deciding whether a request 'states' that it is made under paragraph 5 should consider that

---

95   In relation to which it is no longer possible for the employer to give six months' notice that it is the intended date of retirement. Thus where an oral notification has been given of the retirement date the employee must notify in writing that he or she believes a certain date to be the date on which the employer intends to retire him or her.

96   'A request must be in writing and state that it is made under this paragraph': Sch 6 para 5(3).

97   See the analogous situation related in cases such as *Lavery v Plessey Telecommunications* [1983] ICR 534 dealing with the old law on notification of return after maternity leave under the Employment Protection (Consolidation) Act 1978. See also *Duwuona v John Lewis plc* [1987] ICR 788; *Kolfor Plant Ltd v Wright* [1982] IRLR 311.

the whole of the retirement process represents a derogation from the principle of equal treatment. As such it should be interpreted so as to give effect to that principle.[98] The effect of a strict insistence on the meaning of 'states' would be that the scope of the derogation would become very much broader than is compatible with achieving minimum discrimination. Therefore a request should be said to 'state' that it is made under paragraph 5 of Schedule 6 where it does so either by reference or by implication.

> EXAMPLE: Sheila writes to her employer 'I wish to make a request to carry on working indefinitely after my 65th birthday in accordance with my statutory rights'. This should be sufficient for the request to 'state' that it is made under paragraph 5 if the above breadth of interpretation is adopted.

Repeated requests

9.77   The regulations[99] prevent the employee from making repeat requests in relation to any one intended date of retirement. They also stipulate that the employee may not make a request in relation to a date which supersedes another date as the intended date of retirement in two situations:

1) where a **date later** than the relevant date is **agreed** between the parties or notified by the employer by proper notice and falls six months or less after the relevant date, or an earlier date than the relevant date is agreed;

2) where the **contract of employment has continued** pending the employer giving notice of his or her decision on continuation of employment after the intended date of retirement, and the day following the day on which notice actually given has become the intended date of retirement.[100]

9.78   Thus the employee can make a fresh request where there has been an agreement to extend the contract by more than six months. This provides an incentive for the employer to grant extensions of less than six months. However, the combination of the notice requirements of paragraph 2 (six months' notice must be given) and the effect of not complying with the notice requirements on the determination of the

---

98   See chapter 2.
99   Sch 6 para 5(4).
100   Para 10(3)(b).

reason for dismissal (and hence on whether the dismissal is an act of discrimination) means that most employers will not go down this route.

9.79   There are consequences for the employee who is given an extension of less than six months. No further request can be made in respect of that extension.

> EXAMPLE: Greg's employer, the Gurkha restaurant, has served him less than six months' notice of intention to retire him on his 65th birthday. He therefore makes a request to continue working indefinitely. This is refused and Gurkha extends the contract by four months, giving the new date of dismissal. Greg suspects that this has only been done because of a belief that his capability will diminish after 65. However, he cannot make any further formal request which will give rise to a duty to meet and discuss it in respect of the new date.

The timescale within which the request must be made

9.80   Paragraph 5 makes further procedural requirements. The request is only valid if it is made within certain time periods:

1) if the employer gave 6+ months' notice (but no more than 12), the employee must make the request more than 6 (but not more than 12) months before the intended date of retirement;
2) if the employer did not give 6 months' notice, the employee must simply make the request before intended date of retirement. However notice given more than 6 months before the intended date of retirement will not count, for the obvious reason that the employer can still give 6 months' notice.[101]

Consideration of the request

9.81   The statutory choreography now moves on to the consideration of the request. The employer to whom a paragraph 5 request is made has a duty to consider that request in accordance with the following requirements.[102] The duty to consider a request has been the subject of some discussion. Originally there was a requirement that the employer should consider the request in good faith. This was removed in

101   Sch 6 para 5(5).
102   Sch 6 para 6.

subsequent drafts of the regulations, giving rise to the fear that consideration does not need even to be in good faith. Nevertheless there must be some content to the concept of consideration. At the least it must mean that the employer will take account of what is put before him and weigh them rationally.

9.82 The concept of consideration arises in the context of a measure intended to implement the Framework Directive. As a result at the very least it cannot permit consideration of the request to be discriminatory.

9.83 The act of consideration can itself be an act of discrimination under regulation 7. The only effect that regulation 30 has is to remove the *dismissal* from the ambit of the regulations. The following procedural steps taken under the regulations may themselves form the basis of allegations of discrimination:

1) The decision to dismiss by using the retirement procedure. If the reason the procedure is used involves discriminatory factors, the employer can be held liable for the consequences.
2) The act of extending the contract may be an act of discrimination on the grounds of age if stereotypical considerations have played a role. Thus if the length of the extension is determined by matters related to age considerations, this may constitute an act of discrimination.[103]

> EXAMPLE: Helen and Pauline are of an age. Both apply for extensions beyond the normal retirement age. Pauline looks younger than Helen. Their employer, Michael Milton, decides that Helen can have a four-month extension, but Pauline can have an indefinite extension because he thinks her more capable (although their performance objectively measured is the same). Helen can claim that the length of her extension would have been greater (or indefinite) if her age characteristics were different.

9.84 If the employer has a duty to consider the employee's request, the employer must hold a meeting to discuss the request with the employee within a reasonable period after receiving it.[104] The employer and the employee must take all reasonable steps to attend[105] but there is no

---

103 See further the checklists at the end of this chapter.
104 Para 7(1).
105 Para 7(2) one of the consequences of the procedure not being followed in this respect is that the dismissal is deemed to be unfair. However, the employee who failed to attend a meeting will probably be held to have contributed to the dismissal.

duty to hold the meeting if the employer and the employee agreed to an extension of employment[106] before the reasonable period expires.[107] The duty to hold a meeting does not apply if it is not practicable to hold it within the reasonable period and the employer considers the request by means of any representations made by the employee.[108] The employer must give the employee notice of his or her decision on the request as soon as reasonably practicable after the date of the meeting/consideration of representations.[109] This may mean that if the employee is on email, the notification should be given as soon as the decision is made. The notice given by the employer at this point must state (if it is the case) that the request is accepted.[110] If so, the employer must state in the notice that the employment will continue for a further period (and if so how long it is, or the expiry date), or will continue indefinitely. If the request is refused, the notice must confirm that the employer wishes to retire the employee and state the date on which the dismissal is to take effect. The employer's notice must be in writing and dated.[111]

Appeals

9.85   The employee can appeal against the employer's notice. The employee can appeal the refusal of the request, or against the period of future employment granted.[112] The employee's appeal notice must set out the grounds of appeal and must be given as soon as is reasonably practicable after the date of the employer's notice of decision on the request. The employer must then hold a meeting with the employee to discuss the appeal within a reasonable period after the date of the employee's notice of appeal. The employer and the employee must take all reasonable steps to attend the meeting. If the employer and the employee agree before expiry of the reasonable period that the employee's employment will continue (indefinitely or for a finite period determined by period or date), or if it is not practicable to hold it within the reasonable period (and the employer considers the employee's

---

106 Indefinitely or for a defined period.
107 Para 7(3). The employer must give notice of the new date to the employee. If that is not done, then there is still a duty to meet.
108 Para 7(5).
109 Para 7(6).
110 Sch 6 para 7(7)(a).
111 Sch 6 para 7(8).
112 Sch 6 para 8(1).

representations) there is no need for a meeting. The employer must give the employee notice of his or her decision on the appeal as soon as is reasonably practicable after the meeting or consideration date. The technical requirements for the employer's decision on appeal notice are that it must state if the appeal is accepted and how long (including indefinitely) the employment will continue (by period or by reference to date). If the appeal is refused, the employer must confirm his or her wish to retire the employee and the date on which the dismissal is to take effect. All these notices must be written and dated.[113]

Representation

9.86   At decision or appeal meetings the employee has the right to be accompanied.[114] The employee has the right to be accompanied by one companion chosen by the employee. The companion must be a worker employed by the employer. The companion must be permitted to address the meeting, but not to answer questions on behalf of the employee, and must be permitted to confer with the employee during the meeting. If the companion will not be available for the meeting time proposed by the employer and the employee proposes an alternative meeting time (within seven days of the original meeting time) which is convenient for the employer and the employee and the companion, the employer must postpone the meeting to the time proposed by the employee. The employer must permit the companion time off during working hours for the purposes of accompanying the employee pursuant to a properly made request. Such time will in appropriate cases count as time off for carrying out trade union duties.

Dismissal before consideration

9.87   If the employer has a duty to consider the employee's request, but the employer carries out the contemplated dismissal anyway before considering the request, there will be consequences.[115] If the operative date of termination would fall on or before the date identified in the employer's notice of decision[116] the contract of employment continues in force for all purposes (including determination of continuous employment) until the day after the day on which the employer finally does give

---

113   The appeal process is set out in Sch 6 para 8.
114   Sch 6 para 9.
115   Sch 6 para 10.
116   Given under para 7(6) as soon as practicable after the decision.

notice of the decision. In other words, the employer must give notice of his decision or the contract continues. The consequences are illustrated at para 9.56.

Complaints to the employment tribunal

Failure to notify

9.88   A person who has been dismissed after the procedure has been employed may wish to make a complaint to the employment tribunal. The employee may wish to complain that the dismissal was discriminatory. If the proper procedure under paragraph 2 has been followed this will not be possible. If the reason for dismissal has been determined to be retirement, this will also not be possible. However, where the reason for dismissal includes other matters, the tribunal will have jurisdiction to hear an unlawful discrimination complaint relating to the dismissal.

9.89   Where the employer has failed to comply with the primary notice duty to give between 6 and 12 months' notification of the intention to retire the employee, the employee can present a complaint to that effect to the employment tribunal.[117] That complaint must be presented within three months beginning with the last day for compliance with paragraph 2 (ie six months before intended date of retirement). If the employee did not know at that point in time what the intended date of retirement was, the three months will run from the first date on which the employee knew or *should have known* the intended date of retirement.[118]

9.90   This provision presents certain problems. The date on which the employee should have known the intended date of retirement is not dependant on notification by the employer at all. Therefore where the employee suspects that his 65th birthday will be the retirement date, but the employer has not given any notification and the six months is passing, time will run from the date on which the tribunal concludes the employee should have known his 65th birthday was to be the intended retirement date.

9.91   Time may be extended if it was not reasonably practicable to present the complaint within three months. If the tribunal concludes, for example, that the reason for dismissal was retirement despite the lack of paragraph 2 notification of the intention to retire the employee, and the respondent has otherwise followed the consideration process,

---

117   Sch 6 para 11(2). The statutory grievance procedure does not apply to such a complaint.

118   Para 11(2)(b).

it will still be open to the employee to make a claim that there has been insufficient notification of the intention to retire him or her.

9.92   If the employment tribunal finds that the complaint is well founded, it must order the employer to pay compensation to the employee of such amount, not exceeding eight weeks' pay, as it considers just and equitable. However, the concept of a week's pay is that in the ERA 1996, so the compensation is very limited indeed. There is an argument that the regulations provide for the notification periods as part of the justification for introducing a justified piece of age discrimination – namely retirement age dismissals. The remedies for the breach of the notification period should therefore be dissuasive of future breaches.

Refusal of right to be accompanied

9.93   Where the complaint is that the employer refused the employee the right to be accompanied (or that the employer threatened to fail to comply with the right for the employee to be accompanied), the complaint must be presented within three months of the date on which that occurred. The tribunal may extend time if it was not reasonably practicable for the employee to present within three months. There is a maximum compensation of two weeks' pay, limited in accordance with the ERA 1996.[119]

9.94   The employee has the right not to be subjected to any detriment by any act by the employer done on the ground that he (tried to) exercise the right to be accompanied. The companion has the right not to be subjected to any detriment by any act *or deliberate failure to act,* by the employer on the ground that he (tried to) accompany the employee. The provisions of section 48 ERA apply as to contraventions of that Act. However, if the detriment is dismissal an employee can claim automatically unfair dismissal if the reason or principal reason for dismissal is that he or she exercised or sought to exercise his or her right to be accompanied, or was the companion to an employee (seeking to) exercise his or her right to be accompanied. Interim relief is available in such circumstances. The claimant needs to lodge the complaint immediately after the dismissal for continuation of the contract to be ordered as there is a seven-day time limit on such applications.

---

119   Sch 6 para 12. The statutory grievance procedure does not apply to such a complaint (see Schedules 3 and 4 Employment Act 2002).

Transitional provisions relating to the duty to consider

9.95 The commencement date for the regulations is 1 October 2006. Specific transitional provisions are made to assist employers worried about the introduction of new notice duties.

Notice given before commencement, employee aware dismissal for retirement

9.96 The following rules apply where the date on which the notice of dismissal given by an employer ('the expiry date') expires before 1 April 2007 and the employer has given[120] notice of dismissal before either the minimum contractual notice for the employee or if the contractual period exceeds four weeks. The employer must have made the employee aware before 1 October 2006 that he or she considers that the employee is being retired on the expiry date.

EXAMPLE: Robin has a contract which gives him 12 months' notice of dismissal. He is given notice on 1 August 2006 that his employment will come to an end on 1 February 2007. He is also told verbally that this is a retirement dismissal. He has been made aware that his employment will terminate on that date. The employer appears to be in breach of contract by failing to give requisite notice.

9.97 In these circumstances the employer is treated as complying with the duty to give six months' notice if the employer gives the employee written notice of the employee's right to make a paragraph 5 request.[121] Similarly, in those circumstances the employee's request is treated as being made under paragraph 5 provided it is made after the employer notified the employee of his right to make a request. The request must satisfy the technical requirements in paragraph 5, and must be made where practicable at least four weeks before the expiry date[122] or if that is not practicable, as soon as reasonably practicable (before or after the expiry date) after the employer notifies the employee of the right to

---

120 Before 1 October 2006.
121 Sch 7 para 2(2).
122 The 'expiry date' is the date on which the notice of dismissal given by the employer expires.

make a request. However, a request made more than four weeks after the expiry date will not count.

9.98 If the employer does not, on or as soon as is practicable after 1 October 2006, notify the employee in writing of the employee's right to make a paragraph 5 request,[123] there is a duty to notify the employee in accordance with paragraph 4, but with the following modifications.[124] The employer will be deemed to have failed to have notified in accordance with paragraph 2 (the six-month notice), and the duty under paragraph 4 is treated as a duty to notify at any time before the expiry date. So the employer can, right up to the expiry date, comply with the duty to notify the employee of his right to make a request to carry on working beyond retirement.

9.99 The request by the employee is treated as a paragraph 5 request if it is made before any paragraph 4 notification from the employer. It is also treated as compliant if it is made after the employer's paragraph 4 notification and (if practicable) at least four weeks before the expiry date. Where that is not practicable, it must be made as soon as reasonably practicable (before or after[125] expiry date) after the employer notified the employee of his right to make a request.[126]

9.100 Where the employer gives notice of dismissal to the employee before 1 October 2006 and the expiry date is before 1 April 2007, but either:

a) the notice the employer gives is less than the contractual notice period (or four weeks if the contractual notice is greater than four weeks); or

b) the employer has not made the employee aware, before 1 October 2006, that the employer considers that the employee is being retired on the expiry date, then the duties concerning requesting and considering are modified in the following ways.

9.101 First, the six-month duty to notify does not apply. Second, the duty to notify that does apply is the continuing duty under paragraph 4 modified as if the employer had failed to comply with the six-month duty, and as if the duty was one to consider at any time before the expiry date. The employee's request to continue working is treated as a paragraph 5 request in these circumstances if it is in writing, states the nature of the extension sought, and states that it is a request under paragraph 5

123 Although the employer is not under the duty to give six months' notice
124 Sch 7 para 2(3).
125 Not more than four weeks after.
126 Sch 7 para 2.

of Schedule 6 to the regulations. The employee's request must be made before any notification is given by the employer or if it is given after, where practicable, it must be made at least four weeks before the expiry date or as soon as reasonably practicable after the employer notifies the employee of the right to make the request.[127]

Notice given after 1 October 2006, but expiring before 1 April 2007

9.102　Where the notice is given after the commencement date and it is at least the contractual notice or the ERA statutory minimum notice and the expiry date is before 1 April 2007, if the employer notifies the employee in writing of the latter's right to make a paragraph 5 request before or at the same time as giving notice of dismissal, the employer is treated as complying with paragraph 2 (six months' notice) and the employee's written request specifying the time extension sought is treated as a paragraph 5 request where it is made after the employer notified the employee of the right to request. In addition it must be made, where practicable, at least four weeks before the expiry date or as soon as reasonably practicable after the employer notifies the employee of his right to make a request (but not more than four weeks after the expiry date).[128]

Short notice given after commencement

9.103　If the notice given on or after commencement of the regulations is for a shorter period than the contractual notice or the statutory minimum notice and expires before 1 April 2007, the following rules apply:

- There is no duty to give at least six months' notice of the intention to retire the employee.
- The employer is subject only to the continuing duty to notify the employee of the right to request.
- The duty to consider is one which continues up to the expiry date.
- The employee's request is treated as a paragraph 5 request where it is in writing, specifies the extension period/date and is made before the paragraph 4 notification is given or after it is given. If practicable, it must be given at least four weeks before the expiry date or if that is not practicable after the notification of the right to request (but not more than four weeks after the expiry date).[129]

127　But not later than four weeks after the expiry date.
128　Sch 7 para 4.
129　Sch 7 para 5.

No appeal rights

9.104 During the transitional period, if these modifications to procedure apply, the procedural rules relating to appeals[130] do not apply. However, the employer is under a duty to consider any request which has any one of the following features:

a) it is made after the employer notified the employee of the right to make a request;[131]
b) it is made before notification under paragraph 4 of Schedule 6 of the right to request but (if practicable) four weeks before the expiry date (or as soon as reasonably practicable after notification (but no more than four weeks after the expiry date).[132]

9.105 These must be considered in accordance with the procedural requirements set out in paragraphs 7–9 of Schedule 6 (the appeal provisions).

9.106 The effect of these provisions is that although for unfair dismissal purposes there may be no consideration of the request, there will be no remedy for the lack of appeal rights under paragraph 10 of Schedule 9.

Checklist for unfair dismissal for failure to follow procedure

Section 98ZG (1) applies if the reason (or principal reason) for a dismissal is retirement of the employee. The employee must be regarded as unfairly dismissed if, and only if, there has been a failure on the part of the employer to comply with any of the following obligations:

a) failure to give notification of the intended date of retirement;[133]
b) the duty to consider the request to carry on working past retirement;[134]
c) the duties:[135]
   i) to hold a meeting to discuss the request;
   ii) to hold the meeting within a reasonable period after receiving the request;
   iii) to take all reasonable steps to attend the meeting;

---

130 Contained in Sch 6 para 10.
131 Para 2(2)(b).
132 Para 2(3)(c), para 3(2)(c), para 4(2)(b), (3)(c) or para 5(2)(c).
133 Sch 6 para 4 (notification of retirement, if not already given under para 2).
134 Sch 6 para 6 (consideration of request).
135 Contained in Sch 6 para 7.

    iv) considering the employee's representations if it is not practicable to hold the meeting within a reasonable time;

    v) to give notice of the decision;

    vi) to give notice of the decision as soon as is reasonably practicable after the meeting/consideration;

    vii) to give notice of the extension date on which the contract will come to an end;

    viii)   to confirm, if the request is refused, that the employer wishes to retire the employee;

    ix) to confirm the date on which the dismissal is to take effect (if the request is refused);

    x) to notify the employee of the right to appeal if the request is refused or a shorter extension is granted than was sought by the employee;

d) the duties relating to appeal hearings:

    i)   hold a meeting with the employee to discuss an appeal within a reasonable period after the date of the notice of appeal;

    ii) to take reasonable steps to attend the meeting;

    iii) to consider representations if it is not practicable to hold the meeting within a reasonable period after the appeal;

    iv) to give notice of the appeal decision as soon as is reasonably practicable after the decision;

    v) if the decision is to grant a further period of employment, to confirm that and to confirm the date on which the employment will come to an end;

    vi) if the decision is to refuse the appeal, to state as much, and to confirm the date on which the dismissal will take effect.[136]

If any of these duties is not observed, the dismissal becomes unfair. Dismissal is said to be unfair if and only if there is a breach of one of these duties. The effect of this and section 98(3A) is that the employee may be able to show that there is more than one reason for the dismissal and may be able to show that the dismissal is discriminatory. However, the fairness of the dismissal, where retirement is the principal reason, is determined by reference to whether there has been a breach of one of the above duties.

<hr>

136 Para 8 (duty to consider appeal against decision to refuse request not to be retired).

Checklist for discrimination in the retirement process

(1) The use and manner of the above process – bad faith. Consideration/no consideration/harassment during request to continue working process
(2) Reliance by employer on stereotypes or assumptions when considering a request.
(3) Omission of steps in the above procedure.
(4) Failing to grant any/the requested extension as a result.
(5) If retirement is not 'the reason' for dismissal.

CHAPTER 10

Pensions

10.23   Remedies

10.4   Members and prospective members

10.4   Remedies in employment tribunals

> **Key points**
> - It is unlawful for occupational pension schemes to discriminate against members or prospective members of a scheme on the basis of age.
> - Pension benefits accrued and discriminatory practices up to 1 October 2006 will not be affected by the Age Regulations 2006.
> - Trustees will be obliged to disapply any discriminatory rules under their scheme; trustees are also given power to amend any scheme rules that conflict with the regulations.
> - Workers who suffer discrimination on grounds of age in relation to pensions can bring a claim to an employment tribunal against the trustees and/or employer.

Introduction

10.1   On 8 September 2006, after this chapter was written, the Department of Works and Pensions announced that the provisions of the Regulations relating to pensions would not come into force until 1 December 2006. The aim of the delay was two fold: (a) to give industry more time to adjust to the new rules; (b) to have a short consultation period to assess whether any amendments are required to provide greater clarity for schemes and employers. We have left the content of this chapter, but will provide an update at www.ace.org.uk/agediscriminationlaw once the consultation takes place. It is not clear how extensive any changes will be. There are a number of areas in relation to pensions which will need to be explored as the Employment Equality (Age) Regulations 2006 become more familiar to practitioners. If an employer has a normal retirement age of 60 it will have to justify maintaining that age after 1 October 2006 by reference to a legitimate aim and show that the normal retirement age was a proportionate means of achieving that aim. Often this will not be possible. This raises questions for the employer and trustees of the pension scheme (or managers). If there is an attempt to raise the pensionable age to match the default retirement age (65), this can only be done in respect of pensionable service after the date of the change. Another area of potential difficulty is partnership pensions. Partnerships are covered by regulation 17 of the Employment Equality (Age) Regulations 2006. Their pension arrangements are affected if the partners are members of an occupational scheme or are required to pay a certain amount of their profits into a pension arrangement[1] or if payments are made by the partnership to retired partners. It is likely that such arrangements will have to be justified objectively unless one of the exemptions discussed below applies. In many cases such exemptions are unlikely to apply.

10.2   The Department of Trade and Industry (DTI) published specific pensions guidance on the age regulations: *The impact of Age Regulations on pension schemes* (DTI guidance published in April 2006). This has no statutory force but may be of some guidance. It is not a statutory code to which regard must be had.

The prohibition on discrimination in relation to pensions

10.3   The regulations prohibit direct and indirect discrimination and harassment. Regulation 11 of the age regulations prohibits direct discrimination and indirect discrimination against pension scheme members or prospective pension scheme members[2] by the trustees or managers of an occupational pension scheme (OPS) on the grounds of age.

10.4   Regulation 11 provides that it is unlawful for the trustees or managers of an OPS to discriminate against a member or prospective member of the scheme in carrying out any of their functions in relation to it (including in particular their functions relating to the admission of members to the scheme and the treatment of members of it). However, trustees or managers of an OPS may discriminate on the grounds of age against a member or prospective member of the scheme in relation to rights accrued or benefits payable in respect of periods of service prior to the coming into force of the regulations on 1 December 2006.[3]

> EXAMPLE: Alistair is 18. The rules of the company pension scheme will not permit him to join the scheme until he is 21. On the face of it, this is discriminatory on the grounds of age. However, his birthday is on 2 October 2006. He can only make a claim in respect of denied rights after 1 December 2006.[4]

---

1   Whether or not an occupational or personal pension.
2   Definition at para 10.63 below.
3   Reg 11(1).
4   However, see the exceptions below.

10.5 Where a specific justification or exemption does not apply, the trustees and managers of a pension scheme will have to be able to show objective justification for any discrimination in the rules. One question which will become increasingly important is whether such schemes can objectively justify ceasing pension accrual or employer contributions at 65, despite the fact that the scheme member continues in employment.

10.6 It is unlawful for the trustees or managers of an occupational pension scheme, in relation to the scheme, to subject to harassment a member or prospective member of it.[5]

10.7 Schedule 2 to the regulations deals with pension schemes. The Schedule has effect for the purposes of defining terms in the regulations and exempting certain rules and practices in or relating to pension schemes from Parts 2 and 3 of the regulations.[6]

10.8 Every OPS is treated as including a non-discrimination rule.[7] Trustees or managers of an OPS have power to alter the scheme so as to secure conformity with the non-discrimination rule. The Schedule also makes provision in relation to the procedures, and remedies which may be granted, on complaints relating to occupational pension schemes presented to an employment tribunal under regulation 36.

Occupational Pension Schemes

10.9 'Occupational pension scheme' means an occupational pension scheme within the meaning of Pension Schemes Act 1993 s1(1). This provides:

> 'occupational pension scheme' means any scheme or arrangement which is comprised in one or more instruments or agreements and which has, or is capable of having, effect in relation to one or more descriptions or categories of employments so as to provide benefits, in the form of pensions or otherwise, payable on termination of service, or on death or retirement, to or in respect of earners with qualifying service in an employment of any such description or category.

10.10 The regulations cover all occupational pension schemes (including stakeholder pension scheme classified as an occupational pension). It makes no difference whether they are registered or unregistered, salary related, defined contribution, hybrid or if it provides life cover only.

5 Reg 11(2).
6 Reg 11(3)(a)–(e)
7 Reg 11(3) and Sch 2.

Non-discrimination rule

10.11   Every scheme is treated as including a provision ('the non-discrimination rule') containing a requirement that the trustees or managers of the scheme refrain from doing any act which is unlawful by virtue of regulation 11.[8] The other provisions of the scheme are to have effect subject to the non-discrimination rule.[9] This means that the non-discrimination rule will override any other duty contained in the provisions of the scheme. In order to ensure that the scheme managers or trustees may act to give effect to the requirements of regulation 11, they may by resolution make such alterations to the scheme. That power is restricted however. The following conditions must be fulfilled:

- they do not otherwise have power to make such alterations to the scheme as may be required to secure conformity with the non-discrimination rule; or
- if they have such power but the procedure for doing so:
  - is liable to be unduly complex or protracted; or
  - involves the obtaining of consents which cannot be obtained, or can only be obtained with undue delay or difficulty.

10.12   It is only necessary to get the employer's consent to the changes made by the trustees if the employer's consent is required under the scheme's power of amendment. The existence of the power appears to be based on a judgment being made about whether the procedure for amendments is unduly complex. Trustees who make amendments where this is not the case will be acting outside the scope of their powers and may become liable to account for the consequences to the beneficiaries of the scheme. Similarly, a judgment is to be made as to whether there will be undue delay or difficulty in obtaining consents. Trustees who act on the basis of legal advice in relation to these matters may be relieved from some of the consequences of an error.

10.13   The point in time at which the amendment is made may not be crucial in any event. The alterations made by such a resolution is permitted to have effect in relation to a period before the alterations are made (but may not have effect in relation to any time before the coming into force of the regulations). In addition such resolutions will be subject to the consent of any employer in relation to the scheme whose consent would be required for such a modification if it were to be made under the scheme rules.[10]

---

8   Sch 2 para 2(1).
9   Sch 2 para 2(2).
10   Sch 2 para 2(4).

10.14 An employer who withholds such consent may be liable to a member of the scheme for discrimination on the grounds of age in withholding the consent.

Exemptions

10.15 Schedule 2 to the age regulations contains a number of exemptions from the age regulations for pension schemes. There are exceptions for rules, practices, actions and decisions relating to occupational pension schemes contained in Part 2 of the Schedule. These relate to admissions to schemes and similar issues. Nothing in Part 2 or Part 3 of the regulations renders it unlawful for an employer, or for trustees or managers, to maintain or use, in relation to a scheme, any of the rules, practices, actions or decisions set out in Part 2.

Admission to schemes

10.16 In relation to admission to a scheme, the following practices are exempted:

a) a minimum or maximum age for admission, including different ages for admission for different groups or categories of worker;

b) a minimum level of pensionable pay for admission, provided that such a minimum is not above the lower earnings limit referred to in Social Security Contributions and Benefits Act 1992 s5(1).[11]

Para 7 rules practices actions and decisions

10.17 In relation to the rules, practices, actions and decisions relating to a minimum or maximum age for admission, including different ages for admission for different groups or categories of worker, 'occupational pension scheme' means an occupational pension scheme within the meaning of Pension Schemes Act 1993 s1(1) under which only retirement-benefit activities within the meaning of Pensions Act 2004 s255(4) are carried out. 'Retirement-benefit activities' means operations related to retirement benefits, and activities arising from operations related to retirement benefits. The reference to 'retirement benefits' means:

a) benefits paid by reference to reaching, or expecting to reach, retirement; and

11 Sch 2 para 7. The lower earnings limit for 2006/07 is £4,368 pa.

b) benefits that are supplementary to such benefits which are provided on an ancillary basis:

   i) in the form of payments on death, disability or termination of employment; or

   ii) in the form of support payments or services in the case of sickness, poverty or need, or death.

The use of age criteria in actuarial calculations

10.18 The use of age criteria in actuarial calculations generally is permitted. The DTI gives an example not explicit in the regulations themselves:

> EXAMPLE: The actuarial calculation of the amount of benefits a member must surrender if they wish to exchange benefits for an additional dependant's pension. Also, the amount of additional dependant's pension a member can 'buy' in exchange for a given amount of pension surrendered. Under the regulations this practice can continue. Defined benefit transfer values and commutation factors[12] may also be exempt if calculated by a scheme actuary.[13]

10.19 The Schedule gives examples of such use:

a) in the actuarial calculation of any age related benefit commencing before any early retirement pivot age[14] or enhancement of such benefit commencing after any late retirement pivot age;

> EXAMPLE: A scheme allows members to take retirement from age 60 on a full pension. However, there is an option for a member to take early retirement before this age. This will be subject to an actuarial reduction. The actuarial reduction is calculated according to how many years the member is from age 60. Under the regulations this practice can continue.

---

12 Commutation factors are used to determine the amount of pension which needs to be foregone in order to provide a lump sum benefit.

13 DTI booklet p16.

14 'Early retirement pivot age' means an age specified in the scheme rules as the earliest age at which age related benefit becomes payable without actuarial reduction (disregarding any special provision as to early payment on grounds of ill health or otherwise).

b) member or employer contributions to a scheme; or

> EXAMPLE: The rules of a money purchase arrangement provide for the rate of employer contributions to differ according to the age of a member. The rate is determined by an actuary, with the aim of producing equal pensions for workers of different ages with the same salary and length of service. Under the Regulations this practice can continue[15].

c) any age related benefit commuted in exchange for the payment of any lump sum.[16]

> EXAMPLE: A scheme uses (actuarially determined) lower conversion rates for older members when calculating by how much a pension should be reduced when a lump sum benefit is taken. Under the Regulations this practice can continue.[17]

Contributions

10.20 Any difference in the rate of member or employer contributions by or in respect of different members is excepted to the extent that this is attributable to any differences in the pensionable pay of those members.[18]

Contributions under money purchase arrangements

10.21 Under a money purchase arrangement it is permissible to have:

a) different rates of member or employer contributions according to the age of the members by or in respect of whom contributions are made where the aim in setting the different rates is:
   i) to equalise the amount of benefit to which members of different ages who are otherwise in a comparable situation will become entitled under the arrangement; or
   ii) to make the amount of benefit to which such members will become entitled under the arrangement more nearly equal;

15 DTI p15.
16 Sch 2 para 8.
17 DTI p16.
18 Sch 2 para 9.

> EXAMPLE: A company operates a money purchase arrangement where the contributions payable by the employer are age-related according to a number of age bands. This practice is exempted where the age-related contributions are intended to provide (more or less) comparable target pensions at retirement, by setting higher contributions for older workers. Under the regulations, this practice can continue.[19]

b) equal rates of member or employer contributions irrespective of the age of the members by or in respect of whom contributions are made.[20]

Contributions under defined benefits arrangements

10.22   Under a defined benefits arrangement,[21] different rates of member or employer contributions according to the age of the members by or in respect of whom contributions are made, are exempted to the extent that:

a) each year of pensionable service entitles members in a comparable situation to accrue a right to defined benefits based on the same fraction of pensionable pay; and

b) the aim in setting the different rates is to reflect the increasing cost of providing the defined benefits in respect of members as they get older.[22]

> EXAMPLE: A company runs a defined benefits arrangement, where employee contributions are based on the ages of members. Older members of the scheme pay higher contributions (compared to younger members) to reflect the fact that it costs the scheme more to provide benefits to older members. The accrual rate is the same for all ages.[23]

19 DTI p17.

20 Sch 2 para 10.

21 'Defined benefits arrangement' has the meaning given by Finance Act 2004 s152(6), whereby an arrangement is a 'defined benefits arrangement' at any time if, at that time, all the benefits that may be provided to or in respect of the member under the arrangement are defined benefits. However, the reference to an arrangement in this context refers to an arrangement in respect of a member under a scheme as defined in Pension Schemes Act 1993 s1(1) rather than in respect of a member under a pension scheme as defined in Finance Act 2004 s150(1).

22 Sch 2 para 11.

23 DTI p17 – the accrual rate (for example, 1/60th or 1/80th) is the same for every member, regardless of age.

Age-related rules, practices, actions and decisions relating to benefit

10.23 A minimum age for entitlement to or payment of any age-related benefit to a member, provided that, in the case of any age-related benefit paid under a defined benefits arrangement before any early retirement pivot age:

a) such benefit is subject to actuarial reduction for early receipt; and

b) the member is not credited with additional periods of pensionable service.[24]

10.24 In this context, OPS means an occupational pension scheme within the meaning of either Pension Schemes Act 1993 s1(1) or Finance Act 2004 s150(5).[25] Further, the meaning of 'member' is modified. Here the term 'member' includes any active, deferred or pensioner member within the meaning of section 151(2)–(4) of the Finance Act 2004 whereby a person is an active member of a pension scheme if there are presently arrangements made under the pension scheme for the accrual of benefits to or in respect of the person. A person is a *pensioner member* if the person is entitled to the present payment of benefits under the scheme and is not an active member. A person is a *deferred member* if the person has accrued rights under the pension scheme and is neither an active member nor a pensioner member.

> EXAMPLE: An occupational pension scheme provides that benefits can be taken on early retirement from age 50. This is exempted, as long as the benefits are not 'enhanced' (ie the benefits must be actuarially reduced and the early retiree must not be credited with 'additional years' of service). Minimum ages for 'enhanced' early retirement benefits will need to be objectively justified.

10.25 From 2010, registered pension schemes may not pay benefits to members before 55.[26]

10.26 Very often the early retirement pivot age is the same as the normal retirement age applicable to the member. Before the early retirement

24 Sch 2 para 12.
25 Ie it means a pension scheme established by an employer or employers and having or capable of having effect so as to provide benefits to or in respect of any or all of the employees of: (a) that employer or those employers, or (b) any other employer, (whether or not it also has or is capable of having effect so as to provide benefits to or in respect of other persons). (Group pensions.)
26 Under the Finance Act 2004.

pivot age a pension can only be paid if it is actuarially reduced, and the member does not get an enhancement. Where the member is active or prospect on 1 December 2006, the scheme can pay an unreduced pension before the early retirement pivot age. Equally, an enhanced payment may be made before the early retirement pivot age.

10.27   In relation to workers who are active or prospective members[27] of a scheme on 1 December 2006, it is permissible to have a minimum age for entitlement to or payment of any age related benefit to such members under defined benefit arrangements before any early retirement pivot age, where such benefit is calculated in one or both of the following ways:

a) it is not made subject to actuarial reduction for early receipt;
b) it results from crediting the member with additional periods of pensionable service.[28]

10.28   Here an OPS means an occupational pension scheme within the meaning of either Pension Schemes Act 1993 s1(1) or Finance Act 2004 s150(5).[29]

> EXAMPLE: Under a defined benefit scheme, existing members who retire early, eg on redundancy, may leave on an 'early retirement' package. This will allow them to receive the pension that they would have received if they had continued working until the age at which workers normally retire. In other words, the pension will not be actuarially reduced for early payment (and the member may be credited with 'additional years of service'). Such arrangements can continue for existing and prospective members but not for new joiners.

10.29   It is permissible to have an early retirement pivot age or a late retirement pivot age, including different such ages for different groups or categories of member.[30]

---

27 In the context of paragraph 13 'active member' includes anyone who is an active member for the purposes of Finance Act 2004 s151(2) whereby a person is an *active member* of a pension scheme if there are presently arrangements made under the pension scheme for the accrual of benefits to or in respect of the person.
28 Sch 2 para 13.
29 See above.
30 Sch 2 para 14.

> EXAMPLE: A scheme sets ages from which members have the right to be paid full scheme retirement benefits without actuarial reduction. Under the regulations, this practice can continue. It will also be possible to set different ages for different groups to take their benefits, eg an earlier age for senior executives and a later one for the rest of the workforce.

10.30 An area where these regulations may have an impact is in the selection of staff for redundancy. If there is a provision for enhanced payments on redundancy above a particular age, then unless the redundant member was active or prospect on 1 December 2006, the trustees or managers may not make a payment of an unreduced pension to the member before the early retirement pivot date. However, if the staff are members of the scheme on 1 December 2006 it would be possible for them to receive an enhanced early retirement pension. Otherwise reduced pensions would have to be paid. The employer will have to be careful about using this factor as a part of a selection criterion.

10.31 The enhancement of any age-related benefit in the event of a member's retirement before any early retirement pivot age on ill health grounds is permitted, where that enhancement is calculated by reference to the years of pensionable service which that member would have completed if he or she had continued in pensionable service up to the age specified for that purpose in the scheme rules.[31]

> EXAMPLE: Two workers in the same scheme both take ill health retirement. One is aged 52 and the other is aged 42. Both have worked for the company for the same length of time and earned the same salary. Each receives the pension that he would have received if he had worked to age 60. The older worker could potentially complain that he has suffered discrimination because his pension has not been 'enhanced' as much as the younger worker's pension. This exemption prevents the older worker bringing such a claim.[32]

10.32 Any other ill health pension enhancement must be objectively justified.

10.33 Any rule, practice, action or decision whereby a male member who reaches pensionable age is not entitled or is no longer entitled to any

---

31 Sch 2 para 15.
32 DTI p19.

additional amount of pension which would have been payable to such a member before pensionable age in the circumstances prescribed for the purposes of Pensions Act 1995 s64(2) by Occupational Pension Schemes (Equal Treatment) Regulations 1995 reg 13.[33]

> EXAMPLE: A bridging pension is paid to retired men aged 60–64 to compensate for the fact that they do not yet qualify for the basic state pension. Men over 65 cannot complain under the regulations that they no longer qualify for such a pension.[34]

10.34   The reduction of any pension payable in consequence of a member's death to any dependant of the member where that dependant is more than a specified number of years younger than the member is permitted.[35]

> EXAMPLE: A scheme provides that where a dependant spouse is more than ten years younger than the member, the spouse's pension is reduced. Under the regulations, a spouse cannot complain about this practice.[36]

10.35   In relation to pensioner members who have retired on ill health grounds before any early retirement pivot age, discontinuation of any life assurance cover once any such members reach the normal retirement age which applied to them at the time they retired, or in relation to members to whom no such normal retirement age applied, once such members reach the age of 65.[37]

> EXAMPLE: A company provides life cover to ill health retirees which ceases at age 65. Ill health retirees over 65 cannot complain under the regulations that they are no longer provided with life assurance cover.[38]

---

33 Sch 2 para 16.
34 DTI p19.
35 Sch 2 para 17.
36 DTI p19.
37 Sch 2 para 18.
38 DTI p19.

Exemption for other rules, practices, actions and decisions relating to benefit

10.36 This exemption applies to any difference in the amount of any age-related benefit or death benefit payable under a defined benefits arrangement to or in respect of members with different lengths of pensionable service to the extent that the difference in amount is attributable to their differing lengths of service, provided that, for each year of pensionable service, members in a comparable situation are entitled to accrue a right to benefit based upon the same fraction of pensionable pay.[39]

> EXAMPLE: A defined benefits scheme can provide a higher pension to a member with 20 years of pensionable service than to one with only 10 years of service, where pensions are based on accrual of eg 1/60th of final salary for each year of pensionable service. This exemption does not cover arrangements where accrual rates increase after a certain number of years of service eg from 1/60th to 1/40th.[40]

10.37 Any difference in the amount of any age related benefit or death benefit payable from a scheme to or in respect of different members is permissible to the extent that the difference in amount is attributable to differences over time in the pensionable pay of those members.[41]

> EXAMPLE: A scheme provides for members who retire at normal retirement date to receive a pension equivalent to 1/60th of final pensionable salary for each complete year of pensionable service. Two members are retiring after both being in pensionable service for 10 years each. Member A is on a final pensionable salary of £40,000 and member B is on £25,000. It will not be discriminatory for member A to receive a higher pension than member B (ie 10/60ths x 40 versus 10/60ths x 25).[42]

10.38 Any limitation of the amount of any age-related benefit or death benefit payable from a scheme is permissible where the limitation results

---

39 Sch 2 para 19.
40 DTI p20.
41 Sch 2 para 20.
42 DTI p20.

from imposing a maximum number of years of service by reference to which such benefit may be calculated.[43]

> EXAMPLE: A scheme will be able to cease benefits accruing after a stated period of service. So maximum benefits can for example, be limited to a maximum of 40 years service.[44]

10.39   Any rule, practice, action or decision whereby any age-related benefit or death benefit is only payable to or in respect of members who have completed a minimum period of service, provided that such a minimum period is not longer than two years' qualifying service within the meaning of Pension Schemes Act 1993 s71(7).[45]

> EXAMPLE: A scheme will be able to continue to operate a vesting period of up to two years.[46]

10.40   By Pensions Schemes Act 1993 s101AA (as amended by Pensions Act 2004 s264), early leavers with three months' pensionable service may have a cash transfer sum to another pension arrangement as an alternative to the existing right to a refund of member contributions less tax. This exemption relates to the member's right to a deferred pension. It does not allow employers or trustees to limit the cash transfer sum to members above or below a certain age in these circumstances. Any such limitation would have to be justified as the proportionate means of achieving a legitimate aim therefore.

10.41   Any limitation on the amount of any age-related benefit or death benefit payable from a scheme is permissible where the limitation results from imposing a minimum level of pensionable pay by reference to which any such benefit may be calculated, provided that such a minimum is not above the lower earnings limit referred to in Social Security Contributions and Benefits Act 1992 s5(1).[47]

> EXAMPLE A scheme will be able to decide to only provide benefits for members provided their pensionable pay is above the lower earnings limit (for 2006/07 this is the equivalent of £4,368 per annum).[48]

43   Sch 2 para 21.
44   DTI p20.
45   Sch 2 para 22.
46   DTI p20.
47   Sch 2 para 23.
48   DTI p20.

10.42 Any limitation on the amount of any age-related benefit or death benefit payable from a scheme is exempted where the limitation results from imposing a maximum level of pensionable pay by reference to which such benefit may be calculated.[49]

> EXAMPLE: A scheme will be able to continue to offer benefits payable to its members by reference to a maximum level of pensionable pay specified in the scheme rules. (For example, the earnings cap for 2005/06 was £105,600 and for 2006/07 it will be £108,600.)

Closure of schemes

10.43 The regulations exempt the closure of a scheme, from a particular date, to workers who have not already joined it.[50]

> EXAMPLE: A company can close its defined benefits arrangement to new joiners but continue to allow existing members to remain in the scheme for future accrual (or for a deferred pension). The company may decide to offer alternative pension arrangements to new joiners[51].

Other rules, practices, actions and decisions

10.44 Increases of pensions in payment which are made to members over 55 but not to members below that age.[52]

> EXAMPLE: A scheme rule can provide that no annual pension increase or a lower increase will be paid to early retirees until they reach age 55.[53]

10.45 Any difference in the rate of increase of pensions in payment for members of different ages to the extent that the aim in setting the different rates is to maintain the relative value of members' pensions.[54]

---

49 Sch 2 para 24.
50 Sch 2 para 25.
51 DTI p21.
52 Sch 2 para 26.
53 DTI p21.
54 Sch 2 para 27.

> EXAMPLE: A scheme may pay a higher increase to pensioners at
> or above a certain age (eg 75) if those older pensioners have
> been worse affected than younger pensioners by increases in
> the cost of living since their retirement.[55]

10.46　Any difference in the rate of increase of pensions in payment for members whose pensions have been in payment for different lengths of time to the extent that the aim in setting the different rates is to maintain the relative value of members' pensions.[56]

> EXAMPLE: A scheme could decide to pay a higher pensions
> increase to pensioners who retired more than ten years ago than
> to more recent retirees. This would be in order to allow less
> recent retirees to catch up with the increases in the cost of living
> since their retirement.[57]

10.47　The application of an age limit for transfer of the value of a member's accrued rights into or out of a scheme, provided that any such age limit is not more than one year before the member's normal pension age.[58]

> EXAMPLE: A scheme with a normal pension age of 65 will be
> able to specify in its rules that it will not allow transfers to be
> paid out of the scheme or accepted by the scheme after age 64.

Registered pension schemes

10.48　Any rules, practices, actions or decisions relating to entitlement to or payment of benefits under a registered pension scheme are exempted from the regulations insofar as compliance is necessary to secure any tax relief or exemption available under Part 4 of the Finance Act 2004 or to prevent any charge to tax arising under that part of that Act, whoever is liable in relation to such charge.[59] However, this exemption does not apply to any rules, practices, actions or decisions setting a

---

55　DTI p21.
56　Sch 2 para 28.
57　DTI p21.
58　Sch 2 para 29.
59　Sch 2 para 30(1).

minimum age for entitlement to or payment of any age-related benefit.[60]

> EXAMPLE: A scheme may provide that a pension payable to any dependant children on death-in-service ceases at age 23. Under the regulations, older members will not be able to complain that they are likely to be disadvantaged by this rule (ie if their children are less likely to be under age 23).

10.49 In this context, OPS means an occupational pension scheme within the meaning of either Pension Schemes Act 1993 s1(1) or Finance Act 2004 s150(5).[61]

Exception for rules, practices, actions and decisions relating to contributions by employers to personal pension schemes

10.50 Nothing in Part 2 or Part 3 of the regulations renders it unlawful for an employer, in relation to the payment of contributions to any personal pension scheme in respect of a worker, to maintain or use any of the rules, practices, actions or decisions set out below.[62] These relate to contributions by employers.

10.51 This is the only point at which the regulations touch on personal pension schemes. Conditions of access to personal pensions and employer contributions to a personal pension scheme should not be restricted on the grounds of age, unless there is objective justification. It is highly unlikely that a refusal to make contributions on the grounds of age could be objectively justified.

Contributions by employers

10.52 Different rates of contributions by an employer according to the age of the workers in respect of whom the contributions are made are permissible where the aim in setting the different rates is:

- to equalise the amount of benefit to which workers of different ages who are otherwise in a comparable situation will become entitled under their personal pension schemes; or

60 Sch 2 para 30(2).
61 For the latter, see above at para 10.24.
62 In Sch 2 Part 3.

- to make the amount of benefit to which such workers will become entitled under their personal pension schemes more nearly equal.[63] The DTI explains that this exemption for personal pension schemes (such as group personal pension schemes) mirrors that for occupational pension schemes.[64]

10.53 Any difference in the rate of contributions by an employer in respect of different workers is exempted to the extent that this is attributable to any differences in remuneration payable to those workers.[65]

EXAMPLE: A company pays employer contributions of 6% of pay to workers who earn £30,000 or more per annum, and contribution of 5% to workers who earn less than £30,000. The difference in the employer contribution rate is exempted.[66]

Benefits based on length of service

10.54 In addition to the above exemptions, regulation 32 provides an exemption which may be relied upon in respect of benefits[67] based on length of service. This provides that nothing in Part 2 or Part 3 renders it unlawful for a person ('A'), in relation to the award of any benefit by him, to put a worker ('B') at a disadvantage when compared with another worker ('C'), if and to the extent that the disadvantage suffered by B is because B's length of service is less than that of C.[68]

10.55 On the face of it, this would apply to any person in the role of A. However, the award of benefits must be by A rather than anyone else. The managers or trustees of a pension fund would not be in this position. However, if a trustee or pension manager were responsible for awarding the benefit, the wording of the regulation would appear to exempt them. The wording of the following paragraphs of the regulation suggest, however, that B works for A.

---

63 Sch 2 para 31.
64 See the example at para 10.21 relating to Sch 2 para 10.
65 Sch 2 para 32.
66 DTI p22.
67 'Benefit' does not include any benefit awarded to a worker by virtue of his ceasing to work for A (reg 32(7)).
68 Reg 32(1).

10.56   The DTI guidance suggests that trustees may not rely on this regulation.

> EXAMPLE: An employer only allows workers to join an occupational pension scheme after four years service. This will be permitted under regulation 32. Note: trustees cannot rely on this exemption. So they will need objectively to justify any scheme rules which indirectly discriminate against younger members by favouring members with long service.[69]

10.57   Paragraph 3 of Schedule 2 to the Age Regulations 2006, permits the employer to rely upon the exemptions in Schedule 2 insofar as Parts 2 and 3 of the regulations apply.

10.58   If B's length of service exceeds five years,[70] it must reasonably appear to A that the way in which he uses the criterion of length of service, in relation to the award in respect of which B is put at a disadvantage, fulfils a business need of his undertaking (for example, by encouraging the loyalty or motivation, or rewarding the experience, of some or all of his workers).[71] B clearly works for A in this regulation.

> EXAMPLE: A company increases employer contributions after an employee has been with the company for ten years. If an employer can show the reason for the difference in contributions is to fulfill a business need, this practice is exempted.[72]

10.59   There are specific rules for calculating the worker's length of service in these circumstances. A must calculate:

a) the length of time the worker has been working for him doing work which he reasonably considers to be at or above a particular level (assessed by reference to the demands made on the worker, for example, in terms of effort, skills and decision-making); or
b) the length of time the worker has been working for him in total;

and on each occasion on which he decides to use the criterion of length of service in relation to the award of a benefit to workers, it is for him

69   DTI p23.
70   'Year' means a year of 12 calendar months (reg 32(7)).
71   Reg 32(2).
72   DTI p23.

to decide which of these definitions to use to calculate their lengths of service.[73]

10.60   Note that the regulations suggest that the employer must make a decision at the time he or she decides to use length of service to differentiate between benefits conferred on different employee as to which of the definitions is used. That means that the claimant should immediately ask about this decision in the questionnaire in any case which may involve differentiation on the basis of length of service in relation to benefits. The documents demonstrating which calculation definition was used should also be sought if they are not disclosed as a matter of course by the respondent.[74]

10.61   For the purposes of this calculation of the length of time a worker has been working for him:

- A must calculate the length of time in terms of the number of weeks during the whole or part of which the worker was working for him or her;

- A may discount any period during which the worker was absent from work (including any period of absence which at the time it occurred was thought by A or the worker to be permanent) unless in all the circumstances (including the way in which other workers' absences occurring in similar circumstances are treated by A in calculating their lengths of service) it would not be reasonable for him or her to do so;

- A may discount any period of time during which the worker was present at work ('the relevant period') where:

  a) the relevant period preceded a period during which the worker was absent from work; and

  b) in all the circumstances (including the length of the worker's absence, the reason for his absence, the effect his absence has had on his ability to discharge the duties of his or her work, and the way in which other workers are treated by A in similar circumstances) it is reasonable for A to discount the relevant period.

---

73 Reg 32(3). This raises very difficult issues akin to those raised by equal value claims of the assessment of the particular level of work by reference to the demands made on the worker for example in terms of effort skills and decision making. However, the method mentioned is merely indicative, and the employer simply has to be able to show that his view that the worker is at that particular level is a reasonable one. It is likely therefore that employers will opt to use the second method in many cases.

74 See chapter 11 for the procedure for disclosure.

10.62 For the purposes of calculating the total time the worker has worked for A (method b) above), a worker shall be treated as having worked for A during any period during which he worked for another if:

a) that period is treated as a period of employment with A for the purposes of the 1996 Act by virtue of the operation of section 218 of that Act;[75] or

b) were the worker to be made redundant[76] by A, that period and the period he has worked for A would amount to 'relevant service' within the meaning of section 155 of that Act.[77]

Remedies

10.63 The employment tribunal has jurisdiction to hear complaints brought by members of schemes and prospective members of schemes[78] against the trustees or managers of the pension scheme.

Members and prospective members

10.64 A prospective member of a scheme is defined as any person who, under the terms of his or her employment, or the scheme rules, or both:

a) is able, at his or her own option, to become a member of the scheme;

b) shall become so able if he or she continues in the same employment for a sufficient period of time;

75 The provisions dealing with the effect of a change of employer on continuity of employment.

76 Ie dismissed for redundancy within the meaning of ERA 1996.

77 In relation to any person to whom the Redundancy Payments (Continuity of Employment in Local Government, etc) (Modification) Order 1999 SI No 2277 (as amended) applies, section 155 has effect as if continuity was measured as 'employed in relevant service'. In this context 'relevant service' means one of two things. First it can mean continuous employment by an employer specified in the Redundancy Payments (Continuity of Employment in Local Government etc) (Modification) Order 1999 Sch 2. Alternatively, if immediately prior to the relevant event a person has been successively employed by two or more local government employers (specified in Sch 2 Part II), such aggregate period of service with such employers as would be continuous employment if they were a single employer. It does not matter therefore whether the employee is a local authority worker, the same rules for calculation of continuity apply.

78 Reg 36.

c) shall be so admitted to it automatically unless he makes an election not to become a member; or

d) may be admitted to it subject to the consent of any person.[79]

10.65 For all but one purpose, the term 'member' is defined as:

a) any active member;[80] or

b) deferred member[81] or pensioner member.[82]

10.66 Where under regulation 36 a member or prospective member of a scheme presents to an employment tribunal a complaint that the trustees or managers of the scheme:

a) have committed against him an act which is unlawful by virtue of regulation 11 or regulation 24 which prohibits discrimination in respect of relationships which have come to an end; or

b) are to be treated as having committed against him or her such an act,[83]

the employer in relation to the scheme shall, for the purposes of the rules governing procedure, be treated as a party and be entitled to appear and be heard in accordance with those rules.

---

79 Sch 2 para 1(5).

80 This means a person who is in pensionable service under the scheme (see Pensions Act 1995 s124(1)) but in paragraph 13 it includes anyone who is an active member for the purposes of Finance Act 2004 s151(2) whereby a person is *an active member* of a pension scheme if there are presently arrangements made under the pension scheme for the accrual of benefits to or in respect of the person.

81 'Deferred member', in relation to an occupational pension scheme, means a person (other than an active or pensioner member) who has accrued rights under the scheme. A 'pensioner member' is a person who in respect of his pensionable service under the scheme or by reason of transfer credits, is entitled to the present payment of pension or other benefits (see Pensions Act 1995 s124(1)).

82 But in para 12 member includes any active, deferred or pensioner member within the meaning of Finance Act 2004 s151(2)–(4) whereby a person is an *active member* of a pension scheme if there are presently arrangements made under the pension scheme for the accrual of benefits to or in respect of the person. A person is a *pensioner member* if the person is entitled to the present payment of benefits under the scheme and is not an active member. A person is a *deferred member* if the person has accrued rights under the pension scheme and is neither an active member nor a pensioner member.

83 By virtue of reg 25(liability of employers and principals) or reg 26 (aiding unlawful acts).

Remedies in employment tribunals

10.67 Where an employment tribunal finds that a complaint relating to:

a) the terms on which persons become members of the scheme;
b) the terms on which members of the scheme are treated,

by a member or prospective member of a scheme against the trustees, managers or an employer is well founded but the complainant is not a pensioner member[84] of the scheme then the following rules apply.[85] The tribunal may, without prejudice to the generality of its power to make order declaring rights of the complainant and respondent,[86] make an order declaring that the complainant has the following rights:

a) where the complaint relates to the terms on which persons become members of the scheme, to be admitted to the scheme;
b) where the complaint relates to the terms on which members of the scheme are treated, to membership of the scheme without discrimination.

10.68 Such an order may be made in respect of a specific period.[87] It may also make such provision as the employment tribunal considers appropriate as to the terms on which, or the capacity in which, the complainant is to enjoy admission or membership. However, the employment tribunal may not make an order requiring the respondent to pay to the complainant compensation of an amount corresponding to any damages he or she could have been ordered by a county court or by a sheriff court an order for compensation,[88] whether in relation to arrears of benefits or otherwise, except:

a) for injury to feelings;
b) where a respondent fails without reasonable justification to comply with a recommendation made by the tribunal (when the tribunal can award damages).[89]

---

84 'Pensioner member', in relation to an occupational pension scheme, means a person who in respect of his or her pensionable service under the scheme or by reason of transfer credits, is entitled to the present payment of pension or other benefits (see Pensions Act 1995 s124(1)).
85 Sch 2 para 6(1).
86 Under reg 38(1)(a).
87 Other than one pre-dating 1 October 2006.
88 Under regs 38(1)(b) and 39.
89 By virtue of reg 38(3).

10.69   It should be remembered that if the claimant has a complaint relating to the pension scheme which has been through the internal scheme dispute resolution procedure the claimant can still make a complaint to the Pensions Ombudsman provided that a complaint has not already been made to the employment tribunal.[90] Regulation 35 states nothing in the regulations prevents a complaint to the ombudsman.

---

90 Pension Schemes Act 1993 s146 – the complaint must be brought within three years.

CHAPTER 11

Bringing a claim

Key points

- All claims under the Age Regulations 2006 should be brought before the employment tribunal except those claims relating to allegations of discrimination brought against qualifications bodies or claims against institutions of further and higher education.
- Claims against qualification bodies and educational establishments are brought in the county or sheriff court.
- Claimants should make use of the questionnaire procedures available to them. Unreasonable failure by the respondent to reply within eight weeks of service could lead to adverse inferences being drawn against the respondent.
- Claimants should be aware of strict time periods within which they must initiate proceedings.
- The statutory dismissal, disciplinary and grievance procedures apply to most aspects of discrimination claims. There are serious consequences for both employers and employees who do not follow them.
- In certain circumstances, the time limits for applying to the tribunals is extended. In particular, if a grievance is brought within the normal limitation period (usually three months), time is automatically extended for presenting a claim by a further three months.
- The burden of proof provisions are consistent with most other areas in discrimination. Guidelines have been provided and advisers should consider how they apply in each case.
- Tribunals are governed by the Employment Tribunals (Constitution and Rules of Procedure) Regulations 2004. These provisions are not easily worded. Some guidance is offered in this section.
- Costs, wasted costs and time preparation orders are available in the employment tribunals under the new rules. However, they remain the exception rather than the rule.

Jurisdiction

Employment tribunals

11.1 Employees must bring claims of age discrimination arising out of their employment before the employment tribunals.[1] This includes claims brought against the employer itself, as well as individual employees, where those individuals are considered to be personally responsible for discrimination or harassment.[2] In addition, with the exception of allegations of discrimination brought against qualifications bodies[3] or claims against institutions of further and higher education,[4] all other claims alleging age discrimination pursuant to Part 2 of the regulations should be brought before the employment tribunal.[5]

County and sheriff courts: education-related claims only

11.2 Claims alleging age discrimination within educational establishments (not schools) are brought before the county/sheriff courts. Discrimination or harassment which takes place within, or arising out of and is closely connected to a relationship, which takes place in the setting of institutions of further and higher education, or universities, pursuant to regulation 23 must be litigated before the county court, in England and Wales,[6] or before the sheriff court in Scotland.[7] Such claims are treated as any other form of tortuous claim in civil proceedings, or in Scotland as a claim in reparation for breach of statutory duty.[8] Note that claims arising out of employment in further or higher education institutions should be brought before the employment tribunal in the normal way.

Questionnaire procedure

11.3 The regulations provide special assistance for claimants in relation to age discrimination claims. Regulation 41 provides that a person who

1 Reg 36.
2 See chapter 4.
3 Pursuant to reg 19.
4 Pursuant to reg 23.
5 Reg 36(1) and (2).
6 Reg 39(2)(a).
7 Reg 39(2)(b).
8 Reg 39(1).

considers that he or she may have been discriminated against or been the subject of harassment may serve on the respondent a series of questions in the form set out in Schedule 3 or forms to the like effect with such variation as the circumstances require. The respondent may, if he or she so wishes, reply to such questions by way of the form set out in Schedule 4 or in similar form with such variation as the circumstances require. Significantly, regulation 41(2) states that where the person questions the respondent, whether in accordance with that procedure or not,

a) the questions, and any reply by the respondent (whether in accordance with the formal procedure set out in regulation 41(1) or not) shall be admissible as evidence in the proceedings;

b) if it appears to the court or tribunal that the respondent deliberately, and without reasonable excuse, omitted to reply within eight weeks of service of the questions or that his reply is evasive or equivocal, the court or tribunal may draw any inference from that fact that it considers it just and equitable to draw, including an inference that he or she committed an unlawful act.

11.4   This is a very powerful device indeed. What it means is that if the claimant asks a question, inferences can be drawn from an evasive or equivocal response, or indeed a failure to respond, and it stresses the importance of doing so. In *Dattani v Chief Constable of West Mercia*[9] the Employment Appeals Tribunal (EAT) considered whether the equivalent Race Relations Act (RRA) 1976[10] provision covered replies given in a form other than that prescribed. The EAT held that a 'respondent, asked a direct question in writing by an aggrieved person, who fails to respond, or does so evasively, ought to be treated in the same way irrespective of whether a question has been asked under the statutory procedure'.[11] In remitting the case to the employment tribunal, the EAT required the employment tribunal to consider whether it was appropriate to draw inferences, and if so what inferences from alleged inconsistencies in/between the following documents:

a) the Notice of Appearance;

b) further particulars;

c) a letter from the respondent giving an explanation relating to the alleged discrimination.

9   [2005] IRLR 327.
10   RRA 1976 s65.
11   Para 44.

11.5　What is interesting about this approach is the way the EAT required the pleaded case to be inspected in the same way as the evidence relating to the case. A claimant should be astute therefore in conducting the comparisons. On a very basic level, the importance of placing the claimant's questions and the respondent's answers next to each other cannot be over emphasised. There is still, remarkably, a tendency among respondents to treat responses to the questionnaire as something of an occult pleading art where the letter and not the spirit of the question is to be met. By placing the material next to each other a claimant can quickly see what has and (often more significantly) what has not been said in response to the questions.

11.6　The tribunal can therefore draw inferences from any of the documents. The impact of regulation 41 is that the tribunal may draw adverse inferences from any reply to a direct question. In strategic terms this means that where advisers are dealing with a case before proceedings have been issued, such as at the grievance stage, consideration should be given to the placing of questions relating to the suspected discrimination.[12] The respondent will then either have to give an answer which can then be relied upon and may limit the scope of the defence later in any proceedings, give an evasive answer, which will simply create problems in answering any claim later on, or fail to give an answer. In the latter situation the respondent will run the risk of being seen not to take the grievance seriously, and again inferences may be drawn from this. The aggrieved person, however, will lose any prospect of a tribunal drawing inferences if it is quite apparent from the volume and nature of the questions asked that the reason they were not answered was that they were disproportionate, irrelevant or time-wasting. Some discretion therefore needs to be exercised in the selection of the questions asked.

11.7　So, as in all other discrimination claims, claimants, or their advisers, should make use of the questionnaire procedure through which valuable information about the respondent's defence can be elicited. The EAT in *Dattani* stated: 'The procedure is most useful so aggrieved persons may understand the nature of any suspected unfavourable treatment prior to launching Tribunal proceedings. It facilitates the presentation at an early stage of material focussing upon factual

---

12　Note however that a questionnaire itself will not be regarded as a grievance for the purposes of the Employment Act 2002 (Dispute Resolution) Regulations 2004 SI No 752 and for the purposes of compliance with Employment Act 2002 s32, Sch 2 Part 2 para 6; *Holc-Gale v Makers UK Ltd* [2006] ICR 462; [2006] IRLR 178.

matters which may be in dispute, and explanations for various forms of treatment.'[13] It is an effective way to obtain information, and it is tactically significant in view of the potential inferences that can be drawn. Questionnaires, in practice, also permit claimants, or their advisers to seek documents or other evidence long before the disclosure stage. This may be a useful tool at the earliest stages when deciding even whether to bring a claim at all. Any person who considers that he or she has been discriminated against or harassed unlawfully, under the age regulations, is entitled to, and should serve a formal or informal questionnaire on the respondent, whether the claim is brought in the employment tribunal or in the county/sheriff court. The inferential significance of the document asking the questions can be increased by reminding the respondent of the prospect of inferences being drawn from a lack of response or evasion in response.

Time limits for serving questionnaires

11.8   As a rule of thumb, questionnaires should be served at the earliest opportunity. In practice, advisers may find that they can only serve the questionnaires at the same time as lodging the ET1. In claims before the employment tribunal, the claimant has 21 days, beginning on the day on which the ET1 was lodged, to serve the questionnaire, where an ET1 has been lodged in the tribunal.[14] If the questionnaire has not been served in that three-week time frame, the tribunal's leave to serve the questionnaire out of time must be sought. However, the tribunal has discretion to refuse permission, or restrict the number of questions that may be asked.[15] If permission is given, the questionnaire must be served within the period directed by the tribunal.[16] If permission is not given, claimants should consider whether further information or particular documents can be sought through the disclosure process or by way or written questions. If the questionnaire is

---

13   Para 43.
14   Reg 41(4)(b)(i).
15   If the application has to be made out of time, it should be done in accordance with ordinary application procedures. The proposed questionnaire should be included. The tribunal will consider representations (or hold a case management hearing). In deciding whether or not to grant leave, the tribunal will take into account such matters as prejudice, delay, prolixity, oppression and irrelevance (*Williams v Greater London Citizens Advice Bureaux Service* [1989] ICR 545, EAT). These issues should therefore be addressed in the application (or response to the representations made by the respondent).
16   Reg 41(4)(b)(ii).

served before an ET1 has been lodged, it must be served within three months beginning when the act complained of was done.[17]

11.9   Where claims are brought concurrently under the age discrimination and disability discrimination regulations, advisers should be aware that the period within which disability questionnaires should be served is 28 days.[18] All other discrimination claims require the questionnaire to be served within 21 days of the date of presentation of the ET1.[19]

11.10   In relation to any claim brought before a county or sheriff court, the questionnaire should be served within six months beginning when the act complained of was done, if it is served before proceedings have been instituted.[20] If proceedings have been instituted, the court's leave is required and the questionnaire then must be served in accordance with directions.[21]

Manner of service

11.11   The questionnaire may be served by personal delivery or by post at the last known residence or place of business of either the respondent (or prospective respondent), or where that person is acting by a solicitor, to the solicitor's address for service. Any reply may also be delivered personally or sent by post at the claimant's address as stated by him or her in the questionnaire itself.[22] For certainty, it is preferable to send questionnaires by recorded delivery. Where the questionnaires are sent directly to the respondent, they should be marked for the specific attention of an individual, or where the name is not known, the key position which should normally be someone within the legal, or human resources department, or in small companies, the managing director.

Format of the questionnaire/reply

11.12   The format of the questionnaire is set out in Schedule 3 to the regulations.[23] A standard form reply is found in Schedule 4 to the

---

17   Reg 41(4)(a).
18   DDA 1995; Disability Discrimination (Questions and Replies) Order 2004 SI No 1168.
19   Sex Discrimination (Questions and Replies) Order 1975 SI No 2048; Race Relations (Questions and Replies) Order 1977 SI No 842; Sexual Orientation Regulations 2003 SI No 1661 reg 33(4); Religion or Belief Regulations 2003 SI No 1660 reg 33(4); Equal Pay Act 1970 s7B.
20   Reg 41(3)(a).
21   Reg 41(3)(b).
22   Reg 41(5).
23   See appendix A.

regulations.[24] Although there is no obligation to use those forms, it is preferable to follow the suggested format.

11.13   Questions should be drafted clearly and concisely. Ambiguous, trawling questions are unhelpful, since the respondent will be able to give equally evasive answers and could argue that it is reasonable to do so. Consideration needs to be given to what exactly the claimant wants to know, and should know, and whether tactical questions should be asked which would put pressure on the respondent at the earliest stage. If questions are poorly drafted, or vague, a respondent may try to argue that no inference should be drawn since it was not reasonable to expect them to understand what was being asked. It is important to consider the pleaded case when drafting the questions. Questions and statements of fact should be consistent in both the questionnaire and the pleadings, otherwise it can expose the claimant to accusations of changing his or her story.[25]

11.14   It can be helpful to ask for statistical evidence, and this will sometimes be necessary in claims of indirect discrimination. Advisers need to break down requests for this kind of information.

11.15   There are generally three areas which have formed the basis of questions:

a) specific aspects of the claimant's claim, with direct reference to the pleaded case;

b) questions about potential comparators, or other individuals, to find out whether there are patterns, inconsistencies or similarities in treatment;

c) statistical or general questions about the place of employment which provide a broader overview of working conditions and treatment. Advisers should consider whether claims brought under the age discrimination legislation may be brought simultaneously under any other discrimination legislation and elicit questions on all fronts within the questionnaire process.

11.16   To these could now be added questions which assist in relation to age-specific matters and justification:

d) questions aimed at identifying an age group or group identified by an age-related characteristic;

---

24   See appendix A.

25   In *Virdee v ECC Quarries Ltd* [1978] IRLR 295, the respondents failed to answer eight out of nine questions pursuant to the Race Relations Act questionnaire served by the claimant. Their failure was considered to be deliberate and evasive, and therefore enabling the tribunal to infer that substantive unlawful discrimination had taken place.

e) the youngest age of a person who has been affected by a policy, criterion or practice (PCP) (or the oldest age);

f) the age differentials between people who have received different treatment;

g) the aims of the respondent in treating the aggrieved person in the way he or she was treated;

h) why it was considered that this treatment was appropriate;

i) what other courses of action were considered and if any were, why they were rejected in favour of the action adopted by the employer.

The reply

11.17   The respondent is entitled to reply to the questionnaire, and has eight weeks to do so. However, the tribunal or court cannot compel any reply. Nevertheless, if it appears to the court or tribunal that the respondent has deliberately, and without any reasonable excuse, failed to reply to the questionnaire, within eight weeks of service, or that the reply is evasive or equivocal, the court or tribunal may draw any inference from that fact that it considers just or equitable to draw. This may include an inference that the respondent did commit an unlawful act of discrimination or harassment.[26] The authorities suggest that tribunals should make use of the ability to draw inferences and should take seriously any defects in the reply, or failures to respond at all.[27] Increasingly, claims are listed before tribunals at very short notice. It is therefore a good idea to have as much information about the defence at the earliest stage; there is nothing to prevent claimants exerting pressure on respondents to provide replies within 14 or 21 days, since many respondents are unaware of the lengthy eight-week time scale which they are entitled to use. However, the tribunal will not necessarily draw inferences about not responding within the suggested earlier timescale, although it is worth making that argument if it would have been reasonable to have responded earlier.

11.18   Respondents may seek to argue that certain information is confidential, privileged or subject to the Data Protection Act 1998. There may be practical ways around this problem, such as deleting names from lists or in serious cases, an undertaking by advisers not to disclose names. It may be possible to seek the consent of the relevant

---

26   Reg 41(2)(b).

27   See *Igen Ltd and others v Wong; Chamberlin Solicitors and another v Emokpae; Brunel University v Webster* [2005] IRLR 258, CA.

individuals.[28] Where those methods are insufficient or inappropriate, disclosure is permitted for the purpose of actual or prospective legal proceedings under the Data Protection Act 1998.[29]

11.19   There is no obligation on an employer to answer an unreasonable question such as the name and address of a successful applicant for a post.[30]

Pleading the Claim Form

11.20   What details need to be included in the Claim Form? In employment tribunals, claim forms are known as ET1s, and the response forms are known as ET3s. Their use is compulsory. There are prescribed sections which need to be completed. When completing the forms, advisers should ensure that they deal with the sections indicating whether a grievance has been lodged (and if not, why not) and whether the claim involves discrimination (ticking each and every box that applies).

11.21   Tribunals have the power to screen out claims which appear not to contain the requisite information or where there appears to have been a breach of Employment Act 2002 s32 to have used the grievance procedures appropriately. The tribunal secretariat will forward such claims to a chair who can decide whether to accept or reject a claim form on paper.

11.22   In a discrimination claim an employment tribunal can only make findings of liability on causes of action which have been pleaded. A tribunal is not entitled to consider all the evidence and make findings of liability on incidents arising from the evidence. In order to obtain a remedy the claimant must have pleaded the incident or facts on which a finding of liability may be made.[31] Advisers who do not set out the discrimination case with sufficient precision run the risk of being found to be negligent because a cause of action may be lost to the claimant by sloppy pleading.[32]

---

28 An employer can dispose of consent where reasonable to do so pursuant to Data Protection Act 1998 s7(4).

29 Section 35(2).

30 *Oxford v Department of Health and Social Security* [1977] ICR 884.

31 *Chapman v Simon* [1994] IRLR 124. This is the classic statement of the principle, applied by the Court of Appeal in *Nagarajan v Swiggs (No 2)* [1998] IRLR 73 and in *Ali* (below).

32 We recommend that the incidents on which the discrimination claim is to be based and for which remedies are claimed should be set out in numbered paragraphs separately so that there can be no doubt.

11.23   The statement of case, whether in courts or tribunals, should contain at least the following detail:

- The nature of the claim, specifying each substantive act of discrimination, and whether the individuals acts are said to constitute a continuing act and/or pattern of harassment.
- The causative link on which a claim is based, so that if a claim is said to be for unfair dismissal, it will not be taken to include a claim for victimisation on grounds of age where there is no hint of that in the pleaded case.[33] The advice is clear: Thought must be given to what complaints are being brought to the tribunal or court, and they must all be set out cogently.
- The different types of allegations, ie whether the facts pleaded are said to be direct or indirect discrimination, harassment or victimisation.[34]
- Note that in *Ali v Office of National Statistics*[35] the Court of Appeal held that where there was a generalised claim of discrimination pleaded, which did not make any mention (either directly or indirectly in the facts set out) of indirect discrimination, permission to amend the claim at a later stage would be required as it would be treated as a new claim, subject to the 'just and equitable' test. This stresses the importance of considering whether a discrimination claim is to be brought as direct or indirect or both at the outset. In some age cases it will be necessary to set out the role age plays in the definition of the age group or how the age characteristic is related to age.
- Whether the alleged discriminatory acts are said to be on the grounds of age, and/or any other unlawful form of discrimination.
- Where possible, dates of acts of discrimination, including details of the perpetrator and the context (where appropriate) of the discriminatory act.
- Where the case includes a claim for constructive unfair dismissal, state the reasons for resignation clearly and whether/why that is said to be related to the claimant's age. Similar detail should be provided for allegations of detriment related to age.

---

33   *Housing Corporation v Bryant* [1999] ICR 123, CA.
34   *Smith v Zeneca (Agrochemicals) Ltd* [2000] ICR 800.
35   [2005] IRLR 201, disapproving suggestions in *Quarcoopome v Sockshop Holdings Ltd* [1995] IRLR 353, EAT that a catch-all reference to 'discrimination' in the originating application would be sufficient to cover all forms of discrimination.

- If a dismissal is said to be both discriminatory and unfair, both should be pleaded.[36]
- When setting out the discriminatory detriment suffered by the claimant, it is advisable to specify that employees of a different age/age group were not or would not have been subjected to such a detriment.
- If there is a clear comparator at this stage, it is advisable to mention that individual.[37]
- The statement should be concise, tight and fact-based. The time for adding opinion, or speculation is later in the witness statements.
- Do not add uncertain detail, unless it is unavoidable. Inconsistent or inaccurate material can be used against witnesses or the claimant in cross-examination as a matter of credibility.

11.24 The EAT has ruled that when considering whether the details of the claim have been provided (or other required information), the tribunal chair is exercising a judicial function (as opposed to the secretary's administrative function).[38] As such, the chair must have the interests of justice firmly in mind. The test for 'details of the claim' emerges as being 'whether it can be discerned from the claim as presented that the claimant is complaining of an alleged breach of an employment right which falls within the jurisdiction of the ET. It follows that if that test is met, there is no scope for either the Secretary or a Chairman interpreting "details of the claim" as being "sufficient particulars of claim"'.[39]

Limitation periods

11.25 Claims brought before the employment tribunal must be presented within three months (or any extended time limit under the statutory dispute resolution procedures) beginning when the act complained of

---

36 A breach of discrimination regulations does not mean that the claimant was automatically unfairly dismissed *HJ Heinz Co Ltd v Kenrick* [2000] ICR 491. Thus an amendment may be necessary to add such a claim which will not be considered to be implicit in pleadings citing only the discrimination element (see *Harvey v Port of Tilbury (London) Ltd* [1999] ICR 1030; [1999] IRLR 693).

37 However, claimants should also ensure that they have made it clear that they also rely on a hypothetical comparator in the alternative.

38 *Grimmer v KLM* [2005] IRLR 596UKEAT 0070/05/MAA.

39 Para 15 of the judgment, ibid.

was done.[40] Claims brought before the county/sheriff courts must be instituted within six months beginning when the act complained of was done.[41] Advisers should bear in mind the following points relating to limitation:

- Time limits are jurisdictional.[42] This means that time points can be taken at any stage in the proceedings, including by a tribunal or court of its own motion. This has happened in the course of an appeal.[43] Any claim which is presented after the expiry of the time limit cannot be considered, unless the tribunal exercises its discretion to extend time. It is therefore vital that advisers are aware of the three month limitation period and lodge claims before that time.

- Even if respondents are content to allow a claim to be judged on its merits, rather than incurring the expense of an additional preliminary hearing on time, the tribunal is compelled to deal with time points, as they arise. It may be arguable, by either or both sides, however, that issues of time can be better dealt with at a substantive hearing rather than at a preliminary hearing. This is especially true when arguments are likely to relate to questions of continuing acts, so that the facts the tribunal or court must hear to decide the time point are the same or similar to those in the substantive claim. There is authority to support the proposition that time points should be dealt with at the time of the substantive hearing, and there is a presumption that parties are entitled to have the whole of their cases heard.[44]

- Where issues of fact need to be resolved, it may be preferable to have a full tribunal rather than simply a tribunal sitting alone.[45] However, the Employment Tribunal Procedure Rules provide that pre-hearing reviews will be conducted by a chairman sitting alone unless a party has made a request in writing not less than ten days before the date of the hearing, and a chairman considers that one or more

---

40   Reg 42(1).
41   Reg 42(2).
42   *Westward Circuits Ltd v Read* [1973] 2 All ER 1013; *Rodgers v Bodfari (Transport) Ltd* [1973] IRLR 172; *Dedman v British Building and Engineering Appliances Ltd* [1974] 1 All ER 205 for examples of cases dealing with jurisdictional nature of unfair dismissal time limits.
43   *Landon v Lill* EAT/1486/00.
44   *Sutcliffe v Big C's Marine Ltd* [1998] IRLR 428, EAT.
45   See *Sutcliffe* ibid.

substantive issues of fact are likely to be determined, so that it is desirable for the pre-hearing review to be conducted by a tribunal.[46] Accordingly, advisers need to remember to request a full tribunal at least ten days before a pre-hearing reviews is listed, and set out all the reasons why the chairman should make an order as to having a full tribunal determine the issue.

- If the issue of time is decided at a pre-hearing review, both sides are entitled to call evidence and make submissions. The onus is on the claimant, and there is no presumption that time will be extended.[47] The claimant therefore should give his or her evidence first.[48]
- Where the statutory dispute resolution procedures apply, in certain situations described further below, the primary period of time will be extended automatically.
- In some situations, notably where a grievance has not been lodged (see paras 11.41–11.44 below), the tribunal may be precluded from hearing a claim because it is brought before the relevant time period has commenced.

Calculating time periods

11.26 Two sets of time limits may be of importance. Under the Employment Rights Act (ERA) 1996, claims for unfair dismissal carry a three month time limit running from the effective date of termination of the employment. The principle for extending time is that it must not have been reasonably practicable to have presented within that time limit and that claim must have been presented within a reasonable time thereafter. By contrast the claim that the dismissal was an act of unlawful age discrimination will be governed by the time limits set under the regulations. These carry with them a principle of extension under which the tribunal may in its discretion extend time if it considers it just and equitable to do so.

11.27 In the case of a discrimination complaint, time begins to run on the day that the act complained of was done. In the case of an unfair dismissal time runs from the effective date of termination. In both cases the easiest way to work out when the time period expires is to take

---

46 Employment Tribunals (Constitution and Rules etc) Regs 2004 SI No 1861 r 18(1), Sch 1.

47 *Robertson v Bexley Community Centre, t/a Leisure Link* [2003] IRLR 434.

48 The claimant should prepare a witness statement dealing with the matters discussed at para 11.37 below.

the day of the month immediately before the day of the act complained of, such as the date of dismissal, and run forward by three months. For example, if the date of dismissal is 5 August 2006, the final date for presentation (in accordance with the normal time limit, and without any extensions of time under the Statutory Dispute Resolution Procedures) will be 4 November 2006.

11.28   Where a claimant claims that a dismissal was unfair by reasons of age discrimination, the first step for the purposes of claiming unfair dismissal is to establish the effective date of termination (EDT). It may be straightforward, such as the date the dismissal took effect. That date will generally be the one on which the cause of action for discrimination purposes will be fully constituted. Claimants usually will want to argue that any ongoing discrimination or harassment culminated in the date of dismissal. This enables them to claim that there has been a continuing act terminating on that date. If an employee has been summarily dismissed, irrespective of any payment for a period of notice, the EDT is the date of the dismissal or when he ceases to work.[49] Where an employer gives notice to terminate a contract of employment, but does not require the employee to work their notice period, the EDT is the date on which the notice expires. Where a claimant claims constructive unfair dismissal, and gives a notice period, the EDT is the date on which the notice takes effect.[50] Those will be the relevant dates for the purposes of unfair dismissal. For the purposes of discrimination, it is necessary to establish when the cause of action was fully constituted. This will generally be when the detriment has occurred to the claimant. In dismissal cases frequently that will be the date of dismissal.[51]

---

49 ERA 1996 s111.

50 ERA 1996 s97(1)(a).

51 But see *Cast v Croydon College* [1998] ICR 500; [1998] IRLR 318 sometimes the act of discrimination will be constituted in advance of the dismissal – for example when the decision was communicated on the basis of which, subsequently, the employee resigns. See also *Commissioner of Police of the Metropolis v Harley* [2001] ICR 927; [2001] IRLR 263 in this respect. However this also means that where the detriment caused by the act of less favourable treatment does not occur for some time, time will only start to run then. In *Metropolitan Police Service v Shoebridge* [2004] ICR 1690, the EAT, held that an employee was entitled to bring a sex victimisation claim against his former employers, some 14 months after the termination of his employment, where he alleged that unsolicited statements made by those employers to his subsequent employers had resulted in the loss of his new job.

Continuing acts

11.29 In common with the other discrimination legislation, a claimant may wish to argue that a particular act of discrimination or harassment forms part of an act continuing over a period of time. In those circumstances, that act is treated as done at the end of the period, for the purposes of limitation.[52] This would cover a continuing policy or state of affairs as well as a continuing course of discriminatory conduct or harassment.[53]

11.30 The leading case on whether an act continues over a period of time is *Hendricks v Metropolitan Commissioner*.[54] The Court of Appeal stated that the focus should be on the substance of complaints that an individual or employer is responsible for an ongoing situation or a continuing state of affairs, rather than adopting a strict approach considering whether the acts, or series of acts constitutes a policy, rule, practice, scheme or regime. Ms Hendricks therefore was required to show that there was a sufficient link between the incidents so as to demonstrate that the acts generally extended over a period of time as distinct from a succession of unconnected or isolated specific acts, for which time would begin to run from the date when each specific act was committed. An example of a continuing act would be a rule that only people aged 30 or below could attend paid training courses would amount to continuing discrimination. Examples of isolated acts would include a decision not to promote or transfer an individual. Each fresh such decision (where there had been a series of applications or requests) would amount to a new act of discrimination, from which time would begin to run. However, where a manager simply refers back to his or her previous decisions refusing the decision, rather than making a fresh decision, time is likely to run from the earlier decision.[55] The *Hendricks* case does give some leeway to argue that the continuing sequence of individual refusals, particularly if combined with other discriminatory behaviour, may amount to a continuing act, for time purposes.

11.31 Where the making of the contract, or the inclusion of a particular term within the contract is itself argued to be the unlawful act, that act will be treated as extending over the duration of the contract.[56] In practice, this means that the last day for bringing such a claim will be three months from the effective date of termination of the contract.

52 Reg 42(4)(b).
53 *Barclays Bank v Kapur* [1991] IRLR 136.
54 [2003] IRLR 96.
55 *Owusu v London Fire and Civil Defence Authority* [1995] IRLR 574, EAT; *Cast v Croydon College* [1998] IRLR 318, CA.
56 Reg 42(4)(a).

11.32   In *Rihal v London Borough of Ealing*[57] where an employer instituted an arrangement which was discriminatory (in that case, on grounds of race), that arrangement did not cease to be discriminatory merely because the manager in charge had changed.

11.33   Advisers may need to be prepared to argue claims in the alternative, claiming that the discriminatory treatment or harassment amounted to a continuing act, but in the alternative that it is just and equitable to extend time to bring a claim.[58]

Deliberate omissions

11.34   A deliberate omission will be treated as done when the person in question decides upon the omission itself.[59] Accordingly, time will run from that date. There is a rather complex provision in the regulations as to the definition of when that person 'decides' upon the omission. In the absence of contrary evidence, a person is taken to decide upon an omission when he or she does an act inconsistent with doing the omitted act.

> EXAMPLE: Raj puts in an application for a job but because his photograph on the application form makes him look older than the type of employee the employer wants, the employer does nothing about the application. The decision on Raj's application should be made at the same time as everyone else's application. Appointing someone else without considering Raj's application is inconsistent with considering Raj's application. Time will run from that point.

11.35   Where that person has not done an inconsistent act, the person is taken to have 'decided' upon the omission when the period expires within which he or she might reasonably have been expected to do the omitted act if it was to be done.[60]

---

57 [2004] IRLR 642.
58 See paras 11.36–11.38 below.
59 Reg 42(4)(c).
60 Reg 42(4)(c). So for example if I apply for a benefit which it normally takes personnel a week to process, but because of my age the personnel officer does nothing about it, time will start to run after that week expires. This can be something of a trap for claimants who will reply when questioned on this point that, of course, the benefit should have been considered immediately. This manifestation of their frustration at the subsequent discrimination frequently translates into a date on which the act of discrimination occurred which is in fact unrealistically early.

Extension of time

11.36 As with all discrimination claims, the tribunal has a broad discretion to grant an extension of time if, in all the circumstances of the case, it considers that it is just and equitable to do so.[61] However, there is no presumption in favour of extension of time, and the onus is always on the claimant to show that time should be extended.[62]

11.37 It is helpful to consider the factors listed in Limitation Act 1980 s33 when seeking to persuade a tribunal or court that time should be extended.[63] These include:

- the length and reasons for the delay;
- the extent to which the cogency of evidence may be affected by the delay;
- conduct of both parties, and in particular the employer's conduct, including whether the employer co-operated with any requests for information;
- the speed with which the claimant acted once he or she was aware of the facts giving rise to their claim;
- steps taken to obtain professional advice once the possibility of action became apparent to the claimant.

11.38 However, although there is no requirement that each and every factor be considered as part of a checklist, advisers will consider and deal with each of these key headings when arguing that time should be extended. The employment tribunal will not, however, be considered to have made a mistake, so long as no 'significant factor' is omitted.[64] Pursuing an internal grievance is one of the factors attributing to the delay that a tribunal should consider, although it is not necessarily determinative.[65]

---

61 Reg 42(3).
62 *Robertson v Bexley Community Centre* [2003] IRLR 434, CA.
63 See *British Coal Corporation v Keeble* [1997] IRLR 336, *Mills and Crown Prosecution Service v Marshall* [1998] IRLR 494, sub nom *DPP v Marshall* [1998] ICR 518, EAT.
64 *Southwark London Borough v Afolabi* [2003] IRLR 220 at para 33, CA.
65 *Robinson v Post Office* [2000] IRLR 804, EAT, approved by the Court of Appeal in *Apelogun-Gabriels v London Borough of Lambeth* [2002] IRLR 116.

Extension of time under the Employment Dispute Regulations 2004

11.39   The Employment Act 2002 (Dispute Resolution) Regulations 2004[66] provide, in certain specified circumstances, for an automatic three month extension of time to the normal time limits for the bringing of any of the claims specified in Schedule 3 or Schedule 4.[67] By virtue of Schedule 8 to the age discrimination regulations, these will now include claims for age discrimination in the employment field.[68] Regulation 15(1)(b) of the Dispute Regulations 2004, in conjunction with regulation 15(3) provides for the automatic extension of time (namely by three months) where:

a)   the employee has presented his or her complaint to the tribunal within the normal time limit, but is barred from so doing either because he or she has not complied with the grievance requirement set out in Employment Act 2002 s32(2), which is to present a grievance in writing to the employer about the subject matter of the complaint, or because he or she has not allowed 28 days to elapse following the submission of her grievance before lodging the ET1 with the tribunal; or

b)   the employee has raised a grievance within the normal time limit, namely three months, but then presents the claim to the tribunal following the expiry of the normal time limit.

11.40   'Normal time limit' is defined in regulation 15(5) and is, for the purposes of claims under the age regulations, the three month period before which the tribunal would need to consider whether it should exercise its discretion or make any findings on jurisdiction.

Statutory dispute resolution procedures

11.41   Employment Act 2002 s32(2) prevents a claimant from bringing a claim to the tribunal where he or she has not lodged a grievance, where the subject matter of the claim requires a grievance to be brought (which is now the case for all claims relating to age discrimination in employment, except where the act of dismissal itself is said to be discriminatory). Section 32(3) prevents the claimant from bringing a claim where he

---

66   SI No 752.
67   Dispute Regs 2004 reg 15.
68   Pursuant to Age Regs 2006 reg 36.

or she is required to bring a grievance where he or she has not allowed 28 days to lapse between the date the grievance was submitted and the date that the ET1 is lodged. Section 32(4) then enables a claimant to validly present a claim one month from the expiry of the 'original' time limit. In practical terms, this means *the claimant is not entitled to bring a claim unless he or she has presented a written grievance to the employer within four months of the date of the date of dismissal, or the day on which the last discriminatory act is said to have been done.*

11.42   In *Spillett v Bupa*,[69] the EAT makes clear that the 'original time limit' is said to be the time limits provided for by legislation, and therefore contemplates that the one month extension *could theoretically apply* to a complaint made outside the primary limitation period where it is just and equitable to do so (or reasonably practicable according to the relevant test required to grant an extension of time).

11.43   It is only in the specific circumstances set out in regulation 15 that time will be extended automatically to provide an automatic extension of three months to the normal time limit, beginning with the day after the day on which it would otherwise have expired.

11.44   The relevant circumstances are:

- Where the disciplinary procedures apply: That the employee presents a complaint to the tribunal after the expiry of the normal time limit for presenting the complaint but had reasonable grounds for believing, when that time limit expired, that a dismissal or disciplinary procedure, whether statutory or otherwise, in respect of matters that consisted of or included the substance of the tribunal complaint.
- Where the grievance procedures apply; and
  - the employee presents his or her ET1 within the normal time limit (three months generally) and the employee had not lodged a grievance *or* the employee has lodged a grievance, but not waited for 28 days to elapse before presenting his or her ET1;
  - the employee has complied with the grievance procedure within the normal time limit (generally three months), but presented his or her ET1 after the expiry of the normal time limit. The following acts are treated as compliance, for the purposes of this regulation:
    - where the grievance is that the employer has taken or is contemplating taking relevant disciplinary action against the employee and one of the reasons for the grievance is:

> – that the relevant disciplinary action amounted to or, if it
> took place, would amount to unlawful discrimination;
> or
> – that the grounds on which the employer took the action
> or is contemplating taking it were or are unrelated to the
> grounds on which he asserted that he took the action or
> is asserting that he is contemplating taking it,

the standard grievance procedure or, as the case may be, modified grievance procedure shall apply but the parties shall be
treated as having complied with the applicable procedure if the
employee has set out the grievance in a written statement and
sent the statement or a copy of it to the employer either before
the appeal meeting in either of the dismissal or disciplinary
procedures (if they are being followed), and if they are not being
followed, before presenting a claim to the tribunal.

Tribunal procedures

11.45 New Rules of Procedure for employment tribunals are found in the
Employment Tribunals (Constitution and Rules of Procedure) Regulations 2004.[70] These apply to England and Wales, and also to Scotland (with some minor differences in terminology and practice, as
clearly set out). The regulations are known as the Employment Tribunals Rules of Procedure (ET Rules) 2004.[71] They set out extensively
the power and the jurisdiction of employment tribunals, but must be
read alongside the Employment Act 2002 and the Dispute Resolution
Regulations 2004, since the tribunal's jurisdiction is now governed to
a large degree by those instruments.

11.46 It is beyond the scope of this book to recite the full extent of the
procedure rules.

11.47 The regulations themselves contain a version of the overriding
objective. The central objective of the rules is to enable tribunals and
chairmen to deal with cases justly.[72] The duty to deal with cases justly
is expressed as a high duty 'so far as practicable' to:

a) ensure that the parties are on an equal footing;
b) deal with cases in ways which are proportionate to the complexity
or importance of the issues;

---

70 SI No 1861.
71 SI No 1861.
72 ET Procedure Regulations 2004 reg 3.

c) ensure that the case is dealt with expeditiously and fairly;
d) saving expenses.

11.48 The chairman is to give effect to that overriding objective *in exercising* any power given to him by the regulations or the rules or *when interpreting* those regulations and rules. The parties are under a duty to assist the tribunal or the chairman to further the overriding objective.

Presenting the claim

11.49 The claim must be presented within the relevant time limit. Rule 61 provides that any notice given or document sent under the rules shall (unless the chairman or tribunal orders otherwise) be in writing and may be given or sent by post/fax (or other means of electronic communication) /personal delivery. If sent in this way the notice or document shall, unless the contrary is proved, be taken to have been received by the addressed party:

- in the case of a document by post, on the day on which the notice etc would be delivered in the ordinary course of post;
- in the case of the document etc transmitted by fax or other electronic communication means, on the day on which the notice or document is transmitted;
- in the case of a document etc delivered in person, the day on which the notice etc is delivered.

11.50 In *Coleridge v HM Prison Service*[73], this rule was recommended as being clear. Care should be taken therefore where the limitation period expires on a weekend or bank holiday. The rule that applies in the EAT, which extends the period of time for doing an act to the next working day, where the period of time expires on a non-working day, does not apply.

11.51 Where the relevant time for presenting a response has passed and the following circumstances apply, a chairman has a discretion to issue a default judgment to determine the claim without hearing if he or she considers it appropriate to do so:

- no response in those proceedings has been presented to the employment tribunal within the relevant time limit;
- although a response has been presented a decision has been made not to accept it (whether by the secretary or by the chairman) and the

73 [2005] UKEAT 0728/04/TM.

employment tribunal office has not received an application for a review under rule 34;

- the claimant has not informed the employment tribunal office in writing either that the claimant does not wish a default judgment to be issued or that the case has settled.[74]

11.52 The default judgment may determine liability alone or liability and remedy but if it determines remedy it shall be such remedy as it appears to the chairman that the claimant is entitled to on the basis of the information before him (rule 8(3)). The judgment is recorded in writing and signed by the chairman.[75] The secretary sends a copy of the judgment to the parties, ACAS, and if the proceedings were referred by a court, to the court. The secretary must also inform the parties of their rights to have the default judgment reviewed under rule 33.

11.53 Both the claimant and the respondent may apply to have such judgments reviewed in accordance with rules 33. If the parties have settled on, or before, the date on which default judgment in the proceedings is issued the default judgment has no effect and the effect of such a settlement is that either party may apply to the tribunal under rule 33 to have the default judgment revoked.

11.54 The only thing that a respondent can do is to make an application for a review of the default judgment or make an application under rule 35 for a preliminary consideration of an application for review. It also may be called as a witness by another person or even sent a copy of the document or corrected entry showing the default judgment (rule 8(4)), a copy of the judgment (rule 29(2)), or a copy of a corrected entry under rule 37.

11.55 Probably the most important rule from a practical point of view is rule 10. The rule also deals with postponements and adjournments, and amendments to the claim or response, witness statement exchange or preparation. The chairman may at any time either on the application of a party or on his or her own initiative make an order in relation to any matter which appears to him or her to be appropriate.[76] That general

---

74 Rule 8(2).
75 Where it is not possible for a judgment, order or reasons to be signed by the chairman due to death, incapacity or absence if the chairman has dealt with the proceedings alone the document shall be signed by the Regional Chairman, Vice President or President when it is practicable for him to do so; and if the proceedings have been dealt with by a tribunal composed of two or three persons, the document shall be signed by the other person or persons. Any person who signs the document shall certify that the chairman is unable to sign.
76 Rule 10(1).

power is made subject to the rules that follow. The rule gives examples of the orders that can be made in rule 10(2). However rule 10(1) expressly provides that the chairman may make 'such other orders as he thinks fit'.

11.56   Rule 10(2)(d) provides that a chairman may make an order requiring any person in Great Britain to disclose documents to a party or to allow a party to inspect such material as might be ordered by a County Court (or in Scotland, by a sheriff). By rule 10(5) such an order which requires a person other than a party to grant disclosure or inspection of material may be made only when the disclosure sought is necessary in order to dispose fairly of the claim or to save expense. The rules clearly envisage that orders may be made against non-parties. It does not, of course, follow from rule 10(5) that these factors are not germane to disclosure between parties.

11.57   In *South Tyneside BC v Anderson*[77] the ET chairman had concluded that his powers to order disclosure were equivalent to those of the county court and therefore referred to the Civil Procedure Rules 1998 (CPR) rule 31, rule 31.5 and the practice directions made for CPR 31. Rule 31.5 provides for standard disclosure, unless the court otherwise directs. Standard disclosure requires disclosure of those documents on which a party relies, those which adversely affect his own claim or another party's claim, those which support another party's case. In the CPR standard disclosure also encompasses those documents which are required to be disclosed by a relevant practice direction. CPR 31.12 provides for specific disclosure. This is an order which requires a party to disclose documents or classes of documents specified in the order, carry out a search to the extent specified in the order and disclose documents located as a result of that search. The CPR practice direction requires evidence to be presented to the court to justify an order for specific disclosure.

11.58   HHJ Wilkie QC held that whilst it did not follow automatically that the ET has to apply the practice direction from the CPR, he took the view that the practice direction contains an important principle namely that in order that disclosure should be as much as, but not more than is necessary for the effective disposal of the litigation, a step by step approach is to be often preferred.

11.59   Making and responding to applications is dealt with in rule 11. At any stage of the proceedings a party may apply for an order to be issued, varied or revoked or for a case management discussion or pre-hearing review to be held.[78]

---

77   UKEAT 0002/2005.
78   Rule 11(1).

11.60   However, an application for an order must be made not less than ten days before the date of the hearing at which it is to be considered (if any) unless it is not reasonably practicable to do so, or the chairman or tribunal considers it in the interests of justice that shorter notice be allowed.[79] The rule appears to impose a muddled test for the exceptions to the ten days period. If the test is reasonable practicability, that is a difficult test to satisfy. However, if the test is simply whether the chairman or tribunal considers it in the interests of justice that shorter notice be allowed, that is a completely discretionary test, which will be applied having regard to the overriding objective.

11.61   The requirements of an application[80] are:

i) that it be in writing;
ii) that the case number be included;
iii) that the reasons for the request be explained;
iv) that there be included an explanation as to why and how any order sought would assist the tribunal or chairman in dealing with the proceedings fairly and efficiently;
v) if it is an application for a Case Management Discussion, that the orders sought should be identified.

Case Management Discussions

11.62   Case Management Discussions (CMDs) are interim hearings and may deal with matters of procedure and management of the proceedings and they may be held in private. They are conducted by a chairman. Significantly, there may be no determination of a person's civil rights or obligations in a CMD. This permits the rules to allow the tribunal to sit in private without having to consider article 6 of the European Convention on Human Rights (ECHR), as codified in the Human Rights Act (HRA) 1998. Article 6 only applies where there is to be a determination of the civil rights and obligations of any party. The rule goes on to point out that the matters listed in rule 10(2) are examples of matters which may be dealt with at case management discussions.

---

79   Rule 11(2).
80   Unless a chairman or tribunal orders otherwise.

Pre-hearing reviews

11.63 A chairman may hold a Pre-Hearing Review (PHR interim hearing),[81] save where a party has made a request in writing, and a chairman considers that substantive issue(s) of fact are likely to be determined at the PHR[82] and issues an order that the PHR is to be conducted by an employment tribunal. The application that the pre-hearing review be conducted by a tribunal must be made not less than ten days before the date on which the pre-hearing review is due to take place.[83]

11.64 The chairman may carry out a preliminary consideration of the proceedings and he may determine any interim or preliminary matter relating to the proceedings and/or issue any order in accordance with rule 10 or do anything else which may be done at a CMD.[84] This means that a CMD is a subset of a PHR, so that listing for a PHR necessarily may include a CMD. However, the reverse does not follow.

11.65 The PHR may result in an order[85] that a deposit be paid, without hearing evidence.[86] However the rules do permit oral or written representations or evidence at PHRs.[87] Note the scope of rule 20. A deposit may be ordered in respect of an issue in a case. The chairman may give judgment on any preliminary issue of substance relating to the proceedings. Judgments or orders made at a pre-hearing review may result in the proceedings being struck out or dismissed or otherwise determined with the result that a hearing is no longer necessary.[88]

11.66 The PHR may result in a judgment or order as to the following:

a) the entitlement of any party to bring or contest particular proceedings;

b) striking out or amending all or part of any claim or response on the grounds that it is scandalous, or vexatious or has no reasonable prospect of success;

c) striking out any claim or response (or part of one) on the grounds that the manner in which the proceedings have been conducted

---

81 Held in public, save where a ruling under rule 16 is made.
82 And considers it desirable that the ET hear it.
83 Rule 18(3).
84 Rule 18(2)(a), (b).
85 Under rule 20.
86 Where this is ordered, the chairman who conducted that pre-hearing review shall not be a member of the tribunal at the hearing in relation to those proceedings (rule 18(9)).
87 Rule 18(2)(d).
88 Rule 18(5).

by or on behalf of the claimant or the respondent (as the case may be) has been scandalous, unreasonable or vexatious;

d) striking out a claim which has not been actively pursued;[89]

e) striking out a claim or response (or part of one) for non-compliance with an order or practice direction;

f) striking out a claim where the chairman or tribunal considers that it is no longer possible to have a fair hearing in those proceedings;

g) making a restricted reporting order.[90]

11.67 The notice requirements for an entitlement/strike out/restricted reporting order to be made are that the secretary sends notice to the party against whom it is proposed that the order or judgment should be made, and it informs him of the order or judgment to be considered. He must be given the opportunity to give reasons why the judgment or order should not be made. However if an opportunity to give reasons orally has been given to that party there is no such obligation on the secretary.[91]

The hearing

11.68 Procedure at a hearing is informal. The tribunal can regulate its own procedure and can admit evidence such as hearsay evidence which it would be more difficult to introduce in other courts. A hearing of the case must be held in public save where an application is made under rule 16.[92] A hearing or part of one may be conducted in private for the purpose of hearing from any person evidence or representations which in the opinion of the tribunal or chairman is likely to consist of information:

a) which the person could not disclose without contravening a prohibition imposed by or by virtue of any enactment;

---

89   There is a special service rule relating to notices of this sort of order: rule 19(2) provides that a notice sent in relation to an order to strike out a claim which has not been actively pursued, unless the contrary is proved, the notice shall be treated as if it were received by the addressee if it has been sent to the address specified in the claim as the address to which notices are to be sent (or to any subsequent replacement for that address which has been notified to the Employment Tribunal Office). Note that this presumption does not appear to apply to the other types of orders that can be made.

90   Subject to rule 50.

91   Rule 19.

92   Or where the proceedings are held under the national security procedure.

b) which has been communicated to the person in confidence, or which he or she has otherwise obtained in consequence of the confidence placed in him or her by another person; or

c) the disclosure of which would, for reasons other than its effect on negotiations with respect to any of the collective bargaining matters mentioned in Trade Union and Labour Relations (Consolidation) Act 1992 s178(2), cause substantial injury to any undertaking of his or any undertaking in which he works.

11.69 Thus matters relating to the psychiatric state of the claimant could be heard in private under this rule if the evidence was being given by a doctor to whom it was communicated in confidence.

Costs, access to justice

Employment tribunals

11.70 Rules 38–48 of the ET Rules 2004 deal with costs, preparation orders and wasted costs. Significantly, there are now provisions for 'preparation time orders' for non-legally represented parties to be made.[93]

11.71 The award of costs remains discretionary in most circumstances. Awards of costs remain the exception rather than the norm in tribunals. However, costs orders may be made against a party who has postponed or adjourned a hearing in respect of any costs incurred or allowances paid by the other party.[94] Common sense prevails in such applications. Factors to be considered (which are not set out in the rules) might include:

- reasons why the postponement/adjournment was sought;
- amount of notice given to other parties and/or the tribunal as to the application for adjournment;
- whether the request is reasonable;
- whether supporting evidence, such as medical notes etc, are available;
- whether the application for postponement/adjournment was contested and why.

11.72 Costs orders may be made against a party who has not complied with an order or practice direction.[95]

---

93 ET Rules 2004 r38(2), Sch 1.
94 Ibid r40(1).
95 Ibid r40(4).

11.73   The tribunal or a chair 'shall consider making a costs order' where, in its opinion:

a) the paying party has in bringing the proceedings, acted vexatiously, abusively, disruptively or otherwise unreasonably; or
b) the paying party or his representative has in conducting the proceedings acted vexatiously, abusively, disruptively or otherwise unreasonably; or
c) the bringing or conducting of the proceedings has been misconceived.[96]

11.74   A costs order must be made in favour of a claimant where the claimant has expressed a wish to be re-instated or re-engaged, which has been communicated to the respondent not less than seven days before the hearing, and the hearing has been adjourned or postponed by the respondent's failure, without special reason, to adduce reasonable evidence as to the availability of the job from which the claimant was dismissed, or of comparable or suitable employment.[97]

11.75   A costs order may be made against or in favour of a respondent who has not had a response accepted in the proceedings in relation to the conduct of any part which he has taken in the proceedings.[98] The EAT has held that it is not possible to award costs against a respondent who fails to submit a Response Form. When an employer fails to enter a response, the tribunal is limited to awarding costs caused or incurred in dealing with one of the matters expressly set out in rule 9, which effectively limits the award of costs in these circumstances to making an application for review of a default judgment.[99]

11.76   Applications in respect of costs orders may be made at any time during the proceedings, or at the end of a hearing orally, or in writing to the employment tribunal office. This should be done at the latest within 28 days from the issuing of the judgment determining the claim.[100] The date of the judgment will be the date on which judgment is given orally at a hearing, or if judgment is reserved, the date on which written judgment is sent to the parties.[101] Applications which are received later than the 28 days will only be entertained if a tribunal or chairman considers it in the interests of justice to do so.

96   Ibid r40(2) and (3).
97   Ibid r39.
98   Reg 38(4).
99   *Sutton v The Ranch Ltd* UKEAT/0072/06.
100   Ibid r38(7).
101   Ibid r38(8).

11.77   If an application for costs is made orally at a hearing, both sides should be given the opportunity to express their views on whether the order should be made. If an application is made in writing, the tribunal secretary must send notice to the party against whom the order may be made, giving them the opportunity to give reasons why the order should not be made.[102]

11.78   If a tribunal or chairman does make a costs award, requests for written reasons should be made orally at the hearing or within 14 days of the date of the costs order, in writing.[103]

11.79   The tribunal or chair may have regard to the paying party's ability to pay when considering whether a costs order should be made, or the amount of such order.[104] However, unless expressly agreed by the parties, the tribunal may not order that an award exceed £10,000. Alternatively, the tribunal may order that the amount (which could exceed £10,000) be subject to detailed assessment in a county court, in accordance with the CPR 1998, or taxed in the sheriff's court in Scotland accordingly.[105]

Preparation time orders

11.80   Preparation time orders may be made where a party has not been legally represented at a hearing or in proceedings which are determined without a hearing, if the receiving party was not legally represented at the time when the proceedings were determined.[106] 'Preparation time' is defined as time spent by the receiving party or his or her employees carrying out preparatory work directly related to the proceedings, and the receiving party's legal or other advisers relating to the conduct of the proceedings, up to *but not including* time spent at any hearing.[107] The provisions governing preparation time orders, and the procedure for applying for them, are broadly the same as those for costs orders.

11.81   The amount of such an award will be assessed by the tribunal or chair by considering the information provided to it by the receiving party on the amount of time spent, as well as the tribunal or chair's own

---

102   Ibid r38(9).
103   Ibid r39(10).
104   Ibid r41(2).
105   Ibid r41(1).
106   Ibid r42(2).
107   Ibid r42(3).

assessment of what would be a reasonable and proportionate amount of time to spend in the circumstances.[108] The hourly rate to be applied is £26 as at 6 April 2006 and will increase by £1 on each subsequent year on 6 April.[109] No preparation time order may exceed £10,000.[110]

11.82   The two regimes governing preparation time orders and costs are mutually exclusive. A tribunal or chair may not make a preparation time order and a costs order in favour of the same party in the same proceedings. However, if the tribunal or chair wishes to make either a costs order or a preparation time order in proceedings, before the claim has been determined, an order may be made that either costs or preparation time be awarded to the receiving party. In such circumstances, the tribunal or chair may decide whether the award should be for costs or preparation time after the proceedings have been determined.[111]

Deposits

11.83   Deposits go to the preparation time order or costs order, if such is made.[112] Any excess above the costs is returned.[113] However, if the party is ordered to pay a deposit in respect of a matter, and has persisted in respect of that matter, there are discretionary consequences should the ultimate tribunal find against the party on that matter. This is the case even where no preparation time or costs order has been made, arising out of the proceedings on the matter. What the tribunal or chair has to consider is whether to make a costs or preparation time order against that party on the ground that he conducted the proceedings relating to the matter unreasonably in persisting in having the matter determined. However, no costs or preparation time order may be made on that ground unless it has considered the document recording the order under rule 20 and is of the opinion that the grounds which caused the tribunal or chair to find against the party in its judgment were substantially the same as the grounds recorded in that document for considering that the contentions of the party had little reasonable prospect of success.[114]

---

108   Ibid r45(1).
109   Ibid r45(4).
110   Ibid r45.
111   Ibid r46(2).
112   Ibid r47(2).
113   Ibid r47(2).
114   Ibid r47(1).

Wasted costs

11.84 There is now provision for a wasted costs order to be made by a tribunal or chair against a party's representative.[115] These are costs incurred by a party as a result of any improper, unreasonable or negligent act or omission on the part of any representative, or which in the light of any act or omission occurring after they were incurred, the tribunal considers it unreasonable to expect that party to pay.[116]

11.85 A 'representative' is defined as a party's legal or other representative, or any employee of such representative, but it does not include a representative who is not acting in pursuit of profit with regard to those proceedings. A person is considered to be acting in pursuit of profit if he is acting on a conditional fee arrangement.[117]

11.86 Wasted costs orders permit the tribunal or chair to disallow or order the representative of a party to meet the whole or part of any wasted costs of any party, including an order that the representative repay to his client any costs which have already been paid. Further, the tribunal or chair may order that the representative pay the secretary of state the whole or part of any allowances, such as witness expenses, to anyone for the purposes of, or in connection with, that person's attendance at the tribunal by reason of the representative's conduct of the proceedings.

11.87 Wasted costs orders may be made in favour of a party whether or not that person is legally represented, so that it would cover the situation of an unregulated representative who is not legally qualified. Such an order may be made also in favour of a representative's own client. However, a wasted costs order may not be made against a representative where that representative is an employee of a party.[118]

11.88 The representative must be given an opportunity to make oral or written representations why the order should not be made, and the representative's ability to pay must be taken into account.[119] When made, the order must specify the amount to be disallowed or paid.

11.89 The tribunal must provide written reasons for making a wasted costs order if a request is made for written reasons within 14 days of the date of the order. There is no provision for this time limit to be extended under rule 10.[120]

115 Ibid r48.
116 Ibid r48(3).
117 Ibid r48(4).
118 Ibid r48(5).
119 Ibid r48(6).
120 Ibid r48(9).

Burden of proof

Employment tribunals

11.90   The burden of proof, which is to be applied in respect of any complaint presented to the employment tribunal,[121] is drafted in exactly the same format as appears in the Sex Discrimination Act 1975, Sexual Orientation Regulations 2003[122] and Religious Belief Regulations 2003:[123]

> Where, on the hearing of the complaint, the complainant proves facts from which the tribunal could, apart from this regulation, conclude in the absence of an adequate explanation that the respondent–
> (a) has committed against the complainant an act to which regulation 36 applies; or
> (b) is by virtue of regulation 25 (liability of employers and principals) or 26 (aiding unlawful acts) to be treated as having committed against the complainant such an act,
> the tribunal shall uphold the complaint unless the respondent proves that he did not commit, or as the case may be, is not to be treated as having committed, that act.[124]

11.91   The Court of Appeal has issued 'revised *Barton* guidelines' (as an annex to the decision) in the case of *Igen v Wong*,[125] and these constitute the most recent guidelines that practitioners should follow.

11.92   The **amended Barton guidelines** are set out below:

> (1) Pursuant to s.63A of the SDA, it is for the claimant who complains of sex discrimination to prove on the balance of probabilities facts from which the tribunal could conclude, in the absence of an adequate explanation, that the respondent has committed an act of discrimination against the claimant which is unlawful by virtue of Part II or which by virtue of s. 41 or s. 42 of the SDA is to be treated as having been committed against the claimant.
> (2) If the claimant does not prove such facts he or she will fail.
> (3) It is important to bear in mind in deciding whether the claimant has proved such facts that it is unusual to find direct evidence of sex discrimination. Few employers would be prepared to admit such discrimination, even to themselves. In some cases the discrimination will not be an intention but merely based on the assumption that 'he or she would not have fitted in'.

---

121   Reg 37(1).
122   Employment Equality (Sexual Orientation) Regulations 2003 SI No 1661.
123   Employment Equality (Religion or Belief) Regulations 2003 SI No 1660.
124   Reg 37(2).
125   *Igen ltd v Wong, Chamberlin Solicitors v Emokpae; Brunel University v Webster, EOC, CRE and DRC intervening* [2005] IRLR 258, CA.

(4) In deciding whether the claimant has proved such facts, it is important to remember that the outcome at this stage of the analysis by the tribunal will therefore usually depend on what inferences it is proper to draw from the primary facts found by the tribunal.

(5) It is important to note the word 'could' in s.63A(2). At this stage the tribunal does not have to reach a definitive determination that such facts would lead it to the conclusion that there was an act of unlawful discrimination. At this stage a tribunal is looking at the primary facts before it to see what inferences of secondary fact could be drawn from them.

(6) In considering what inferences or conclusions can be drawn from the primary facts, the tribunal must assume that there is no adequate explanation for those facts.

(7) These inferences can include, in appropriate cases, any inferences that it is just and equitable to draw in accordance with s.74(2)(b) of the SDA from an evasive or equivocal reply to a questionnaire or any other questions that fall within s.74(2) of the SDA.

(8) Likewise, the tribunal must decide whether any provision of any relevant code of practice is relevant and if so, take it into account in determining, such facts pursuant to s.56A(10) of the SDA. This means that inferences may also be drawn from any failure to comply with any relevant code of practice.

(9) Where the claimant has proved facts from which conclusions could be drawn that the respondent has treated the claimant less favourably on the ground of sex, then the burden of proof moves to the respondent.

(10) It is then for the respondent to prove that he did not commit, or as the case may be, is not to be treated as having committed, that act.

(11) To discharge that burden it is necessary for the respondent to prove, on the balance of probabilities, that the treatment was in no sense whatsoever on the grounds of sex, since 'no discrimination whatsoever' is compatible with the Burden of Proof Directive.

(12) That requires a tribunal to assess not merely whether the respondent has proved an explanation for the facts from which such inferences can be drawn, but further that it is adequate to discharge the burden of proof on the balance of probabilities that sex was not a ground for the treatment in question.

(13) Since the facts necessary to prove an explanation would normally be in the possession of the respondent, a tribunal would normally expect cogent evidence to discharge that burden of proof. In particular, the tribunal will need to examine carefully explanations for failure to deal with the questionnaire procedure and/or code of practice.

11.93 Advisers should be wary of relying heavily on cases pre-dating the *Barton* decision since although many of the principles remain generally useful and applicable, the state of law regarding burden of proof has now changed.

11.94   The formulation of the burden of proof to some degree may make it easier for claimants to prove their case. Tribunals are bound to find that there has been discrimination when the circumstances set out in regulation 37(1) are met and the employer has no satisfactory explanation. In *Adebayo*, Cox J stated that once the burden of proof has passed to the employer, the employer must show that the explanation is non-discriminatory and the real reason for what happened (at para 53).

11.95   Evidence of conduct or actions that took place in the past can be useful illustrations in proving discrimination claims. Statistical evidence can be useful. In *Rihal v London Borough of Ealing*,[126] the Court of Appeal held that in determining whether there were racial grounds for less favourable treatment, a tribunal is obliged to look at all the material put before it which is relevant to determination of the issue, which may include evidence about the conduct of the alleged discriminator before to after the act about which the complaint is made. This means that even if historical matters have not been fully pleaded, a tribunal should be encouraged to look at the full picture emerging from witness statements, documents and submissions as to the historical and present reality, which may allow it to draw inferences of discrimination. The court also stressed that when constructing a picture of how a hypothetical comparator would have been treated, the tribunal may need to look beyond the immediate circumstances of the incident about which complaint is brought. Further, the tribunal should avoid a fragmented approach and consider the cumulative picture, rather than looking at individual incidents in isolation.

11.96   The tribunal must identify what the less favourable treatment is, since it is the treatment itself rather than its consequences which must be different and less favourable.[127]

11.97   When determining whether discrimination has occurred, a tribunal may draw inferences from certain conduct by the Respondent. In *Dattani v Chief Constable of West Mercia Police*,[128] in a case brought under the Race Relations Act 1976, the EAT considered the effect of the new burden of proof[129] on the drawing of inferences. The claimant was of Indian origin. He brought proceedings alleging he had been selected for a transfer against his will, on the basis of his race. The

---

126   [2004] IRLR 642, CA.

127   *Balgobin v Tower Hamlets London Borough Council* [1987] ICR 829.

128   [2005] IRLR 327, EAT.

129   RRA 1976 s54A introduced by the Race Relation Act (Amendment) Regulations 2003, implementing Council Directive 2000/43/EC.

earlier Court of Appeal authority, in which the newer burden of proof was not applicable, *Anya v University of Oxford*[130] was approved in respect of the procedure for drawing adverse inferences. Inferences can be both conclusions in respect of circumstantial evidence drawn from primary facts as well as legal conclusions drawn from those primary and secondary findings. Such inferences can also be drawn from responses, or failure to provide responses, in the earlier questionnaire procedure. In Anya, a black Nigerian doctor applied for a post as a post-doctoral research assistant. He was rejected following an interview and the post went to the other shortlisted candidate who was white. The Court of Appeal held that very little discrimination would be overt or even deliberate. In this case, it was said that it would not be unduly onerous to proceed from a process of selection, if it is accompanied by a difference in race, to a request for an explanation. It was said that in the allocation of jobs by any sensibly-run institution, the explanation would be straightforward. The candidates would all have been interviewed by an unbiased panel on an equal footing, using common criteria which contained no obvious or latent elements capable of favouring one racial group over the other, and the best person for the job was chosen. Where there was evidence that at least one member may not have been unbiased, that may point to the possibility of conscious or unconscious racial bias. The tribunal therefore needs to make findings of primary fact before it can draw any inferences and follow through on its conclusions in a fully reasoned manner.

11.98   In *Sinclair Roche & Temperly v Heard*,[131] the EAT stated that:

> It is apparent that, particularly given the reversal of the burden of proof, it is essential that, if the tribunal satisfies itself that there has been on the face of it unfavourable treatment, it has effectively only reached halfway; it must set out clearly its conclusions as to the nature and extent of such unfavourable treatment, and it must then fully and carefully consider, having thus identified the conduct which requires explaining, what the explanations of the employer were, and why, if such be the case, such explanations provide no answer.

11.99   In *Law Society v Bahl*,[132] Elias J stated, at para 100:

> ... where the alleged discriminator acts unreasonably then a tribunal will want to know why he has acted in that way. If he gives a non-discriminatory explanation, which the tribunal considers to be honestly given, then that is likely to be a full answer to any discrimination claim. It need not be,

---

130 *Anya v University of Oxford* [2001] IRLR 377, CA: See also *Rihal v London Borough of Ealing* [2004] IRLR 642, CA.

131 [2004] IRLR 763, EAT.

because it is possible that he is subconsciously influenced by unlawful discriminatory considerations. But again, there should be proper evidence from which such an inference should be drawn.

11.100 In *EB v BA*,[133] in a case concerning unlawful discrimination in the allocation of work on grounds of gender reassignment, the Court of Appeal held that once the burden of proof had shifted, the consequences of an absence of significant documents from the employers could only be adverse to the employers, rather than the employee since the failure to produce them was not that of the claimant. Absence of significant documents deprived the employers of the opportunity to rebut the case made against it. The Court stressed that employers should not be permitted to escape the (parallel) provisions of Sex Discrimination Act 1976 s63A by leaving it to the employee to prove her case, and that tribunals should bear in mind the objectives of the burden of proof at pre-hearing as well as hearing stage. If an employer adopts a 'you prove it' stance towards the claimants, particularly those with limited or no means, those claimants who seek to challenge large corporations would be at a great disadvantage, effectively minimising the value of the reverse burden of proof.

11.101 Note that it is not normally appropriate for half time submissions of no case to answer to be made in a discrimination claim. In *Logan v Commissioners of Custom & Excise*,[134] the Court of Appeal approved the statement that 'in discrimination cases, it will only be an exceptional or a frivolous case that it would be right to take such a course", referring to the acceding of a half time submission of no case to answer.

County and sheriff courts: education-related claims only

11.102 The burden of proof is exactly the same as for claims brought within the employment tribunal, and is set out in regulation 40.

Funding of claims

11.103 Funding is not usually available for advocacy in the employment tribunal.[135] Public funding is available for proceedings in the EAT in the

---

132 [2004] IRLR 640, EAT, Elias J presiding.
133 [2006] IRLR 47.
134 [2004] IRLR 63, CA.
135 By virtue of Access to Justice Act 1999 Sch 2 para 2.

normal way. In the employment tribunals, the Lord Chancellor can authorise the Legal Services Commission (LSC) to fund representation in excluded proceedings if specific criteria set out by the Lord Chancellor are met or if the LSC requests authorisation to provide funding in individual cases. Guidance on exceptional funding is contained in the LSC Manual Volume 3 Part C of the Funding Code.[136] This provides that the Lord Chancellor is likely to consider exceptional public funding where:

1.1 The services to be funded are excluded from scope and not covered by general directions (which applies to employment tribunal hearings);
1.2 the claimant is financially eligible for Legal Representation; and
1.3 all the relevant criteria of the Funding Code are satisfied; and
1.4 the client has produced evidence to demonstrate clearly that no alternative means of funding is available, whether through conditional fees or otherwise.

11.104 The factors that might persuade the LSC to consider funding include where there is a significant wider public interest in the resolution of the case, and funding will contribute to this. The Framework Directive specifically deals with discrimination in the field of employment and the 2006 regulations will initially create many cases where either the scope of the regulations or the directive will be in question.[137] The next criteria to be considered is the degree of importance of the case to the claimant. A person's age is an intimate aspect of their personality through time. It is true that it is an aspect of ordinariness,[138] but it is precisely for that reason that being the subject of discrimination because of age will be as demeaning as any other ordinary feature of a person's life, like their sex, their race, or their fundamental beliefs about the world. All of these are 'ordinary' in the sense of being matters a person cannot change. Therefore discrimination on the grounds of age will, in certain cases, be of overwhelming importance to the claimant.

11.105 The guidance requires that there be convincing evidence that there are other exceptional circumstances such that without public funding for representation it would be practically impossible for the claimant to bring or defend the proceedings, or lack of public funding would lead to obvious unfairness. Many of the early tribunal cases on age discrimination will satisfy this criterion. The issues of law and of the

---

136 See Guidance 3C-268 para 13.
137 For example there is a clear wide public interest in determining whether regulation 3 covers associative discrimination or not; whether justification of direct discrimination requires a narrower test than that for indirect discrimination etc.
138 See *R (on the application of Carson) v Secretary of State for Work and Pensions* [2005] UKHL 37; [2006] 1 AC 173, para 60.

approach to the evidence are likely to be complex. Issues of EC law are very likely to be relevant to the proper application of the regulations. Without representation the tribunal and the claimant will be placed in difficulty. The case must have prospects of success. If it can be demonstrated that it would be in the wider public interest this will assist in the decision on funding.

11.106   Finally, it is worth remembering how exceptional 'exceptional' is:

> There must be something exceptional about the client or the case such that for the client to proceed without public funding would be practically impossible or would lead to obvious unfairness. I will use as a benchmark those very exceptional cases where the ECHR at Strasbourg has indicated that the right of access to the courts has effectively been denied because of the lack of public funding.[139]

11.107   In the county court, however, public funding is available, and the usual tests of viability of the claim must be met.

Appeals

11.108   Appeals to the EAT are restricted to appeals on a point of law. In order to maintain an appeal, the appellant must be able to show either that the tribunal misdirected itself in law in some way or that it reached a perverse conclusion. This means that the decision was one no reasonable tribunal could have reached. A tribunal will err in law where it fails to apply the correct legal test or where it fails to evaluate the evidence at all on a necessary aspect of the case (as opposed to reaching an adverse conclusion to the would-be appellant). Questions such as whether a person is an employee have been treated as questions of fact (unless they turn wholly on the construction of a document)[140]. Whether a dismissal is a constructive dismissal has been treated as question of fact[141]. Whether a term is to be implied into a contract of employment is a question of law[142]. The question of justification of indirect discrimination has been treated in some cases as a matter of

---

139   LSC Manual, Vol 13, Part C of the Funding Code, para 3C-268, para 15.
140   See for example *O'Kelly v Trusthouse Forte plc* [1984] QB 90, [1983] ICR 728, CA. For construction of contractual documentation errors see *Davies v Presbyterian Church of Wales* [1986] 1 All ER 705, [1986] ICR 280. For the most part the documentation will be only one of several factors and the overall question will remain one of fact: *Carmichael v National Power plc* [1999] ICR 1226, [2000] IRLR 43, HL.
141   *Pedersen v Camden London Borough Council* [1981] ICR 674, [1981] IRLR 173, CA; *Woods v WM Car Services (Peterborough) Ltd* [1982] ICR 693, [1982] IRLR 413, CA.
142   *Courtaulds Northern Spinning Ltd v Sibson* [1988] ICR 451.

fact[143]. However the question of whether the tribunal has used the correct test for justification would be a question of law.

11.109   The time for lodging an appeal with the EAT is as follows:

  (i)   If the ET has given a judgment and written reasons were requested either
        (a) orally at hearing or
        (b) in writing within 14 days of the date when the written record of the judgment was sent to the parties,
        the time limit is 42 days from the date on which the written reasons were sent to the parties.[144]

  (ii) If the written reasons were reserved and given in writing by the tribunal, the time limit is 42 days from the date on which the written reasons were sent to the parties.[145]

  (iii) In the case of an appeal from a judgment of an employment tribunal, where written reasons were not requested as above, and written reasons were not reserved, the time limit is 42 days from the date on which the written record of the judgment was sent to the parties.[146]

  (iv) In the case of an appeal from an order of an employment tribunal, the time limit is 42 days from the date of the order.[147]

Test cases

11.110   Age discrimination cases are going to present advisers with difficult questions of law in the initial years. No Commission currently holds a brief to promote issues of age discrimination law. The burden of developing test case strategies will therefore fall to the unions and advice centres as well as individual solicitors and barristers. Other areas of discrimination law have benefited from a guided approach to test case litigation and organisations like the Discrimination Law Association will prove useful information exchanges for those considering appeals. Claimant advisers will, to a certain extent, also need to know something about the interplay between litigation in this field and the wider campaigning issues surrounding age whether nationally or locally.[148] Campaigning resources are also available from Age Concern England's website.[149]

143 See *Home Office v Holmes* [1984] 3 All ER 549, [1984] ICR 678, EAT; *Greater Glasgow Health Board v Carey* [1987] IRLR 484, EAT.
144 EAT Rules r3(3)(a)(i).
145 Ibid r3(3)(a)(i).
146 Ibid r3(3)(a)(iii).
147 Ibid r3(3)(b).
148 Katie Ghose's book *Beyond the courtroom* (LAG, 2005), provides an excellent starting point for advisers who are interested.
149 See www.ageconcern.org.uk.

CHAPTER 12

Remedies for age discrimination in employment and occupation

Key points

- The claimant can claim a declaration and a recommendation from the tribunal in relation to the discrimination.
- The claimant can claim compensation on a tortious basis for the consequences of discrimination.
- Remedies must be effective, proportionate and dissuasive of further discrimination to be compliant with the directive's requirements.
- Compensation for discrimination can include damages for injury to feelings.
- Compensation for discrimination can include personal injury damages.
- The schedule of loss should identify, quantify and (if necessary) explain the heads of claim.
- There are remedies available for collective discrimination matters.

Introduction

12.1   The Employment Equality (Age) Regulations 2006 provide for remedies for age discrimination in employment and occupation. In the discussion that follows, the need for dissuasive sanctions under the Framework Directive should be kept in mind. Those sanctions must be proportionate, but also effective.[1] The requirement that judicial and/or administrative procedures for the enforcement of obligations under the directive are available should also be the standard against which the effectiveness of any adopted remedy should be judged.[2] The remedies phase should be carefully managed, and the tribunal should not be adverse to giving proper directions including the exchange of witness statements.[3] The claimant may need to ensure that there is full disclosure by the respondent of documents relating to remedies (and in particular compensation) and will have to ensure that full disclosure of documents relating to efforts to mitigate the loss are disclosed.

---

1   See discussion of article 17 of the Directive in chapter 2.
2   Article 9 of the Directive.
3   *Buxton v Equinox Design Ltd* [1999] IRLR 158.

12.2   A claim for age discrimination, like other types of unlawful discrimination claims, may be continued by the claimant's personal representative after a complainant's death.[4]

12.3   A claim for age discrimination is generally subject to the requirements concerning grievances. It is advisable that any age discrimination grievance should state this clearly.[5] Complaints relating to discrimination under the 2006 regulations will not necessarily be easy to identify, so tribunals may take a strict line on this. Chapters 8 and 11 both deal with the grievance regime. In brief, however, the Employment Act 2002 contains penalties for failure to comply with an applicable grievance procedure. First, an employee may not generally bring a claim in an employment tribunal under regulation 36 unless he or she has first submitted a written statement of grievance to his or her employer and waited 28 days.[6] If the claimant has submitted the grievance and brings a claim after at least 28 days but before the applicable grievance procedure has been completed, the tribunal will still hear the claim. However, if the claimant succeeds, the tribunal will decide on who is to blame for the failure to complete the procedure and increase or reduce the compensation award depending on whether the employer or employee has failed to comply with the procedure. The increase or reduction will be between 10% and 50%. The employee can be penalised in this way for failing to exercise a right of appeal under the grievance procedure.[6a]

Potential orders available to tribunals

12.4   Where an employment tribunal finds that a complaint presented to it under its age discrimination jurisdiction[7] is well-founded, it must make such of the following as it considers just and equitable:[8]

a)   an order declaring the rights of the complainant and the respondent in relation to the act to which the complaint relates;

---

4   *Harris (Andrews' Personal Representative) v Lewisham and Guys Mental Health NHS Trust* [2000] IRLR 320 and in Scotland see *Soutar's Executors v James Murray & Co (Cupar) Ltd; Same v Scottish Provident Institution* [2002] IRLR 22 for the principle that common law permits pursuit of a claim on behalf of the dead claimant.

5   See, for example, *Noskiw v Royal Mail Group plc*, ET case no 2602639/04, 7 March 2005 in which failure to mention that a poor pay review was thought to be on the basis of disability discrimination led the ET to reject the claim on the basis that a grievance had not been lodged.

6   EA 2002 s32.

6a See paragraphs 8.101 & following.

7   Reg 36.

8   Reg 38(1).

b) an order requiring the respondent to pay to the complainant compensation of an amount corresponding to any damages he or she could have been awarded by a county court or by a sheriff court if the case fell within that jurisdiction under the regulations;

c) a recommendation that the respondent take within a specified period action appearing to the tribunal to be practicable for the purpose of obviating or reducing the adverse effect on the complainant of any act of discrimination or harassment to which the complaint relates.

12.5   The inclusion of the words *'just and equitable'* in the selection of remedy simply gives a choice to the tribunal as to which remedy it wishes to award.[9] They do not permit the tribunal to refuse to give any remedy. The discretion must be exercised judicially, having regard to relevant (and excluding irrelevant) factors. If the tribunal decides to award compensation, the basis of the award is not discretionary. There is no reference to an award of an amount that seems just and equitable to the tribunal, as there is in relation to unfair dismissal damages. Once a tribunal has decided to award compensation the amount of compensation is to be computed on the basis of the damages that would be recoverable in a county court.

Declarations

12.6   A person may have no financial loss arising out of a breach of statutory duty and yet pursue a claim (for example for unfair dismissal) properly.[10] The power of the tribunal is confined to an order declaring the rights of the complainant and the respondent in relation to the act to which the complaint relates.

Recommendations

12.7   The tribunal has the power to make a recommendation that the respondent take within a specified period action appearing to the tribunal to be practicable for the purpose of obviating or reducing the adverse effect on the complainant of any act of discrimination or harassment to which the complaint relates. The tribunal in other anti-discrimination fields has been fairly restricted in how it uses recommendations.

12.8   In one race victimisation case, the tribunal accepted that because of the tribunal proceedings the claimant was less likely to be offered

9   *Hurley v Mustoe (No 2)* [1983] ICR 422.
10   See eg *Telephone Information Services v Wilkinson* [1991] IRLR 148.

contracts by other clubs. They would see him as a troublemaker. It recommended that the respondent offer the claimant a contract of employment. This was to be on the same terms as the last of a series of fixed-term contracts on which they had employed him. It was considered necessary to obviate or reduce the adverse impact on the claimant. The respondents successfully appealed on the basis that the adverse impact which the recommendation sought to alleviate was that of the proceedings rather than the act of victimisation which had been found.[11]

12.9   Often a tribunal will want to make general recommendations, but these must be put in the reasoning rather than the decision. If they are put in the operative part of the decision they will not fulfil the requirement of the regulation that they should have the purpose of obviating or reducing the adverse effect of discrimination on an individual complainant.[12] The tribunal will not be able to order the employer to cease a discriminatory practice of general application in the workplace.[13] The power to make recommendations does not extend to recommendations to pay to the claimant an amount of money,[14] for example the pay he or she would have received in a position which was refused on grounds of age.

12.10   Having mentioned these restrictions, practitioners should always consider seeking a recommendation in an appropriate case. The recommendation can be a very flexible tool to ensure redress and address the acknowledgement that often claimants seek. A tribunal was held in one case to be entitled to make a recommendation that a Deputy Chief Constable interview police officers (named in the order). They had committed acts of discrimination against the complainant. The recommendation was that the Deputy Chief Constable conduct these interviews and discuss the tribunal's decision on liability with each of them. This was good practice. The knowledge that the wrongdoers

11   *Leeds Rhinos Rugby Club & ors v Sterling* EAT 267/01.

12   *Record Production Chapel Ltd v Turnbull & EOC* EAT 955/83. The recommendation must relate to the individual complainant.

13   See the EAT's decision in *MOD v Jeremiah* [1978] ICR 984.

14   In *Irvine v Prestcold* [1981] IRLR 281 a tribunal made a recommendation 'That the applicant be seriously considered as the most suitable candidate for the position of service administration manager as soon as it falls vacant ... and that in the alternative she should continue to receive the difference in salary referred to above until she has been promoted either to that job or to a job of equivalent status'. The Court of Appeal held that the second part of the recommendation was not proper because it did not specify a period during which action was to be taken and because financial compensation was fully dealt with under the provision relating to compensation.

would have to face the tribunal's findings was said to serve to reduce the injury to feelings suffered by the complainant.[15]

12.11   The effectiveness of recommendations as a remedy under the directive can be challenged because there is no sanction for breach of the order save one. If without reasonable justification the respondent to a complaint fails to comply with a recommendation made by an employment tribunal then, if it thinks it just and equitable to do so:

a) the tribunal may increase the amount of compensation required to be paid to the complainant in respect of the complaint;[16] or

b) if an order for compensation was not made, the tribunal may make such an order.

12.12   An employer may effectively ignore a recommendation in these circumstances. If the tribunal awarded compensation when making the recommendation the only way in which compensation could legitimately be increased is by the award of exemplary, aggravated or punitive damages of some sort.[17] However, before the tribunal makes any such award it must be satisfied that the respondent has without reasonable justification failed to comply with the recommendation. The mere fact of delay in complying with a recommendation will not necessarily mean that the respondent does not have reasonable justification. The tribunal will take account of the practical realities of the workplace. Can the discrimination be eliminated immediately? Does there need to be negotiation with the unions before the practice can be stopped? The early discrimination cases indicated that it would not be unreasonable for there to be a period of time before the discrimination was eliminated.[18]

Collective agreements and rules of undertakings

12.13   It is possible, however, to act quickly to remove the discriminatory effects of a collective agreement in the light of a recommendation of a tribunal. Practitioners who believe that they have a case in which such a term is to be challenged must add a cause of action under Schedule 5.

---

15 *Chief Constable of West Yorkshire Police v Vento (No 2)* [2002] IRLR 177.
16 However, that compensation must be ordered in accordance with tortious principles (see below).
17 See below para 12.111.
18 *Nelson v Tyne & Wear Transport* [1978] ICR 1183, EAT.

12.14   Schedule 5 to the regulations has two parts. The first relates to the validity of contracts. However, the second part applies to:

a) any term of a collective agreement,[19] including an agreement which was not intended, or is presumed not to have been intended, to be a legally enforceable contract;

b) any rule made by an employer for application to all or any of the persons who are employed by him or who apply to be, or are, considered by him for employment;

c) any rule made by a trade organisation[20] or a qualifications body[21] for application to:

   i) all or any of its members or prospective members; or

   ii) all or any of the persons on whom it has conferred professional or trade qualifications[22] or who are seeking the professional or trade qualifications which it has power to confer.

12.15   Any such term or rule is void where:

a) the making of the collective agreement is, by reason of the inclusion of the term, unlawful under the regulations;

b) the term or rule is included or made in furtherance of an act which is unlawful by virtue of the regulations; or

c) the term or rule provides for the doing of an act which is unlawful by virtue of the regulations.

12.16   The voiding rule applies whether the agreement was entered into, or the rule made, before or after the coming into force of the regulations.[23] However, in the case of an agreement entered into, or a rule made, before the date on which they came into force, the voiding rule does not apply in relation to any period before that date so as to render them retrospectively void.[24]

---

19 'Collective agreement' means any agreement relating to one or more of the matters mentioned in section 178(2) of the Trade Union and Labour Relations (Consolidation) Act 1992 (collective agreements and collective bargaining), being an agreement made by or on behalf of one or more employers or one or more organisations of employers or associations of such organisations with one or more organisations of workers or associations of such organisations.

20 See para 3.45 these are trade organisations within the meaning of reg 18.

21 See para 3.48, reg 19.

22 Within the meaning of reg 19.

23 1 October 2006.

24 Sch 5 para 4(3).

12.17   A complaint may be made to the employment tribunal that a term of the collective agreement or an employer's rule is void under the voiding rule if the complainant has reason to believe:[25]

a) that the term or rule may at some future time have effect in relation to him or her; and
b) (where he alleges that it is void because the term or rule provides for the doing of an act which is unlawful age discrimination) that:
   i) an act for the doing of which it provides, may at some such time be done in relation to him or her; and
   ii) the act would be unlawful by virtue of the regulations if done in relation to him or her in present circumstances.

12.18   If the complaint is about any of the following, the complainant must be a person who is, or is genuinely and actively seeking to become, one of the employer's employees.[26] The complaint must be about:

a) a term of a collective agreement made by or on behalf of:
   i) an employer;
   ii) an organisation of employers of which an employer is a member; or
   iii) an association of such organisations or one of which an employer is a member; or
b) a rule made by an employer for application to all or any of the persons who are employed by the employer or who apply to be, or are, considered by the employer for employment.

12.19   If the complaint is about a rule made by a trade organisation or qualification body the complainant must be a person:

a) who is, or is genuinely and actively seeking to become, a member of the organisation or body;
b) on whom the organisation or body has conferred a professional or trade qualification which the organisation or body has power to confer; or
c) who is genuinely and actively seeking such a professional or trade qualification which the organisation or body has power to confer.[27]

12.20   When an employment tribunal finds that a complaint about the rule or term of the agreement presented to it is well-founded the tribunal

25   Sch 5 para 5(1).
26   Sch 5 para 6(1).
27   Sch 5 para 7.

must make an order declaring that the term or rule is void.[28] The order may include provision as respects any period before the making of the order.[29] Thus the order may declare that the term or rule was void at some time prior to the order being made.

12.21　　When a term of a collective agreement or rule which provides for any person to be discriminated against is rendered void,[30] the consequences for the individual contract of employment must be considered. The voiding process is without prejudice[31] to rights[32] conferred by (or in respect of) a contract, where that contract is made[33] in pursuance of that term or rule.[34] The voiding process is thus without prejudice to:

a) the rights of the person to be discriminated against; and
b) the rights of any person who will be treated more favourably in direct or indirect consequence of the discrimination.

12.22　The voiding of the collective rule therefore does not result in the corresponding terms in the individual contract becoming void. On the other hand, the individual whose contract treats him or her less favourably can require levelling up of his or her terms and conditions.[35]

12.23　　In this context a 'collective agreement' means any agreement relating to one or more of the matters mentioned in section 178(2) of the Trade Union and Labour Relations (Consolidation) Act 1992 (collective agreements and collective bargaining). The agreement must be an agreement made by, or on behalf of, one or more employers or one or more organisations of employers or associations of such organisations with one or more organisations of workers or associations of such organisations.

28　Sch 5 para 8.
29　However, it must be after the coming into force of the regulations: Sch 5 para 8(2).
30　By the operation of Sch 5 para 4(2).
31　By Sch 5 para 9.
32　Except insofar as they enable any person to require another person to be treated less favourably than him or herself.
33　Or modified (and either made or modified in whole or in part).
34　Or by reference to it.
35　This accords with the principle that a collective agreement's termination does not remove the contractual terms implied into individual contracts (see *Gibbons v Associated British Ports* [1985] IRLR 376) and *Framptons Limited v Badger & ors* [2006] UKEAT 0138/06/0906 (9 June 2006).

Compensation – financial loss

Introduction

12.24   Before dealing with the construction of a compensation claim on a finding of age discrimination, various points should be noted. First, there is no upper limit on the amount of damages that can be awarded for age discrimination. Second, it is possible for an employment tribunal to make an award of compensation for discrimination on a joint and several basis (for example, against a company and against the managing director of a company who was joined as a respondent). The claimant's view on whether he or she wishes the perpetrator of the act of discrimination joined as a party may be influenced by knowing that the individual can be brought before the tribunal to answer what he or she has done.

12.25   If the tribunal does not make an award on a joint and several basis it may apportion liability between the respondents to such a case.[36] The tribunal must have regard to section 2(1) of the Civil Liability (Contribution) Act 1978 in determining who pays what as between respondents who are responsible for the discrimination. That section provides that 'in any proceedings for contribution ... the amount of the contribution recoverable from any person shall be such as may be found by the court to be just and equitable having regard to the extent of that person's responsibility for the damage in question'. 'Responsibility' refers both to the extent to which each person:

a)   caused the damage; and
b)   each person's relative culpability.

12.26   Therefore, it is not appropriate in most cases for a tribunal to make a 'joint and several' award (which is 100% against each respondent). In particular, it is not permissible for a tribunal to make a joint and several award because of the relative financial resources of the respondent. This may raise problems where the company is insolvent but the director is not, for example, or vice versa.

36   In *Way v Crouch* [2005] IRLR 603 the EAT held that the employment tribunal did not err in law in making an award for compensation for sex discrimination on a joint and several basis against the respondent company and its managing director. However, the employment tribunal did err in making the whole of the compensation order payable jointly and severally by both respondents. If an employment tribunal considers it necessary to make a joint and several award, rather than apportioning liability between the employer respondent and the individual employee respondent, it should make clear its reason for doing so. See also *Miles v Gilbank* [2006] ICR 12.

12.27   Turning to the general principles that the tribunal will apply. By regulation 38 the tribunal may make an order requiring the respondent to pay to the complainant compensation of an amount corresponding to any damages he could have been ordered by a county court or by a sheriff court to pay to the complainant if the complaint had fallen to be dealt with under the jurisdiction of county or sheriff courts. In those courts damages are awarded for a breach of statutory duty. In other words, damages are awarded on the same basis as they would be in a tort case. From this, the following principles flow.

- The claimant ('C' hereafter) should be compensated for any financial loss C would not have suffered if the act of discrimination had not occurred.[37] C can claim for any financial loss which is properly attributable to the unlawful act of discrimination.[38]
- Damages include an award for injury to feelings.[39]
- C's award should include elements for financial loss:
  a) past loss of earnings;
  b) future loss of earnings.
  In this C can claim for discretionary bonuses and other benefits.[40] Lost earnings are calculated net of tax and national insurance.[41] Pension loss can be claimed. The effect of tax should be considered. Interest is payable on awards.
- Certain matters limit or reduce loss:
  a) a break in causation between the act of discrimination and the loss;
  b) C's failure to take reasonable steps to mitigate C's loss;[42]
  c) sums earned from another source – a lower paid job, insurance policy payments (personal health insurance) etc;
  d) accelerated receipt discounts.

12.28   Some of these principles overlap and are difficult to distinguish on any logical basis. We will examine them below. In summary, however, it is convenient for the tribunal if C arranges the schedule under the following headings:

a) Past Loss;
b) Future Loss;
c) Injury to Feelings;

---

37   *MOD v Cannock* [1994] ICR at 935, EAT.
38   *Coleman v Skyrail Oceanic Ltd* [1981] IRLR 398, CA.
39   See reg 39(3).
40   *Cantor Fitzgerald International v Horkulak* [2004] IRLR 942.
41   *British Transport Commission v Gourley* [1956] AC 185.
42   See *Wilding v British Telecommunications plc* [2002] IRLR 524 at para 39.

and if appropriate:

d) Personal Injury;
e) Aggravated Damages;
f) Exemplary Damages.

Indirect discrimination

12.29 Regulation 38(2) provides, in respect of an unlawful act of indirect discrimination that if the respondent proves that the provision, criterion or practice (PCP) was not applied with the intention[43] of treating the complainant unfavourably on grounds of age, an order for compensation may be made only if the employment tribunal:

a) makes such declaration and such recommendation as it would have made if it had no power to make an order for compensation; and

b) where it makes a declaration or a recommendation considers that it is just and equitable to make an order of compensation as well.

12.30 In short the tribunal must decide that it is just and equitable to award compensation. A tribunal should be reminded the purpose of the regulations is to provide effective proportionate and dissuasive sanctions for discrimination and in the normal case the individual will not be properly compensated for the effects of a discriminatory practice simply by a recommendation and a declaration. A person who, when he does the act of imposing the PCP, wants to bring about the state of affairs which constitutes the prohibited result of placing the disadvantaged group at a disadvantage, and knows that that prohibited result will follow from his act, intends the act.[44]

Compensation – general principles

1) The claimant should be compensated for any financial loss C would not have suffered if the act of discrimination had not occurred[45]

12.31 The first question to be settled by the tribunal is whether, but for the act of discrimination, the particular head of loss would have occurred.

---

43 All that is necessary is an intention to apply the PCP and a knowledge of its impact on the disadvantaged age group and C in particular (see *London Underground v Edwards* [1995] IRLR 355).

44 See *Walker v Hussain* [1996] IRLR 1.

45 *MOD v Cannock* [1994] ICR at 935, EAT.

The tribunals have to award compensation on the same basis as the county court[46] would award for a breach of statutory duty. Such damages are awarded on a tortious basis.[47] What must be proved is that the discrimination caused the loss. Once that is done, the loss and damage actually sustained must be made good in full.[48] The objective for the tribunal is restitution in this sense. At this stage of the process the question to be answered is whether, but for the act of discrimination, a particular loss would have occurred.[49]

12.32   An important principle in discrimination cases generally is that C will be tied much more rigorously to the pleadings than in an unfair dismissal case. What this means is that the tribunal will only consider the acts of discrimination that are actually pleaded in the claim form and any amendments or further particulars (and respondent's response).[50] Therefore it is important to set out the acts of discrimination on the basis of which it is said that a remedy may be claimed.[51] These principles have implications for compensation.

Multiple acts, some of which are discrimination

12.33   Respondents may argue in cases where there are multiple acts pleaded as discrimination, some of which are not proved, that certain loss flowed from acts which are either not acts of discrimination, or which were not pleaded as such. The tortious principle that the wrongful act should have contributed in a material way to the loss may assist C in these cases. The loss claimed must be a loss or expense which would probably not have occurred in any event.[52] If there are two acts, A1 which is an act of age discrimination and A2 which is not, both of which result in loss to C, C can only recover that damage which would not have occurred but for A1.

12.34   In age discrimination this will become an acute question where A1 is a decision to employ the retirement procedure against C for discriminatory reasons, and A2 is the dismissal, after the retirement

46 And Sheriff courts in Scotland.
47 'As best as money can do it, the [claimant] must be put into the position she would have been in but for the unlawful conduct of [her employer]' (*Ministry of Defence v Cannock* [1994] ICR at 935 EAT, per Morison J). The discriminator must therefore take his or her individual victim as he or she finds the victim.
48 *Laing Ltd v Essa* [2004] EWCA Civ 2; [2004] ICR 746, para 51.
49 *Kuwait Airways Corporation v Iraqi Airways Co* [2002] 2 WLR 1353 para 69.
50 See *Chapman v Simon* [1994] IRLR 124.
51 See also *Ali v ONS* [2005] IRLR 201.
52 See the principles in the clinical negligence case of *Hotson v East Berkshire Health Authority* [1987] AC 750.

procedure has been followed. C will be able to argue that but for the discriminatory decision, A2 would not have occurred. The consequence of that is that C would have continued in employment beyond age 65.

12.35 There are conflicting authorities on the question of the significance of the ability of the employer to terminate the contract lawfully in discrimination cases. The fact that the employer has the right to dismiss the employee when the latter reaches 65 using the statutory procedure does not necessarily limit the damages that may be awarded to that period. This may be argued on the basis of *MOD v Cannock*:

> ... the hypothesis upon which the victim is compensated is that there had been no accident and therefore no disability and, although the court must take account of the fact that he could have found himself unemployed for a number of reasons, the amount of notice to which the victim was subject in his contract of employment will be unlikely to have any significance in relation to the size of the award.[53]

12.36 It can be argued that the existence of the statutory procedure does not indicate an automatic cut off point for compensation. What must be considered is what chance of continued employment C has lost in that situation. Compensation should then be awarded for the period after the potential dismissal date on a percentage basis.[54] However it will not be an error of law for a tribunal to decline to do so where the facts render the assessment of the chance too difficult. Thus in one case a finding that a fair dismissal would have followed after an unfair dismissal was treated as a finding that there was a 100% chance that the fair dismissal would have occurred (and therefore logically there was a 0% chance of loss after that time).[55]

12.37 The respondent will be able to claim the benefit of the loss of a chance that the loss might have occurred in any event. However advisers should argue that the respondent should produce something more than speculation in order to justify a substantial discount (for example to reflect the chance that the worker would not have remained in employment with the respondent over the long term).

12.38 There will be some acts which clearly break the causal chain. If A1 is a failure to promote a young shopworker C, but A2 is the fact that C is filmed taking money from the till, for which C is dismissed, compensation from A1 will clearly cease when A2 has its consequences (dismissal). However there will be cases where the act of discrimination influences the behaviour of C.

---

53 P 930.
54 See below para 12.45.
55 *O'Donoghue v Redcar & Cleveland Borough Council* [2001] IRLR 615.

> EXAMPLE: C is passed over for promotion because of being over
> 50, and there is no justification. The respondent may try to argue
> that C's decision to take early retirement breaks causation. How-
> ever, if C produces evidence that the decision to take early retire-
> ment was the result of the act of discrimination, C should be
> able to recover for any loss arising from that decision.

*2) A claimant can claim for any financial loss which is properly
attributable to the unlawful act of discrimination*[56]

12.39   The basis of the award is that the complainant may recover compensation for all damage that flows directly and naturally from the
unlawful age discrimination.[57] The second stage in the process of
attribution of loss to the act of discrimination is to evaluate whether
the respondent ought to be held liable. In other words, whether C's
loss should be within the scope of the respondent's liability, given the
reasons why the law has recognised the cause of action in age discrimination.[58]

12.40   In policy terms, the loss must be recognised in law and not be prohibited by reasons of illegality[59] or public policy.[60] In *Dimond* loss was
irrecoverable where it would have arisen out of an unenforceable agreement with a third party. In *Hewison* a seaman was injured as a result
of negligence for which his employer was responsible. However, he had
fraudulently concealed his epilepsy and, had that been disclosed, he
would not have been able to continue to work for the employer. The
Court of Appeal would not allow him recover damages for lost earnings
as a seaman as he had deceived his employer about his epilepsy and
could only have had a continuing loss of employment earnings if he had
continued to deceive his employer. Clarke LJ considered that the right
approach was to ask whether the claimant's unlawful act was a collat-
eral illegality in the performance of the contract, or part of the claimant's
case. Tuckey LJ said at §51:

> Illegality may affect a tort claim in many ways ranging from an essential
> part of the story giving rise to liability to some remote aspect of quantum.
> For this reason I favour a broad test of the kind proposed by Clarke L.J. viz:

---

56   *Coleman v Skyrail Oceanic Ltd* [1981] IRLR 398, CA.
57   See *Laing Ltd v Essa* (above) para 37.
58   See *Kuwait Airways Corporation v Iraqi Airways Co* [2002] 2 WLR 1353 para 70
     cited in *Laing v Essa* (above).
59   See *Hewison v Meridian Shipping PTE* [2003] ICR 766.
60   See *Dimond v Lovell* [2002] 1 AC 384.

is the claim or the relevant part of it based substantially (and not therefore collaterally or insignificantly) on an unlawful act? Such a broad test has the merit of simplicity. It does not involve the judge having to make very specific and difficult value judgments about precisely how serious the misconduct is or whether it would result in imprisonment or whether the claimant's loss is disproportionate to his misconduct.

12.41 In most employment cases the loss of earnings will depend on the contract of employment. If this is unlawful, no loss will be recoverable arising from it. However, arguably injury to feelings damages should be awarded in those situations and in appropriate situations lost earnings will still be capable of being awarded.

12.42 In *Hall v Woolston Hall Leisure Ltd*[61] the Court of Appeal held that despite C's acquiescence in failure to deduct tax and National Insurance, C should be awarded compensation despite the illegality of the contract since Council Directive 76/207 unambiguously guaranteed the principle of fair treatment between men and women with regard to working conditions and the court had a duty to interpret the national law so as to give effect to the directive and provide the individual with an effective remedy. The Court of Appeal pointed out that the tribunal had failed to adopt the correct approach because it had approached the sex discrimination complaint as based on the contract of employment. The Court of Appeal found that the illegality concerned only the means by which wages were paid. There was no causal link between C's acquiescence in that matter and her complaint of sex discrimination which concerned her dismissal on becoming pregnant. There were no public policy reasons for not awarding compensation.[62]

12.43 The decision of the Court of Appeal in *Laing v Essa* suggests that it is not necessary for a claimant who has been discriminated against to show that the particular type of loss was reasonably foreseeable.[63] We will return to that case in the context of injury to feelings where that principle holds good for sure. There is a risk that the decision will be

---

61 [2001] ICR 99.

62 However, if the discrimination is so closely connected with the deliberate illegality of the employment contract C would be precluded from pursuing a discrimination claim (see *Vakante v Addey and Stanhope School Governing Body* [2004] ICR 279).

63 See judgment of Clarke LJ and Pill LJ. However the case should be treated with some caution as it appears to assume that a statutory discrimination tort can only be committed intentionally, and there is a divergence between the scope of the judgments of Clarke LJ and Pill LJ, the latter linking his conclusions firmly to the facts of the case, the former appearing not to do so. The better view is that both LJs intended to link the conclusions to the facts which dealt with the consequences of racial abuse.

confined to its own facts or at least to situations in which the tort of direct discrimination is carried out deliberately. In *Vince-Cain v Orthet (No 2)*[64] *Essa* was referred to by the EAT which noted that Pill LJ decided that loss (in that case psychiatric illness) does not have to be reasonably foreseeable, but must have arisen in accordance with the normal rules on causation, intervening acts and mitigation.[65] The appeal then appears to have proceeded on the basis that the principles in *Essa* were of general application. *Essa* appears to have been firmly based on the facts that there had been direct racial abuse. The nature of that tort was intentional and so analogies with intentional torts were apt. However, the Court of Appeal also considered that it was possible for a different approach to be taken to the issue of foreseeablility even within the same tort.[66]

12.44   Generally, in the context of a statutory tort, C must have suffered a type of damage which was reasonably foreseeable and attributable to the respondent's unlawful act. In the light of *Essa* it is likely that foreseeability of loss will play a lesser role. However the case potentially opens up the possibility of a difference of approach between those cases in which an intentional or deliberate act of age discrimination is committed and those in which the tort is either unintentional or unconscious. The simpler approach and the one which clearly implements the requirement that there should be effective proportionate and dissuasive sanctions for breach of the 2006 regulations is that foreseeability is not an element in the calculation of loss. On that basis it is sufficient that the act of discrimination probably caused or contributed to the complainant's loss.

Lost chances

12.45   The act of age discrimination may mean that C has lost a chance of obtaining a past or future benefit. C is entitled to claim a loss of a real or substantial chance of a benefit or profit:

> ... in assessing damages which depend upon its view as to what will happen in the future or would have happened in the future if something had not happened in the past, the court must make an estimate as to what are the chances that a particular thing will or would have happened and reflect those chances, whether they are more or less than even, in the amount of damages which it awards.[67]

64   [2005] ICR 374; [2004] IRLR 857.
65   *Essa*, para 43.
66   *Essa*, para 34.
67   *Mallett v McMonagle* [1970] AC 166 per Lord Diplock at p176.

12.46 In cases in which C's loss depends upon the hypothetical action of another person, C need only show that there was a substantial chance of the other person acting in such a way as to confer a benefit on C.[68] Here a claimant need only show that there was a significant chance, which can be less than likely that the benefit would have been achieved. Thus in one personal injury case the court concluded that, had it not been for his injuries, C would have had a two-thirds chance of obtaining promotion as a principal lecturer. The judge stated at p293:

> Where the question is one of what might have been the situation in a hypothetical state of facts, then, to the extent that a chance of the event necessary to an award of damages fall significantly below 100%, the award should be discounted in my view.[69]

12.47 In *Ministry of Defence v Cannock*[70] the EAT confirmed that the proper approach to what might have been if discrimination had not taken place is to use a percentage approach. However, claimant advisers need to consider carefully what evidence will convince the tribunal. Thus it may be sensible to ensure that the tribunal has statistical evidence to enable it to evaluate the chance the loss of which is being assessed. Equally, however, statistics may be a poor guide in an area of social change and advisers should be careful to place them in context. The following guidance can be given:

1) Statistics relating to the time a person remains in employment with that employer or similar employers may be useful, but (particularly around current retirement ages) may not reflect non-discriminatory approaches to the consideration of requests to continue to work after retirement.

2) The age discrimination legislation was introduced to change social attitudes to matters such as retirement and career progression. The right to request to continue working is aimed at retaining more persons over retirement age.[71]

3) Evidence of ambition, dedication and determination in the face of adversity – ie ability to stay in a job – should be properly marshalled.

4) Evidence as to the future prospects of the employee should be obtained if appropriate.

---

68 See *Allied Maples v Simmons and Simmons* [1995] 1 WLR 1602 per Stuart Smith LJ.
69 *Anderson v Davis* [1993] PIQR Q87, Bell QC. This was approved in *Doyle v Wallace* [1998] PIQR Q146.
70 [1994] ICR 918.
71 See *Chief Constable of West Yorkshire Police v Vento (No 2)* [2003] ICR 318 at 322, paras 15–16.

12.48   *Loss of earnings in cases of discrimination in job application.* Clearly, where the discrimination is a failure to evaluate an application for employment properly, there will be a question whether C would have got the job, even if C had not been the object of discrimination. It is important in all cases of discrimination to ensure that the tribunal applies itself properly to this head. A lost chance of stable employment in a company with a low turnover of staff may be a substantial head of claim even if the chance of obtaining the job was itself low. Advisers should consider the following points:

1) Is there clear evidence that C would have obtained the job so that it can be proved on the balance of probabilities?
2) If the evidence is not clear, for example because C was denied the opportunity to undertake an assessment which would have been evaluated, has C lost a chance of obtaining the job which must be evaluated?
3) Is there a standard training/probationary period after which new employees receive either a pay rise or promotion automatically?
4) If not, what were the prospects of the respondent for promotion during the first few years of employment? Again C will have lost a chance of promotion by the act of discrimination which has a value to be assessed (for example by reference to the numbers getting promotion).
5) What is the turnover of staff within the respondent? The answer to this type of question will demonstrate the likelihood of C remaining in the employment so as to benefit from promotion opportunities.

12.49   *Lost opportunities in promotion/training cases.* Similar points can be made in relation to the effect of discrimination in promotion cases, but there is likely to be more information available to C, in terms of appraisals and skills assessments. In training cases the range of lost opportunities may extend to opportunities outside the employer if C has been deprived of a recognised transferable skill or qualification making them less attractive to an employer in the labour market for a better range of jobs. The better way of compensating this loss, it is suggested, is to consider how long it would be before the relevant skill/qualification can be obtained and treat it as a factor in the period of future loss and in relation to mitigation. Clearly if C has obtained a job which pays the same as the one previously held, but could have obtained a better paid job had training been given, that lost chance remains after the new job appears to extinguish the loss from the old job.

12.50   *Lost chances of earnings.* In many situations C will complain that as a result of the discrimination of the respondent C has lost the chance of obtaining a particular salary or band of salaries. C must be able to show that the lost chance was not fanciful or speculative, but 'real' or 'substantial'. This means, it is suggested, that it must be more than merely minimal.[72] Thus in cases involving qualification bodies,[73] the damages could include damages for lost earnings for having to defer entry to work in an industry.[74]

12.51   The burden of proof of the lost chance is on C, who must therefore raise sufficient evidence of the lost chance. It is sensible therefore to ensure that C's schedule of loss foreshadows any unusual lost chance that may be claimed. The witness statement should also deal, in detail, with the circumstances raising the issue of the lost chance.

12.52   If issues that might render the chance less likely exist which do not relate to the discrimination of the respondent, it is sensible to marshal evidence that the other cause would not have prevented C realising the chance in any event. So, for example, if C suffers some ill health C would have to be able to show that this would not have prevented him or her from obtaining the benefit in question. One area in age discrimination where this principle may play a role is in relation to the notification procedure for retirement.[75] If the employer knew that he or she was going to retire C at a year before the intended retirement age, but did not tell C until later than six months before the retirement date (subsequently refusing to have a meeting with C to discuss C's request to continue working), so that the employer did not tell the employee in good time, and the dismissal is unfair, there is an argument that C should be compensated for the loss of an opportunity to gain a new job earlier.[76] For highly skilled persons coming up to the retirement age this may be a significant head of claim.

Proper attribution – multiple acts of discrimination

12.53   In many cases there will be several instances of discrimination. The tribunal must determine the role each such act played in relation to the loss suffered. If C was not promoted as a result of being thought too youthful on several occasions, the tribunal may have to establish what the consequences of each failure to promote would have been. Advisers should consider separate tables for each such consequence.

---

72   See *Kitchen v RAFA* [1958] 2 All ER 241.
73   Reg 19.
74   See, for example, *Oades v Park* [1994] CLY (Current Law) 1623.
75   See chapter 9.
76   *Elkouil v Coney Island Ltd* [2002] IRLR 174, EAT.

EXAMPLE: If C had received promotion to the position of supervisor there is evidence that most people remain as a supervisor
for about two years and thereafter become managers. The tribunal would have to assess the lost chance of subsequently
becoming a manager even if this is below 50%, say 40%.

C subsequently did not receive promotion to a specialist supervisor position. Again this was a result of age discrimination. C can
claim that C has lost a chance of becoming a specialist supervisor (which pays more) and subsequent chance of becoming a
specialist manager. However, C's chances of obtaining such promotion are lower than in the first example (say 20%) because
the competition was more difficult.

12.54   The adviser will have to give separate calculations based on both scenarios as they are obviously alternatives to one another. However, the
tribunal will also have to calculate the way in which various contingencies impact on one another. Thus there may be a 75% chance that
C would have remained in employment for 5 years, but for the discriminatory dismissal. Had C done so there was a 25% chance of being
promoted one year later. For the period from dismissal C should receive
75% of current earnings until the date on which the loss of a chance of
promotion occurred. From that time the tribunal can calculate 25%
of the difference between 100% of earnings in the first post and 100%
of the earnings in the promotion post, and then award 75% of the
product.[77]

EXAMPLE: C is 64 and has been served with notice of intention
to dismiss for retirement on C's 65th birthday. C makes a request
to continue working. At the meeting to consider that request the
employer makes it clear to C that C's application is not being
seriously considered by the employer because of C's age attributes (the employer thinks that C looks too old for the shop) and

77   See *MOD v Hunt* [1996] ICR 554 at 561: 'on the evidence in a particular case,
    may conclude that there was an 80 per cent chance that a woman would have
    availed herself of maternity leave before returning to service but only a 40 per
    cent chance that she would have proceeded to complete the full period of her
    engagement thereafter. In quantifying loss of earnings, this would require an
    industrial tribunal to apply the 80 per cent figure to the first period. However,
    for the subsequent period the appropriate calculation would be cumulative,
    this is to say 40 per cent of the 80 per cent and not 40 per cent of the original
    100 per cent'. And see *MOD v Wheeler* [1998] ICR 242.

> refuses to listen to what C has to say because the employer says that no matter what C says now, in six months' time C will be thinking of C's Spanish retirement home rather than work. The discrimination (based on C's perceived age characteristics rather than chronological age) is a failure to take the application to work beyond retirement seriously. The tribunal must consider the chances of C working beyond retirement age if the request had been taken seriously by the employer.

12.55 Employers will argue that since they can lawfully dismiss C at age 65 provided the statutory scheme is followed, loss cannot extend beyond that point. However, the better argument is that where discriminatory considerations are brought to bear on the consideration of whether to grant a request to continue working that is an act of age discrimination which should sound in damages and is unaffected by the existence of the statutory procedure in the same way that the right to damages for discrimination is not curtailed by the right of the employer to terminate the contract by notice.

Constructing the schedule of loss

12.56 We will now set out an approach to constructing the schedule of loss in an age discrimination case and the particular problems that may arise. Many cases are successfully prosecuted in the tribunals only to fail to recover the sums that should have been awarded because insufficient attention was paid to effective construction of the schedule. Naturally the circumstances of any case will vary, so it is important to remember the principal purpose of the schedule which is to identify, quantify and (if necessary) explain the heads of claim. The schedule should aim to provide the tribunal with a template on which it can work to assess the compensation.

12.57 The claimant's adviser should, if in doubt, include an item of claim only if it is arguably recoverable. The schedule should be realistic, as including unreasonable items may make it more difficult for a settlement to be achieved. The schedule should only claim losses for which there is evidence. The tribunal is obliged to calculate the value of a loss on the available evidence.[78] If the schedule leaves the tribunal to guess, it will do so, but often conservatively. It is advisable, therefore, to consider issues relating to compensation with C from the start of the case.

---

78 See eg *Eden v West & Co* [2002] EWCA Civ 991.

12.58   The claimant should be asked to produce the following, which should then be referred to in the witness statement dealing with compensation:

- payslips;
- P60 or P45, as appropriate;
- details of additional overtime, bonus payments or profit-related pay etc insofar as they do not appear in the pay slips or notifications;
- pension details;
- contract of employment – which may indicate benefits.

12.59   The claimant should be asked for details of:

- promotional opportunities from the job which has been lost or from the job into which promotion was sought;
- any comparators that might be able to show how C's employment would have progressed (for example, two apprentices from the same cohort of apprentices).

12.60   Consideration should be given to using an employment expert if C is not able to continue in C's chosen occupation as a result of the discrimination, but with training can earn. Another situation in which an expert could be considered is where evidence will be needed concerning a professional job with a hierarchical structure, and clear opportunities for career progression.

Past losses

12.61   Compensation for loss of earnings, both past and future, may be awarded. The calculation of past losses is relatively easy. Take the net monthly or weekly pay. This is best calculated as the amount C actually took home, as it will include overtime and other amounts earned during a comparable period. The tribunal will award net earnings from the date on which loss flowing from the act of discrimination occurred until the date of the compensation hearing (past loss).

12.62   The first step must be to establish what the net earnings were. These will include what C had a reasonable expectation of receiving such as pay increases, back-dated pay increases; contractual or non-contractual overtime,[79] and tips, whether paid by the customers directly from (the now rare) tronc.[80] If C is claiming the benefit of a back-dated

---

79   *Mullet v Brush Electrical Machines Ltd* [1977] ICR 829.
80   *Palmanor Ltd v Cedron* [1978] ICR 1008.

pay rise it must be shown that C would have received it on a balance of probabilities. Of course compensation can only be awarded on a lawful basis so that if a person was paid less than the minimum wage, compensation must be calculated on the basis of the minimum wage level.[81]

12.63 If the case concerns a promotion which would have taken place but for the discrimination, the approach to assessing the chance of promotion is discussed above at para 12.49 onwards.

Future loss

12.64 It has been traditional in discussions of compensation to consider retirement age as the end-point for compensation. Of course one of the effects of the new legislation may be to call this principle into question. The calculation of future loss requires consideration and justification of the following elements:

1) Why should the tribunal accept that C will remain unemployed or unpromoted for any particular period? For example, it may be that a secondment of the sort denied only becomes available periodically.

2) What evidential basis is there to show what C's situation would have been had the discrimination not taken place?

3) What is the appropriate figure to reflect the period of loss together with any vicissitudes of life (known as the multiplier)?

4) What is the appropriate figure to be multiplied?[82]

12.65 In a simple dismissal case where there is a short-term future loss (for example because the employee has long declared an intention to retire at 68, but was subject to a discriminatory retirement at 65), the future loss will be easily reckoned. In that case C will recover part of the three years as past loss, and probably the remainder (subject to mitigation arguments) as future loss.

12.66 Where the period of future loss is long, however, the compensation awarded by the tribunal will represent a lump sum. That lump sum will over compensate C unless it is discounted to reflect that it is received much sooner than it otherwise would be received. The tribunals have also discounted such long awards to reflect the vicissitudes of life, such as the risk of death. Respondents who seek to emphasise this in cases of older workers who are claiming a longer period of future loss should be challenged to produce any proper basis

---

81 *Paggetti v Cobb* [2002] IRLR 861.
82 These are sometimes referred to as the multiplier and multiplicand. The latter is the yearly net earnings and benefits.

for the assertion that someone in C's state of health will not live an ordinary life span or that unusually high discounts should be given to reflect the risk of C dying before the sums would be earned.

12.67   In these types of cases it may be worth looking at the actuarial tables known as the Ogden tables, which give standardly accepted statistics on mortality and other matters relevant to compensation. The tables provide an aid for those assessing the lump sum appropriate as compensation for a continuing future pecuniary loss. They set out multipliers, which enable the user to assess the present capital value of future annual loss (net of tax) calculated on the basis of various assumptions explained in the tables. Accordingly, to find the present capital value of a given annual loss it is necessary to select the appropriate table, find the appropriate multiplier and then multiply the amount of the annual loss or expense by that figure. The relevant tables for employment cases are likely to be tables 3–14. In these tables, assumptions are made about the retirement age. The age of 65 is assumed in tables 9 and 10. The age of 70 is assumed in tables 11 and 12, and 75 in tables 13 and 14. These are likely to be of the most guidance.[83]

12.68   To find the appropriate figure for the present value of a particular loss or expense, first choose that table which relates to the period of loss for which the individual claimant is to be compensated and to the sex of the claimant. Thus if the loss is to age 70, you would choose T11 or T12. When you look at these tables you will see columns with percentages ranging from 0% upwards. One of these columns is 2.5%. This is the current annual rate of return (at the time of writing) and is to be used.

12.69   These tables make reasonable provision for the levels of mortality which members of the population of England and Wales alive today may expect to experience in future. The tables do not take account of the other risks and vicissitudes of life, such as the possibility that the claimant would for periods have ceased to earn due to ill health or loss of employment. Nor do they take account of the fact that many people cease work for substantial periods to care for children or other dependants. Section B of the Explanatory Notes to the tables suggests ways in which allowance may be made to the multipliers for loss of earnings, to allow for certain risks other than mortality. These are principally the risk of illness or unemployment. The risk of antici-

---

83   Where a retirement age which does not correlate to any of these (for example because it is in between two tables) is in issue, see para 14 of the explanatory notes to the tables, part A.

pated unemployment is expressed by means of tables referable to the sex of the claimant.[84] If there is a higher than average risk of unemployment due to economic conditions use the 'low' column. The figure which results, from consideration of the age of C, is then further adjusted by reference to the following factors:

a) what occupation was C in? Some carry a greater risk of illness than others;[85]

b) where does C live? The figure should be adjusted accordingly.[86]

The figure thus derived is applied to the multiplier first selected by use of one of tables 11 upwards.

12.70   To summarise, the method to obtain the future loss lump sum is:

1) Choose the tables relating to the appropriate period of loss.

2) Choose the table, relating to that period, appropriate to the sex of the claimant and retirement (tables 1–26).

3) Choose the appropriate rate of return (currently 2.5%) C will not simply receive compensation for the period over which the loss is sustained. The lump sum received by C will be discounted by a percentage to reflect early receipt of some of it at a rate, currently 2.5% (at the time of writing).[87]

4) Find the figure under the column in the table chosen given against the age at trial of C.

5) Adjust the figure to take account of contingencies other than mortality, as specified in Section B above.

6) Multiply the annual loss (net of tax) or expense by that figure.[88]

Clearly the longer the loss claimed, the less certain the loss.

---

84   See Ogden tables p12.

85   See Ogden tables p13.

86   See Ogden tables p13: For persons resident in the South East, East Anglia, South West and East Midlands, the figure which will subsequently modify the multiplier should be increased by a maximum of the order of 0.01 up to age 40, rising to 0.03 at age 55. For persons resident in the North, North West, Wales and Scotland, that figure should be reduced by a maximum of the order of 0.01 at age 25, 0.02 at age 40 and 0.05 at age 55.

87   In other words, the court will assume that in respect of any loss occurring in the future the claimant will be able to invest his or her money now to achieve an annual net rate of return of 2.5% after inflation has been accounted for.

88   See Ogden tables p14.

12.71   The use of the Ogden tables[89] was considered in *Kingston-upon-Hull City Council v Dunnachie (No 3)*[90] where the EAT held that employment tribunals should only rely on Ogden tables when calculating future loss of earnings and benefits in unfair dismissal claims[91] where a prima facie career long loss was established. Whether there is such loss should be addressed by reference to 'old job facts' and 'new job facts'. 'Old job facts' include whether the applicant would have remained in the job anyway and, if so, for how long, whether he would have been promoted and whether his earnings would have remained stable.[92] 'New job facts' require the tribunal to ask:

i)   whether the applicant would be likely to obtain a new job and, if so, what job would be likely to be obtained, by what date and at what remuneration;[93]

ii) is there a pay differential between the old and the new job and, if so, whether that differential would be affected by the applicant getting a better paid job in the future or being promoted or receiving pay increases.[94]

12.72   The tribunal must not abdicate from the job of deciding what, on the balance of probabilities is likely to happen, and the Ogden tables, coupled with a substantial discount, should not be a substitute or alternative for such an exercise. The EAT pointed out various dangers in using the tables in their current form for calculating tribunal loss:

---

89   The Actuarial Tables with explanatory notes for use in personal injury and fatal accident cases (the Ogden tables) are prepared by the Government Actuary's Department and published by The Stationery Office (ISBN 0 11 5600825, price £12.50). The Ogden tables can be found fully set out in Professional Negligence Bar Association's 'Facts & Figures'; in Personal Injury Damages Statistics by Rodney Nelson-Jones; and can be downloaded from the Government Actuary's website at www.gad.gov.uk, current reference: www.gad.gov.uk/Publications/docs/ogdentables5thed.pdf.

90   [2004] ICR 227; [2003] IRLR 843 at para 28 ff.

91   Although in *Birmingham City Council v Jaddoo* [2004] UKEAT 448/04/2810 the EAT stated that it was firmly of the view that this approach applies to all tribunal cases and not just unfair dismissal claims.

92   Were there apparent factors, whether personal (health, family situations, location) or economic (new technology, fall-off in orders, lay-offs, redundancies) which on the available evidence, including the experience of the employment tribunal as industrial jury, that should be taken into account? Would he or she have taken early retirement, or considered a second career?

93   After using reasonable mitigation.

94   Would the loss be eliminated in the future by promotion, new job or pay increase?

1) The tables take account of insufficient contingencies simply to be applied. Contingencies need to be considered when considering the factors about the old job and the new job factors.
2) There are dangers of double counting and the tables do not deal with the effect of tax adequately.[95]

12.73 *Dunnachie (No 3)* also gave guidance on the use of the tables:

i) the tribunal should not consider the use of the Ogden tables until a career-long loss (or differential loss) has been prima facie established, to which it is then appropriate to apply those Ogden tables which apply to loss to the relevant retirement age, as a useful tool;

ii) a rate of return of 2.5% (or such rate as may from time to time be substituted by way of statutory instrument under the Damages Act) should be adopted, if the tables are to be used;[96]

iii) if such tables are to be useful, it may be that other tables than the present, for example giving answers for loss up to retirement for each year between 50 and 70, could be produced under the supervision of the employment tribunal service;[97]

iv) the tribunals should give directions in any case where future loss is sought, along the lines of the schedules and counter-schedules in the High Court. Each party can set out its respective case as to the old job facts and the new job facts as a start. If there were to be any agreed schedules incorporating one set of figures, then it is essential that the basis of such agreement should be set out, ie whether the figures were agreed simply as figures or whether they were wholly agreed to be recoverable, subject only to liability.

12.74 The EAT then gave guidance to the parties on the preparation for hearings in which the tables are to be used:

i) A party seeking to rely on the Ogden tables should indicate in advance whether it wishes to rely on the tables and if so which table, preferably by way of a schedule submitted within 14 days of the presentation of a notice of appearance. Such schedule should set out the suggested multiplicand, by reference to relevant old job facts and new job facts, the relevant period relied upon and what if any discount is to be made from the multiplier.

95 See *Dunnachie (No 3)* para 31.
96 See also *Bentwood Bros (Manchester) Ltd v Shepherd* [2003] EWCA Civ 380 if it is suggested that a discount of 5% is appropriate.
97 In the 5th edition of the Ogden tables the age of retirement is assumed to be 50 in tables 3 and 4; 55 in tables 5 and 6; 60 in tables 7 and 8; 65 in tables 9 and 10; 70 in tables 11 and 12; and 75 in tables 13 and 14.

ii) The other party, upon receipt of such a schedule, should submit a counter-schedule of loss within 14 days of receiving the first party's schedule, giving the same particulars.

iii) In a case in which such steps have not been complied with, a chairman should be robust in issuing orders for further particulars and/or disclosure well in advance of the hearing, so that each party knows what case is to be met and what evidence needs to be called.

iv) The tables should not be used by an employment tribunal without giving the parties the opportunity to put forward their case.

v) The use of actuarial evidence outside the tables should be discouraged.[98]

> EXAMPLE: In *Dunnachie* reference was made to the case of a dismissal near to the retirement age. In the *Kennard* case[99] the applicant was aged 58 at the time of the remedies hearing. He was disabled and had been employed by the respondent for 16 years on what was described as a good salary taking into account his disability. The tribunal had regard to his age and his handicap on the labour market to reach the conclusion that there was no possibility that he would secure comparably paid employment. The tribunal accepted that he would have remained in employment until age 65. Compensation to the normal retiring age was said to be exceptional. The tribunal also felt it was just and equitable to calculate the applicant's loss by relying on the Ogden tables. The calculation, in the schedule of loss, reduced the applicant's losses by an appropriate percentage, to take account of contingencies other than mortality, for example the chance that the applicant might have been dismissed or made redundant, prior to age 65. That percentage made sufficient allowance for the possibility that the applicant might not have remained in employment until retirement. The tribunal entertained and then dismissed the argument that it should make a greater reduction for those contingencies than the percentage suggested in the Ogden tables.

98   *Dunnachie No 3* para 24. In the context of age discrimination this last guidance may be inappropriate until better actuarial information is available concerning the years around the current retirement assumptions are available.

99   *Kennard v Royal British Legion Industries* 1100479/2001/R, Employment Tribunal.

> It then:
>
> i) calculated that the applicant's continuing annual net loss of earnings; and
> ii) applied an appropriate multiplier, at a rate of return at 2.5%, with a discount for factors other than mortality.
>
> This produced a figure for loss of earnings to age 65.

12.75 It was felt in *Dunnachie* that the use of the Ogden tables would be justified where C was nearing retirement. The basis for this feeling may have been that in such a case it is more apparent that there is a career long loss (ie to retirement age). That is a conclusion that may have to be revisited if the 2006 regulations do change thinking about retirement (and the ages at which people retire).

12.76 Where C is not nearing retirement, the tribunal will consider whether a whole career loss can be made out. In most cases that will be unlikely. The question for the tribunal will then be how long into the future C's loss will last, having regard to its own knowledge of local employment conditions (if relevant to the type of employment being considered). However, where age discrimination has been found it is important that the tribunal does not make assumptions concerning the impact that age will have on ability or the type of job that can be obtained. The tribunal will, undoubtedly recognise the fact that it is more difficult for an older person to obtain work at the same level as the job from which they were dismissed.

12.77 Where the tribunal has more information its predication about future loss is likely to be more accurate. Thus it is likely to award a longer period of future loss where a person has a job which pays less well than if the same person is looking for work. The starting point is that C will obtain the same type of job at the same type of pay. The tribunal will not make that assumption if C has a job. The question will then become how long it will take for that differential to be made up. Generally tribunals will recognise that this takes longer.

Pensions

12.78 There are two methods of compensation generally used for pension losses. If the break in pensionable employment is likely to be short, the tribunal will award the contributions for the period of loss. If the break is not likely to be short-term the tribunal will determine the cost for C to purchase equivalent pension benefits.[100] The requirement to have an

100 Quotes from insurance companies will provide evidence of these.

appropriate approach to calculation of such losses in the context of the higher maximum levels of the compensatory award was expressed by the EAT in *Clancy v Cannock Chase Technical College* [2001] IRLR 331. In *Clancy* the EAT upheld an appeal from a decision of the employment tribunal that the loss for pension rights should be assessed only on the basis of the lost contributions from the employer. The EAT stressed that such an approach inadequately compensated the former employee because it took no account of the real losses suffered by him because of the entitlement, as of right, to a lump sum under the scheme.

12.78A   Guidelines on calculating pension losses are contained in *Employment Tribunals – Compensation for loss of pension rights* (London, HMSO) written by Colin Sara, David Pugsley and Douglas Crump.[100a] These are merely guidelines however so that a tribunal may depart from them without error of law.[100b] Different considerations apply to:

Money purchase schemes: the pension is directly related to the contributions made by the employer and employee. The loss is the loss of the employer's contributions to the pension from the date of the dismissal.

Final salary schemes: these relate the salary not directly to the contributions but to the years of service of the employee, his age and final salary. Generally members are entitled to 1/60th of the final salary for each year of service. The contribution of the employee will be 5% of salary. The employer provides the rest of the contribution (on average 10% of salary). The employee is entitled to a deferred pension at retirement age created by the salary at the date of dismissal and the years of service at that date. It rises by 5% per year and the loss is the difference between that deferred pension which the employee would have been entitled to receive if he had not been unfairly dismissed, less any pension received in new employment.

12.78B   In each case the loss falls under three headings:

(i) loss of pension rights from the date of dismissal to the date of hearing (these are the employer's notional contributions for the requisite period – 10% in the absence of contrary evidence);
(ii) loss of future pension rights
(For final salary schemes the employer's contributions are used to determine loss – a multiplier is then applied taking account of all foreseeable contingencies in the case (see below));

100a www.employmenttribunals.gov.uk/about_us/document/comp_loss_
pension_rights.pdf (3rd edn).
100b *Bingham v Hobourn Engineering Ltd* [1992] IRLR 298.

(iii) loss of enhancement of accrued pension rights. For money purchase scheme the accured sums simply continue to be invested ordinarily. For final salary scheme no compensation is awarded under the guidelines for employees in the public sector schemes or those with less than 5 years until retirement. Similarly if the contract would have been terminated shortly after the actual termination no compensation should be awarded for this element. In other cases use the Government Actuary's Department table based upon the C's age, length of service and anticipated age of retirement.[100c] The result should then be reduced for the likelihood that the applicant would have been dismissed before the pension became due. It is for the tribunal to determine the appropriate percentage in all the circumstances.

12.79 Note that in relation to compensation for age discrimination in breach of the pension provisions, paragraph 6 of Schedule 2 applies. The compensation provisions under regulation 38 do not apply therefore to remedies for breach of the pension equal treatment rule.[101]

Disadvantage in the labour market

12.80 Suppose that the discrimination has been a failure to give training to C which will mean that in future C will be disadvantaged if dismissed or if C resigns. If there is a substantial, rather than negligible, risk that a termination may take place, an award under this head should be made to reflect the fact that the act of discrimination has placed the C at a disadvantage in the labour market.[102] This will arise where the training can only be obtained from the specific employer (or a small group of employers).[103] If the training is readily available an award

---

100c http://www.employmenttribunals.gov.uk/about_us/document/comp_loss_pension_rights.pdf appendix 4.

101 See chapter 10.

102 *Moeliker v A Reyrolle & Co Ltd* [1997] 1 WLR 132 per Browne LJ. Browne LJ corrected his judgment in that case in *Cook v Consolidated Fisheries* [1977] ICR 635 to point out that the head of damages arises not only when the C is in employment at the time of trial but can arise where at the time of trial the C is unemployed. However, it will generally only arise when C is unemployed at time of trial.

103 For example, the training of pilots on specific types of aircraft ('typing').

may not be appropriate, but recovery of training costs might be. Other examples of when a '*Smith v Manchester*' award is appropriate include where C is ill as a result of the discrimination or harassment. Such an award tends to be a lump sum payment to reflect the likelyhood of future disadvantage.

Principles reducing recoverable loss

Matters which break the causal chain

12.81   C must prove that the loss is caused by the act of discrimination. In some cases a dismissed employee will have obtained a new job, the pay and benefits from which extinguish the financial loss caused by the act of discrimination. On the face of it, that would break the causal relationship between the act of discrimination and any subsequent loss (for example, if C loses the new job).

12.82   The tribunal must consider the question of loss at the date of the compensation hearing. If the employee has been unemployed since dismissal, the starting point is of course that C should receive C's entire loss. However where C has obtained secure and permanent employment at a lower level of earnings, C's loss will be reduced by that amount. Where C takes a job which is for a limited time, C may after that job is finished revert to claiming full loss, giving credit for the earnings received from the temporary employment. However, as soon as C obtains permanent employment which pays the same or more than the pre-dismissal earnings this does break the chain of causation. That means that if the earnings are greater than the previous job, C does not have to give credit for those earnings, but by the same token if C loses that job C cannot revive the loss if C loses the permanent post.[105] The burden of proof on matters of causation is on C.

105   See *Dench v Flynn & Partners* [1998] IRLR 653, approving *Whelan v Richardson* [1998] IRLR 114. The remarks in *Dench* concerning causation must be seen in the context of the compensatory award for unfair dismissal which is an award of such sum as the tribunal considers just and equitable, rather than an award on tortious principles. Therefore the better approach is to allow such loss as can continue to be attributed to the discriminatory act. In most cases obtaining permanent employment will break that causal link. However, in certain situations placing C in the situation C would have been in had the discrimination not occurred will require consideration of all the influences and causes of the second period of unemployment. If the second period of unemployment can fairly be said to be attributable to the act of discrimination, it should be recoverable.

12.83   In *HM Prison Service v Beart (No 2)*,[106] the Court of Appeal held that the tribunal was correct in awarding compensation to the claimant for disability discrimination in respect of future loss of earnings without treating the fact that she had been unfairly dismissed as the operative cause of any loss after it took effect. The Court rejected the argument that the fact of dismissal, albeit unfair, terminated the employer's liability for the earlier wrong of disability discrimination so that all further losses had to be assessed under the unfair dismissal regime with its statutory cap on compensation. An employer cannot rely upon a subsequent wrong that it has committed in order to reduce the damages that would otherwise flow from an earlier wrongful act.

Contributory fault

12.84   An award of compensation for age discrimination is compensation 'of an amount corresponding to any damages he could have been ordered by a County Court or by a Sheriff Court to pay to the Complainant if the complaint had fallen to be dealt with under tortious principles for a breach of statutory duty'. It follows that the award of compensation in an age discrimination case is subject to the Law Reform (Contributory Negligence) Act 1945 which allows for reduction in compensation in tortious claims where C's conduct itself amounts to negligence or breach of a legal duty and contributed to the damage.[107]

Mitigation of loss

12.85   Credit must be given for earnings actually received by C since the act of discrimination (as above). However, the respondent may sometimes argue that C has not mitigated the loss flowing from the act of discrimination by obtaining further work either at the same level of earnings as the loss flowing from that act.[108] or at a lower level.[109] The respondent can argue that credit must be given for such sums as C would have had if C had acted to mitigate the loss.

---

106   [2005] IRLR 568.
107   *Way v Crouch* (above) para 11 of the judgment. Cf the EAT in *The Blackpool Fylde and Wyre Society for The Blind v Begg* [2005] UKEAT 0035 where HHJ McMullen felt the statutory commissions should intervene before a conclusion was reached on this point which he regarded as requiring to be reasoned.
108   Thus extinguishing the loss for which the respondent is liable.
109   Thus diminishing the loss for which the respondent is liable and leaving a residual (and potentially continuing) loss.

12.86   The rule is that C must act as a reasonable person would if C had no hope of seeking compensation from the respondent. The burden of proof of the failure is on the respondent. There is a difference between an event which breaks causation (burden on C to show causation of loss) and an event representing a failure to mitigate (burden on the respondent). It is important that the respondent should set out a clear case as to which is being argued before the tribunal.[110] Careful attention should be paid to the respondent's pleadings to see which is being asserted. This is because two different tests are to be employed.[111] If causation is being challenged the tribunal must simply make a decision on whether the event broke causation in any relevant sense. However, if mitigation is being argued the tribunal needs to find the specifics referred to below. It is appropriate to use the principles developed in unfair dismissal cases to determine these issues.[112]

12.87   C must take all reasonable steps to mitigate the loss consequent on the discrimination. The standard of reasonableness is not high in view of the fact that the respondent is a wrongdoer.[113] As was said in

---

110   See *Williams v North Tyneside Council* [2006] UKEAT 0415/05/3101.

111   'The process is a three-stage one, requiring, initially, factual quantification of losses claimed; secondly, but equally importantly, the extent to which any or all of those losses are attributable to the dismissal or action taken by the employer, which is usually the same thing, the word "attributable" implying that there has to be a direct and natural link between the losses claimed and the conduct of the employer in dismissing, on the basis that the dismissal is the causa causans of the particular loss and not that it simply arises by reason of a causa sine qua non, i.e. but for the dismissal the loss would not have arisen. If that is the only connection, the loss is too remote. The third part of the assessment in terms of the reference to the phrase "just and equitable" requires a Tribunal to look at the conclusions they draw from the first two quarters and determine whether, in all the circumstances, it remains reasonable to make the relevant award. It must again be emphasised, however, what has to be considered under the third test already has to have passed the second. Finally, it has to be observed that while the facts relating to a question of mitigation will frequently bear upon the question of causative link, mitigation is essentially an equitable plea to be judged in the context of reasonableness at common law and thus on not too fine a balance.' *Simrad Ltd v Scott* [1997] IRLR 147. This test was qualified in *IBC Vehicles v Khanum UKEAT* [1999] UKEAT 685/98/1509: the tribunal must decide whether a decision to retrain was reasonable and directly caused by the dismissal. The authorities are conflicting and opaque on the distinction between causation and mitigation.

112   *MOD v Cannock* [1994] ICR 918.

113   *Banco de Portugal v Waterlow & Sons Ltd* [1932] AC 452. The reasonableness of the employee's behaviour will be judged in the context of the surrounding circumstances: *Fyfe v Scientific Funishings Ltd* [1989] ICR 648.

Wilding v British Telecommunications plc[114] it was not enough for the respondent:

> ... to show that it would have been reasonable to take the steps he has proposed. He must show that it was unreasonable of the innocent party not to take them. This was a real distinction. It reflects the fact that if there is more than one reasonable response open to the wronged party, the wrongdoer has no right to determine his choice. It is only where the wrongdoer can show affirmatively that the other party acted unreasonably in relation to his duty to mitigate that the defence will succeed.

12.88　Thus where a dismissed employee had back problems which were so severe that he signed on sick (and subsequently obtained invalidity benefit) it was found that he was not acting unreasonably in so doing. He was genuinely seeking to mitigate his loss despite the fact that this lowered the chances of his obtaining work.[115] By contrast, it was held to be an error for a tribunal to assess the loss of a person in poor health by determining when it was likely that he would obtain alternative employment as though he were fully fit. The employers must take their employee as they find him or her.[116]

12.89　Where C decided to undergo a 12-month post graduate course of study at Bath University after his dismissal, a tribunal was entitled to allow loss of earnings from the termination of his employment until the date he started the course. The EAT held that by deciding to embark upon the course C effectively took himself out of the labour market. That made the start of the course an appropriate cut off point for compensation. Future loss at the termination of the university course was considered so remote as to be incapable of calculation.[117] However, a decision to retrain will not necessarily break the causal link between the discrimination and the loss.[118] Such ques-

---

114　[2002] IRLR 524 per Sedley LJ.

115　*Wilson v Glenrose* UKEAT 444 91 2107.

116　*Fougere v Phoenix Motor Company Ltd* [1976] ICR 495.

117　*Holroyd v Graveur Cylinders Ltd* [1984] IRLR 259. However, that approach would have to be qualified by the consideration that in many cases in today's labour market, it will be necessary for an employee to acquire new skills. It is worth considering whether there are factors that limit the type of employment that C may undertake without retraining. Retraining will (even to a degree level) sometimes be a reasonable act of mitigation. In *Glen Henderson Ltd v Nisbet* EAT 34/90, the cost of a five-week Business Enterprise Course was recovered. The claimant had taken the course with a view to becoming self-employed.

118　See *IBC Vehicles Ltd v Khanum* EAT/685/98 cited in *Williams v North Tyneside Council* [2006] UKEAT 0415 05 3101.

tions should be treated as issues of mitigation of loss, rather than of causation.[119]

12.90   In a particular case, C may have established that as a result of age discrimination C has lost earnings for a period which will be unlimited save for the steps that should be taken in mitigation of loss. One of those steps may be training. If it is reasonable to engage in training as a way of mitigating loss, causation will not be broken. However, if it was not reasonable to engage in the training, it is not a step of mitigation. If one then asks the question whether the training breaks the causal link, that will come down to the question of whether the undertaking of training has the effect of removing C from the employment market. It may or may not, depending on whether C has continued to take active steps during the training period to seek work.

12.91   If the tribunal finds that the claimant has not taken reasonable steps to lessen the loss, the tribunal must then decide whether:

a) the effect of reasonable steps would be that the claimant would have obtained a job/promotion at the same or greater pay and benefits than the loss flowing from the act of discrimination; or

b) the effect of reasonable steps would be that C would have obtained a less well-paid job.

12.92   There seems in principle no reason why these eventualities should not be treated as lost chances. However, that is not the approach adopted in relation to the whole period of loss:

> In order to show a failure to mitigate, it has to be shown that [if] a particular step had been taken, [C] would, after a particular time, on balance of probabilities have gained employment; from then onward the loss flowing from the unfair dismissal would have been extinguished or reduced by his income from that other source. In fixing the amount to be deducted for failing to mitigate, it is necessary for the tribunal to identify what steps should have been taken; the date on which that step would have produced an alternative income and, thereafter, to reduce the amount of compensation by the amount of the alternative income which would have been earned. Since that is the principle of mitigation, a reduction of a percentage of a total sum representing compensation for the whole period is inappropriate.[120]

12.93   This means that the respondent must prove the particular job that would have been obtained and the level of earnings that would have

119 This was the approach taken by the employment tribunal and analysed by the EAT in *Orthet Ltd v Vince-Cain* [2004] IRLR 857.

120 *Gardener-Hill v Rowland Berger Technics Ltd* [1982] IRLR 498, 500; see also *Peara v Enderlin Ltd* [1979] ICR 804.

been derived from that job. If the respondent can only show that C could have obtained a less well-paid job then the tribunal should reduce the loss from the date that it is found that there has been a failure to mitigate.

12.94 Where C has been unfairly dismissed in an act of age discrimination, there will still be scope for the argument (depending on the circumstances) that an unreasonable failure to accept an offer of re-instatement made at an early stage, should result in C being unable to claim any loss at all.[121]

12.95 The Court of Appeal has summarised these principles:[122]

> As was made clear in the judgment of the EAT, (at paragraph 64) the various authorities referred to by the Tribunal (see paragraph 22 and 23 above) and *Payzu –v- Saunders* are apt to establish the following principles which (in a form which I have somewhat recast) were accepted as common ground between the parties. (i) It was the duty of Mr Wilding to act in mitigation of his loss as a reasonable man unaffected by the hope of compensation from BT as his former employer; (ii) the onus was on BT as the wrongdoer to show that Mr Wilding had failed in his duty to mitigate his loss by unreasonably refusing the offer of re-employment; (iii) the test of unreasonableness is an objective one based on the totality of the evidence; (iv) in applying that test, the circumstances in which the offer was made and refused, the attitude of BT, the way in which Mr Wilding had been treated and all the surrounding circumstances should be taken into account; and (v) the court or tribunal deciding the issue must not be too stringent in its expectations of the injured party. I would add under (iv) that the circumstances to be taken into account included the state of mind of Mr Wilding.

12.96 The test for whether C has mitigated is reasonableness and not whether any new job represents suitable alternative employment in the sense used in relation to redundancy payments.[123]

12.97 Certain steps of mitigation may in fact increase the loss. Such increased loss will be recoverable if the taking of the step was reasonable.[124] Thus in retraining cases it may be possible to recover the tuition fees. In *Aon Training Ltd v Dore*[125] the Court of Appeal held that the employment tribunal had erred in quantifying the claimant's losses arising from his dismissal (partly for reasons relating to his disability) solely on the basis of the interest on loans which he took out in order

---

121 *Sweetlove v Redbridge & Waltham Forest Area Health Authority* [1979] ICR 477.
122 *Wilding v British Telecommunications plc* [2002] ICR 1079.
123 *Bessenden Properties Ltd v Corness* [1973] IRLR 365.
124 *Gardiner-Hill v Roland Berger Technics* [1982] IRLR 498.
125 [2005] IRLR 891.

to set up his own business rather than seeking alternative employment. Where a dismissed employee attempts to mitigate his loss by setting up his own business and the employment tribunal is satisfied that mitigation in that way was reasonable, the conventional way to assess compensation is to calculate what sum represents the loss of remuneration. The tribunal should then consider the costs incurred in mitigating that loss and such, if reasonably incurred, should be added to the loss. From that sum should be deducted the earnings from the new business.

Compensation – non-financial loss

Injury to feelings

12.98   'Injury' must be proved. However, 'no tribunal will take much persuasion that the anger, distress and affront caused by the act of discrimination has injured the claimant's feelings'.[126] One of the interesting issues for C's advisers will be whether the same low level of compensation for injury to feelings for age discrimination will be seen as when other strands of anti-discrimination compensation have come into force. One aspect of age discrimination which may cause difficulty in this regard is a deep philosophical distinction that appears to be given some currency, to the effect that it is necessary to distinguish between those grounds of discrimination which prima facie appear to offend our notions of the respect due to the individual (such as gender) and those which merely require some rational justification (potentially including age).[127] The directive emphasises the dignity of the individual[128] suggesting that awards for injury to feelings should be on a par with those related to other discrimination strands.

---

126   *Ministry of Defence v Cannock* [1994] ICR 918.

127   *Massachusetts Board of Retirement v Murgia* (1976) 438 US 285 cited in *R (on the application of Carson) v Secretary of State for Work and Pensions* [2005] UKHL 37; [2006] 1 AC 173 at paras 14–17 and para 60: 'There is nothing intrinsically demeaning about age. It may be disheartening for a man to be told that he cannot continue in his chosen job after 50, and it is certainly demeaning for a woman air hostess to be told that she cannot continue as cabin crew after the age of 40 (see *Defrenne v Société Anonyme Belge de Navigation Aérienne* (Case 43/75) [1976] ECR 455). But Mlle Defrenne was discriminated against on the ground of sex, not age. In relation to normal retirement ages lines have to be drawn somewhere as *Murgia* explains': per Lord Walker of Gestingthorpe.

128   See chapter 5 and the discussion of *Mangold*.

12.99   Awards for injury to feelings are designed to compensate the injured party fully but not to punish the guilty party. An award should not be inflated by feelings of indignation at the guilty party's conduct. An award should not be so low as to diminish respect for the policy of the anti-discrimination legislation – on the other hand, awards should not be so excessive that they might be regarded as untaxed riches. Awards should bear some broad general similarity to the range of awards in personal injury cases.[129] Tribunals should bear in mind the value in everyday life of the sum they have in mind and the need for public respect for the level of the awards made aggravated damages, which are intended to deal with cases where the injury to the complainant was inflicted by conduct that was high-handed, malicious, insulting or oppressive,[130] and should be kept separate from injury to feelings damages.[131]

12.100   The Court of Appeal gave detailed guidance on injury to feelings awards in *Vento v Chief Constable of West Yorkshire Police.*[132] This is still the leading case on the assessment of non-pecuniary damages in discrimination cases. The court set out three bands of damages for injury to feelings:[133]

- **Top:** £15,000 to £25,000 for most serious cases, such as where there has been a lengthy campaign of discriminatory harassment.
- **Middle:** £5,000 to £15,000 for serious cases which do not merit an award in the highest band.
- **Lower:** £500 to £5,000 for less serious cases, e.g. isolated or one-off occurrence. Awards of less than £500 are to be avoided. Similarly, the Sheriff Court in *Purves v Joydisc Ltd*[134] held that £750 was the very minimum award for the slightest injury to feelings.[135]

By reference to inflation, the £25,000 upper limit in *Vento* should now be around £27,200; the lower limit of £500 should be about £550.[136]

---

129   In *Armitage and ors v Johnson* [1997] IRLR 162 EAT.
130   See eg *Alexander v Home Office* [1988] IRLR 190, CA.
131   *Scott v Commissioners of Inland Revenue* [2004] IRLR 713.
132   [2003] IRLR 102.
133   At para 65.
134   [2003] IRLR 420.
135   However, see *Greig v Initial Security Ltd* EAT 0036/05 which appears to reject this idea.
136   See also eg *Moyhing v Barts and London NHS Trust* DLA E News 68 July 2006.

12.101   The issue of an award for injury to feelings will turn very much on the evidence presented to the tribunal and the extent to which they are persuaded. It is very difficult to interfere with a tribunal's award.[137]

Matters to be taken into account

12.102   A salutary principle for bullying or high handed respondents is that subsequent events, such as the way a grievance is treated may add to the injury to feelings,[138] (as may overly aggressive cross examination in the course of the tribunal hearing). The way cases are dispersed among the bands gives some idea of the factors to be considered, but it should be emphasised that each case should be placed on its merits as opposed to a comparison being conducted:[139]

- **Top band:** *Gilbank v Miles:*[140] £25,000 awarded for an 'inhumane and sustained campaign of bullying and discrimination' 'targeted, deliberate, repeated and consciously inflicted' and 'not only demonstrated ... a total lack of concern for the welfare of the claimant herself, but a callous disregard ... for the life of her unborn child'.[141]
- **Middle band:** *Wallington v S and B Car Hire Kent Ltd:*[142] £7,000 for

137   *Skyrail Oceanic Ltd v Coleman* [1991] ICR 864, the EAT should only interfere with an award if the tribunal 'acted on a wrong principle of law or ... misapprehended the facts or... made a wholly erroneous estimate of the damage suffered'. This applies to all heads of loss. In *Vento* this was formulated as a perversity test.

138   *British Telecommunications plc v Reid* [2004] IRLR 327.

139   See IDS Brief 808, July 2006.

140   [2006] IRLR 538.

141   See also *Hall v Broadacres Housing Association Ltd* Employment Tribunal Case No 2506939/03 (IDS Diversity at Work No 12): £24,000, for 'heartless indifference' shown to a disabled person who 'was made for years to feel like a pariah and a beggar' when his needs were ignored (resulting in pain from her disability); *Goddard v Wilkinson Hardware Stores Ltd* Employment Tribunal Case No 3104507/03 (IDS Diversity at Work No 14), young female worker confided details of psychiatric matters to older trusted manager, who after offering initial support sought to exploit her vulnerability for sexual favours. This went on for two years.

142   EAT 0240/03 and see *Carney v Rouf and anor* UKEAT 0353/04 £8500 on appeal for a barmaid who suffered persistent sexual harassment; *Harwood v Sargent t/a Brewers Arms Hotel* Employment Tribunal Case No 1801300/05 £6,000 for an 18-year-old waitress kissed on the lips against her wishes by her much older manager; *Osborne-Clarke (as personal representative of Nigel Osborne Clarke deceased) v Commissioners of Inland Revenue* Employment Tribunal Case No 1400656/04 (IDS Diversity at Work No 17): £15,000. Hearing-impaired man discriminated against including disciplinary charges. Deeply affected by them. Subsequently committed suicide. Impossible to speculate why, as other matters preyed on his mind as well, but discrimination was a clear factor.

dismissal the day before going on maternity leave. The manner of the dismissal was very serious although it was an one-off incident.

- **Lower band:** *Doshoki v Draeger Ltd:*[143] £1200 (increased from £750): prior to his dismissal nine months after the start of his employment, Doshoki had been subjected on several separate occasions to taunts, such as 'Oh shut up Ayatollah' and had also been described as a 'eunuch' and an 'Arab' at training sessions.

12.103 Awards can be made against individual respondents (*Armitage and Marsden and HM Prison Service v Johnson*[144] involved awards of £500 each upheld against two prison officers), subject to the principles in *Way v Crouch*.

12.104   Compensation for injury to feelings must of course be limited to the injury to feelings arising directly from the act of discrimination. Often respondents' representatives will seek to trawl medical records to see if there are any other competing or pre-existing causes for conditions such as anxiety or depression.

Taxation of injury to feelings awards

12.105 In *Walker v Adams (Inspector of Taxes)*[145] C had been constructively dismissed due to religious discrimination and was awarded compensation for his dismissal. Any payments made directly or indirectly in relation to the termination of employment fell to be assessed under income tax legislation as income. The inspector accepted that the award for injury to feelings was outside its scope but found that the remainder amounted to a taxable payment in connection with his employment. In *Orthet Ltd v Vince-Cain*[146] the EAT held that an employment tribunal had been entitled to make an award of £15,000 for injury to feelings with-

---

143 [2002] IRLR 340. See also *Appleby v DWP* Current Law 03/2083 234958 (Lambeth County Court): £850 an interviewer became irritated and frustrated at C's inability to hear. C felt humiliated but had not claimed that it had caused him any lasting damage or that his life had been particularly affected. The incident had taken place in a private room, so he had not been humiliated in the full gaze of the public waiting area. *Bartley v Raven Building Services* Employment Tribunal Case No 2305483/01: £4,000 awarded to a man of black Jamaican origin. A hod carrier frequently referred to him and his black colleagues as 'black bastards' and distinguished Bartley and his black colleagues from other colleagues by referring to them in Bartley's presence as 'your friends'.

144 [1997] IRLR 162.

145 [2003] STC (SCD) 269.

146 [2004] IRLR 857.

out reference to the tax implications of that award. Although the EAT held that the matter was unclear it stated that if an award for injury to feelings was to be taxed C might seek a review of the tribunal's decision. This seems sensible given the *concession* based nature of the current position adopted by the Inland Revenue and the absence of other authority.

Personal injury

12.106　It is clear from the decision in *Sheriff v Klyne Tugs (Lowestoft) Ltd*[148] that discrimination claims with a personal injury (PI) element (usually psychiatric) can be brought in the employment tribunal. If it is arguable that the discrimination is the material cause of the injury, the claim *must* be brought in the tribunal, the common law courts lacking jurisdiction to determine employment discrimination claims. There may be disadvantages to the complainant with having damages assessed here, such as the restricted costs jurisdiction. However, that also means a much lower costs risk for a claimant in a difficult case. Other advantages to both parties include the relatively swift employment tribunal outcome. The applicable interest rates are higher in the employment tribunal. In valuing pain, suffering and loss of amenity, the usual sources for PI comparators should be consulted, such as the *JSB Guidelines* (7th edn, 2004); volumes such as *Kemp and Kemp* and the *Butterworths Personal Injury Litigation Service;* and online sources of PI quantum reports such as Current Law and Lawtel.

12.107　　In the employment tribunal interest is due pursuant to the Employment Tribunal (Interest on Awards in Discrimination Cases) Regulations 1996[149] from the date of the act of discrimination (on awards for injury to feelings and PSLA) and usually from the time midpoint on all other awards (past pecuniary losses currently at a rate of 6% pa). The employment tribunal must consider interest and should give reasons if it decides not to award interest as above. A failure to include interest can be corrected as a 'slip' (on the employment tribunal's own motion or on application) under rule 37(1) of the Employment Tribunal Rules of Procedure 2004.[150] In the courts, by contrast, interest on PSLA runs at only 2% per annum from the date of service of the proceedings; and only on pecuniary losses is the Special Investment Account rate applicable currently 6%.

148　[1999] ICR 1170.
149　SI No 2803.
150　SI No 1861.

12.108   If the judgment sum remains unpaid after 14 days, then interest is payable from the day after judgment at the Judgments Act 1838 rate (currently 8%, at the time of writing), under the Employment Tribunals (Interest) Order 1990.[151]

12.109   The heads of damages listed below may sometimes arise as part of a claim where personal injury has been caused by discrimination. The same principles are relevant as in other personal injury claims and are covered in the leading personal injury practitioners' texts such as *Kemp and Kemp* and *Butterworths Personal Injury Litigation Service:*

12.110 • care, whether provided professionally or by family and friends;
        • private medical treatment, eg to mitigate the effects of depressive illness;
        • housing, equipment etc, only in very rare cases will victims of discrimination require adapted or new accommodation or equipment.

Aggravated damages

12.111 The award of aggravated damages can be made where the complainant's sense of injury from the wrongful act is justifiably heightened by the manner in which or the motive for which the respondent did it.[154] Where the respondent has behaved in a 'high-handed, malicious, insulting or oppressive manner', aggravated damages may be awarded.[155] C must have suspected or known of the insulting behaviour in order to justify aggravated damages. In *ICTS Ltd v Tchoula*[156] (EAT), Judge Clark considered that aggravated damages (like injury to feelings) are compensatory and not punitive, and that whether they were awarded separately or as part of an award for injury to feelings was a matter of form, not substance. However in *Scott v Commissioners of Inland Revenue*[157] the Court of Appeal disagreed, holding that aggravated damages are separate from damages for injury to feelings. In *Zaiwalla & Co*

---

151   SI No 479.
152   In *Laing Ltd v Essa* [2004] ICR 746; [2004] IRLR 313.
153   *Orthet Ltd v Vince-Cain* [2005] ICR 374; [2004] IRLR 857.
154   *Broome v Cassell* [1972] AC 1027.
155   *Alexander v Home Office* [1998] IRLR 190. See also *Armitage & Prison Service v Johnson* [1997] IRLR 162.
156   [2000] IRLR 643.
157   [2004] IRLR 713.

v Walia[158] the EAT confirmed that aggravated damages can be awarded as a matter of principle in discrimination cases marked by a respondent's oppressive conduct of the proceedings themselves.

Exemplary damages

12.112 Exemplary damages punish the respondent. Until *Kuddus v Chief Constable of Leicestershire*[159] it had been thought that such damages were only available with certain types of causes of action:

a) where there has been oppressive, unconstitutional conduct by respondents who were servants of the government;

b) where the conduct has been calculated to make a profit which may exceed the compensation to the complainant;

c) where statute expressly authorises it.

12.113 In *Kuddus* the House of Lords reviewed the authorities and held that exemplary damages should not be restricted to cases where exemplary damages would have been available before 1964. It held that it was the features of the behaviour rather than the cause of action which must be looked at. In *Virgo Fidelis Senior School v Boyle*[160] the EAT held that such damages were possible under the Employment Rights Act (ERA) 1996, so there appears no reason why, if the other conditions are satisfied, they should not be awarded in discrimination cases. Two circumstances in particular seem to call for them in that context:

a) where servants of the state have acted in an oppressive arbitrary or unconstitutional manner; or

b) where the respondent's conduct is calculated to make a profit exceeding the compensation that might be paid to C.

12.114 Exemplary damages will be rare because they should only be awarded when a compensatory award is an inadequate punishment to the wrongdoer. In awarding exemplary damages regard should be had to the means of the respondent. The award is unlikely to be less than £5,000; for an award to be as much as £25,000 the respondent must be 'particularly deserving of condemnation; £50,000 is to be regarded as the absolute maximum[161] though this figure should also be up-rated for inflation.

---

158 [2002] IRLR 697.

159 [2001] 2 WLR 1789.

160 [2004] ICR 1210; [2004] IRLR 268.

161 *Thompson v Metropolitan Police Commissioner* [1998] QB 498.

Tax: grossing up and settlement

12.115 Subject to important exceptions, sections 401–404 of the Income Tax (Earnings and Pensions) Act 2003 renders an employee or ex-employee liable to income tax on such 'payments and other benefits [as are] received directly or indirectly in consideration or in consequence of, or otherwise in connection with ... the termination of [his] employment'. Such payments or benefits are treated as 'employment income of the employee or former employee ... for the relevant tax year'. One exception relates to the first £30,000 of the 'payment or benefit'.[162] Another is a payment or other benefit provided '(a) in connection with the termination of the employment by the death of the employee or (b) on account of injury to or disability of the employee'.[163] This was held to include injury to feelings damages.[164] Such damages are therefore non-taxable. As such it does not form part of the damages to be grossed up.[164a]

12.116 It is suggested that the following is the correct method:

Suppose the employment tribunal awards C £10,000 for injury to feelings and £90,000 for pecuniary losses. Applying the Orthet reasoning, only the £90,000 would be subject to grossing up. Of that sum, the first £30,000 is exempt by reason of section 403(1) of ITEPA 2003. Note that, to the extent that it exceeds the £30,000 threshold, the payment counts as 'employment income' for the tax year in which it was received (section 403(1)–(2)). Assume for simplicity that the money is paid today, and that C has no other 'employment income' in this tax year. On C's taxable £60,000 C will pay the following tax in the year ending 2007:

	2006/2007 TAX BANDS	Tax payable	C will pay on 60,000
Personal allowance (0%)	£5,035	Nil	Nil
Lower rate (10%)	£2,150	£215	£215
Basic rate (22%)	£31,150	£6,853	£6,853
Higher rate (40%)	£38,335 +	40% on excess	£9,082

---

162 Income Tax (Earnings and Pensions) Act (ITEPA) 2003 s403(1).
163 Section 406.
164 *Orthet v Vince-Cain* (above).
164a See para 12.105.

> So an extra £7068 (ie 215 + 6,853) will indemnify C from lower rate
> tax. That has to be added in to produce the balance which is
> taxable at higher rate (60,000 − 31,150 − 2,150 − 5,035 + 7,068 =
> £28,733). In order to receive that £28,733 balance in C's hand after
> 40% tax C should get:
> 100/60 x 28,733 = £47,888.33
> So her £90,000 becomes £116,223 after grossing-up (ie £30,000
> + £5,035 + £2,150 + £31,150 + £47,888), an extra £26,223.

Settlements and tax

12.117   The Inland Revenue's Extra-Statutory Concession A81 observes that any
costs recovered by an employee in a settlement with his former
employer are also assessable to income tax as a 'payment or benefit'.[165]
The Revenue has agreed, however, that in certain circumstances tax will
not be charged on such costs. The relevant circumstances are in cases
which settle without recourse to the court (presumably including the
employment tribunal) and where payments by the employer:

- are made direct to the employee's solicitor;
- are in full or partial discharge of costs incurred only in connection
  with the termination of the employee's employment; and
- are made in accordance with a specific term to that effect in the
  compromise agreement/COT3.

12.118   Where the dispute does go to court (presumably including tribunals),
there is no tax charge imposed on payment of costs (even when made
direct to the employee) where payment is in accordance with a court
order (either a judgment or a consent order); but payments must relate
only to legal costs and not to other miscellaneous costs. So in a pre-hearing settlement context, it is important to record in the settlement
agreement that payments are made in accordance with these requirements. More generally, if the compensation payment is structured
this way, it will obviously reduce the overall sum which is subject to tax
or other deductions.

Interest

12.119   Where an amount of compensation falls to be awarded the tribunal has
a discretion to include in the award, interest on that amount subject to,
and in accordance with, the provisions of the Employment Tribunals

165   ITEPA 2003 ss401–406.

(Interest on Awards in Discrimination Cases) Regulations 1996.[166] These provide for interest on loss of use of money awarded which relates to loss accruing before the hearing date. The 1996 Regulations provide for interest on injury to feelings. The principles for calculation for awards of injury to feelings damages are:

1) determine the date of the act of discrimination;
2) determine the calculation date, ie the date on which the remedies decision is made;
3) apply the current rate of interest (6%[167]).

12.120 In relation to other compensation for past loss:

1) determine the date of the act of discrimination;
2) determine the calculation date;
3) find the date which is the mid-point between those two;
4) apply the current rate of interest to the period from 3, to the calculation date.

12.121 There is no power to award interest for a matter which occurs after the calculation date. Where the award is in the county court, the 1996 regulations do not apply and interest is awarded under the County Courts Act 1984 and there is a risk that injury to feelings could be compensated at the 2% rate awarded for general damages in personal injury cases. However, the county court has a discretion in this matter and its attention should be drawn to the rate considered appropriate in employment cases.

Issues relating to age discrimination

12.122 Age discrimination cases will raise some difficult compensation questions. Consider the following example:

---

166 SI No 2803.
167 But periods prior to 1 August 1999 attract 8% and from then to 1 February 2002 the rate is 7%; since that time it is 6%.

EXAMPLE: Alan is 64 and applies for a job. He is refused that job because they do not want 'an old codger like him' working for them. He successfully wins his tribunal because regulation 7(4) does not apply to him and the tribunal rejects the idea that there was justified direct discrimination because the employer did not think they would get sufficient work out of Alan before retirement was forced on him at 65.

Alan could lawfully be dismissed at age 65, but would be able to request to continue working. Equally, the employer could simply, when Alan was 64½, tell him that they no longer wanted someone of his age working for them, serve six months' notice of retirement on him and when he presents his request to work (or at the subsequent meeting) tell him that they were not prepared to keep him on after that age. Such treatment would be lawful.

When considering Alan's compensation for the refusal to give him the job, how is the tribunal to deal with this?

12.123 In *HM Prison Service v Beart (No 2)*,[168] the Court of Appeal held that the employment tribunal was right to award compensation to the claimant for disability discrimination in respect of future loss of earnings without treating the fact that she had been unfairly dismissed as the operative cause of any loss after it took effect (see para 12.83).

12.124 Where the employer follows the correct formal procedure, the act of dismissal would not be a wrongful act. Consequently the tribunal will have to decide whether C has lost a chance of continuing to work after the retirement age in the case of persons approaching retirement age.

County court

12.125 Regulation 39 provides that a claim by C that the respondent has committed against C an act of the following nature or is liable as employer or principal or as someone who has aided an unlawful act. The county court has jurisdiction over any act of discrimination or harassment that is unlawful by virtue of regulation 23, which relates to institutions of further and higher education. The county court also has jurisdiction where the act of discrimination or harassment arises out of and is closely connected to a relationship between the claimant and the respondent which has come to an end but during the course of which an act of discrimination against, or harassment of, the claimant by the respondent would have been unlawful by virtue of regulation 23.[170] Regulation 39 provides that such acts 'may be made the subject of civil proceedings in like manner as any other claim in tort or (in Scotland) in reparation for breach of statutory duty'. Thus the full range of remedies are available, including injunctions. As discussed above, damages in respect of an unlawful act may include compensation for injury to feelings whether or not they include compensation under any other head.[171] An act of discrimination or harassment which would have been unlawful includes, in the case of a relationship which has come to an end before the coming into force of these regulations, reference to an act of discrimination or harassment which would, after the coming into force of these regulations, have been unlawful.[172]

---

170   And so is unlawful under reg 24.
171   Reg 39(4).
172   Reg 39(5).

Discrimination in education

Key points
- Most educational establishments, except schools, are covered by the Age Regulations 2006.
- This includes universities, colleges of higher and further education and other similar institutions.
- In respect of applicants for courses and degrees, there is some limited provision to bring a claim, which can only be for discrimination in the 'terms' on which the applicant is offered admission, or by refusing the applicant admission.
- There is no provision made to combat discrimination in 'arrangements' for admission.
- In respect of students at establishments, they have a right not to be discriminated against in the provision of, access to and against the refusal of benefits.
- Students have a right not to be discriminated against by excluding them, or by subjecting them to other detriments on grounds of their age.
- Harassment against students or prospective students who have applied for admission is unlawful.
- This section may affect younger students as much as older individuals.
- Vocational training providers are also covered by the regulations, insofar as they are not employers providing training to their employees.

Educational establishments

13.1   Universities, institutions and colleges of higher and further education, and colleges of further education in Scotland all will now be affected by the Employment Equality (Age) Regulations 2006. Schools, however, are not covered.

13.2   The education provisions, set out chiefly in regulation 23, largely mirror those found in respect of equality within the education setting elsewhere, with one significant omission in respect of 'arrangements' for admission.

13.3   It is unlawful for the governing bodies of relevant educational establishments to discriminate against a person:[1]

a) in the terms on which it offers to admit the person to the establishment as a student;

1 Reg 23(1).

b) by refusing or deliberately not accepting an application for the person's admission to the establishment as a student; or

c) where the person is a student of the establishment:

   i) in the way it affords the person access to any benefits;

   ii) by refusing or deliberately not affording the person access to them; or

   iii) by excluding the person from the establishment or subjecting him or her to any other detriment.

13.4   When considering education provisions, it is always useful to have recourse to commensurate provisions under employment law, where the law is more broadly developed.

13.5   It is significant that there is *no provision for anti-discrimination in respect of the 'arrangements'* the institution makes in order to decide to whom a place is awarded. On its face, this would permit discrimination in respect of discriminatory policies regarding prospective applicants, application forms, arrangements for interview, including times of interviews, medical testing etc. This leaves exposed a considerable lacuna.

EXAMPLE: A university has a policy not to grant any places to students under the age of 18 and over the age of 25. On its face, this would be a discriminatory policy on grounds of age, but there is no clear provision to prevent this.

EXAMPLE: An 'arrangement' might include the time and location of an interview. A 15-year-old applying for a place at a further education institute may not have access to a car, since he would not be able to drive himself, and if the location and time of the interview are remote and either early or late, this may affect his ability to be interviewed.

EXAMPLE: Application forms properly would be considered under 'arrangements'. If the date of birth of a candidate is required on the form, the answer may negatively influence people assessing whether to shortlist candidates. For example, a 50-year-old man applying for a place on a college course, competing with 16–18-year-olds may be disadvantaged by prejudices about his age.

13.6   Since these concerns about arrangements have informed the final draft of the employment provisions, as well as in relation to vocational training providers, it is surprising that they have not been mirrored in respect of education. Although there is no provision made in either of the sex or race discrimination legislation for 'arrangements' in respect of both schools and post-16 educational establishments, the disability framework does govern arrangements for admissions. Advisers should be aware of the overlap if the lacuna in age can be overcome by use of the alternative equality provisions.

13.7   Further, it may be necessary to argue a broad interpretation of regulation 23(1)(b) where it is made unlawful for a governing body of an educational establishment to discriminate on grounds of age by refusing or deliberately not accepting an application for admissions. In the example given above of a discriminatory policy in respect of the ages of students who are allowed to apply for admission, it could be argued that the deliberate refusal of admission would cover those students adversely impacted by the rule. It would not, however, be easily arguable, within the framework as set out in regulation 23, that the policy itself was discriminatory.

13.8   The provisions relating to discrimination towards students of the establishments are familiar from the similar provisions under regulation 7 (employment).

13.9   An example of where there may be discrimination in relation to access to benefits is that people under a certain age may not be able to go on educational trips abroad. Of course, there may be legitimate reasons enabling the establishment to properly justify their decision or action so that there would be no unlawful discrimination.

13.10   Exclusion is not defined but it is assumed it will be given the broad meaning found under the education and other discrimination provisions generally. In *Anyanwu and another v South Bank Students' Union and South Bank University*,[2] the two claimants were students of black African origin at South Bank University. They were elected as full-time salaried officers of the student union. Following investigations of serious misconduct against them, they were expelled from the university. This led to them being barred from the student union building and the student union treated their employment as being at an end. They brought proceedings for leave to apply for judicial review of their expulsion from the university and claims for race discrimination before the employment tribunal. They claimed that the students union

2   [2001] IRLR 305, HL.

discriminated against them by dismissing them, and the university knowingly aided this unlawful act within the meaning of Race Relations Act 1976 s33(1). The case was appealed up to the House of Lords, where the appeal turned on the correct interpretation and application of section 33(1). However, the interest of this case for the purposes of this chapter lies in the breadth of the facts. The students considered both their dismissal and their treatment by the student union to be discriminatory. Under the age discrimination regulations, such a claim could be brought under the employment provisions of regulation 7 as well as the education provisions under regulation 23.

13.11   'Subjection to any other detriment' should be understood broadly as a catch-all provision, which applies only to students of the establishment, not applicants or prospective students. See the comments made in chapter 8 about the breadth of this subsection, under the commensurate provisions in employment law.

13.12   There is a specific defence for establishments if the training would only fit a person for employment which, by virtue of the provisions made for genuine occupational requirement, the employer could lawfully refuse to offer the person seeking training.[3] It is difficult to imagine where such a situation may arise, although potentially, there may be issues relating to genuine health and safety requirements or age limits.

13.13   The difficulty can be exemplified in this way: If an acting academy refused to train a teenager to play older roles on the grounds that the teenager would never be selected (which may be the type of situation which this exception was intended to cover), it would still always be difficult to justify. As has been said in respect of the employment provisions, in an age where excellent make-up and techniques exist to alter the form, face and voice of actors, it would not be a given that youngsters could not play roles of older characters, and vice versa.

13.14   Possible situations where the defence could be pleaded would include professions which may exclude individuals over a certain age, due to fitness and health, such as active fire-fighters or pilots

13.15   It is unlawful for the governing body of the establishment to harass a student at the establishment, or to harass someone who has applied for admission to the establishment.[4] For a full discussion on what would constitute harassment, chapter 4 should be referred to in greater detail.

3 Reg 23(3).
4 Reg 23(2).

Relationships which have come to an end

13.16   By virtue of regulation 4, educational establishments can be affected even subsequent to the degree or college course, where it subjects a former student to a detriment, or subjects him to harassment. The most common example would be in respect of a failure to provide a reference, where such non-provision was on grounds of age, or to provide a discriminatory reference on grounds of age.

> EXAMPLE: Tim, who is 20, asks his former university tutor to give a reference to a prospective employer. The tutor agrees and writes 'Given his young age, he is reasonably mature'. Or Sanjay, aged 52, who was an adult learner at college, is given a post-studies reference that states 'given that he has been around the block a few times, he cottoned on reasonably quickly'.

Vocational training providers

13.17   Vocational training, and the providers of such training, falls within the scope of the regulations, within regulation 20. The scope of regulation 20 is set out in chapter 3. Training providers will not be able to set age limits for entry to training or training courses, unless they can show that there is a real need to apply such limits.

13.18   A 'training provider' is defined loosely as 'any person who provides, or makes arrangements for the provision of training'.[5] However, it does not include training provided by employers for persons he employs,[6] the governing bodies of institutions of further and higher education[7] or a proprietor of schools in relation to any registered pupil.[8] Training providers could include:[9]

- employers (but not for persons he employs);
- private, public or voluntary sector training bodies; and
- adult education programmes.

---

5   Reg 20(4)(e).
6   Reg 20(4).
7   Reg 20(4), and see further the cross-reference to reg 23.
8   Reg 20(4).
9   Taken from DTI Age Legislation Fact Sheet No 4.

13.19   'Training' means:[10]

a) all types and all levels of training which would help fit a person for any employment;
b) vocational guidance;
c) facilities for training;
d) practical work experience provided by an employer to a person whom he or she does not employ; and
e) any assessment related to the award of any professional or trade qualification.

13.20   The definition of 'training' has been left broad, and in theory could cover all manner of schemes. Certainly obvious training, such as nursing, teaching and crafts apprenticeships would be covered. It might cover even more distant forms of training such as driving, since it would be arguable that driving skills would assist a person in later employment.

13.21   'Vocational guidance' is likely to cover advice given by local initiative schemes, school leaver schemes, careers officers etc.

13.22   Regulation 20 ensures that access to training is not hampered on grounds of age by the inclusion of facilities for training. Providers would need to be aware of choice of location – can the young as well as the more elderly access such facilities? Facilities at the venue which may be affected by age-related concerns have to be considered.

13.23   It is unlawful for a training provider to discriminate against any person seeking or undergoing training:[11]

a) in the arrangements the provider makes for the purpose of determining to whom he or she should offer training;
b) in the terms on which the training provider affords the person access to any training;
c) by refusing or deliberately not affording the person such access;
d) by terminating the person's training; or
e) by subjecting the person to any other detriment during his or her training.

> EXAMPLE: A 16-year-old girl applies for a vocational training course to improve her skill set in order to obtain employment. She is refused entry because she is too young. This would be unlawful unless it could be objectively justified.

10   Reg 20(4).
11   Reg 20(1).

> EXAMPLE: A solicitor's firm offers practical work experience.
> Jonathan, who is 38, is turned down on grounds that he is 'too
> mature' to undertake that experience.

13.24   There is an exception made if the training would only fit a person for
employment which, by virtue of the provisions made for genuine occupational requirement, the employer could lawfully refuse to offer the
person seeking training. As for the commensurate provision in regulation 23 for educational establishments, it is difficult to imagine where
or how often such a situation may arise.

13.25   Harassment by the training provider in relation to a person seeking
or undergoing training is also unlawful.[12]

Education funding

13.26   One of the key controversies with respect to education is whether
the regulations extend to the funding of education. During the consultation process the Government had suggested that student maintenance would be outside the scope of the regulations but it gave no
indication that the funding of tuition would be excluded. This is of
more than theoretical interest because a number of adult education
funding entitlements have age limits. Further Education is generally
free up to the age of 19, while fees are charged in most cases for older
adults. However apprenticeships are free up to the age of 25 and in 2006
the Department for Education and Skills proposed that this age cut-off
should also apply to free entitlement to A Level equivalent qualifications.
It had been assumed that these policies would need to be objectively justified.

13.27   Before the regulations came into force the Department for Education and Skills published guidance which asserted that funding for
tuition was not however within the scope of the Directive:[13]

> **What about funding? Isn't that access?**
>
> Article 3.3 of the Directive clearly states that the Directive does not
> apply to payments of any kind made by state schemes. The power
> to make provision for support for students is set out in s22 of the

---

12 Reg 20(2).
13 Age and Vocational Training, A guide for providers of vocational training, 2006:
www.dti.gov.uk.

Teaching and Higher Education Act 1998. The grants and loans for tuition fees and maintenance paid to students under the Education (Student Support) Regulations 2006 (which are made under section 22) are from public funds. Student support in the UK is therefore a 'state scheme'. As such funding falls outside scope of the Directive it is not covered by the age regulations.

Maintenance loans for students affect maintenance during study, not admission to a course of study. They are not related to access and fall outside the scope of the Directive.

Bursaries and scholarships are also not covered, because they are incentives, as opposed to relating directly to access.

What about learning programmes supported by Government funding that has age limits?

Age limits set in relation to Government funding are outside the scope of the Directive, as explained above. However, any decision to deny access to a training course to people outside that age group would need to be objectively justified by the training provider.

What does this mean for a training provider?

What this means is illustrated by the following two examples:

Training Provider X run an IT course which receives Government funding for participants under 25. The training provider only admits people within this age limit and refuses places to anybody 26 or over on grounds of their age. This would have to be objectively justified.

Training Provider Y also run an IT course which receives Government funding for participants under 25, who are offered free/subsidised places. However, rather than denying access to people aged 26 or over they instead require them to pay for their own place on the course.

This would not need to be objectively justified.

For further information on objective justification, please refer to pages 30 and 31 of the Acas guidance.

13.28   It is highly controversial to suggest that a Government funding programme is outside the scope of the regulations on the basis of article 3.3, which refers to payments directly to individuals (social security and social protection). If this interpretation is upheld it would create a huge loophole in the regulations, by potentially exempting any Government-funded employment support, such as education, careers guidance and Jobcentre Plus programmes. It seems likely that this interpretation of the directive will be the subject of early litigation.

CHAPTER 14

Future developments in age equality legislation

14.69   Risk in financial services

When should people of the same age be treated alike? • Are price increases related to age proportionate to the increasing risk? • Should providers be allowed to exclude people from a product rather than simply increasing their prices to reflect extra risk?

14.80   Market segmentation

14.83   Age discrimination and human rights

Key points
- The Age Regulations 2006 look set to be the first of several pieces of legislation on age equality. This chapter looks at changes that can be expected over the next few years.
- Further legislation is likely to come from three sources:
  - a review of the 'default' mandatory retirement age scheduled for 2011;
  - further EU legislation;
  - developments in domestic equality legislation.
- The chapter looks at the key areas where change is possible:
  - a new framework for equality law and tighter age employment legislation;
  - age discrimination legislation on goods and services;
  - age discrimination legislation on volunteering;
  - an age equality duty in the public sector.

The 2011 review of the default retirement age

14.1   When the government announced in December 2004 that the age regulations would include a default mandatory retirement, it committed to reviewing the policy in 2011. The decision to hold a review was preferred over an alternative proposal, circulating within Whitehall, to automatically repeal the default retirement provisions in 2011 (a 'sunset' clause).[1] The outcome of the review should not therefore be viewed as a foregone conclusion. Although several ministers have indicated that they would prefer retirement ages to end, determined business lobbying could once again lead to mandatory retirement being retained. Furthermore, by 2011 there could be a change of government and the Conservative opposition has not taken an official position on the retirement issue.

14.2   Any change in the law resulting from a 2011 review would take time, as several months would be needed to conduct the review itself, and further time would then be required to amend the legislation. It is also likely that there would be an implementation period to give employers the chance to prepare.

14.3   The *Coming of age* consultation set out in some detail the basis on which the review would be conducted:

---

1   Sunday Times, 28 November 2004.

Extract from *Coming of age – monitoring and review*
[Until 2011] we will collect relevant information from a number of sources to ensure that our decision is based on evidence ...

This section summarises how we will take the decision, and what we will do in the period leading up to the decision. More details, particularly on the information sources that we will use as the basis for our decision, are available in the Regulatory Impact Assessment...

What will the review consider?
The default retirement age is necessary because many businesses need it for reasons of workforce planning, and because not having a default retirement age could have adverse effects on pensions and other employment benefits.

In 2011, our decision on whether to keep or abolish the default retirement age will focus mainly on two factors:

• whether, in the light of the evidence, the default retirement age remains appropriate and necessary to facilitate workforce planning and to avoid adverse effects on pensions and other employment benefits; and
• the influence of any other social policy objectives.

What information will we collect to help us make the decision?
We will look at the evidence on longevity, and employment patterns of older workers in particular. Changes to longevity are important because they might be expected to have implications for the labour market. With rising longevity more individuals might be expected to seek to work for longer; to help support longer retirements; and, with older people a growing proportion of the overall population employers might be expected to look to them as an increasingly important labour supply. Through such channels, changes to longevity could indirectly bear on the costs and benefits of maintaining a fixed retirement age. Other areas to be examined will include:

• information relevant to workforce planning: such as evolution of employers' use of age in workforce planning – both in businesses that have retirement ages and in the growing number of those that do not;

- information relevant to pensions: such as trends in life expectancy, individual savings patterns and financial planning, and any changes to occupational pensions (what the changes are, why they have occurred, and any conclusions we can draw about the effect on pensions of removing the default retirement age);
- information relevant to other employment benefits: such as any changes to employment benefits (what the changes are, why they have occurred, and any conclusions we can draw about the effect on employment benefits of removing the default retirement age); and
- other relevant information: such as changes in people's expectations of retirement ages, changes by employers to their retirement ages (and the reasons for doing so), changes in participation rates in the labour market of those over 65 compared with other age groups (and the effect of the new duty to consider on this), changes in the numbers of requests to work beyond normal retirement age as well as in the percentages of accepted requests, and changes in patterns of work for older workers (including part-time work and other forms of flexible working).

We will use both independent information sources and informal discussions with our main stakeholders to monitor the developments in these areas between now and 2011.

Independent sources of information

This will involve the use of surveys (both surveys that use statistical information and surveys that use case studies) and official databases.

Some examples of the surveys we will use are the Labour Force Survey (LFS), the survey of Factors Affecting the Labour Market Participation of Older Workers (FALMPOW), the DTI/ DWP Survey of Employment Practices and the Employers' Pension Provision Survey (EPPS).

More detail on the complete list of surveys, the information we expect to get from them and the methods for interpreting the information is in the Regulatory Impact Assessment (see chapter 10).

> *Informal contacts with stakeholders*
> The main organisations with an interest in the Age Regulations are representatives of employers, employees and age equality organisations.
>
> These include Age Concern, British Chambers of Commerce, the Confederation of British Industry, the Chartered Institute of Personnel and Development, the Chartered Management Institute, Employers Forum on Age, the Federation of Small Businesses, Help the Aged, Third Age Employment Network and Trades Union Congress.
>
> We have developed our policy on age discrimination (including retirement ages) following extensive consultation with these stakeholders. We will continue to stay in close contact with them during the period leading up to the formal review. Their views will help us gauge the extent to which we are achieving the desired cultural change, which will influence the decision. In addition, stakeholders may be able to give anecdotal feedback on the impact of the legislation "in the real world". They may also be able to provide us with additional data from any surveys or monitoring activities that they carry out.

14.4   By 2011 it is probable that the age regulations will already have been replaced by primary legislation in the shape of a single Equality Act (see below). It would be possible for that bill to include a provision to repeal the default retirement provisions through secondary legislation. If this course is not followed the government would have to wait for suitable primary legislation, following the outcome of the review, in order to overturn the retirement provisions.

EU legislation

14.5   In the short term, further EU age equality legislation is a fairly remote prospect. However over the next decade there is a reasonable chance of further age equality law as part of wider moves to tackle discrimination.

14.6   Future EU legislation could either introduce further protection with respect to employment or broaden the scope of protection. The European Commission is responsible for monitoring the implementation of the article 13 directives and may if necessary develop proposals to 'revise and update' them.[2] Over time the Commission is expected to monitor the impact of article 6 and related Court of Justice case-law. If article 6 leads to widespread exemptions from the principle of equal treatment, so that there is clear evidence that the Framework Directive is not offering effective protection from age discrimination, the Commission will come under increasing pressure to introduce proposals for tougher law. However, it is likely to be many years from the directive's implementation date of December 2006 before the Commission feels it has the evidence to justify additional employment legislation.

14.7   Article 13 also gives the union power to legislate on age equality in areas beyond employment.[3] Unlike the framework directive, the 2000 race directive covered all issues where the union had competence including the supply of goods, facilities and services. Since then an article 13 gender directive covering discrimination in goods and services was approved in 2004. The gender directive was passed because EU actors and member states believed that similar protection should exist for gender and race equality. To date the same commitment has not been extended to other grounds of equality, with the European Commission resisting pressure for a similar directive with respect to disability.

14.8   As for age equality, the Commission seems un-persuaded by the case for further legislation at present. In the 2004 green paper[4] it emphasised the challenges of effectively implementing the existing directives and the important role of non-legislative action. The green paper said:

> Interest groups and experts are actively lobbying for a number of additional initiatives. These include, for example, action to tackle age discrimination in the provision of goods and services, to broaden the level of protection with regard to sexual orientation, or to address the specific needs of certain minorities, such as the Roma.

> While acknowledging these demands for further action, the Commission is conscious of the need to ensure effective implementation of the current legal framework. It is also important to note that legislation is not the only tool available at European, national or regional level to address discrimination. In practice, support for non-discrimination requires full use to be made of a wide range of policy and funding instruments. Concerted action by the various stakeholders will also be crucial to the success of these efforts.

2 *Equality and non-discrimination in an enlarged European Union: green paper,* European Commission, 2004.

3 EC Treaty, Article 13.

4 *Equality and non-discrimination in an enlarged European Union: green paper,* European Commission, 2004.

14.9   In summer 2005 the Commission published a strategy *Non-discrimination and Equal Opportunities for All* which confirmed this position but announced a scoping study in advance of possible future legislation:

Extract from *Non-discrimination and equal opportunities for all – a framework strategy*, May 2005
Some respondents highlighted the need for additional measures to complement the current legal framework, including the possibility of further EC legislation based on Article 13 of the EC Treaty. Others felt that this was premature and underlined the need to take into account the principle of subsidiarity, as well as weighing up the potential economic costs and benefits of further legislative action.

The Commission acknowledges the demands from certain stakeholders to take action to address the differences in the level and scope of protection against discrimination on different grounds. Given the need for additional efforts to ensure the proper functioning of the existing legal framework, as well as the economic and political concerns highlighted in some responses to the Green Paper consultation, the Commission is not proposing to come forward at this stage with further legislative proposals based on Article 13 of the Treaty.

However, the Commission will undertake an in-depth study into the relevance and feasibility of possible new measures to complement the current legal framework. This study will examine national provisions, which go beyond the requirements of the EC Directives, in Member States and in some third countries. It will consider the relative merits of legislative and non-legislative measures. It will also produce a synthesis of cost/benefit analyses of different policy options carried out at the national level. The results of the study will be made available in autumn 2006. On the basis of this material, the Commission will assess the feasibility of possible new initiatives to complement the current legal framework.

14.10   Despite the Commission's caution, older people's NGOs from across Europe have been campaigning for legislative action on goods and services. The discrimination expert group of AGE, the European Platform for Older People commissioned Robin Allen QC to draft a proposal for a directive to stimulate discussion.[5] The 'directive' was launched at a meeting of MEPs in Autumn 2006 with the backing of ten NGOs from across the union.

14.11   If the Commission reports favourably on the case for a goods and services directive, and NGOs lobby member states effectively, it is possible that a directive could become law over a three- to five-year period. However, with article 13 directives requiring unanimity, and with little political interest in age discrimination in goods and services, campaigners face a significant uphill struggle to secure backing for a new law.

The Discrimination Law Review and the single equality Act

14.12   In the UK the extension of age equality law is likely to come via domestic channels before the slow-moving EU processes deliver change. The introduction of the article 13 directives and the Race Relations (Amendment) Act 2000 led to a phase of rapid, incremental law making on equality issues. These developments have led to a period of consolidation and review, with a promised single equality bill in the lifetime of the 2005 Parliament.

14.13   For several years experts in discrimination law have been calling for a single equality bill that would consolidate the mass of equality legislation that had built up over a thirty-year period. The non-governmental organisation (NGO) Justice believes there are 39 Acts, 80 Statutory Instruments, 15 Codes of Practice, 6 Codes of Guidance and 16 EC Directives and Recommendations with relevance to equality law.[6] The most influential contribution to the calls for a single equality Act was the Independent Review of the Enforcement of Anti-Discrimination Legislation, led by Sir Bob Hepple QC. It recommended a single equality Act in its 2000 report *Equality: a new framework.*[7] In 2000 Lord Lester introduced a private member's bill which aimed to implement many of the review's proposals.

5   *Proposed European Directive addressing age discrimination in goods, facilities and services*, Age Concern England, DaneAge, LBL, Kuratorium Deutsche Altershilfe, 2006.

6   www.justice.org.uk.

7   B Hepple, M Coussey, T Choudhury, *Equality: a new framework*, Hart, 2000.

14.14   Pressure for consolidating legislation grew further with new legislative developments between 2000 and late 2004:

- the introduction of employment discrimination law covering sexual orientation and religion or belief (with consultation continuing on the age regulations);
- amendments to existing race and disability law to bring it into line with the directives;
- a decision to establish the Commission for Equality and Human Rights (CEHR), driven mainly by the widening of equality law to cover all the grounds listed in article 13;
- the extension of the public sector duty to promote race equality to cover disability and a firm commitment to introduce a similar duty for gender;
- a commitment to outlaw discrimination in goods and services on grounds of religion or belief.

14.15   The complexity of all this new legislation led to pressure for harmonisation and simplification. Meanwhile several of the interest groups who were hostile or sceptical with respect to the CEHR argued that it should not begin work until there was coherent equality legislation for it to police.[8]

14.16   Other campaigners were less interested in a single act than in securing specific legislative changes on issues affecting their community. Lobbies for particular equality interests pointed to the example of recent progress in one field or another to make the case for further legislation on their own issues. Legislative improvements for one equality 'strand' therefore had the effect of 'ratcheting up' expectations in other areas. One result of this was that the 2005 Equality Bill which had originally been intended only to establish the CEHR, included an assortment of substantive equality law: a public sector gender equality duty; goods and services discrimination law with respect to religion or belief and (following late amendments) sexual orientation. But there were still calls for new law, for example from campaigners for older people and representatives of the trans-gender community. The proposal for a single equality Act was seen as a mechanism for achieving a settlement that would satisfy those interest groups who felt they had been 'left behind'.

14.17   The Labour government was relatively amenable to pressure for a single Equality Bill. This was for a range of reasons including the personal commitment of ministers and officials holding relevant posts;

8   for example the 1990 Trust, *A Vision of Equality*, 2003.

the need to offer lobby groups gains in order to secure their support for the establishment of the CEHR; and the proximity of a General Election which inevitably led to politicians reviewing what they had to offer to different sections of the community. The promise of a future single equality bill was also a way of appeasing campaigners who were unable to secure immediate legal reform, such as older people's organisations.

14.18 The government gradually committed to a single equality act in the lead-up to the 2005 General Election. In November 2004 the government responded to the white paper consultation on the CEHR and fell just short of a commitment to review existing legislation:

> Many stakeholders expressed concerns about imbalances in the current legislative provision for the different equality areas in their responses to the consultation on the CEHR. The Government have long recognised these concerns. We are beginning to consider the best mechanisms for reviewing the current discrimination legislation framework, as part of its continuing work in reviewing barriers to equality, taking into account the interests of the many different stakeholders who would be affected by any changes to the current position. The CEHR will clearly have an important role to play in this review and will separately be empowered to recommend changes to discrimination legislation as it sees fit.[9]

14.19 Then shortly before the General Election on 25 February 2005 ministers announced there would be two reviews that together were intended to lead towards a single equality Act.[10] The Equalities Review was to be carried out by an independent panel led by Trevor Phillips[11] and supported by a Cabinet Office secretariat. It had a remit to:

- investigate the social, economic, cultural and other factors that limit or deny people the opportunity to make the best of their abilities;
- provide an understanding of the long term and underlying causes of disadvantage that need to be addressed by public policy;
- make practical recommendations on key policy priorities for: the government and public sector; employers and trade unions; civic society and the voluntary sector; and
- inform both the modernisation of equality legislation, towards a Single Equality Act; and the development of the new CEHR.

---

9 Lords Hansard, 18 November 2004: Column WS76.
10 'Review of causes of discrimination announced', press release, 25 February 2005, Department of Trade and Industry and Cabinet Office.
11 Chair of the Commission for Racial Equality, and since appointed Chair designate of the Commission for Equality and Human Rights. He is leading the review in a personal capacity.

14.20   The second review, the Discrimination Law Review was an in-house Whitehall project, working in parallel to, and informed by, the Equalities Review. It was to be led by the Department of Trade and Industry and involve all the government departments with an interest in equality issues. Its aim was to work on the 'development of a simpler, fairer legal framework and assess how anti-discrimination legislation could be modernised to fit the needs of Britain in the 21st Century'.[12]

14.21   The 2005 Labour Party manifesto formalised the ministerial commitment to move towards a single equality act in the lifetime of the 2005 parliament:

> In the next Parliament we will establish a Commission on Equality and Human Rights to promote equality for all and, tackle discrimination, and introduce a Single Equality Act to modernise and simplify equality legislation.[13]

Terms of reference of the Discrimination Law Review

The Discrimination Law Review (DLR) will address long-held concerns about inconsistencies in the current anti-discrimination legislative framework. The Review is considering the fundamental principles of discrimination legislation and its underlying concepts. The Discrimination Law Review will consider the opportunities for creating a clearer and more streamlined equality legislation framework, which produces better outcomes for those who experience disadvantage.

This work will begin alongside the independent Equalities Review, which will carry out an investigation into the causes of persistent discrimination and inequality in British society. The Discrimination Law Review will consider the recommendations of the Equalities Review, which will report to the Prime Minister in early 2007.

Key areas of this work will include:

- a consideration of the fundamental principles of discrimination legislation and its underlying concepts and a comparative analysis of the different models for discrimination legislation;
- an investigation of different approaches to enforcing discrimination law so that a spectrum of enforcement options can be considered;

---

12   www.womenandequalityunit.gov.uk/dlr/
13   *Britain forward not back*, The Labour Party, 2005.

- an understanding of the evidence of the practical impact of legislation – both within the UK and abroad – in tackling inequality and promoting equality of opportunity;
- an investigation of new models for encouraging and incentivising compliance;
- consideration of the opportunities for creating a simpler, fairer and more streamlined legislative framework in a Single Equality Act. Any proposals will have due regard to better regulation principles and take into account the need to minimise bureaucratic burdens on business and public services. A key priority will be seeking to achieve greater consistency in the protection afforded to different groups while taking into account evidence that different legal approaches may be appropriate for different groups.

The Discrimination Law Review will be grounded in a comprehensive analysis of the efficacy of Great Britain's current equality enactments and the requirements of European equality legislation. The Review will not consider changes to the substantive rights contained in the Human Rights Act (HRA) but will take account of views expressed on interactions between the HRA and the equality enactments.

Building on the model developed for the work to establish the Commission for Equality and Human Rights, the Discrimination Law Review will be led by the Women & Equality Unit in DTI with the close involvement of Ministers and officials in key Departments including the Department for Work & Pensions, the Home Office and the Department for Constitutional Affairs and in the Devolved Administrations.

The Discrimination Law Review Team will regularly update and consult the Equalities Review Panel and the expert Reference Group, co-chaired by the Chairs of the Disability Rights Commission and the Equal Opportunities Commission, as its work progresses. The Team will also engage more widely with key interests, including equality stakeholders, employers, business and trade unions. It will report to the Minister for Women & Equality with close engagement by Ministers across Whitehall, and at official level between the Secretariat to the Equalities Review and the Discrimination Law Review Team.

> This will ensure that a full range of views on the reform of the current framework is reflected in any proposals that are brought forward.
>
> The Review will begin immediately. Its anticipated product is a series of proposals for a coherent, modern, outcome-focused framework for this area of the law with a view to bringing forward a Single Equality Bill.
>
> The Government remains committed to establishing the new Commission for Equality and Human Rights on the current timetable, with the new body becoming operational in 2007.

14.22   In setting up the DLR and promising a single equality Act, ministers were careful not to commit to further age equality legislation. At the same time, the government published a strategy for an ageing society and the Labour Party produced a mini-manifesto for older people. A short section on discrimination in insurance promised a review but no legislation:

> Some individuals and organisations feel that there is a problem with discrimination in pricing of and access to general insurance for older people. However, insurance companies use a variety of sources of information to assess risk, and, in many cases, premiums will vary according to actuarial data. The Government will consider with the industry whether there are cases where the criticisms made in relation to discrimination are justified.[14]

14.23   Later in 2005 there was similar reticence to commit to age legislation during the Equality Bill's passage through parliament.

14.24   Despite this public caution, ministers made it clear that they were sympathetic to the case for further age legislation. There was recognition that the 'age lobby' was the only major group of equality campaigners who had not progressed their legislative goals since 2000. From the outset scoping the case for further age equality law was a major focus of the Discrimination Law Review's work.

14.25   Between summer 2005 and spring 2006, teams of officials developed options for legislation that would outlaw age discrimination in goods and services and also for the introduction of an integrated public sector equality duty covering six grounds of discrimination. The cautious tone but detailed engagement was made clear by Meg Munn MP, the Parliamentary Under-Secretary for Equality, in a speech on 27 April 2006:

---

14 *Opportunity Age: meeting the challenges of ageing in the 21st century*, Department for Work and Pensions, 2005.

A great deal of detailed work is being undertaken in the review. One of the issues we are considering very carefully is the issue of unfair age discrimination in the provision of goods, facilities and services ... Discrimination is a complex area. It's important therefore that we understand the issues properly before we make proposals. We do not want negative unintended consequences. We will also frame our proposals to strike the right balance between tackling harmful discrimination, and retaining the ability of both the public and private sectors to differentiate on age where this is appropriate ... To conclude, we are considering very carefully the issue of age discrimination in goods, facilities and services. We want to bring forward proposals that are workable, that tackle unfair discrimination whilst retaining age differentials where this is appropriate.[15]

14.26   The original expectation was that the Equalities Review would report to the Prime Minister in summer 2006 and, at the same time, the DLR would launch a green paper consultation to inform the drafting of an equality bill. The timing of both reviews slipped considerably. Neither project was up and running until summer 2005 and the Equalities Review did not publish even an interim report until March 2006. At the time of writing its final report was expected in early 2007. However further uncertainty arose when Trevor Phillips was appointed chair designate of the CEHR, since the work of the review and the 'shadow' commission was now likely to overlap.

14.27   Initially the DLR made faster progress than the Equalities Review and by late spring 2006 was ready to launch a green paper. However, at this point there was a cabinet reshuffle and a reorganisation of the machinery of government (DCLG). Lead responsibility for equality and race relations transferred to the newly created Department for Communities and Local Government. The change of department and a new secretary of state – Ruth Kelly – led to progress on the review being slowed. Ministers asked officials to develop fresh proposals for the green paper that would take account of the new department's emerging strategy for tackling inequality. The DLR was 're-coupled' to the Equalities Review (which also transferred to the DCLG), with Ruth Kelly's announcement of 12 July that 'the thinking on the discrimination law review will be developed in the context of the equalities review'.[16] At the time of writing the green paper was expected in early 2007. For there to be a reasonable chance of the government fulfilling its manifesto commitment to pass a single equality act during the lifetime of the Parliament rapid

15 Speech by Meg Munn MP at the Opportunity Age at Work Conference, 27 July 2005.
16 Uncorrected oral evidence, 12 July 2006, House of Commons communities and local government select committee, session 2005/06.

progress is needed. A complicated piece of law is unlikely to pass during the fourth session of the parliament (between November 2008 and a General Election that is likely to take place in the first half of 2009). This means that the government's bill will need to be ready for publication in time for the parliament's third Queen's Speech in November 2007. A period of nine months from the launch of a green paper to the publication of a bill is an achievable but tight timescale. Any further slippage could jeopardise the chance of an Equality Act.

A new framework for equality law and enhanced employment protection?

14.28   A single equality Act can be expected to lead to the harmonisation and simplification of equality law across all strands, including age. One of the review's main activities has been 'exploring the scope for harmonisation/alignment of the current law'.[17] This is likely to lead to new common definitions on concepts such as direct discrimination, indirect discrimination and genuine occupational requirement. However, while there will almost certainly be some changes to the 2006 regulations, these are likely to be modest. In particular, there are unlikely to be changes to the 'age specific' elements of the regulations, such as the objective justification of direct discrimination, or to the numerous exemptions, including the default retirement age. There are several reasons for believing that changes to the regulations will be modest:

- Although the DLR was tasked to look at 'the fundamental principles of discrimination legislation' there appears to be little appetite within government for change to the basic framework of the law. For example there has been little enthusiasm for options such as extending the concept of 'reasonable adjustment' beyond disability[18]; reshaping equality law to ground it in human rights principles such as dignity; or introducing private sector duties to promote equality.
- The age regulations are the most up to date examples of British equality law. They have been designed to comply with recent EU law and are intended to be consistent with legislation on other strands wherever possible (eg the 2003 sexual orientation and religion or belief regulations). Changes in definitions are likely to lead to other legislation falling into line with the age regulations rather than vice versa.

17   www.womenandequalityunit.gov.uk/dlr/
18   An approach which has worked well in Canada.

- The DLR is working to an 'unwritten' rule that decisions made during the development of the 2003 and 2006 employment equality regulations will not be overturned. This means the bill the government presents to parliament is unlikely to narrow the scope for direct discrimination or remove the default retirement age exemption. This is partly a pragmatic decision to prevent contentious decisions being re-opened. Another explanation is that by 2007 there will be little experience of how the new law is working and no definitive case-law.

14.29   This official reticence means that any scope for enhancing employment protection is likely to arise during the passage of a bill through Parliament. For example, it is possible that parliamentarians might support the immediate repeal of the default retirement age provisions, notwithstanding the planned 2011 review.

Discrimination against volunteers

14.30   Age discrimination is fairly widespread in organisations working with volunteers. In the late 1990s one-fifth of volunteering organisations admitted using upper age limits.[19] Organisations have said consistently that the main reason they discriminate is because of concerns regarding insurance (although the insurance industry says that insurance products should not restrict organisations' use of older volunteers).

14.31   Since the 1990s there have been voluntary initiatives to improve age diversity in volunteering, including the launch in 2004 of a campaign and code of practice. The code's requirements included removing arbitrary upper age limits, objective selection criteria based on the volunteering tasks, and a commitment to seek out insurance that would not require organisations to discriminate. The code was signed by 240 organisations, however stories of age discrimination continued, and as with many campaigns momentum flagged after the launch. In 2006 the campaign was re-launched by Volunteering England and Volunteering in the Third Age, a government-funded initiative.[20]

14.32   In recent years the policies of volunteering organisations appear to have improved, no doubt in response to these campaigns as well as growing awareness of the forthcoming employment regulations. However changes in policy have not always been reflected in practice. Age

19   National Centre for Volunteering, *Issues in Volunteering Management: a report of a survey*, 1998.
20   www.volunteering.org.uk/campaignsandpolicies/agediscrimination

Concern carried out an internet survey in 2005, which received 234 responses from large and small organisations. This revealed that only 5% of organisations today have a formal 'retirement' date for volunteers, while 13% ask individuals to stop on grounds of age on a case-by-case basis. However this improvement in organisational policies was not reflected in the profile of volunteers in many organisations, with a quarter of respondents saying they had no volunteers over 70.

14.33   During the consultations on the implementation of the Framework Directive there was discussion about its application to unpaid workers. The directive's wide definition of employment and occupation led organisations like Age Concern to argue that unpaid workers would be covered in many instances.[21] The DTI, however, concluded that the regulations should only cover unpaid workers whose work formed part of a training course, or who were crown office holders.

14.34   It is possible that there will be litigation on whether the directive offers protection to other unpaid workers, owing to its wide definition of employment and occupation ('conditions for access to employment, to self-employment or to *occupation*' and 'access to all types and to all levels of vocational guidance/training ... including *practical work experience*'). It is certainly arguable that volunteering can in some instances be considered an occupation, a condition for accessing employment, or an example of practical work experience.

14.35   Although many organisations support the principle of discrimination protection for volunteers, there would be disquiet if this was achieved by blurring the distinction between volunteers and employees. This is because there is concern that volunteers could be vested with full employment rights, leading to major financial costs and potentially to a restriction on the use of volunteers. In recent years there have been a number of cases under the Disability Discrimination Act (DDA) 1995 where the claimants have argued that volunteers should be treated as employees for the purposes of the legislation. However, in 2004 the Employment Appeals Tribunal (EAT) gave clear guidance on the distinction between a volunteer and an employee.[22]

14.36   Campaigners that advocate discrimination protection for volunteers have been searching for a mechanism that makes a clear distinction between volunteers and employees. One promising avenue proposed at an Age Concern seminar in 2006 is to offer protection by defining volunteering as a 'facility' offered by an organisation, that

---

21   *Age Concern's response to Equality and Diversity: Age Matters*, Age Concern England, 2003.

22   *South East Sheffield Citizen's Advice Bureau v Grayson* [2004] IRLR 353.

would be covered by legislation outlawing discrimination in goods, facilities and services.[23]

14.37   There is scope to push for the outlawing of age discrimination in volunteering during the DLR process. In a speech on volunteering in later life, the minister for the third sector, Ed Milliband, did not rule out including volunteering in the scope of the legislation.[24] However, volunteering was not a major focus of discussions prior to the green paper, so it is likely that proponents of legislation in this area will need to mount a credible campaign if provisions are to be included in the eventual equality bill.

A duty to promote age equality[25]

14.38   Over the last decade there has been a major shift in the shape of equality legislation in the UK. The equality laws introduced in the 1970s (and subsequent legislation modelled on these statutes, including the 2006 age regulations) focused on outlawing specific acts of discrimination, where unequal treatment could be proved in the courts. The experiences of organisations who have sought to combat discrimination have shown however that a wider range of approaches are needed. Giving individuals rights in law to challenge discrimination they face cannot in itself achieve a society in which people are free from prejudice and from the barriers people and institutions put in their way.

14.39   As a result, in recent years anti-discrimination laws have been supplemented by a new approach that requires organisations to take proactive steps to deliver equality of opportunity and root-out disadvantage. This has been implemented through a new generation of statutory 'equality duties' for public bodies. These were first applied to race equality and to the equality provisions of the new devolved institutions. Legislation has now been passed to extend the duties to disability (from December 2006) and gender (from April 2007).[26] So, as the CEHR begins work there will be a three-strand framework for public sector equality duties. Age equality issues risk being marginalised as the energies of public services, regulators and the CEHR are likely to focus

23 *Tackling Age Discrimination Beyond the Workplace*, Age Concern Seminar Series, Age Concern England, 2006.
24 speech by Ed Milliband MP at the Older Volunteers: Opportunity of a Lifetime conference, 6 June 2006.
25 For more detail on proposals for an age equality duty see A Harrop and E Saltmarshe, *An Age Equality Duty*, Age Concern England, 2004.
26 Disability Discrimination Act 2005; Equality Act 2006.

on achieving equality in the areas where legal obligations exist. There could be precious little room for voluntary initiatives on age equality.

> ### Equality duties in the UK
> Equality duties are legal obligations placed on organisations requiring them to consider equality of opportunity in all aspects of their work. There are now a number of examples of equality duties, with varying legal requirements, but sharing several key characteristics.
>
> *Public bodies* – all the existing duties apply to public bodies - or to providers of public services, including voluntary and private contractors (there is a separate debate about whether duties should be placed on private organisations, with regard to employment, following the model that has been in place for many years in Northern Ireland with respect to religion).
>
> *Employment, services and functions* – Equality duties generally apply to everything an organisation does. This includes employment, service delivery, procurement and public functions that are not services, such as planning control and law enforcement.
>
> *'Positive' Promotion of Equality of Opportunity* – Equality duties are intended to go beyond narrow requirements not to discriminate. They instead require bodies to actively promote equality of opportunity. This should entail taking positive steps to address disadvantage suffered by different groups and integrate consideration of equality into all areas of an organisation's work. The aim of securing equal outcomes should influence the basic assumptions on which organisations work and the development of policy at its earliest stage. Equality duties are sometimes called 'positive duties' to differentiate them from 'negative' duties barring illegal discrimination. The legal formula for these duties has been to require public bodies to have 'due regard' to equality in carrying out their functions. Some commentators have suggested this obligation is too weak as it does not necessarily mandate action. [EDF report]
>
> *Examples of equality duties*
> The **Race Equality Duty** was introduced by the Race Relations (Amendment) Act 2000, following the Stephen Lawrence inquiry. It replaced a more limited equality duty for local authorities intro-

duced by the Race Relations Act 1976. It is a duty placed on public bodies throughout Great Britain to have due regard for the need to 'eliminate racial discrimination' and to 'promote equality of opportunity and good relations between persons of different racial groups'. The duty includes specific requirements for public bodies to monitor employment outcomes and develop 'race equality schemes' itemising the steps they will take to address race equality.

The **Disability Equality Duty** was contained in the Disability Discrimination Act 2005 and comes into force in December 2006. The general duty is more detailed than the race duty and specifically refers to treating disabled people more favourably where necessary. The duty to promote good relations is replaced by responsibilities relating to public attitudes and participation by disabled people. The specific duties require that an equality scheme is published and implemented (as long as this is not unreasonable or impracticable), with authorities required to report on progress each year. Every three years certain Secretaries of State have a duty to report on disability equality in their area of responsibility.

The **Gender Equality Duty** was part of the Equality Act 2006 and comes into force in April 2007. The general duty has requirements relating to eliminating unlawful discrimination and harassment and promoting equality of opportunity between men and women. At the time of writing secondary legislation setting out the specific duties has not been brought into force. The Government has indicated that the legislation will be less prescriptive about the content of equality schemes than was the case for the race and disability duties. There will be a requirement to monitor progress and report annually but not a specific duty to implement a scheme. Authorities will also have a specific requirement to carry out gender impact assessments on significant new areas of policy and practice.

In **Northern Ireland, Wales** and **London** there are duties for devolved public bodies to promote equality of opportunity, including age equality. The duties vary considerably. The Northern Ireland duty mandates action in detail, while in London and Wales the only subsidiary requirement is to report annually.

> Recent legislation in **England** and **Scotland** has introduced
> equality duties for specific bodies, such as Scottish housing
> authorities and English Learning and Skills Councils. These
> duties are weak because there are no detailed specific duties
> to back up the general requirement, and inspectorates have not
> policed their implementation.

14.40   The intention behind equality duties is that they move the focus away from individual acts of discrimination to a comprehensive 'whole system' approach, with organisations expected to promote equality in everything they do. The aim is to 'design-in' equality from the outset of their policy-making and service planning and see that it is implemented at every level of operational practice. This is partly to ensure that equality can be advanced without the need for confrontational litigation, where often it is only the confident and articulate who are able to secure justice. But achieving equality of opportunity also goes beyond the elimination of discrimination, as legally defined. Discrimination is narrowly understood with reference to 'equal treatment', but equality of opportunity means much more. In its widest sense equal opportunity involves securing the equal participation in society of all, based on respect for the dignity of each individual.

14.41   There are strong arguments for promoting age equality through the introduction of a public sector duty. In its 2004 report, *An age equality duty,* Age Concern argued that a duty could help Britain adapt to an ageing population and longer life expectancies, by equipping public bodies to contribute to four challenges:

1. A culture of equality and respect must replace the ageism of today.
2. Public services must be re-shaped to meet the diverse needs and aspirations of older people, and of people of every age who need to prepare for a long and varied later life.
3. The labour market must change to accommodate older people who want and need to work for more years before choosing to retire.
4. People of all ages must feel at home, valued and secure in a diverse society.

14.42   Many of the concerns raised by the Stephen Lawrence inquiry regarding 'institutional racism' are just as applicable to age. For example, the outcomes organisations or systems achieve for people of different ages often vary unjustifiably, even where this is not the intention of the people providing services. In these instances, unequal treatment is often linked to people's unacknowledged attitudes or the ageist culture of an organisation. On top of this there are explicit examples of overt discrimination in policies and rules. While some of these should become unlawful through the implementation of the age regulations, or in future if goods and services legislation is introduced, others may be permitted through objective justification or exemptions. On the other hand an age equality duty could be used to require policy makers to assess and monitor age-related rules, and could over time lead to discriminatory practices being dispensed with. For example, under the age regulations there is nothing to stop public employers dismissing all employees on their 65th birthday; with an age duty these employers would be required to 'age-proof' this decision and would be expected to remove a mandatory retirement age if they could not find an adequate rationale for its continuation.

14.43   In its 2004 report Age Concern identified the following ways an age equality duty could have a positive impact on the lives of older people:

* **Involvement** – Older people will be asked for their views and involved in decisions affecting them.
* **Equal access** – Age-related barriers to services will be stripped away unless they can be justified with evidence and a clear rationale.
* **Responsive and personalised services** – Older people will not be seen as a single uniform group. Services would be tailored to meet their needs as individuals.
* **Accountability and improvement** – Monitoring outcomes against agreed targets will create transparency and drive improvement in services.
* **Opportunities to work** – Promoting age equality in employment, procurement and service delivery will break down barriers to the workplace.
* **Information and advocacy** – Delivering equality in access, quality and choice will require that improved information, advice and support is offered to older people.
* **An end to two-tier services** – Equality in service delivery and employment opportunities will not be affected by whether a service is delivered by public, voluntary or private agencies.

14.44   An additional argument in support of an age equality duty is that voluntary initiatives in the public sector to address age equality have had limited impact. The most important age equality initiative relating to public service delivery is the Department of Health's National Service Framework for Older People. It applies both to health services and social care. Standard One of the NSF states:

NHS services will be provided, regardless of age, on the basis of clinical need alone. Social care services will not use age in their eligibility criteria or policies, to restrict access to available services.[27]

14.45   In 2006 the Healthcare Commission, the Commission for Social Care Inspection and the Audit Commission reported on progress in delivering the National Service Framework (NSF).[28] The inspectorates concluded that the NSF has led to a reduction in explicit age discrimination, except with respect to mental health services. However, their report identified major challenges in the day-to-day treatment of older service users.

Age equality in health and social care – findings from *Living well in later life*

Progress has been made in tackling age discrimination through equal access to services depending on need. However, some examples of ageist practice or behaviour were still found in some services. In some acute hospitals, for example, older people were receiving poor treatment because of their age.

Although age discrimination audits had been carried out, this is only the first step in ensuring that older people can be confident that they will not be discriminated against because of their age. There was little evidence of staff receiving training to help them challenge ageist attitudes.

Many of the older people involved in this review had experienced ageist treatment, with some highlighting a negative change in attitude and availability of services following the transition from one service to another when they reached the age of 65.

Organisations had their own policies to promote equality and ensure fair access to services, but these were rarely brought together within a coordinated programme. Older people highlighted a number of cases where they had received an inferior service, or had been prevented from using a service, purely on the grounds of their age. For example, one leisure centre had barred older people from using its equipment because an older man had suffered a heart attack during an exercise session. In a day

---

27   National Service Framework for Older People, Department of Health, 2001.
28   *Living Well in Later Life: A review of progress against the national service framework for older people*, Healthcare Commission, 2006.

centre, which catered for people with physical disabilities and older people, there was preferential funding for the group with physical disabilities, resulting in the older people having fewer activities and a less varied programme.

Conclusions

Despite these changes there is still evidence of ageism among staff across all services. This ranges from patronising and thoughtless treatment from staff, to the failure of some mainstream public services, such as transport, to take the needs and aspirations of older people seriously. Many older people find it difficult to challenge ageist attitudes and their reluctance to complain can often mean that nothing changes.

We found that some older people experienced poor standards of care on general hospital wards, including poorly managed discharge from hospitals, repeated moves from one ward to another for non-clinical reasons, being cared for in mixed-sex bays or wards and meals being taken away before they could eat them due to a lack of support at meal times.

All users of health and social care services need to be treated with dignity and respect.

However, some older people can be particularly vulnerable and it is essential that extra attention is given to making sure that care givers treat them with dignity at all times and in all situations. To fail to do this is an infringement of their human rights.

There is a deep rooted cultural attitude to ageing, where older people are often presented as being incapable and dependent particularly in the media. As there is an increasingly ageing population, there is a need for policy makers and those who plan and deliver public services to consider the impact of ageism and to take action to address this.

Recommendations

While progress has been made by health and local authorities in systematically tackling age discrimination, through audits of policy, and the reviewing of eligibility criteria, there is still evidence of age discrimination and ageist attitudes, which have had an impact on the lives of older people. These include the

> discrimination older people sometimes experience when receiv-
> ing care services that fail to treat them with dignity and respect.
> Managers of NHS trusts, social services and providers of inde-
> pendent health and social care had to ensure that the human
> rights of older people are upheld at all times.

14.46   The DLR seems likely to propose that an age equality duty should be
introduced as part of the single equality act. In April 2006 Meg Munn
MP confirmed that the DLR would: 'consider how to ensure that duties
are focused on outcomes and that any proposal for an integrated duty
across all the discrimination strands include age'.[29]

14.47   Not only are the potential benefits of a duty well recognised, but an
age duty would have none of the complexities of legislation outlawing discrimination in goods and services; since the law requires an
authority to only *promote* equality of opportunity there would not be an
obligation to take action that would severely undermine its operations.
Equally importantly, there is likely to be little opposition to an age duty
which does not effect the private sector (except as contractors). This
leaves a number of questions about the shape a new duty should take.

Can a single equality duty ensure age issues are promoted?

14.48   A new age equality duty will almost certainly form part of an integrated
single equality duty. There are clear attractions to requiring public services to address equality issues through a cross-strand approach, perhaps under-pinned by human rights. The compliance costs would
probably be lower and it will be possible to focus on issues of multiple
disadvantage or to prioritise the most acute inequalities, regardless of
the ground on which they are based. However there is also a risk that age
will be marginalised without specific legal requirements and issues
specific to age might not receive the necessary attention in a generic duty.
For example it would be tempting for a public body to prioritise hate
crime motivated by racism over abuse and neglect of older people in
institutional settings, even though the latter is likely to lead to far more
death and injury. One option that has been proposed is that there is a
general duty to promote equality, underpinned by specific duties for
each equality strand. For example an age duty should probably include
specific duties relating to involving and consulting age-groups (young
and old) whose voices are not being heard in decision-making.

29   Speech by Meg Munn MP at the Opportunity Age at Work Conference, 27 July
2005.

Should an age duty include requirements to promote good relations?

14.49 The new gender duty does not include a duty to promote good relations between men and women, unlike the race and disability duties. By contrast the Equality Act 2006 gives the CEHR a duty to promote good relations between different 'groups' defined by seven different attributes including age and gender:

> Section 10(1) The Commission shall, by exercising the powers conferred by this Part–
> (a) promote understanding of the importance of good relations–
>   (i) between members of different groups, and
>   (ii) between members of groups and others,
> (b) encourage good practice in relation to relations–
>   (i) between members of different groups, and
>   (ii) between members of groups and others,
> (c) work towards the elimination of prejudice against, hatred of and hostility towards members of groups, and
> (d) work towards enabling members of groups to participate in society.

14.50 This definition combines elements of the public sector good relations duties for race and disability. It would be quite possible to apply it to a new generic equality duty. There would certainly be value in encouraging public bodies to promote the participation of older people in society, the elimination of prejudice towards different age groups, and the encouragement of good practice in relations between different age groups. The disadvantage of this approach might be that a complicated new duty on good relations could reduce the attention paid to discrimination and inequality.

Which services should be covered by duties?

14.51 The general race duty only applies to named public bodies, while the gender and disability duties apply to any public authority. The flexibility of the latter definition is welcome, but it creates some difficulties because the meaning of 'public authority' is itself unclear, at least with respect to the Human Rights Act (HRA) 1998. This follows litigation on the status of providers of services under contract. The case-law has found that in some instances private services can count as public authorities (examples have included prisons, hospitals and housing associations) but that other services discharging statutory obligations are not themselves public authorities. This is a key issue for age equality because the main class of provider that have been exempted from HRA

1998 obligations are residential care homes (eg Leonard Cheshire[30]). The Commission for Racial Equality (CRE) has attempted to deal with the limited scope of the race duty by issuing clear guidance on how the duty must be exercised with respect to procurement.[31] However with the increasing out-sourcing of services there are clear advantages in directly transferring equality obligations to third-party providers. This is an issue the DLR has been considering and the Department of Constitutional Affairs is expected to hold a separate consultation on the definition of public authorities under the HRA 1998.

How to minimise process and focus on outcomes?

14.52   The race duty has been accused of being excessively process-driven, while the new gender duty makes few stipulations about processes and focuses on outcomes. The disability duty is probably the toughest of the three, with the detail of what should be included in an equality scheme specified, and a requirement that the scheme must be implemented. However, in recent years the appetite for micro-managing public services from Whitehall has diminished and it is likely that a generic equality duty will not include overly-prescriptive specific duties. The challenge will be to ensure that moving from a focus on process to outcomes is not viewed by public services as an excuse for ignoring their equality obligations. This will be a key early challenge for the CEHR, working in conjunction with public sector inspectorates.

See appendix C for general and specific duties under the RRA, DDA and SDA.

Age discrimination in goods and services

14.53   It is reasonably likely that the single equality bill will include provisions to outlaw age discrimination in goods, facilities and services in one shape or another (and if this happened the law would also no doubt cover accommodation and public functions). However, the devil will be in the detail. The government's reticence in committing to goods and services age discrimination law has mainly stemmed from the complexity of the issues. Age discrimination in goods and services takes many forms, and poses considerable questions that do not

30   [2002] EWCA Civ 266; [2002] 2 All ER 936.
31   *Public procurement and race equality – guidelines for public authorities,* Commission for Racial Equality, 2003.

arise in other aspects of discrimination. Like the European Commission, the UK government decided to carry out a thorough scoping exercise before promising legislation.

14.54 However, the problems are not intractable and age discrimination in goods and services has been outlawed in several jurisdictions. At appendix C there are extracts from the relevant legislation for Ireland and Australia. In framing their legislation both countries had to grapple with the question of when differential treatment should be considered legitimate, and as a result both acts include lists of exemptions. It is inevitable that any legislation in Great Britain would also include scope for exemptions. This could take the form of detailed lists of exemptions, with specific criteria for a practice to qualify as legitimate under each example. Or the law could follow the model of the Framework Directive and include a general provision for objective justification. Perhaps the most likely outcome is that the Government follows the model it has adopted for the employment regulations and provides for both objective justification and exemptions.

14.55 The reason objective justification or exemptions are likely to be needed become clear once the issues surrounding age discrimination in goods, facilities and services are analysed. Some age discrimination arises directly from prejudice and stereotyping. There are however other examples of age discrimination which are not directly related to prejudice, and often seem to have a rational basis. This is where discrimination in goods of services gets complicated.

Prejudice-based discrimination

14.56 There are clear examples of discrimination in service provision that are simply the result of prejudice and stereotyping. To take a straightforward example, older people are sometimes excluded from gyms or bars because of the ageism of staff or management. This sort of exclusion is offensive but its effects are relatively trivial.

14.57 Examples of prejudice-based discrimination tend to be more serious when they relate to the essential public services. The findings from the *Living well in later life*[32] show significant evidence of older users of public services receiving 'second class services' by being patronised, treated without respect, expected to wait longer; or receiving a lower level of service. The cause of this treatment is often stereotyping and prejudice from the public workers providing the service. In turn

---

32 *Advancing equality for men and women: government proposals to introduce a public sector duty to promote gender equality*, Department of Trade and Industry, 2005.

this can be the result of poor training, processes or standards adopted by organisations.

14.58   The first objective of any credible goods and services legislation should be to outlaw these sorts of prejudice-driven practices across both the private and public sectors.

Rationing resources

14.59   In the public sector there are several examples of age discrimination where cost rather than prejudice is the main driver of discrimination:

- On grounds of cost, older people are often required to live in residential homes when they have care needs that would be catered for at home in the case of younger adults.
- Mental health services for older people are chronically under-funded compared to similar services for other adults.
- There are age restrictions on certain healthcare procedures, such as automatic invitations for some types of diagnostic screening.
- There is an upper age limit on access to disability benefits to pay for mobility.

14.60   It is interesting that many of these examples of discrimination relate to disability and reflect differences in expectations about what older and younger disabled people can expect. But regardless of the history behind these forms of discrimination it will cost very large sums of public money to achieve age equality (or alternatively it would involve 'levelling down' for younger adults). Where the costs run into billions of pounds, it is not surprising that the government is reluctant to act – given the other possible uses for the money – no matter how committed it is to the principle of equality.

14.61   The issues here are similar to those facing service providers under the DDA 1995 with respect to reasonable adjustments. Although campaigning organisations will argue for full and immediate equality, in practice the government may decide that cost should be the basis for a reasonable justification for age discrimination in service delivery. Alternatively, a period of gradual implementation might be proposed or the most costly areas simply exempted from the legislation.

State benefits and concessions

14.62   Few people are opposed to the state treating people differently once they have reached State Pension Age. After all, receiving the state pension and other age-related benefits is essential to guarantee our ability to retire. The difficult question is deciding which benefits and concessions are legitimate. It can be argued that many are not essential for retirement. For example, why should older people have free bus travel or medical prescriptions when younger people of the same income do not? This problem has become particularly acute now that pensioners are on average no poorer than other adults. Old age is a very poor proxy for low income. In any case, these days, many benefits are means tested; why should others be available just because of age?

14.63 In thinking about future legislation it is possible to come at the problem from a pragmatic or principle-led perspective. The practical approach is to say that concessions and benefits based on age are very popular with older people and rarely resented by others. They may serve little rationale but it would serve no political purpose to remove them; so they should be exempted from restrictions on discrimination. It is very likely that politicians drawing up a single equality bill will follow this pragmatic course.

14.64 This is the route that has been followed in both Ireland and Australia. The Irish legislation says: 'imposing or maintaining a reasonable preferential fee, charge or rate in respect of anything offered or provided to or in respect of ... persons in a specific age group does not constitute' discrimination. Meanwhile the Australian law has a section on positive discrimination which permits discrimination where '(a) the act provides a bona fide benefit to persons of a particular age; or (b) the act is intended to meet a need that arises out of the age of persons of a particular age; or (c) the act is intended to reduce a disadvantage experienced by people of a particular age.' Arguably, this provision begs more questions than it answers, since 'bona fide' is likely to be a contestable concept that is determined by the social context.

14.65 The alternative principle-led approach would be to separate out concessions for which there is a logical explanation and remove the rest. For instance, a future equality bill could permit age-related concessions and benefits where they achieve results that would not be possible by simply paying people the equivalent in money. So, giving older people free bus travel or prescriptions can be said to encourage them to take-up services that are important to their quality of life which they might not otherwise use, even if they had the money available (for example because they prefer to put the money in savings). There is of course no evidence that this sort of assessment has been made in the past. Older people have received advantageous treatment compared to other age groups because they were seen as 'deserving' or as a powerful interest group with significant electoral power.

14.66   In the discussions around the DLR it has interestingly been older people's organisations who sought intellectually coherent justifications for concessions and benefits, not wishing to appear to be putting their own constituency's interests ahead of those of society as a whole. The government has appeared to be much more happy to strike a pragmatic compromise.

Medical ethics

14.67   Age can also be a relevant predictor of risk or ability to benefit for clinical decisions, although it is very rare for it to be a determining factor. Legislation on age discrimination in goods and services in Ireland and Australia both make explicit reference to clinical judgment.[33] The issue has recently been a subject to controversy in England, following the publication of draft guidance on 'social value judgements' by the National Institute for Health and Clinical Excellence.[34] The guidance endorsed the recommendations of a citizens' council which sought to develop guidance on the basis of public attitudes. The council's recommendations were that:

> health should not be valued more highly in some age groups rather than others; individuals' social roles, at different ages, should not influence considerations of cost effectiveness; however, where age is an indicator of benefit or risk, age discrimination is appropriate.

14.68   Older people's organisations reacted with fury to the latter recommendation, mainly because it was not accompanied by any further guidance or contextual information.[35] After a public spat the much longer final recommendations were a significant improvement:

> The Institute's general principle is that patients should not be denied NHS treatment simply because of their age. NICE acknowledges that treatments can produce different benefits at different ages and that age itself may be the only identifiable indicator. Nonetheless, wherever practical, NICE's advisory bodies should avoid issuing guidance that refers to age if this is being used as a presumed proxy for some aspect of patients' health status.
>
> Where NICE guidance refers to age it should only occur when all the following conditions are met:
>
> • the evidence indicates that age is a good proxy for some aspect of patients' health status and/or the likelihood of adverse effects of the treatment, and

33   *Living Well in Later Life: A review of progress against the national service framework for older people,* Healthcare Commission, 2006.

34   *Social value judgements, guidelines for the institute and its advisory bodies, draft for consultation,* National Institute for Health and Clinical Excellence, 2005.

35   Press release, 5 May 2005, Age Concern England.

- there is no practical way of identifying patients other than by their age (there is, for example, no routinely available diagnostic test to measure the relevant aspect of their health status), and
- it is logically and/or biologically plausible that, because of their age, patients will respond differently to the treatment in question.

In such instances NICE and its advisory bodies should explain within the guidance the reasons for using age as an indicator. The use of arbitrary age cut-offs intended to indicate (for example) 'old age', 'childhood' or 'adolescence' should be avoided. Where it is necessary to indicate an age cut-off, and where the treatment is appropriate only for people in a particular age group, then a reason for using this specific cut-off should be provided.

Principle
NICE clinical guidance should only recommend the use of a therapeutic or preventive measure for a particular age group when there is clear evidence of differences in the clinical effectiveness of the measure in different age groups that cannot be identified by any other means.

Risk in financial services

14.69   Age is one of the most common criteria for assessing risk for a range of financial products. For example it would be impossible to sell a pension annuity without taking someone's age into account, because otherwise there would no way of estimating their life expectancy. Age can also be a proxy for risk of ill health for a *group*, so it may be a relevant factor for calculating insurance premiums for products such as private medical insurance, life assurance, motor insurance and travel insurance (age is not an accurate predictor of the health of particular *individuals*).

14.70   Most observers in the UK agree that age (like gender but unlike race or sexuality) should be a legitimate criterion for pricing risk-based products in certain circumstances.[36] But this raises further questions:

When should people of the same age be treated alike?

14.71   Age is a poor proxy for features such as personal health or income. For example older people with high incomes have been outraged when they have been refused credit. Others are angry when the cost of motor insurance rises sharply when they have an excellent driving record and no health problems. Equally, why should responsible young men buying motor insurance be penalised because of a minority of

36 Interestingly in other European jurisdictions with different traditions with respect to financial services there is more disagreement on this point (with regard to gender and age).

'hot-heads'? The issue here is determining when it is appropriate for insurers to find alternative or additional information about their clients, rather than relying simply on their age.

Are price increases related to age proportionate to the increasing risk?

14.72   Many older people accept that insurance premiums will rise gradually with age but are angry by sudden price hikes when they hit thresholds such as 75. This has opened the controversial question of whether insurers should be required to reveal some of the commercially sensitive data upon which they base their pricing decisions, in order to show that premiums accurately reflect differences in costs.

Should providers be allowed to exclude people from a product rather than simply increasing their prices to reflect extra risk?

14.73   This is perhaps the most controversial issue being debated in the run up to the discrimination law Green Paper. Many people can see the logic in linking price to risk, but feel it is unfair that they cannot obtain a quote at all. Blanket age-based exclusions from financial services are surprisingly common, for example in motor insurance and travel insurance. Often exclusions are motivated by convenience, since it is easier to have one price for everyone while excluding high-risk groups, instead of calculating risk-based premiums. This is particularly common when a financial service is being bundled in as a subsidiary part of another product (examples include bank accounts, credit cards, package holidays, and car hire).

14.74   Financial services companies argue that, in a free market, providers should have the right to choose which segments of the market they operate in. They believe that the market will offer a better deal for everyone if providers are allowed to compete for the custom of particular groups, such as women, different age-groups or people who represent particularly good or bad risks. There are two opposing arguments – one relating to equal treatment, the other to competitiveness. The first argument is that people's age should be treated just like someone's race or sexual orientation; it is now unacceptable for these characteristics to form the rationale for excluding people from everyday services. Second, equality campaigners argue that where the majority of providers refuse to quote there is market failure, and people are trapped with very few companies to choose from and little price competition. For people over 75 or 80 who want to buy holiday insurance or change their motor insurance this certainly seems to be the case, since only a few niche providers operate such as SAGA and Age Concern Insurance.

14.75　There is an interesting parallel to this debate with respect to gender discrimination. The Sex Discrimination Act (SDA) 1975 has been interpreted as permitting wide leeway, including complete exclusions from products:

> **Section 45**
> Nothing in Parts II to IV shall render unlawful the treatment of a person in relation to an annuity, life assurance policy, accident insurance policy, or similar matter involving the assessment of risk, where the treatment–
>
> (a) was effected by reference to actuarial or other data from a source on which it was reasonable to rely, and
> (b) was reasonable having regard to the data and any other relevant factors.

14.76　By contrast, article 13 of the Gender Directive 2004 is much tighter and clearly rules out discriminatory exclusions:

> **Article 5 (2)**
> Notwithstanding paragraph 1, Member States may decide before 21 December 2007 to permit proportionate differences in individuals' premiums and benefits where the use of sex is a determining factor in the assessment of risk based on relevant and accurate actuarial and statistical data. The Member States concerned shall inform the Commission and ensure that accurate data relevant to the use of sex as a determining actuarial factor are compiled, published and regularly updated. These Member States shall review their decision five years after 21 December 2007, taking into account the Commission report referred to in Article 16, and shall forward the results of this review to the Commission.

14.77　Campaigners for older people have argued that following the approach in the gender directive for age would pose few problems financial companies will anyway need to implement these provisions for gender, so age could be included with few additional difficulties.

14.78　A further indication that the exclusion from financial services could be a major issue comes from recent Republic of Ireland case-law. The Equal Status Act 2000 includes an exemption for risk-based financial products which was considered to be fairly broad. Section 5(2)d of the act states that discrimination does not occur if:

> ... differences in the treatment of persons in relation to annuities, pensions, insurance policies or any other matters related to the assessment of risk where the treatment–

(i)   is effected by reference to–
   (a) actuarial or statistical data obtained from a source on which it is reasonable to rely, or
   (b) other relevant underwriting or commercial factors, and
(ii) is reasonable having regard to the data or other relevant factors.

14.79   However, in October 2003 the Equality Tribunal ruled, in the case of *Ross v Royal and Sun Alliance*, that a refusal to quote did not lie within the scope of the exemption. The insurer, in failing to produce actuarial or statistical data to support their policy, had not satisfied the requirement that the data had to come 'from a source on which it is reasonable to rely'. In addition the decision to have an 'across the board' policy, rather than considering individual requests, was held not to be 'reasonable having regard to the data or other relevant factors'.[37]

Market segmentation

14.80   Excluding customers from financial services is one example of market segmentation. There are a wide range of commercial practices where age is used as a criteria for offering services, where the motivation is not on the face of it prejudice, but a rational commercial decision. For example:

- *Exclusions* – Some businesses exclusively target products to people of certain ages. This can be because the age of clients is itself a defining characteristic of the service (for example dating services or group-based holidays such as SAGA or Club 18–30). Or it can be because a provider can offer low prices by only serving a particular segment of a market (the example of only offering an insurance product to people under a certain age).
- *Concessions* – Companies ranging from hairdressers, to cinemas or train operators offer discounts to older people, often to encourage them to use their services during off-peak periods when demand is low. Some of these companies also offer age-based concessions as corporate social responsibility (although the idea long pre-dates the terminology!) to the benefit of the community.

14.81   These sorts of practices sometimes cause outrage, as we have seen in the case of financial services. But other practices are widely welcomed (for example, concessions for older people using services off-peak) or at least do not create significant opposition (eg holidays exclusively

37   *Ross v Royal and Sun Alliance*, DEC-S2003-116; www.equalitytribunal.ie/index.asp?locID=94&docID=440.

for one age group or another). Policy-makers could decide that all of these sorts of practices should be unlawful. Or they could attempt to rise to the challenge of determining which practices are reasonable and which are discriminatory, in their intention or effect. To do this the DLR will first need to tease out the difference between prejudice and market segmentation. For example products based on the preferences of their clients, such as group holidays for older people, can be considered little different to restrictions which are based directly on prejudice such as when a gym assuming its patrons will not want older users. Second practices would need to be evaluated from the perspective of the harm they cause people who do not benefit (be this an excluded minority or the majority). In the case of concessions for older people, other age groups are potentially disadvantaged although they are at least able to use the service at a higher price. In the case of people being excluded altogether from an insurance product, holiday or whatever, the harm caused will depend on whether they are able to find an alternative and at what price.

14.82   Once again it seems likely that the answer to these difficult questions will be a 'fudge'. The discrimination law green paper is likely to propose exemptions along the lines of those found in the Irish or Australian legislation. They are likely to focus more on preserving the status quo where it is not causing significant offence, rather than reaching an evidence based demarcation of what is and is not discrimination. SAGA and Club 18-to-30 holidays may seem out of place in a brave new world of age equality, but the chances are that will be around for as long as they have clients coming back for more.

Age discrimination and human rights

14.83   In looking at future developments there is one further issue, relating not to new legislation but to the future development of case-law: to what extent can human rights legislation be expected to offer protection from age discrimination? This is a particularly relevant to the question of discrimination with respect to goods and services, both because there is no current discrimination law covering this area, and because the discriminator may often be a public authority, with obligations under the European Convention on Human Rights (ECHR).

14.84   Running through all of the aspects of these chapters is the fundamental question: why should there be protection against discrimination on the grounds of age? The directive gives a very clear answer in that it is founded on the belief that participation in economic activity ensures continued dignity at every stage of a working life. A key tool that advisers will have to use in respect of the areas mentioned in this chapter, where the directive does not provide protection, is the HRA 1998.[38] However, in this area there occasionally appears to be uncertainty whether protection should be given for discrimination on the grounds of age.

14.85   The House of Lords in *Carson*[39] examined the concept of discrimination under the ECHR. Lord Walker stated that discrimination is regarded as particularly objectionable because it disregards fundamental notions of human dignity and equality before the law. He gave the example of race and sex discrimination. This, he acknowledged, demeans the victim by using a sexual or racial stereotype as a sufficient ground for unfavourable treatment, rather than treating the victim as an individual to be judged on his or her own merits. Lord Walker cited Baroness Hale in *Ghaidan v Godin-Mendoza*[40] who pointed out that sex and race discrimination was wrong in the context of employment choices (such as who should be employed) because the race or sex of the person was simply irrelevant to the choice that had to be made (how well the person could do the job). Baroness Hale went on to point out that:

> It was wrong because it depended on stereotypical assumptions about what a woman or a black person might be like, assumptions which had nothing to do with the qualities of the individual involved: even if there were any reason to believe that more women than men made bad customers this was no justification for discriminating against all women. It was wrong because it was based on an irrelevant characteristic which the woman or the black person did not choose and could do nothing about.

14.86   In *Carson* Lord Walker went on to consider the grounds for discrimination in article 14 ECHR. 'Status' in article 14 means:

> a personal characteristic ... by which persons or groups of persons are distinguishable from each other.[41]

---

38 See F Butler *Rights for Real*, Age Concern England, 2006.
39 See *Regina (Carson) v Secretary of State for Work and Pensions* [2005] 2 WLR 1369, [2005] UKHL 37.
40 [2004] 2 AC 557, 604, at para 130.
41 *Kjeldsen, Busk Madsen and Pedersen v Denmark* (1976) 1 EHRR 711, and *R (S) v Chief Constable of the South Yorkshire Police* [2004] 1 WLR 2196, 2213, para 48, per Lord Steyn. Cited at paras 53 and 54 of Carson.

14.87 Clearly age falls into this concept of 'status' and therefore differentiation on the basis of age in respect of the other convention rights will be protected against, unless there is an objective and reasonable justification for the difference.

14.88 The state, in *Carson*, argued that a distinction was drawn between the 'most sensitive grounds' which can only be justified by very weighty reasons, and the others.[42] Lord Walker went on to make remarks on the sensitive categories, which, he acknowledged, include race, sex, sexual orientation, illegitimacy, nationality and religion. In relation to 'place of residence' Lord Walker distinguished this ground from the other grounds on the basis that it was a matter of choice. However, so are religion and potentially nationality. It was submitted in that case that age was a characteristic requiring very weighty reasons to justify differentiation using them as grounds. This submission was rejected.

14.89 Lord Walker said:

> 60 Age is a personal characteristic, but it is different in kind from other personal characteristics. Every human being starts life as a tiny infant, and none of us can do anything to stop the passage of the years. As the High Court of Australia said (in a different context) in *Stingel v The Queen* (1990) 171 CLR 312, 330: 'the process of development from childhood to maturity is something which, being common to us all, is an aspect of ordinariness.' There is nothing intrinsically demeaning about age. It may be disheartening for a man to be told that he cannot continue in his chosen job after 50, and it is certainly demeaning for a woman air hostess to be told that she cannot continue as cabin crew after the age of 40: see *Defrenne v Sabena (Case 43/75)* [1976] ICR 547. But Mlle Defrenne was discriminated against on the ground of sex, not age. In relation to normal retirement ages lines have to be drawn somewhere, as Murgia explains.

14.90 This passage, it is respectfully suggested, conflates several concepts. First, age is a non-volitional personal characteristic. The passage conflates age (the possession of a chronological age) with the process of ageing. Second, there is nothing intrinsically demeaning about any of the protected categories. The reason they are protected is that on occasion they are used as a method of differentiation when in fact they are irrelevant to the decision to be made. It is not a necessary feature of protection that the characteristic be intrinsically or otherwise demeaning. It is sufficient if a general characteristic is taken irrelevantly as a ground for differentiation (the consequence of which may be that the person is demeaned by reliance on that characteristic). Therefore, whilst it is true that there is nothing intrinsically demeaning

42 *Carson* para 57.

about age, nothing follows from that in terms of the importance of age as a means of differentiation abuse of which should be prohibited. The fact that something is an 'aspect of ordinariness', far from pointing away from the need for protection, points to the need to protect against discrimination which is based on taking that aspect of ordinariness and using it irrelevantly to form a basis for less favourable treatment of the person possessing it.

14.91   Advisers should argue that age falls on the continuum of rights far more toward the core elements of what makes up a human individual than, for example, nationality or religion. It is something over which a person has no choice, which is not relevant to judgments about a person's abilities in most employment situations and which forms the basis of many stereotypical judgements. A person may change his or her religious beliefs, or philosophical opinions with the reading of successive books. A person may acquire a nationality by choice on occasions. It is illogical to treat age as less of a sensitive ground for justified discrimination than either of these. Age is an immutable characteristic in the sense that I cannot change my date of birth. In that sense possession of an age is a characteristic which an individual cannot change and is irrelevant to decision making. Protection against discrimination based on it should require very weighty reasons.

14.92   However, in Carson the House of Lords was convinced that:

> 15. Article 14 expresses the Enlightenment value that every human being is entitled to equal respect and to be treated as an end and not a means. Characteristics such as race, caste, noble birth, membership of a political party and (here a change in values since the Enlightenment) gender, are seldom, if ever, acceptable grounds for differences in treatment. In some constitutions, the prohibition on discrimination is confined to grounds of this kind and I rather suspect that article 14 was also intended to be so limited. But the Strasbourg court has given it a wide interpretation, approaching that of the Fourteenth Amendment, and it is therefore necessary, as in the United States, to distinguish between those grounds of discrimination which prima facie appear to offend our notions of the respect due to the individual and those which merely require some rational justification: *Massachusetts Board of Retirement v Murgia* (1976) 427 US 307.

> 16. There are two important consequences of making this distinction. First, discrimination in the first category cannot be justified merely on utilitarian grounds, e g that it is rational to prefer to employ men rather than women because more women than men give up employment to look after children. That offends the notion that everyone is entitled to be treated as an individual and not a statistical unit. On the other hand, differences

in treatment in the second category (e g on grounds of ability, education, wealth, occupation) usually depend upon considerations of the general public interest. Secondly, while the courts, as guardians of the right of the individual to equal respect, will carefully examine the reasons offered for any discrimination in the first category, decisions about the general public interest which underpin differences in treatment in the second category are very much a matter for the democratically elected branches of government.

17. There may be borderline cases in which it is not easy to allocate the ground of discrimination to one category or the other and, as I have observed, there are shifts in the values of society on these matters. *Ghaidan v Godin-Mendoza* [2004] 2 AC 557 recognised that discrimination on grounds of sexual orientation was now firmly in the first category. Discrimination on grounds of old age may be a contemporary example of a borderline case. But there is usually no difficulty about deciding whether one is dealing with a case in which the right to respect for the individuality of a human being is at stake or merely a question of general social policy. In the present case, the answer seems to me to be clear.[43]

14.93   Lord Hoffmann's judgment appears to express uncertainty about where within this categorisation of rights old age discrimination falls. It is submitted that any logical attempt to categorise the ECHR rights must take account of the way in which ageing is increasingly seen as creating rights. The House of Lords in Carson appears to have failed to take into account materials such as Implementation of the International Plan of Action on Ageing and related activities[44], the Political Declaration and Madrid International Plan of Action on Ageing, 2002[45] both of which emphasise the importance of the dignity of older persons and included in the UN's action plan the recommendation that older persons should be enabled to continue with income-generating work for as long as they want and for as long as they are able to do so productively. These UN documents emphasise the importance of the status of age as a characteristic. An approach that justifies discrimination on the grounds of age in the field of human rights on simply utilitarian grounds sits at best uneasily with such plans of action.

14.94   The House of Lords instead looked at the way in which, in the 1970s, the United States approached age discrimination in the context of mandatory retirement ages. The Supreme Court in *Murgia*[46]

43   Paras 14–17 per Lord Hoffmann.
44   A/RES/46/91.
45   A/CONF.197/9.
46   *Massachusetts Board of Retirement v Murgia* (1976) 427 US 307.

considered the requirement that uniformed state police officers were obliged to retire at 50. The Supreme Court held that this requirement did not need strict scrutiny but only a rational basis. This was that the police force had to be 'fit enough to carry out arduous and demanding duties'. The House of Lords, considering this case remarked in passing that in relation to normal retirement ages a line has to be drawn somewhere.

14.95   The House concluded that differential payment of jobseeker's allowance on the ground of age could be rationally justified since persons under the age of 25 could legitimately be regarded as having lower earnings expectations and lower living costs so as to permit their being treated differently for the purpose of social security payments, the giving effect to that distinction again being a matter for the legislature.

14.96   It is suggested that in relation to mandatory retirement ages, the position adopted in *Murgia* can no longer be sustained even in the United States and in 1986 mandatory retirement ages were abolished there. It is not clear that the US position has remained the same since *Murgia*. In particular, the concept of age discrimination has recently been extended to include indirect discrimination. The treatment of all discrimination on the grounds of age as justifiable by utilitarian reasons is therefore less sustainable. The new structure of US age discrimination law permits a proper distinction to be drawn between indirect discrimination (where there is less likely to be an affront to dignity) and direct discrimination. The level of scrutiny to be afforded to direct discrimination cases accordingly may be higher now than was envisaged in *Murgia* in 1976.

14.97   Advisers will have to be able to show how the facts of a particular case engaging article 14 address the issues of the individual's dignity. To the extent that they do not, justification of age discrimination in relation to human rights cases will have a very low threshold.

14.98   Most of the articles of the ECHR have application to the position of older people particularly. Thus article 2 impinges on end of life issues, and access to life saving treatment. Medical law issues, such as clinical negligence may be affected by article 2. For example, in *R (on the application of Burke) v General Medical Council*[47] Mr Burke suffered from a progressive, degenerative brain condition and was likely to need artificial nutrition and hydration (ANH). He was concerned that the General Medical Council's guidance on life-prolonging treatment

---

47   See [2005] EWCA Civ 1003; [2006] QB 273; [2005] 3 WLR 1132.

allowed doctors to withdraw ANH at a time when his death might not be imminent but he would be incapacitated. He challenged the guidance, claiming that it was incompatible with the ECHR and was successful at first instance. On appeal, the Court of Appeal held that article 2 would plainly be violated if a doctor were to bring about the death of a competent patient by withdrawing life prolonging treatment contrary to that patient's wishes. There was also a positive obligation to enforce article 2. However so far as the guidance related to the claimant's predicament, there was no ground for declaring any part of it unlawful. If a competent patient indicated a wish to be kept alive by the provision of ANH, any doctor who deliberately brought that patient's life to an end by discontinuing the supply of ANH would be guilty of murder. A clinical decision could not override the competent patient who expressed the wish to remain alive. The doctors would not be able to seek authorisation from the court for such action. Good practice but not law might require medical practitioners to seek such a declaration where the legality of proposed treatment was in doubt. This was not however, something that they were required to do as a matter of law.

14.99   The prohibition on degrading treatment in article 3 will have particular application in the context of 'elder abuse'. Whether conduct reaches the minimum threshold to constitute degrading treatment will depend on the features of the individual claimant, the vulnerability of an elderly person will be a feature lowering the threshold.[48] Similarly, restrictions on the movements of elderly people in care homes may raise issues relating to article 5 depending on the severity of the restrictions. Issues of care may also give rise to infringements of article 8 which guarantees the right to respect for private and family life. Article 8 also covers areas of concern such as consent to medical care. The other rights may also be engaged (eg freedom of association (article 11), freedom of thought and religion (article 9)). The right to peaceful enjoyment of property may also give rise to particular issues for the young and elderly (article 1 protocol 1).

14.100   Section 6 of the HRA 1998 provides that 'it is unlawful for a public authority to act in a way which is incompatible with a Convention right'. Claims are brought in the county court for breach of statutory duty, or in the administrative court by way of judicial review.

14.101   Section 3 of the HRA 1998 requires that, so far as it is possible to do so, primary legislation and subordinate legislation must be read

---

48 See the systemic issues concerning manual handling and the need of elderly residents for human touch discussed in *R on the application of v East Sussex County Council* [2003] EWHC 167; (2003) 6 CCLR 194, para 68 onwards.

and given effect in a way that is compatible with the Convention rights.[49]

14.102   The section 6 duties apply to public authorities. A private body carrying out state functions (such as detention) may be for the purposes of that function considered a public authority and subject to the section 6 duty.[50]

14.103   ECHR cases in which age has played a role have usually been those discrimination cases where another ground has been operative. For example, *L v Austria*[51] and similar cases on the age of consent was based on discrimination on the grounds of sex. However, age itself will constitute a status for the purposes of article 14 of the convention. Therefore, where another human right under the convention is engaged[52] the court may make a finding of a breach of article 14 if there has been direct or indirect discrimination on the grounds of age for which there is no objective and reasonable justification.

14.104   Advisors are most likely, therefore, to have to argue about whether there is an objective and reasonable justification for any age discrimination in relation to the other convention rights.

14.105   In the light of the Carson decision advisers will have to become skilled at demonstrating the ways in which differential treatment affects the dignity of the individual claimant in cases involving non-employment age discrimination. A unifying strand of much of today's anti-discrimination measures is the need for respect for the dignity of the individual.[53] Many of the cases that will arise under the HRA 1998 in respect of age discrimination will form part of campaigns to inform and change attitudes towards the impact of age discrimination at all age levels. Advisers may find themselves involved in local or national campaigning involving test cases as a result.[54]

49   See *Ghaidan v Godin-Mendoza* [2004] UKHL 30; [2004] 2 AC 557 and *Fleming (t/a Bodycraft) v Customs and Excise Commissioners* [2006] EWCA Civ 70; [2006] STC 864.

50   *R (on the application of A) v Partnerships in Care Ltd* [2002] EWHC 529; [2002] 1 WLR 2610 and *R (on the application of Heather) v Leonard Cheshire Foundation* [2002] EWCA Civ 366, [2002] 2 All ER 936 both indicate that in many situations affecting elderly residents of care homes human rights legislation will not protect them. This is because the care home will not be regarded as standing in the shoes of the local authority. See also *R (on the application of Johnson and others) v Havering London Borough Council* [2006] EWHC 1714.

51   EHRLR [2007] forthcoming.

52   Ie whether the facts in the case touch the enjoyment of the right guaranteed by the other convention right.

53   See *Dignity discourse in discrimination law: a better approach to equality?* Moon & Allen [ref] 2006.

54   See Katie Ghose *Beyond the courtroom*, LAG, 2005 for an excellent guide through this potentially difficult area.

APPENDICES

Employment Equality (Age) Regulations 2006[1]

PART 1: GENERAL

1 Citation, commencement and extent

(1) These Regulations may be cited as the Employment Equality (Age) Regulations 2006, and shall come into force on:

    (a) subject to sub-paragraphs (b) and (c), on 1st October 2006;

    (b) for the purposes of regulation 7 (Applicants and Employees) and regulation 24 (Relationships which have come to an end), in so far as either regulation relates to arrangements for—

        (i) the payment of pension contributions;

        (ii) admission to a pension scheme; and

        (iii) the provision of any benefits relating to pensions,

    on 1st December 2006, and

    (c) for the purposes of regulation 11 (Pension Schemes) and Schedule 2 (Pension Schemes), on 1st December 2006.

(2) Any amendment, repeal or revocation made by these Regulations has the same extent as the provision to which it relates.

(3) Subject to that, these Regulations do not extend to Northern Ireland.

2 Interpretation

(1) In these Regulations, references to discrimination are to any discrimination falling within regulation 3 (discrimination on grounds of age), regulation 4 (discrimination by way of victimisation) or regulation 5 (instructions to discriminate) and related expressions shall be construed accordingly, and references to harassment shall be construed in accordance with regulation 6 (harassment on grounds of age).

(2) In these Regulations–

'1996 Act' means the Employment Rights Act 1996;

'act' includes a deliberate omission;

'benefit', except in regulation 11 and Schedule 2 (pension schemes), includes facilities and services;

'commencement date' means 1st October 2006;

'Crown employment' means–

    (a) service for purposes of a Minister of the Crown or government department, other than service of a person holding a statutory office; or

---

1 As amended by the Employment Equality (Age) (Amendment) Regulation 2006 SI No 2408. © Crown Copyright. Reproduced with the permission of the Controller of HMSO and the Queen's Printer for Scotland.

(b)   service on behalf of the Crown for purposes of a person holding a statutory office or purposes of a statutory body;

'detriment' does not include harassment within the meaning of regulation 6;

'employment' means employment under a contract of service or of apprenticeship or a contract personally to do any work, and related expressions (such as 'employee' and 'employer') shall be construed accordingly, but this definition does not apply in relation to regulation 30 (exception for retirement) or to Schedules 2, 6, 7 and 8;

'Great Britain' includes such of the territorial waters of the United Kingdom as are adjacent to Great Britain;

'Minister of the Crown' includes the Treasury and the Defence Council;

'proprietor', in relation to a school, has the meaning given by section 579 of the Education Act 1996;

'relevant member of the House of Commons staff' means any person who was appointed by the House of Commons Commission or who is a member of the Speaker's personal staff;

'relevant member of the House of Lords staff' means any person who is employed under a contract of employment with the Corporate Officer of the House of Lords;

'school', in England and Wales, has the meaning given by section 4 of the Education Act 1996, and, in Scotland, has the meaning given by section 135(1) of the Education (Scotland) Act 1980, and references to a school are to an institution in so far as it is engaged in the provision of education under those sections;

'service for purposes of a Minister of the Crown or government department' does not include service in any office mentioned in Schedule 2 (Ministerial offices) to the House of Commons Disqualification Act 1975;

'statutory body' means a body set up by or in pursuance of an enactment, and 'statutory office' means an office so set up; and

'worker' in relation to regulations 32 and 34 and to Schedule 2, means, as the case may be–

(a)   an employee;

(b)   a person holding an office or post to which regulation 12 (office-holders etc) applies;

(c)   a person holding the office of constable;

(d)   a partner within the meaning of regulation 17 (partnerships);

(e)   a member of a limited liability partnership within the meaning of that regulation;

(f)   a person in Crown employment;

(g)   a relevant member of the House of Commons staff;

(h)   a relevant member of the House of Lords staff.

(3)   In these Regulations references to 'employer', in their application to a person at any time seeking to employ another, include a person who has no employees at that time.

3   Discrimination on grounds of age

(1)   For the purposes of these Regulations, a person ('A') discriminates

against another person ('B') if–

(a) on grounds of B's age, A treats B less favourably than he treats or would treat other persons, or

(b) A applies to B a provision, criterion or practice which he applies or would apply equally to persons not of the same age group as B, but–

    (i) which puts or would put persons of the same age group as B at a particular disadvantage when compared with other persons, and

    (ii) which puts B at that disadvantage,

and A cannot show the treatment or, as the case may be, provision, criterion or practice to be a proportionate means of achieving a legitimate aim.

(2) A comparison of B's case with that of another person under paragraph (1) must be such that the relevant circumstances in the one case are the same, or not materially different, in the other.

(3) In this regulation–

(a) 'age group' means a group of persons defined by reference to age, whether by reference to a particular age or a range of ages; and

(b) the reference in paragraph (1)(a) to B's age includes B's apparent age.

4 Discrimination by way of victimisation

(1) For the purposes of these Regulations, a person ('A') discriminates against another person ('B') if he treats B less favourably than he treats or would treat other persons in the same circumstances, and does so by reason that B has–

(a) brought proceedings against A or any other person under or by virtue of these Regulations;

(b) given evidence or information in connection with proceedings brought by any person against A or any other person under or by virtue of these Regulations;

(c) otherwise done anything under or by reference to these Regulations in relation to A or any other person; or

(d) alleged that A or any other person has committed an act which (whether or not the allegation so states) would amount to a contravention of these Regulations,

or by reason that A knows that B intends to do any of those things, or suspects that B has done or intends to do any of them.

(2) Paragraph (1) does not apply to treatment of B by reason of any allegation made by him, or evidence or information given by him, if the allegation, evidence or information was false and not made (or, as the case may be, given) in good faith.

5 Instructions to discriminate

For the purposes of these Regulations, a person ('A') discriminates against another person ('B') if he treats B less favourably than he treats or would treat other persons in the same circumstances, and does so by reason that–

(a) B has not carried out (in whole or in part) an instruction to do an act which is unlawful by virtue of these Regulations, or

(b) B, having been given an instruction to do such an act, complains to A or to any other person about that instruction.

6   Harassment on grounds of age

(1) For the purposes of these Regulations, a person ('A') subjects another person ('B') to harassment where, on grounds of age, A engages in unwanted conduct which has the purpose or effect of–

(a) violating B's dignity; or

(b) creating an intimidating, hostile, degrading, humiliating or offensive environment for B.

(2) Conduct shall be regarded as having the effect specified in paragraph (1)(a) or (b) only if, having regard to all the circumstances, including in particular the perception of B, it should reasonably be considered as having that effect.

PART 2: DISCRIMINATION IN EMPLOYMENT AND VOCATIONAL TRAINING

7   Applicants and employees

(1) It is unlawful for an employer, in relation to employment by him at an establishment in Great Britain, to discriminate against a person–

(a) in the arrangements he makes for the purpose of determining to whom he should offer employment;

(b) in the terms on which he offers that person employment; or

(c) by refusing to offer, or deliberately not offering, him employment.

(2) It is unlawful for an employer, in relation to a person whom he employs at an establishment in Great Britain, to discriminate against that person–

(a) in the terms of employment which he affords him;

(b) in the opportunities which he affords him for promotion, a transfer, training, or receiving any other benefit;

(c) by refusing to afford him, or deliberately not affording him, any such opportunity; or

(d) by dismissing him, or subjecting him to any other detriment.

(3) It is unlawful for an employer, in relation to employment by him at an establishment in Great Britain, to subject to harassment a person whom he employs or who has applied to him for employment.

(4) Subject to paragraph (5), paragraph (1)(a) and (c) does not apply in relation to a person–

(a) whose age is greater than the employer's normal retirement age or, if the employer does not have a normal retirement age, the age of 65; or

(b) who would, within a period of six months from the date of his application to the employer, reach the employer's normal retirement age or, if the employer does not have a normal retirement age, the age of 65.

(5) Paragraph (4) only applies to a person to whom, if he was recruited by

the employer, regulation 30 (exception for retirement) could apply.

(6) Paragraph (2) does not apply to benefits of any description if the employer is concerned with the provision (for payment or not) of benefits of that description to the public, or to a section of the public which includes the employee in question, unless–

(a) that provision differs in a material respect from the provision of the benefits by the employer to his employees; or

(b) the provision of the benefits to the employee in question is regulated by his contract of employment; or

(c) the benefits relate to training.

(7) In paragraph (2)(d) reference to the dismissal of a person from employment includes reference–

(a) to the termination of that person's employment by the expiration of any period (including a period expiring by reference to an event or circumstance), not being a termination immediately after which the employment is renewed on the same terms; and

(b) to the termination of that person's employment by any act of his (including the giving of notice) in circumstances such that he is entitled to terminate it without notice by reason of the conduct of the employer.

(8) In paragraph (4) 'normal retirement age' is an age of 65 or more which meets the requirements of section 98ZH of the 1996 Act.

8   Exception for genuine occupational requirement etc

(1) In relation to discrimination falling within regulation 3 (discrimination on grounds of age)–

(a) regulation 7(1)(a) or (c) does not apply to any employment;

(b) regulation 7(2)(b) or (c) does not apply to promotion or transfer to, or training for, any employment; and

(c) regulation 7(2)(d) does not apply to dismissal from any employment,

where paragraph (2) applies.

(2) This paragraph applies where, having regard to the nature of the employment or the context in which it is carried out–

(a) possessing a characteristic related to age is a genuine and determining occupational requirement;

(b) it is proportionate to apply that requirement in the particular case; and

(c) either–

(i) the person to whom that requirement is applied does not meet it, or

(ii) the employer is not satisfied, and in all the circumstances it is reasonable for him not to be satisfied, that that person meets it.

9   Contract workers

(1) It is unlawful for a principal, in relation to contract work at an establishment in Great Britain, to discriminate against a contract worker–

    (a)   in the terms on which he allows him to do that work;

    (b)   by not allowing him to do it or continue to do it;

    (c)   in the way he affords him access to any benefits or by refusing or deliberately not affording him access to them; or

    (d)   by subjecting him to any other detriment.

(2)   It is unlawful for a principal, in relation to contract work at an establishment in Great Britain, to subject a contract worker to harassment.

(3)   A principal does not contravene paragraph (1)(b) by doing any act in relation to a contract worker where, if the work were to be done by a person taken into the principal's employment, that act would be lawful by virtue of regulation 8 (exception for genuine occupational requirement etc).

(4)   Paragraph (1) does not apply to benefits of any description if the principal is concerned with the provision (for payment or not) of benefits of that description to the public, or to a section of the public to which the contract worker in question belongs, unless that provision differs in a material respect from the provision of the benefits by the principal to his contract workers.

(5)   In this regulation–

'principal' means a person ('A') who makes work available for doing by individuals who are employed by another person who supplies them under a contract made with A;

'contract work' means work so made available; and

'contract worker' means any individual who is supplied to the principal under such a contract.

10   **Meaning of employment and contract work at establishment in Great Britain**

(1)   For the purposes of this Part ('the relevant purposes'), employment is to be regarded as being at an establishment in Great Britain if the employee–

    (a)   does his work wholly or partly in Great Britain; or

    (b)   does his work wholly outside Great Britain and paragraph (2) applies.

(2)   This paragraph applies if–

    (a)   the employer has a place of business at an establishment in Great Britain;

    (b)   the work is for the purposes of the business carried on at that establishment; and

    (c)   the employee is ordinarily resident in Great Britain–

        (i)   at the time when he applies for or is offered the employment, or

        (ii)   at any time during the course of the employment.

(3)   The reference to 'employment' in paragraph (1) includes–

    (a)   employment on board a ship only if the ship is registered at a port of registry in Great Britain, and

    (b)   employment on an aircraft or hovercraft only if the aircraft or hovercraft is registered in the United Kingdom and operated by a person who has his principal place of business, or is ordinarily resident, in Great Britain.

(4)   Subject to paragraph (5), for the purposes of determining if employment concerned with the exploration of the sea bed or sub-soil or the exploitation of their natural resources is outside Great Britain, this regulation has effect as if references to Great Britain included–

(a)   any area designated under section 1(7) of the Continental Shelf Act 1964 except an area or part of an area in which the law of Northern Ireland applies; and

(b)   in relation to employment concerned with the exploration or exploitation of the Frigg Gas Field, the part of the Norwegian sector of the Continental Shelf described in Schedule 1.

(5)   Paragraph (4) shall not apply to employment which is concerned with the exploration or exploitation of the Frigg Gas Field unless the employer is–

(a)   a company registered under the Companies Act 1985;

(b)   an oversea company which has established a place of business within Great Britain from which it directs the exploration or exploitation in question; or

(c)   any other person who has a place of business within Great Britain from which he directs the exploration or exploitation in question.

(6)   In this regulation–

'the Frigg Gas Field' means the naturally occurring gas-bearing sand formations of the lower Eocene age located in the vicinity of the intersection of the line of latitude 59 degrees 53 minutes North and of the dividing line between the sectors of the Continental Shelf of the United Kingdom and the Kingdom of Norway and includes all other gas-bearing strata from which gas at the start of production is capable of flowing into the above-mentioned gas-bearing sand formations;

'oversea company' has the same meaning as in section 744 of the Companies Act 1985.

(7)   This regulation applies in relation to contract work within the meaning of regulation 9 as it applies in relation to employment; and, in its application to contract work, references to 'employee', 'employer' and 'employment' are references to (respectively) 'contract worker', 'principal' and 'contract work' within the meaning of regulation 9.

11   Pension schemes

(1)   It is unlawful, except in relation to rights accrued or benefits payable in respect of periods of service prior to the coming into force of this Regulation, for the trustees or managers of an occupational pension scheme to discriminate against a member or prospective member of the scheme in carrying out any of their functions in relation to it (including in particular their functions relating to the admission of members to the scheme and the treatment of members of it).

(2)   It is unlawful for the trustees or managers of an occupational pension scheme, in relation to the scheme, to subject to harassment a member or prospective member of it.

(3)   Schedule 2 (pension schemes) shall have effect for the purposes of–

(a)   defining terms used in this regulation and in that Schedule;

(b)   exempting certain rules and practices in or relating to pension schemes from Parts 2 and 3 of these Regulations;

(c)   treating every occupational pension scheme as including a non-discrimination rule;

(d)   giving trustees or managers of an occupational pension scheme power to alter the scheme so as to secure conformity with the non-discrimination rule;

(e)   making provision in relation to the procedures, and remedies which may be granted, on certain complaints relating to occupational pension schemes presented to an employment tribunal under regulation 36 (jurisdiction of employment tribunals).

12   Office-holders etc

(1)   It is unlawful for a relevant person, in relation to an appointment to an office or post to which this regulation applies, to discriminate against a person–

(a)   in the arrangements which he makes for the purpose of determining to whom the appointment should be offered;

(b)   in the terms on which he offers him the appointment; or

(c)   by refusing to offer him the appointment.

(2)   It is unlawful, in relation to an appointment to an office or post to which this regulation applies and which is an office or post referred to in paragraph (8)(b), for a relevant person on whose recommendation (or subject to whose approval) appointments to the office or post are made, to discriminate against a person–

(a)   in the arrangements which he makes for the purpose of determining who should be recommended or approved in relation to the appointment; or

(b)   in making or refusing to make a recommendation, or giving or refusing to give an approval, in relation to the appointment.

(3)   It is unlawful for a relevant person, in relation to a person who has been appointed to an office or post to which this regulation applies, to discriminate against him–

(a)   in the terms of the appointment;

(b)   in the opportunities which he affords him for promotion, a transfer, training or receiving any other benefit, or by refusing to afford him any such opportunity;

(c)   by terminating the appointment; or

(d)   by subjecting him to any other detriment in relation to the appointment.

(4)   It is unlawful for a relevant person, in relation to an office or post to which this regulation applies, to subject to harassment a person–

(a)   who has been appointed to the office or post;

(b)   who is seeking or being considered for appointment to the office or post; or

(c)   who is seeking or being considered for a recommendation or approval in relation to an appointment to an office or post referred to in paragraph (8)(b).

(5)   Paragraphs (1) and (3) do not apply to any act in relation to an office or post where, if the office or post constituted employment, that act would be lawful by virtue of regulation 8 (exception for genuine occupational requirement etc); and paragraph (2) does not apply to any act in relation to an office or post where, if the office or post constituted employment, it would be lawful by virtue of regulation 8 to refuse to offer the person such employment.

(6)   Paragraph (3) does not apply to benefits of any description if the relevant person is concerned with the provision (for payment or not) of benefits of that description to the public, or a section of the public to which the person appointed belongs, unless–

(a)   that provision differs in a material respect from the provision of the benefits by the relevant person to persons appointed to offices or posts which are the same as, or not materially different from, that which the person appointed holds; or

(b)   the provision of the benefits to the person appointed is regulated by the terms and conditions of his appointment; or

(c)   the benefits relate to training.

(7)   In paragraph (3)(c) the reference to the termination of the appointment includes a reference

(a)   to the termination of the appointment by the expiration of any period (including a period expiring by reference to an event or circumstance), not being a termination immediately after which the appointment is renewed on the same terms and conditions; and

(b)   to the termination of the appointment by any act of the person appointed (including the giving of notice) in circumstances such that he is entitled to terminate the appointment without notice by reason of the conduct of the relevant person.

(8)   This regulation applies to–

(a)   any office or post to which persons are appointed to discharge functions personally under the direction of another person, and in respect of which they are entitled to remuneration; and

(b)   any office or post to which appointments are made by (or on the recommendation of or subject to the approval of) a Minister of the Crown, a government department, the National Assembly for Wales or any part of the Scottish Administration,

but not to a political office or a case where regulation 7 (applicants and employees), 9 (contract workers), 15 (barristers), 16 (advocates) or 17 (partnerships) applies, or would apply but for the operation of any other provision of these Regulations.

(9)   For the purposes of paragraph (8)(a) the holder of an office or post–

(a)   is to be regarded as discharging his functions under the direction of another person if that other person is entitled to direct him as to when and where he discharges those functions;

(b) is not to be regarded as entitled to remuneration merely because he is entitled to payments–

    (i) in respect of expenses incurred by him in carrying out the function of the office or post; or

    (ii) by way of compensation for the loss of income or benefits he would or might have received from any person had he not been carrying out the functions of the office or post.

(10) In this regulation–

(a) appointment to an office or post does not include election to an office or post;

(b) 'political office' means–

    (i) any office of the House of Commons held by a member of it;

    (ii) a life peerage within the meaning of the Life Peerages Act 1958, or any office of the House of Lords held by a member of it;

    (iii) any office mentioned in Schedule 2 (Ministerial offices) to the House of Commons Disqualification Act 1975;

    (iv) the offices of Leader of the Opposition, Chief Opposition Whip or Assistant Opposition Whip within the meaning of the Ministerial and other Salaries Act 1975;

    (v) any office of the Scottish Parliament held by a member of it;

    (vi) a member of the Scottish Executive within the meaning of section 44 of the Scotland Act 1998, or a junior Scottish Minister within the meaning of section 49 of that Act;

    (vii) any office of the National Assembly for Wales held by a member of it;

    (viii) in England, any office of a county council, a London borough council, a district council, or a parish council held by a member of it;

    (ix) in Wales, any office of a county council, a county borough council, or a community council held by a member of it;

    (x) in relation to a council constituted under section 2 of the Local Government etc (Scotland) Act 1994 or a community council established under section 51 of the Local Government (Scotland) Act 1973, any office of such a council held by a member of it;

    (xi) any office of the Greater London Authority held by a member of it;

    (xii) any office of the Common Council of the City of London held by a member of it;

    (xiii) any office of the Council of the Isles of Scilly held by a member of it;

    (xiv) any office of a political party;

(c) 'relevant person', in relation to an office or post, means–

    (i) any person with power to make or terminate appointments to the office or post, or to determine the terms of appointment,

     (ii)   any person with power to determine the working conditions of a person appointed to the office or post in relation to opportunities for promotion, a transfer, training or for receiving any other benefit, and

     (iii) any person or body referred to in paragraph (8)(b) on whose recommendation or subject to whose approval appointments are made to the office or post;

(d)   references to making a recommendation include references to making a negative recommendation; and

(e)   references to refusal include references to deliberate omission.

13   Police

(1)   For the purposes of this Part, the holding of the office of constable shall be treated as employment–

    (a)   by the chief officer of police as respects any act done by him in relation to a constable or that office;

    (b)   by the police authority as respects any act done by it in relation to a constable or that office.

(2)   For the purposes of regulation 25 (liability of employers and principals)–

    (a)   the holding of the office of constable shall be treated as employment by the chief officer of police (and as not being employment by any other person); and

    (b)   anything done by a person holding such an office in the performance, or purported performance, of his functions shall be treated as done in the course of that employment.

(3)   There shall be paid out of the police fund–

    (a)   any compensation, costs or expenses awarded against a chief officer of police in any proceedings brought against him under these Regulations, and any costs or expenses incurred by him in any such proceedings so far as not recovered by him in the proceedings; and

    (b)   any sum required by a chief officer of police for the settlement of any claim made against him under these Regulations if the settlement is approved by the police authority.

(4)   Any proceedings under these Regulations which, by virtue of paragraph (1), would lie against a chief officer of police shall be brought against the chief officer of police for the time being or in the case of a vacancy in that office, against the person for the time being performing the functions of that office; and references in paragraph (3) to the chief officer of police shall be construed accordingly.

(5)   A police authority may, in such cases and to such extent as appear to it to be appropriate, pay out of the police fund–

    (a)   any compensation, costs or expenses awarded in proceedings under these Regulations against a person under the direction and control of the chief officer of police;

    (b)   any costs or expenses incurred and not recovered by such a person in such proceedings; and

    (c)   any sum required in connection with the settlement of a claim that has or might have given rise to such proceedings.

(6) Paragraphs (1) and (2) apply to a police cadet and appointment as a police cadet as they apply to a constable and the office of constable.

(7) Subject to paragraph (8), in this regulation–

'chief officer of police'–

    (a) in relation to a person appointed, or an appointment falling to be made, under a specified Act, has the same meaning as in the Police Act 1996;

    (b) in relation to a person appointed, or an appointment falling to be made, under the Police (Scotland) Act 1967, means the chief constable of the relevant police force;

    (c) in relation to any other person or appointment means the officer or other person who has the direction and control of the body of constables or cadets in question;

'police authority'–

    (a) in relation to a person appointed, or an appointment falling to be made, under a specified Act, has the same meaning as in the Police Act 1996;

    (b) in relation to a person appointed, or an appointment falling to be made, under the Police (Scotland) Act 1967, has the meaning given in that Act;

    (c) in relation to any other person or appointment, means the authority by whom the person in question is or on appointment would be paid;

'police cadet' means any person appointed to undergo training with a view to becoming a constable;

'police fund'–

    (a) in relation to a chief officer of police within sub-paragraph (a) of the above definition of that term, has the same meaning as in the Police Act 1996;

    (b) in any other case means money provided by the police authority; and

'specified Act' means the Metropolitan Police Act 1829, the City of London Police Act 1839 or the Police Act 1996.

(8) In relation to a constable of a force who is not under the direction and control of the chief officer of police for that force, references in this regulation to the chief officer of police are references to the chief officer of the force under whose direction and control he is, and references in this regulation to the police authority are references to the relevant police authority for that force.

(9) This regulation is subject to regulation 14.

14   Serious Organised Crime Agency

(1) For the purposes of this Part, any constable or other person who has been seconded to SOCA to serve as a member of its staff shall be treated as employed by SOCA.

(2) For the purposes of regulation 25 (liability of employers and principals)–

    (a) the secondment of any constable or other person to SOCA to serve as a member of its staff shall be treated as employment by SOCA (and not as employment by any other person); and

(b)   anything done by a person so seconded in the performance, or purported performance, of his functions shall be treated as done in the course of that employment.

(3)   In this regulation 'SOCA' means the Serious Organised Crime Agency established under section 1 of, and Schedule 1 to, the Serious Organised Crime and Police Act 2005.

15   Barristers

(1)   It is unlawful for a barrister or barrister's clerk, in relation to any offer of a pupillage or tenancy, to discriminate against a person–

(a)   in the arrangements which are made for the purpose of determining to whom the pupillage or tenancy should be offered;

(b)   in respect of any terms on which it is offered; or

(c)   by refusing, or deliberately not offering, it to him.

(2)   It is unlawful for a barrister or barrister's clerk, in relation to a pupil or tenant in the set of chambers in question, to discriminate against him–

(a)   in respect of any terms applicable to him as a pupil or tenant;

(b)   in the opportunities for training, or gaining experience, which are afforded or denied to him;

(c)   in the benefits which are afforded or denied to him; or

(d)   by terminating his pupillage, or by subjecting him to any pressure to leave the chambers or other detriment.

(3)   It is unlawful for a barrister or barrister's clerk, in relation to a pupillage or tenancy in the set of chambers in question, to subject to harassment a person who is, or has applied to be, a pupil or tenant.

(4)   It is unlawful for any person, in relation to the giving, withholding or acceptance of instructions to a barrister, to discriminate against any person by subjecting him to a detriment, or to subject him to harassment.

(5)   In this regulation–

'barrister's clerk' includes any person carrying out any of the functions of a barrister's clerk;

'pupil', 'pupillage' and 'set of chambers' have the meanings commonly associated with their use in the context of barristers practising in independent practice; and

'tenancy' and 'tenant' have the meanings commonly associated with their use in the context of barristers practising in independent practice, but also include reference to any barrister permitted to work in a set of chambers who is not a tenant.

(6)   This regulation extends to England and Wales only.

16   Advocates

(1)   It is unlawful for an advocate, in relation to taking any person as his pupil, to discriminate against a person–

(a)   in the arrangements which he makes for the purpose of determining whom he will take as his pupil;

(b)   in respect of any terms on which he offers to take any person as his pupil; or

(c)   by refusing to take, or deliberately not taking, a person as his pupil.

(2)   It is unlawful for an advocate, in relation to a person who is his pupil, to discriminate against him–

   (a)   in respect of any terms applicable to him as a pupil;

   (b)   in the opportunities for training, or gaining experience, which are afforded or denied to him;

   (c)   in the benefits which are afforded or denied to him; or

   (d)   by terminating the relationship, or by subjecting him to any pressure to terminate the relationship or other detriment.

(3)   It is unlawful for an advocate, in relation to a person who is his pupil or taking any person as his pupil, to subject such a person to harassment.

(4)   It is unlawful for any person, in relation to the giving, withholding or acceptance of instructions to an advocate, to discriminate against any person by subjecting him to a detriment, or to subject him to harassment.

(5)   In this regulation–

'advocate' means a member of the Faculty of Advocates practising as such; and

'pupil' has the meaning commonly associated with its use in the context of a person training to be an advocate.

(6)   This regulation extends to Scotland only.

17   Partnerships

(1)   It is unlawful for a firm, in relation to a position as partner in the firm, to discriminate against a person–

   (a)   in the arrangements they make for the purpose of determining to whom they should offer that position;

   (b)   in the terms on which they offer him that position;

   (c)   by refusing to offer, or deliberately not offering, him that position; or

   (d)   in a case where the person already holds that position–

      (i)   in the way they afford him access to any benefits or by refusing to afford, or deliberately not affording, him access to them; or

      (ii)   by expelling him from that position, or subjecting him to any other detriment.

(2)   It is unlawful for a firm, in relation to a position as partner in the firm, to subject to harassment a person who holds or has applied for that position.

(3)   Paragraphs (1)(a) to (c) and (2) apply in relation to persons proposing to form themselves into a partnership as they apply in relation to a firm.

(4)   Paragraph (1) does not apply to any act in relation to a position as partner where, if the position were employment, that act would be lawful by virtue of regulation 8 (exception for genuine occupational requirement etc).

(5)   In the case of a limited partnership references in this regulation to a partner shall be construed as references to a general partner as defined in section 3 of the Limited Partnerships Act 1907.

(6)   This regulation applies to a limited liability partnership as it applies to a firm; and, in its application to a limited liability partnership, references to a partner in a firm are references to a member of the limited liability partnership.

(7)   In this regulation, 'firm' has the meaning given by section 4 of the Partnership Act 1890.

(8)   In paragraph (1)(d) reference to the expulsion of a person from a position as partner includes reference–

    (a)   to the termination of that person's partnership by the expiration of any period (including a period expiring by reference to an event or circumstance), not being a termination immediately after which the partnership is renewed on the same terms; and

    (b)   to the termination of that person's partnership by any act of his (including the giving of notice) in circumstances such that he is entitled to terminate it without notice by reason of the conduct of the other partners.

18   Trade organisations

(1)   It is unlawful for a trade organisation to discriminate against a person–

    (a)   in the terms on which it is prepared to admit him to membership of the organisation; or

    (b)   by refusing to accept, or deliberately not accepting, his application for membership.

(2)   It is unlawful for a trade organisation, in relation to a member of the organisation, to discriminate against him–

    (a)   in the way it affords him access to any benefits or by refusing or deliberately omitting to afford him access to them;

    (b)   by depriving him of membership, or varying the terms on which he is a member; or

    (c)   by subjecting him to any other detriment.

(3)   It is unlawful for a trade organisation, in relation to a person's membership or application for membership of that organisation, to subject that person to harassment.

(4)   In this regulation–
'trade organisation' means an organisation of workers, an organisation of employers, or any other organisation whose members carry on a particular profession or trade for the purposes of which the organisation exists;
'profession' includes any vocation or occupation; and
'trade' includes any business.

19   Qualifications bodies

(1)   It is unlawful for a qualifications body to discriminate against a person–

    (a)   in the terms on which it is prepared to confer a professional or trade qualification on him;

(b)   by refusing or deliberately not granting any application by him for such a qualification; or

(c)   by withdrawing such a qualification from him or varying the terms on which he holds it.

(2)   It is unlawful for a qualifications body, in relation to a professional or trade qualification conferred by it, to subject to harassment a person who holds or applies for such a qualification.

(3)   In this regulation–

'qualifications body' means any authority or body which can confer a professional or trade qualification, but it does not include–

(a)   a governing body of an educational establishment to which regulation 23 (institutions of further and higher education) applies, or would apply but for the operation of any other provision of these Regulations, or

(b)   a proprietor of a school;

'confer' includes renew or extend;

'professional or trade qualification' means any authorisation, qualification, recognition, registration, enrolment, approval or certification which is needed for, or facilitates engagement in, a particular profession or trade;

'profession' and 'trade' have the same meaning as in regulation 18.

20   The provision of vocational training

(1)   It is unlawful, in relation to a person seeking or undergoing training, for any training provider to discriminate against him–

(a)   in the arrangements he makes for the purpose of determining to whom he should offer training;

(b)   in the terms on which the training provider affords him access to any training;

(c)   by refusing or deliberately not affording him such access;

(d)   by terminating his training; or

(e)   by subjecting him to any other detriment during his training.

(2)   It is unlawful for a training provider, in relation to a person seeking or undergoing training, to subject him to harassment.

(3)   Paragraph (1) does not apply if the discrimination concerns training that would only fit a person for employment which, by virtue of regulation 8 (exception for genuine occupational requirement etc), the employer could lawfully refuse to offer the person seeking training.

(4)   In this regulation–

'professional or trade qualification' has the same meaning as in regulation 19;

'registered pupil' has the meaning given by section 434 of the Education Act 1996;

'training' means–

(a)   all types and all levels of training which would help fit a person for any employment;

(b)   vocational guidance;

(c)   facilities for training;

(d)   practical work experience provided by an employer to a person whom he does not employ; and

(e)   any assessment related to the award of any professional or trade qualification;

'training provider' means any person who provides, or makes arrangements for the provision of, training, but it does not include–

(a)   an employer in relation to training for persons employed by him;

(b)   a governing body of an educational establishment to which regulation 23 (institutions of further and higher education) applies, or would apply but for the operation of any other provision of these Regulations; or

(c)   a proprietor of a school in relation to any registered pupil.

21   Employment agencies, careers guidance etc

(1)   It is unlawful for an employment agency to discriminate against a person–

(a)   in the terms on which the agency offers to provide any of its services;

(b)   by refusing or deliberately not providing any of its services; or

(c)   in the way it provides any of its services.

(2)   It is unlawful for an employment agency, in relation to a person to whom it provides its services, or who has requested it to provide its services, to subject that person to harassment.

(3)   Paragraph (1) does not apply to discrimination if it only concerns employment which, by virtue of regulation 8 (exception for genuine occupational requirement etc), the employer could lawfully refuse to offer the person in question.

(4)   An employment agency shall not be subject to any liability under this regulation if it proves that–

(a)   it acted in reliance on a statement made to it by the employer to the effect that, by reason of the operation of paragraph (3), its action would not be unlawful; and

(b)   it was reasonable for it to rely on the statement.

(5)   A person who knowingly or recklessly makes a statement such as is referred to in paragraph (4)(a) which in a material respect is false or misleading commits an offence, and shall be liable on summary conviction to a fine not exceeding level 5 on the standard scale.

(6)   For the purposes of this regulation–

(a)   'employment agency' means a person who, for profit or not, provides services for the purpose of finding employment for workers or supplying employers with workers, but it does not include–

(i)   a governing body of an educational establishment to which regulation 23 (institutions of further and higher education) applies, or would apply but for the operation of any other provision of these Regulations; or

(ii)   a proprietor of a school; and

(b)   references to the services of an employment agency include guidance on careers and any other services related to employment.

22   Assisting persons to obtain employment etc

(1)   It is unlawful for the Secretary of State to discriminate against any person by subjecting him to a detriment, or to subject a person to harassment, in the provision of facilities or services under section 2 of the Employment and Training Act 1973 (arrangements for assisting persons to obtain employment).

(2)   It is unlawful for Scottish Enterprise or Highlands and Islands Enterprise to discriminate against any person by subjecting him to a detriment, or to subject a person to harassment, in the provision of facilities or services under such arrangements as are mentioned in section 2(3) of the Enterprise and New Towns (Scotland) Act 1990 (arrangements analogous to arrangements in pursuance of the said Act of 1973).

(3)   This regulation does not apply in a case where–

(a)   regulation 20 (the provision of vocational training) applies or would apply but for the operation of any other provision of these Regulations, or

(b)   the Secretary of State is acting as an employment agency within the meaning of regulation 21 (employment agencies, careers guidance etc).

23   Institutions of further and higher education

(1)   It is unlawful, in relation to an educational establishment to which this regulation applies, for the governing body of that establishment to discriminate against a person–

(a)   in the terms on which it offers to admit him to the establishment as a student;

(b)   by refusing or deliberately not accepting an application for his admission to the establishment as a student; or

(c)   where he is a student of the establishment–

(i)   in the way it affords him access to any benefits,

(ii)   by refusing or deliberately not affording him access to them, or

(iii)   by excluding him from the establishment or subjecting him to any other detriment.

(2)   It is unlawful, in relation to an educational establishment to which this regulation applies, for the governing body of that establishment to subject to harassment a person who is a student at the establishment, or who has applied for admission to the establishment as a student.

(3)   Paragraph (1) does not apply if the discrimination concerns training that would only fit a person for employment which, by virtue of regulation 8 (exception for genuine occupational requirement etc), the employer could lawfully refuse to offer the person in question.

(4)   This regulation applies to the following educational establishments in England and Wales, namely–

(a)   an institution within the further education sector (within the meaning of section 91(3) of the Further and Higher Education Act 1992);

(b)   a university;

(c)   an institution, other than a university, within the higher education sector (within the meaning of section 91(5) of the Further and Higher Education Act 1992).

(5)   This regulation applies to the following educational establishments in Scotland, namely–

(a)   a college of further education within the meaning of section 36(1) of the Further and Higher Education (Scotland) Act 1992 under the management of a board of management within the meaning of Part I of that Act;

(b)   a college of further education maintained by an education authority in the exercise of its further education functions in providing courses of further education within the meaning of section 1(5)(b)(ii) of the Education (Scotland) Act 1980;

(c)   any other educational establishment (not being a school) which provides further education within the meaning of section 1 of the Further and Higher Education (Scotland) Act 1992;

(d)   an institution within the higher education sector (within the meaning of Part 2 of the Further and Higher Education (Scotland) Act 1992);

(e)   a central institution (within the meaning of section 135 of the Education (Scotland) Act 1980).

(6)   In this regulation–

'education authority' has the meaning given by section 135(1) of the Education (Scotland) Act 1980;

'governing body' includes–

(a)   the board of management of a college referred to in paragraph (5)(a), and

(b)   the managers of a college or institution referred to in paragraph (5)(b) or (e);

'student' means any person who receives education at an educational establishment to which this regulation applies; and

'university' includes a university college and the college, school or hall of a university.

24   Relationships which have come to an end

(1)   In this regulation a 'relevant relationship' is a relationship during the course of which an act of discrimination against, or harassment of, one party to the relationship ('B') by the other party to it ('A') is unlawful by virtue of any preceding provision of this Part.

(2)   Where a relevant relationship has come to an end, it is unlawful for A–

(a)   to discriminate against B by subjecting him to a detriment; or

(b)   to subject B to harassment;

where the discrimination or harassment arises out of and is closely connected to that relationship.

(3)   In paragraph (1), reference to an act of discrimination or harassment which is unlawful includes, in the case of a relationship which has come to an end before the date on which the act of discrimination or harassment became unlawful by virtue of these Regulations, reference to an act of discrimination or harassment which would, after that date, be unlawful.

PART 3: OTHER UNLAWFUL ACTS

25 Liability of employers and principals

(1)   Anything done by a person in the course of his employment shall be treated for the purposes of these Regulations as done by his employer as well as by him, whether or not it was done with the employer's knowledge or approval.

(2)   Anything done by a person as agent for another person with the authority (whether express or implied, and whether precedent or subsequent) of that other person shall be treated for the purposes of these Regulations as done by that other person as well as by him.

(3)   In proceedings brought under these Regulations against any person in respect of an act alleged to have been done by an employee of his it shall be a defence for that person to prove that he took such steps as were reasonably practicable to prevent the employee from doing that act, or from doing in the course of his employment acts of that description.

26 Aiding unlawful acts

(1)   A person who knowingly aids another person to do an act made unlawful by these Regulations shall be treated for the purpose of these Regulations as himself doing an unlawful act of the like description.

(2)   For the purposes of paragraph (1) an employee or agent for whose act the employer or principal is liable under regulation 25 (or would be so liable but for regulation 25(3)) shall be deemed to aid the doing of the act by the employer or principal.

(3)   A person does not under this regulation knowingly aid another to do an unlawful act if–

(a)   he acts in reliance on a statement made to him by that other person that, by reason of any provision of these Regulations, the act which he aids would not be unlawful; and

(b)   it is reasonable for him to rely on the statement.

(4)   A person who knowingly or recklessly makes a statement such as is referred to in paragraph (3)(a) which in a material respect is false or misleading commits an offence, and shall be liable on summary conviction to a fine not exceeding level 5 on the standard scale.

PART 4: GENERAL EXCEPTIONS FROM PARTS 2 AND 3

27 Exception for statutory authority

(1)   Nothing in Part 2 or 3 shall render unlawful any act done in order to comply with a requirement of any statutory provision.

(2)   In this regulation 'statutory provision' means any provision (whenever enacted) of–

(a)   an Act or an Act of the Scottish Parliament;

(b)   an instrument made by a Minister of the Crown under an Act;

(c)   an instrument made under an Act or an Act of the Scottish Parliament by the Scottish Ministers or a member of the Scottish Executive.

28   Exception for national security

Nothing in Part 2 or 3 shall render unlawful an act done for the purpose of safeguarding national security, if the doing of the act was justified by that purpose.

29   Exceptions for positive action

(1)   Nothing in Part 2 or 3 shall render unlawful any act done in or in connection with–

(a)   affording persons of a particular age or age group access to facilities for training which would help fit them for particular work; or

(b)   encouraging persons of a particular age or age group to take advantage of opportunities for doing particular work;

where it reasonably appears to the person doing the act that it prevents or compensates for disadvantages linked to age suffered by persons of that age or age group doing that work or likely to take up that work.

(2)   Nothing in Part 2 or 3 shall render unlawful any act done by a trade organisation within the meaning of regulation 18 in or in connection with–

(a)   affording only members of the organisation who are of a particular age or age group access to facilities for training which would help fit them for holding a post of any kind in the organisation; or

(b)   encouraging only members of the organisation who are of a particular age or age group to take advantage of opportunities for holding such posts in the organisation,

where it reasonably appears to the organisation that the act prevents or compensates for disadvantages linked to age suffered by those of that age or age group holding such posts or likely to hold such posts.

(3)   Nothing in Part 2 or 3 shall render unlawful any act done by a trade organisation within the meaning of regulation 18 in or in connection with encouraging only persons of a particular age or age group to become members of the organisation where it reasonably appears to the organisation that the act prevents or compensates for disadvantages linked to age suffered by persons of that age or age group who are, or are eligible to become, members.

30   Exception for retirement

(1)   This regulation applies in relation to an employee within the meaning of section 230(1) of the 1996 Act, a person in Crown employment, a relevant member of the House of Commons staff, and a relevant member of the House of Lords staff.

(2)   Nothing in Part 2 or 3 shall render unlawful the dismissal of a person to whom this regulation applies at or over the age of 65 where the reason for the dismissal is retirement.

(3)   For the purposes of this regulation, whether or not the reason for a dismissal is retirement shall be determined in accordance with sections 98ZA to 98ZF of the 1996 Act.

31   Exception for the national minimum wage

(1)   Nothing in Part 2 or 3 shall render it unlawful for a relevant person ('A') to be remunerated in respect of his work at a rate which is lower than the rate at which another such person ('B') is remunerated for his work where–

(a)   the hourly rate of the national minimum wage for a person of A's age is lower than that for a person of B's age, and

(b)   the rate at which A is remunerated is below the single hourly rate for the national minimum wage prescribed by the Secretary of State under section 1(3) of the National Minimum Wage Act 1998.

(2)   Nothing in Part 2 or 3 shall render it unlawful for an apprentice who is not a relevant person to be remunerated in respect of his work at a rate which is lower than the rate at which an apprentice who is a relevant person is remunerated for his work.

(3)   In this regulation–

'apprentice' means a person who is employed under a contract of apprenticeship or, in accordance with regulation 12(3) of the National Minimum Wage Regulations 1999, is to be treated as employed under such a contract;

'relevant person' means a person who qualifies for the national minimum wage (whether at the single hourly rate for the national minimum wage prescribed by the Secretary of State under section 1(3) of the National Minimum Wage Act 1998 or at a different rate).

32   Exception for provision of certain benefits based on length of service

(1)   Subject to paragraph (2), nothing in Part 2 or 3 shall render it unlawful for a person ('A'), in relation to the award of any benefit by him, to put a worker ('B') at a disadvantage when compared with another worker ('C'), if and to the extent that the disadvantage suffered by B is because B's length of service is less than that of C

(2)   Where B's length of service exceeds 5 years, it must reasonably appear to A that the way in which he uses the criterion of length of service, in relation to the award in respect of which B is put at a disadvantage, fulfils a business need of his undertaking (for example, by encouraging the loyalty or motivation, or rewarding the experience, of some or all of his workers).

(3)   In calculating a worker's length of service for these purposes, A shall calculate–

(a)   the length of time the worker has been working for him doing work which he reasonably considers to be at or above a particular level (assessed by reference to the demands made on the worker, for example, in terms of effort, skills and decision making); or

(b)   the length of time the worker has been working for him in total;

and on each occasion on which he decides to use the criterion of length of service in relation to the award of a benefit to workers, it is for him to decide which of these definitions to use to calculate their lengths of service.

(4)   For the purposes of paragraph (3), in calculating the length of time a worker has been working for him—

(a)   A shall calculate the length of time in terms of the number of weeks during the whole or part of which the worker was working for him;

(b)   A may discount any period during which the worker was absent from work (including any period of absence which at the time it occurred was thought by A or the worker to be permanent) unless in all the circumstances (including the way in which other workers' absences occurring in similar circumstances are treated by A in calculating their lengths of service) it would not be reasonable for him to do so;

(c)   A may discount any period of time during which the worker was present at work ('the relevant period') where—

(i)   the relevant period preceded a period during which the worker was absent from work, and

(ii)   in all the circumstances (including the length of the worker's absence, the reason for his absence, the effect his absence has had on his ability to discharge the duties of his work, and the way in which other workers are treated by A in similar circumstances) it is reasonable for A to discount the relevant period.

(5)   For the purposes of paragraph (3)(b), a worker shall be treated as having worked for A during any period during which he worked for another if—

(a)   that period is treated as a period of employment with A for the purposes of the 1996 Act by virtue of the operation of section 218 of that Act; or

(b)   were the worker to be made redundant by A, that period and the period he has worked for A would amount to 'relevant service' within the meaning of section 155 of that Act.

(6)   In paragraph (5)—

(a)   the reference to being made redundant is a reference to being dismissed by reason of redundancy for the purposes of the 1996 Act;

(b)   the reference to section 155 of that Act is a reference to that section as modified by the Redundancy Payments (Continuity of Employment in Local Government, etc) (Modification) Order 1999.

(7)   In this regulation—

'benefit' does not include any benefit awarded to a worker by virtue of his ceasing to work for A; and

'year' means a year of 12 calendar months.

33   Exception for provision of enhanced redundancy payments to employees

(1)   Nothing in Part 2 or 3 shall render it unlawful for an employer–

    (a)   to give a qualifying employee an enhanced redundancy payment which is less in amount than the enhanced redundancy payment which he gives to another such employee if both amounts are calculated in the same way;

    (b)   to give enhanced redundancy payments only to those who are qualifying employees by virtue of sub-paragraph (a) or (c)(i) of the definition of qualifying employee below.

(2)   In this regulation–

'the appropriate amount', 'a redundancy payment' and 'a week's pay' have the same meaning as they have in section 162 of the 1996 Act;

'enhanced redundancy payment' means a payment of an amount calculated in accordance with paragraph (3) or (4);

'qualifying employee' means–

    (a)   an employee who is entitled to a redundancy payment by virtue of section 135 of the 1996 Act;

    (b)   an employee who would have been so entitled but for the operation of section 155 of that Act;

    (c)   an employee who agrees to the termination of his employment in circumstances where, had he been dismissed–

        (i)   he would have been a qualifying employee by virtue of sub-paragraph (a) of this definition; or

        (ii)   he would have been a qualifying employee by virtue of sub-paragraph (b).

(3)   For an amount to be calculated in accordance with this paragraph it must be calculated in accordance with section 162(1) to (3) of the 1996 Act.

(4)   For an amount to be calculated in accordance with this paragraph–

    (a)   it must be calculated as in paragraph (3);

    (b)   however, in making that calculation, the employer may do one or both of the following things–

        (i)   he may treat a week's pay as not being subject to a maximum amount or as being subject to a maximum amount above the amount laid down in section 227 of the 1996 Act;

        (ii)   he may multiply the appropriate amount allowed for each year of employment by a figure of more than one;

    (c)   having made the calculation as in paragraph (3) (whether or not in making that calculation he has done anything mentioned in sub-paragraph (b)) the employer may increase the amount thus calculated by multiplying it by a figure of more than one.

(5)   For the purposes of paragraphs (3) and (4), the reference to 'the relevant date' in section 162(1)(a) of the 1996 Act is to be read, in the case of a qualifying employee who agrees to the termination of his employment, as a reference to the date on which that termination takes effect.

34   Exception for provision of life assurance cover to retired workers

(1)   Where a person ('A') arranges for workers to be provided with life assurance cover after their early retirement on grounds of ill health, nothing in Part 2 or 3 shall render it unlawful–

   (a)   where a normal retirement age applied in relation to any such workers at the time they took early retirement, for A to arrange for such cover to cease when such workers reach that age;

   (b)   in relation to any other workers, for A to arrange for such cover to cease when the workers reach the age of 65.

(2)   In this regulation, 'normal retirement age', in relation to a worker who has taken early retirement, means the age at which workers in A's undertaking who held the same kind of position as the worker held at the time of his retirement were normally required to retire.

PART 5: ENFORCEMENT

35   Restriction of proceedings for breach of Regulations

(1)   Except as provided by these Regulations no proceedings, whether civil or criminal, shall lie against any person in respect of an act by reason that the act is unlawful by virtue of a provision of these Regulations.

(2)   Paragraph (1) does not prevent the making of an application for judicial review or the investigation or determination of any matter in accordance with Part 10 (investigations: the Pensions Ombudsman) of the Pension Schemes Act 1993 by the Pensions Ombudsman.

36   Jurisdiction of employment tribunals

(1)   A complaint by any person ('the complainant') that another person ('the respondent')–

   (a)   has committed against the complainant an act to which this regulation applies; or

   (b)   is by virtue of regulation 25 (liability of employers and principals) or 26 (aiding unlawful acts) to be treated as having committed against the complainant such an act;

   may be presented to an employment tribunal.

(2)   This regulation applies to any act of discrimination or harassment which is unlawful by virtue of any provision of Part 2 other than–

   (a)   where the act is one in respect of which an appeal or proceedings in the nature of an appeal may be brought under any enactment, regulation 19 (qualifications bodies);

   (b)   regulation 23 (institutions of further and higher education); or

   (c)   where the act arises out of and is closely connected to a relationship between the complainant and the respondent which has come to an end but during the course of which an act of discrimination against, or harassment of, the complainant by the respondent would have been unlawful by virtue of regulation 23, regulation 24 (relationships which have come to an end).

(3) In paragraph (2)(c), reference to an act of discrimination or harassment which would have been unlawful includes, in the case of a relationship which has come to an end before the date on which the act of discrimination or harassment became unlawful by virtue of these Regulations, reference to an act of discrimination or harassment which would, after that date, have be unlawful.

(4) In this regulation, 'enactment' includes an enactment comprised in, or in an instrument made under, an Act of the Scottish Parliament.

37 Burden of proof: employment tribunals

(1) This regulation applies to any complaint presented under regulation 36 to an employment tribunal.

(2) Where, on the hearing of the complaint, the complainant proves facts from which the tribunal could, apart from this regulation, conclude in the absence of an adequate explanation that the respondent–

    (a) has committed against the complainant an act to which regulation 36 applies; or

    (b) is by virtue of regulation 25 (liability of employers and principals) or 26 (aiding unlawful acts) to be treated as having committed against the complainant such an act,

the tribunal shall uphold the complaint unless the respondent proves that he did not commit, or as the case may be, is not to be treated as having committed, that act.

38 Remedies on complaints in employment tribunals

(1) Where an employment tribunal finds that a complaint presented to it under regulation 36 is well-founded, the tribunal shall make such of the following as it considers just and equitable–

    (a) an order declaring the rights of the complainant and the respondent in relation to the act to which the complaint relates;

    (b) an order requiring the respondent to pay to the complainant compensation of an amount corresponding to any damages he could have been ordered by a county court or by a sheriff court to pay to the complainant if the complaint had fallen to be dealt with under regulation 39 (jurisdiction of county and sheriff courts);

    (c) a recommendation that the respondent take within a specified period action appearing to the tribunal to be practicable for the purpose of obviating or reducing the adverse effect on the complainant of any act of discrimination or harassment to which the complaint relates.

(2) As respects an unlawful act of discrimination falling within regulation 3(1)(b) (discrimination on the grounds of age), if the respondent proves that the provision, criterion or practice was not applied with the intention of treating the complainant unfavourably on grounds of age, an order may be made under paragraph (1)(b) only if the employment tribunal–

    (a) makes such order under paragraph (1)(a) (if any) and such recommendation under paragraph (1)(c) (if any) as it would have made if it had no power to make an order under paragraph (1)(b); and

(b) (where it makes an order under paragraph (1)(a) or a recommendation under paragraph (1)(c) or both) considers that it is just and equitable to make an order under paragraph (1)(b) as well.

(3) If without reasonable justification the respondent to a complaint fails to comply with a recommendation made by an employment tribunal under paragraph (1)(c), then, if it thinks it just and equitable to do so–

(a) the tribunal may increase the amount of compensation required to be paid to the complainant in respect of the complaint by an order made under paragraph (1)(b); or

(b) if an order under paragraph (1)(b) was not made, the tribunal may make such an order.

(4) Where an amount of compensation falls to be awarded under paragraph (1)(b), the tribunal may include in the award interest on that amount subject to, and in accordance with, the provisions of the Employment Tribunals (Interest on Awards in Discrimination Cases) Regulations 1996.

(5) This regulation has effect subject to paragraph 6 of Schedule 2 (pension schemes).

39   Jurisdiction of county and sheriff courts

(1) A claim by any person ('the claimant') that another person ('the respondent')–

(a) has committed against the claimant an act to which this regulation applies; or

(b) is by virtue of regulation 25 (liability of employers and principals) or 26 (aiding unlawful acts) to be treated as having committed against the claimant such an act,

may be made the subject of civil proceedings in like manner as any other claim in tort or (in Scotland) in reparation for breach of statutory duty.

(2) Proceedings brought under paragraph (1) shall–

(a) in England and Wales, be brought only in a county court; and

(b) in Scotland, be brought only in a sheriff court.

(3) For the avoidance of doubt it is hereby declared that damages in respect of an unlawful act to which this regulation applies may include compensation for injury to feelings whether or not they include compensation under any other head.

(4) This regulation applies to any act of discrimination or harassment which is unlawful by virtue of–

(a) regulation 23 (institutions of further and higher education); or

(b) where the act arises out of and is closely connected to a relationship between the claimant and the respondent which has come to an end but during the course of which an act of discrimination against, or harassment of, the claimant by the respondent would have been unlawful by virtue of regulation 23, regulation 24 (relationships which have come to an end).

(5) In paragraph (4)(b), reference to an act of discrimination or harassment which would have been unlawful includes, in the case of a relationship which has come to an end before the date on which the act of discrimination or harassment became unlawful by virtue of these Regulations, reference to an act of discrimination or harassment which would, after that date, have be unlawful.

40 Burden of proof: county and sheriff courts

(1) This regulation applies to any claim brought under regulation 39 in a county court in England and Wales or a sheriff court in Scotland.

(2) Where, on the hearing of the claim, the claimant proves facts from which the court could, apart from this regulation, conclude in the absence of an adequate explanation that the respondent–

    (a) has committed against the claimant an act to which regulation 39 applies; or

    (b) is by virtue of regulation 25 (liability of employers and principals) or 26 (aiding unlawful acts) to be treated as having committed against the claimant such an act,

the court shall uphold the claim unless the respondent proves that he did not commit, or as the case may be, is not to be treated as having committed, that act.

41 Help for persons in obtaining information etc

(1) In accordance with this regulation, a person ('the person aggrieved') who considers he may have been discriminated against, or subjected to harassment, in contravention of these Regulations may serve on the respondent to a complaint presented under regulation 36 (jurisdiction of employment tribunals) or a claim brought under regulation 39 (jurisdiction of county and sheriff courts) questions in the form set out in Schedule 3 or forms to the like effect with such variation as the circumstances require; and the respondent may if he so wishes reply to such questions by way of the form set out in Schedule 4 or forms to the like effect with such variation as the circumstances require.

(2) Where the person aggrieved questions the respondent (whether in accordance with paragraph (1) or not)–

    (a) the questions, and any reply by the respondent (whether in accordance with paragraph (1) or not) shall, subject to the following provisions of this regulation, be admissible as evidence in the proceedings;

    (b) if it appears to the court or tribunal that the respondent deliberately, and without reasonable excuse, omitted to reply within eight weeks of service of the questions or that his reply is evasive or equivocal, the court or tribunal may draw any inference from that fact that it considers it just and equitable to draw, including an inference that he committed an unlawful act.

(3) In proceedings before a county court in England or Wales or a sheriff court in Scotland, a question shall only be admissible as evidence in pursuance of paragraph (2)(a)–

     (a)   where it was served before those proceedings had been instituted, if it was so served within the period of six months beginning when the act complained of was done;

     (b)   where it was served when those proceedings had been instituted, if it was served with the leave of, and within a period specified by, the court in question.

(4)   In proceedings before an employment tribunal, a question shall only be admissible as evidence in pursuance of paragraph (2)(a)–

     (a)   where it was served before a complaint had been presented to the tribunal, if it was so served within the period of three months beginning when the act complained of was done;

     (b)   where it was so served when a complaint had been presented to the tribunal, either–

         (i)   if it was served within the period of twenty-one days beginning with the day on which the complaint was presented, or

         (ii) if it was so served later with leave given, and within a period specified, by a direction of the tribunal.

(5)   A question and any reply thereto may be served on the respondent or, as the case may be, on the person aggrieved–

     (a)   by delivering it to him;

     (b)   by sending it by post to him at his usual or last-known residence or place of business;

     (c)   where the person to be served is a body corporate or is a trade union or employers' association within the meaning of the Trade Union and Labour Relations (Consolidation) Act 1992, by delivering it to the secretary or clerk of the body, union or association at its registered or principal office or by sending it by post to the secretary or clerk at that office;

     (d)   where the person to be served is acting by a solicitor, by delivering it at, or by sending it by post to, the solicitor's address for service; or

     (e)   where the person to be served is the person aggrieved, by delivering the reply, or sending it by post, to him at his address for reply as stated by him in the document containing the questions.

(6)   This regulation is without prejudice to any other enactment or rule of law regulating interlocutory and preliminary matters in proceedings before a county court, sheriff court or employment tribunal, and has effect subject to any enactment or rule of law regulating the admissibility of evidence in such proceedings.

(7)   In this regulation 'respondent' includes a prospective respondent.

42   Period within which proceedings to be brought

(1)   An employment tribunal shall not consider a complaint under regulation 36 unless it is presented to the tribunal before the end of the period of three months beginning when the act complained of was done.

(2)   A county court or a sheriff court shall not consider a claim brought under regulation 39 unless proceedings in respect of the claim are

instituted before the end of the period of six months beginning when the act complained of was done.

(3) A court or tribunal may nevertheless consider any such complaint or claim which is out of time if, in all the circumstances of the case, it considers that it is just and equitable to do so.

(4) For the purposes of this regulation and regulation 41 (help for persons in obtaining information etc)—

    (a) when the making of a contract is, by reason of the inclusion of any term, an unlawful act, that act shall be treated as extending throughout the duration of the contract; and

    (b) any act extending over a period shall be treated as done at the end of that period; and

    (c) a deliberate omission shall be treated as done when the person in question decided upon it,

and in the absence of evidence establishing the contrary a person shall be taken for the purposes of this regulation to decide upon an omission when he does an act inconsistent with doing the omitted act or, if he has done no such inconsistent act, when the period expires within which he might reasonably have been expected to do the omitted act if it was to be done.

PART 6: SUPPLEMENTAL

43 Validity of contracts, collective agreements and rules of undertakings

Schedule 5 (validity of contracts, collective agreements and rules of undertakings) shall have effect.

44 Application to the Crown etc

(1) These Regulations apply—

    (a) to an act done by or for purposes of a Minister of the Crown or government department; or

    (b) to an act done on behalf of the Crown by a statutory body, or a person holding a statutory office,

as they apply to an act done by a private person.

(2) These Regulations apply to Crown employment as they apply to employment by a private person, and shall so apply as if references to a contract of employment included references to the terms of service and references to dismissal included references to termination of Crown employment.

(3) Paragraphs (1) and (2) have effect subject to paragraph (4) and regulations 13 (police) and 14 (Serious Organised Crime Agency).

(4) These regulations do not apply to service in any of the naval, military or air forces of the Crown.

(5) Regulation 10(3) (meaning of employment and contract work at establishment in Great Britain) shall have effect in relation to any ship, aircraft or hovercraft belonging to or possessed by Her Majesty in right of the government of the United Kingdom as it has effect in relation to a ship, aircraft or hovercraft specified in regulation 10(3)(a) or (b).

(6)   The provisions of Parts 2 to 4 of the Crown Proceedings Act 1947 shall apply to proceedings against the Crown under these Regulations as they apply to proceedings in England and Wales which by virtue of section 23 of that Act are treated for the purposes of Part 2 of that Act as civil proceedings by or against the Crown, except that in their application to proceedings under these Regulations section 20 of that Act (removal and transfer of proceedings) shall not apply.

(7)   The provisions of Part 5 of the Crown Proceedings Act 1947 shall apply to proceedings against the Crown under these Regulations as they apply to proceedings in Scotland which by virtue of the said Part are treated as civil proceedings by or against the Crown, except that in their application to proceedings under these Regulations the proviso to section 44 of that Act (proceedings against the Crown in the Sheriff Court) shall not apply.

45   Application to House of Commons staff

(1)   Subject to paragraphs (2) and (3), these Regulations apply in relation to employment as a relevant member of the House of Commons staff as they apply in relation to other employment.

(2)   These Regulations apply to employment as such a member as they apply to employment by a private person, and shall so apply as if references to a contract of employment included references to the terms of employment of such a member and references to dismissal included references to termination of such employment.

(3)   In relation to employment as such a member, subsections (6) to (12) of section 195 of the 1996 Act (person to be treated as employer of House of Commons staff) apply, with any necessary modifications, for the purposes of these Regulations.

46   Application to House of Lords staff

(1)   These Regulations apply in relation to employment as a relevant member of the House of Lords staff as they apply in relation to other employment.

(2)   Section 194(7) of the 1996 Act (continuity of employment) applies for the purposes of this regulation.

47   Duty to consider working beyond retirement

Schedule 6, which sets out the procedure to be followed if an employee (within the meaning of that Schedule) is to be retired, shall have effect.

48   Duty to consider working beyond retirement–transitional provisions

Schedule 7, which sets out transitional provisions in relation to the duty to consider working beyond retirement, shall have effect.

49   Amendments, transitionals, repeals and revocations

(1)   Schedule 8, which contains amendments to and repeals of legislation and related transitional provisions, shall have effect.

(2)   Schedule 9, which contains repeals and revocations, shall have effect.

SCHEDULE 1

NORWEGIAN PART OF THE FRIGG GAS FIELD

Regulation 10(4)

1   The part of the Norwegian sector of the Continental Shelf described in this Schedule is the area defined by–

(a)   the sets of lines of latitude and longitude joining the following surface co-ordinates–

Longitude	Latitude
02 degrees 05 minutes 30 seconds E	60 degrees 00 minutes 45 seconds N
02 degrees 05 minutes 30 seconds E	59 degrees 58 minutes 45 seconds N
02 degrees 06 minutes 00 seconds E	59 degrees 58 minutes 45 seconds N
02 degrees 06 minutes 00 seconds E	59 degrees 57 minutes 45 seconds N
02 degrees 07 minutes 00 seconds E	59 degrees 57 minutes 45 seconds N
02 degrees 07 minutes 00 seconds E	59 degrees 57 minutes 30 seconds N
02 degrees 07 minutes 30 seconds E	59 degrees 57 minutes 30 seconds N
02 degrees 07 minutes 30 seconds E	59 degrees 55 minutes 30 seconds N
02 degrees 10 minutes 30 seconds E	59 degrees 55 minutes 30 seconds N
02 degrees 10 minutes 30 seconds E	59 degrees 54 minutes 45 seconds N
02 degrees 11 minutes 00 seconds E	59 degrees 54 minutes 45 seconds N
02 degrees 11 minutes 00 seconds E	59 degrees 54 minutes 15 seconds N
02 degrees 12 minutes 30 seconds E	59 degrees 54 minutes 15 seconds N
02 degrees 12 minutes 30 seconds E	59 degrees 54 minutes 00 seconds N
02 degrees 13 minutes 30 seconds E	59 degrees 54 minutes 00 seconds N
02 degrees 13 minutes 30 seconds E	59 degrees 54 minutes 30 seconds N
02 degrees 15 minutes 30 seconds E	59 degrees 54 minutes 30 seconds N
02 degrees 15 minutes 30 seconds E	59 degrees 53 minutes 15 seconds N
02 degrees 10 minutes 30 seconds E	59 degrees 53 minutes 15 seconds N
02 degrees 10 minutes 30 seconds E	59 degrees 52 minutes 45 seconds N
02 degrees 09 minutes 30 seconds E	59 degrees 52 minutes 45 seconds N
02 degrees 09 minutes 30 seconds E	59 degrees 52 minutes 15 seconds N
02 degrees 08 minutes 30 seconds E	59 degrees 52 minutes 15 seconds N
02 degrees 08 minutes 30 seconds E	59 degrees 52 minutes 00 seconds N
02 degrees 07 minutes 30 seconds E	59 degrees 52 minutes 00 seconds N
02 degrees 07 minutes 30 seconds E	59 degrees 51 minutes 30 seconds N
02 degrees 05 minutes 30 seconds E	59 degrees 51 minutes 30 seconds N
02 degrees 05 minutes 30 seconds E	59 degrees 51 minutes 00 seconds N
02 degrees 04 minutes 00 seconds E	59 degrees 51 minutes 00 seconds N
02 degrees 04 minutes 00 seconds E	59 degrees 50 minutes 30 seconds N
02 degrees 03 minutes 00 seconds E	59 degrees 50 minutes 30 seconds N
02 degrees 03 minutes 00 seconds E	59 degrees 50 minutes 00 seconds N

(b)   a line from the point 02 degrees 03 minutes 00 seconds E 59 degrees 50 minutes 00 seconds N west along the parallel of latitude 59 degrees 50 minutes 00 seconds N until its intersection with the Dividing Line;

(c)   a line from the point of intersection specified in sub-paragraph (b) along the Dividing Line until its intersection with the parallel of latitude 60 degrees 00 minutes 45 seconds N;

(d)   a line from the point of intersection specified in sub-paragraph (c) east along the parallel of latitude 60 degrees 00 minutes 45 degrees N until its intersection with the meridian 02 degrees 05 minutes 30 seconds E.

2   In this Schedule, the 'Dividing Line' means the dividing line as defined in an Agreement dated 10th March 1965 and made between the government of the United Kingdom of Great Britain and Northern Ireland and the government of the Kingdom of Norway as supplemented by a Protocol dated 22 December 1978.

SCHEDULE 2

PENSION SCHEMES

Regulation 11(3)

PART 1 PENSION SCHEMES–GENERAL

Interpretation

1(1)   In this Schedule, subject to sub-paragraphs (2) and (3), 'occupational pension scheme' means an occupational pension scheme within the meaning of section 1(1) of the Pension Schemes Act 1993.

(2)   In relation to rules, practices, actions and decisions identified at paragraph 7(a), 'occupational pension scheme' means an occupational pension scheme within the meaning of section 1(1) of the Pension Schemes Act 1993 under which only retirement-benefit activities within the meaning of section 255(4) of the Pensions Act 2004 are carried out.

(3)   In relation to rules, practices, actions and decisions identified at paragraphs 12, 13 and 30, 'occupational pension scheme' means an occupational pension scheme within the meaning of either section 1(1) of the Pension Schemes Act 1993 or section 150(5) of the Finance Act 2004.

(4)   In this Schedule, 'scheme' means an occupational pension scheme, construed in accordance with sub-paragraphs (1) to (3).

(5)   In this Schedule, in relation to a scheme–

'active member' has the meaning given by section 124(1) of the Pensions Act 1995, but in paragraph 13 also includes an active member within the meaning of section 151(2) of the Finance Act 2004;

'age related benefit' means benefit provided from a scheme to a member–

(a) on or following his retirement (including early retirement on grounds of ill health or otherwise),

(b) on his reaching a particular age, or

(c) on termination of his service in an employment;

'death benefit' means benefit payable from a pension scheme, in respect of a member, in consequence of his death;

'deferred member' has the meaning given by section 124(1) of the Pensions Act 1995;

'defined benefits arrangement' has the meaning given by section 152(6) of the Finance Act 2004, but the reference in that section to an arrangement shall be read as referring to an arrangement in respect of a member under a scheme as defined in section 1(1) of the Pension Schemes Act 1993 rather than in respect of a member under a pension scheme as defined in section 150(1) of the Finance Act 2004;

'dependant' means dependant as defined in the scheme rules;

'early retirement pivot age' means an age specified in the scheme rules as the earliest age at which age related benefit becomes payable without actuarial reduction (disregarding any special provision as to early payment on grounds of ill health or otherwise);

'employer' has the meaning given by section 318(1) of the Pensions Act 2004;

'employer contribution' means any contribution to a scheme by an employer in respect of a member;

'employment' includes any trade, business, profession, office or vocation, whether or not a person is employed in it under a contract of employment or is self employed;

'late retirement pivot age' means an age specified in the scheme rules above which benefit becomes payable with actuarial enhancement;

'managers' has the meaning given by section 124(1) of the Pensions Act 1995;

'member' means any active member, deferred member or pensioner member, but in paragraph 12 includes any active, deferred or pensioner member within the meaning of section 151(2) to (4) of the Finance Act 2004;

'member contribution' means any contribution to a scheme by a member;

'money purchase arrangement' has the meaning given by section 152(2) of the Finance Act 2004, but the reference in that section to an arrangement shall be read as referring to an arrangement in respect of a member under a scheme as defined in section 1(1) of the Pension Schemes Act 1993 rather than in respect of a member under a pension scheme as defined in section 150(1) of the Finance Act 2004;

'non-discrimination rule' means the rule in paragraph 2(1);

'normal pension age' has the meaning given by section 180 of the Pension Schemes Act 1993;

'normal retirement age', in relation to a member, means the age at which workers in the undertaking for which the member worked at the time of his retirement, and who held the same kind of position as the member held at his retirement, were normally required to retire;

'pensionable age' has the meaning given by section 122(1) of the Social Security Contributions and Benefits Act 1992;

'pensionable pay' means that part of a member's pay which counts as pensionable pay under the scheme rules;

'pensionable service' has the meaning given by section 124(1) of the Pensions Act 1995;

'pensioner member' has the meaning given by section 124(1) of the Pensions Act 1995; and

'prospective member' means any person who, under the terms of his employment or the scheme rules or both–

(a)   is able, at his own option, to become a member of the scheme,

(b)   shall become so able if he continues in the same employment for a sufficient period of time,

(c)   shall be so admitted to it automatically unless he makes an election not to become a member, or

(d)   may be admitted to it subject to the consent of any person.

(6)   In their application to a scheme which is divided into two or more sections, the provisions of this Schedule shall apply as if each section of the scheme was a separate scheme.

(7)   In this Schedule–

'personal pension scheme' has the meaning given by section 1(1) of the Pension Schemes Act 1993;

'registered pension scheme' has the meaning given by section 150(2) of the Finance Act 2004; and

references to contributions under a money purchase arrangement shall be construed as including amounts credited to a member's account whether or not they reflect payments actually made under the scheme.

(8)   Any term used in regulation 11 (pension schemes) shall have the same meaning in that regulation as it has in this Schedule.

Non-discrimination rule

2(1)   Every scheme shall be treated as including a provision ('the non-discrimination rule') containing a requirement that the trustees or managers of the scheme refrain from doing any act which is unlawful by virtue of regulation 11.

(2)   The other provisions of the scheme are to have effect subject to the non-discrimination rule.

(3)   The trustees or managers of a scheme may–

(a)   if they do not (apart from this sub-paragraph) have power to make such alterations to the scheme as may be required to secure conformity with the non-discrimination rule, or

(b)   if they have such power but the procedure for doing so–

(i)   is liable to be unduly complex or protracted, or

(ii)   involves the obtaining of consents which cannot be obtained, or can only be obtained with undue delay or difficulty,

by resolution make such alterations to the scheme.

(4)   Alterations made by a resolution such as is referred to in sub-paragraph (3)–

(a)   may have effect in relation to a period before the alterations are made (but may not have effect in relation to any time before 1st December 2006), and

(b)   shall be subject to the consent of any employer in relation to the scheme whose consent would be required for such a modification if it were to be made under the scheme rules.

Exception for rules, practices, actions and decisions relating to occupational pension schemes

3   Nothing in Part 2 or 3 of these Regulations shall render it unlawful for an employer, or for trustees or managers, to maintain or use, in relation to a scheme, any of the rules, practices, actions or decisions set out in Part 2 of this Schedule.

Exception for rules, practices, actions and decisions relating to contributions by employers to personal pension schemes

4   Nothing in Part 2 or 3 of these Regulations shall render it unlawful for an employer, in relation to the payment of contributions to any personal pension scheme in respect of a worker, to maintain or use any of the rules, practices, actions or decisions set out in Part 3 of this Schedule.

Procedure in employment tribunals

5   Where under regulation 36 (jurisdiction of employment tribunals) a member or prospective member of a scheme presents to an employment tribunal a complaint that the trustees or managers of the scheme–

(a)   have committed against him an act which is unlawful by virtue of regulation 11 (pension schemes) or 24 (relationships which have come to an end); or

(b)   are by virtue of regulation 25 (liability of employers and principals) or 26 (aiding unlawful acts) to be treated as having committed against him such an act,

the employer in relation to the scheme shall, for the purposes of the rules governing procedure, be treated as a party and be entitled to appear and be heard in accordance with those rules.

Remedies in employment tribunals

6(1)   This paragraph applies where–

(a)   under regulation 36 (jurisdiction of employment tribunals) a member or prospective member of a scheme ('the complainant') presents to an employment tribunal a complaint against the trustees or managers of the scheme or an employer;

(b)   the complainant is not a pensioner member of the scheme;

(c)   the complaint relates to the terms on which persons become members of the scheme, or the terms on which members of the scheme are treated; and

(d)   the tribunal finds the complaint to be well-founded.

(2)   Where this paragraph applies, the employment tribunal may, without prejudice to the generality of its power under regulation 38(1)(a) (power to make order declaring rights of complainant and respondent), make an order declaring that the complainant has a right–

(a)   where the complaint relates to the terms on which persons become members of the scheme, to be admitted to the scheme;

(b)   where the complaint relates to the terms on which members of the scheme are treated, to membership of the scheme without discrimination.

(3)   An order under sub-paragraph (2)–

(a)   may be made in respect of such period as is specified in the order (but may not be made in respect of any time before 1st December 2006);

(b)   may make such provision as the employment tribunal considers appropriate as to the terms on which, or the capacity in which, the complainant is to enjoy such admission or membership.

(4)   Where this paragraph applies, the employment tribunal may not make an order for compensation under regulation 38(1)(b), whether in relation to arrears of benefits or otherwise, except–

(a)   for injury to feelings;

(b)   by virtue of regulation 38(3).

PART 2: EXCEPTED RULES, PRACTICES, ACTIONS AND DECISIONS RELATING TO OCCUPATIONAL PENSION SCHEMES

Admission to schemes

7   In relation to admission to a scheme–

(a)   a minimum or maximum age for admission, including different ages for admission for different groups or categories of worker;

(b)   a minimum level of pensionable pay for admission, provided that such a minimum is not above the lower earnings limit referred to in section 5(1) of the Social Security Contributions and Benefits Act 1992.

The use of age criteria in actuarial calculations

8   The use of age criteria in actuarial calculations, for example in the actuarial calculation of–

(a)   any age related benefit commencing before any early retirement pivot age or enhancement of such benefit commencing after any late retirement pivot age;

(b)   member or employer contributions to a scheme; or

(c) any age related benefit commuted in exchange for the payment of any lump sum.

Contributions

9 Any difference in the rate of member or employer contributions by or in respect of different members to the extent that this is attributable to any differences in the pensionable pay of those members.

Contributions under money purchase arrangements

10 Under a money purchase arrangement–
(a) different rates of member or employer contributions according to the age of the members by or in respect of whom contributions are made where the aim in setting the different rates is–
  (i) to equalise the amount of benefit to which members of different ages who are otherwise in a comparable situation will become entitled under the arrangement, or
  (ii) to make the amount of benefit to which such members will become entitled under the arrangement more nearly equal;
(b) equal rates of member or employer contributions irrespective of the age of the members by or in respect of whom contributions are made.

Contributions under defined benefits arrangements

11 Under a defined benefits arrangement, different rates of member or employer contributions according to the age of the members by or in respect of whom contributions are made, to the extent that–
(a) each year of pensionable service entitles members in a comparable situation to accrue a right to defined benefits based on the same fraction of pensionable pay, and
(b) the aim in setting the different rates is to reflect the increasing cost of providing the defined benefits in respect of members as they get older.

Age related rules, practices, actions and decisions relating to benefit

12 A minimum age for entitlement to or payment of any age related benefit to a member, provided that, in the case of any age related benefit paid under a defined benefits arrangement before any early retirement pivot age–
(a) such benefit is subject to actuarial reduction for early receipt, and
(b) the member is not credited with additional periods of pensionable service.

13 In relation to workers who are active or prospective members of a scheme on 1st December 2006, a minimum age for entitlement to or payment of any age related benefit to such members under defined benefit arrangements before any early retirement pivot age, where such benefit is calculated in one or both of the following ways–
(a) it is not made subject to actuarial reduction for early receipt;

(b)   it results from crediting the member with additional periods of pensionable service.

14   An early retirement pivot age or a late retirement pivot age, including different such ages for different groups or categories of member.

15   The enhancement of any age related benefit in the event of a member's retirement before any early retirement pivot age on ill health grounds, where that enhancement is calculated by reference to the years of pensionable service which that member would have completed if he had continued in pensionable service up to the age specified for that purpose in the scheme rules.

16   Any rule, practice, action or decision whereby a male member who reaches pensionable age is not entitled or is no longer entitled to any additional amount of pension which would have been payable to such a member before pensionable age in the circumstances prescribed for the purposes of section 64(2) of the Pensions Act 1995 by regulation 13 of the Occupational Pension Schemes (Equal Treatment) Regulations 1995.

17   The reduction of any pension payable in consequence of a member's death to any dependant of the member where that dependant is more than a specified number of years younger than the member.

18   In relation to pensioner members who have retired on ill health grounds before any early retirement pivot age, discontinuation of any life assurance cover once any such members reach the normal retirement age which applied to them at the time they retired, or in relation to members to whom no such normal retirement age applied, once such members reach the age of 65.

Other rules, practices, actions and decisions relating to benefit

19   Any difference in the amount of any age related benefit or death benefit payable under a defined benefits arrangement to or in respect of members with different lengths of pensionable service to the extent that the difference in amount is attributable to their differing lengths of service, provided that, for each year of pensionable service, members in a comparable situation are entitled to accrue a right to benefit based upon the same fraction of pensionable pay.

20   Any difference in the amount of any age related benefit or death benefit payable from a scheme to or in respect of different members to the extent that the difference in amount is attributable to differences over time in the pensionable pay of those members.

21   Any limitation of the amount of any age related benefit or death benefit payable from a scheme where the limitation results from imposing a maximum number of years of service by reference to which such benefit may be calculated.

22   Any rule, practice, action or decision whereby any age related benefit or death benefit is only payable to or in respect of members who have completed a minimum period of service, provided that such a minimum period is not longer than 2 years qualifying service within the meaning of section 71(7) of the Pension Schemes Act 1993.

23   Any limitation on the amount of any age related benefit or death benefit payable from a scheme where the limitation results from imposing a minimum level of pensionable pay by reference to which any such benefit may be calculated, provided that such a minimum is not above the lower earnings limit referred to in section 5(1) of the Social Security Contributions and Benefits Act 1992.

24   Any limitation on the amount of any age related benefit or death benefit payable from a scheme where the limitation results from imposing a maximum level of pensionable pay by reference to which such benefit may be calculated.

Closure of schemes

25   The closure of a scheme, from a particular date, to workers who have not already joined it.

Other rules, practices, actions and decisions

26   Increases of pensions in payment which are made to members over 55 but not to members below that age.

27   Any difference in the rate of increase of pensions in payment for members of different ages to the extent that the aim in setting the different rates is to maintain the relative value of members' pensions.

28   Any difference in the rate of increase of pensions in payment for members whose pensions have been in payment for different lengths of time to the extent that the aim in setting the different rates is to maintain the relative value of members' pensions.

29   The application of an age limit for transfer of the value of a member's accrued rights into or out of a scheme, provided that any such age limit is not more than one year before the member's normal pension age.

Registered pension schemes

30(1)   Subject to sub-paragraph (2), any rules, practices, actions or decisions relating to entitlement to or payment of benefits under a registered pension scheme insofar as compliance is necessary to secure any tax relief or exemption available under Part 4 of the Finance Act 2004 or to prevent any charge to tax arising under that Part of that Act, whoever is liable in relation to such charge.

(2)   Sub-paragraph (1) does not apply to any rules, practices, actions or decisions setting a minimum age for entitlement to or payment of any age related benefit.

PART 3: EXCEPTED RULES, PRACTICES, ACTIONS AND DECISIONS RELATING TO CONTRIBUTIONS BY EMPLOYERS TO PERSONAL PENSION SCHEMES

Contributions by employers

31   Different rates of contributions by an employer according to the age of the workers in respect of whom the contributions are made where the aim in setting the different rates is—

(a)   to equalise the amount of benefit to which workers of different ages who are otherwise in a comparable situation will become entitled under their personal pension schemes, or

(b)   to make the amount of benefit to which such workers will become entitled under their personal pension schemes more nearly equal.

32   Any difference in the rate of contributions by an employer in respect of different workers to the extent that this is attributable to any differences in remuneration payable to those workers.

SCHEDULE 3

QUESTIONNAIRE OF PERSON AGGRIEVED

Regulation 41(1)

To   name of person to be questioned)

of

                                            (address)

1(1)   I   (name of questioner)

of

                                            (address)

consider that you may have discriminated against me [subjected me to harrassment] contrary to the Employment Equality (Age) Regulations 2006.

(2)   (Give date, approximate time and a factual description of the treatment received and of the circumstances leading up to the treatment.)

(3)   I consider that this treatment may have been unlawful because

                            (complete if you wish to give reasons, otherwise delete).

2   Do you agree that the statement in paragraph 1(2) above is an accurate description of what happened? If not, in what respect do you disagree or what is your version of what happened?

3   Do you accept that your treatment of me was unlawful discrimination [harrassment]? If not–

(a)   why not,

(b)   for what reason did I receive the treatment accorded to me, and

(c)   how far did considerations of age affect your treatment of me?

4   (Any other questions you wish to ask.)

5   My address for any reply you may wish to give to the questions raised above is [that set out in paragraph 1(1) above] [the following address

                          (signature of questioner)

                                      (date)

NB–By virtue of regulation 41 of the Employment Equality (Age) Regulations 2006 this questionnaire and any reply are (subject to the provisions of that regulation) admissible in proceedings under the Regulations. A court or tribunal may draw any such inference as is just and equitable from a failure without reasonable excuse to reply within eight weeks of service of this questionnaire, or from an evasive or equivocal reply, including an inference that the person questioned has committed an unlawful act.

SCHEDULE 4

REPLY BY RESPONDENT

Regulation 41(1)

To   (name of questioner)
of
                                                                      (address)
1   I   (name of person questioned)
of

                                                                      (address)
hereby acknowledge receipt of the questionnaire signed by you and dated
which was served on me on   (date).
2   [I agree that the statement in paragraph 1(2) of the questionnaire is an accurate description of what happened.]
[I disagree with the statement in paragraph 1(2) of the questionnaire in that

3   I accept/dispute that my treatment of you was unlawful discrimination [harrassment].
[My reasons for so disputing are

The reason why you received the treatment accorded to you and the answers to the other questions in paragraph 3 of the questionnaire are
                                                                            ]
4   (Replies to questions in paragraph 4 of the questionnaire.)
5   [I have deleted (in whole or in part) the paragraph(s) numbered above, since I am unable/unwilling to reply to the relevant questions in the correspondingly numbered paragraph(s) of the questionnaire for the following reasons   ]
                                                      (signature of questioner)
                                                                      (date)

SCHEDULE 5

VALIDITY OF CONTRACTS, COLLECTIVE AGREEMENTS AND RULES OF UNDERTAKINGS

Regulation 43

PART 1: VALIDITY AND REVISION OF CONTRACTS

1(1)   A term of a contract is void where–

(a)   the making of the contract is, by reason of the inclusion of the term, unlawful by virtue of these Regulations;

(b)   it is included in furtherance of an act which is unlawful by virtue of these Regulations; or

(c)   it provides for the doing of an act which is unlawful by virtue of these Regulations.

(2)   Sub-paragraph (1) does not apply to a term the inclusion of which constitutes, or is in furtherance of, or provides for, unlawful discrimination against, or harassment of, a party to the contract, but the term shall be unenforceable against that party.

(3)   A term in a contract which purports to exclude or limit any provision of these Regulations is unenforceable by any person in whose favour the term would operate apart from this paragraph.

(4)   Sub-paragraphs (1), (2) and (3) shall apply whether the contract was entered into before or after the date on which any term of the contract became unlawful by virtue of these Regulations, but in the case of a contract made before the date on which a term became unlawful, those sub-paragraphs do not apply to that term in relation to any period before that date.

2(1)   Paragraph 1(3) does not apply–

(a)   to a contract settling a complaint to which regulation 36(1) (jurisdiction of employment tribunals) applies where the contract is made with the assistance of a conciliation officer within the meaning of section 211 of the Trade Union and Labour Relations (Consolidation) Act 1992;

(b)   to a contract settling a complaint to which regulation 36(1) applies if the conditions regulating compromise contracts under this Schedule are satisfied in relation to the contract; or

(c)   to a contract settling a claim to which regulation 39 (jurisdiction of county or sheriff courts) applies.

(2)   The conditions regulating compromise contracts under this Schedule are that–

(a)   the contract must be in writing;

(b)   the contract must relate to the particular complaint;

(c)   the complainant must have received advice from a relevant independent adviser as to the terms and effect of the proposed contract and in particular its effect on his ability to pursue a complaint before an employment tribunal;

(d)   there must be in force, when the adviser gives the advice, a contract of insurance, or an indemnity provided for members of a profession or professional body, covering the risk of a claim by the complainant in respect of loss arising in consequence of the advice;

(e)   the contract must identify the adviser; and

(f)   the contract must state that the conditions regulating compromise contracts under this Schedule are satisfied.

(3)   A person is a relevant independent adviser for the purposes of sub-paragraph (2)(c)–

(a)   if he is a qualified lawyer;

(b)   if he is an officer, official, employee or member of an independent trade union who has been certified in writing by the trade union as competent to give advice and as authorised to do so on behalf of the trade union; or

(c)   if he works at an advice centre (whether as an employee or a volunteer) and has been certified in writing by the centre as competent to give advice and as authorised to do so on behalf of the centre.

(4)   But a person is not a relevant independent adviser for the purposes of sub-paragraph (2)(c) in relation to the complainant–

(a)   if he is employed by, or is acting in the matter for the other party, or is a person who is connected with the other party;

(b)   in the case of a person within sub-paragraph (3)(b) or (c), if the trade union or advice centre is the other party or a person who is connected with the other party; or

(c)   in the case of a person within sub-paragraph (3)(c), if the complainant makes a payment for the advice received from him.

(5)   In sub-paragraph (3)(a) 'qualified lawyer' means–

(a)   as respects England and Wales, a barrister (whether in practice as such or employed to give legal advice), a solicitor who holds a practising certificate, or a person other than a barrister or solicitor who is an authorised advocate or authorised litigator (within the meaning of the Courts and Legal Services Act 1990; and

(b)   as respects Scotland, an advocate (whether in practice as such or employed to give legal advice), or a solicitor who holds a practising certificate.

(6)   A person shall be treated as being a qualified lawyer within sub-paragraph (5)(a) if he is a Fellow of the Institute of Legal Executives employed by a solicitors' practice.

(7)   In sub-paragraph (3)(b) 'independent trade union' has the same meaning as in the Trade Union and Labour Relations (Consolidation) Act 1992.

(8)   For the purposes of sub-paragraph (4)(a) any two persons are to be treated as connected–

(a)   if one is a company of which the other (directly or indirectly) has control; or

(b)   if both are companies of which a third person (directly or indirectly) has control.

(9)   An agreement under which the parties agree to submit a dispute to arbitration–

    (a)   shall be regarded for the purposes of sub-paragraphs (1)(a) and (b) as being a contract settling a complaint if–

        (i)   the dispute is covered by a scheme having effect by virtue of an order under section 212A of the Trade Union and Labour Relations (Consolidation) Act 1992, and

        (ii)   the agreement is to submit it to arbitration in accordance with the scheme, but

    (b)   shall be regarded as neither being nor including such a contract in any other case.

3(1)   On the application of a person interested in a contract to which paragraph 1(1) or (2) applies, a county court or a sheriff court may make such order as it thinks fit for–

    (a)   removing or modifying any term rendered void by paragraph 1(1), or

    (b)   removing or modifying any term made unenforceable by paragraph 1(2);

but such an order shall not be made unless all persons affected have been given notice in writing of the application (except where under rules of court notice may be dispensed with) and have been afforded an opportunity to make representations to the court.

(2)   An order under sub-paragraph (1) may include provision as respects any period before the making of the order (but after the date on which the inclusion of any term which is the subject of the order becomes unlawful by virtue of these Regulations).

PART 2: COLLECTIVE AGREEMENTS AND RULES OF UNDERTAKINGS

4(1)   This Part of this Schedule applies to–

    (a)   any term of a collective agreement, including an agreement which was not intended, or is presumed not to have been intended, to be a legally enforceable contract;

    (b)   any rule made by an employer for application to all or any of the persons who are employed by him or who apply to be, or are, considered by him for employment;

    (c)   any rule made by a trade organisation (within the meaning of regulation 18) or a qualifications body (within the meaning of regulation 19) for application to–

        (i)   all or any of its members or prospective members; or

        (ii)   all or any of the persons on whom it has conferred professional or trade qualifications (within the meaning of regulation 19) or who are seeking the professional or trade qualifications which it has power to confer.

(2)   Any term or rule to which this Part of this Schedule applies is void where–

(a)   the making of the collective agreement is, by reason of the inclusion of the term, unlawful by virtue of these Regulations;

(b)   the term or rule is included or made in furtherance of an act which is unlawful by virtue of these Regulations; or

(c)   the term or rule provides for the doing of an act which is unlawful by virtue of these Regulations.

(3)   Sub-paragraph (2) shall apply whether the agreement was entered into, or the rule made, before or after the date on which any term of the agreement or rule became unlawful by virtue of these Regulations; but in the case of an agreement entered into, or a rule made, before the date on which a term, or rule, became unlawful, that sub-paragraph does not apply to that term or rule in relation to any period before that date.

5   A person to whom this paragraph applies may present a complaint to an employment tribunal that a term or rule is void by virtue of paragraph 4 if he has reason to believe–

(a)   that the term or rule may at some future time have effect in relation to him; and

(b)   where he alleges that it is void by virtue of paragraph 4(2)(c), that–

   (i)   an act for the doing of which it provides, may at some such time be done in relation to him, and

   (ii)   the act would be unlawful by virtue of these Regulations if done in relation to him in present circumstances.

6   In the case of a complaint about–

(a)   a term of a collective agreement made by or on behalf of–

   (i)   an employer,

   (ii)   an organisation of employers of which an employer is a member, or

   (iii)   an association of such organisations of one of which an employer is a member, or

(b)   a rule made by an employer within the meaning of paragraph 4(1)(b),

paragraph 5 applies to any person who is, or is genuinely and actively seeking to become, one of his employees.

7   In the case of a complaint about a rule made by an organisation or body to which paragraph 4(1)(c) applies, paragraph 5 applies to any person–

(a)   who is, or is genuinely and actively seeking to become, a member of the organisation or body;

(b)   on whom the organisation or body has conferred a professional or trade qualification (within the meaning of regulation 19) which the organisation or body has power to confer; or

(c)   who is genuinely and actively seeking such a professional or trade qualification which the organisation or body has power to confer.

8(1)   When an employment tribunal finds that a complaint presented to it under paragraph 5 is well-founded the tribunal shall make an order declaring that the term or rule is void.

(2)   An order under sub-paragraph (1) may include provision as respects any period before the making of the order (but after the date on which the inclusion of the term or rule became unlawful by virtue of these Regulations).

9   The avoidance by virtue of paragraph 4(2) of any term or rule which provides for any person to be discriminated against shall be without prejudice to the following rights (except in so far as they enable any person to require another person to be treated less favourably than himself), namely–

(a)   such of the rights of the person to be discriminated against; and

(b)   such of the rights of any person who will be treated more favourably in direct or indirect consequence of the discrimination,

as are conferred by or in respect of a contract made or modified wholly or partly in pursuance of, or by reference to, that term or rule.

10   In this Schedule 'collective agreement' means any agreement relating to one or more of the matters mentioned in section 178(2) of the Trade Union and Labour Relations (Consolidation) Act 1992 (collective agreements and collective bargaining), being an agreement made by or on behalf of one or more employers or one or more organisations of employers or associations of such organisations with one or more organisations of workers or associations of such organisations.

SCHEDULE 6

DUTY TO CONSIDER WORKING BEYOND RETIREMENT

Regulation 47

Interpretation

1(1)   In this Schedule–

'dismissal' means a dismissal within the meaning of section 95 of the 1996 Act;

'employee' means a person to whom regulation 30 (exception for retirement) applies and references to 'employer' shall be construed accordingly;

'intended date of retirement' has the meaning given by sub-paragraph (2);

'operative date of termination' means (subject to paragraph 10(3))–

(a)   where the employer terminates the employee's contract of employment by notice, the date on which the notice expires, or

(b)   where the employer terminates the contract of employment without notice, the date on which the termination takes effect;

'request' means a request made under paragraph 5; and

'worker' has the same meaning as in section 230(3) of the 1996 Act.

(2)   In this Schedule 'intended date of retirement' means–

(a)   where the employer notifies a date in accordance with paragraph 2, that date;

(b) where the employer notifies a date in accordance with paragraph 4 and either no request is made or a request is made after the notification, that date;

(c) where,

(i) the employer has not notified a date in accordance with paragraph 2,

(ii) a request is made before the employer has notified a date in accordance with paragraph 4 (including where no notification in accordance with that paragraph is given),

(iii) the request is made by an employee who has reasonable grounds for believing that the employer intends to retire him on a certain date, and,

(iv) the request identifies that date,

the date so identified;

(d) in a case to which paragraph 3 has applied, any earlier or later date that has superseded the date mentioned in paragraph (a), (b) or (c) as the intended date of retirement by virtue of paragraph 3(3);

(e) in a case to which paragraph 10 has applied, the later date that has superseded the date mentioned in paragraph (a), (b) or (c) as the intended date of retirement by virtue of paragraph 10(3)(b).

Duty of employer to inform employee

2(1) An employer who intends to retire an employee has a duty to notify the employee in writing of–

(a) the employee's right to make a request; and

(b) the date on which he intends the employee to retire,

not more than one year and not less than six months before that date.

(2) The duty to notify applies regardless of–

(a) whether there is any term in the employee's contract of employment indicating when his retirement is expected to take place,

(b) any other notification of, or information about, the employee's date of retirement given to him by the employer at any time, and

(c) any other information about the employee's right to make a request given to him by the employer at any time.

3(1) This paragraph applies if the employer has notified the employee in accordance with paragraph 2 or 4 or the employee has made a request before being notified in accordance with paragraph 4 (including where no notification in accordance with that paragraph is given), and–

(a) the employer and employee agree, in accordance with paragraph 7(3)(b) or 8(5)(b), that the dismissal is to take effect on a date later than the relevant date;

(b) the employer gives notice to the employee, in accordance with paragraph 7(7)(a)(ii) or, where the employee appeals, paragraph 8(9)(a)(ii), that the dismissal is to take effect on a date later than the relevant date; or

(c)   the employer and employee agree that the dismissal is to take effect on a date earlier than the relevant date.

(2)   This Schedule does not require the employer to give the employee a further notification in respect of dismissal taking effect on a date–

   (a)   agreed as mentioned in sub-paragraph (1)(a) or notified as mentioned in sub-paragraph (1)(b) that is later than the relevant date and falls six months or less after the relevant date; or

   (b)   agreed as mentioned in sub-paragraph (1)(c) that is earlier than the relevant date.

(3)   If–

   (a)   a date later than the relevant date is agreed as mentioned in sub-paragraph (1)(a) or notified as mentioned in sub-paragraph (1)(b) and falls six months or less after the relevant date, or

   (b)   a date earlier than the relevant date is agreed as mentioned in sub-paragraph (1)(c),

the earlier or later date shall supersede the relevant date as the intended date of retirement.

(4)   In this paragraph, 'the relevant date' means the date that is defined as the intended date of retirement in paragraph (a), (b) or (c) of paragraph 1(2).

Continuing duty to inform employee

4   Where the employer has failed to comply with paragraph 2, he has a continuing duty to notify the employee in writing as described in paragraph 2(1) until the fourteenth day before the operative date of termination.

Statutory right to request not to retire

5(1)   An employee may make a request to his employer not to retire on the intended date of retirement.

   (2)   In his request the employee must propose that his employment should continue, following the intended date of retirement–

   (a)   indefinitely,

   (b)   for a stated period, or

   (c)   until a stated date;

and, if the request is made at a time when it is no longer possible for the employer to notify in accordance with paragraph 2 and the employer has not yet notified in accordance with paragraph 4, must identify the date on which he believes that the employer intends to retire him.

   (3)   A request must be in writing and state that it is made under this paragraph.

   (4)   An employee may only make one request under this paragraph in relation to any one intended date of retirement and may not make a request in relation to a date that supersedes a different date as the intended date of retirement by virtue of paragraph 3(3) or 10(3)(b).

   (5)   A request is only a request made under this paragraph if it is made–

   (a)   in a case where the employer has complied with paragraph 2, more than three months but not more than six months before the intended date of retirement, or

(b)   in a case where the employer has not complied with paragraph 2, before, but not more than six months before, the intended date of retirement.

An employer's duty to consider a request

6   An employer to whom a request is made is under a duty to consider the request in accordance with paragraphs 7 to 9.

Meeting to consider request

7(1)   An employer having a duty under paragraph 6 to consider a request shall hold a meeting to discuss the request with the employee within a reasonable period after receiving it.

(2)   The employer and employee must take all reasonable steps to attend the meeting.

(3)   The duty to hold a meeting does not apply if, before the end of the period that is reasonable–

(a)   the employer and employee agree that the employee's employment will continue indefinitely and the employer gives notice to the employee to that effect; or

(b)   the employer and employee agree that the employee's employment will continue for an agreed period and the employer gives notice to the employee of the length of that period or of the date on which it will end.

(4)   The duty to hold a meeting does not apply if–

(a)   it is not practicable to hold a meeting within the period that is reasonable, and

(b)   the employer complies with sub-paragraph (5).

(5)   Where sub-paragraph (4)(a) applies, the employer may consider the request without holding a meeting provided he considers any representations made by the employee.

(6)   The employer shall give the employee notice of his decision on the request as soon as is reasonably practicable after the date of the meeting or, if sub-paragraphs (4) and (5) apply, his consideration of the request.

(7)   A notice given under sub-paragraph (6) shall–

(a)   where the decision is to accept the request, state that it is accepted and–

(i)   where the decision is that the employee's employment will continue indefinitely, state that fact, or

(ii)   where the decision is that the employee's employment will continue for a further period, state that fact and specify the length of the period or the date on which it will end,

(b)   where the decision is to refuse the request, confirm that the employer wishes to retire the employee and the date on which the dismissal is to take effect,

and, in the case of a notice falling within paragraph (b), and of a notice referred to in paragraph (a) that specifies a period shorter than the period proposed by the employee in the request, shall inform the employee of his right to appeal.

(8) All notices given under this paragraph shall be in writing and be dated.

Appeals

8(1) An employee is entitled to appeal against–

    (a) a decision of his employer to refuse the request, or

    (b) a decision of his employer to accept the request where the notice given under paragraph 7(6) states as mentioned in paragraph 7(7)(a)(ii) and specifies a period shorter than the period proposed by the employee in the request,

by giving notice in accordance with sub-paragraph (2) as soon as is reasonably practicable after the date of the notice given under paragraph 7(6).

(2) A notice of appeal under sub-paragraph (1) shall set out the grounds of appeal.

(3) The employer shall hold a meeting with the employee to discuss an appeal within a reasonable period after the date of the notice of appeal.

(4) The employer and employee must take all reasonable steps to attend the meeting.

(5) The duty to hold a meeting does not apply if, before the end of the period that is reasonable–

    (a) the employer and employee agree that the employee's employment will continue indefinitely and the employer gives notice to the employee to that effect; or

    (b) the employer and employee agree that the employee's employment will continue for an agreed period and the employer gives notice to the employee of the length of that period or of the date on which it will end.

(6) The duty to hold a meeting does not apply if–

    (a) it is not practicable to hold a meeting within the period that is reasonable, and

    (b) the employer complies with sub-paragraph (7).

(7) Where sub-paragraph (6)(a) applies, the employer may consider the appeal without holding a meeting provided he considers any representations made by the employee.

(8) The employer shall give the employee notice of his decision on the appeal as soon as is reasonably practicable after the date of the meeting or, if sub-paragraphs (6) and (7) apply, his consideration of the appeal.

(9) A notice under sub-paragraph (8) shall–

    (a) where the decision is to accept the appeal, state that it is accepted and–

        (i) where the decision is that the employee's employment will continue indefinitely, state that fact, or

        (ii) where the decision is that the employee's employment will continue for a further period, state that fact and specify the length of the period or the date on which it will end,

(b)   where the decision is to refuse the appeal, confirm that the employer wishes to retire the employee and the date on which the dismissal is to take effect.

(10)   All notices given under this paragraph shall be in writing and be dated.

Right to be accompanied

9(1)   This paragraph applies where–

(a)   a meeting is held under paragraph 7 or 8, and

(b)   the employee reasonably requests to be accompanied at the meeting.

(2)   Where this paragraph applies the employer must permit the employee to be accompanied at the meeting by one companion who–

(a)   is chosen by the employee;

(b)   is a worker employed by the same employer as the employee;

(c)   is to be permitted to address the meeting (but not to answer questions on behalf of the employee); and

(d)   is to be permitted to confer with the employee during the meeting.

(3)   If–

(a)   an employee has a right under this paragraph to be accompanied at a meeting,

(b)   his chosen companion will not be available at the time proposed for the meeting by the employer, and

(c)   the employee proposes an alternative time which satisfies sub-paragraph (4),

the employer must postpone the meeting to the time proposed by the employee.

(4)   An alternative time must–

(a)   be convenient for employer, employee and companion, and

(b)   fall before the end of the period of seven days beginning with the first day after the day proposed by the employer.

(5)   An employer shall permit a worker to take time off during working hours for the purpose of accompanying an employee in accordance with a request under sub-paragraph (1)(b).

(6)   Sections 168(3) and (4), 169 and 171 to 173 of the Trade Union and Labour Relations (Consolidation) Act 1992 (time off for carrying out trade union duties) shall apply in relation to sub-paragraph (5) above as they apply in relation to section 168(1) of that Act.

Dismissal before request considered

10(1)   This paragraph applies where–

(a)   by virtue of paragraph 6 an employer is under a duty to consider a request;

(b)   the employer dismisses the employee;

(c)   that dismissal is the contemplated dismissal to which the request relates; and

(d)   the operative date of termination would, but for sub-paragraph (3), fall on or before the day on which the employer gives notice in accordance with paragraph 7(6).

(2)   Subject to sub-paragraph (4), the contract of employment shall continue in force for all purposes, including the purpose of determining for
any purpose the period for which the employee has been continuously
employed, until the day following that on which the notice under paragraph 7(6) is given.

(3)   The day following the day on which that notice is given shall supersede–

(a)   the date mentioned in sub-paragraph (1)(d) as the operative date
of termination; and

(b)   the date defined as the intended date of retirement in paragraph
(a), (b) or (c) of paragraph 1(2) as the intended date of retirement.

(4)   Any continuation of the contract of employment under sub-paragraph
(2) shall be disregarded when determining the operative date of termination for the purposes of sections 98ZA to 98ZH of the 1996 Act.

Complaint to employment tribunal: failure to comply with paragraph 2

11(1) An employee may present a complaint to an employment tribunal that
his employer has failed to comply with the duty to notify him in paragraph 2.

(2)   A tribunal shall not consider a complaint under this paragraph unless
the complaint is presented–

(a)   before the end of the period of three months beginning with–

(i)   the last day permitted to the employer by paragraph 2 for
complying with the duty to notify, or

(ii)   if the employee did not then know the date that would be
the intended date of retirement, the first day on which he
knew or should have known that date; or

(b)   within such further period as the tribunal considers reasonable in
a case where it is satisfied that it was not reasonably practicable for
the complaint to be presented before the end of that period of
three months.

(3)   Where a tribunal finds that a complaint under this paragraph is well-
founded it shall order the employer to pay compensation to the employee
of such amount, not exceeding 8 weeks' pay, as the tribunal considers
just and equitable in all the circumstances.

(4)   Chapter 2 of Part 14 of the 1996 Act (calculation of a week's pay) shall
apply for the purposes of sub-paragraph (3); and in applying that Chapter the calculation date shall be taken to be the date on which the complaint was presented or, if earlier, the operative date of termination.

(5)   The limit in section 227(1) of the 1996 Act (maximum amount of a
week's pay) shall apply for the purposes of sub-paragraph (3).

Complaint to employment tribunal: denial of right to be accompanied

12(1) An employee may present a complaint to an employment tribunal that
his employer has failed, or threatened to fail, to comply with paragraph
9(2) or (3).

(2)   A tribunal shall not consider a complaint under this paragraph in relation to a failure or threat unless the complaint is presented–

(a)   before the end of the period of three months beginning with the date of the failure or threat; or

(b)   within such further period as the tribunal considers reasonable in a case where it is satisfied that it was not reasonably practicable for the complaint to be presented before the end of that period of three months.

(3)   Where a tribunal finds that a complaint under this paragraph is well-founded it shall order the employer to pay compensation to the worker of an amount not exceeding two weeks' pay.

(4)   Chapter 2 of Part 14 of the 1996 Act (calculation of a week's pay) shall apply for the purposes of sub-paragraph (3); and in applying that Chapter the calculation date shall be taken to be the date on which the relevant meeting took place (or was to have taken place).

(5)   The limit in section 227(1) of the 1996 Act (maximum amount of a week's pay) shall apply for the purposes of sub-paragraph (3).

Detriment and dismissal

13(1)   An employee has the right not to be subjected to any detriment by any act by his employer done on the ground that he exercised or sought to exercise his right to be accompanied in accordance with paragraph 9.

(2)   A worker has the right not to be subjected to any detriment by any act, or any deliberate failure to act, by his employer done on the ground that he accompanied or sought to accompany an employee pursuant to a request under paragraph 9.

(3)   Section 48 of the 1996 Act shall apply in relation to contraventions of sub-paragraph (1) or (2) above as it applies in relation to contraventions of certain sections of that Act.

(4)   Sub-paragraph (2) does not apply where the worker is an employee and the detriment in question amounts to dismissal (within the meaning of Part 10 of the 1996 Act).

(5)   An employee who is dismissed shall be regarded for the purposes of Part 10 of the 1996 Act as unfairly dismissed if the reason (or, if more than one, the principal reason) for the dismissal is that he–

(a)   exercised or sought to exercise his right to be accompanied in accordance with paragraph 9, or

(b)   accompanied or sought to accompany an employee pursuant to a request under that paragraph.

(6)   Sections 128 to 132 of the 1996 Act (interim relief) shall apply in relation to dismissal for the reason specified in sub-paragraph (5)(a) or (b) above as they apply in relation to dismissal for a reason specified in section 128(1)(b) of that Act.

SCHEDULE 7

DUTY TO CONSIDER WORKING BEYOND RETIREMENT

Regulation 48

1   In paragraphs 2 to 6–

    (a) 'the expiry date' means the date on which notice of dismissal given by an employer expires; and

    (b) words and expressions shall have the same meanings as they do in Schedule 6.

2(1) This paragraph applies in a case where–

    (a) an employer has given notice of dismissal to the employee before the commencement date of–

        (i) at least the period required by the contract of employment; or

        (ii) where the period required by the contract exceeds four weeks, at least four weeks;

    (b) the expiry date falls before 1st April 2007; and

    (c) the employer has made the employee aware, before the commencement date, that the employer considers that the employee is being retired on the expiry date.

(2)   Where this paragraph applies and the employer on or as soon as is practicable after the commencement date notifies the employee in writing of the employee's right to make a request under paragraph 5 of Schedule 6–

    (a) the employer shall be treated as complying with the duty in paragraph 2 of Schedule 6;

    (b) a request shall be treated as being a request made under paragraph 5 of Schedule 6 provided it–

        (i) is made after the employer notified the employee of his right to make a request;

        (ii) satisfies the requirements of sub-paragraphs (2) and (3) of paragraph 5 of Schedule 6; and

        (iii) is made–

            (aa) where practicable, at least four weeks before the expiry date; or

            (bb) where that is not practicable, as soon as reasonably practicable (whether before or after the expiry date) after the employer notified the employee of his right to make a request, but not more than four weeks after the expiry date.

(3)   Where this paragraph applies and the employer does not, on or as soon as is practicable after the commencement date, notify the employee in writing of the employee's right to make a request under paragraph 5 of Schedule 6–

    (a) the duty to notify in accordance with paragraph 2 of Schedule 6 does not apply;

    (b) the duty to notify in accordance with paragraph 4 of Schedule 6 applies as if–

      (i)   the employer had failed to notify in accordance with paragraph 2 of that Schedule; and

      (ii)   the duty was one to notify at any time before the expiry date;

  (c)   a request shall be treated as being a request made under paragraph 5 of Schedule 6 if it satisfies the requirements of sub-paragraphs (2) and (3) of that paragraph and is made–

      (i)   before any notification given in accordance with paragraph 4 of Schedule 6; or

      (ii)   after such notification and–

          (aa) where practicable, at least four weeks before the expiry date; or

          (bb) where that is not practicable, as soon as reasonably practicable (whether before or after the expiry date) after the employer notified the employee of his right to make a request, but not more than four weeks after the expiry date.

3(1)   This paragraph applies in a case where the employer has given notice of dismissal to the employee before the commencement date and–

  (a)   the expiry date falls before 1st April 2007, but

  (b)   the period of notice given is shorter than the minimum period of notice required by paragraph 2(1)(a) or the employer has not complied with paragraph 2(1)(c).

(2)   Where this paragraph applies–

  (a)   the duty to notify in accordance with paragraph 2 of Schedule 6 does not apply;

  (b)   the duty to notify in accordance with paragraph 4 of Schedule 6 applies as if–

      (i)   the employer had failed to notify in accordance with paragraph 2 of that Schedule; and

      (ii)   the duty was one to notify at any time before the expiry date;

  (c)   a request shall be treated as being a request made under paragraph 5 of Schedule 6 if it satisfies the requirements of sub-paragraphs (2) and (3) of that paragraph and is made–

      (i)   before any notification given in accordance with paragraph 4 of Schedule 6; or

      (ii)   after such notification and–

          (aa) where practicable, at least four weeks before the expiry date; or

          (bb) where that is not practicable, as soon as reasonably practicable (whether before or after the expiry date) after the employer notified the employee of his right to make a request, but not more than four weeks after the expiry date.

4(1)   This paragraph applies in a case where–

  (a)   notice of dismissal is given on or after the commencement date of at least–

      (i)   the period required by the contract of employment; or

(ii)   if longer, the period required by section 86 of the 1996 Act; and

(b)   the expiry date falls before 1st April 2007.

(2)   Where this paragraph applies and the employer notifies the employee in writing of the employee's right to make a request under paragraph 5 of Schedule 6 before, or on the same day as, the day on which notice of dismissal is given–

    (a)   the employer shall be treated as complying with the duty in paragraph 2 of Schedule 6;

    (b)   a request shall be treated as being a request made under paragraph 5 of Schedule 6 provided it–

        (i)   is made after the employer notified the employee of his right to make a request;

        (ii)   satisfies the requirements of sub-paragraphs (2) and (3) of paragraph 5 of Schedule 6; and

        (iii)   is made–

           (aa)   where practicable, at least four weeks before the expiry date; or

           (bb)   where that is not practicable, as soon as reasonably practicable (whether before or after the expiry date) after the employer notified the employee of his right to make a request, but not more than four weeks after the expiry date.

(3)   Where this paragraph applies but the employer does not notify the employee in writing of the employee's right to make a request under paragraph 5 of Schedule 6 before, or on the same day as, the day on which notice of dismissal is given–

    (a)   the duty to notify in accordance with paragraph 2 of Schedule 6 does not apply;

    (b)   the duty to notify in accordance with paragraph 4 of Schedule 6 applies as if–

        (i)   the employer had failed to notify in accordance with paragraph 2 of that Schedule; and

        (ii)   the duty was one to notify at any time before the expiry date;

    (c)   a request shall be treated as being a request made under paragraph 5 of Schedule 6 if it satisfies the requirements of sub-paragraphs (2) and (3) of that paragraph and is made–

        (i)   before any notification given in accordance with paragraph 4 of Schedule 6; or

        (ii)   after such notification and–

           (aa)   where practicable, at least four weeks before the expiry date; or

           (bb)   where that is not practicable, as soon as reasonably practicable (whether before or after the expiry date) after the employer notified the employee of his right to make a request, but not more than four weeks after the expiry date.

5(1)   This paragraph applies in a case where–

    (a)   notice of dismissal is given on or after the commencement date and is for a period shorter than–

        (i)   the period required by the contract of employment; or

        (ii)   if longer, the period required by section 86 of the 1996 Act; and

    (b)   the period of notice expires on a date falling before 1st April 2007.

(2)   Where this paragraph applies–

    (a)   the duty to notify in accordance with paragraph 2 of Schedule 6 does not apply;

    (b)   the duty to notify in accordance with paragraph 4 of Schedule 6 applies as if–

        (i)   the employer had failed to notify in accordance with paragraph 2 of that Schedule; and

        (ii)   the duty was one to notify at any time before the expiry date;

    (c)   a request shall be treated as being a request made under paragraph 5 of Schedule 6 if it satisfies the requirements of sub-paragraphs (2) and (3) of that paragraph and is made–

        (i)   before any notification given in accordance with paragraph 4 of Schedule 6; or

        (ii)   after such notification and–

            (aa)   where practicable, at least four weeks before the expiry date; or

            (bb)   where that is not practicable, as soon as reasonably practicable (whether before or after the expiry date) after the employer notified the employee of his right to make a request, but not more than four weeks after the expiry date.

6   In every case to which paragraph 2, 3, 4 or 5 applies–

    (a)   paragraph 10 of Schedule 6 does not apply; and

    (b)   the employer is under a duty to consider any request which complies with the requirements of paragraph 2(2)(b), 2(3)(c), 3(2)(c), 4(2)(b), 4(3)(c) or 5(2)(c) in accordance with paragraphs 7 to 9 of Schedule 6.

SCHEDULE 8

AMENDMENTS TO LEGISLATION AND RELATED TRANSITIONAL PROVISIONS

Regulation 49(1)

PART 1: PRIMARY LEGISLATION

The Mines and Quarries Act 1954

1 The Mines and Quarries Act 1954 is amended as follows.

2(1) In section 42(1) (charge of winding and rope haulage apparatus when persons are carried) omit the words 'who has attained the age of twenty-two years'.

(2) In section 43(2) (charge of winding and rope haulage apparatus when persons are not carried) omit the words 'who has attained the age of eighteen years'.

(3) In section 44 (charge of conveyors at working faces) omit the words 'who has attained the age of eighteen years'.

The Parliamentary Commissioner Act 1967

3 The Parliamentary Commissioner Act 1967 is amended as follows–

4(1) Section 1 (appointment and tenure of office) is amended in accordance with this paragraph.

(2) In subsection (2) omit the words from ', and any person' to 'during good behaviour'.

(3) After subsection (2) insert–

'(2A) A person appointed to be the Commissioner shall hold office until the end of the period for which he is appointed.

(2B) That period must be not more than seven years.

(2C) Subsection (2A) is subject to subsections (3) and (3A).'.

(4) For subsection (3) substitute–

'(3) A person appointed to be the Commissioner may be–

(a) relieved of office by Her Majesty at his own request, or

(b) removed from office by Her Majesty, on the ground of mis-behaviour, in consequence of Addresses from both Houses of Parliament.'.

(5) After subsection (3A) insert–

'(3B) A person appointed to be the Commissioner is not eligible for re-appointment.'.

5(1) Section 3A (appointment of acting Commissioner) is amended in accordance with this paragraph.

(2) After subsection (1) insert–

'(1A) A person appointed to act as the Commissioner ('an acting Com-missioner') may have held office as the Commissioner.

(1B) A person appointed as an acting Commissioner is eligible for appointment as the Commissioner unless he has already held office as the Commissioner.'.

(3)   In subsection (2) for the words 'under this section' substitute 'as an acting Commissioner'.

(4)   For subsection (3) substitute–

'(3)   A person appointed as an acting Commissioner shall, while he holds office, be treated for all purposes, except for the purposes of section 1 and 2, and this section of this Act, as the Commissioner.'.

6   The amendments made to the Parliamentary Commissioner Act 1967 apply in relation to appointments made on or after the commencement date.

The Pilotage Act 1987

7(1)   The Pilotage Act 1987 is amended in accordance with this paragraph.

(2)   In section 3(2) (authorisation of pilots) omit the word 'age,'.

The Social Security Contributions and Benefits Act 1992

8   The Social Security Contributions and Benefits Act 1992 is amended as follows.

9(1)   Section 163(1) (interpretation of Part 11 and supplementary provisions) is amended in accordance with this paragraph.

(2)   In the definition of 'employee' omit paragraph (b) and the word 'and' preceding it.

(3)   For the definition of 'employer' substitute–

''employer', in relation to an employee and a contract of service of his, means a person who–

(a)   under section 6 above is liable to pay secondary Class 1 contributions in relation to any earnings of the employee under the contract, or

(b)   would be liable to pay such contributions but for–

(i)   the condition in section 6(1)(b), or

(ii)   the employee being under the age of 16:'.

10(1) Section 171(1) (interpretation of Part 12 and supplementary provisions) is amended in accordance with this paragraph.

(2)   In the definition of 'employee' omit paragraph (b) and the word 'and' preceding it.

(3)   For the definition of 'employer' substitute–

''employer', in relation to a woman who is an employee, means a person who–

(a)   under section 6 above is liable to pay secondary Class 1 contributions in relation to any of her earnings; or

(b)   would be liable to pay such contributions but for–

(i)   the condition in section 6(1)(b), or

(ii)   the employee being under the age of 16;'.

applies in relation to any case where the expected week of confinement begins on or after 14th January 2007.

11(1) Section 171ZJ (Part 12ZA: supplementary) is amended in accordance with this paragraph.

(2)   In subsection (1) for the definition of 'employer' substitute
        ''employer', in relation to a person who is an employee, means a person
        who–
        (a)   under section 6 above is, liable to pay secondary Class 1 contri-
               butions in relation to any of the earnings of the person who is an
               employee; or
        (b)   would be liable to pay such contributions but for–
               (i)   the condition in section 6(1)(b), or
               (ii)   the employee being under the age of 16;'.

(3)   In subsection (2) omit paragraph (b) and the word 'and' preceding it.

(4)   This paragraph applies in relation to an entitlement to–
        (a)   statutory paternity pay (birth) in respect of children whose expected
               week of birth begins on or after 14th January 2007;
        (b)   statutory paternity pay (adoption) in respect of children–
               (i)   matched with a person who is notified of having been
                      matched on or after the commencement date; or
               (ii)   placed for adoption on or after the commencement date.

12(1) Section 171ZS (Part 12ZB: supplementary) is amended in accordance
        with this paragraph.

(2)   In subsection (1) for the definition of 'employer' substitute–
        ''employer', in relation to a person who is an employee, means a person
        who–
        (a)   under section 6 above is liable to pay secondary Class 1 contribu-
               tions in relation to any of the earnings of the person who is an
               employee; or
        (b)   would be liable to pay such contributions but for–
               (ii)   the condition in section 6(1)(b), or
               (ii)   the employee being under the age of 16;'.

(3)   In subsection (2) omit paragraph (b) and the word 'and' preceding it.

(4)   This paragraph applies in relation to an entitlement to statutory adop-
        tion pay in respect of children–
        (a)   matched with a person who is notified of having been matched on
               or after the commencement date; or
        (b)   placed for adoption on or after that commencement.

13(1) In Schedule 11 omit paragraph 2(a) (period of entitlement not to arise
        if at the relevant date the employee is over 65).

(2)   Sub-paragraph (1) applies in relation to a period of incapacity for work
        which–
        (a)   begins on or after the commencement date, or
        (b)   begins before and continues on or after the commencement date.

(3)   But in a case falling within sub-paragraph (2)(b), sub-paragraph (1)
        does not affect the application of paragraph 1 of Schedule 11 to the
        1992 Act in relation to the part of the period of incapacity for work that
        falls before the commencement date.

The Health Service Commissioners Act 1993

14   The Health Service Commissioners Act 1993 is amended as follows.

15(1)   Schedule 1 (the English Commissioner) is amended in accordance with this paragraph.

(2)   For paragraph 1 (appointment of Commissioners) substitute the following new paragraphs–

'1

Her Majesty may by Letters Patent appoint a person to be the Commissioner.

1A

Subject to paragraphs 1C and 1D a person appointed to be the Commissioner shall hold office until the end of the period for which he is appointed.

1B

That period must be not more than seven years.

1C

A person appointed to be the Commissioner may be relieved of office by Her Majesty at his own request.

1D

A person appointed to be the Commissioner may be removed from office by Her Majesty, on the ground of misbehaviour, in consequence of Addresses from both Houses of Parliament.

1E

A person appointed to be the Commissioner is not eligible for re-appointment.'.

(3)   In paragraph 2 (appointment of acting Commissioners)–

(a)   after sub-paragraph (1) insert–

'(1A)A person appointed to act as the Commissioner ('an acting Commissioner') may have held office as the Commissioner.

(1B) A person appointed as an acting Commissioner is eligible for appointment as the Commissioner unless he has already held office as the Commissioner.';

(b)   in sub-paragraph (2) for the words 'under this paragraph' substitute 'as acting Commissioner,'; and

(c)   for sub-paragraph (3), substitute–

'(3)   A person appointed as an acting Commissioner shall, while he holds office, be treated for all purposes, except for the purposes of paragraphs 1, 4 to 10 and this paragraph, as the Commissioner.'.

16   The amendments made to the Health Service Commissioners Act 1993 apply in relation to appointments made on or after the commencement date.

The Statutory Sick Pay Act 1994

17(1)   The Statutory Sick Pay Act 1994 is amended in accordance with this paragraph.

(2)   In section 1(2) omit the words after paragraph (b).

The Employment Tribunals Act 1996

18   The Employment Tribunals Act 1996 is amended as follows.

19(1)   Section 18(1) (conciliation) is amended in accordance with this paragraph.

(2)   At the end of paragraph (p), omit 'or'.

(3)   After paragraph (q), insert

'or

(r) under regulation 36 of the Employment Equality (Age) Regulations 2006.'.

20(1)   Section 21(1) (jurisdiction of Appeal Tribunal) is amended in accordance with this paragraph.

(2)   At the end of paragraph (q), omit 'or'.

(3)   After paragraph (r) insert–

'or

(s) the Employment Equality (Age) Regulations 2006.'.

The Employment Rights Act 1996

21   The 1996 Act is amended as follows.

22(1)   Section 98 (fairness of dismissal: general) is amended as follows.

(2)   In subsection (2), after paragraph (b) insert–

'(ba) is retirement of the employee,'.

(3)   After subsection (2) insert–

'(2A) Subsections (1) and (2) are subject to sections 98ZA to 98ZF.'.

(4)   After subsection (3) insert–

'(3A) In any case where the employer has fulfilled the requirements of subsection (1) by showing that the reason (or the principal reason) for the dismissal is retirement of the employee, the question whether the dismissal is fair or unfair shall be determined in accordance with section 98ZG.'.

(5)   In subsection (4) for 'Where' substitute 'In any other case where'.

23   After section 98 insert–

'Retirement

98ZA No normal retirement age: dismissal before 65

(1)   This section applies to the dismissal of an employee if–

(a)   the employee has no normal retirement age, and

(b)   the operative date of termination falls before the date when the employee reaches the age of 65.

(2)   Retirement of the employee shall not be taken to be the reason (or a reason) for the dismissal.

98ZB No normal retirement age: dismissal at or after 65

(1)   This section applies to the dismissal of an employee if–

(a)   the employee has no normal retirement age, and

(b)   the operative date of termination falls on or after the date when the employee reaches the age of 65.

(2) In a case where–
- (a) the employer has notified the employee in accordance with paragraph 2 of Schedule 6 to the 2006 Regulations, and
- (b) the contract of employment terminates on the intended date of retirement,

retirement of the employee shall be taken to be the only reason for the dismissal by the employer and any other reason shall be disregarded.

(3) In a case where–
- (a) the employer has notified the employee in accordance with paragraph 2 of Schedule 6 to the 2006 Regulations, but
- (b) the contract of employment terminates before the intended date of retirement,

retirement of the employee shall not be taken to be the reason (or a reason) for dismissal.

(4) In a case where–
- (a) the employer has not notified the employee in accordance with paragraph 2 of Schedule 6 to the 2006 Regulations, and
- (b) there is an intended date of retirement in relation to the dismissal, but
- (c) the contract of employment terminates before the intended date of retirement,

retirement of the employee shall not be taken to be the reason (or a reason) for dismissal.

(5) In all other cases where the employer has not notified the employee in accordance with paragraph 2 of Schedule 6 to the 2006 Regulations, particular regard shall be had to the matters in section 98ZF when determining the reason (or principal reason) for dismissal.

98ZC Normal retirement age: dismissal before retirement age

(1) This section applies to the dismissal of an employee if–
- (a) the employee has a normal retirement age, and
- (b) the operative date of termination falls before the date when the employee reaches the normal retirement age.

(2) Retirement of the employee shall not be taken to be the reason (or a reason) for the dismissal.

98ZD Normal retirement age 65 or higher: dismissal at or after retirement age

(1) This section applies to the dismissal of an employee if–
- (a) the employee has a normal retirement age,
- (b) the normal retirement age is 65 or higher, and
- (c) the operative date of termination falls on or after the date when the employee reaches the normal retirement age.

(2) In a case where–
- (a) the employer has notified the employee in accordance with paragraph 2 of Schedule 6 to the 2006 Regulations, and

(b)   the contract of employment terminates on the intended date of retirement,

retirement of the employee shall be taken to be the only reason for the dismissal by the employer and any other reason shall be disregarded.

(3)   In a case where–

(a)   the employer has notified the employee in accordance with paragraph 2 of Schedule 6 to the 2006 Regulations, but

(b)   the contract of employment terminates before the intended date of retirement,

retirement of the employee shall not be taken to be the reason (or a reason) for dismissal.

(4)   In a case where–

(a)   the employer has not notified the employee in accordance with paragraph 2 of Schedule 6 to the 2006 Regulations, and

(b)   there is an intended date of retirement in relation to the dismissal, but

(c)   the contract of employment terminates before the intended date of retirement,

retirement of the employee shall not be taken to be the reason (or a reason) for dismissal.

(5)   In all other cases where the employer has not notified the employee in accordance with paragraph 2 of Schedule 6 to the 2006 Regulations, particular regard shall be had to the matters in section 98ZF when determining the reason (or principal reason) for dismissal.

98ZE Normal retirement age below 65: dismissal at or after retirement age

(1)   This section applies to the dismissal of an employee if–

(a)   the employee has a normal retirement age,

(b)   the normal retirement age is below 65, and

(c)   the operative date of termination falls on or after the date when the employee reaches the normal retirement age.

(2)   If it is unlawful discrimination under the 2006 Regulations for the employee to have that normal retirement age, retirement of the employee shall not be taken to be the reason (or a reason) for dismissal.

(3)   Subsections (4) to (7) apply if it is not unlawful discrimination under the 2006 Regulations for the employee to have that normal retirement age.

(4)   In a case where–

(a)   the employer has notified the employee in accordance with paragraph 2 of Schedule 6 to the 2006 Regulations, and

(b)   the contract of employment terminates on the intended date of retirement,

retirement of the employee shall be taken to be the only reason for dismissal by the employer and any other reason shall be disregarded.

(5)   In a case where–

(a)   the employer has notified the employee in accordance with paragraph 2 of Schedule 6 to the 2006 Regulations, but

(b)   the contract of employment terminates before the intended date of retirement,

retirement of the employee shall not be taken to be the reason (or a reason) for dismissal.

(6)   In a case where–

(a)   the employer has not notified the employee in accordance with paragraph 2 of Schedule 6 to the 2006 Regulations, and

(b)   there is an intended date of retirement in relation to the dismissal, but

(c)   the contract of employment terminates before the intended date of retirement,

retirement of the employee shall not be taken to be the reason (or a reason) for dismissal.

(7)   In all other cases where the employer has not notified the employee in accordance with paragraph 2 of Schedule 6 to the 2006 Regulations, particular regard shall be had to the matters in section 98ZF when determining the reason (or principal reason) for dismissal

98ZF Reason for dismissal: particular matters

(1)   These are the matters to which particular regard is to be had in accordance with section 98ZB(5), 98ZD(5) or 98ZE(7)–

(a)   whether or not the employer has notified the employee in accordance with paragraph 4 of Schedule 6 to the 2006 Regulations;

(b)   if the employer has notified the employee in accordance with that paragraph, how long before the notified retirement date the notification was given;

(c)   whether or not the employer has followed, or sought to follow, the procedures in paragraph 7 of Schedule 6 to the 2006 Regulations.

(2)   In subsection (1)(b) 'notified retirement date' means the date notified to the employee in accordance with paragraph 4 of Schedule 6 to the 2006 Regulations as the date on which the employer intends to retire the employee.

98ZG Retirement dismissals: fairness

(1)   This section applies if the reason (or principal reason) for a dismissal is retirement of the employee.

(2)   The employee shall be regarded as unfairly dismissed if, and only if, there has been a failure on the part of the employer to comply with an obligation imposed on him by any of the following provisions of Schedule 6 to the 2006 Regulations–

(a)   paragraph 4 (notification of retirement, if not already given under paragraph 2),

(b)   paragraphs 6 and 7 (duty to consider employee's request not to be retired),

(c)   paragraph 8 (duty to consider appeal against decision to refuse request not to be retired).

98ZH Interpretation

In sections 98ZA to 98ZG–

'2006 Regulations' means the Employment Equality (Age) Regulations 2006;

'intended date of retirement' means the date which, by virtue of paragraph 1(2) of Schedule 6 to the 2006 Regulations, is the intended date of retirement in relation to a particular dismissal;

'normal retirement age', in relation to an employee, means the age at which employees in the employer's undertaking who hold, or have held, the same kind of position as the employee are normally required to retire;

'operative date of termination' means–

(a)   where the employer terminates the employee's contract of employment by notice, the date on which the notice expires, or

(b)   where the employer terminates the contract of employment without notice, the date on which the termination takes effect.

Other Dismissals

24   In section 108 (qualifying period of employment) in subsection (3) (cases where no qualifying period of employment is required)–

(a)   at the end of paragraph (l) omit 'or'; and

(b)   after paragraph (m) insert–

'or

(n) paragraph (a) or (b) of paragraph 13(5) of Schedule 6 to the Employment Equality (Age) Regulations 2006 applies.'.

25   Omit section 109 (upper age limit on unfair dismissal right).

26(1)   Section 112 (remedies for unfair dismissal: orders and compensation) is amended as follows.

(2)   In subsection (5)(a) after 'section' insert '98ZG or'.

27(1)   Section 119 (basic award) is amended as follows.

(2)   Omit subsections (4) and (5).

28(1)   Section 120 (basic award: minimum in certain cases) is amended as follows.

(2)   In subsection (1A) after 'section' insert '98ZG or'.

29   In section 126(1) (acts which are both unfair dismissal and discrimination), for paragraph (b) substitute–

'(b) any one or more of the following–

(i)   the Sex Discrimination Act 1975;

(ii)   the Race Relations Act 1976;

(iii)   the Disability Discrimination Act 1995;

(iv)   the Employment Equality (Sexual Orientation) Regulations 2003;

(v)   the Employment Equality (Religion or Belief) Regulations 2003;

(vi)   the Employment Equality (Age) Regulations 2006.'.

30   Section 156 (upper age limit) is repealed.

31 Section 158 (pension rights) is repealed.

32(1) Section 162 (amount of a redundancy payment) is amended in accordance with this paragraph.

(2) Subsections (4), (5) and (8) are repealed.

(3) In subsection (6), for the words 'Subsections (1) to (5)' substitute 'Subsections (1) to (3)'.

33 In relation to any case where the date that is the relevant date by virtue of section 153 of the 1996 Act falls before the commencement date, paragraphs 30 to 32 do not apply.

34(1) Section 209 (powers to amend Act) is amended as follows.

(2) In subsection (5) omit '109(1),'.

35(1) Section 211 (period of continuous employment) is amended in accordance with this paragraph.

(2) In paragraph (a) of subsection (1) for the words 'subsections (2) and' substitute 'subsection'.

(3) Subsection (2) is repealed.

The Employment Act 2002

36(1) The Employment Act 2002 is amended in accordance with this paragraph.

(2) At the end of each of the following Schedules–

    (a) Schedule 3 (tribunal jurisdictions to which section 31 applies for adjustment of awards for non-completion of statutory procedure);

    (b) Schedule 4 (tribunal jurisdictions to which section 32 applies for complaints where the employee must first submit a statement of grievance to employer); and

    (c) Schedule 5 (tribunal jurisdictions to which section 38 applies in relation to proceedings where the employer has failed to give a statement of employment particulars),

    insert–

'Regulation 36 of the Employment Equality (Age) Regulations 2006 (discrimination in the employment field)'.

The Equality Act 2006

37 The Equality Act 2006 is amended as follows.

38(1) Section 14(1) (codes of practice) is amended in accordance with this paragraph.

(2) At the end of paragraph (g) omit 'and'.

(3) After paragraph (h) insert

    'and

    (i) Parts 2 and 3 of the Employment Equality (Age) Regulations 2006.'.

39(1) Section 27(1) (conciliation) is amended in accordance with this paragraph.

(2) At the end of paragraph (f) omit 'or'.

(3) After paragraph (g) insert–

    'or

(h) regulation 39 of the Employment Equality (Age) Regulations 2006 (Jurisdiction of County and Sheriff Courts).'.

40(1)   Section 33(1) (equality and human rights enactments) is amended in accordance with this paragraph.

(2)   At the end of paragraph (g) omit 'and'.

(3)   After paragraph (h) insert–
'and

(i)   the Employment Equality (Age) Regulations 2006.'.

PART 2: OTHER LEGISLATION

41(1)   The Coal and Other Mines (Locomotives) Regulations 1956, Schedule 1 to the Coal and Other Mines (Locomotives) Order 1956 is amended in accordance with this paragraph.

(2)   In regulation 17(1) (drivers of locomotives) omit the words 'and no appointed driver shall operate a locomotive hauling persons in vehicles unless he has attained the age of–

(a)   in the case of a mine of shale, eighteen years;

(b)   in the case of any other mine, twenty-one years'.

42(1)   The Stratified Ironstone, Shale and Fireclay Mines (Explosives) Regulations 1956 are amended in accordance with this paragraph.

(2)   In regulation 3 (qualification of shot firers) omit the words 'he has attained the age of twenty-one years; and'.

43(1)   The Miscellaneous Mines (Explosives) Regulations 1959 are amended in accordance with this paragraph.

(2)   Omit regulation 6(2).

(3)   In regulation 8(2) (control of issue of detonators) omit the words 'has attained the age of eighteen years and'.

44(1)   The Lynemouth Mine (Diesel Vehicles and Storage Battery Vehicles) Special Regulations 1961 are amended in accordance with this paragraph.

(2)   In regulation 15 after the words 'Regulations 17' insert 'as amended by the Employment Equality (Age) Regulations 2006'.

45(1)   The South Crofty Mine (Locomotive) Special Regulations 1965 are amended in accordance with this paragraph.

(2)   In regulation 11(2) omit the words 'has attained the age of twenty-one years and'.

46(1)   The Glebe Mine (Locomotives and Diesel Vehicles) Special Regulations 1967 are amended in accordance with this paragraph.

(2)   In regulation 15(2) omit the words 'has attained the age of eighteen years and'.

47(1)   The Winsford Rock Salt Mine (Diesel Vehicles and Storage Battery Vehicles) Special Regulations 1971 are amended in accordance with this paragraph.

(2)   In regulation 14(2) omit the words 'is under the age of twenty-one years and'.

48(1)   The Thoresby Mine (Cable Reel Load-Haul-Dump Vehicles) Special Regulations 1978 are amended in accordance with this paragraph.

(2)   In regulation 17 after the words 'Regulations 17' insert 'as amended by the Employment Equality (Age) Regulations 2006'.

49   The Statutory Sick Pay (General) Regulations 1982 are amended as follows.

50(1)   Regulation 16 (meaning of 'employee') is amended in accordance with this paragraph.

(2)   In paragraph (1)–
   (a)   at the beginning insert the words 'Subject to paragraph (1ZA),', and
   (b)   omit the words 'over the age of 16'.

(3)   After paragraph (1) insert–
   '(1ZA) Any person under the age of 16 who would have been treated as an employed earner or, as the case may be, would have been treated otherwise than as an employed earner by virtue of the Social Security (Categorisation of Earners) Regulations 1978 had he been aged 16 or over, shall be treated as if he is aged 16 or over for the purposes of paragraph (1).'.

51(1)   Regulation 17(2) (meaning of 'earnings') is amended in accordance with this paragraph.

(2)   At the end of sub-paragraph (a) insert ' (or would have been so excluded had he not been under the age of 16)'.

(3)   At the end of sub-paragraph (b) insert ' (or where such a payment or amount would have been so excluded and in consequence he would not have been entitled to statutory sick pay had he not been under the age of 16)'.

52   The Statutory Maternity Pay (General) Regulations 1986 are amended as follows.

53(1)   Regulation 17 (meaning of 'employee') is amended in accordance with this paragraph.

(2)   In paragraph (1)–
   (a)   at the beginning insert the words 'Subject to paragraph (1A),', and
   (b)   omit the words 'over the age of 16'.

(3)   After paragraph (1) insert–
   '(1A) Any woman under the age of 16 who would have been treated as an employed earner or, as the case may be, would have been treated otherwise than as an employed earner by virtue of the Social Security (Categorisation of Earners) Regulations 1978 had she been aged 16 or over, shall be treated as if she is aged 16 or over for the purposes of paragraph (1).'.

54(1)   Regulation 20(2) (Meaning of 'earnings') is amended in accordance with this paragraph.

(2)   At the end of sub-paragraph (a) insert ' (or would have been so excluded had she not been under the age of 16)'.

(3)   At the end of sub-paragraph (b) insert ' (or where such a payment or amount would have been so excluded and in consequence she would not have been entitled to statutory maternity pay had she not been under the age of 16)'.

(4)   This paragraph applies in relation to any case where the expected week of confinement begins on or after 14th January 2007.

55(1)   The Coal and Other Safety-Lamp Mines (Explosives) Regulations 1993 are amended in accordance with this paragraph.

(2)   In regulation 4(4) (appointment of shotfirers and trainee shotfirers) omit the words 'he is at least 21 years of age and'.

56(1)   The Employment Tribunals (Interest on Awards In Discrimination Cases) Regulations 1996 are amended in accordance with this paragraph.

(2)   In sub-paragraph (b) of the definition of 'an award under the relevant legislation' in regulation 1(2) (interpretation)–

(a)   after 'regulation 30(1)(b) of the Employment Equality (Sexual Orientation) Regulations 2003' omit 'or'; and

(b)   after 'regulation 30(1)(b) of the Employment Equality (Religion or Belief) Regulations 2003' insert–

'or regulation 38(1)(b) of the Employment Equality (Age) Regulations 2006'.

57(1)   The Employment Protection (Continuity of Employment) Regulations 1996 are amended in accordance with this paragraph.

(2)   In regulation 2 (application)–

(a)   omit the word 'or' at the end of paragraph (e); and

(b)   after paragraph (f) insert–

', or

(g)   a decision taken arising out of the use of the statutory duty to consider procedure contained in Schedule 6 to the Employment Equality (Age) Regulations 2006.'.

58(1)   The National Minimum Wage Regulations 1999 are amended in accordance with this paragraph.

(2)   Omit regulation 12(2)(a).

(3)   Omit paragraphs (2) to (6) of regulation 13.

(4)   In regulation 13(7) for the words 'Paragraphs (1) and (2) do' substitute 'Paragraph (1) does'.

(5)   In relation to any case where, before the commencement date, a worker within the meaning of regulation 12(2) has attained the age of 26, sub-paragraph (2) does not apply.

59   The Statutory Paternity Pay and Statutory Adoption Pay (General) Regulations 2002 are amended as follows.

60(1)   Regulation 32 (Treatment of persons as employees) is amended in accordance with this paragraph.

(2)   In paragraph (1)–

(a)   at the beginning insert the words 'Subject to paragraph (1A),', and

(b)   omit the words 'over the age of 16'.

(3)   After paragraph (1) insert–

'(1A) Any person under the age of 16 who would have been treated as an employed earner or, as the case may be, would have been treated otherwise than as an employed earner by virtue of the Social Security (Categorisation of Earners) Regulations 1978 had he been aged 16 or over, shall be treated as if he is aged 16 or over for the purposes of paragraph (1).'.

61(1) Regulation 39(2) (Meaning of 'earnings') is amended in accordance with this paragraph.

(2) At the end of sub-paragraph (a) insert ' (or would have been so excluded had he not been under the age of 16)'.

(3) At the end of sub-paragraph (b) insert ' (or where such a payment or amount would have been so excluded and in consequence he would not have been entitled to statutory paternity pay or, as the case may be, statutory adoption pay had he not been under the age of 16)'.

62(1) Schedule 1A (occupational pension schemes) to the Employment Equality (Religion or Belief) Regulations 2003 is amended in accordance with this paragraph.

(2) In paragraph 1(1)–
   (a) in the definition of 'active member', 'deferred member', 'managers', 'pensioner member' and 'trustees or managers', omit the words 'as at the date of the coming into force of these Regulations', and
   (b) in the definition of 'occupational pension scheme' omit the words 'as at the date of the coming into force of these Regulations'.

(3) In paragraph 1(2) omit the words 'as at the date of the coming into force of these Regulations'.

63(1) Schedule 1A (occupational pension schemes) to the Employment Equality (Sexual Orientation) Regulations 2003 is amended in accordance with this paragraph.

(2) In paragraph 1(1)–
   (a) in the definition of 'active member', 'deferred member', 'managers', 'pensioner member' and 'trustees or managers', omit the words 'as at the date of the coming into force of these Regulations', and
   (b) in the definition of 'occupational pension scheme' omit the words 'as at the date of the coming into force of these Regulations'.

(3) In paragraph 1(2) omit the words 'as at the date of the coming into force of these Regulations'.

64(1) The Employment Act 2002 (Dispute Resolution) Regulations 2004 are amended in accordance with this paragraph.

(2) In regulation 4(1) (dismissals to which the dismissal and disciplinary procedures do not apply)–
   (a) omit the word 'or' at the end of sub-paragraph (f); and
   (b) after sub-paragraph (g) insert–
   ', or
   (h) the reason (or, if more than one, the principal reason) for the dismissal is retirement of the employee (to be determined in accordance with section 98ZA to 98ZF of the 1996 Act)'.

SCHEDULE 9
REPEALS AND REVOCATIONS
Regulation 49(2)

(1)   Repeals

Short title and chapter	Extent of repeal
Marriage (Scotland) Act 1977 (c 15)	In section 9(1) the proviso, In section 12 the proviso, and In section 17 the proviso
Education (Scotland) Act 1980 (c 44)	Section 89
Solicitors (Scotland) Act 1980 (c 46)	Section 6(1)(a)
Weights and Measures Act 1985 (c 72)	Section 73(3)
Electricity Act 1989 (c 29)	In Schedule 10, paragraph 9(3)
Judicial Pensions and Retirement Act 1993 (c 8)	In Schedule 6, paragraph 66
Scottish Public Services Ombudsman Act 2002 (asp 11)	In Schedule 1, paragraph 4(1)(c). In Schedule 1, in paragraph 4(3), the words in brackets
Freedom of Information (Scotland) Act 2002 (asp 13)	Section 42(4)(b). In section 42(5), the words in brackets

(2)   Revocations

Title and reference	Extent of revocation
Coal and Other Mines (Sidings) Regulations 1956, Schedule to the Coal and Other Mines (Sidings) Order 1956 (SI 1956/1773)	Regulation 21 In regulation 22, the definition of locomotive
The Management and Administration of Safety and Health in Mines Regulations 1993 (SI 1993/1897)	Regulation 17(2)

Council Directive 2000/78/EC

of 27 November 2000 establishing a general framework for equal treatment in employment and occupation[1]

THE COUNCIL OF THE EUROPEAN UNION,

Having regard to the Treaty establishing the European Community, and in particular Article 13 thereof,

Having regard to the proposal from the Commission,[2]

Having regard to the Opinion of the European Parliament,[3]

Having regard to the Opinion of the Economic and Social Committee,[4]

Having regard to the Opinion of the Committee of the Regions,[5]

Whereas:

(1) In accordance with Article 6 of the Treaty on European Union, the European Union is founded on the principles of liberty, democracy, respect for human rights and fundamental freedoms, and the rule of law, principles which are common to all Member States and it respects fundamental rights, as guaranteed by the European

Convention for the Protection of Human Rights and Fundamental Freedoms and as they result from the constitutional traditions common to the Member States, as general principles of Community law.

(2) The principle of equal treatment between women and men is well established by an important body of Community law, in particular in Council Directive 76/207/EEC of 9 February 1976 on the implementation of the principle of equal treatment for men and women as regards access to employment, vocational training and promotion, and working conditions.[6]

(3) In implementing the principle of equal treatment, the Community should, in accordance with Article 3(2) of the EC Treaty, aim to eliminate inequalities, and to promote equality between men and women, especially since women are often the victims of multiple discrimination.

---

1 L 303/16 EN Official Journal of the European Communities, 2 December 2000. Only European Community Legislation printed in the paper edition of the *Official Journal of the European Union* is deemed authentic.

2 OJ C 177 E, 27.6.2000, p42.

3 Opinion delivered on 12 October 2000 (not yet published in the Official Journal).

4 OJ C 204, 18.7.2000, p82.

5 OJ C 226, 8.8.2000, p1.

6 OJ L 39, 14.2.1976, p40.

(4)   The right of all persons to equality before the law and protection against discrimination constitutes a universal right recognised by the Universal Declaration of Human Rights, the United Nations Convention on the Elimination of All Forms of Discrimination against Women, United Nations Covenants on Civil and Political Rights and on Economic, Social and Cultural Rights and by the European Convention for the Protection of Human Rights and Fundamental Freedoms, to which all Member States are signatories. Convention No 111 of the International Labour Organisation (ILO) prohibits discrimination in the field of employment and occupation.

(5)   It is important to respect such fundamental rights and freedoms. This Directive does not prejudice freedom of association, including the right to establish unions with others and to join unions to defend one's interests.

(6)   The Community Charter of the Fundamental Social Rights of Workers recognises the importance of combating every form of discrimination, including the need to take appropriate action for the social and economic integration of elderly and disabled people.

(7)   The EC Treaty includes among its objectives the promotion of coordination between employment policies of the Member States. To this end, a new employment chapter was incorporated in the EC Treaty as a means of developing a coordinated European strategy for employment to promote a skilled, trained and adaptable workforce.

(8)   The Employment Guidelines for 2000 agreed by the European Council at Helsinki on 10 and 11 December 1999 stress the need to foster a labour market favourable to social integration by formulating a coherent set of policies aimed at combating discrimination against groups such as persons with disability. They also emphasise the need to pay particular attention to supporting older workers, in order to increase their participation in the labour force.

(9)   Employment and occupation are key elements in guaranteeing equal opportunities for all and contribute strongly to the full participation of citizens in economic, cultural and social life and to realising their potential. (10) On 29 June 2000 the Council adopted Directive 2000/43/EC[7] implementing the principle of equal treatment between persons irrespective of racial or ethnic origin. That Directive already provides protection against such discrimination in the field of employment and occupation.

(11)   Discrimination based on religion or belief, disability, age or sexual orientation may undermine the achievement of the objectives of the EC Treaty, in particular the attainment of a high level of employment and social protection, raising the standard of living and the quality of life, economic and social cohesion and solidarity, and the free movement of persons.

(12)   To this end, any direct or indirect discrimination based on religion or belief, disability, age or sexual orientation as regards the areas covered

by this Directive should be prohibited throughout the Community. This prohibition of discrimination should also apply to nationals of third countries but does not cover differences of treatment based on nationality and is without prejudice to provisions governing the entry and residence of third-country nationals and their access to employment and occupation.

(13) This Directive does not apply to social security and social protection schemes whose benefits are not treated as income within the meaning given to that term for the purpose of applying Article 141 of the EC Treaty, nor to any kind of payment by the State aimed at providing access to employment or maintaining employment.

(14) This Directive shall be without prejudice to national provisions laying down retirement ages.

(15) The appreciation of the facts from which it may be inferred that there has been direct or indirect discrimination is a matter for national judicial or other competent bodies, in accordance with rules of national law or practice. Such rules may provide, in particular, for indirect discrimination to be established by any means including on the basis of statistical evidence.

(16) The provision of measures to accommodate the needs of disabled people at the workplace plays an important role in combating discrimination on grounds of disability.

(17) This Directive does not require the recruitment, promotion, maintenance in employment or training of an individual who is not competent, capable and available to perform the essential functions of the post concerned or to undergo the relevant training, without prejudice to the obligation to provide reasonable accommodation for people with disabilities.

(18) This Directive does not require, in particular, the armed forces and the police, prison or emergency services to recruit or maintain in employment persons who do not have the required capacity to carry out the range of functions that they may be called upon to perform with regard to the legitimate objective of preserving the operational capacity of those services.

(19) Moreover, in order that the Member States may continue to safeguard the combat effectiveness of their armed forces, they may choose not to apply the provisions of this Directive concerning disability and age to all or part of their armed forces. The Member States which make that choice must define the scope of that derogation.

(20) Appropriate measures should be provided, ie effective and practical measures to adapt the workplace to the disability, for example adapting premises and equipment, patterns of working time, the distribution of tasks or the provision of training or integration resources.

(21) To determine whether the measures in question give rise to a disproportionate burden, account should be taken in particular of the financial and other costs entailed, the scale and financial resources of the organisation or undertaking and the possibility of obtaining public funding or any other assistance.

(22)   This Directive is without prejudice to national laws on marital status and the benefits dependent thereon.

(23)   In very limited circumstances, a difference of treatment may be justified where a characteristic related to religion or belief, disability, age or sexual orientation constitutes a genuine and determining occupational requirement, when the objective is legitimate and the requirement is proportionate. Such circumstances should be included in the information provided by the Member States to the Commission.

(24)   The European Union in its Declaration No 11 on the status of churches and non-confessional organisations, annexed to the Final Act of the Amsterdam Treaty, has explicitly recognised that it respects and does not prejudice the status under national law of churches and religious associations or communities in the Member States and that it equally respects the status of philosophical and non-confessional organisations. With this in view, Member States may maintain or lay down specific provisions on genuine, legitimate and justified occupational requirements which might be required for carrying out an occupational activity.

(25)   The prohibition of age discrimination is an essential part of meeting the aims set out in the Employment Guidelines and encouraging diversity in the workforce. However, differences in treatment in connection with age may be justified under certain circumstances and therefore require specific provisions which may vary in accordance with the situation in Member States. It is therefore essential to distinguish between differences in treatment which are justified, in particular by legitimate employment policy, labour market and vocational training objectives, and discrimination which must be prohibited.

(26)   The prohibition of discrimination should be without prejudice to the maintenance or adoption of measures intended to prevent or compensate for disadvantages suffered by a group of persons of a particular religion or belief, disability, age or sexual orientation, and such measures may permit organisations of persons of a particular religion or belief, disability, age or sexual orientation where their main object is the promotion of the special needs of those persons.

(27)   In its Recommendation 86/379/EEC of 24 July 1986 on the employment of disabled people in the Community,[8] the Council established a guideline framework setting out examples of positive action to promote the employment and training of disabled people, and in its Resolution of 17 June 1999 on equal employment opportunities for people with disabilities,[9] affirmed the importance of giving specific attention inter alia to recruitment, retention, training and lifelong learning with regard to disabled persons.

(28)   This Directive lays down minimum requirements, thus giving the Member States the option of introducing or maintaining more favourable provisions. The implementation of this Directive should

8   OJ L 225, 12.8.1986, p43.
9   OJ C 186, 2.7.1999, p3.

not serve to justify any regression in relation to the situation which already prevails in each Member State.

(29) Persons who have been subject to discrimination based on religion or belief, disability, age or sexual orientation should have adequate means of legal protection. To provide a more effective level of protection, associations or legal entities should also be empowered to engage in proceedings, as the Member States so determine, either on behalf or in support of any victim, without prejudice to national rules of procedure concerning representation and defence before the courts.

(30) The effective implementation of the principle of equality requires adequate judicial protection against victimisation.

(31) The rules on the burden of proof must be adapted when there is a prima facie case of discrimination and, for the principle of equal treatment to be applied effectively, the burden of proof must shift back to the respondent when evidence of such discrimination is brought. However, it is not for the respondent to prove that the plaintiff adheres to a particular religion or belief, has a particular disability, is of a particular age or has a particular sexual orientation.

(32) Member States need not apply the rules on the burden of proof to proceedings in which it is for the court or other competent body to investigate the facts of the case. The procedures thus referred to are those in which the plaintiff is not required to prove the facts, which it is for the court or competent body to investigate.

(33) Member States should promote dialogue between the social partners and, within the framework of national practice, with non-governmental organisations to address different forms of discrimination at the workplace and to combat them.

(34) The need to promote peace and reconciliation between the major communities in Northern Ireland necessitates the incorporation of particular provisions into this Directive.

(35) Member States should provide for effective, proportionate and dissuasive sanctions in case of breaches of the obligations under this Directive.

(36) Member States may entrust the social partners, at their joint request, with the implementation of this Directive, as regards the provisions concerning collective agreements, provided they take any necessary steps to ensure that they are at all times able to guarantee the results required by this Directive.

(37) In accordance with the principle of subsidiarity set out in Article 5 of the EC Treaty, the objective of this Directive, namely the creation within the Community of a level playing-field as regards equality in employment and occupation, cannot be sufficiently achieved by the Member States and can therefore, by reason of the scale and impact of the action, be better achieved at Community level. In accordance with the principle of proportionality, as set out in that Article, this Directive does not go beyond what is necessary in order to achieve that objective,

HAS ADOPTED THIS DIRECTIVE:

CHAPTER I

GENERAL PROVISIONS

Article 1

Purpose

The purpose of this Directive is to lay down a general framework for combating discrimination on the grounds of religion or belief, disability, age or sexual orientation as regardsemployment and occupation, with a view to putting into effect in the Member States the principle of equal treatment.

Article 2

Concept of discrimination

1. For the purposes of this Directive, the 'principle of equal treatment' shall mean that there shall be no direct or indirect discrimination whatsoever on any of the grounds referred to in Article 1.

2. For the purposes of paragraph 1:

   (a) direct discrimination shall be taken to occur where one person is treated less favourably than another is, has been or would be treated in a comparable situation, on any of the grounds referred to in Article 1;

   (b) indirect discrimination shall be taken to occur where an apparently neutral provision, criterion or practice would put persons having a particular religion or belief, a particular disability, a particular age, or a particular sexual orientation at a particular disadvantage compared with other persons unless:

      (i)   that provision, criterion or practice is objectively justified by a legitimate aim and the means of achieving that aim are appropriate and necessary, or

      (ii) as regards persons with a particular disability, the employer or any person or organisation to whom this Directive applies, is obliged, under national legislation, to take appropriate measures in line with the principles contained in Article 5 in order to eliminate disadvantages entailed by such provision, criterion or practice.

3. Harassment shall be deemed to be a form of discrimination within the meaning of paragraph 1, when unwanted conduct related to any of the grounds referred to in Article 1 takes place with the purpose or effect of violating the dignity of a person and of creating an intimidating, hostile, degrading, humiliating or offensive environment. In this context, the concept of harassment may be defined in accordance with the national laws and practice of the Member States.

4. An instruction to discriminate against persons on any of the grounds referred to in Article 1 shall be deemed to be discrimination within the meaning of paragraph 1.

5. This Directive shall be without prejudice to measures laid down by national law which, in a democratic society, are necessary for public security, for the maintenance of public order and the prevention of criminal offences, for the protection of health and for the protection of the rights and freedoms of others.

Article 3

Scope

1. Within the limits of the areas of competence conferred on the Community, this Directive shall apply to all persons, as regards both the public and private sectors, including public bodies, in relation to:
    (a) conditions for access to employment, to self-employment or to occupation, including selection criteria and recruitment conditions, whatever the branch of activity and at all levels of the professional hierarchy, including promotion;
    (b) access to all types and to all levels of vocational guidance, vocational training, advanced vocational training and retraining, including practical work experience;
    (c) employment and working conditions, including dismissals and pay;
    (d) membership of, and involvement in, an organisation of workers or employers, or any organisation whose members carry on a particular profession, including the benefits provided for by such organisations.

2. This Directive does not cover differences of treatment based on nationality and is without prejudice to provisions and conditions relating to the entry into and residence of third country nationals and stateless persons in the territory of Member States, and to any treatment which arises from the legal status of the third-country nationals and stateless persons concerned.

3. This Directive does not apply to payments of any kind made by state schemes or similar, including state social security or social protection schemes.

4. Member States may provide that this Directive, in so far as it relates to discrimination on the grounds of disability and age, shall not apply to the armed forces.

Article 4

Occupational requirements

1. Notwithstanding Article 2(1) and (2), Member States may provide that a difference of treatment which is based on a characteristic related to any of the grounds referred to in Article 1 shall not constitute discrimination where, by reason of the nature of the particular occupational activities concerned or of the context in which they are carried out, such a characteristic constitutes a genuine and determining occupational requirement, provided that the objective is legitimate and the requirement is proportionate.

2.   Member States may maintain national legislation in force at the date of adoption of this Directive or provide for future legislation incorporating national practices existing at the date of adoption of this Directive pursuant to which, in the case of occupational activities within churches and other public or private organisations the ethos of which is based on religion or belief, a difference of treatment based on a person's religion or belief shall not constitute discrimination where, by reason of the nature of these activities or of the context in which they are carried out, a person's religion or belief constitute a genuine, legitimate and justified occupational requirement, having regard to the organisation's ethos. This difference of treatment shall be implemented taking account of Member States' constitutional provisions and principles, as well as the general principles of Community law, and should not justify discrimination on another ground.

Provided that its provisions are otherwise complied with, this Directive shall thus not prejudice the right of churches and other public or private organisations, the ethos of which is based on religion or belief, acting in conformity with national constitutions and laws, to require individuals working for them to act in good faith and with loyalty to the organisation's ethos.

Article 5

Reasonable accommodation for disabled persons

In order to guarantee compliance with the principle of equal treatment in relation to persons with disabilities, reasonable accommodation shall be provided. This means that employers shall take appropriate measures, where needed in a particular case, to enable a person with a disability to have access to, participate in, or advance in employment, or to undergo training, unless such measures would impose a disproportionate burden on the employer. This burden shall not be disproportionate when it is sufficiently remedied by measures existing within the framework of the disability policy of the Member State concerned.

Article 6

Justification of differences of treatment on grounds of age

1.   Notwithstanding Article 2(2), Member States may provide that differences of treatment on grounds of age shall not constitute discrimination, if, within the context of national law, they are objectively and reasonably justified by a legitimate aim, including legitimate employment policy, labour market and vocational training objectives, and if the means of achieving that aim are appropriate and necessary.

Such differences of treatment may include, among others:

(a)   the setting of special conditions on access to employment and vocational training, employment and occupation, including dismissal and remuneration conditions, for young people, older workers and persons with caring responsibilities in order to promote their vocational integration or ensure their protection;

(b)   the fixing of minimum conditions of age, professional experience or seniority in service for access to employment or to certain advantages linked to employment;

(c)   the fixing of a maximum age for recruitment which is based on the training requirements of the post in question or the need for a reasonable period of employment before retirement.

2.   Notwithstanding Article 2(2), Member States may provide that the fixing for occupational social security schemes of ages for admission or entitlement to retirement or invalidity benefits, including the fixing under those schemes of different ages for employees or groups or categories of employees, and the use, in the context of such schemes, of age criteria in actuarial calculations, does not constitute discrimination on the grounds of age, provided this does not result in discrimination on the grounds of sex.

Article 7

Positive action

1.   With a view to ensuring full equality in practice, the principle of equal treatment shall not prevent any Member State from maintaining or adopting specific measures to prevent or compensate for disadvantages linked to any of the grounds referred to in Article 1.

2.   With regard to disabled persons, the principle of equal treatment shall be without prejudice to the right of Member States to maintain or adopt provisions on the protection of health and safety at work or to measures aimed at creating or maintaining provisions or facilities for safeguarding or promoting their integration into the working environment.

Article 8

Minimum requirements

1.   Member States may introduce or maintain provisions which are more favourable to the protection of the principle of equal treatment than those laid down in this Directive.

2.   The implementation of this Directive shall under no circumstances constitute grounds for a reduction in the level of protection against discrimination already afforded by Member States in the fields covered by this Directive.

CHAPTER II

REMEDIES AND ENFORCEMENT

Article 9

Defence of rights

1.   Member States shall ensure that judicial and/or administrative procedures, including where they deem it appropriate conciliation procedures, for the enforcement of obligations under this Directive are

available to all persons who consider themselves wronged by failure to apply the principle of equal treatment to them, even after the relationship in which the discrimination is alleged to have occurred has ended.

2. Member States shall ensure that associations, organisations or other legal entities which have, in accordance with the criteria laid down by their national law, a legitimate interest in ensuring that the provisions of this Directive are complied with, may engage, either on behalf or in support of the complainant, with his or her approval, in any judicial and/or administrative procedure provided for the enforcement of obligations under this Directive.

3. Paragraphs 1 and 2 are without prejudice to national rules relating to time limits for bringing actions as regards the principle of equality of treatment.

Article 10

Burden of proof

1. Member States shall take such measures as are necessary, in accordance with their national judicial systems, to ensure that, when persons who consider themselves wronged because the principle of equal treatment has not been applied to them establish, before a court or other competent authority, facts from which it may be presumed that there has been direct or indirect discrimination, it shall be for the respondent to prove that there has been no breach of the principle of equal treatment.

2. Paragraph 1 shall not prevent Member States from introducing rules of evidence which are more favourable to plaintiffs.

3. Paragraph 1 shall not apply to criminal procedures.

4. Paragraphs 1, 2 and 3 shall also apply to any legal proceedings commenced in accordance with Article 9(2).

5. Member States need not apply paragraph 1 to proceedings in which it is for the court or competent body to investigate the facts of the case.

Article 11

Victimisation

Member States shall introduce into their national legal systems such measures as are necessary to protect employees against dismissal or other adverse treatment by the employer as a reaction to a complaint within the undertaking or to any legal proceedings aimed at enforcing compliance with the principle of equal treatment.

Article 12

Dissemination of information

Member States shall take care that the provisions adopted pursuant to this Directive, together with the relevant provisions already in force in this field, are brought to the attention of the persons concerned by all appropriate means, for example at the workplace, throughout their territory.

Article 13

Social dialogue

1. Member States shall, in accordance with their national traditions and practice, take adequate measures to promote dialogue between the social partners with a view to fostering equal treatment, including through the monitoring of workplace practices, collective agreements, codes of conduct and through research or exchange of experiences and good practices.
2. Where consistent with their national traditions and practice, Member States shall encourage the social partners, without prejudice to their autonomy, to conclude at the appropriate level agreements laying down anti-discrimination rules in the fields referred to in Article 3 which fall within the scope of collective bargaining. These agreements shall respect the minimum requirements laid down by this Directive and by the relevant national implementing measures.

Article 14

Dialogue with non-governmental organisations

Member States shall encourage dialogue with appropriate nongovernmental organisations which have, in accordance with their national law and practice, a legitimate interest in contributing to the fight against discrimination on any of the grounds referred to in Article 1 with a view to promoting the principle of equal treatment.

CHAPTER III

PARTICULAR PROVISIONS

Article 15

Northern Ireland

1. In order to tackle the under-representation of one of the major religious communities in the police service of Northern Ireland, differences in treatment regarding recruitment into that service, including its support staff, shall not constitute discrimination insofar as those differences in treatment are expressly authorised by national legislation.
2. In order to maintain a balance of opportunity in employment for teachers in Northern Ireland while furthering the reconciliation of historical divisions between the major religious communities there, the provisions on religion or belief in this Directive shall not apply to the recruitment of teachers in schools in Northern Ireland in so far as this is expressly authorised by national legislation.

CHAPTER IV

FINAL PROVISIONS

Article 16

Compliance

Member States shall take the necessary measures to ensure that:

(a)   any laws, regulations and administrative provisions contrary to the principle of equal treatment are abolished;

(b)   any provisions contrary to the principle of equal treatment which are included in contracts or collective agreements, internal rules of undertakings or rules governing the independent occupations and professions and workers' and employers' organisations are, or may be, declared null and void or are amended.

Article 17

Sanctions

Member States shall lay down the rules on sanctions applicable to infringements of the national provisions adopted pursuant to this Directive and shall take all measures necessary to ensure that they are applied. The sanctions, which may comprise the payment of compensation to the victim, must be effective, proportionate and dissuasive. Member States shall notify those provisions to the Commission by 2 December 2003 at the latest and shall notify it without delay of any subsequent amendment affecting them.

Article 18

Implementation

Member States shall adopt the laws, regulations and administrative provisions necessary to comply with this Directive by 2 December 2003 at the latest or may entrust the social partners, at their joint request, with the implementation of this Directive as regards provisions concerning collective agreements. In such cases, Member States shall ensure that, no later than 2 December 2003, the social partners introduce the necessary measures by agreement, the Member States concerned being required to take any necessary measures to enable them at any time to be in a position to guarantee the results imposed by this Directive. They shall forthwith inform the Commission thereof.

In order to take account of particular conditions, Member States may, if necessary, have an additional period of 3 years from 2 December 2003, that is to say a total of 6 years, to implement the provisions of this Directive on age and disability discrimination. In that event they shall inform the Commission forthwith. Any Member State which chooses to use this additional period shall report annually to the Commission on the steps it is taking to tackle age and disability discrimination and on the progress it is making towards implementation. The Commission shall report annually to the Council.

When Member States adopt these measures, they shall contain a reference to this Directive or be accompanied by such reference on the occasion of their official publication. The methods of making such reference shall be laid down by Member States.

Article 19

Report

1. Member States shall communicate to the Commission, by 2 December 2005 at the latest and every five years thereafter, all the information necessary for the Commission to draw up a report to the European Parliament and the Council on the application of this Directive.

2. The Commission's report shall take into account, as appropriate, the viewpoints of the social partners and relevant non-governmental organisations. In accordance with the principle of gender mainstreaming, this report shall, *inter alia*, provide an assessment of the impact of the measures taken on women and men. In the light of the information received, this report shall include, if necessary, proposals to revise and update this Directive.

Article 20

Entry into force

This Directive shall enter into force on the day of its publication in the *Official Journal of the European Communities*.

Article 21

Addressees

This Directive is addressed to the Member States.

Done at Brussels, 27 November 2000.

For the Council
The President
É GUIGOU

Goods and services age discrimination legislation in other countries

REPUBLIC OF IRELAND

Equal Status Act 2000 ss 3, 5, 9, 15 and 16

The act relates to non-employment discrimination across nine grounds (as amended by the Equality Act 2004)

3(1) For the purposes of this Act discrimination shall be taken to occur–

(a) where a person is treated less favourably than another person is, has been or would be treated in a comparable situation on any of the grounds specified in subsection (2) (in this Act referred to as the 'discriminatory grounds') which–

　(i) exists,

　(ii) existed but no longer exists,

　(iii) may exist in the future, or

　(iv) is imputed to the person concerned,

(b) where a person who is associated with another person–

　(i) is treated, by virtue of that association, less favourably than a person who is not so associated is, has been or would be treated in a comparable situation, and

　(ii) similar treatment of that other person on any of the discriminatory grounds would, by virtue of paragraph (a), constitute discrimination, or

(c) where an apparently neutral provision puts a person referred to in any paragraph of section 3(2) at a particular disadvantage compared with other persons, unless the provision is objectively justified by a legitimate aim and the means of achieving that aim are appropriate and necessary.

(2) As between any two persons, the discriminatory grounds (and the descriptions of those grounds for the purposes of this Act) are:

(a) that one is male and the other is female (the 'gender ground'),

(b) that they are of different marital status (the 'marital status ground'),

(c) that one has family status and the other does not or that one has a different family status from the other (the 'family status ground'),

(d) that they are of different sexual orientation (the 'sexual orientation ground'),

(e) that one has a different religious belief from the other, or that one has a religious belief and the other has not (the 'religion ground'),

(f) subject to subsection (3), that they are of different ages (the 'age ground'),

(g) that one is a person with a disability and the other either is not or is a person with a different disability (the 'disability ground'),

(h) that they are of different race, colour, nationality or ethnic or national origins (the 'ground of race'),

(i) that one is a member of the Traveller community and the other is not (the 'Traveller community ground'),

(j) that one–

    (i) has in good faith applied for any determination or redress provided for in Part II or III,

    (ii) has attended as a witness before the Authority, the Director or a court in connection with any inquiry or proceedings under this Act,

    (iii) has given evidence in any criminal proceedings under this Act,

    (iv) has opposed by lawful means an act which is unlawful under this Act, or

    (v) has given notice of an intention to take any of the actions specified in subparagraphs (i) to (iv), and the other has not (the 'victimisation ground').

(3) (a) Treating a person who has not attained the age of 18 years less favourably or more favourably than another, whatever that person's age shall not be regarded as discrimination on the age ground.

    (b) Paragraph (a) does not apply in relation to the provision of motor vehicle insurance to licensed drivers under that age.

(3A) In any proceedings statistics are admissible for the purpose of determining whether discrimination has occurred by virtue of subsection (1)(c).

(4) The Minister shall, not later than two years after the commencement of this section, review the operation of this Act to assess whether there is a need to add to the discriminatory grounds specified in *subsection* (2).

5(1) A person shall not discriminate in disposing of goods to the public generally or a section of the public or in providing a service, whether the disposal or provision is for consideration or otherwise and whether the service provided can be availed of only by a section of the public.

(2) Subsection (1) does not apply in respect of–

    (a) an activity referred to in section 7(2),

    (b) a service related to a matter provided for under section 6, or a service offered to its members by a club in respect of which section 8 applies,

    (c) differences in the treatment of persons on the gender ground in relation to services of an aesthetic, cosmetic or similar nature, where the services require physical contact between the service provider and the recipient,

(d) differences in the treatment of persons in relation to annuities, pensions, insurance policies or any other matters related to the assessment of risk where the treatment–

    (i) is effected by reference to–

        (a) actuarial or statistical data obtained from a source on which it is reasonable to rely, or

        (b) other relevant underwriting or commercial factors,

    and

    (ii) is reasonable having regard to the data or other relevant factors,

(e) differences in the treatment of persons on the religion ground in relation to goods or services provided for a religious purpose,

(f) differences in the treatment of persons on the gender, age or disability ground or on the basis of nationality or national origin in relation to the provision or organisation of a sporting facility or sporting event to the extent that the differences are reasonably necessary having regard to the nature of the facility or event and are relevant to the purpose of the facility or event,

(g) differences in the treatment of persons on the gender ground where embarrassment or infringement of privacy can reasonably be expected to result from the presence of a person of another gender,

(h) differences in the treatment of persons in a category of persons in respect of services that are provided for the principal purpose of promoting, for a bona fide purpose and in a bona fide manner, the special interests of persons in that category to the extent that the differences in treatment are reasonably necessary to promote those special interests,

(i) differences in the treatment of persons on the gender, age or disability ground or on the ground of race, reasonably required for reasons of authenticity, aesthetics, tradition or custom in connection with a dramatic performance or other entertainment,

(j) an age requirement for a person to be an adoptive or foster parent, where the requirement is reasonable having regard to the needs of the child or children concerned,

(k) a disposal of goods by will or gift, or

(l) differences, not otherwise specifically provided for in this section, in the treatment of persons in respect of the disposal of goods, or the provision of a service, which can reasonably be regarded as goods or a service suitable only to the needs of certain persons.

9(1) For the purposes of section 8, a club shall not be considered to be a discriminating club by reason only that–

(a) if its principal purpose is to cater only for the needs of–

    (i) persons of a particular gender, marital status, family status, sexual orientation, religious belief, age, disability, nationality or ethnic or national origin,

    (ii) persons who are members of the Traveller community,

or

        (iii) persons who have no religious belief,
            it refuses membership to other persons,

(b) it confines access to a membership benefit or privilege to members within the category of a particular gender or age, where–

    (i) it is not practicable for members outside the category to enjoy the benefit or privilege at the same time as members within the category, and

    (ii) arrangements have been made by the club which offer the same or a reasonably equivalent benefit or privilege both to members within the category and to members outside the category,

(c) it has different types of membership, access to which is not based on any discriminatory ground,

(d) for the purpose of reducing or eliminating the effect of any rule or practice of the club (whether adopted before or after the commencement of this section) restricting access to particular types of membership to persons of a particular gender it offers concessionary rates, fees or membership arrangements to persons who were or are disadvantaged by any such rule or practice, or

(e) it provides different treatment to members in the category of a particular gender, age, disability, nationality or national origin in relation to sporting facilities or events and the different treatment is relevant to the purpose of the facilities or events and is reasonably necessary.

(2) For the purposes of section 8, a club shall not be considered to be a discriminating club by reason only that it–

(a) has, for the principal purpose of promoting equality, a reserved place or places on its board or committee of management for persons who are members of a particular category, or

(b) takes other measures for the principal purpose of obtaining a more equal involvement in club matters of persons who are members of a particular category.

15(1) For greater certainty, nothing in this Act prohibiting discrimination shall be construed as requiring a person to dispose of goods or premises, or to provide services or accommodation or services and amenities related to accommodation, to another person ('the customer') in circumstances which would lead a reasonable individual having the responsibility, knowledge and experience of the person to the belief, on grounds other than discriminatory grounds, that the disposal of the goods or premises or the provision of the services or accommodation or the services and amenities related to accommodation, as the case may be, to the customer would produce a substantial risk of criminal or disorderly conduct or behaviour or damage to property at or in the vicinity of the place in which the goods or services are sought or the premises or accommodation are located.

(2) Action taken in good faith by or on behalf of the holder of a licence or other authorisation which permits the sale of intoxicating liquor, for the sole purpose of ensuring compliance with the provisions of the Licensing Acts, 1833 to 1999, shall not constitute discrimination.

16(1)   Imposing or maintaining a reasonable preferential fee, charge or rate in respect of anything offered or provided to or in respect of persons together with their children, married couples, persons in a specific age group or persons with a disability does not constitute–
   (a)   discrimination for the purposes of section 5 or 6, or
   (b)   a discriminatory rule, policy or practice for the purposes of section 8(2)(a).

   (2)   Treating a person differently does not constitute discrimination where the person–
   (a)   is so treated solely in the exercise of a clinical judgment in connection with the diagnosis of illness or his or her medical treatment, or
   (b)   is incapable of entering into an enforceable contract or of giving an informed consent and for that reason the treatment is reasonable in the particular case.

AUSTRALIA

Age Discrimination Act 2004 ss28, 33–37, 39–42, 44

This federal act relates to employment and non-employment issues. It supplements existing legislation in some states and territories.

Goods, services and facilities

28   It is unlawful for a person who, whether for payment or not, provides goods or services, or makes facilities available, to discriminate against another person on the ground of the other person's age:
   (a)   by refusing to provide the other person with those goods or services or to make those facilities available to the other person; or
   (b)   in the terms or conditions on which the firstmentioned person provides the other person with those goods or services or makes those facilities available to the other person; or
   (c)   in the manner in which the firstmentioned person provides the other person with those goods or services or makes those facilities available to the other person.

Positive discrimination

33   This Part does not make it unlawful for a person to discriminate against another person, on the ground of the other person's age, by an act that is consistent with the purposes of this Act, if:
   (a)   the act provides a bona fide benefit to persons of a particular age; or
   Example: This paragraph would cover a hairdresser giving a discount to a person holding a Seniors Card or a similar card, because giving the discount is an act that provides a bona fide benefit to older persons.
   (b)   the act is intended to meet a need that arises out of the age of persons of a particular age; or

Example: Young people often have a greater need for welfare services (including information, support and referral) than other people. This paragraph would therefore cover the provision of welfare services to young homeless people, because such services are intended to meet a need arising out of the age of such people.

(c)   the act is intended to reduce a disadvantage experienced by people of a particular age.

Example: Older people are often more disadvantaged by retrenchment than are other people. This paragraph would therefore cover the provision of additional notice entitlements for older workers, because such entitlements are intended to reduce a disadvantage experienced by older people.

Charities

34(1)   This Part does not:

(a)   affect a provision in a charitable instrument that confers charitable benefits, or enables charitable benefits to be conferred, wholly or in part on persons of a particular age; or

(b)   make unlawful any act done to give effect to such a provision.

Religious bodies

35   This Part does not affect an act or practice of a body established for religious purposes that:

(a)   conforms to the doctrines, tenets or beliefs of that religion; or

(b)   is necessary to avoid injury to the religious sensitivities of adherents of that religion.

Voluntary bodies

36(1)   This Part does not make it unlawful for a voluntary body to discriminate against a person, on the ground of the person's age, in connection with:

(a)   the admission of persons as members of the body; or

(b)   the provision of benefits, facilities or services to members of the body...

Superannuation, insurance and credit–actuarial data etc.

37   Superannuation and insurance

(1)   Subsections (2) and (3) apply to the following:

(a)   an annuity;

(b)   a life insurance policy;

(c)   a policy of insurance against accident or any other policy of insurance;

(d)   membership of a superannuation or provident fund;

(e)   membership of a superannuation or provident scheme.

(2)   This Part does not make it unlawful for a person to discriminate against another person, on the ground of the other person's age:

(a)   in respect of the terms or conditions on which the annuity, policy or membership is offered to, or may be obtained by, the other person; or

(b)   by refusing to offer the annuity, policy or membership to the other person;

if the condition in subsection (3) is satisfied.

(3)   The condition is satisfied if:

(a)   the discrimination:

(i)   is based upon actuarial or statistical data on which it is reasonable for the firstmentioned person to rely; and

(ii)   is reasonable having regard to the matter of the data and other relevant factors; or

Note: The Commission and the President can require the disclosure of the source of the actuarial or statistical data (see section 54).

(b)   in a case where no such actuarial or statistical data is available and cannot reasonably be obtained—the discrimination is reasonable having regard to any other relevant factors.

Credit

(4)   This Part does not make it unlawful for a person to discriminate against another person, on the ground of the other person's age:

(a)   in respect of the terms or conditions on which credit is provided to, or may be obtained by, the other person; or

(b)   by refusing to offer credit to the other person;

if the condition in subsection (5) is satisfied.

(5)   The condition is satisfied if the discrimination:

(a)   is based upon actuarial or statistical data on which it is reasonable for the firstmentioned person to rely; and

(b)   is reasonable having regard to the matter of the data.

Note: The Commission and the President can require the disclosure of the source of the actuarial or statistical data (see section 54).

Direct compliance with laws, orders etc.

39   Acts, regulations and instruments mentioned in Schedule 1

(1)   This Part does not make unlawful anything done by a person in direct compliance with:

(a)   an Act mentioned in Schedule 1; or

(b)   a regulation or any other instrument mentioned in Schedule 1.

Other Acts or regulations – 2 year exemption period

(2)   This Part does not make unlawful anything done by a person, in direct compliance with any other Commonwealth Act or regulation, during the period:

(a)   beginning on the day on which this Act commences; and

(b)   ending 2 years after that day.

(3)   To avoid doubt, subsection (2) does not affect the operation of any other provision in this Division.

State and Territory Acts, regulations and instruments

(4)   This Part does not make unlawful anything done by a person in direct compliance with:

(a)   an Act of a State or Territory; or

(b)   a regulation or any other instrument made under an Act of a State or Territory.

(5)   Subsection (4) does not apply in relation to an Act, regulation or other instrument of a State or Territory if the Act, regulation or instrument is specified in regulations made for the purposes of this subsection.

(6)   To avoid doubt, section 49A of the Acts Interpretation Act 1901 does not prevent a regulation made for the purposes of subsection (5) from specifying an Act, regulation or instrument as in force at a particular time or as in force from time to time.

Court orders

(7)   This Part does not make unlawful anything done by a person in direct compliance with an order of a court.

Workplace relations

(8)   This Part does not make unlawful anything done by a person in direct compliance with any of the following:

(a)   an order or award of a court or tribunal having power to fix minimum wages;

(b)   a certified agreement (within the meaning of the Workplace Relations Act 1996);

(c)   an Australian workplace agreement (within the meaning of the Workplace Relations Act 1996).

Taxation laws

40   This Part does not make unlawful anything done by a person in direct compliance with a taxation law (within the meaning of the Income Tax Assessment Act 1997).

Pensions, allowances and benefits etc.

41(1)   This Part does not make unlawful anything done by a person in direct compliance with:

(a)   the A New Tax System (Family Assistance) Act 1999; or

(b)   the A New Tax System (Family Assistance) (Administration) Act 1999; or

(c)   the Child Support (Assessment) Act 1989; or

(d)   the Child Support (Registration and Collection) Act 1988; or

(e)   the Defence Service Homes Act 1918; or

(f)   the Disability Services Act 1986; or

(fa) the Military Rehabilitation and Compensation Act 2004; or

(fb) the Military Rehabilitation and Compensation (Consequential and Transitional Provisions) Act 2004; or

(fc) Part XI of the Safety, Rehabilitation and Compensation Act 1988; or

(g)   the Social Security Act 1991; or

(h)   the Social Security (Administration) Act 1999; or

(i)   the Social Security (International Agreements) Act 1999; or

(j)   the Veterans' Entitlements Act 1986.

(2)   This Part does not make unlawful anything done by a person in direct compliance with a regulation under an Act mentioned in paragraph (1)(a), (b), (c), (d), (f), (g), (h) or (i).

(2A)   This Part does not make unlawful anything done by a person in direct compliance with a determination in force under subparagraph 169(1)(a)(i) of the A New Tax System (Family Assistance) (Administration) Act 1999.

(2B)   This Part does not make unlawful anything done by a person in direct compliance with a regulation, scheme or other instrument under the Military Rehabilitation and Compensation Act 2004 or the Military Rehabilitation and Compensation (Consequential and Transitional Provisions) Act 2004.

(3)   This Part does not make unlawful anything done by a person in direct compliance with the CDEP Scheme (within the meaning of the Social Security Act 1991).

(3A)   This Part does not make unlawful anything done by a person in direct compliance with a determination in force under subparagraph 209(1)(a)(i) of the Social Security (Administration) Act 1999.

(4)   This Part does not make unlawful anything done by a person in direct compliance with a determination in force under paragraph 88A(1)(c) of the Veterans' Entitlements Act 1986.

(5)   This Part does not make unlawful anything done by a person in direct compliance with the Approved Guide to the Assessment of Rates of Veterans' Pensions (within the meaning of the Veterans' Entitlements Act 1986).

Health

Exempted health programs

42(1)   This Part does not make an exempted health program (see subsection (6)) unlawful.

Example: A program for providing free influenza vaccines to older people, based on evidence showing that older people are at greater risk of complications as a result of influenza than are people of different ages, would be covered by this subsection.

(2)   This Part does not make unlawful anything done by a person in accordance with an exempted health program.

Example: A person providing free influenza vaccines to older people in accordance with an exempted health program would be covered by this subsection.

Individual decisions–health or medical goods or services

(3)   This Part does not make it unlawful for a person to discriminate against another person, on the ground of the other person's age, by taking the other person's age into account in making a decision relating to health goods or services or medical goods or services, if:

        (a)   taking the other person's age into account in making the decision is reasonably based on evidence, and professional knowledge, about the ability of persons of the other person's age to benefit from the goods or services; and

(b)   the decision is not in accordance with an exempted health program.

Note: The exemption in subsection (2) covers anything done by a person in accordance with an exempted health program.

(4)   The evidence mentioned in paragraph (3)(a) is the evidence that was reasonably available at the time the decision was made.

Administration of certain health legislation

(5)   This Part does not make unlawful anything done by a person in relation to the administration of:

(a)   the Health Insurance Act 1973, or a regulation or any other instrument made under that Act, to the extent that the thing done relates to:

(i)   the release of, or the giving of access to, information held by the Chief Executive Officer of Medicare Australia; or

(ii)   the issue of a medicare card; or

(b)   the National Health Act 1953, or a regulation or any other instrument made under that Act, to the extent that the thing done relates to the release of, or the giving of access to, information held by the Chief Executive Officer of Medicare Australia; or

(c)   the Therapeutic Goods Act 1989, or a regulation or any other instrument made under that Act.

Definitions

(6)   In this section:

evidence includes medical, clinical and scientific evidence.

exempted health program means a program, scheme or arrangement that:

(a)   relates to health goods or services or medical goods or services; and

(b)   to the extent that it applies to people of a particular age, is reasonably based on evidence of effectiveness, and on cost (if cost has been taken into account in relation to the program, scheme or arrangement).

The evidence of effectiveness mentioned in paragraph (b) is evidence that is reasonably available from time to time about matters (such as safety, risks, benefits and health needs) that:

(c)   affect people of the age mentioned in that paragraph (if no comparable evidence is reasonably available from time to time in relation to people of a different age); or

(d)   affect people of the age mentioned in that paragraph in a different way to people of a different age (in all other cases).

medicare card has the meaning given by subsection 84(1) of the National Health Act 1953.

Commission may grant exemptions

44(1)   The Commission may, on application by:

    (a)   a person:

        (i)   on that person's own behalf; or

        (ii)   on behalf of that person and another person or other persons; or

        (iii)   on behalf of another person or other persons; or

    (b)   2 or more persons:

        (i)   on their own behalf; or

        (ii)   on behalf of themselves and another person or other persons; or

        (iii)   on behalf of another person or other persons;

by instrument, grant to the person or persons to whom the application relates, as the case may be, an exemption from the operation of a provision of Division 2 or 3, as specified in the instrument.

(2)   The Commission may, on application by a person to, or in respect of, whom an exemption from a provision of Division 2 or 3 has been granted under subsection (1), being an application made before the expiration of the period to which the exemption was granted, grant a further exemption from the operation of that provision.

(3)   An exemption granted under this section:

    (a)   may be granted subject to such terms and conditions as are specified in the instrument; and

    (b)   may be expressed to apply only in such circumstances, or in relation to such activities, as are specified in the instrument; and

    (c)   is to be granted for a specified period not exceeding 5 years.

Duties on public authorities under race, disability and gender legislation

The general duties

Race – Race Relations Act 1976 (amended in 2000)
Section 71(1) Every body or other person specified in Schedule 1A or of a description falling within that Schedule 'shall, in carrying out its functions, have due regard to the need:
(a)   to eliminate unlawful age discrimination; and
(b)   to promote equality of opportunity and good relations between persons of different ages.

Disability – Disability Discrimination Act 1995 (amended in 2005)
Section 49A(1) Every public authority shall in carrying out its functions have due regard to–
(a)   the need to eliminate discrimination that is unlawful under this Act;
(b)   the need to eliminate harassment of disabled persons that is related to their disabilities;
(c)   the need to promote equality of opportunity between disabled persons and other persons;
(d)   the need to take steps to take account of disabled persons' disabilities, even where that involves treating disabled persons more favourably than other persons;
(e)   the need to promote positive attitudes towards disabled persons; and
(f)   the need to encourage participation by disabled persons in public life.

Gender – Sex Discrimination Act 1975 (amended in 2006)
Section 76(1) A public authority shall in carrying out its functions have due regard to the need–
(a)   to eliminate unlawful discrimination and harassment, and
(b)   to promote equality of opportunity between men and women.

The specific duties

Race
The main components of the specific duties are to prepare a race equality scheme and to monitor employment outcomes. They are set out in the Race Relations Act 1976 (Statutory Duties) Order 2001.

Race equality schemes

2(1)   A body or other person specified in Schedule 1 to this Order shall, before 31st May 2002, publish a Race Equality Scheme, that is a scheme showing how it intends to fulfil its duties under section 71(1) of the Race Relations Act and this Order. (2) A Race Equality Scheme shall state, in particular

(a)   those of its functions and policies, or proposed policies, which that person has assessed as relevant to its performance of the duty imposed by section 71(1) of the Race Relations Act; and

(b)   that person's arrangements for

(i)   assessing and consulting on the likely impact of its proposed policies on the promotion of race equality;

(ii)   monitoring its policies for any adverse impact on the promotion of race equality;

(iii)   publishing the results of such assessments and consultation as are mentioned in sub-paragraph (i) and of such monitoring as is mentioned in sub-paragraph (ii);

(iv)   ensuring public access to information and services which it provides; and

(v)   training staff in connection with the duties imposed by section 71(1) of the Race Relations Act and this Order.

(3)   Such a person shall, within a period of three years from 31st May 2002, and within each further period of three years, review the assessment referred to in paragraph (2)(a).

Monitoring by employers

5(1)   A person to which this article applies shall,

(a)   before 31st May 2002, have in place arrangements for fulfilling, as soon as is reasonably practicable, its duties under paragraph (2); and

(b)   fulfil those duties in accordance with such arrangements.

(2)   It shall be the duty of such a person to monitor, by reference to the racial groups to which they belong,

(a)   the numbers of –

(i)   staff in post, and

(ii)   applicants for employment, training and promotion, from each such group, and

(b)   where that person has 150 or more full-time staff, the numbers of staff from each such group who -

(i)   receive training;

(ii)   benefit or suffer detriment as a result of its performance assessment procedures;

(iii)   are involved in grievance procedures;

(iv)   are the subject of disciplinary procedures; or

(v)   cease employment with that person.

(3)   Such a person shall publish annually the results of its monitoring under paragraph (2).

Disability

The requirements of the specific duties are set out in the Disability Discrimination (Public Authorities) (Statutory Duties) Regulations 2005:

Preparation and publication of a Disability Equality Scheme

2(1)   A public authority listed in Schedule 1 shall, on or before the relevant publication date, publish a Disability Equality Scheme ('Scheme'), that is, a scheme showing how it intends to fulfil its section 49A(1) duty and its duties under these Regulations.

(2)   Such an authority shall involve in the development of the Scheme disabled people who appear to that authority to have an interest in the way it carries out its functions.

(3)   A Scheme shall include a statement of–

    (a)   the ways in which such disabled people have been involved in its development;

    (b)   that authority's methods for assessing the impact of its policies and practices, or the likely impact of its proposed policies and practices, on equality for disabled persons;

    (c)   the steps which that authority proposes to take towards the fulfilment of its section 49A(1) duty;

    (d)   that authority's arrangements for gathering information on the effect of its policies and practices on disabled persons and in particular its arrangements for gathering information on–

        (i)   their effect on the recruitment, development and retention of its disabled employees,

        (ii)   their effect, in the case of an authority specified in Part II, III or IV of Schedule 1, on the educational opportunities available to, and on the achievements of, disabled pupils and students, and

        (iii)   the extent to which, in the case of an authority specified in Part I of Schedule 1, the services it provides and those other functions it performs take account of the needs of disabled persons; and

    (e)   that authority's arrangements for making use of such information to assist it in the performance of its section 49A(1) duty and, in particular, its arrangements for–

        (i)   reviewing on a regular basis the effectiveness of the steps referred to in sub-paragraph (c), and

        (ii)   preparing subsequent Schemes.

(4)   Such an authority shall review its Scheme and publish a revised Scheme–

    (a)   not later than the end of the period of three years beginning with the date of publication of its first Scheme; and

(b)   subsequently at intervals of not more than three years beginning with the date of publication of the last revision of the Scheme.

(5)   Such an authority may comply with the duty to publish under paragraph (1) or (4) by setting out its Scheme as part of another published document or within a number of other published documents.

(6)   In this regulation, "the relevant publication date" means–

  (a)   in the case of a public authority listed in Part I or II of Schedule 1, 4th December 2006;

  (b)   in the case of a public authority listed in Part III of Schedule 1, 3rd December 2007;

  (c)   in the case of a public authority listed in Part IV of Schedule 1, 1st April 2007.

Implementation of the Disability Equality Scheme

3(1)   A public authority listed in Schedule 1 shall within the period of three years beginning with the date when a Scheme prepared for the purposes of regulation 2 is published–

  (a)   take the steps which it has been required to set out in the Scheme by virtue of regulation 2(3)(c); and

  (b)   put into effect its arrangements, which it has been required to set out in the Scheme by virtue of regulations 2(3)(d) and (e), for–

    (i)   gathering information, and

    (ii)   making use of such information.

(2)   Nothing in this regulation imposes any duty on an authority where, in all the circumstances, it would be unreasonable or impracticable for it to perform the duty.

Annual reporting

4(1)   A public authority listed in Schedule 1 shall publish a report–

  (a)   not later than the end of the period of one year beginning with the date of publication of its first Scheme; and

  (b)   subsequently at intervals of not more than one year beginning with the date of publication of the last report.

(2)   The report shall contain a summary of–

  (a)   the steps the authority has taken for the purposes of regulation 3(1)(a);

  (b)   the results of the information-gathering it has carried out for the purposes of regulation 3(1)(b)(i); and

  (c)   the use it has made of such information it has gathered for the purposes of regulation 3(1)(b)(ii).

(3)   Such an authority may comply with the duty to publish under paragraph (1) by setting out its report within another published document.

Duty on public authorities listed in Schedule 2 [ie Secretaries of State and the National Assembly of Wales]

5(1)   A reporting authority shall, in respect of its policy sector, publish a report–

    (a)   not later than 1st December 2008; and

    (b)   subsequently not later than the end of each successive period of three years beginning with 1st December 2008.

(2)   The report shall–

    (a)   give an overview of progress towards equality of opportunity between disabled persons and other persons made by public authorities operating in the policy sector; and

    (b)   set out the reporting authority's proposals for the coordination of action by public authorities operating in that sector so as to bring about further progress towards equality of opportunity between disabled persons and other persons.

(3)   In paragraph (1)–

'reporting authority' means a person specified in Schedule 2;

'policy sector' means the sector of public activity in which the reporting authority carries out public functions.

Gender

At the time of writing the regulations setting out the specific duties for gender had not been laid before Parliament. The 2005 consultation paper Advancing Equality for Men and Women: Government proposals to introduce a public sector duty to promote gender equality proposed the following duties.

A public authority must:

- draw up a scheme identifying gender equality goals and showing the action it will take to implement them;
- consult employees and stakeholders as appropriate in drawing up their gender equality schemes;
- publish their gender equality scheme setting out goals and planned outcomes;
- monitor progress and publish annual reports on progress; and
- review their gender equality scheme every three years.

Public authorities must:

(I)   Conduct and publish gender impact assessments, consulting appropriate stakeholders, covering:

- all primary legislation and significant secondary legislation; and
- all major proposed developments in employment/policy/services.

(II)   Develop and publish arrangements for identifying developments that justify conducting a formal gender impact assessment.

Acas guidance: Age and the workplace

Putting the Employment Equality (Age) Regulations 2006 into practice with your employment relations needs[1]

1   © Crown Copyright. Published October 2006. This document can be downloaded in full from www.acas.org.uk.

Introduction

From 1 October 2006 the Employment Equality (Age) Regulations make it unlawful to discriminate against workers, employees, job seekers and trainees because of their age. This booklet describes the regulations and gives you guidance on how to implement them.

> **Terms in this guide – workers and employees**
> **Workers** are covered in the regulations and in this guidance. Workers often undertake roles similar to employees but do not have contracts of employment like employees. Workers include office holders, police, barristers and partners in a business. Our guidance uses the term **'employee'** throughout to cover all workers except under length of service issues, retirement, and right to request which are for a narrower range of employees.

Fairness at work and good job performance go hand in hand

Tackling discrimination helps to attract, motivate and retain staff and enhances your reputation as an employer. Eliminating discrimination helps everyone to have an equal opportunity to work and to develop their skills.

Employees who are subjected to discrimination, harassment or victimisation may:

- be unhappy, less productive and less motivated
- resign
- make a complaint to an employment tribunal.

In addition employers may find:

- their reputation as a business and as an employer may be damaged
- the cost of recruitment and training will increase because of higher employee turnover
- they may be liable to pay compensation following a claim to an employment tribunal – there is no upper limit to the amount of this compensation.

There is already legislation to protect people against discrimination on the grounds of sex, race, disability, gender reassignment, sexual orientation and religion or belief.

The new regulations should pose few difficulties in organisations where people are treated fairly and with consideration.

This guidance aims to:

- help employers and vocational training providers fulfil their obligations under the Employment Equality (Age) Regulations 2006
- make employees, job seekers and trainees aware of how they will be affected by the regulations.

What the regulations say – in summary

These regulations apply to all employers, private and public sector vocational training providers, trade unions, professional organisations, employer organisations and trustees and managers of occupational pension schemes. In this context an employer is anyone who has employees or who enters into a contract with a person for them to do work. The regulations cover recruitment, terms and conditions, promotions, transfers, dismissals and training. They do not cover the provision of goods and services.

The regulations make it unlawful on the grounds of age to:

- discriminate directly against anyone – that is, to treat them less favourably than others because of their age – unless objectively justified

- discriminate indirectly against anyone – that is, to apply a criterion, provision or practice which disadvantages people of a particular age unless it can be objectively justified

- subject someone to harassment. Harassment is unwanted conduct that violates a person's dignity or creates an intimidating, hostile, degrading, humiliating or offensive environment for them having regard to all the circumstances including the perception of the victim

- victimise someone because they have made or intend to make a complaint or allegation or have given or intend to give evidence in relation to a complaint of discrimination on grounds of age

- discriminate against someone, in certain circumstances, after the working relationship has ended.

Employers could be responsible for the acts of employees who discriminate on grounds of age. This makes it important to train staff about the regulations.

Upper age limits on unfair dismissal and redundancy have been removed.

There is a national default retirement age of 65, making compulsory retirement below 65 unlawful unless objectively justified.

Employees have the right to request to work beyond 65 or any other retirement age set by the company. The employer has a duty to consider such requests.

There are limited circumstances when discrimination may be lawful (see section on genuine occupational requirements, objective justifications, exceptions and exemptions).

This guide does not use the precise legal terms contained within the regulations – reference needs to be made to the regulations.

GUIDANCE FOR EMPLOYERS

What do the regulations mean?

A brief explanation of the regulations

Direct discrimination

Direct discrimination is less favourable treatment because of someone's age.

For example it is unlawful on the grounds of age to:

- decide not to employ someone
- dismiss them
- refuse to provide them with training
- deny them promotion
- give them adverse terms and conditions
- retire an employee before the employer's usual retirement age(if there is one) or retire an employee before the default retirement age of 65 without an objective justification (see below).

Example: Whilst being interviewed, a job applicant says that she took her professional qualification 30 years ago. Although she has all the skills and competences required of the job holder, the organisation decides not to offer her the job because of her age. This is direct discrimination.

NOTE: A job applicant can make a claim to an employment tribunal, it is not necessary for them to have been employed by the organisation to make a claim of discrimination.

Indirect discrimination

Indirect discrimination means selection criteria, policies, benefits, employment rules or any other practices which, although they are applied to all employees, have the effect of disadvantaging people of a particular age unless the practice can be justified. Indirect discrimination is unlawful whether it is intentional or not.

Lawful discrimination

There are limited circumstances when it is lawful to treat people differently because of their age.

It is not unlawful to discriminate on the grounds of age if:

- there is an objective justification for treating people differently – for example, it might be necessary to fix a maximum age for the recruitment or promotion of employees (this maximum age might reflect the training requirements of the post or the need for a reasonable period of employment before retirement)
- where a person is older than, or within six months of, the employer's normal retirement age, or 65 if the employer doesn't

have one, there is a specific exemption allowing employers to refuse to recruit that person.

- the discrimination is covered by one of the exceptions or exemptions given in the regulations – for example pay related to the National Minimum Wage
- there is a genuine occupational requirement (GOR) that a person must be of a certain age – for example, if you are producing a play which has parts for older or younger characters.

For more details see the section on genuine occupational requirements, objective justifications, exceptions and exemptions.

Harassment

Harassment includes behaviour that is offensive, frightening or in any way distressing. It may be intentional bullying which is obvious or violent, but it can also be unintentional, subtle and insidious. It may involve nicknames, teasing, name calling or other behaviour which is not with malicious intent but which is upsetting. It may be about the individual's age or it may be about the age of those with whom the individual associates. It may not be targeted at an individual(s) but consist of a general culture which, for instance, appears to tolerate the telling of ageist jokes.

You may be held responsible for the actions of your employees – as well as the employees being individually responsible. If harassment takes place in the workplace or at a time and place associated with the workplace, for example a work-related social gathering, you may be liable. You may be ordered to pay compensation unless it can be shown that you took reasonable steps to prevent harassment. Individuals who harass may also be ordered to pay compensation.

It is good practice to protect your workers from harassment by third parties, such as service users and customers.

When you are investigating claims of harassment, consider all the circumstances before reaching a conclusion. Harassment is often subjective so think carefully about the complainant's perception of what has happened to them. Ask yourself if what has taken place could 'be reasonably considered to have caused offence?'

Example: A young employee is continually told he is 'wet behind the ears' and 'straight out of the pram' which he finds humiliating and distressing. This is harassment.

Example: An employee has a father working in the same workplace. People in the workplace often tell jokes about 'old fogies' and tease the employee about teaching 'old dogs new tricks'. This may be harassment on the grounds of age, even though it is not the victim's own age that is the subject of the teasing.

Victimisation

Victimisation is when an individual is treated detrimentally because they have made a complaint or intend to make a complaint about discrimination or harassment or have given evidence or intend to give evidence relating to a complaint about discrimination or harassment.

They may become labelled 'troublemaker', denied promotion or training, or be 'sent to Coventry' by their colleagues. If this happens or if you fail to take reasonable steps to prevent it from happening, you may be ordered to pay compensation. Individuals who victimise may also be ordered to pay compensation.

> **Example:** An employee claims discrimination against their employer on the grounds of age. A work colleague gives evidence on their behalf at the employment tribunal. When the work colleague applies for promotion her application is rejected even though she is able to show she has all the necessary skills and experience. Her manager maintains she is a 'troublemaker' because she had given evidence at the tribunal and should not be promoted. This is victimisation.

Discrimination, harassment or victimisation following the end of a working relationship covers issues such as references either written or verbal.

> **Example:** A manager is approached by someone from another organisation. He says that Ms 'A' has applied for a job and asks for a reference. The manager says that he cannot recommend her as she was not accepted by other staff because she was 'too young and inexperienced'. This is direct discrimination because of age.

An equality policy and action plan

You can start to address fairness at work by writing an equality policy or updating an existing one – with an action plan to back it up. You may already have equal opportunity or diversity policies which cover age but, if not, age should now be included. It is good practice in drawing up a policy to consult with your workforce or their representatives.

To make sure age discrimination is eliminated in your workforce draw up an action plan to review your policies for:

- recruitment, selection and promotion
- training
- pay, benefits and other conditions
- bullying and harassment
- retirement.

Also consider the make up of your workforce and whether positive action is required to tackle any age imbalance (guidance on positive action can be found below).

Ensure that all employees know about your equality policy and what is expected of them; a communications strategy should be a key part of your action plan.

Employees are often attracted to an organisation if it has a robust equality policy. Although not a legal necessity, such a policy makes applicants feel confident and discourages those who do not embrace equality of opportunity.

Acas can help you to draw up and implement an equality policy and to train you and your employees to use it. For further information see the Acas booklet *Tackling discrimination and promoting equality – good practice guidance for employers.*

Recruitment

Base your decisions about recruitment on the skills required to do the job. Provide training to help those making judgements to be objective and avoid stereotyping people because of their age. See also the section on Lawful discrimination.

Application form

Remove age/date of birth from the main application form and include it in a diversity monitoring form to be retained by HR/Personnel. In addition review your application form to ensure that you are not asking for unnecessary information about periods and dates. Asking for age-related information on an application form could allow discrimination to take place.

Monitor your decisions for any evidence of age bias, particularly after shortlisting (see below).

Job description and person specification

A job description outlines the duties required of a particular post holder. A person specification gives the skills, knowledge and experience required to carry out these duties.

Avoid references, however oblique, to age in both the job description and the person specification. For example, avoid asking for 'so many years' experience. This may rule out younger people who have the skills required but have not had the opportunity to demonstrate them over an extended period. A jobseeker could challenge any time requirement and you may have to justify it (see below).

> **Example:** Scrape and Co, a local driving school have been advertising for instructors who must be qualified and have a minimum of 10 years driving experience. Effectively this would prevent people under 28 applying for this job and could therefore be discriminatory. Scrape would need to justify this 10 year experience criterion if challenged by a jobseeker under 28 especially as only four years experience is formally required to qualify as a driving instructor.

Educational and vocational qualifications have changed and developed over the years. Make sure that the qualifications you specify are not disadvantaging people at different ages.

Ask yourself:

- are the qualifications really necessary?
- are they still current?
- are there other ways of specifying the skill level you require?

If you are going to be specific about qualifications be sure you can justify their need and make it clear you will consider equivalent or similar level alternative qualifications.

Advertising

It makes sound business sense to attract a wide field of applicants – if you rely on the friends or family of current staff you will miss the opportunity to tap into the diverse skills of your local community.

Advertise in a way that will be accessible to a large audience. For instance, avoid using a publication or employment agency that is focused on a niche market. This may limit the diversity of applicants and may constitute indirect discrimination.

> **Example:** An advertisement placed only in a magazine aimed at young people may indirectly discriminate against older people because they are less likely to subscribe to the magazine and therefore less likely to find out about the vacancy and apply.

Write your job advert using the information in the job description and person specification. Avoid using language that might imply that you would prefer someone of a certain age, such as 'mature', 'young' or 'energetic'.

> **Example:** Try to avoid stereotyping. For example, which vacancy is asking for an older person and which a younger person?
>
> 1 'We require an enthusiastic person, flexible enough to fit in with our fast moving market place, not afraid of challenging the status quo and in touch with latest thinking'.
>
> 2 'Our ideal candidate will need to manage competing demands. He or she should be reflective, and have boardroom presence and gravitas'.

Be clear about what skills you actually need for the post – and what skills are merely desirable or reflect the personal preferences of the selector. Recruit and/or promote for these essential skills and aptitudes – you can always decide not to recruit or promote someone if the applicant does not have these necessary skills or abilities.

As well as considering the language you use in adverts think also about the hidden messages that may be present in any promotional literature that you have, particularly the pictures.

Graduates

If you ask for graduates, remember that the term can be interpreted as code for someone in their early twenties. Graduates can be almost any age. Make it clear that you are interested in the qualification and not the age of the applicant.

> **Example:** A local engineering company is looking for a new Personnel Officer and asks for applicants to be graduates and hold the CIPD qualification. As many more people attend university today than say 25 years ago, there is a lower chance that older Personnel Officers will be university graduates even though holding the CIPD qualification and having considerable practical experience. This graduate requirement might thus be indirect age discrimination if the employer is unable to justify it. Remember also that the CIPD qualification was formerly the IPM qualification.

If you limit your recruitment to university 'milk rounds' only, you may find that this is indirect age discrimination as this practice would severely restrict the chances of someone over say, 25 applying for your vacancies. If challenged you would need to objectively justify this practice (see section on genuine occupational requirements, objective justifications, exceptions and exemptions).

Consider enhancing any 'milk round' programme with a broader recruitment strategy, using other avenues to capture a wider pool of applicants of differing ages.

Shortlisting

If you have removed age-related material from your application form then you will generally not know a person's age although applicants may make reference to their age on the form so this is not always the case.

Whether or not you know someone's age, it is important that those doing the shortlisting, ideally more than one person, base their decisions on skills and ability alone. They should be trained, reminded of their responsibility not to discriminate on age grounds and use the requirements of the person specification to judge applicants.

Before moving on to the next stage of the recruitment process, check that no bias, deliberate or unintentional, has influenced decisions. In all organisations this check should be carried out by someone who has not been involved in the shortlisting. In all instances, you should record your decisions and retain these records, ideally for 12 months.

Interviewing

Interviews should preferably not be carried out by one person on their own. When interviewing, try to avoid:

- asking questions related to age, for example, 'how would you feel about managing older/younger people?'
- throw-away comments such as 'you're a bit young for a post of this responsibility' or 'don't you think someone like you should be looking for something with more responsibility'.

Focus on the applicant's competence and where more than one demonstrates the required competence the applicant who is more competent or offers the best skill mix should be appointed.

Check decisions for any bias and make sure interviewers have received training in the skills required and equal opportunities/diversity.

Again, in all instances, record your decisions and retain these records, ideally for 12 months from the date of the interviews.

Working with employment agencies

If you use a recruitment agency you need to be sure the agency acts appropriately and in accordance with your company's equality and diversity policies.

If you tell an employment agency to discriminate on age grounds because you consider you have objective justification for doing so, then the regulations enable the agency to rely on this justification if challenged. In such circumstances the agency should obtain this justification in writing from the employer and if at all unhappy to raise that with the employer.

Vocational training

As well as training provided by employers for their own employees, the regulations also cover organisations providing vocational education and training to the wider community. For the purpose of anti-discrimination law, all forms of vocational training including general educational provision at further, higher and other adult education institutions are covered.

This means that vocational training providers will not be able to set age limits or age related criteria:

- for entry to training; or
- in the terms under which they provide training, for example when offering help with costs to encourage participation among under represented groups of people.

As an employer, training provider, college or university you need to consider the following questions:

- do you set a minimum or maximum age for entry generally or in relation to admission or access to particular courses? If so, what are the justifications for these?

- even if you do not have formal minimum or maximum ages, is age taken into account when you consider applications for admission or access, eg do you offer preferential fee discount arrangements based on age?

In either case, you need to consider:

- can you objectively justify any age-related criterion, eg what evidence have you in support of restricting such financial help to a particular age group?
- what legitimate aim does any age-related criterion help you achieve, eg have you clear evidence that demonstrates particular age groups would be excluded from your learning provision if they had to pay full fees?
- are your age-related criteria a proportionate means of achieving that aim?
- is there another way of achieving that aim without resorting to discrimination?

The EU Employment Directive allows for the setting of age requirements relating to institutions of further and higher education and in respect of access to vocational training if they can be objectively justified, for example on the grounds of vocational integration.

Retaining good staff

Many factors motivate employees and make them want to stay with an organisation. People are more likely to feel positive about an organisation if they are treated fairly and with consideration regardless of their age.

Promotion and training

Opportunities for promotion and training should be made known to all employees and be available to everyone on a fair and equal basis.

Where employees apply for internal transfers take care with informal and verbal references between departmental heads, supervisors, etc. These references are covered by the regulations and should be fair and non-discriminatory.

Job-related training or development opportunities should be available to all employees regardless of age – monitor the training to make sure no particular age group is missing out.

Review the style and location of training to ensure:

- there are no barriers to any particular age group participating
- it is suitable for people of all ages
- everyone is encouraged to participate.

For example, if you are using computer-based training, do not assume everyone will be fully competent using a PC.

Age discrimination awareness

However large or small an organisation, it is good practice for them to have an Equality Policy and to train all employees and update them on a regular basis. This will help to reduce the likelihood of discrimination, harassment and victimisation taking place and may help to limit liability if a complaint is made.

All employees should understand:

- what the terms 'discrimination' and 'harassment' mean
- why discrimination and harassment are hurtful, unlawful and totally unacceptable.

Tell all employees about your company policy on age discrimination and train those who make decisions that affect others. Training should apply not only to those who recruit and select but also to those involved in day-to-day decisions about work allocation, performance appraisal, etc. Supervisors and managers also need training in recognising and dealing with bullying and harassment.

Performance appraisal

Check any performance appraisal system you have to ensure that it is working fairly and without bias. Many people have preconceptions about age and these can influence the judgements we make about people. If these preconceptions appear in performance appraisals through use of inappropriate comments – such as 'does well despite their age' or 'shows remarkable maturity for their age' – they will undermine the whole basis of a fair appraisal system. Such comments could also lead to further discrimination when decisions about promotion or work allocation are being made.

> **Example:** Two candidates have done equally well for the post on offer, so the selectors decide to review previous assessments to try and draw a fair distinction between them. On one they read: 'Despite his many years with the company John remains capable and enthusiastic' and 'John does very well at work considering his age'.

There are no such comments on Mark's assessments.

Which candidate now has a question mark against them?

Treat all employees the same when setting objectives or measuring performance. Ignoring shortfalls in performance because an employee is nearing retirement may be discriminatory – particularly if the same shortfalls are addressed in younger employees.

Redundancy selection

Check that your selection processes for redundancy are free of age discrimination. This means that practices such as last in first out (LIFO), and using length of service in any selection criteria are likely to be age discriminatory.

Policies and procedures

Review policies and procedures for age bias, including those covering:

- sick absence
- leave and holidays
- discipline and grievances
- staff transfers
- flexible working
- use of computers
- individual space requirements (ergonomic policies).

Annex 3 shows you how to use an age impact assessment to carry out these kinds of reviews.

Bullying and harassment

Every individual member of staff has the right to be treated fairly and with dignity and respect. Harassment occurs when someone engages in unwanted conduct which has the purpose or effect of violating someone else's dignity or creating an intimidating, hostile, degrading, humiliating or offensive environment.

It is not the intention of the perpetrator which defines whether a particular type of conduct is harassment but the effect it has on the recipient.

Bullying is just as unacceptable as any other form of harassment.

People can become targets of harassment because of their age. Harassment could take the form of:

- inappropriate comments – for example, by suggesting someone is too old ('over the hill') or too young ('wet behind the ears')
- offensive jokes
- exclusion from informal groups such as social events.

Example: George is in his 60s and works in an office with a team of younger colleagues in their 20s and 30s. The team, including the manager, often go out socialising. They do not ask George because they feel that he wouldn't like the venues they choose for such events. However, George finds out that many workplace issues and problems are discussed and resolved during these informal meetings. George feels undervalued and disengaged by this unintended action. This is a form of harassment, even though unintended, as George is being excluded from the team. To prevent this, the manager ought to consider office-based meetings to consult more fully with all staff in decision-making to prevent George feeling excluded because of his age.

Dealing with harassment

Make sure your anti-harassment policy covers age. You may have a stand alone policy or one that is part of a wider equal opportunities policy (for more detailed information see the Acas booklet *Tackling discrimination and promoting equality*).

If managers see unacceptable behaviour **whether or not a complaint is made** they need to treat the matter seriously and take action to eliminate the behaviour in question. This may involve just pointing out to someone the effect that their behaviour has on others and getting them to stop. If this informal approach fails, or in more serious cases, or where the person being harassed prefers it will be necessary to take formal action within the normal disciplinary procedures of the company or within the guidelines laid down by a specific anti-harassment policy.

For further information see the Acas leaflet *Bullying and harassment at work: a guide for managers and employers*.

Retirement

> **Pension age** is when an employee can draw down their pension; for many, but not all, it is also the time when they can retire if they wish.
>
> **Retirement age** in this guidance is either the employer's normal retirement age (if there is one) or the default retirement age of 65.
>
> **Normal retirement age** means the age at which the employer requires employees in the same kind of position to retire.

The regulations set a default retirement age of 65 (to be reviewed in 2011). This means you can retire employees or set retirement ages within your company at or above 65. Retirements or retirement ages below the default retirement age need to satisfy the test of objective justification (see below).

However, you do not have to have a fixed retirement age. Indeed, there are many business benefits to adopting a flexible approach to the employment and work patterns of older workers. Employees have the right to request to continue working beyond their retirement date and you have a duty to give consideration to such requests.

Think about each request on an individual basis – taking into account opportunities to vary the employee's hours or the duties they perform. You are under no obligation to agree to such requests.

Fair retirement

A fair retirement is one that:

- takes effect on or after the default retirement age (or on or after the employer's normal retirement age – if there is one); and
- where the employer has given the employee written notice of the date of their intended retirement and told them about their right to request to continue working. (See below for the timing requirements of this notice.)

If the employer's normal retirement age is below the age of 65, it must be objectively justified.

For the retirement to be classed as 'fair' you need to have informed the employee in writing of their intended retirement date and of their right to make a request to work beyond retirement age at least six months in advance (but no more than 12 months before the intended date). If they do make such a request, you must have followed the correct procedure for dealing with it. Annex 5 sets out a guidance flowchart for fair retirements.

Working beyond retirement date – notification of right to request to continue working

You should notify the employee in writing of their right to request to go on working beyond their retirement date (at least six months in advance but no more than 12 months before the intended date).

When you write to the employee it is good practice to set out how you will manage the retirement process. Remind them of your obligation to give consideration to any request to work after the normal retirement age and in order not to raise the expectations of the employee, explain that you are entitled to refuse the request. You are not required to give a reason for your decision as – if you have followed the retirement procedure correctly (see Annex 5) – the reason for their dismissal will always be retirement.

However giving reasons and a more detailed explanation of your retirement policy may enable the employee to leave with dignity and respect and help you maintain good workplace relationships with other employees. This would be in line with normal good practice recommended by Acas.

If you choose to give reasons, take the time to consider what you are going to say and how you are going to say it. You must be careful not to suggest that you might be discriminating against the employee on the grounds of race, gender, disability, sexual orientation or religion or belief.

If the employee has been properly notified (as above) and wishes to continue working, they must request to do so no less than three months before the intended retirement date.

If you fail to notify the employee six months in advance of retirement, you may be liable for compensation and you have an ongoing duty (up until two weeks before the retirement dismissal) to inform the employee of both the intended date and their right to request working longer. Failure to do this will make the dismissal automatically unfair.

If you fail to inform the employee of their intended retirement date and of their right to request to continue working, the employee will still be able to make a request not to retire at any stage until dismissal. If the employee does make a request the employment must continue until the day after the employer notifies the employee of their decision on the request.

Employees should be able to retire with dignity so try and use as much tact and sensitivity as possible.

Dealing with the request

If the employee requests in writing not to be retired this request must be considered before the employee is retired. Failure to do so will make the dismissal automatically unfair. You must meet the employee to discuss their request within a reasonable period of receiving it (unless agreeing to the request or it is not practicable to hold a meeting) and inform them in writing of your decision as soon as is reasonably practicable. The employee's employment continues until you have informed them of your decision on the request.

As preparation for this meeting, it is good practice for you to reflect on the positive reasons why you should grant an extension, in particular:

- savings to the organisation in recruitment and training costs
- retaining the valuable experience and knowledge of the employee.

Try to avoid making stereotypical assumptions about the capabilities of the employee. At the meeting the employee has a right to be accompanied by a colleague. There is the same right in relation to any subsequent appeal meeting.

The individual accompanying the employee must be:

- chosen by the employee
- a worker or trade union representative employed by the same employer as the employee
- permitted to address the meeting but not answer questions on behalf of the employee; and
- permitted to confer with the employee during the meeting.

The employee may appeal against your decision as soon as is reasonably practicable after receiving notification of your decision. If the employee does appeal, the appeal meeting should be held as soon as is reasonable. The employee may appeal the decision if you refuse the request in its entirety or if you accept it but decide to continue employing the employee for a shorter period than the employee requested. The appeal meeting can be held after the retirement has taken effect.

This procedure must be repeated each time an individual nears an extended point for retirement. Annex 6 sets out a guidance framework for retirement and the duty to consider.

As long as employers follow this procedure correctly they may rely on their normal retirement age (if they have one) or the default retirement age without the dismissal being regarded as unfair or age discriminatory. Where a dismissal is for reasons of retirement, the statutory dismissals procedure does not apply.

Transitional arrangements

There are transitional arrangements produced by the Department for Trade and Industry (DTI) for employees who are retiring on or shortly after 1 October 2006. These arrangements are available at the DTI website and are summarised at Annex 12 of this guide (see below).

Know your employees

You will probably have information that shows the ages of your employees. It makes sense to analyse this information (probably in age bands – see Annex 4) to get an age profile of your workforce.

This profile will help you decide whether there is a need for any remedial action.

For example, do you need to:

- plan for a retirement peak?
- take positive action to rectify any obvious imbalance in the age bands?

You can also use this profile to check that your entire workforce is getting access to training and other facilities.

Staff attitude surveys and exit interviews can also give you valuable insights into how people view their work and you as an employer, and help you to create a positive working environment.

It is important to monitor in this way if you wish to claim an objective justification or, when reviewing service related benefits, 'conclude' a business benefit (see section on genuine occupational requirements, objective justifications, exceptions and exemptions). In considering these matters you should always use evidence in your decision-making rather than merely continuing old working practices or relying on 'gut feeling' as these may be based on unfounded assumptions.

Annex 4 sets out a framework for age monitoring.

Positive action

You can take positive action to prevent or compensate for disadvantages linked to age.

This might involve:

- giving people of a particular age access to vocational training; or
- encouraging people of a particular age to take up employment opportunities.

Where it reasonably appears to the person undertaking such positive action that it will prevent or compensate for disadvantages linked to age that they have or may suffer.

For example, you might place advertisements where they are more likely to be seen by people in a disadvantaged group. Or you might limit access to a computer training course to those over 60 because they may have had less exposure to such training in the past.

Positive action on age can help you to attract people from all age groups in your local community.

> **Example:** Green and Co, a transport company, see from their internal monitoring processes that the company has a mature age profile with disproportionately few workers under 40. Not wanting to miss out on the talents of all the local community, they

include a statement in their next adverts saying 'We welcome applications from everyone irrespective of age but, as we are under-represented by people under 40, would especially welcome applications from these jobseekers. Appointment will be on merit alone'.

Objective justifications, exceptions, exemptions and genuine occupational requirements

Treating people differently because of their age will only be justifiable in the following exceptional circumstances.

Objective justification

You may treat people differently on the grounds of their age if you have an **objective justification.**

An objective justification allows employers to set requirements that are directly age discriminatory. Remember that different treatment on grounds of age will only be possible exceptionally for good reasons (see below).

You will need to provide real evidence to support any claim of objective justification. Assertion alone will not be sufficient and each case must be considered on its individual merits.

Both direct and indirect discrimination will be justified if it is:

- a proportionate means (of)
- achieving a legitimate aim.

What is proportionate?

This means:

- what you are doing must actually contribute to a legitimate aim, eg if your aim is to encourage loyalty then you ought to have evidence that the provision or criterion you introduce is actually doing so
- the discriminatory effect should be significantly outweighed by the importance and benefits of the legitimate aim
- you should have no reasonable alternative to the action you are taking. If the legitimate aim can be achieved by less or non-discriminatory means then these must take precedence.

What is a legitimate aim?

A legitimate aim might include:

- economic factors such as business needs and efficiency
- the health, welfare and safety of the individual (including protection of young people or older workers)
- the particular training requirements of the job.

A legitimate aim must correspond with a real need of the employer – economic efficiency may be a real aim but saving money because discrimination is cheaper than non-discrimination is not legitimate. The legitimate aim cannot be related to age discrimination itself.

The test of objective justification is not an easy one and it will be necessary to provide evidence if challenged. Remember assertions alone will not be enough.

Example: Jones and Company are unsure if they need an objective justification. To help make the decision they ask themselves:

- Why do we want to do this?
- Can we set out the reason clearly on paper?
- Do we have evidence to support us in this reason?
- Are we certain this is real hard evidence and not just based on assumptions?
- Is there an alternative less or non-discriminatory way of achieving the same result?

The HR director seeks a second opinion from the Board and keeps all records of how the decision was made in case it is reviewed in the future.

In a smaller company, you could consult your partner or colleague.

Exceptions and exemptions

There are also **exceptions** to or **exemptions** from the age regulations in the following areas:

- pay and other employment benefits based on length of service
- pay related to the National Minimum Wage
- acts under statutory authority
- enhanced redundancy
- life assurance
- retirement (see separate section below)
- occupational pension systems (not covered in this guidance).

Payments and benefits based on length of service

In many cases employers require a certain length of service before increasing or awarding a benefit such as holiday entitlement. Without the exemptions contained in the regulations this could often amount to indirect age discrimination because some age groups are more likely to have completed the length of service than others.

Any benefit earned by five years service or less will be exempt.

Employers may use pay scales that reflect growing experience or limit the provision of non-pay benefits to those who have served a qualifying period, subject to the five-year limit.

The use of length of service of more than five years for all types of employment benefits is lawful if:

- awarding or increasing the benefit is meant to reflect a higher level of experience of the employee, or to reward loyalty, or to increase or maintain the motivation of the employee;

- the employer has reasonable grounds for concluding that using length of service in this way fulfils a business need of his undertaking.

In order to meet these requirements employers would need evidence from which they can conclude there is a benefit to the organisation. This could include information the employer might have gathered through monitoring, staff attitude surveys or focus groups for example.

National Minimum Wage

Nothing in the regulations will alter the provisions of the National Minimum Wage. The exemption linked to the National Minimum Wage will allow employers using exactly the same age bands, ie 16 and 17, 18 to 21 and 22 and over, to pay at or above the national minimum rates provided those in the lower age group(s) are paid less than the adult minimum wage.

This will allow an employer to pay those aged 22 and over more than those aged under 22 as long as those under 22 are paid less than the minimum adult rate; likewise an employer may pay those aged 18 to 21 more than those under 18 as long as those under 18 are paid less than the minimum adult rate. The exemption does not allow employers to pay different rates to those in the same age category. Apprentices not entitled to the National Minimum Wage may continue to be paid at a lower rate than those that are.

Acts under statutory authority

Age criteria are widely used in legislation, notably to qualify for various licences. Where this is the case the employer must follow the criteria laid down by statute and will not be contravening the age regulations by doing so.

Enhanced redundancy payments

The statutory redundancy scheme has not substantially changed (except in respect of the years worked when an employee was below 18 or over 64). Both the statutory authority exemption and this regulation make it clear that, even though statutory redundancy payments are calculated using age-related criteria, such payments are lawful.

The exemption linked to statutory redundancy payments is for an employer who wants to make more generous redundancy payments than under the statutory scheme. It allows the employer to use one of the methods specified, based on the statutory redundancy scheme, to calculate the amount of redundancy payment. An employer can use a different method of their own to calculate the amount of redundancy payment, but if it is based on length of service and if an employee brings a discrimination claim under the regulations, the employer will have to objectively justify it in so far as age discrimination arises.(This is because the exception for pay and benefits based on length of service does not apply to redundancy payments).

The exemption allows the employer to either raise or remove the maximum amount of a week's pay so that a higher amount of pay is used in the calculation, or multiply the total amount calculated by a figure of more than one, or both. Having done this, the employer may again multiply the total by a figure of more than one.

The exemption also allows an employer to make a redundancy payment to an employee who has taken voluntary redundancy, and an employee with less than two years continuous employment. In such cases, where no statutory redundancy payment is required, an employer may make a payment equivalent to the statutory minimum payment, or if they so wish an enhanced payment as above.

Life assurance cover

Some employers provide life assurance cover for their workers. If a worker retires early due to ill health, the employer may continue to provide that life assurance cover for that worker. This exemption allows an employer to stop doing so when the worker reaches the age at which he would have retired had he not fallen ill. If there was no normal retirement age at which the worker would have retired, the employer can stop providing life assurance cover when the worker reaches 65.

Genuine occupational requirement (GOR)

In very limited circumstances, it will be lawful for an employer to treat people differently if it is a genuine occupational requirement that the job holder must be of a particular age. When deciding if this applies, it is necessary to consider the nature of the work and the context in which it is carried out. Jobs may change over time and you should review whether the requirement continues to apply, particularly when recruiting.

> **Example:** An organisation advising on and promoting rights for older people may be able to show that it is essential that its chief executive – who will be the public face of the organisation – is of a certain age. The age of the holder of the post may be a genuine occupational requirement.

GUIDANCE FOR THE INDIVIDUAL

What do I do if I think I have suffered discrimination or harassment?

Expressing your concerns

If you think you are being harassed or discriminated against it is a good idea to make it clear to the person who is harassing you that their behaviour is unwelcome and that you want it to stop. However, you do not have to do this, particularly if you are feeling bullied or intimidated. If you do choose to address your concerns to the person, be clear and assertive but take care that you are not perceived to be bullying the individual. Some people may find it helpful to ask a friend, colleague, welfare officer or trade union representative to be with them in a support role.

If speaking to the person in question has failed to stop the problem, you should talk to your manager or your trade union representative. If it is your manager or supervisor who is harassing you, speak to someone higher up. Employers should deal with such complaints quickly, thoroughly and sympathetically.

It is usually best to try and sort things out quickly and as close to the problem as possible. If your organisation has a personnel or human resources department or an equality adviser you might find it helpful to talk to them. Discrimination can happen accidentally or through thoughtlessness. Harassment can be unintentional. Often, once a manager understands the problem, he or she will be willing to try and put things right.

Using the grievance procedure

If your manager is unable to help you, or refuses to help you, you must use your organisation's grievance procedure if you wish to proceed with your complaint. All organisations should have a grievance procedure by law. You also have a legal right to be accompanied by a trade union representative or a work colleague at any hearing into your grievance.

If you are not satisfied with the result of a grievance procedure, you have a right of appeal which should be heard, if the organisation's size allows it, by someone different from the person who conducted the original grievance hearing. You have a right to be accompanied by a trade union representative or a work colleague during the appeal hearing.

Making a claim to an employment tribunal

When you have tried all these things, or if your employer does not have a grievance procedure, or if you feel too intimidated to use the internal procedures, you may be able to bring a complaint to an employment tribunal under the age regulations. You do not have to hand in your notice to bring such a complaint. As part of your employment tribunal claim, you can require your employer to answer a set of questions about discrimination in your workplace. A questionnaire is available on the DTI website (www.dti.gov.uk) and from jobcentres and citizens advice bureaux.

You and any witnesses have a right not to be victimised for following up a grievance or complaining to an employment tribunal under these regulations provided the complaint was made in good faith.

If you have been dismissed because you objected to conduct towards you, you may be able to bring a complaint of unfair dismissal to an employment tribunal.

Complaints to an employment tribunal must normally be brought within three months of the act you are complaining about. Care should be taken to ensure that the three month point is not exceeded during any internal grievance/appeals process.

Retirement

You now have the right to request to continue working beyond your expected retirement date. If you do so your employer must give consideration to your request if you have made it in time and if they turn it down you have the right to appeal to the employer. If you do not make the request to continue working no less than three months before your expected date of retirement you may lose your opportunity to continue working.

You will not automatically be allowed to work beyond your expected retirement. Your employer does not have to agree to your request or give you a reason for turning it down.

If you want to continue working beyond your expected retirement date, but perhaps with alternative or variable working patterns take the initiative and discuss this with your employer at an early stage. Your employer does not have to agree to vary your job but early discussion could help highlight the mutual benefits of a different pattern of work or combination of duties.

Take advantage of training and development opportunities in the years approaching retirement. It will help you to make a stronger case for continuing to work. Your employer should inform you of their intended retirement date for you and your right to request to continue working at least six months, but no more than 12 months, before the intended date. If your employer does not do this you may have the right to eight weeks pay as compensation.

If you ask to continue working, your employer should hold a meeting with you to consider your request. You have a right to be accompanied by a work colleague or trade union representative at the meeting. The trade union representative must also be a work colleague. You must be told the result of your request as soon as is reasonably practicable after the meeting. You can appeal against the decision if your request is not met. You will need to give your employer notice of the appeal as soon as is reasonably practicable after you have received his decision.

There will no longer be an upper age limit on unfair dismissal claims. The statutory redundancy payments scheme is also being adjusted to remove upper and lower age limits as is statutory sick pay and maternity pay.

FURTHER GUIDANCE FOR EMPLOYERS

Some frequently asked questions

Q   Do the regulations only cover older employees?

A   No. The regulations cover workers of all ages – young and old.

Q   Can I ask for a candidate's date of birth on the application form?

A   Yes. But asking for age-related information on an application form could allow discrimination to take place. Remove the date of birth/age from the main application form and include it in a diversity monitoring form to be retained by HR/personnel. In addition review your application form to ensure that you are not asking for unnecessary information about periods and dates.

Q   Am I responsible for what an employment agency does?

A   Yes. If you use a recruitment agency you need to be sure the agency acts appropriately and in accordance with your company's equality and diversity policies.

Q   Do I have to do anything new or different now the legislation is in force?

A   Yes. Include age in your equality policy. Consider adding all forms of discrimination and harassment (sex, race, disability, gender reassignment, sexual orientation and religion or belief) to your disciplinary rules. These rules should also include bullying.

   Make sure all employees are aware (through training, noticeboards, circulars, contracts of employment, etc) that it is not only unacceptable to discriminate, harass or victimise someone on the grounds of age, it is also unlawful. Make it clear that you will not tolerate such behaviour.

   Individuals should know what to do if they believe they have been discriminated against or harassed, or if they believe someone else is being discriminated against or harassed. This should be included in the grievance procedure.

   Reminder: The Employment Act 2002 requires all employers, however large or small, to have both a disciplinary and a grievance procedure.

   Check your policies for retirement and redundancy. Upper age limits on unfair dismissal claims and redundancy payments have been removed. There is a default retirement age of 65, making compulsory retirement below 65 unlawful unless objectively justified.

   Give serious consideration to the benefits of flexible working. All employees also have the right to request to work beyond 65 or any other retirement age set by the organisation. You have a duty to consider such requests.

Q   Must I have an equality policy?

A   No. However, an equality policy is the best way of demonstrating that you take discrimination seriously and have steps in place to tackle it. The policy should set the minimum standard of behaviour expected of all employees through recruitment right through to retirement. It also spells out what employees can expect from the organisation. It gives employees confidence that they will be treated with dignity and respect, and may be used as an integral part of a grievance or disciplinary process if necessary. If you would like help putting an equality policy in place Acas can help – call our helpline on 08457 47 47 47.

Q **Do these regulations cover all workers?**

A Yes. The regulations apply to all workers, including office holders, police, barristers and partners in a business. They also cover related areas such as membership of trade organisations, the award of qualifications, the services of careers guidance organisations, employment agencies and vocational training providers, including further and higher education institutions.

The regulations also cover anyone who applies to an organisation for work, or who already works for an organisation – whether they are directly employed, work under some other kind of contract, or are an agency worker. You will also be responsible for the behaviour of your employees towards an individual working for someone else but on their premises, for example someone from another organisation repairing a piece of your equipment.

Employees are sometimes harassed by third parties, such as customers or clients. Where possible you should protect your employees from such harassment and take steps to deal with actual or potential situations of this kind. This will enhance your reputation as a good employer and make the organisation a welcoming and safe place to work.

Many organisations provide visitors and visiting workers with guidance on health and safety matters. It may be appropriate to include some comments on your organisation's attitude to harassment.

However the default retirement age and the duty to consider procedure apply only to a narrower group of employees – this does not include office holders, partners, barristers etc. Refer to the regulations for the precise definition.

Q **I am a partner, am I covered by the regulations?**

A Yes, you are covered by the regulations except for the provisions covering retirement and the right to request. Partnerships will need to objectively justify their decisions on age issues and for retirement. It would be sensible for partners to have clear records of these decisions at partnership meetings to show they meet business objectives, are properly considered and regularly reviewed. Such records may help support any case for objective justification.

Q **No one in my organisation has ever complained of discrimination or harassment so I don't need to do anything new, do I?**

A People do not always feel able or confident enough to complain, particularly if the harasser is a manager or senior executive. Sometimes they will simply resign. One way to find out is to undertake exit interviews when people leave and to ask them if they have ever felt harassed, bullied or discriminated against in the workplace. If it is possible, exit interviews should be undertaken by someone out of the individual's line of management, for instance a personnel officer.

Discrimination includes harassment which can take place without management being aware of it. Make sure all your employees understand that harassment means any unwanted behaviour that makes someone feel intimidated, degraded, humiliated or offended.

This includes teasing, tormenting, name calling and gossip and it applies to whoever the perpetrator may be. The victim's perception of the effect of the behaviour is also important. Take all possible steps to make sure employees understand that they and their management teams will not tolerate such behaviour and that they will deal with whoever is causing the problem.

Q   **Should I take positive action to promote age diversity?**

A   Your business could benefit from employing people of different ages. The law allows you to introduce positive action measures where you can demonstrate that employees of a particular age are at a career disadvantage or are under represented in the organisation (see below).

ANNEXES

ANNEX 1: AN AGE HEALTHCHECK

Purpose

These questions are designed to kick start the planning and thinking process in your organisation. The answers to these questions should tell you if:

- any key personnel decisions are influenced by age
- your recruitment is attracting people from everyone in the local community.

The checklist

1   Look at your records to establish your company age profile – insert 16–21, 22–30, 31–40, 41–50, 51–60, 60–65, 65+ (These age bands are for illustration only; you may wish to choose different ones to suit your company circumstances.) Compare this to census data available from websites, libraries, business and Chambers of Commerce. What do you find?

2   Look at your application forms for recent recruitments and compare with your age profile. Are you missing out on potential talent? **Yes/No**

3   Is your equality and diversity policy visibly supported by your board and chief executive? **Yes/No**

4   Do you train employees to recognise and tackle age discrimination? **Yes/No**

5   Is age ever used as a factor in staff recruitment/selection or training and development? **Yes/No**
     If yes, can it be justified? **Yes/No**

6   Do you offer variable and alternative working patterns to employees regardless of age? **Yes/No**

7   Are your managers aware of what behaviour could be perceived as harassment on the grounds of age? **Yes/No/Not Sure**

8   Do you have an action plan to ensure you are compliant with the age regulations? **Yes/No**

ANNEX 2: AGE ACTION PLAN – SOME POTENTIAL QUICK WINS

Purpose

To make your action plan successful:

- Agree who is responsible for the plan
- Launch it with the support of the head of your organisation
- Agree who should be involved and consulted, for example line managers, personnel staff, trade unions, other stakeholders
- Make sure your partners and suppliers support your action plan
- Agree and publish timescales for when you will do things and prioritise key objectives
- Get feedback from employees and address their concerns/questions.

Some quick win areas for the action plan

1 Recruitment, promotion and selection

- Remove ageist language (see page 12) from job and promotion adverts and focus on the needs of the job. In the short-term make someone responsible for 'vetting' the wording
- In performance assessments challenge phrases that make assumptions about an individual and focus on actual performance
- Look at where you advertise and how you advertise to ensure you reach the whole labour market
- Train selectors in anti-age discrimination
- Monitor and publish your results to show you mean business.

2 Hearts and minds

- Deliver a programme of age awareness training to all employees to focus on:
  – tackling deep seated stereotypes; and
  – bullying and harassment.
- Review company literature for age bias, look to how your organisation might be perceived by younger or older employees. If someone feels fully engaged with an organisation they are likely to be more productive.

3 Retirement and knowledge management

- Recognise that senior employees have a wealth of experiences that are valuable and can help the organisation. Set up a system to capture this knowledge.
- Make your retirement policy well known and treat requests to stay after retirement as an opportunity to retain knowledge.

ANNEX 3: PRACTICAL IMPACT ASSESSING FOR AGE BIAS IN POLICIES

Purpose

Impact assessments are designed to measure the impact of policies and processes on different groups of people. They can help to inform planning and decision-making.

Ask yourself:

- What is the purpose of a policy or practice?
- What is it achieving?
- Do any age groups benefit and, if so, how?
- Do any age groups appear to lose out and, if so, how?
- Using this information can I objectively justify any difference in benefit? If not, should I change the policy?

To answer these questions you will need to look at:

- Your monitoring data (see section 'Know your staff' and Annex 4)
- Anecdotal views from managers and employee representatives about the way a policy is working locally
- Attitude surveys, focus groups, exit interviews and specific research and evaluation exercises you may wish to carry out
- What has worked elsewhere and why by comparing your data with that of other business groups/employer organisations.

This process will give you evidence of different outcomes by age groups. It is important to remember that not all differences are necessarily wrong and you need to ask the question 'is it justifiable for this to continue?' Our guidance on objective justification can give some pointers here.

We would suggest that it would be good practice to undertake these assessments openly in the organisation as a sign of your commitment to tackle unwitting age discrimination.

ANNEX 4: AGE MONITORING – A FRAMEWORK

Monitoring the effect of the anti-age discrimination regulations can help you to:

- identify any problems
- gather evidence that might be needed by the courts for objective justification of any age discrimination (see page 30).

The following age bands might provide a useful starting point for gathering your information: 16–21, 22–30, 31–40, 41–50, 51–60, 60–65, 65+

Keep records on how all your employees fit into these age bands. Also keep data on employees who:

- Apply for jobs (and those who are successful)
- Apply for training (and those who receive training)
- Apply for promotion (and those who are successful)
- Are being assessed to measure their performance
- Are involved in disciplinary and grievance processes (and the outcomes of these processes)
- Leave the organisation.

Another source of monitoring information are staff attitude surveys that can be used in concluding a business benefit when considering the exemptions surrounding service-related benefits.

Staff consultation groups and trade unions can also be valuable sources of information that can add to raw data figures.

ANNEX 5: FAIR RETIREMENT FLOWCHART

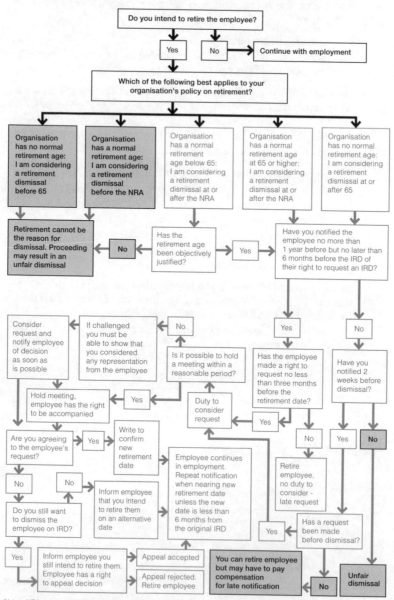

Notes: NRA means normal retirement age IRD means intended retirement date

ANNEX 6: REQUEST TO WORK BEYOND RETIREMENT FLOWCHART

Annex 6: Request to work beyond retirement flowchart

Employer – Pre-Retirement

If you intend to retire the employee you must inform the employee of the retirement date, in writing, no more than one year but no later than six months before the intended retirement and that they have a right to request to work beyond the retirement age.

Employee – Responding to your employer's notification

When your employer has notified you of your intended retirement date and your right to request, if you want to request working beyond retirement age you must inform your employer no less than three months before the intended retirement date. Your request to your employer must be in writing and state whether you wish to continue work:

• indefinitely

• for a stated period

• or until a certain date.

You may only make one request in relation to each intended retirement date. If your employer has failed to notify you of your intended retirement date six months before that date, you may still make a request not to retire at any time before you retire.

Employer – Responding to your employee's request

When you receive your employee's request you must normally hold a meeting with your employee to discuss the request. If you accept there is no need to hold a meeting; simply amend the employee's contract of employment to reflect the new intended retirement date, and if required, the new employment pattern.

If after considering the request, you decide that you do wish to continue with the retirement you should hold a meeting with the employee. This will enable the employee to put their case to you. The employee has a right to be accompanied at the meeting.

The companion can be:

• chosen by the employee; but must be

• a worker or trade union representative employed by you or the organisation.

The companion can:

• address the meeting but not answer questions on behalf of the employee

• confer with the employee during the meeting.

The meeting must be held within a reasonable period after the request has been received from the employee. If the meeting cannot be held within a reasonable period, you may inform the employee of your decision in writing as long as you have considered any representation made by the employee.

Employee – The meeting to consider your request

If your employer does not accept your request, they must still offer you a meeting to discuss it. This is your opportunity to put your case before your employer. You have a right to be accompanied at the meeting.

The companion can be:

• chosen by you; but must be

• a worker or trade union representative employed by the same employer.

The companion can:

• address the meeting but not answer questions on your behalf

• confer with you during the meeting.

It is important to remember that your companion cannot answer questions on your behalf. You must take all reasonable steps to attend the meeting, although if it is not possible to hold the meeting within a reasonable period your employer may inform you of their decision in writing.

(continued)

Annex 6: Request to work beyond retirement flowchart (continued)

The meeting

The meeting is an opportunity for the employee to put their case before the employer. At the end of the meeting the employer may decide that whilst they cannot accept the employee's stated request, there may be a compromise solution. It is perfectly acceptable for the employer to propose alternative working patterns and retirement dates, other than those proposed by the employee, if the employer is persuaded by the employee's case not to be retired.

Employer – Post-meeting action

If, after the meeting, you decide to accept the employee's request you should inform them that you have accepted the request and state the new employment pattern and when the new intended retirement date will be.

Where the decision is to refuse the request you should confirm with them that you still wish to retire them – either on the original intended retirement date or an alternative later date.

Any decision should be given in writing and should be dated. The employee has a right to appeal the employer's decision, or a decision on a new intended retirement date if it is shorter than the intended retirement proposed by the employee in the employee's initial request.

Employee – Post-meeting

The employer will inform you as soon as is reasonable after the meeting of their decision. If the employer rejects your request or proposes a new intended retirement date that is less than that in your original request, you may ask for an appeal meeting.

Appeal meeting

The appeal meeting is the final opportunity for the employee to put their case before the employer. At the end of the meeting the employer may decide that whilst they cannot accept the employee's stated request, there may be a compromise solution. It is perfectly acceptable for the employer to propose alternative working patterns and retirement dates, other than those proposed by the employee, if the employer is persuaded by the employee's case not to be retired.

Employer – Post-appeal meeting action

If, after the meeting you decide to accept the employee's request, you should inform them that you have accepted the appeal and state the new employment pattern and when the new intended retirement date will be.

Where the decision is to reject the appeal you should confirm with them that you still wish to retire them and the date that the dismissal is to take effect.

Any decision should be given in writing and should be dated.

Employee – Post-appeal meeting

The employer will inform you as soon as is reasonable after the appeal meeting of their decision. If your request is accepted, or a compromise solution is reached, the employer should inform you in writing of that decision.

If your appeal is rejected the employer is obliged to inform you of this in writing and of the date of your retirement. The employer does not need to give a reason why your application has been rejected.

ANNEX 7: EXAMPLE OF A LETTER INFORMING EMPLOYEE OF THEIR RETIREMENT DATE

Letter to inform employee of their retirement date and of their right to make a request.

Note to employer: You must inform the employee no more than one year but no later than six months before their retirement date what the intended retirement date is and that they have a right to request not to be retired. Failure to inform the employee of the date and their right may mean that the dismissal is unfair. This letter should only be used if you are complying with the above time limits. If you do not, you are under an obligation to consider a request made by the employee at any time before retirement takes effect. You can get additional guidance on retirement from Acas.

Dear: Staff Number:

Date:

1   I am writing to inform you that your retirement date will be [insert date] and that you have a right to request not to be retired.

1a I will give careful consideration to any request you may make to work beyond this date and will inform you if I cannot let you. I am not required by law to give a reason.

2   Your request not to be retired must be returned to [insert name] no later than three months before the date stated in paragraph 1. Failure to do so will mean that you lose your statutory right to have your request considered and you will be retired on the retirement date above.

Name: Signature:

Date:

ANNEX 8: EXAMPLE OF A LETTER INFORMING EMPLOYEE OF A MEETING TO DISCUSS A REQUEST NOT TO RETIRE

Note to employer: The meeting to discuss the request should be held within a reasonable period after the request has been received. The employee has a right to be accompanied at the meeting.

The companion can be:

- chosen by the employee
- a worker employed by you or the organisation.

The companion can:

- address the meeting but not answer questions on behalf of the employee
- confer with the employee during the meeting.

Dear: Staff Number:

Date:

I am writing to inform you that after receiving your request not to be retired that there will be a meeting to discuss your request. The meeting will be held on [insert date] at [insert time] at [insert location].

You have a right to be accompanied at the meeting by a fellow worker or a trade union representative. Your companion may be someone that you have chosen, but they must work for [insert name of organisation]. Your companion can address the meeting but not answer questions on your behalf although you may confer with your companion during the meeting.

After the meeting if it is decided to continue your employment beyond the intended retirement date of [insert date] you will receive written notification reflecting these agreed changes to your contract.

If no agreement is reached you will receive further notification confirming your intended retirement date and informing you of your right to appeal.

Name: Signature:

Date:

ANNEX 9: EXAMPLE OF A LETTER CONFIRMING RETIREMENT ON THE INTENDED DATE

Note to employer: If after the meeting to discuss the employee's request not to be retired, you decided that you still wish to retire the employee, you must inform them as soon as is reasonably practicable. You must also inform them that they have a right to appeal.

Dear: Staff Number:

Date:

I am writing to inform you that after our meeting held on [insert date] to discuss your request not to be retired, that [insert organisation] still intends to retire you on [insert intended retirement date].

You have a right to appeal this decision. If you wish to appeal you must inform [insert name] as soon as is reasonable. Failure to do so may mean that you lose the right to an appeal meeting and [insert organisation's name] may consider your appeal without holding a meeting but they will consider any previous representations that you have made.

Name: Signature:

Date:

ANNEX 10: EXAMPLE OF A LETTER TO EMPLOYEE NOTIFYING THE RESULT OF THEIR APPEAL

Note to employer: You must hold the appeal meeting to discuss the employee's appeal not to be retired as soon as is reasonably practicable. If it is not reasonably practicable to hold an appeal meeting within a period that is reasonable you may consider the appeal without holding a meeting as long as you consider any representations that the employee has made.

Dear: Staff Number:

Date:

I am writing to inform you that after our meeting held on [insert date] to discuss your appeal not to be retired, that [insert organisation] still intends to retire you on [insert intended retirement date].

Name: Signature:

Date:

ANNEX 11: EXAMPLE OF A LETTER TO EMPLOYEE CONFIRMING NEW RETIREMENT DATE

Note to employer: You should use this letter if you accept the employee's request or appeal.

Dear: Staff Number:

Date:

I am writing to inform you that following our meeting to consider your request not to be retired/appeal meeting [delete as appropriate] [insert organisation] has agreed that your new intended retirement date shall be [insert date].

As agreed at the meeting to discuss your request not to be retired/appeal meeting [delete as appropriate] your new working pattern will be as follows. [Delete this paragraph if no new working pattern is agreed].

Name: Signature:

Date:

ANNEX 12: RETIREMENT – TRANSITIONAL ARRANGEMENTS APPLICABLE UP TO 1 APRIL 2007

Transitional arrangements apply to retirements from 1 October 2006 to 31 March 2007 because the DTI recognises that:

Where an employee is due to retire soon after 1 October 2006 the procedures for ensuring a retirement dismissal is fair are summarised below.

Notice given before 1 October 2006

If the employee is given notice before 1 October that they are to be retired after 1 October 2006 but before 1 April 2007:

- notice must be at least the period required by the contract of employment;

or

- where the employee is already serving a long period of notice required by the contract that exceeds four weeks, the employer must give at least four weeks notice before the 1 October 2006 to ensure the employee is aware and given the statutory minimum period of notice for retirement.

The employer must write to the employee as soon as practicable telling them of their right to request working longer.

The employee can make such a request after their contract has been terminated but not more than four weeks afterwards.

A meeting to discuss the request, and any subsequent appeal meeting, must be held within a reasonable period. The employee can ask to be accompanied by a companion.

Notice given after 1 October 2006

If the employee is given notice after 1 October that they are to be retired before 1 April 2007 the employer must:

- write to the employee notifying them of the intended retirement date
  – giving the longer of contractual or statutory notice; and
- tell them in writing that they have a right to request working longer.

An employee who wants to exercise this right should make a written request:

- where possible, four weeks before the intended retirement date; or
- as soon as reasonably practicable after being notified of the 'right to request'.

The request can be made after the employee's contract has been terminated but not more than four weeks after termination. A meeting to discuss the request, and any subsequent appeal meeting, must be held within a reasonable period. The employee can ask to be accompanied by a companion.

Anyone retiring on or after 1 April 2007 will be subject to the full retirement procedure set out in the Employment Equality (Age) Regulations 2006 and described in this guidance.

Questionnaire

THE EMPLOYMENT EQUALITY (AGE) REGULATIONS 2006: THE QUESTIONNAIRE[1]

Questionnaire contents: The facts of the questionnaire and the questions asked are designed to illustrate generic questions which could be asked about:

1   Retirement processes
2   Appointment to posts
3   Harassment and
4   General matters such as equal opportunities policies on age.

Essentially each questionnaire will be particular to its own facts. In general advisers should pose questions designed to ascertain who the relevant decision makers were and what reasons they had for the suspect decisions. Information about comparators should be obtained (for example the person who got the promotion, or the benefits received by younger or older workers.[2]

This booklet is in four parts:

Part 1: Introduction

Part 2: Questionnaire of the person aggrieved: The Complainant (*regulation 41*).

Part 3: Reply by respondent (*regulation 41*).

Appendix: Notes on the scope of The Employment Equality (Age) Regulations 2006.

---

1   © Crown Copyright. This questionnaire can be downloaded from www.dti.gov.uk/employment/discrimination/age-discrimination/index.html. The draft answers to the questions have been added by the authors of this work and are not part of the original form.

2   Advisers may find Tamara Lewis's Age Questionnaires useful: Guide to writing questionnaires under the Age Regulations. Available from Central London Law Centre from November 2006. Tel 020 7839 2998.

PART 1: INTRODUCTION

General

- The purpose of this introduction is to explain the questions procedure under Regulation 41 of the Employment Equality (Age) Regulations 2006.
- The procedure is intended to help a person (*referred to in this booklet as the complainant*) who thinks he/she has been discriminated against by another (*the respondent*) to obtain information from that person about the treatment in question in order to:
  - decide whether or not to bring legal proceedings; and
  - if proceedings are brought, to present his/her complaint in the most effective way.
- We have devised a questionnaire which the complainant can send to the respondent. There is also a matching reply form for use by the respondent – both are included in this booklet. The questionnaire and reply form are designed to assist both the complainant and respondent to identify information which is relevant to the complaint. It is not obligatory for the questionnaire and reply form to be used: the exchange of questions and replies may be conducted, for example, by letter.
- The complainant and respondent should read this booklet thoroughly before completion and retain a copy of the information supplied.
- Guidance for the complainant on the preparation of the questionnaire is set out in Part 2.
- Guidance for the respondent on the use of the reply form is set out in Part 3.
- The notes at the end of this booklet explain the main provisions of the Employment Equality (Age) Regulations 2006. You can obtain further information about the legislation from the DTI website http://www.dti.gov.uk/employment/discrimination/age-discrimination/index.html or about your rights and responsibilities from the Acas good practice guide entitled *Age and the Workplace*. The Acas guidance is available via their website www.acas.org.uk.
- Employees who require help or advice about completing this booklet can get advice from Citizens Advice Bureaux, law centres and, where appropriate, Trade Unions. They may also seek independent legal advice from a solicitor. Employees and employers can seek practical advice from Acas via their national helpline (08457 47 47 47).
- You can obtain copies of this booklet ('*URN 06/1403*') as well as copies of the Acas guide mentioned above free of charge. See reverse of booklet for details.

Purpose of the questions procedure

The questionnaire can provide the complainant with more information so that he or she can make a better informed decision about whether to bring a complaint and if they do will be able to present it more effectively.

- If the respondent's answers satisfy the complainant there may be no need for legal proceedings.
- If the respondent's answers do not satisfy the complainant, they should help to identify what is agreed and what is in dispute between the parties. For example, the answers should reveal whether the parties disagree on the facts of the case, or, if they agree on the facts whether they disagree on how the regulations apply. In some cases, this may lead to a settlement of the grievance, making legal proceedings unnecessary.
- If the complainant institutes proceedings against the respondent, the proceedings should be simpler because the matters in dispute will have been identified in advance.

What happens if the respondent does not reply or replies evasively

The respondent cannot be compelled to reply to the complainant's questions. However, if the respondent does not reply within eight weeks, or replies in an evasive or equivocal manner without a reasonable excuse, a court or tribunal may draw adverse inferences from that, should the complainant bring proceedings against him/her. The respondent's attention is drawn to these possible consequences in the note at the end of the questionnaire.

Period within which proceedings must be brought

There are different time limits for bringing a complaint under the Regulations. A complaint to an employment tribunal must be presented within 3 months of the alleged act. Where a complaint is brought against an institution of Higher Education or Further Education the complaint must be brought in the county or sheriff court within 6 months of the alleged act. A court or tribunal has a discretion to accept a late complaint if it would be just and equitable to do so.

Employment tribunal proceedings

In order to be admissible as evidence in any ensuing employment tribunal proceedings, the complainant's questionnaire must be served on the respondent either:

(a)   before a complaint about the treatment concerned is made to an employment tribunal; or

(b)   if a complaint has already been made to a tribunal, within 21 days beginning when the complaint was received by the tribunal.

However, where the complainant has made a complaint to a tribunal and the period of 21 days has expired, a questionnaire may still be served provided the permission of the tribunal is obtained. This may be done by sending to the Secretary of the Tribunals a written application, which must state the names of the complainant and the respondent and set out the grounds of the application. However, every effort should be made to serve the questionnaire within the period of 21 days as the permission of the tribunal to serve the questionnaire after the expiry of that period will not necessarily be obtained.

County or Sheriff Court proceedings

In order to be admissible in any ensuing county or sheriff court proceedings, the complainant's questionnaire must be served on the respondent before proceedings in respect of the treatment concerned are brought, but not more than 6 months after the treatment. However, where proceedings have been brought, a questionnaire may still be served provided the permission of the court has been obtained. In the case of county court proceedings, this may be done by obtaining the appropriate form from the county court office, completing it and sending it to the court, with the appropriate fee, and the respondent. In the cases of sheriff court proceedings, this may be done by making an application to a sheriff.

PART 2: QUESTIONNAIRE OF PERSON AGGRIEVED: THE COMPLAINANT

Note:

- Before filling in this questionnaire, we advise you to prepare what you want to say on a separate piece of paper.
- If you have insufficient room on the questionnaire for what you want to say, continue on an additional piece of paper, which should be sent with the questionnaire to the respondent.

Enter the name of the person to be questioned (the respondent)	To	
Enter the respondent's address	of	
Enter your name (you are the complainant)	1.1	
Enter your address	of	

Please give as much relevant information as you can about the treatment you think may have been unlawful discrimination. You should mention the circumstances leading up to that treatment and, if possible, give the date, place and approximate time it happened. You should bear in mind that at paragraph 4 of this questionnaire you will be asking the respondent whether he/she agrees with what you say here.

I am now just 65. I worked for the Respondent for six years as PA to Mr Miller for five years. On several occasions over the past year, he has made remarks about Mrs Green my co-worker's appearance such as 'here's Whitney dressed as Britney' because he said she was wearing kids' fashion. He always told me that people should wear clothes which are appropriate to their age. On my 64th birthday I was pre-sented with a card with a tombstone on it by him and from that time on he has regularly made jokes about my health and imminent death (which I found rather distasteful).

Two months ago I was given a letter telling me that Mr Miller wanted to retire me. He told me at the time 'you can ask to carry on working, it's your right, but I have to tell you there's no point'. I then got a letter from Mr Miller. He said that I had the right to ask to con-tinue working if I wrote saying so. I did write asking to carry on working indefinitely. I have occupied that post for six years and my appraisals have been excellent throughout that time. However when asked to talk to Mr Miller about carrying on work-ing, he put me off for a month before having a meeting with me although we saw each other every day. I never got a satisfactory expla-nation why we could not meet to discuss my continuing to work.

At the meeting he told me that it was time for me to retire. I pointed out that my work was fine, my health was fine and that on all of my appraisals I had been rated excel-lent. I pointed out that I was rated the same as my younger counter-parts who work for other senior managers. Mr Miller said, to my surprise: 'look Abe, you know I'm not prejudiced but we all know that there's a reason for the retirement age. You'll start to slow down and I will keep on needing a dynamic go getter for my PA. It's kinder this way'. I said 'Walter, you know that my work is good enough and I will be good for another five years.' He agreed with this, but said that he just wanted to 'trade me in for a younger model'. He laughed. I told him I needed to work because I needed to finish building my pension. He would not listen. I pointed out that lots of the PAs in the Company generally continued working after 65. He said that the company's normal retirement age was 65.

Mr Miller had been making remarks about getting rid of me because I was 'over the hill' for the past year. I applied for other vacancies in the company but was not interviewed. I was told by Mrs Drabble of HR that I shouldn't bother trying to get another post within the company as there were alot of younger workers trying to redeploy. There were redundancies being made.

Mr Miller wrote to me recently saying that he was not prepared to extend my contract and that I would be retiring on my 65th birthday. He refused to give a reason for this decision and gave no reason in the letter. I think he made the decision because he thinks that people over 65 are less capable than younger employees.

I complained to Mr Barney about Mr Miller's behaviour. He was always making jokes about my age. Next thing I knew I was getting a call from Ms Drabble of HR who told me that I needn't jump on the discrimination band wagon. She said that my retirement was quite lawful and so I couldn't complain about the meeting or Mr Miller's attitude. She urged me to go quietly or things could get nasty.

I saw that I could appeal against the retirement decision. I wrote an appeal pointing out that my work was as good as a younger person's and that there was no reason to insist on my retirement. I asked to carry on working indefinitely. However at my appeal meeting Mrs Cuthbert and Mr McGrough told me that I had not made a proper request to continue working and that they did not have to listen to me.

Nevertheless they invited me to tell them why I should not be dismissed and I explained about the quality of my work. They said that Mr Miller was within his rights to retire me. They said that the company's insurance premiums for health insurance would rocket if they started keeping everyone who wanted to continue to work after 65. I was 65 two weeks ago and my contract ended that day. I think that the company unfairly dismissed me and that I was dismissed because of my age or my appearance. I look older than some of my co-workers (of a similar age) who have been kept on after a request. I used to smoke.

Yesterday I got a letter telling me that I would not be receiving the leaver's bonus. I understand that Mrs Green told Mrs Cuthbert that she had seen me coming out of the local law centre recently. I think she suspected me of having taken action to complain about their age discrimination.

In paragraph 1.3 you are telling the respondent that you think the treatment you have described in 1.2 may have been unlawful discrimination/ harassment] by them against you. You do not have to complete 1.3. If you do not wish or are unable to do so, you should delete the word 'because'. If you wish to complete paragraph 1.3, but feel you need more information about the Employment Equality (Age) Regulations 2006 before doing so, see the notes attached.

If you do decide to complete paragraph 1.3, you may find it useful to indicate what kind of discrimination/ harassment you think the treatment may have been ie. whether it was:

    direct discrimination;
    indirect discrimination;
    harassment; or
    victimisation;

and which provision of the regulations you think may make unlawful the kind of discrimination you think you may have suffered.

This is the first of your questions to the respondent. You are advised not to alter it.

This is the second of your questions to the respondent. You are advised not to alter it

1.3   I consider that this treatment may have been unlawful because

2.   Do you agree that the statement in 1.2 above is an accurate description of what happened? If not, in what respect do you disagree or what is your version of what happened?

3.   Do you accept that your treatment of me was unlawful discrimination/ harassment by you against me? If not:

   a) why not,
   b) for what reason did I receive the treatment accorded to me, and
   c) how far did considerations of age affect your treatment of me?

- The questions at paragraph 3 are especially important if you think you may have suffered direct discrimination, or indirect discrimination because they ask the respondent whether your age had anything to do with your treatment. They do not ask specific questions relating to victimisation. Questions at paragraph 4 provide you with the opportunity to ask other questions you think may be of importance. For example, if you think you have been discriminated against by having been refused a job, you may want to know what the qualifications were of the person who did get the 4. job and why that person got the job.

  If you think you have been victimised you may find it helpful to include the following questions:

- Was the reason for my treatment the fact that I had done or intended to do, or that you suspected I had done or intended to do, any of the following:
- brought proceedings under the Employment Equality (Age) Regulations 2006;
- gave evidence or information in connection with proceedings under the regulations;
- did something else under or by reference to the regulations; or
- made an allegation that someone acted unlawfully under the regulations

4.   Any other questions you may wish to ask:

In reply to each of the following questions, if your answer is in the negative sense, please explain why this is the case

4.1.   Do you have an equal opportunities policy incorporating rules prohibiting age discrimination? If so please supply a copy.

4.2.   If you have equal opportunities materials relating to age, do you publish in these materials a standard form letter which an employee may use to notify you formally of his or her request to continue working and which specifies that the request is made under the Employment Equality (Age) Regulations 2006?

4.3.   Do you conduct monitoring of your work force by age?

4.4. How many employees fall into each of the following age categories:

(a) 65 and over;
(b) 55-64
(c) 40-54
(d) 20-39

4.5. For each such category, please state how many personal assistants are there in the category?

4.6. How many PAs are there in your employment

4.7. Over the past five years, how many PAs have been dismissed? For each such dismissal please state the age of the person dismissed and the reason for the dismissal?

4.8. What is the normal retirement age for personal assistants in your employment?

4.9. If you have indicated an age as a normal retirement age for PAs, please indicate the facts upon which you rely for that particular age being the normal retirement age for this class of employee.

4.10. Please state what training on avoidance of age discrimination and bullying and harassment is given to managers in your employment.

4.11. Is it accepted that Mr Miller gave me a birthday card with a tombstone on it for my 64th birthday? Do you accept that this was unwanted conduct related to my age, which had the effect of undermining my dignity at work and of creating a hostile environment?

4.12. Have there been any grievances or complaints made, brought or sustained against

Mr Miller in respect of (alleged or substantiated) discrimination on the grounds of age or otherwise? If so when did they occur? What was the nature of the complaint?

4.13. Do you accept that Ms Drabble discouraged me from applying for any vacant posts within the Company on the grounds of my age? If not, what was the reason? If so, do you accept that this was unlawful? If not, why do you say that this treatment was lawful?

4.14. On what date did you inform me in writing of the intended date of retirement and of my right to make a request to work beyond retirement age?

4.15. Do you accept that you sent me two letters conveying information concerning the intention to dismiss me for retirement in one and informing me of my right to ask to carry on working in the second? If not, when do you say and how do you say I was informed of these matters?

4.16. Do you accept that you did not supply a letter which would enable me to make a formal request to continue working? If so, why did you fail to do this?

4.17. Why did Mr Miller wait for a month before having the meeting concerning my request to continue working?

4.18. Do you accept that Mr Miller did not hold the meeting within a reasonable period? If not why do you say that the period was reasonable?

4.19. Do you agree that Mr Miller, at the meeting, told me that it was time for me to retire? What did he mean by this?

4.20 Do you accept that Mr Miller did not consider my work record in reaching the decision whether to permit me to continue working? If not, how did Mr Miller take my work record into account in deciding to reject my request?

4.21. Do you accept that the decision to reject my request was based on my age? If not, what was it based upon?

4.22. Do you accept that Mr Miller told me that he needed a 'dynamic PA' which he assumed could not be me because of my age?

4.23. If Mr Miller believed that I could not be dynamic (or would not be in the future) on what basis did he reach this conclusion?

4.24. Do you accept that Mr Miller did not notify me of his intention to retire me was not given more than 6 months? If not why not?

4.25. What were the reasons for refusing my request to continue working beyond 65?

4.26. Please explain why you refused to provide reasons for refusing my request to continue working past 65?

4.27 Do you accept that I am capable of performing the essential requirements of the job of PA? If not why not?

4.28. Do you accept that my work performance is the equivalent of other PAs who are younger than me? If not why not?

4.29. Do you accept that I have not been subject to any capability procedure within the last five years?

4.30. Do you accept that I have not had above average sickness absence over that same period?

4.31. Do you accept that I will probably not have above average sickness absence of the next 5 years? If not please state each and every matter on which you rely to suggest that I am likely to have more than average sickness absence over that period?

4.32. Do you accept that I made it clear to Mr Miller at the meeting to discuss my request to carry on working that I needed to work to complete my pension payments? If not what do you say happened at that meeting?

4.33. When considering whether or not to grant my request to continue work after age 65, what factors did you take into account:

(1) In favour of granting my request?

(2) In favour of refusing my request?

(3) What consideration was given to my financial need to continue working?

4.34. Why did Mrs Drabble tell me not to jump on the discrimination band wagon?

4.35 Why did Mrs Drabble tell me to go quietly or things would get nasty?

4.36. Why did you reject my appeal against the decision to

refuse my request to carry on working?

4.37. Why did you refuse to provide reasons for the decision to reject my appeal against Mr Miller's decision?

4.38. Do you accept that the rejection of my appeal constituted an act of unlawful age discrimination? If not why not?

4.39. Did you contact the company's insurers to ask them whether premiums would be affected by my retention in employment? If so, please indicate what information you supplied to them (providing copies of all such information and correspondence)? Please explain how much the premium would have been raised by and from when?

4.40. If you did not contact the insurance company concerning me, on what information did you base the remark that insurance premiums would increase if the company retained people over 65?

4.41. Please provide details of the vacancy listings for the post of personal assistant, including job description and person specification; please state who produced the job description and person specification?

4.42. What review was carried out before advertising to ensure that the requirements of the post are age compliant?

4.43. In respect of each of the applications I made for alternative posts, please tell me who considered my application?

4.44. Why, in each case, was my application not processed further, providing all relevant documentation?

4.45. Please give the following details of the successful candidate in each case:
(1) Age
(2) Qualifications, and/or experience

4.46. If you accept that I was treated less favourably on the grounds of my age in respect of any of these posts, please state (a) why I was treated in that way and (b) whether, and if so how, you argue that my treatment was justified?

4.47. What evidence, if any, did you rely in concluding that age was a relevant consideration in appointing to any of these posts.

4.48. Why did you fail to pay me the leaver's bonus?

4.49. Was the reason you failed to pay me that bonus was because Mrs Green had told Mrs Cuthbert that she had seen me coming out of the local law centre and you suspected me of having taken action to complain about the age discrimination to which I had been subjected?

5. My address for any reply you may wish to give to the questions I have raised is:
At 1 above ☐   below ☐
(please tick appropriate box)

| The questionnaire must be signed and dated. If it is to be signed on behalf of (rather than by) the complainant, the person signing should:

• describe himself/herself e.g. 'solicitor acting for (name of complainant)'; and
• give business address (or home address, if appropriate). | Signed

![ ]

Address *(if appropriate)*

![ ]

Date

![ ] |

How to serve the papers
- We strongly advise that you retain and keep in a safe place a copy of the completed questionnaire.
- Send the person to be questioned the **whole** of this document either to their usual last known residence or place of business or if you know they are acting through a solicitor, to that address. If your questions are directed at a limited company or other corporate body or a trade union or employers' association, you should send the papers to the secretary or clerk at the registered or principal office. You should be able to find out where this is by enquiring at your public library. However, if you are unable to do so you will have to send the papers to the place where you think it is most likely they will reach the secretary or clerk. It is your responsibility to see that they receive them.
- You can deliver the papers in person or send them by post.
- If you send them by post, we advise you to use the recorded delivery service (this will provide you with proof of delivery).

By virtue of regulation 41 of the Employment Equality (Age) Regulations 2006 this questionnaire and any reply are (subject to the provisions of that regulation) admissible in proceedings under the Regulations. A court or tribunal may draw any such inference as is just and equitable from a failure without reasonable excuse to reply within eight weeks of service of this questionnaire, or from an evasive or equivocal reply, including an inference that the person questioned has committed an unlawful act.

PART 3 REPLY: THE RESPONDENT

Note:

- Before completing this reply form, we advise you to prepare what you want to say on a separate piece of paper.
- If you have insufficient room on the reply form for what you want to say, continue on an additional piece of paper, which should be attached to the reply form and sent to the complainant.

Enter the name of the person you are replying to (the complainant)	To [ ]
Enter the complainant's address	of [ ]
Enter your name (you are the respondent)	1. [ ]
Enter your address	of [ ]
Complete as appropriate	hereby acknowledge the receipt of the questionnaire signed by you and dated which was served on me (date) [ ]
Please tick relevant box: If you disagree with the complainant's statement of events, you should explain in what respects you disagree, or your version of what happened, or both.	2. ☐ I agree that the statement in 1.2 of thje questionnaire is an accurate description of what happened. ☐ I disagree with the statement in 1.2 of the questionnaire in that: [ ]

Please tick relevant box: you are answering question at paragraph 3 of the complainant's questionnaire here. If in answer to paragraph 2 of the questionnaire you have agreed that the statement is an accurate description of what happened by dispute that it is unlawful discrimination, you should state your reasons. If you have disagreed with the facts in the complainant's statement of events, you should answer the question on the basis of your version of the facts. We advise you to look at the attached notes and also the relevant parts of the Employment Equality (Age) Regulations 2006. You will need to know:

- *how the regulations define discrimination and in what situations the regulations make discrimination unlawful – see paragraph 1 of the attached notes; and*
- *what exceptions the regulations provide – see paragraph 3 of the attached notes.*

If you think that an exception (eg. the exception for employment where a person's age is a genuine occupational qualification) applies to the treatment described in paragraph 1.2 of the complainant's questionnaire, you should mention this in paragraph 3a, with an explanation about why you think the exception applies.

3a.

☐ I accept that my treatment of you was unlawful discrimination [harassment] by me against you

☐ I dispute that my treatment of you was unlawful discrimination [harassment] by me against you. My reasons for so disputing are:

3b.
The reason why you received the treatment accorded to you and the answers to the other questions in paragraph 3 of the questionnaire are:

4. Replies to questions in paragraph 4 of the questionnaire:

Delete the whole of this sentence if you have answered all the questions in the complainant's questionnaire. If you are unable or unwilling to answer the questions please tick the appropriate box and give your reasons for not answering them.

5. I have deleted (*in whole or in part*) the paragraphs answered all the questions in the complainant's numbered above

☐ Since I am unable
☐ Since I am unwilling
to reply to the relevant questions in the complainant's questionnaire for the reasons given in the box below.

The reply form must be signed and dated. If it is to be signed on behalf of (rather than by) the respondent the person signing should:
- *describe himself/herself eg. 'solicitor acting for (name of respondent)' or 'personnel manager of (name of firm)'; and*
- *give business address (or home address if appropriate).*

Signed

Address *(if appropriate)*

Date

How to serve the reply form on the complainant
- If you wish to reply to the questionnaire we strongly advise that you do so without delay.
- You should retain, and keep in a safe place, the questionnaire sent to you and a copy of your reply.
- You can serve the reply either by delivering it in person to the complainant or by sending it by post.
- If you send it by post, we advise you to use the recorded delivery service (this will provide you with evidence of delivery).
- You should send the reply form to the address indicated in paragraph 5 of the complainant's questionnaire.

APPENDIX: NOTES ON THE SCOPE OF THE EMPLOYMENT EQUALITY (AGE) REGULATIONS 2006

Definitions of discrimination

1.   The different kinds of discrimination covered by the regulations are summarised below:

Direct discrimination (Regulation 3) occurs where, because of B's age, A treats B less favourably than he treats or would treat other persons unless A can objectively justify that treatment.

Indirect discrimination (Regulation 3) arises where:

* A applies to B a provision, criterion or practice which A applies equally to persons not of the same age group as B;
* that provision, criterion or practice puts persons of B's age group at a particular disadvantage when compared to other persons; and
* B suffers that disadvantage.

The Directive allows direct or indirect discrimination if it is 'objectively justified' i.e. if it pursues a 'legitimate aim' and is a 'proportionate' means of achieving that aim.

Victimisation (Regulation 4) arises where a person is treated less favourably than other persons in the same circumstances are or would be treated, because they have made a complaint or intend to make a complaint about discrimination or harassment or have given evidence or intend to give evidence relating to a complaint about discrimination or harassment.

Harassment (Regulation 6) arises where on grounds of age, A engages in unwanted conduct which has the purpose or effect of violating B's dignity or creating an intimidating, hostile, degrading, humiliating or offensive environment for B. Harassment may be intentional bullying which is obvious or violent, but it can also be unintentional, subtle and insidious. It may involve nicknames, teasing, name calling or other behaviours, which is not with malicious intent but of those with whom the individual associates. It may not be targeted at an individual but consist of a general culture which, for instance, appears to tolerate the telling of ageist jokes.

How to find out more about the provisions of the regulations

2.   The DTI has prepared Notes on the Regulations which explain the provisions in the Regulations. The notes give general explanations only and should not be regarded as a complete or authoritative statement of the law. You can access the Notes on the Regulations by   visiting the DTI website at www.dti.gov.uk/employment/discrimination/age-discrimination/index.html. Acas has also published good practice guidance entitled Age and the Workplace. The Acas guide can be found on its website at www.acas.org.uk.

Exceptions

3. The Regulations provide that the following practices shall not constitute unlawful age discrimination;

- **Pay and other employment benefits based on length of service (Regulation 32).** This allows employers to continue to award certain benefits to employees using the criterion of length of service.
- **Pay related to the National Minimum Wage (Regulation 31).** This allows employers to base their pay structures on the national minimum wage legislation.
- **Acts under the statutory authority (Regulation 27).** This ensures that the Regulations do not render unlawful any act which is done in order to comply with the requirement of any other statutory provisions.
- **Enhanced redundancy (Regulation 33).** This allows employers to base their redundancy schemes on the statutory redundancy scheme.
- **Life assurance (Regulation 34).** This allows employers to cease life assurance cover to workers who have had to retire early on grounds of ill health.
- **Retirement (Regulation 30).** This allows an employer to dismiss an employee where the reason for the dismissal is retirement (whether or not the reason for a dismissal is a retirement shall be determined in accordance with sections 98ZA to 98ZF of the Employment Rights Act 1996).
- **Occupational and personal pensions (Regulation 11).** Schedule 2 contains exemptions for practices which typically exist in occupational pension schemes, and for relevant practices in personal pension schemes.
- **Genuine Occupational Requirements (Regulation 8).** This allows an employer, when recruiting for a post, to treat job applicants differently on grounds of their age if possessing a characteristic related to age is a genuine occupational requirement (ìGORî) for that post. An employer may also rely on this exception when promoting, transferring or training persons for a post, and when dismissing persons from a post, where a GOR applies in respect of that post.
- **Positive action (Regulation 29).** This permits positive action in certain circumstances. It can be relied upon in the absence of evidence showing that a particular age group is under-represented in jobs or trade organisations. The positive action should ìprevent or compensate for disadvantages linked to ageî among the relevant section of people to whom the positive action relates.

Produced by:
Employment Relations Directorate
Department of Trade and Industry
1 Victoria Street
London SW1H 0ET

Telephone: 020 7215 5000
For help or advice about completing this form employees can contact the Citizens Advice Bureaux, law centres and, where appropriate, Trade Unions. They may also seek independent legal advice from a solicitor.

URN 06/1403

Copies and further information is also available on the DTI website at http://www.dti.gov.uk/employment/discrimination/age-discrimination/index.html and at Jobcentre Plus Offices and Citizens Advice Bureaux.

Letter to employer requesting extension of contract beyond normal retirement age

Date:

Dear

1. I am writing to you in response to your notification that I am due to be retired on [date] in your letter of [date]

    or:

    I believe that you intend to retire me on [date] but have not notified me of this fact.

2. I am requesting that my contract of employment does not end on [date].

3. I propose that it is extended [indefinitely]

    or

    until I reach age [state preferred age of retirement]

    or

    for [x years/months].

4. I am making this request under paragraph 5 of Schedule 6 of the Employment Equality (Age) Regulations 2006.

5. As I understand the procedure you now have a duty to consider my request and to hold a meeting with me to discuss it within a reasonable period of time.

6. The reasons for my request to defer my retirement are as follows:

    [e.g.] My job consists, as you know, of [state duties undertaken in practice]. I have the ability to continue to do my job and in the previous appraisals I have received [state markings or commendations]. I believe that I can continue to serve this company well and bring to bear my experience and ability to its benefit.

    ...

    [if other staff have been retained beyond retirement age: [e.g.] I believe that [name] was not required to retire at [state age of proposed retirement]. I believe that my situation is no different in any material respect to that of [name], and I believe that I can provide the same level of service as [name] has done since being retained past retirement].

    I look forward to meeting you and discussing the above reasons.

Signed: Dated:

Useful organisations

Advice UK
12th Floor
New London Bridge House
25 London Bridge Street
London SE1 9SG
Website: www.adviceuk.org.uk
E-mail: general@adviceuk.org.uk
Tel: 020 7407 4070
To find an independent advice agency in your area.

ACAS
Brandon House
180 Borough High Street
London SE1 1LW
Website: www.acas.org.uk
Tel: 08457 47 47 47
For advice and information on your rights at work. Also provide conciliation services in employment disputes.

Age Concern England
Astral House
1268 London Road
London SW16 4ER
Website: www.ageconcern.org.uk
Email: ace@ace.org.uk
Tel: 0800 00 99 66

Age Concern Cymru
13/14 Neptune Court
Vanguard Way
Cardiff CF24 5PJ
Website: www.accymru.org.uk
E-mail: enquiries@accymru.org.uk
Tel: 029 2043 1555

Age Concern Northern Ireland
3 Lower Crescent
Belfast BT7 1NR
Website:
http://www.ageconcernni.org
Email: info@ageconcernni.org
Tel: 028 9024 5729

Age Concern Scotland
National Organisation
Leonard Small House
113 Rose Street
Edinburgh EH2 3DT
Website:
www.ageconcernscotland.org.uk
E-mail: enquiries@acscot. Org.uk
Tel: 0131 2203345

Age partnership group
E-mail:
Christine.ashdown@dwp.gsi.gov.uk
Group of some of the listed organisations. Their publication BE READY and CD provides training and good practice guidance in relation to age discrimination issues in all areas.

Age Positive

Department for Work and Pensions
Room W8d
Moorfoot
Sheffield S1 4PQ
Website: www.agepositive.gov.uk
E-mail: agepositive@dwp.gsi.gov.uk
Tel: 0114 267 7230
*Government campaign promoting age
diversity in employment.*

Age Positive Cymru

Website: www.agepositive.gov.uk
E-mail:
Melissa.rajan@geronimopr.com

Association of British Insurers

511 Gresham St
London EC2V 7HQ
Website: www.abi.org.uk.
E-mail: info@abi.org.uk
Tel: 020 7600 3333

Better Government for Older People

207-221 Pentonville Road
London N1 9UZ
Website: www.bgop.org.uk
E-mail: information@bgop.org.uk
Tel: 0870 770 3292

British Chambers of Commerce

65 Petty France
London SW1H 9EU
Website: www.chamberonline.co.uk
E-mail:
Info@britishchambers.org.uk
Tel: 020 7654 5800

Campaign Against Age Discrimination in Employment

Website: www.caade.net

Carers UK

20-25 Glasshouse Yard
London EC1A 4JT
Website: www.carersuk.org
E-mail: info@carersuk.org
Tel (Carers line): 0808 808 7777
(Wed and Thurs: 10am-12pm and
2pm–4pm.)
*Campaigning organisation providing
information and advice for carers.
Carers UK leads the ACE National
(Action for Carers and Employment)
partnership www.acecarers.org.uk*

Carers Scotland

91 Mitchell Street
Glasgow G1 3LN
Website: www.carerscotland.org
E-mail: info@carerscotland.org
Tel: 0141 221 9141

Carers Wales

River House
Ynsbridge Court
Gwaelod-y-Garth
Cardiff CF15 9SS
Website: www.carerswales.org
E-mail: info@carerswales.org.uk
Tel: 029 2081 1370

Carers Northern Ireland

58 Howard Street
Belfast BT1 6PJ
Website: www.carersni.org
E-mail: info@carersni.demon.co.uk
Tel: 028 9043 9843

CBI

Centre Point
103 New Oxford Street
London WC1A 1DU
Website: www.cbi.org.uk
E-mail: Thomas.moran@cbi.org.uk
Tel: 020 7395 7400

Centre for Research on the Older Worker
Senate House
University of Surrey
Guildford GU2 7XH
Website:
www.surrey.ac.uk/ education/crow
E-mail:
enquiries@managers.org.uk

Chartered Management Institute
Management House,
Cottingham Road
Corby
Northamptonshire NN17 1TT
Website: www.managers.org.uk
E-mail:
enquiries@managers.org.uk
Tel: 01536 204222

CIPD
151 The Broadway
London SW19 1JQ
Website: www.cipd.co.uk
E-mail: cipd@cipd.co.uk
Tel: 0208 612 6200

Citizens Advice
Myddelton House
115-123 Pentonville Road
London N1 9LZ
Website: www.adviceguide.org.uk

Combined Pension Forecasting team
Room TB014
Tyneview Park
Newcastle upon Tyne NE98 1BA
Website:
www.thepensionservice.gov.uk
/employer/what-they-are.asp
Tel: 0870 010 1684

Commission for Equality and Human Rights (CEHR)
Website: www.cehr.org.uk

Commission for Racial Equality (CRE)
St Dunstan's House
201-211 Borough High Street
London SE1 1GZ
Website: www.cre.gov.uk
E-mail: info@cre.gov.uk
Tel: 020 7939 0000

CRE Scotland
The Tun
12 Jackson's Entry
off Holyrood Road
Edinburgh EH8 8PJ
Website: www.cre.gov.uk/scotland/
index.html
E-mail: Scotland@cre.gov.uk
Tel: 0131 5242000

CRE Wales
3rd Floor Capital Tower
Greyfriars Road
Cardiff CF10 SAG
Website: www.cre.gov.uk/wales/
index.html
Tel: 02920 729 200

Community Legal Service
Website: clsdirect.org.uk
Tel: 0845 345 4 345 (Helpline)

Directgov
Website: direct.gov.uk

Disability Rights Commission
Freepost MID02164
Stratford upon Avon CV37 9BR
Website: www.drc-gb.org
E-mail: enquiry@drc-gb.org
Tel: 08457 622 633 (8am to 8pm
Monday to Friday)

Department for Trade and Industry

1 Victoria Street
London SW1H OET
Website: www.dti.gov.uk
E-mail:
Dti.enquiries@dti.gsi.gov.uk
Tel: 0207 215 5000

EEF

The Manufacturers' Organisation
Broadway House
Tothill Street
London SW1H9NQ
Website: www.eef.org.uk
E-mail: enquiries@eef-fed.org.uk
Tel: 020 7222 7777

Employers' Forum on Age

Floor 3
Downstream
1 London Bridge
London SE1 9BG
Website: www.efa.org.uk
E-mail: efa@efa.org.uk
Tel: 0845 456 2495

Employment Agency Standards Inspectorate

Department of Trade and Industry
(4140)
1 Victoria Street
London SW1H 0ET
Enquiry line on 0845 9555105
(Monday – Friday 9:30am- 4:30pm).
Minicom – 020 7215 6740
For complaints against employment agencies.

Employment Tribunals Service

Customer Services Team
3rd Floor, Alexandra House
14-22 The Parsonage
Manchester, M3 2JA
Website: www.employment
tribunals.gov.uk
Public Enquiry Line: 0845 795 9775
Minicom: 0845 757 3722

Equal Opportunities Commission (EOC)

Arndale House
Arndale Centre
Manchester M4 3EQ
Website: www.eoc.org.uk
E-mail: info@eoc.org.uk
Tel: 0845 601 5901

EOC Scotland

St Stephens House
259 Bath Street
Glasgow G2 4JL
Website: www.eoc.org.uk
E-mail: Scotland@eoc.org.uk
Tel: 0845 601 5901

EOC Wales

Windsor Lane
Cardiff CF10 3GE
Website: www.eoc.org.uk
E-mail: wales@eoc.org.uk
Tel: 029 2034 3552

Financial Services Authority (FSA):

25 The North Colonnade
London E14 5HS
Website: www.fsa.gov.uk
Consumer helpline: 0845 606 1234.
Independent regulator of the financial services industry. Provides information for consumers, including on pensions.

FiftyOn
Second Floor
Ryder Court
14 Ryder Street
London SW1Y 6QB
Website: www.fiftyon.co.uk
E-mail: info@fiftyon.co.uk
Tel: 020 7451 0231

FSB
2 Catherine Place
London SW1E 6HF
Website: www.fsb.org.uk
Tel: 020 7592 8100

Help the Aged
207-211 Pentonville Road
London N1 9UZ
Website: www.helptheaged.org.uk
E-mail: info@helptheaged.org.uk
Tel: 020 7278 1114

Highlands & Islands Equality Forum
Unit 2
Fairways Business Park
Castle Heather
Inverness IV2 6AA
Website: www.hief.org.uk
E-mail: hief@scvo.org.uk

HSE
Rose Court
2 Southwark Bridge
London SE1 9HS
Website: www.hse.gov.uk
E-mail: Hseinformationservices
@natbrit.com
Tel: 0845 345 0055

Law Centres Federation:
Duchess House
18-19 Warren Street
London W1P†5DB
Website: www.lawcentres.org.uk
Tel: 020 7387 8570

Law Society
113 Chancery Lane
London WC2A 1PL
Website: www.lawsociety.org.uk
Find a solicitor helpline:
0870 606 6575

Learning and Skills Council
Website: http://www.lsc.gov.uk/
National/default.htm

Life academy
9 Chesham Road
Guildford
Surrey GU1 3LS
Website: http://www.life-academy.
co.uk/
E-mail: info@life-academy.co.uk
Tel: 01483 301170

Local Government Employers
Website: http://www.lge.gov.uk/
E-mail: info@lge.gov.uk
Tel: 020 7187 7373

National Association of Pension Funds
NOIC House
4 Victoria Street
London SW1H ONX
Website: www.napf.co.uk
E-mail: Scott.garner@napf.co.uk
Tel: 020 7808 1313

National Association for Voluntary and Community Action (NAVCA)
117 Arundel Street
Sheffield S1 2NU
Website: www.navca.org.uk
Tel: 0114 278 6636

NIACE

Renaissance House
20 Princess Road West
Leicester LE1 6TP
Website: www.niace.org.uk
E-mail: enqiries@niace.org.uk
Tel: 0116 204 4200/4201

Pensions Advisory Service

11 Belgrave Road
London
SW1V 1RB
Website: www.opas.org.uk
Tel: 0845 601 2923
An independent voluntary organisation providing information and guidance on state, company, stakeholder and personal pension schemes.

Pension Protection Fund

Knollys House
17 Addiscombe Road
Croydon CR0 6SR
Website: www.pensionprotection-fund.gov.uk
Tel: 0845 600 2541
A fund to compensate members of pension schemes on the insolvency of employers.

Pension Service

Website:
www.thepensionservice.gov.uk.
Tel: 0845 731 3233

Policy Research Institute on Ageing and Ethnicity

31-32 Park Row
Leeds LS1 5JD
Website: www.priae.org
Tel: 0113 285 5990

PRIME

Astral House
1268 London Road
London SW16 4ER
Website:
www.primeinitiative.org.uk
E-mail: prime@ace.org.uk
Tel: 020 8765 7833
Not-for-profit company dedicated to helping people over 50 set up in business.

Small Business Service

Kingsgate House
66-74 Victoria Street
London SW1E 6SW
Website: www.sbs.gov.uk
Tel: 020 7215 5000

TAEN (The Age and Employment Network)

207-221 Pentonville Road
London N1 9UZ
Website: www.taen.org.uk
E-mail: taen@helptheaged.org.uk
Tel: 020 7843 1590

Third Age Foundation

Britannia House
1-11 Glenthorne Road
London W6 0LH
Website: www.thirdage.org.uk
E-mail: Sylvia@thirdage.org.uk
Tel: 020 8748 9898
Helps older people to find a new direction and learn IT skills.

Trades Union Congress
Congress House
Great Russell Street
London WC1B3LS
Contact on age discrimination:
Lucy Anderson
Website: www.tuc.org.uk
E-mail: Landerson@tuc.org.uk
Tel: 020 7636 4030

And
www.Worksmart.org.uk
TUC website giving information on
employment rights. The site
includes the Union Finder search
function allowing you to find if a
union is recognised by your
employer, or to find a union relevant
to the sector you work in.

Union finder helpline –
0870 600 4 882

Union Learning Fund
Website:
www.learningservices.org.uk
/unionlearningreps/cont acts.htm
Tel: 0151 2367678

Union Learning Fund for Wales
Website: www.wales.gov.uk/
subieducationtraining/content/
adult_training/wulf-intro-e.htm
Tel: 02920 826685

**Union Learning Fund for
Scotland**
Website: www.scotland.gov.uk/
library5/education/ sulf5-OO.asp
Tel: 0141 242 0220

Index